Mozley and Whiteley's
Law Dictionary

Mozley & Whiteley's Law Dictionary

Ninth Edition

By John B Saunders Esq

OF LINCOLN'S INN, BARRISTER

London
BUTTERWORTHS
1977

ENGLAND:
> BUTTERWORTH & CO. (PUBLISHERS) LTD.
> > LONDON: 88 KINGSWAY, WC2B 6AB

AUSTRALIA:
> BUTTERWORTHS PTY. LTD.
> > SYDNEY: 586 PACIFIC HIGHWAY, CHATSWOOD, NSW 2067
> > Also at MELBOURNE, BRISBANE,
> > ADELAIDE and PERTH

CANADA:
> BUTTERWORTH & CO. (CANADA) LTD.
> > TORONTO: 2265 MIDLAND AVENUE, SCARBOROUGH M1P 4S1

NEW ZEALAND:
> BUTTERWORTHS OF NEW ZEALAND LTD.
> > WELLINGTON: 26/28 WARING TAYLOR STREET, 1

SOUTH AFRICA:
> BUTTERWORTH & CO. (SOUTH AFRICA) (PTY.) LTD.
> > DURBAN: 152–154 GALE STREET

USA:
> BUTTERWORTH & CO. (PUBLISHERS) INC.
> > BOSTON: 19 CUMMINGS PARK, WOBURN, MASS 01801

Casebound 0 406 62523 9
Limp 0 406 62524 7

PRINTED BY THOMSON LITHO LTD., EAST KILBRIDE, SCOTLAND

Preface to the Ninth edition

It is seven years since the last edition of this work was published, and during those years many changes have taken place, making necessary a considerable revision of the dictionary. The United Kingdom is now increasingly becoming subject to European Community law; local government in England and Wales has been reorganised by the Local Government Act 1972; the Sex Discrimination Act 1975 has taken its place upon the statute book; national insurance and social security legislation has been consolidated, for the time being, in the Social Security Act 1975; whilst political considerations have led to further alteration in the law relating to industrial relations. In almost every direction new laws are coming into being and old laws are being amended.

It is against this constantly moving background that this new edition has been prepared, the entries having been revised up to 31st December 1976.

Some Scottish and Canadian definitions have been added.

J.B.S.

May 1977

Extract from Authors' Preface to First edition

THE primary object of this Work is to give an exposition of legal terms and phrases of past and present use. But, as the mere exposition of a word or phrase would often be barren and unsatisfactory, we have in many cases, especially when dealing with the legal terms of the present day, added an exposition of the law bearing upon the subject-matter of the Title.

To many of the Titles which have reference to the historical portions of the law, we have appended the law-Latin or Norman-French words which were used as their equivalent by the mediaeval lawyers when writing (as they often did) in one or other of those languages respectively.

There is a difference in the practice of lexicographers as to the order of Titles consisting of more than one word. Some place the order according to the letters of the Title considered as a whole; others regulate the order by the letters of the first word. This being so, it may be as well to state that we have adopted the latter principle. Thus, "Writ of Right" has precedence over "Writer to the Signet," because "Writ" would precede "Writer" if the words stood alone, notwithstanding that "e" (the fifth letter in "writer") precedes in the alphabet "o" (the first letter of "of ").

We append to this Preface a list of the abbreviations used in the course of the Book. We do not in this list include authorities which are referred to in full, nor any series of Legal Reports. A catalogue of all the Reports, with the abbreviations generally used to denote them, will be found under the Title "Reports", pp. 302–319.

List of Abbreviations

[*As to* REPORTS, *see pp.* 302–319]

A Concise Law Dictionary

A

A 1. In shipping phraseology, this denotes a first-class vessel.

A and B lists. [CONTRIBUTORY.]

A FORTIORI (from a stronger [reason]), all the more.

A MENSA ET THORO. From table and bed. [JUDICIAL SEPARATION.]

A POSTERIORI. [A PRIORI.]

A PRIORI. An argument derived from considerations of an abstract character, or which have but a remote and possibly indirect (though none the less real) bearing upon the point under discussion, is called an argument *a priori*; whereas an argument derived from actual observation or other direct consideration is called an argument *a posteriori*.

A.R. *Anno regni*—in the year of the reign.

A, TABLE. [TABLE A.]

A VERBIS LEGIS NON RECEDENDUM EST (from the words of the law there should not be any departure). A rule to be applied in the interpretation of Acts of Parliament whereby the words of the statute are to be the primary guide for the court rather than the intention of the legislature.

A VINCULO MATRIMONII. From the bond of matrimony.

AB ANTIQUO. From ancient time.

AB INITIO (from the beginning), specially in relation to trespass. If a man abuse the authority given him by the law, he becomes, by the common law, a trespasser *ab initio*, so that the legality of his first proceedings is vitiated by his subsequent illegal acts.

AB INTESTATO (from an intestate). Succession *ab intestato* means the succession to the property of a person dying intestate, *i.e.*, without a will.

ABANDONMENT. 1. In marine insurance, abandonment is the act of cession, by which, in case of the constructive total loss of a vessel or goods in the progress of a voyage, the owners give up to the insurers or underwriters what remains of the vessel or goods on condition of receiving the whole amount of insurance. Notice of such abandonment must be given to the underwriters within reasonable time after the loss. See Marine Insurance Act 1906. [TOTAL LOSS.]

2. Service of a notice of discontinuance under R.S.C. 1965, Ord. 21 enables a party to abandon an action in the High Court.

3. Abandonment of a child or young person is a misdemeanour under s. 1 of the Children and Young Persons Act 1933. As to when a child is deemed to be abandoned, see s. 2 (9) of the Children Act 1948, as substituted by the Children Act 1975.

ABATEMENT sometimes signifies the act of the abator, and sometimes the result of the act to the thing abated.

1. *In Commerce* it means a deduction made from payments due, and it is also used to denote the allowance sometimes made at the custom-house for damages received by goods in warehousing or during importation.

2. *Abatement amongst Creditors* takes place where the assets of a debtor are not sufficient to pay his creditors in full, so that they are compelled to share the assets in proportion to their debts.

3. *Abatement amongst Legatees* in like manner is enforced where there are not

ABATEMENT—*continued.*

sufficient assets to pay the legacies in full. But pecuniary or general legacies abate proportionally before specific legacies and before demonstrative legacies until the fund out of which the latter are payable is exhausted; and in addition a legacy may be expressly preferred to another of the same class.

4. *Abatement of an Action or Suit* takes place when, from some supervenient cause, one of the parties thereto is no longer before the court; so that, unless his place be supplied, there is no one to proceed therein.

Now by R.S.C., 1965, Ord. 15, where a party dies or becomes bankrupt, but the action survives, it shall not abate by reason of the death or bankruptcy.

5. *Abatement of Freehold* was where a person died seised of an inheritance, and before the heir or devisee entered, a stranger, who had no right, made entry and got possession of the freehold: this entry was called an abatement, and he an abator. [Disseisin; Intrusion; Ouster.]

6. *Abatement, Pleas in,* were those showing ground for quashing the proceedings. They did not dispute the cause of action, but only pointed out an error, unconnected with the merits of the case, *e.g.*, misnaming or misdescription of parties, which unless remedied was fatal to the suit. Now abolished in both civil and criminal proceedings.

7. *Abatement of Nuisances, i.e.,* their removal. A self-remedy allowed to one injured by a nuisance. The abatement must be done peaceably and without causing unnecessary damage.

A local authority must serve an abatement notice on any person responsible for the existence of a nuisance prejudicial to the health of the inhabitants of the neighbourhood. If an abatement notice is not complied with, a court of summary jurisdiction may make a nuisance order requiring the defendant to comply with the abatement notice. See the Public Health Act 1936, ss. 92–100.

ABBREVIATURE. A short draft.

ABDICATE. 1. To renounce or give up the throne or government.

2. (Roman Law.) To disinherit.

ABDUCTION. The leading away of any person. More strictly the taking away

of a wife from her husband, a child from its parent, a ward from her guardian and a female servant from her master. In some cases the act is criminal, and in others a civil action will lie against the aggressor; and see Sexual Offences Act 1956, ss. 19, 20, as to girls under the ages of 16 and 18 years respectively. [Heiress.]

ABEARANCE. Behaviour. [Good Behaviour.]

ABET (Fr. *Bouter*; Lat. *Impellere, Excitare*). To encourage or set on. Thus an abettor of a crime is one who, being present either actually or constructively, aids in the commission of the offence. A person who supplies the instrument for a crime or anything essential to its commission aids in the commission of it; if he does so knowingly and with intent to aid, he abets it as well and is guilty of aiding and abetting: *National Coal Board* v. *Gamble*, [1959] 2 Q.B. 11. Aiding and abetting almost inevitably involves a situation in which the secondary party and the main offender are together at some stage discussing the plans which they may be making in respect of the alleged offence, and are in contact so that each knows what is passing through the mind of the other: *A.-G.'s Reference (No. 1 of 1975)*, [1975] 2 All E.R. 684, C.A. [Accessory.]

ABEYANCE (probably from the Fr. *Bayer*, to expect).

1. An estate is said to be in *abeyance* when there is no person *in esse* in whom it can vest; though the law considers it as always potentially existing, and ready to vest whenever a proper owner appears. This estate has also been called *in nubibus* (in the clouds) and *in gremio legis* (in the bosom of the law). The fee simple of the glebe of a parson is said to be in abeyance.

2. The doctrine of abeyance of a peerage relates to the state of suspense into which a peerage falls when co-heirship occurs in the succession.

ABJURATION, OATH OF. The oath formerly required to be taken by every person holding any office in the state; and whereby the person taking it *abjured* any allegiance to the Pretender. Abolished. For present form of oath of allegiance, see the Promissory Oaths Act 1868, s. 2.

ABJURATION OF THE REALM. [Sanctuary.]

ABODE. A man's residence, where he lives with his family and sleeps at night. It may include a place where the person in question works and has his business.

ABORTION. A miscarriage, or the premature expulsion of the contents of the womb before the term of gestation is completed. To procure abortion was a felony but it has now been legalised under certain circumstances by the Abortion Act 1967. [CHILD DESTRUCTION.]

ABRIDGMENT. A short comprehensive treatise or digest of the law, *e.g.*, the works of Fitzherbert, Brooke and Rolle, Viner, Comyns and Bacon.

ABROGATE. To annul or repeal.

ABSCOND. To go out of the jurisdiction of the courts, or to conceal oneself to avoid legal process. It is an act of bankruptcy (*q.v.*).

ABSCONDING DEBTOR. See the Bankruptcy Act 1914, s. 23.

ABSENCE. 1. Non-appearance of a party to an action.

2. Unheard of for seven years, a presumption of death; absence of husband or wife for seven years is under certain circumstances a defence to an indictment for bigamy, and a ground for divorce under the Matrimonial Causes Act 1973, s. 19 (3). The fact that the parties to a marriage have lived apart continuously for at least five years will be sufficient reason for a divorce: see s. 1 (2) of the Act of 1973.

ABSOLUTE. Complete, unconditional. A rule or order absolute is one which is complete and can be put into force at once, in contradistinction to a rule or order *nisi*, which is made on the application of one party only (*ex parte*) to be made absolute unless the other party appear and show cause why it should not be made absolute. As to applications generally, see R.S.C., 1965, Ord. 8 [DECREE ABSOLUTE.]

ABSOLUTE TITLE. Under the Land Registration Act 1925, land may be registered with an absolute title. The first registration of any person as proprietor of freehold land with such a title vests in the person so registered an estate in fee simple in possession in the land, together with all rights, privileges, and appurtenances, belonging or appurtenant thereto, subject to the following rights and interests:—

(a) To the incumbrances, and other entries, if any, appearing on the register; and

(b) Unless the contrary is expressed on the register, to such overriding interests, if any, as affect the registered land; and

(c) Where the first proprietor is not entitled for his own benefit to the registered land, as between himself and the persons entitled to minor interests, to any minor interests of such persons of which he has notice,

but free from all other estates and interests whatsoever, including estates and interests of the Crown (Land Registration Act 1925, s. 5).

For the effect of registration of leaseholds with an absolute title, see *ibid.*, s. 9.

ABSTRACT OF TITLE. A summary or abridgment of the deeds constituting the title of an estate, furnished by a vendor or mortgagor to an intending purchaser or mortgagee.This is usually perused by the purchaser's or mortgagee's solicitor and verified by an examination of the original deeds. This is followed by requisitions on title (*q.v.*).

An *Abstract-in-Chief* is one made direct from a document and not from a mere recital of it. Under the Law of Property Act 1925, s. 10, abstracts of title are not to include an instrument relating only to interests or powers, which will be overreached by the conveyance of the land to which title is being shown. See also specimens contained in Sched. VI to the Act. [CURTAIN CLAUSES; TITLE.]

ABUNDANS CAUTELA NON NOCET. Excess of caution does no harm.

ABUSE OF DISTRESS. The using of animal or chattel distrained. This renders the distrainer liable as for a conversion.

ABUSE OF PROCESS is the malicious and improper use of some regular legal proceeding to obtain some advantage over an opponent.

ABUTTALS, or **ABBUTTALS** (Fr. *Abutter*). The buttings or boundings of lands, showing to what other lands, highways or places they belong, or are abutting.

ACCELERATION. The hastening of the vesting in possession of a reversion or remainder by the determination of the prior particular estate by surrender, etc., before its natural termination.

ACCEPTANCE. "A thing in good part, and as it were a kind of agreeing to some act done before, which might have been undone and avoided if such acceptance had not been." *Cowel.*

1. *If*, for instance, a lease for more than three years be made verbally, acceptance of rent from the lessee if he obtained possession will create a tenancy from year to year binding upon the lessor; and on the same principle, acceptance of rent may confirm a lease, which has been put an end to by notice, the acceptance here operating as a withdrawal, waiver or abandonment of the notice. This did not apply if the premises were within the Rent Restriction Acts. See now the Rent Act 1968.

2. A buyer is deemed to have accepted goods when he intimates to the seller that he has accepted them, or when the goods have been delivered to him, and he does any act in relation to them which is inconsistent with the ownership of the seller, or when after the lapse of a reasonable time he retains the goods without intimating to the seller that he has rejected them. Sale of Goods Act 1893, s. 35.

3. Acceptance of an offer may be made by express words or may be inferred from conduct showing an unqualified intention to accept. A mere intention to accept not shown by words or conduct is insufficient.

ACCEPTANCE OF A BILL is an engagement by the drawee (*i.e.*, the person on whom the bill is drawn) to pay the bill according to the tenor of his acceptance. After the acceptance the drawee is called the *acceptor*. The acceptance must be in writing, and it is usually made by the acceptor's writing the word "accepted" across the bill and signing his name. See Bills of Exchange Act 1882, s. 17.

ACCEPTANCE SUPRA PROTEST, or an *acceptance for honour*, is an acceptance of a bill for the honour of the drawer or an indorser, when the drawee refuses to accept. It is made by some friend of the drawer or indorser to prevent the bill being sent back upon him as unpaid, after a protest (*supra protest*) has been drawn up declaratory of its dishonour by the drawee. This operates not as an engagement to pay absolutely, but only to pay in the event of its being presented to, and dishonoured by, the drawee when it arrives at maturity, on its then being protested for non-payment, and afterwards duly presented for payment to the "acceptor for honour." See Bills of Exchange Act 1882, ss. 65–68.

ACCEPTING SERVICE is where the solicitor for a defendant on his behalf accepts service of a writ or other process of a court, and undertakes to appear, so as to avoid the necessity of such writ or process being served on his client. [SERVICE, 3.] This undertaking the courts will enforce, if necessary, by attachment. [ATTACHMENT.]

ACCEPTOR. A person who accepts a bill of exchange. [ACCEPTANCE OF A BILL; BILL OF EXCHANGE.]

ACCESS, approach, or the means of approaching. (1) The presumption of a child's legitimacy is rebutted if it be shown that the husband had not access to his wife within such a period of time before the birth as admits of his having been the father; but neither husband nor wife may give evidence to prove non-access. (2) A parent may, following divorce proceedings on the making of a custodianship order, be given, by the court, a right of access to see a child or children. See *e.g.* s. 34 of the Children Act 1975.

ACCESSION. 1. A mode of acquiring property by right of occupancy, founded on the civil law; whereby the original owner of anything which receives an accession by natural or artificial means, as by the growth of vegetables, etc., the pregnancy of animals, etc., is entitled to it under such its state of improvement; but if the thing itself, by such operation, is changed into a different species, as by making wine, oil, or bread, out of another's grapes, olives, or wheat, it belongs to the new operator; who is only to make a satisfaction to the former proprietor for the materials which he has so converted.

2. In international law, accession is occasionally used as a technical expression denoting the absolute or conditional acceptance, by one or several states, of a treaty already concluded between other sovereignties.

3. The word means also the coming of a king or queen to the throne on the death of the prior occupant thereof.

ACCESSORY is he who is not the chief actor in an offence, nor present at its performance, but is some way concerned therein, either *before* or *after* the fact committed. An accessory *before* the fact is one who being absent at the time of the crime committed, yet procures, counsels, or commands another to commit a crime. An accessory *after* the fact is he that receives, favours, aids, assists, or comforts any man who has committed an offence, of which the accessory knows; as by furnishing means of escape or concealment, or assisting to rescue or protect him.

The former law relating to accessories after the fact was replaced by s. 4 of the Criminal Law Act 1967, which provides penalties for assisting any person who has committed an arrestable offence, with intent to impede his apprehension or prosecution.

ACCIDENT. As a ground for seeking the assistance of a court of equity, accident means not merely inevitable casualty, or the act of God, or, as it is called, *Vis major*, but also such unforeseen events, misfortunes, losses, acts, or omissions as are not the result of negligence or misconduct.

Against the consequences arising from the accidental loss, or destruction, of a deed, the courts will grant relief. In the case of the loss of a negotiable instrument, see Bills of Exchange Act 1882, ss. 69, 70.

In the Social Security Act 1975 the word is used in the popular and ordinary sense and means a mishap or untoward event not expected or designed.

ACCOMMODATION BILL. A bill to which a person has put his name, whether as drawer, acceptor, or indorser, without consideration, for the purpose of accommodating some other party who desires to raise money on it. The accommodation party thus becoming liable upon it, may, if compelled to pay, have his remedy over against the person accommodated. [ACCEPTANCE OF A BILL: BILL OF EXCHANGE.]

ACCOMMODATION LAND. Land bought by a builder or speculator who erects houses thereon and then leases portions thereof upon an improved ground rent.

ACCOMMODATION WORKS. Works such as gates, bridges, etc., which the railways are required to make and maintain for the accommodation of the owners and occupiers of land adjoining the railway.

ACCOMPLICE. A person associated with another in the commission of a criminal offence, whether as principal or accessory before or after the fact, or committing, procuring, or aiding and abetting. See *Davies* v. *Director of Public Prosecutions*, [1954] 1 All E.R. 507, H.L.

ACCORD AND SATISFACTION. An agreement between the party injuring and the party injured, by reason of any trespass or breach of contract; which when performed is a bar to all actions on account of the injury, the party injured having thereby received satisfaction for, or redress of, the injury. [SATISFACTION.]

ACCOUNT or **ACCOMPT.** 1. Open, or current: Where the balance is not struck or is not accepted by all the parties. Formerly an "action of account" lay to obtain a statement, but now recourse is usually had to the Chancery Division, where the account may be obtained summarily under R.S.C., 1965, Ord. 43.

2. Stated: An account no longer open or current, but closed by the statement, agreed to by both the parties, of a balance due to the one or other of them. Action will usually be brought thereon in the Queen's Bench Division and the writ indorsed with a statement of claim enabling the plaintiff to take summary proceedings under R.S.C., 1965, Ord. 14.

3. Settled: Where discharged. Sometimes used to mean an account stated.

ACCOUNTABLE RECEIPT. A written acknowledgment of the receipt of money or goods to be accounted for by the receiver.

ACCOUNTANT-GENERAL. [PAYMASTER-GENERAL.]

ACCRETION. Generally synonymous with accruer. [ACCRUE.] But the word is specially used to denote an accession to an owner of land on the sea shore, or fresh land recovered from the sea by alluvion or dereliction.

As to the annexation of accretions from the sea by adjoining parishes, see s. 72 of the Local Government Act 1972. [ALLUVION; DERELICTION.]

ACCROACH, or **ACCROCHE** (Fr. *accrocher*, to fix or hook), means attempting to exercise royal power.

ACCRUE. *Lit.* to grow to, as interest accrues to principal. It also means to arise, as when a cause of action is said not to have accrued to the plaintiff within six years, *actio non accrevit infra sex annos.*

ACCUMULATION. When the interest of a fund, instead of being paid over to some person or persons, is itself invested as often as it accrues, so as to be reserved for the benefit of some person or persons in the future, the income is said to be accumulated. Restrictions are imposed upon accumulation, partly by the rules against perpetuities [PERPETUITY], and partly by the Law of Property Act 1925, ss. 164–166.

ACCUMULATIVE JUDGMENT OR SENTENCE. A sentence passed on a person already under sentence for a crime; the second sentence to commence after the expiration of the first and not to run concurrently.

ACKNOWLEDGMENT. 1. Of debt, if in writing signed by the debtor or his agent, will prevent the limitation period from running except as from the date of such acknowledgment. Similarly, as regards acknowledgment of title to land. Limitation Act 1939, ss. 23, 24.

2. Of signature to a will by testator. If the signature be not made in the presence of two witnesses its subsequent acknowledgment in their presence will satisfy the Wills Act 1837.

ACKNOWLEDGMENT OF DEEDS, BY MARRIED WOMEN. This was formerly required in cases where a married woman conveyed her separate property by deed. The necessity for such acknowledgment was abolished by the Law of Property Act 1925, s. 167.

ACKNOWLEDGMENT OF RIGHT TO PRODUCTION OF DOCUMENTS. If a vendor retains any portion of the property to which title-deeds relate he is entitled to retain the deeds, and will give to the purchaser an acknowledgment of right to production and to copies, and an undertaking for safe custody. If the whole property is disposed of but to two or more separate purchasers, the largest purchaser will take the deeds and give acknowledgment and undertaking. See s. 64 of the Law of Property Act 1925, which deals with the effect of an acknowledgment.

ACQUIESCENCE. Consent either express or implied. A means by which a right may be lost, though the party entitled thereto might have asserted it successfully had he presented his claim in due time.

ACQUISITIVE PRESCRIPTION. Prescription whereby a right is acquired, otherwise called positive prescription. [PRESCRIPTION.]

ACQUITTAL (Fr. *Acquitter*; Lat. *Acquietare*, to discharge, or keep in quiet).

1. A deliverance, and setting free from the suspicion or guilt of an offence. Thus he that is discharged of a criminal offence by judgment, on its merits, if subsequently charged with the same, or legally the same offence, may plead *autrefois acquit.*

2. To be free from entries and molestations by a superior lord for services issuing out of lands. [QUIT RENT; RENT.]

ACQUITTANCE. A discharge in writing of a sum of money, or other duty which ought to be paid or done. If under seal, it is called a release.

ACT IN PAIS (Fr. *Pais*, or *Pays* country). An act done "in the country," *e.g.*, an ordinary conveyance, as distinguished from an act done in court, which is a matter of record. [MATTER, 2.]

ACT OF ATTAINDER. An Act of Parliament passed for attainting a person, or rendering a person liable to the consequences of attainder. [ATTAINDER.]

ACT OF BANKRUPTCY. An act or event done or suffered by a person, which would be available within three months as the ground for a petition by a creditor or creditors to the amount of £200 for a receiving order against the debtor's estate. Enumerated in Bankruptcy Act 1914. [ADJUDICATION; BANKRUPT.]

ACT OF GOD. A phrase which may be defined as an extraordinary occurrence or circumstance which could not have been foreseen and which could not have been guarded against; an accident due to natural causes, as *e.g.* a destructive storm, or a sudden and unforeseen death (*cf.* VIS MAJOR).

ACT OF GRACE. An Act of Parliament proceeding from the Crown in the first instance instead of receiving royal assent after passing through parliament, *e.g.*, an Act at the commencement of a reign granting pardons. In Scotland an Act so termed was passed in 1696 for providing maintenance for debtors imprisoned by their creditors.

ACT OF INDEMNITY. [INDEMNITY ACT.]

ACT OF LAW. An event happening otherwise than by act of party. Specially title so acquired. Thus, before 1926, the eldest son of an intestate succeeded to his father's real estate by act of law. Also remedy given by law, *viz.*, retainer by executor, or remitter (*q.v.*).

ACT OF PARLIAMENT. A statute; a law made by the legislature, the Queen, lords, and commons in parliament assembled.

See, however, the provisions of the Parliament Acts 1911 and 1949.

Acts of parliament are of three kinds:—
1. Public.
2. Local or special.
3. Private or personal.

[STATUTE.]

ACT OF SETTLEMENT, 1700, by which the crown was settled (on the death of Queen Anne) upon Sophia, Electress of Hanover, and the heirs of her body being Protestants.

ACT OF STATE. An act done by the sovereign power of a country that cannot be challenged in the courts; the exercise of the Royal Prerogative. [PREROGATIVE.]

ACT OF SUPREMACY, 1558, by which the supremacy of the Crown in matters ecclesiastical was established.

ACT OF UNIFORMITY. An Act regulating public worship. Such Acts, were passed in 1548, 1551, 1558, and 1662; the latter, of the reign of Charles II, legalising the Book of Common Prayer at present in use in the Church of England.

The Act of 1551 was repealed in 1969. Those of 1548 and 1558 were repealed, so far as unrepealed, by the Church of England (Worship and Doctrine) Measure 1974. The latter Measure also repealed the Act of Uniformity 1662, except for ss. 10, 15. The effect of the Measure of 1974 is that the General Synod of the Church of England may sanction alternative forms of service but the forms of service contained in the Book of Common Prayer *must* continue to be available for use.

ACTA EXTERIORA INDICANT INTERIORA SECRETA. Acts indicate the intention.

ACTIO PERSONALIS MORITUR CUM PERSONA. [ACTIONS PERSONAL.]

ACTION (Lat. *Actio*). The lawful demand of one's right. It is defined by Justinian, *jus prosequendi in judicio quod alicui debetur*; a right of prosecuting, in a judicial proceeding, that which is due to any one. Now generally used to denote the actual pursuit of this right, or the means of its exercise. In this view, *i.e.*, with reference to the right enforced or redress obtained, actions are divided into *civil* and *penal*, and also into *real, personal,* and *mixed.* [ACTIONS CIVIL AND PENAL; ACTIONS MIXED; ACTIONS REAL AND PERSONAL.]

ACTION OF THE WRIT. A phrase used when the defendant pleaded some matter by which he showed that the plaintiff had no cause to have the writ he brought, though it might well be that he might have another writ or action for the same matter. Now obsolete.

ACTION ON THE CASE (Lat. *Actio super casum*). A remedy, given by the Statute of Westminster the Second, 1285, for wrongs and injuries causing indirect damage, *e.g.* trespass, and so called because commenced by newly-framed writs in which the plaintiff's whole case or cause of complaint was set forth at length. [TRESPASS.]

ACTIONS CIVIL AND PENAL. A *civil* action is brought to enforce a civil right merely, as if a man seeks to recover a sum of money formerly lent, etc. A *penal* action aims at some penalty or punishment in the party sued, be it corporal or pecuniary; specially an action brought for recovery of the penalties given by statute. [QUI TAM ACTIONS.] *Criminal* actions, usually styled prosecutions, are of a public nature, in the name of the Queen, against one or more individuals accused of a crime. [ACTION.]

ACTIONS MIXED partook of the nature both of real and personal actions, for therein real property was demanded and also personal damages for a wrong sustained. These suits are all abolished. Arrears of rent may be recovered by the landlord by ordinary action, in which the possession of the property may also be

ACTIONS MIXED—*continued.*
recovered. [ACTIONS REAL AND PERSONAL.]

ACTIONS PERSONAL. 1. An action for a personal right, *i.e.*, for a bodily injury or an injury to the reputation. The Law Reform (Miscellaneous Provisions) Act 1934, modifies the effect of the maxim *actio personalis moritur cum persona* (a personal action dies with the person) by making it the general rule that on the death of any person all causes of action subsisting against or vesting in him shall survive against or for the benefit of his estate. But there is no survival of causes of action for defamation or seduction or for inducing one spouse to leave the other.

2. As opposed to real action. [ACTIONS REAL AND PERSONAL.]

ACTIONS POPULAR. [QUI TAM ACTIONS.]

ACTIONS REAL AND PERSONAL.
1. Real actions were the old feudal actions brought for the recovery of land or any freehold interest therein. By an Act of 1833, all the real and mixed actions then in existence were abolished, with four exceptions therein specified. And, of these four, one (the action of "ejectment") was entirely remodelled by the Common Law Procedure Act of 1852, and by the Judicature Act and rules thereunder was superseded by an ordinary action for recovery of land ; and the three others (writ of dower, writ of right of dower, and *quare impedit*), by the Common Law Procedure Act of 1860, were assimilated in their procedure to personal actions. Dower is now abolished.

2. *Actions personal*, as opposed to actions real, are such whereby a man claims a debt, or personal duty, or damages in lieu thereof; and likewise whereby a man claims a satisfaction or damage for some injury done to his person or property. The former are said to be founded on contracts, or to arise *ex contractu vel quasi ex contractu*; the latter upon torts or wrongs, or to arise *ex delicto vel quasi ex delicto*. Of the former nature are all actions for debts, and claims of that nature, non-delivery of goods, and non-performance of agreements; of the latter, all actions for trespass, assaults, defamatory words, and the like. [ACTIONS PERSONAL.]

ACTIVE TRUST. A trust requiring active duties on the part of the trustee. The Statute of Uses (repealed by the Law of Property Act 1925) did not apply to these. [BARE TRUSTEE TRUST.]

ACTOR. The proctor or advocate in civil courts or causes. *Actor* was also a plaintiff, as contrasted with *reus*, a defendant. *Cowel.*

ACTS OF COURT. Legal memoranda in the nature of pleadings formerly used in the Admiralty Courts.

ACTS OF SEDERUNT are ordinances for regulating judicial procedure in the Court of Session in Scotland.

ACTS OF UNION. The incorporation of Wales into the realm was effected by two statutes of Henry VIII, 1535 and 1542. The Union with Scotland Act 1706 united England and Scotland in the reign of Queen Anne. The Union with Ireland Act 1800 (George III) united Great Britain with Ireland from 1st January, 1801 ; but much of the Act was virtually repealed by legislation consequential upon the establishment of the Irish Free State (Eire) in 1922.

ACTUARY (Lat. *Actuarius*). 1. A clerk or scribe who registered the canons and constitutions of a convocation.

2. Now usually a person who calculates the risks and premiums for fire, life, and other insurances.

ACTUS REUS. "I desire to make an observation on the expression *actus reus*. . . . Strictly speaking, though in almost universal use, it derives, I believe, from a mistranslation of the Latin aphorism: *Actus non facit reum nisi mens sit rea.* Properly translated, this means, 'An act does not make *a man* guilty of a crime, unless his mind be also guilty.' It is thus not the *actus* which is *reus*, but the man and his mind respectively. Before the understanding of the Latin tongue has wholly died out of these islands, it is as well to record this as it has frequently led to confusion." *Haughton* v. *Smith*, [1973] 3 All E.R. 1109, H.L., *per* Lord Hailsham of St. Marylebone, L.C.

AD MEDIUM FILUM AQUAE. To the centre line of the stream.

AD MEDIUM FILUM VIAE. To the centre of the road.

AD HOC. Where there is no settlement or trust for sale under which equitable interests can be overreached (*i.e.*, a purchaser takes free from them) the estate owner can overreach them by creating a trust for sale or a settlement for the purpose (*ad hoc*). It is provided by the Law of Property Act 1925, s. 2 (2), as amended by the Law of Property (Amendment) Act 1926, Schedule, that where a legal estate which is burdened with an equitable interest is subject to a trust for sale, the equitable interest, even though it has priority to the trust for sale, shall be overreached by a conveyance under the trust, provided that the trustees are either (*a*) two or more individuals approved or appointed by the court or the successors in office of the individuals so approved or appointed; or (*b*) a trust corporation. This statutory innovation enables a trust for sale to be created, where none already exists, with the object of overreaching an equity. This is called an "*ad hoc*" trust for sale. For example, if land is held by a beneficial owner in his own right (*i.e.*, subject neither to a strict settlement nor to a trust for sale) but burdened by the payment of a rent charge, which impedes the passing of an absolute title to a purchaser, all that the owner need do is to take advantage of the statute by creating a trust for sale with trustees of the specified kind. The effect of a conveyance by the trustees will then be to create a trust in the proceeds of sale in favour of the chargee, and to give an absolute title to the purchaser.

An alternative method open to the owner is to create an "*ad hoc*" settlement (Settled Land Act 1925, s. 21). He must execute a vesting deed declaring that the legal estate is vested in him upon trust to give effect to all equitable interests affecting the estate, and the deed must appoint as trustees, either a trust corporation, or two or more persons approved or appointed by the court. The result is that the land becomes settled land within the meaning of the Settled Land Act, and the owner as tenant for life under the settlement can make a conveyance to a purchaser which will overreach equitable interests to the same extent and within the same limits as where a conveyance is made by approved trustees for sale.

AD IDEM. Tallying in the essential point. There must be *consensus ad idem* in a valid contract.

AD [...] one ho[...] that so[...] the ki[...]

[...] app[...] beh[...] lit[...]

[...] common la[...] to hold a seco[...] authority is also give[n] Coroners Act 1887.

AD OSTIUM ECCLESIAE (at [...] door of the church). One of the five species of dower formerly recognised. After Edward IV it fell into total disuse and was abolished in 1833.

AD QUOD DAMNUM. 1. A writ which, at common law, used to be sued out before the Crown granted certain liberties, as a fair, market, or such-like, which might be prejudicial to others.

2. A writ to be sued out whenever it was proposed to alter the course of a common highway, for the purpose of inquiring whether the change might in any way be prejudicial to the public.

3. A similar writ was given by a statute of 1299 (Edward I), preliminary to a licence being granted by the Crown to alienate in mortmain.

All are now obsolete.

AD SECTAM (at the suit of). Used, generally, in its abbreviated forms *ads.* and *ats.*, in the designation of the title of an action when the defendant's name is placed first. Thus, the suit *Brown* v. *Smith* may also be described Smith *ats.* Brown.

AD TERMINUM QUI PRAETERIT. A writ of entry which formerly lay for the lessor or his heirs after the term granted had expired, and the lands were withheld. Other remedies were provided by the Landlord and Tenant Act 1730, and the Distress for Rent Act 1737; and the writ itself was abolished. [DOUBLE RENT; DOUBLE VALUE.]

AD VALOREM (according to the value). A duty, the amount of which depends upon the value of the property taxed, is called an *ad valorem* duty.

INSPICIENDUM, *do*. 1. A writ formerly dow was suspected of child, in order to produce eir to an estate, to examine ere with child or not. Now

rase was also used sometimes to e the order of a court (before whom an was capitally convicted and ed in stay of execution that she was k with child), directing a jury of mat- ns to inquire into the fact. [JURY OF MATRONS.]

AD VITAM AUT CULPAM (for life or until misbehaviour). [QUAMDIU BENE SE GESSERIT.]

ADAPTATION. In the case of a literary or dramatic work, this means (*a*) the conversion of a non-dramatic into a dramatic work, or vice-versa; (*b*) a translation of the work; (*c*) the conversion of the work into picture form; or (*d*) in relation to a musical work, an arrangement or transcription of the work. Copyright Act 1956, s. 2 (6).

ADDITION. A title given to a man besides his proper name and surname; that is to say, of what estate, degree, or mystery he is, and of what town, hamlet, or country.

ADDRESS FOR SERVICE. Address given by one party to an action or proceedings for service of notices, etc., by the other. As to address to be given by plaintiff, see R.S.C., 1965, Ord. 6.

ADEMPTION OF A LEGACY is the implied revocation of a bequest in a will by some subsequent act of the testator; as when a specific chattel is bequeathed, and the testator afterwards sells it; or when a parent bequeaths a legacy to his child, and afterwards makes a provision for the child in satisfaction thereof. [SATISFACTION.]

ADHERENCE. The action by which, in Scotland, the mutual obligation of marriage may be enforced by either party. It corresponds to the former English action for the restitution of conjugal rights.

ADHERENT. Being *adherent* to the Queen's enemies, as by giving them aid, intelligence, or the like, constitutes high treason, by the Treason Act 1351.

ADJOURN. To put off the hearing of a case to a future day or *sine die*. Usually in discretion of the court.

ADJOURNED SUMMONS. A summons taken out in the chambers of a judge of the Chancery Division may be "adjourned" from the master to the judge in chambers, or if of sufficient importance direct into open court to be argued by counsel.

ADJUDICATION. 1. The giving of judgment; a sentence or decree; as in the expression, it was adjudged for the plaintiff, etc.

2. An adjudication of bankruptcy, or that A B was adjudicated a bankrupt following the making of a receiving order if no composition was accepted. [BANKRUPT.]

3. By Commissioners of Inland Revenue as to amount of stamp duty chargeable upon a document where in case of doubt application has been made to them under s. 12 of the Stamp Act 1891. A stamp indicating their decision is impressed or affixed. There is an appeal to the High Court.

ADJURATION. A swearing or binding upon oath.

ADJUSTMENT, in marine insurance, is the settling of the amount of the loss, and of the indemnity which the assured is entitled to receive, and, in the case of several underwriters, of the proportion which each underwriter is liable to pay in respect thereof. Average (*q.v.*) may be the subject of adjustment. Marine Insurance Act 1906.

ADMEASUREMENT OF DOWER (Lat. *Admensuratio dotis*). A writ, now abolished, which lay for the heir against a widow, who held from the heir or his guardian more land as dower than she was by law entitled to. [DOWER.]

ADMEASUREMENT OF PASTURE (Lat. *Admensuratio pasturae*). An old writ which lay for surcharge of pasture. [SURCHARGE OF COMMON.]

ADMINISTRATION has several significations. The Queen's ministers, or collectively the ministry, are not infrequently called the *Administration*, as charged with the administration or management of public affairs. The administration of justice by judges, magistrates, etc.

The affairs of a bankrupt may be said to be *administered* by his trustee; and the affairs of an absent person, by his agent, factor, or attorney, etc. But the word is specially used in reference to the following case:—

The administration of a deceased's estate; that is, getting in the debts due to the deceased, and paying his creditors to the extent of his assets, and otherwise distributing his estate to the persons who are by law entitled thereto. The person charged with this duty is spoken of as "executor" or "administrator," according as he has been appointed by the deceased in his will, or by the Chancery Division. See also the Administration of Estates Act 1925, and the Judicature Act 1925. Also applied to the execution of a trust. [ADMINISTRATION SUIT; ADMINISTRATOR; EXECUTION; EXECUTOR.]

ADMINISTRATION SUIT. A suit instituted in Chancery for the administration of a deceased's estate. This suit may be instituted by an executor or administrator, or any person interested in the deceased's estate as creditor, legatee, next of kin, etc. Where, however, there is no doubt as to the solvency of a deceased's estate, the proper course for a creditor is not to institute an administration suit, but to sue the deceased's representative at law. Administration proceedings are now usually taken by originating summons (q.v.).

It may be for general administration or for the furnishing of particulars, accounts, or certain other limited purposes. R.S.C., 1965, Ord. 85.

ADMINISTRATOR is one to whom the administration of the estate of a deceased is committed by letters of administration from the Chancery Division of the High Court of Justice, in cases where the deceased left no will. After 1925, administration is not to be granted to more than four persons in respect of the same property, and if there is a minority or if a life interest arises under the intestacy, administration must be granted either to a Trust Corporation, with or without an individual, or to not less than two individuals—see s. 160 of the Judicature Act 1925. If the administrator dies his executors are not administrators, but a new administration may be granted, of such of the goods as remain to be administered, to some person, who is then called an administrator *de bonis non.* So administration may be granted *durante absentia,* when the executor acting under a will is out of the realm; or *pendente lite,* where the validity of the will itself is questioned; or *cum testamento annexo,* where the testator has left a will and has not appointed an executor, or has appointed an executor who is either unable or unwilling to act. If a stranger, that is not administrator nor executor, takes the goods of the deceased, and administers of his own wrong, he shall be charged and sued not as an administrator, but as an executor *de son tort.* [EXECUTOR DE SON TORT.] There is also another sort of administrator, where one makes his will, and makes an infant his sole executor. Here administration will be committed to his guardian or to such other person as the Court thinks fit, during the minority of the executor, *durante minore aetate.* (See the Judicature Act 1925, s. 165.) And this administration ceases when the infant comes of age. Also administration *ad colligenda bona,* for temporary purposes in case of perishables, etc. See, generally, the Judicature Act 1925, and the Administration of Estates Act 1925. The word "administrator" is also used to designate the officer appointed by the Crown to administer the property of a person convicted of treason or felony. [ADMINISTRATION.]

ADMINISTRATIVE LAW. The body of law which deals with the powers of the executive or administrative organs of the state. It relates particularly to their legislative, judicial and quasi-judicial powers.

ADMINISTRATRIX. A woman to whom administration is granted. [ADMINISTRATION; ADMINISTRATOR.]

ADMIRAL, or Lord High Admiral, was formerly defined as a high officer that had the government of the navy, and the hearing and determining of all causes, as well civil as criminal, belonging to the sea; and for that purpose had a court called the Admiralty. His functions in the government of the navy, however, were committed to the Lords, or Lords Commissioners, of the Admiralty, who were appointed by letters patent to perform them, and of whom one was First Lord. See now, as to the functions of the Defence Council and the Admiralty Board, the Defence (Transfer of Functions) Act 1964.

ADMIRALTY. The Probate, Divorce and Admiralty Division of the High Court of Justice, created by the Judicature Act, 1873, so far as regards admiralty, succeeded to the *civil* jurisdiction of the High Court of Admiralty. It had jurisdiction over claims for salvage, damage arising by collision or otherwise on the high seas and other maritime causes. There were two divisions of the jurisdiction of the Admiralty Division of the High Court, the Prize Court and the Instance Court. The admiralty jurisdiction of the High Court was later set out in s. 1 of the Administration of Justice Act 1956, and included jurisdiction to hear claims to the possession and ownership of ships or stores therein, claims for damage done or received by a ship, claims for death or injury arising from any defect, etc., in a ship, claims for loss of or damage to cargo or goods, etc.

Part I of the Administration of Justice Act 1956 was amended by the Administration of Justice Act 1970, which established a new Admiralty Court as part of the Queen's Bench Division of the High Court.

Proceedings on indictment for *criminal* offences within the jurisdiction of the Admiralty are now brought before the Crown Court established by the Courts Act 1971.

As to county court jurisdiction, see s. 55 of the County Courts Act 1959.

ADMISSION is when the patron presents to a vacant benefice, and the bishop, upon examination, admits the clerk. In the same sense a man is said to be admitted to a corporation, or to the freedom of a city, on having complied with the preliminary conditions. The admission of a solicitor is when, having served his articles and been examined, he is, on conforming to certain regulations, admitted to the privileges of his profession. Personal attendance before the Master of the Rolls is not now necessary.

ADMISSIONS, in *evidence*, are the testimony which the party admitting bears to the truth of a fact against himself. In practice these are usually made in writing by the solicitors in an action, in order to save the expense of formal proof. R.S.C., 1965, Ord. 27 [NOTICE TO ADMIT.] By the Judicature Act all allegations in pleadings not specifically denied are taken to be admitted.

ADMITTANCE. The admission, either on a surrender or on descent, of the tenant by the lord of the manor into the possession of a copyhold estate; whereby the tenant's title to his estate was said to be perfected. Copyholds were abolished by Part V of Law of Property Act 1922, taking effect as from 1st January, 1926. [SURRENDER, 3.]

ADMITTENDO CLERICO. A writ, now obsolete, which lay after judgment in action of *quare impedit*, and was directed to the bishop, requiring him to admit his, the patron's, clerk. [QUARE IMPEDIT.]

ADMONITION. A judical reprimand to an accused person on being discharged from further prosecution. Specially in ecclesiastical proceedings—the lightest punishment. [MONITION.]

AMORTIZATION. [AMORTIZATION.]

ADOPTION. An act by which the rights and duties of the natural parents of a child are extinguished, and equivalent rights and duties (*e.g.*, as to custody, maintenance, education, etc.) become vested in the adopter or adopters, to whom the child then stands in all respects as if born to them in lawful wedlock. See generally Part I of the Children Act 1975.

ADOPTION SOCIETY. A body of persons whose functions consist of or include the making of arrangements for the adoption of children. Adoption societies must be approved and registered under the provisions of the Adoption Act 1958 and Part I of the Children Act 1975.

ADOPTIVE ACTS. Acts of Parliament which come into operation in particular districts upon being adopted, in manner prescribed therein, by the local authorities or inhabitants of that district.

ADPROMISOR (Roman Law), an accessory to a promise, as guarantor.

ADULT. A person who has attained the age of seventeen may be tried summarily on information as an adult under s. 19 of the Magistrates' Courts Act 1952.

ADULTERATION. The admixture with an article intended for food or medicinal use of any other substance, whether noxious or harmless, or the abstraction of any constituent part whereby the quality, substance or nature of the article is injuriously affected and the purchaser is prejudiced. The law relating to the adulteration of food and drugs was consolidated by the Food and Drugs Act 1955.

ADULTERY. Voluntary sexual intercourse during the subsistence of the marriage between one spouse and a person of the opposite sex not the other spouse. It is one of various facts which may be put before a divorce court in proof that a marriage has irretrievably broken down. See s. 1 of the Matrimonial Causes Act 1973.

ADVANCE ON FREIGHT. A sum paid in advance by the charterer of a ship or his agent on account of freight to become due. [FREIGHT.]

ADVANCEMENT. That which is given to a child by a father, or other person standing *in loco parentis*, in anticipation of what the child might inherit. As to powers of advancement, see s. 32 of the Trustee Act 1925. [PORTION; SATISFACTION.]

ADVANCEMENT CLAUSE. Frequently inserted in wills or settlements authorising the trustees to realise a portion (say one-half) of a beneficiary's share for his advancement, *e.g.*, purchase of a business. See now s. 32 of the Trustee Act 1925 under which the amount so paid is not to exceed one-half of the presumptive or vested share of the beneficiary. The maintenance clause formerly inserted dealt only with the *income* of the share, and is now covered by the Trustee Act 1925, s. 31.

ADVENTURE. The sending to sea of a ship or goods at the risk of the sender. Almost obsolete term. [CONSIGNMENT.]

ADVENTURE, BILL OF. A writing signed by a merchant stating that the property in goods shipped in his name belongs to another at whose risk the goods are and covenanting to account for the produce.

ADVERSE POSSESSION. Where one person is in possession of property under any title, and another person claims to be the rightful owner of the property under a different title, the possession of the former is said to be an "adverse possession" with reference to the latter. A rightful owner neglecting to assert his claim within a given period (defined, according to the circumstances of the case, by the Limitation Act 1939) is henceforth barred of his right thereto. [LIMITATION; OCCUPANCY.] This is to be distinguished from prescription (*q.v.*).

ADVERSE WITNESS. A witness hostile to the party calling him, who may, with the leave of the court, cross-examine him.

ADVERTISEMENT. Includes any notice, circular, label, wrapper, invoice or other document, and any public announcement made orally or by any means of producing or transmitting light or sound: Food and Drugs Act 1955, s. 135. It is an offence under the Act to publish any advertisement which falsely describes any food or drug, or which is calculated to mislead as to its nature, substance or quality.

As to advertisements in television programmes, see ss. 8, 9 of the Independent Broadcasting Authority Act 1973. Illuminated signs and hoardings are included in the expression by s. 290 (1) of the Town and Country Planning Act 1971.

ADVICE, LETTER OF. A notification by one person to another in respect of a business transaction in which they are mutually engaged, *e.g.*, by consignor to consignee, of goods having been forwarded to him; or by one merchant to another of the drawing of bills upon him.

ADVICE ON EVIDENCE. Advice given by counsel, after the close of pleadings, on the evidence that it will be necessary to call to support his client's case.

ADVISORY, CONCILIATION AND ARBITRATION SERVICE. A body set up under the Employment Protection Act 1975, Part I, to promote the improvement of industrial relations. As well as arbitrating in trade disputes and giving free advice it may issue codes of practice.

ADVOCATE. A person privileged to plead for another in court. Formerly, in England, confined to those who practised in the Ecclesiastical and Admiralty Courts, but now that these courts have been thrown open to all barristers-at-law, the title has lost its distinctive meaning. In Scotland, barristers practising before the Supreme

ADVOCATE—*continued.*
Court are called advocates. [ADVOCATES, FACULTY OF.]

ADVOCATE, QUEEN'S. Formerly a member of the College of Advocates, appointed by letters patent, who had to advise the Crown in questions involving ecclesiastical and international law. The College of Advocates was abolished in 1857.

ADVOCATE, LORD. [LORD ADVOCATE.]

ADVOCATES, FACULTY OF. In Scotland the barristers practising before the Supreme Court are called *advocates.* The Faculty of Advocates is a corporate body, consisting of the members of the bar in Edinburgh, founded in 1532, the members of which are entitled to plead in every court in Scotland, and in the House of Lords.

ADVOW, or **AVOW** (Lat. *Advocare*; Fr. *Avouer*). To justify or maintain an act formerly done. [REPLEVIN.]

ADVOWEE, or **AVOWEE** (Lat. *Advocatus*), is he who had a right to present to a benefice. So *advowee paramount* was, by the Statute of Provisors, 1351 (repealed), taken for the king, the highest patron.

ADVOWSON (Lat. *Advocatio*). The right to present to a benefice (Stat. West 2, 1285), the *jus patronatus* of the Canon Law. Advowsons are either *appendant* or *in gross,* or partly the one and partly the other. An advowson is *appendant* when it is annexed to the possession of a manor and passes with it; *in gross,* belonging to the person of its owner. Or if a partial right of presentation be granted to a stranger, the advowson may be *appendant* for the term of the lord, and *in gross* for the term of the stranger. Advowsons are also said to be *presentative* or *collative.* An advowson is *presentative* when the patron has the right to present his clerk to the bishop, and to demand his institution if he be qualified; *collative* when the bishop and patron are one and the same person so that the bishop performs by one act (*collation*), the separate acts of presentation and institution. There was formerly a third species, *viz., donative,* when the patron by a *donation* could place the clerk into possession without presentation, institution, or induction; but all

donative benefices were converted into *presentative* by the Benefices Act 1898. As to restrictions on the sale of advowsons, see the Benefices Act 1898 (Amendment) Measure 1923. [APPROPRIATION.]

ADVOWTRY. Adultery.

AERODROME. Any area of land or water designed, equipped, set apart or commonly used for affording facilities for the landing and departure of aircraft including any area or space which is designed, equipped or set apart for affording facilities for the landing and departure of aircraft capable of descending or climbing vertically: Civil Aviation Act 1949, s. 63, as substituted by the Civil Aviation Act 1968, s. 28.

AFFIDAVIT (Lat. *Affido*). A statement in writing and on oath, sworn before some one who has authority to administer it.

AFFIDAVIT OF DOCUMENTS. [DISCOVERY.]

AFFIDAVIT OF INCREASE. An affidavit filed for the purposes of taxation of costs, verifying such payments, *e.g.,* counsels' and witnesses' fees, which do not appear on the face of the proceedings. This affidavit is ordinarily only required in practice where the opposite party disputes any of the alleged payments or the taxing officer specially requires it.

AFFIDAVIT TO HOLD TO BAIL. An old form of procedure under the Judgments Act 1838, whereby a debtor about to abscond could be held to bail in an amount not exceeding the amount in the cause of action. Replaced by the provision for arrest under s. 6 of the Debtors Act 1869 itself now limited by the Administration of Justice Act 1970.

AFFILIATION. The process by which a single woman or married woman living apart from her husband applies to a justice of the peace for a summons to be served on the man alleged by her to be the father of a child born, or to be born, to her. The summons is to appear before a magistrates' court for the petty sessions area, who are to hear the evidence on both sides. If the woman's evidence is corroborated in some material particular by other testimony, to the satisfaction of the justices, they may adjudge the man to be the *putative father* of the child in question, and make an affiliation order on him for the payment to the mother of a weekly sum of money for its maintenance up to 13 or 16 years of age. See the Affiliation Proceedings Act 1957, and the Maintenance Orders Act 1968.

AFFINITY. The relationship resulting from marriage, between the husband and the blood relations of the wife; and also between the wife and the blood relations of the husband. By s. 1 of the Marriage Act 1949 marriages between certain degrees of kindred and affinity are prohibited. The prohibited degrees of relationship are set out in Sched. 1 to that Act. [CONSANGUINITY.]

AFFIRM. To ratify or confirm a former law or judgment. Hence a court of appeal is said to affirm the judgment of the court below. To *affirm* also means to make a solemn declaration, equivalent to a statement upon oath. [AFFIRMATION.]

AFFIRMANTI NON NEGANTI INCUMBIT PROBATIO. The burden of proof is on him who alleges, and not on him who denies.

AFFIRMATION. The testimony given either in open court, or in writing, of those who are permitted to give their evidence without having an oath administered to them, as all persons objecting to take an oath are now enabled by law to do. Oaths Act 1888.

AFFIRMATIVE, THE (as opposed to the negative), is some positive fact or circumstance which is alleged to be or to have been, and which is generally therefore to be proved, according to the rule of law "that the affirmative of the issue must be proved." [RIGHT TO BEGIN.]

AFFOREST. To turn ground into forest.

AFFRAY (Fr. *Effrayer*, to affright or scare). The essence of the common law offence of affray was formerly thought to be that two or more persons fought together to the terror of the Queen's subjects. It is not, as previously thought, a necessary ingredient of the offence that it should be committed in a public place. See *Button* v. *Director of Public Prosecutions*, [1965] 3 All E.R. 587, H.L. Nor need two or more persons fight together: one person acting alone may cause an affray. See *Taylor* v. *Director of Public Prosecutions*, [1973] 2 All E.R. 1108, H.L.

AFFREIGHTMENT (Lat. *Affretamentum*). The freight of a ship. The contract of affreightment is either by charterparty or bill of lading (*q.v.*). [FREIGHT.]

AFORETHOUGHT. A word used to define the premeditation which generally distinguishes murder from manslaughter. It matters not in law for how short a time this premeditation may have been conceived in the mind. [MALICE.]

AFTER-MATH. The second crop of grass; or the right to have the last crop of grass or pasturage.

AGAINST THE FORM OF THE STATUTE. A phrase used to indicate that the matter complained of, whether in an action or an indictment, was prohibited by statute. Now, although the words are still commonly used, they are not of essential importance.

AGE. The periods of life when men and women are enabled by law to do that which before, for want of age and consequently of judgment, they could not legally do. [DOLI CAPAX; FULL AGE; INFANT.]

AGENCY, DEED OF. A revocable and voluntary trust for payment of the settlor's debts.

AGENT. A person authorised, expressly or impliedly, to act for another, who is thence called the principal, and who is, in consequence of, and to the extent of, the authority delegated by him, bound by the acts of his agent. This term includes most kinds of agents, such as factors and brokers, and the stewards of landowners. It is also usually applied to designate the London solicitor acting on the instructions of the solicitor in the country. Agents may be either *general*, who can bind their principals in all matters of a class, or *special*, in a particular transaction only. The agent is not usually personally liable. [DEL CREDERE COMMISSION.]

AGENT OF NECESSITY. A person who pledges the credit of another when urgent reasons make it necessary to do so, *e.g.*, the master of a ship purchasing goods necessary for the continuance of his voyage, or (formerly) a deserted wife ordering necessaries for herself and her children. Such acts are binding upon the principal.

The power of a wife to pledge her husband's credit, as agent of necessity, in

AGENT OF NECESSITY—*continued.* respect of either household necessaries or legal costs, was abolished by s. 41 of the Matrimonial Proceedings and Property Act 1970, itself now repealed by the Matrimonial Causes Act 1973. The authority which a wife has while still running her husband's household is not affected.

AGGRAVATED ASSAULTS. Distinguished from common assaults, *e.g.*, offences against boys under 14, or women. See the Offences against the Person Act 1861, s. 43.

AGGRAVATED BURGLARY. [BURGLARY.]

AGGRAVATION, or *matter of aggravation*, is that which is introduced into a pleading for the purpose of increasing the amount of damages, but which does not affect the right of action itself.

AGIO. The difference in value between metallic and paper money, or between different kinds of metallic money.

AGIST (Fr. *Giste*, a bed or resting-place; Lat. *Stabulari*). Agistment now generally means the taking in by any one (not as formerly by officers of the king's forest only) of other men's cattle to graze in his ground at a certain rate per week, or the payment made for so doing. See s. 19 of the Agricultural Holdings Act 1948, as to privilege of agisted cattle from distraint. There is also an *agistment* of sea-banks, *viz.*, where lands are charged to keep up the sea-banks, and are hence termed *terræ agistatæ*.

AGNATES (Lat. *Agnati*), in Scotch law, are relations on the father's side; as cognates (*cognati*) are relations through the mother. A distinction derived from the Roman law, according to which the *agnati* were the legal relations, and the *cognati* the natural relations.

AGREEMENT (said to be from the Latin *Aggregatio mentium*) is the consent or joining together of two minds in respect of anything done or to be done; also the written evidence of such consent. An agreement, or *contract*, exists either where a promise is made on one side, and assented to on the other; or where two or more persons enter into an engagement with each other, by a promise on either side. [CONTRACT.]

AGRICULTURAL BUILDINGS. Buildings (other than dwellings) occupied together with agricultural land or being or forming part of a market garden, and in either case used solely in connection with agricultural operations thereon. For the full definition see s. 26 (4) of the General Rate Act 1967 as extended by the Rating Act 1971.

AGRICULTURAL HOLDING. The aggregate of the agricultural land comprised in a contract of tenancy. See the Agricultural Holdings Act 1948, s. 1.

AGRICULTURAL LAND. Land let substantially for agricultural purposes, and so used for the purposes of a trade or business. Agricultural Holdings Act 1948, s. 1. It is also defined by s. 26 (3) of the General Rate Act 1967, as extended by the Rating Act 1971, to mean any land used as arable meadow or pasture ground only, land used for a plantation or wood, etc., certain cottage gardens, orchards, allotments, livestock buildings, buildings occupied in connection with beekeeping, etc., but excluding other classes of land such as parks, pleasure grounds and race-courses.

AGRICULTURE. Includes horticulture, fruit growing, seed growing, dairy farming and livestock breeding and keeping, the use of land as grazing land, meadow land, osier land, market gardens and nursery grounds and the use of land for woodlands where that is ancillary to the farming of land for other agricultural purposes. See the Agriculture Act 1947, s. 109.

AGRICULTURE, FISHERIES AND FOOD, MINISTRY OF. Constituted by the Ministry of Agriculture and Fisheries Act 1919, which replaced the old Board of Agriculture and Fisheries and its President by a "Ministry" and a "Minister". [BOARD OF AGRICULTURE AND FISHERIES.]

AID (Fr. *Aide*; Lat. *Auxilium*). Sometimes signified a *subsidy* (11 Edw. 3, st. 2, 1337), but more usually a service or payment due from tenants to their lords. This *aid* was demanded for three purposes, *viz.*, to ransom the lord's person, if taken prisoner; to make the lord's eldest son a knight; and to give a marriage portion to the lord's eldest daughter. This imposition, a relic of the old feudal laws, was abolished by the Tenures Abolition Act 1660.

AID AND ABET. [ABET.]

AID AND COMFORT. The giving of aid and comfort to the Queen's enemies in her realm, or elsewhere, is treason under the Treason Act 1351.

AIDER BY VERDICT is where a defect or error in any pleading in an action, which might in the first instance have been objected to by the opposite party, is, after verdict, no longer open to objection; or, in other words, is *cured by the verdict.*

AIR. The enjoyment of air free and unpolluted is a natural right, and interference with such right is actionable unless such interference is by virtue of an easement.

AIR FORCE. Established by the Air Force (Constitution) Act 1917, and now regulated by the Air Force Act 1955, as amended by the Armed Forces Act 1971.

AIR NAVIGATION. For the law regulating flying and the use of aircraft, see principally the Civil Aviation Acts 1949 to 1971, which deal with aerodromes, accidents, dangerous flying, etc., and which provide that flight of an aircraft over property at a reasonable height shall not constitute trespass. For carriage by air see the Carriage by Air Act 1961; and as to the constitution, etc., of the British Airways Board, which exercises general control over B.O.A.C. and B.E.A., see the Civil Aviation Act 1971.

Former enactments relating to civil aerodromes belonging to the British Airports Authority were consolidated in the Airports Authority Act 1975.

AIR TRAVEL RESERVE FUND. A fund set up by the Air Travel Reserve Fund Act 1975, from which payments may be made in respect of losses or liabilities incurred by customers of air travel organisations who are unable to meet their financial commitments.

AIRCRAFT. Any machine for flying, whether propelled by mechanical means or not, and including any description of balloon: Air Force Act 1955, s. 223.

AIRWAY, a passage for the admission of air into a mine.

ALBA FIRMA, or White Rents. A rent payable in white or silver money, and so called to distinguish it from the *reditus*

nigri, or black-mail, which was payable in work, grain and the like. Also called Blanch-firmes.

ALBUS LIBER. An ancient book which contains a compilation of the laws and customs of the City of London.

ALDERMAN (Sax. *Ealdorman,* signifying literally, elder man). An officer who formerly presided with the bishop in the *schyregemote,* taking cognizance of civil questions, while the latter attended to disputes of a spiritual nature. He was *ex officio* a member of the *witanagemote.* His importance declined when the bishop left the shiremote, and the trial of causes was gradually transferred to the superior courts. There were anciently aldermen of the county, and aldermen of the hundred, etc., etc.; and one officer indeed had the title of *aldermannus totius Angliæ.* By the Local Government Act 1888, the title of alderman, which had become confined to the persons associated with the mayor in the government of a city or town corporate, was revived for a proportion of the members of the county councils created by the same Act.

Now, by s. 249 of the Local Government Act 1972, the title of honorary alderman may be conferred on any person who has, in the opinion of a county or district council, rendered eminent services to that council as a past member. No alderman may now serve *as such* on any council.

ALE SILVER. A tribute or rent paid yearly to the Lord Mayor of London by those who sell ale within the liberty of the City.

ALEATORY CONTRACT. One the effect of which depends on an uncertain event.

ALIBI (elsewhere). When an accused person, in order to show that he could not have committed the offence with which he is charged, sets up as his defence that he was *elsewhere* at the time when the crime is alleged to have taken place, this defence is called an *alibi.*

ALIEN (Lat. *Alienus*). Generally a person born outside the dominions of the crown of England, that is, out of the allegiance of the Queen. But to this rule there are some exceptions. Thus, the children of the sovereign, and the heirs of the

ALIEN—*continued.*

Crown, wherever born, have always been held natural-born subjects; and the same rule applies to the children of our ambassadors born abroad. And by various statutes the restrictions of the common law have been gradually relaxed, so that many, who would formerly have come under the definition of an alien, may now be regarded as natural-born subjects to all intents and purposes. See the British Nationality Acts, 1948 to 1965 [CITIZEN OF THE UNITED KINGDOM AND COLONIES; NATURAL-BORN SUBJECTS; NATURALIZATION.] With regard to alien immigration, see the Immigration Act 1971.

ALIEN AMI. An alien born in, or the subject of, a friendly state.

ALIEN ENEMY. An alien born in, or the subject of, a hostile state.

ALIENAGE, DECLARATION OF. It is provided by s. 19 of the British Nationality Act 1948, that any citizen of the United Kingdom and Colonies of full age and capacity who also is a citizen of a dominion or of Eire or is a national of a foreign country may make a declaration of renunciation of citizenship of the United Kingdom and Colonies, which is registered at the Home Office.

ALIENATION. A transferring of property, or the voluntary resignation of an estate by one man, and its acceptance by another.

ALIENE, TO (Fr. *Aliener*, Lat. *Alienare*, to alienate, to put away from one's self). To transfer property to another. Generally used of landed property.

ALIENI JURIS (of another's right). An expression applicable to those who are in the keeping or subject to the authority of another, and have not full control of their person and property. In English law there are generally reckoned three classes of such persons; infants (*i.e.*, minors), married women (in some cases) and persons suffering from mental disorder. [SUI JURIS.]

ALIMENTARY TRUSTS (commonly called protective trusts). Trusts giving a protected interest for life or any less period to a beneficiary. It is usual, *e.g.*, in marriage settlements, to give the husband a determinable life interest so as to ensure that his interest shall be not lost in the event of

his bankruptcy or alienation. On the happening of such an event the trustees may, in their absolute discretion, apply the income of the fund for the benefit of the wife and issue of the husband. For general form of such trusts, see s. 33 of the Trustee Act 1925.

ALIMONY (Lat. *Alimonia*). The former term for an allowance for the support of a wife while the marriage relation continued to exist but the parties had separated. This was called permanent alimony. In causes between husband and wife the husband might be ordered to allow his wife alimony during the suit: called alimony *pendente lite*. See now, as to financial provision, property adjustment orders, and maintenance pending suit, Part II of the Matrimonial Causes Act 1973.

ALIO INTUITU. With another intention, that is, with a purpose other than the ostensible one.

ALITER (otherwise). A phrase used for the sake of brevity in pointing out a distinction.

ALIUD EST CELARE—ALIUD TACERE. Silence is not equivalent to concealment.

ALIUNDE (from another source, from another place, in another way). Thus if, when a case is not made out in the method anticipated, it may be proved *aliunde*, that is, by other and different evidence.

ALL FOURS. A phrase, often used in our courts of justice, to signify that a case or a decision agrees in all its circumstances with some other case or decision.

ALLEGATION. The assertion or statement of a party to a suit or other proceeding (civil or criminal) which he undertakes to prove. Especially is the word used in ecclesiastical suits, in which if a defendant has any circumstances to offer in his defence, he must do so by way of "defensive allegation."

ALLEGIANCE. "The tie which binds the subject to the sovereign, in return for that protection which the sovereign affords the subject." *Bl.* Allegiance is either *natural* and perpetual, or *local* and temporary; the former being such as is due from all men born within the sovereign's dominions immediately upon their birth; the latter, such as is due from an alien, or stranger born, during the time that he continues within the

Queen's dominion and protection and, in certain circumstances, even after he leaves it. For form of oath of allegiance, see the Promissory Oaths Act 1868, s. 2. [ALIEN; NATURAL-BORN SUBJECTS; OATH OF ALLEGIANCE.]

ALLOCATION (Lat. *Allocatio*). Properly a placing or adding to; in law an allowance formerly made upon an account in the Exchequer.

ALLOCATUR (it is allowed). The certificate of the master, or taxing officer of a court, after a solicitor's bill has been *taxed* by him, that the amount certified by him is allowed as costs, or, as they are then called, "taxed costs." [TAXATION OF COSTS.]

ALLODIUM. Free lands, which formerly paid no fines or services, and were not holden of any superior. Opposed to *feuds*, or lands held of a lord in consideration of services to be rendered.

ALLONGE. A slip of paper applied to a bill of exchange, upon which indorsements are written where there is no room for them on the bill itself. Bills of Exchange Act 1882, s. 32 (1).

ALLOTMENT. Share of land assigned on partition or under an enclosure award. As to provision of allotment gardens, etc., for labourers and others, see the Allotments Acts 1908 to 1950.

ALLOTMENT LETTER, of shares in a joint stock company concluding the contract to take shares. Must be stamped.

ALLOTMENT NOTE. A writing by a seaman, whereby he makes an assignment of part of his wages in favour of his wife, father or mother, grandfather or grandmother, brother or sister. Every allotment note must be in an approved form. The allottee, that is, the person in whose favour it is made, may recover the amount before justices of the peace. See the Merchant Shipping Acts 1894 to 1974; Merchant Shipping (Seamen's Allotment) Act 1911.

ALLUVION. Land that is gained from the sea by the washing up of sand and earth, so as in time to make *terra firma*. [DERELICTION.]

ALMONER, or **ALMNER.** An officer of the Queen's house whose duties are now considered fully performed by an attendance at the distribution of royal alms on Maundy Thursday; that is, the Thursday before Easter.

ALMSHOUSE. A house provided for the reception or relief of poor persons. To make a place an almshouse it is not necessary that the inmates should be entirely destitute, or that it should supply all their wants: *Mary Clark Home Trustees* v. *Anderson*, [1904] 2 K.B. 645.

ALODIUM. [ALLODIUM.]

ALTERATION in deeds or other documents generally vitiates the instrument if made in a material part after execution. In deeds presumed to have been made before or at time of execution; in wills, after execution; and see Wills Act 1837, s. 21. As to bills of exchange, see the Bills of Exchange Act 1882.

ALUMNUS. A foster child. One educated at a school or college is called an *alumnus* thereof.

AMALGAMATION. In company law the union by merger of two or more companies. See the Companies Act 1948, s. 208.

AMBASSADOR. A representative sent by one sovereign power to another, with authority conferred on him by letters of credence to treat on affairs of state; the highest rank among diplomatic officials. His person is protected from civil arrest, and his goods from seizure under distress or execution, by the Diplomatic Privileges Act 1964.

AMBIDEXTER. Properly a man that can equally use both his hands; but in a legal sense a juror who takes bribes from both the parties to an action to promote their respective interests. [EMBRACERY.]

AMBIGUITY. Uncertainty of meaning in the words of a written instrument. Where the doubt arises upon the face of the instrument itself, as where a blank is left for a name, the ambiguity is said to be *patent*, as distinguished from a *latent* ambiguity, where the doubt is introduced by collateral circumstances or extrinsic matter, the meaning of the words alone being *prima facie* sufficiently clear and intelligible.

AMBULATORIA EST VOLUNTAS DEFUNCTI USQUE AD VITÆ SUPREMUM EXITUM. The will of a person who dies is revocable up to the last moment of life.

AMENDMENT. A correction of any errors in writ or pleadings in actions or prosecutions. Large powers of amendment have been given by modern statutes. For amendment in civil proceedings, see R.S.C. 1965, Ord. 20, and County Court Rules; and in criminal proceedings, see the Indictments Act 1915, s. 5. Leave of court is usually necessary for amendment of writ in civil proceedings, but there are large powers of amendment of claim or counterclaim without leave.

AMERCIAMENT, or **AMERCEMENT.** A punishment in the nature of a fine; but in old times a fine was a penalty certain, imposed under some statute by a court of record; an amerciament was imposed by a jury at their discretion, whereby the offending party stood *at the mercy* of the lord.

AMICUS CURIÆ (a friend of the court). A bystander, usually a barrister, who informs a judge in court on a point of law or fact on which the judge is doubtful or mistaken.

AMMUNITION. Includes grenades, bombs and other like missiles, whether capable of use with a firearm or not; also containers of noxious liquid or gas: Firearms Act 1968, s. 5 (1), (2).

AMNESTY. An act of pardon by which crimes against the Government up to a certain date are so condoned that they can never be brought into charge. It originates with the Crown, and may be general, to all concerned, or particular.

AMORTIZATION (Fr. *Amortissement*) (1) an alienation of lands and tenements in the former action in mortmain [MORTMAIN ACTS]; (2) the redemption of stock by a sinking fund.

AMOVEAS MANUS, or **OUSTER LE MAIN.** [MONSTRANS DE DROIT.]

AMPLIATION (Lat. *Ampliatio*). An enlargement; but, in a legal sense, a deferring of judgment, until the cause be further examined.

ANALYST. [PUBLIC ANALYST.]

ANCESTOR (Lat. *Antecessor*), in a legal sense, is not exclusively applied to the *ancestor* of a family; but extends to any person from whom an estate was inherited.

ANCHORAGE. A duty paid by the owners of ships for the use of the haven where they cast anchor.

ANCIENT DEMESNE, or **ANTIENT DEMESNE.** A tenure existing in certain manors, which were in the hands of the Crown at the time of Edward the Confessor, or William the Conqueror. Some of the tenants of these crown manors were for a long time pure and absolute villeins, dependent on the will of the lord. Others were in a great measure enfranchised by the royal favour, and had many immunities and privileges granted to them.

Tenants in antient demesne differed from copyholders in so far as their services were fixed and determinate. The tenure was abolished in 1922.

ANCIENT LIGHTS. Windows through which the access and use of light have been actually enjoyed without interruption for twenty years, unless enjoyed by express consent or agreement in writing: Prescription Act 1832. The period was temporarily extended from twenty to twenty-seven years by the Rights of Light Act 1959.

ANCIENT MONUMENTS. Monuments of historic, architectural, traditional, artistic or archaeological interest which have been acquired by the State or by local authorities and are protected by the provisions of the Ancent Monuments Acts 1913 to 1972.

The Act of 1972 (Field Monuments Act 1972) was passed to protect such remains (threatened in modern times by agricultural and earth-moving machinery) as burial mounds, prehistoric earthworks, hill forts, etc.

ANCIENT WRITINGS. Deeds and other documents which are more than thirty years old. These when put in evidence "prove themselves," that is, they do not ordinarily require proof of their execution when coming from the proper custody.

ANCILLARY (Lat. *Ancilla*, a slave). Auxiliary, or subordinate.

ANCIPITIS USUS (of doubtful use). A phrase used, especially with reference to the law of contraband, of articles of doubtful use, *i.e.*, which might be contraband or not according to circumstances.

ANGLING. Fishing. Angling in the daytime (that is, in the period beginning one hour before sunrise and ending one hour after sunset) is not *per se* an offence under the Theft Act 1968; but angling in the daytime in water which is private property or in which there is any private right of fishery is an offence for which the angler is liable to a fine.

ANIMALS either (1) *domitæ naturæ*, of a tame nature, which are the subject of absolute ownership, considered personal property and may be the subject of theft; or (2) *feræ naturæ*, of a wild nature, which are to be regarded as property, but they cannot be stolen unless they have been reduced into possession by or on behalf of another person. See s. 4 (4) of the Theft Act 1968. Qualified ownership may be acquired in them either *per industriam*, by taming or keeping them under control, *propter impotentiam*, by their being too weak to get away, or *propter privilegium*, by franchise from the Crown, *e.g.*, in warren.

The common law rules imposing strict liability in tort for damage done by an animal on the ground that the animal is regarded as *feræ naturæ*, or that its vicious or mischievous propensities are known or presumed to be known, were replaced by ss. 2–5 of the Animals Act 1971. Those sections cover, respectively: liability for damage done by dangerous animals; liability done by dogs to livestock; liability for damages and expenses due to trespassing livestock; and exceptions from liability.

ANIMUS CANCELLANDI. ANIMUS REVOCANDI. The intention of cancelling. The intention of revoking, specially in relation to will.

ANIMUS FURANDI. The intention of stealing—at common law it must be present at the time of taking.

ANIMUS MANENDI. The intention of remaining, which is material for the purpose of ascertaining a person's *domicile* [DOMICIL.]

ANIMUS REVERTENDI. The intention of returning.

ANIMUS REVOCANDI. [ANIMUS CANCELLANDI.]

ANNATES. [FIRST FRUITS.]

ANNEXATION (*Canada*.) The placing of a thing on land in such circumstances that it becomes part of the land, *e.g.*, a building not of a temporary nature.

ANNI NUBILES. The marriageable age of a woman. At one time the age of consent was fourteen for a male and twelve for a female, but now, by s. 2 of the Marriage Act 1949, a marriage solemnised between persons either of whom is under the age of sixteen is void. Parental consents are required to the marriage of persons under eighteen; see the Family Law Reform Act 1969.

ANNOISANCE. A nuisance. As used in the Bridges Act 1530, now repealed (except as to London) by the Highways Act 1959. [NUISANCE.]

ANNUAL GENERAL MEETING. [MEETING.]

ANNUAL RETURN. A return that must be filed annually by a company with the Registrar of Companies, together with a copy of the balance sheet, auditors' report, etc. The return must be made within forty-two days of the annual general meeting. See ss. 126 *et seq.* of, and Sch. VI to, the Companies Act 1948.

ANNUAL VALUE. A value placed upon hereditaments for the purpose of assessing liability to income tax or rates.

ANNUITY. A yearly sum payable. If charged upon real estate it is more properly called a rent charge. And see ss. 1 (2) and 121, 122, of the Law of Property Act 1925, and s. 31 of the Trustee Act 1925. Annuities created after 1925 are not entered (as formerly) on the Register of Annuities, but are registered as general equitable charges under the Land Charges Act 1972.

A life annuity is an annual payment, *e.g.* under the terms of a will, during the continuance of any life or lives.

ANNULMENT OF ADJUDICATION IN BANKRUPTCY. This may be (1) where a composition has been subsequently accepted (see s. 31 of the Bankruptcy Act 1914), (2) where court is of opinion debtor ought not to have been adjudged, or (3) where the debts are paid in full (see s. 29). The effect is not to render everything done under the bankruptcy null and void, *ab initio*; but merely to stop all further proceedings in the bankruptcy, generally leaving everything done under it, up to the annulment, in full force and operation. There are also provisions for annulment of a receiving order and of a composition or scheme of arrangement.

ANNUS LUCTUS (the year of grief). The year after a husband's death, within which his widow was, by the civil law, not permitted to marry.

ANTARCTICA. The area south of the sixtieth parallel of south latitude, excluding any part of the high seas but including all ice shelves south of that parallel: Antarctic Treaty 1967, s. 10.

ANTE LITEM MOTAM. Before a suit is put in motion.

ANTE-DATE. To date a document before the day of its signature or execution. As to bills of exchange, see the Bills of Exchange Act 1882, s. 13 (2).

ANTENATI. Born before a certain period, especially before marriage.

ANTE-NUPTIAL. Before marriage.

ANTICIPATION, RESTRAINT ON. Before 1936 a married woman could be restrained either by will or settlement from alienating her separate property by way of anticipation. In furtherance of the policy of conferring upon a married woman full proprietary capacity, the restraint on anticipation was abolished as regards instruments executed on or after 1st January, 1936, by the Law Reform (Married Women and Tortfeasors) Act 1935, and accordingly any instrument executed on or after that date is void in so far as it purports to attach to the enjoyment of any property by a woman any restriction upon anticipation or alienation which could not have been attached to the enjoyment of the property by a man. Restraints existing after 1st January, 1936, were finally abolished by the Married Women (Restraint upon Anticipation) Act 1949.

ANTIGRAPHY. A copy or counterpart of a deed.

ANTINOMY. Conflict between two laws or the provisions of a law.

ANTIQUA (or **VETERA**) **STATUTA** (ancient statutes). The Acts of Parliament from Richard I to Edward III.

APOGRAPH. A copy, an inventory.

APOLOGY in actions for libel may operate as a defence, or in mitigation of damages. See the Libel Act 1843, ss. 1, 2; and see R.S.C. 1965, Ord. 82, r. 7.

APPARATOR, or **APPARITOR.** A messenger who cited offenders to appear in the spiritual courts, and served the process thereof.

APPARENT HEIR, or **HEIR APPARENT.** One whose right of inheritance is indefeasible, provided he outlive his ancestor. [HEIR APPARENT.]

APPEAL. 1. A complaint to a superior court of an injustice done by an inferior one. The party complaining is styled the appellant, the other party the respondent. In *civil* causes, appeals from the county court, from the Chancery, Queen's Bench and Family Divisions of the High Court, lie to the Court of Appeal (civil division); from the Court of Appeal, to the House of Lords. The Judicial Committee of the Privy Council is also the ultimate court of appeal in ecclesiastical matters, and from certain Commonwealth courts. Appeal from a master or district registrar lies to judge in chambers, and thence to divisional court, or, in some cases (*e.g.*, on practice or procedure, or in the Chancery Division), to the Court of Appeal. Leave is in many cases necessary for appeal, *e.g.*, usually from interlocutory orders, and the rules as to time for appeal and notice must be complied with. And see s. 31 of the Judicature Act 1925, which deals with restrictions on appeals. As to appeals in *criminal* cases, these are now to the Court of Appeal (criminal division), the former Court of Criminal Appeal having been abolished by the Criminal Appeal Act 1966. See also the Criminal Appeal Act 1968. [CERTIORARI; COURT FOR CONSIDERATION OF CROWN CASES RESERVED; COURT OF ERROR; NEW TRIAL; SPECIAL CASE.]

2. An accusation by a private subject (appellor) against another (appellee) for some heinous crime, demanding punishment on account of the particular injury suffered, rather than for the offence against the public. Now obsolete.

APPEARANCE. As regards the defendant in an action, appearance is entered by his delivering to the proper officer of the court a memorandum importing either that he appears to defend the action in person, or that some solicitor, whose name is given, appears on his behalf. This must usually be done within eight days from the service of the writ or summons. Provision is also made in the case of persons under disability for appearance by guardian, next friend, etc. In county court no appearance is entered except in Admiralty actions, but in case of default summons (for a certain sum) notice of the defence must be given within eight days, otherwise judgment may be obtained by default. In the High Court, failure of defendant to appear will in some cases (*e.g.*, liquidated claims) give the plaintiff right to final judgment; in others (*e.g.*, claims for damages), interlocutory judgment; in others (*e.g.*, Chancery actions), the action must still proceed. See R.S.C. 1965, Ord. 12.

APPELLANT. [APPEAL.]

APPELLATE JURISDICTION. The jurisdiction exercised by a court of justice in appeals.

APPENDANT. Annexed to, or belonging to, some principal thing or corporeal hereditament. Thus advowsons and commons may be *appendant* to a manor, and common of fishing *appendant* to a freehold; and *appendants* are naturally and originally annexed to the principal, as distinguished from *appurtenances*, which may be created at any time, and either by express grant or prescription.

APPENDIX. A printed book which is annexed to the "Case" of each party to an appeal to the Privy Council or House of Lords. It contains the documents and evidence in the courts below.

APPOINTED DAY. The day appointed for bringing into force an Act of Parliament or part thereof.

APPOINTEE. A person to whom or in whose favour what is technically termed "a power of appointment" is exercised. [APPOINTMENT; POWER.]

APPOINTMENT. Besides its ordinary meaning, this word is specially used of the appointment, under a *power of appointment*, limiting an estate or interest in lands or other property for the benefit of some person or persons. Under the Law of Property Act 1925, s. 1 (7), every power of appointment (not being a power vested in a legal mortgagee or in an estate owner in right of his estate), operates only in equity. [POWER.]

APPORTIONMENT. The dividing of a legal right into its proportionate parts, according to the interests of the parties concerned. The word is generally used with reference to the adjustment of rights between two persons having successive interests in the same property, such as a tenant for life and the reversioner. By the common law, if the interest of a person in the rents and profits of land ceased between one day of payment and another (as by the death of a tenant for life), the sum which had accrued since the last day of payment was lost to him or his representatives, and went to the person entitled to the reversion. By the Apportionment Act 1870 it was provided that all rents, annuities, dividends, and other periodical payments in the nature of income, shall be considered as accruing from day to day, and shall be apportionable in respect of time accordingly. See s. 140 of the Law of Property Act 1925, which relates to the apportionment of conditions on severance of the reversionary estate in any land comprised in a lease.

APPRAISEMENT. Valuation. A commission of appraisement to value treasuretrove, waifs, and estrays, seized by the king's officer, was issued after the filing of an information in the King's Exchequer (now Queen's Bench), and a proclamation for the owner (if any) to come in and claim the effects. After the return of the commission, a second proclamation was made; and if no claimant appeared, the goods were condemned to the use of the Crown. Appraisement of goods seized by way of distress for rent, etc., was formerly necessary before the goods could be sold, but this is not now so unless the tenant requires it.

APPRENTICE (Fr. *Apprendre*, to learn). One who is bound by deed indented, or indentures, to serve his master and be maintained and instructed by him. Defined by s. 19 of the Family Allowances Act 1965 (repealed by the Child Benefit Act 1975) as a person undergoing full-time training for any trade, business, profession, office, employment or vocation, and not in receipt of more than limited earnings.

APPROBATE AND REPROBATE. To take advantage of the beneficial parts of a deed, and reject the rest. This the law does not in general permit. [ELECTION.]

APPROPRIATION. 1. The perpetual annexation of an ecclesiastical benefice to the use of some spiritual corporation, sole or aggregate, being the patron of the living.

APPROPRIATION—*continued.*
The patrons retained the tithes and glebe in their own hands, without presenting any clerk, they themselves undertaking to provide for the service of the church. [VICAR.] When the monasteries and religious houses were dissolved, the appropriations belonging to them became vested in the Crown, and many of these were afterwards granted out to subjects, and came into the hands of lay persons, called by way of distinction *lay impropriators.*

2. The application of a particular payment for the purpose of paying a particular debt. The debtor at the time of paying has the right of appropriation, but, as a general rule, the creditor may apply the payment if the debtor does not; if neither does so the law usually appropriates earliest payment to earliest debt (*Clayton's case*).

3. Any part of the real or personal estate of a deceased person may be appropriated in its actual condition in or towards satisfaction of a legacy or share of residue. See s. 41 of the Administration of Estates Act 1925.

4. Section 1 of the Theft Act 1968 provides that a person is guilty of theft if he dishonestly "appropriates" property belonging to another with the intention of permanently depriving the other of it. [THEFT.] In this connection "appropriation" is defined (by s. 3) as any assumption by a person of the rights of an owner. This includes any later assumption of such rights after having come into the possession of the property lawfully or without actually having stolen it, as *e.g.* wrongful appropriation by a bailee.

APPROPRIATOR. A spiritual corporation entitled to the profits of a benefice.

APPROVE (Lat. *Approbare*). To improve; especially of land.

APPROVED SCHOOL. A school for delinquent children approved by the Home Secretary under the Children and Young Persons Acts 1933 to 1963. Provision was made for the discontinuance of approved schools upon the establishment of *Community Homes* under the Children and Young Persons Act 1969.

APPROVED SOCIETY. Under the former National Health Insurance Act 1936, any body of persons, corporate or unincorporate, registered or established under any Act of Parliament or by Royal Charter or having a "prescribed" constitution, approved for the distribution of national health insurance benefits. The Social Security Act 1975 does not make use of the approved societies.

APPROVEMENT. 1. The improvement or partial inclosure of a common. Consent of the Secretary of State for the Environment is now necessary: Law of Commons Amendment Act 1893. For further restrictions on approvements, see the Law of Property Act 1925, s. 194.

2. The profits arising from the improvement of land approved.

3. The act of an approver. [APPROVER.]

APPROVER (Lat. *Approbator*). A person, formerly called an *appellor*, who, when indicted of treason or felony, and arraigned for the same, did confess the fact before plea pleaded, and appeal or accuse others, his accomplices, of the same crime, in order to obtain his pardon. This could only be done in capital offences. If the accused, or, as he was called, the *appellee*, were found guilty, he suffered the judgment of the law, and the approver had his pardon *ex debito justitiæ*; but if the jury acquitted the appellee, the approver received judgment to be hanged, upon his own confession of the indictment. [QUEEN'S EVIDENCE.]

APPURTENANCES, or **THINGS APPURTENANT** (Lat. *Pertinentia*). Things both corporeal and incorporeal belonging to another thing as the principal, but which have not been naturally or originally so annexed, but have become so by grant or prescription, such as hamlets to a manor, common of pasture, turbary, piscary, and the like. [APPENDANT.]

Common appurtenant may arise not only from long usage but from grant, and it may extend to beasts not generally commonable, thus differing in some degree from *common appendant.*

Appurtenance, in relation to a dwelling or to a school, college, or other educational establishment, includes all land occupied therewith and used for the purpose thereof: General Rate Act 1967, s. 19.

ARBITRATION is where two or more parties submit all matters in dispute to the judgment of *arbitrators*, who are to decide the controversy; and if they do not agree, it is usual to add, that another person be called in as *umpire*, to whose sole judgment it is then referred: or frequently there is only one arbitrator originally appointed. The decision, in any of these cases, is called an *award*; but sometimes, when the umpire gives the decision, it is termed *umpirage*. The Arbitration Act 1950 consolidated the earlier law with respect to arbitration.

Arbitration agreements with an international element may be recognised and enforced in the United Kingdom by Convention: Arbitration Act 1975. [ADVISORY, CONCILIATION AND ARBITRATION SERVICE.]

ARCHBISHOP. The chief of all the clergy in his province. He has the inspection of the bishops of that province, as well as of the inferior clergy; or, as the law expresses it, the power to *visit* them. There are two archbishops for England: Canterbury, styled Primate of all England; and York, Primate of England.

ARCHDEACON. An ecclesiastical officer subordinate to the bishop throughout the whole of a diocese or in some particular part of it. He is usually appointed by the bishop, and has a kind of episcopal authority. He *visits* the clergy, and has his separate court for punishment of offenders by spiritual censures, and for hearing all other causes of ecclesiastical cognizance. As a general rule, the jurisdictions of the archdeacon and the bishop are concurrent, but with appeal from former to latter. He also examines for ordination, induction, etc.

ARCHES, COURT OF, is a court of appeal belonging to the Archbishop of Canterbury, whereof the judge, who sits as deputy to the archbishop, is called the *Dean of the Arches*, because he anciently held his court in the church of St. Mary-le-Bow (*Sancta Maria de Arcubus*). This court was afterwards held in the hall at Doctor's Commons, and subsequently at Westminster. Its proper jurisdiction is only over the thirteen peculiar parishes belonging to the archbishop in London, but the office of Dean of the Arches having been for a long time united with that of the archbishop's principal official, he now, in right of the last-mentioned office (as does also the official principal of the Archbishop of York, who since the Public Worship Regulation Act 1874 is the same judge as for Canterbury), receives and determines appeals from the sentences of all inferior ecclesiastical courts within the province. Many original suits are also brought before him, in respect of which the inferior judge has waived his jurisdiction. [LETTERS OF REQUEST.]

From the Court of Arches and from the parallel court of appeal in the province of York, an appeal lies to the Judicial Committee of the Privy Council.

ARMS AND ARMOUR. (1) In legal language extended to anything that a man, in his anger or fury, took into his hand to cast at, or strike, another. In all actions of trespass as opposed to trespass on the case, it was formerly necessary to allege that the acts complained of were done *vi et armis*, "with force and arms," the force being the gist of the complaint.

(2) Armorial bearings. [COURT OF CHIVALRY; HERALDS' COLLEGE.]

ARMY. The military forces of the country, now regulated by the Army Act 1955 and the Armed Forces Act 1971.

ARRAIGN, ARRAIGNMENT (Lat. *Ad rationem ponere*, to call to account). To arraign is to call a prisoner to the bar of the court, to answer the matter charged upon him in the indictment. The prisoner is to be called to the bar by his name; the indictment is to be read to him, after which it is to be demanded of him whether he be guilty of the crime whereof he stands indicted, or not guilty. He may then either confess, plead not guilty, or stand mute. [MUTE; PEINE FORTE ET DURE.]

ARRANGEMENTS between debtors and creditors outside the law of bankruptcy must be in accordance with the Deeds of Arrangement Act 1914. As to registration of deeds of arrangement affecting land, see the Land Charges Act 1972, s. 7 [COMPOSITION, 2.] As to arrangements within the bankruptcy law, see the Bankruptcy Act 1914, s. 16.

ARRAY is the setting forth in order of a jury of men that are impanelled upon a cause, whence comes the verb *to array* a panel, that is, to set forth in order the men that are impanelled. Hence it is said to "challenge the array," and to "quash the array." [CHALLENGE.]

ARREARS. Money owing after time for payment, *e.g.*, interest, rent.

ARRENTATION (Spanish, *Arrendar*). The licensing an owner of lands in the forest to enclose them with a low hedge and little ditch, according to the assize of the forest, under a yearly rent. *Saving the arrentations* was reserving the power to grant such licences. *Cowel.*

ARREST. A restraint of a man's person, obliging him to be obedient to the law. An arrest is the beginning of imprisonment, whereby a man is first taken, and restrained of his liberty, by power or colour of a lawful warrant; also it signifies the decree of a court, by which a person is arrested. An arrest consists of the actual seizure or touching of the person's body with a view to his detention, and the mere pronouncing of words of arrest is insufficient unless the person sought to be arrested submits to the process.

Any person may, without warrant, arrest anyone whom he, with reasonable cause, suspects to be committing an arrestable offence. See, generally, as to arrest without warrant, s. 2 of the Criminal Law Act 1967. As to the use of force in making an arrest, see *ibid.*, s. 3.

Arrest without warrant is also allowed in certain other criminal cases. When a person is arrested without warrant, he must be informed of the reason.

A warrant of arrest may also be obtained in Admiralty proceedings to detain the ship or other *res* the subject of the action.

ARREST OF JUDGMENT. A staying or withholding of judgment, although there has been a verdict in the case, on the ground that there is some error on the face of the record, from which it appears that the plaintiff has at law no right to recover in the action, or that the prisoner should not be sentenced.

ARRESTABLE OFFENCE. An offence for which the sentence is fixed by law or for which a person (not previously convicted) may be sentenced to imprisonment for five years, or the attempt to commit any such offence. A person committing or suspected to be committing an arrestable offence may be arrested without warrant. See s. 2 of the Criminal Law Act 1967.

ARRESTMENT. The Scotch term for the arrest of a person or the seizure of his effects, analogous to the English attachment.

ARSON. The malicious and wilful burning of a house or other building. Formerly a common law offence only, it was made a statutory offence, with liability to imprisonment for life, by the Criminal Damage Act 1971.

ART AND PART means where a person is guilty of aiding and abetting a criminal in the perpertration of a crime.

ART UNIONS. Voluntary associations for the purchase of paintings and other works of art to be distributed by chance or otherwise amongst the members. Excepted from the law against lotteries if complying with the Art Unions Act 1846.

ARTICLED CLERK. A person bound by articles to serve with a practising solicitor, previously to being admitted himself as a solicitor. The period of service under articles is in general five years; but in certain cases it is only four or three years. Solicitors Act 1974.

ARTICLES. A word used in various senses.

1. Agreements between different persons expressed in writing, sealed or unsealed, are often spoken of as "articles." A contract made in contemplation of marriage is in general spoken of as "marriage articles," if it contemplates a further instrument, *i.e.*, settlement, to carry out the intention of the parties. So also "articles of partnership," "articles of association," etc. The use of the term is somewhat capricious. [ARTICLED CLERK.]

2. Rules are sometimes spoken of as "articles"; as, for instance, "articles of war," "articles of the navy," "articles of a constitution," "articles of religion," the Thirty-nine Articles drawn up by Convention in 1562, which must be subscribed to on taking holy orders.

3. The complaint of the promoter in an ecclesiastical cause is called "articles." So, an impeachment by the House of Commons is expressed in what are called "articles of impeachment."

4. The paragraphs of an order or instrument made under statutory powers.

ARTICLES OF ASSOCIATION. Regulations governing the mode of conducting the business of an incorporated company and its internal organisation. These must usually accompany the Memorandum of Association, which sets out the objects and capital, etc., of the company. In the case of a company limited by shares, Table A of the Companies Act 1948 may be taken as the articles of the company. [TABLE A.]

ARTICLES OF RELIGION. [ARTICLES, 2.]

ARTICLES OF THE PEACE. A form of complaint by a person who fears that another may do him some bodily hurt. Articles of peace might formerly be exhibited in the High Court; but since 1938 the procedure is only available in courts of summary jurisdiction. Upon the articles being sworn to by the complainant, sureties of the peace are taken on the part of the party complained against. And the court may require bail for such time as they shall think necessary for the preservation of the peace. See now the Magistrates' Courts Act 1952, s. 91. [KEEPING THE PEACE.]

ARTIFICIAL PERSONS. [PERSON.]

ARTISTIC WORK. Paintings, sculptures, drawings, engravings and photographs, irrespective of artistic quality; also works of architecture, and works of artistic craftsmanship generally. See s. 3 of the Copyright Act 1956.

AS AGAINST. An expression indicating a partial effect or influence. Thus an action may be dismissed as against certain parties to it, who have been wrongfully made parties, while maintained against others.

AS OF. A judgment *as of* Trinity Sittings is a judgment not delivered in Trinity Sittings, but having the same legal effect.

ASSAULT (Fr. *Assailler*) is defined by Blackstone "to be an attempt or offer to beat another, without touching him": and though no actual suffering is proved, yet the party injured may have redress by action for damages as a compensation for the injury, or nominally by criminal prosecution. A *battery* is the unlawful beating of another, and includes the least touching of another's person wilfully or in anger. Practically, however, the word assault is used to include the battery. [BATTERY.]

ASSAY (Fr. *Essayer*). A proof, a trial. Thus the *assay* of weights and measures is

the examination of them by officials.

The *assay* of metals is the testing of the fineness of the precious metals and their alloys. The principal assay offices are: (1) The Wardens and Commonalty of the Mystery of Goldsmiths of the City of London; (2) the Incorporation of Goldsmiths of the City of Edinburgh; (3) the Guardians of the Standard of Wrought Plate in Birmingham; and (4) the Guardians of the Standard of Wrought Plate within the town of Sheffield. [CARAT; HALLMARK.]

ASSEMBLY, UNLAWFUL. [UNLAWFUL ASSEMBLY.]

ASSENT. Consent. The executor's assent to a bequest is essential to perfect a legatee's title. After Land Transfer Act 1897 (repealed), the legal estate in realty could be transferred to the devisee, by assent by personal representative. Fuller provisions as to assents are now contained in s. 36 of the Administration of Estates Act 1925. To pass the legal estate it must be in writing, signed by the personal representative, and must name the person in whose favour it is given. The statutory covenant against incumbrances may be implied if the assent is expressed to be given "as personal representative." (See s. 36 (3).)

ASSESSED TAXES. Assessed or charged in respect of particular subjects, *e.g.*, income tax.

ASSESSMENT. The annual value placed upon hereditaments by an assessment committee for the purpose of levying local rates.

ASSESSORS. Persons who assess the public rates or taxes, also persons who assist a judge with their special knowledge of the subject which he has to decide: as, *e.g.*, "legal assessors," "nautical assessors," "mercantile assessors."

By s. 98 of the Judicature Act 1925 the High Court or Court of Appeal may call in the aid of one or more assessors specially qualified, and may try and hear the matter in question with their assistance. Largely employed in the Admiralty court and before the Judicial Committee of the Privy Council in ecclesiastical matters (Appellate Jurisdiction Act 1876, s. 14).

ASSET (Fr. *Assez*, enough). By *assets* is meant such property as is available for the

ASSET—*continued.*

payment of the debts of an individual or company, or of a person deceased.

Assets of a deceased person are divided into *real assets*, consisting of what is called *real estate*, and *personal assets*, consisting of what is called *personal estate*, which are administered according to different rules.

Assets of a deceased person are also divided into *legal*, such as a creditor of the deceased might make available in an action at law for the payment of his debt; and equitable assets such as could be made available to a creditor in a court of equity only. They include such real assets as the testator has left expressly for the payment of his debts. The importance of the distinction has now ceased to exist, as, since 1870, specialty and simple contract creditors rank *pari passu* against legal as well as equitable assets, and by the Land Transfer Act 1897, s. 2 (repealed), the executor or administrator might sell lands for any lawful purpose of administration, though there was no charge for payment of debts. Now, under s. 32 of the Administration of Estates Act 1925, the real and personal estate, whether legal or equitable, of a deceased person, are made assets for the payment of his debts, whether by specialty or simple contract. This section virtually abolishes any distinction between legal and equitable assets. Realty and personalty are alike equally liable for the payment of debts, and vest in the personal representatives, who have power of sale. See generally the Administration of Estates Act 1925, as amended by the Administration of Estates Act 1971. [MARSHALLING OF ASSETS.]

ASSETS, ADMINISTRATION OF. 1. Where the estate is insolvent, see the Administration of Estates Act 1925, s. 34 (1), and Part I of the First Schedule.

2. Where the estate is solvent, see the Administration of Estates Act 1925, s. 34 (3), and Sched. I, Part II.

ASSIGN, (Lat. *Assignare*), has two significations: (1) to make over a right or interest to another; (2) to point out, or set forth. In the former sense is the assignment of a lease, or of a debt or *chose in action* (*q.v.*); in the latter sense—to assign error, to assign perjury, to assign waste, etc.

Assign, as a substantive, is used in the sense of assignee. [ASSIGNEE.]

ASSIGNEE, or ASSIGN. One who is appointed by another to do any act in his own right, or who takes the rights or title of another by assignment, as distinguished from a *deputy* who acts in the right of another. Such an assignee may be either *by deed*, i.e., by act of party, as when a lessee assigns his lease to another; or *in law*, he whom the law so makes, without any appointment of the person, as an administrator who is the assignee in law to the intestate. An assignee of land is not at common law bound by or entitled to the benefit of covenants which do not run with the land.

Assignees in bankruptcy were those in whom the property of a bankrupt became vested for the benefit of the creditors. They have now been replaced, under the Bankruptcy Act 1914, by *official receivers* and *trustees in bankruptcy.*

ASSIGNMENT OF DOWER. The act by which the share of a widow in her deceased husband's real estate was ascertained and set apart to her.

ASSIGNMENT OF ERRORS. The statement of the case of the plaintiff in error, setting forth the errors complained of. [ERROR.]

ASSIGNOR. One who transfers or assigns property to another [ASSIGNEE.]

ASSISTED PERSON. A person who engages in litigation and who is assisted out of public funds under the Legal Aid Act 1974. [LEGAL AID.]

ASSIZE (Lat. *assideo*, to sit together) signified, originally, the jury who were summoned by virtue of a writ of assize, who tried the cause and "sat together" for that purpose. By a figure it was made to signify the court of jurisdiction which summoned this jury together by a commission of assize, or *ad assisas capiendas*; and hence the judicial assemblies held by the Queen's commission in every county to deliver the gaols, and to try causes at *nisi prius*, were termed in common speech the *assizes*. [ASSIZE COURTS.]

It was also an *ordinance* or *statute*, as the "Assize of Bread and Ale," the "Assize of Clarendon," and "Assize of Arms"; and was sometimes used to denote generally anything reduced to a certainty in respect to number, quantity, quality, weight or measure.

ASSIZE COURTS were composed of two or more commissioners, called judges of assize, who were sent by special commission from the Crown, on *circuits* all round the kingdom, to try such matters as were then under dispute. These judges of assize were the successors of the ancient "justices in eyre," *justiciarii in itinere*. They sat by virtue of four several authorities: (1) Commission of *Oyer and Terminer*, which gave them power to deal with treasons, murders, felonies, etc., and this was their largest commission; (2) of *gaol delivery*, which required them to try every prisoner in gaol, for whatsoever offence he was there; (3) of *nisi prius*, which empowered them to try, by a jury of twelve men of the county in which the venue was laid, all civil causes in which issue had been joined in one of the divisions of the High Court of Justice; and (4) *Commission of peace* in every county of their circuit, by which all justices of the peace, having no lawful impediment, were bound to be present at the assizes, to attend the judges. If any made default, the judges might set a fine upon him at their pleasure and discretion. The sheriff of every shire was also to attend in person, or by sufficient deputy.

In 1971 the Crown Court was established by the Courts Act of that year. The Crown Court superseded the criminal jurisdiction of courts of assize and all the judicial jurisdiction of quarter sessions. The assize courts were accordingly abolished. [CROWN COURT.]

ASSIZE OF DARREIN PRESENT-MENT (or last presentation). A writ directed to the sheriff to summon an assize or jury, to inquire who was the last patron that presented to a church then vacant, of which the plaintiff complained that he was deforced (*i.e.*, unlawfully deprived) by the defendant; and according as the assize determined that question, a writ issued to the bishop, to institute the clerk of that patron in whose favour the determination was made. It was abolished in 1833, and the action of *quare impedit* was substituted. Since 1860 no *quare impedit* can be brought, but an action may be commenced in the Queen's Bench Division of the High Court.

ASSIZE OF MORT D'ANCESTOR. [MORT D'ANCESTOR.]

ASSIZE OF NOVEL DISSEISIN. A writ which lay to recover possession of lands, of which the claimant had been lately disseised (that is, dispossessed). Abolished in 1833.

ASSIZE, WRIT OF. A real action, now abolished, used for the purpose of regaining *possession* of lands whereof the demandant or his ancestors had been unjustly deprived by the tenant or possessor of the freehold, or those under whom he claimed. It proved the title of the demandant by showing his or his ancestor's possession, and it was not necessary (as it was in a writ of entry) to show the unlawful commencement of the tenant's possession. [ENTRY, WRIT OF.]

ASSOCIATE. An officer in each of the superior courts of common law, whose duty was to keep the records and documents of the court to which he was attached, to attend its *nisi prius* sittings, and in each case to enter the verdict and to make up the *postea* or formal entry of the verdict, and deliver the record to the party entitled thereto. By the Judicature Act 1873, s. 77 (repealed), associates were made officers of the Supreme Court of Judicature, and, by the Judicature (Officers) Act 1879 (repealed), were styled "Masters of the Supreme Court." Duties of associates are now carried out by clerks in the Crown Office and Associates Department of the Central Office of the Supreme Court.

ASSOCIATION, ARTICLES OF. [ARTICLES OF ASSOCIATION.]

ASSOCIATION, MEMORANDUM OF. [MEMORANDUM OF ASSOCIATION.]

ASSUMPSIT (he has undertaken). A voluntary promise, by which a man, for a consideration, *assumed* and took upon him to perform to pay anything to another.

This word now is chiefly applied to the action which lay where a party claimed *damages* for breach of *simple contract*, *i.e.*, a promise not under seal. [COVENANT; DEBT.]

ASSURANCE. 1. The legal evidences of the transfer of property are called the *common assurances* of the kingdom. They are also called *conveyances*, and are in general effected by an instrument called a *deed*.

2. Insurance. [INSURANCE.]

ASYLUM. 1. A place in which offenders could find refuge. To seek *political asylum* means to ask admission to another country in order to obtain refuge from political persecution or harassment. Thus s. 3 of the Extradition Act 1870 provides that a fugitive criminal shall not be surrendered if the offence in respect of which his surrender is demanded is one of a political character.

2. An institution for the retention and treatment of lunatics. Either public or private, but all are now subject to Government regulation. Now called mental hospitals.

AT ARM'S LENGTH. When a person is not, or having been, ceases to be, under the influence or control of another, he is said to be "at arm's length" with him, *e.g.*, *cestui que trust* and trustee.

ATOMIC ENERGY. [EUROPEAN ATOMIC ENERGY COMMUNITY.]

ATS. [AD SECTAM.]

ATTACHMENT. The taking into the custody of the law the person or property of one already before the court, or of one whom it is sought to bring before it. This is done by means of a judicial writ, called a *writ of attachment.* An attachment differs from an *arrest* or *capias*, as it may extend to a man's goods as well as to his person; and from a *distress*, as it may extend to his person as well as his goods. The process of attachment is the method which has always been used by the superior courts of justice for the punishment of all "contempts of court." See R.S.C., 1965, Ord. 52.

ATTACHMENT OF DEBTS. [GARNISHEE.]

ATTACHMENT OF EARNINGS. A county court may make an attachment of earnings order to secure payment under a High Court or a county court maintenance order, the payment of a judgment debt (other than a debt of less than £5) or payments under an administration order. A consolidated attachment order may be made to cover two or more judgment debts. The debtor must give particulars of his earnings and anticipated earnings, and attend the court hearing at which the deduction rate from earnings will be decided. The employer must then, under the court order, deduct the specified amounts from the debtors wages or salary, and pay them to the collecting officer of the court: Attachment of Earnings Act 1971.

ATTAINDER. When a person convicted of treason or felony was sentenced to death for the same, or when judgment for outlawry for treason or felony was pronounced against any one, he was said to be *attainted*, and the fact was called an *attainder*. His property was forfeited and his blood was said to be corrupted. This result was abolished by the Forfeiture Act 1870; though nothing is to affect the law of forfeiture consequent upon outlawry.

ATTAINT, WRIT OF. A writ, abolished in 1825, which was in the nature of an appeal, and was the principal remedy for the reversal of an improper verdict. The practice of setting aside verdicts upon motion and granting *new trials* superseded the use of attaints.

ATTEMPT to commit a crime. One of the series of acts necessary to the commission of the crime, and directly approximating thereto. Not punishable more heavily than if the attempted crime had been completed: Powers of Criminal Courts Act 1973, ss. 18 (2), 30 (2).

ATTENDANT TERM. A term held "upon trust to attend an inheritance"; that is, an estate for years in land held in trust for the party entitled to the inheritance thereof on the expiration of the term of years; thus giving protection to him against any unknown incumbrance created *since* the creation of the term, but before the party became entitled to the inheritance. By the Satisfied Terms Act 1845, any attendant term becoming satisfied after the Act immediately ceased. But that Act did not apply to terms created out of leaseholds. That Act was repealed and replaced by s. 5 of the Law of Property Act 1925, and the latter section applies to terms created out of leaseholds as well as to terms created out of freeholds (sub-s. 2). See also Sched. I, Part II, para. 1, to the Law of Property Act 1925. [OUTSTANDING TERM.]

ATTERMINING. The purchasing or gaining longer time for the payment of a debt. *Cowel.*

ATTESTATION. The subscription by a person of his name to a deed, will, or other document executed by another, for the purpose of testifying to its genuineness.

1. **Deed or document** *inter vivos*. A deed ought to be duly attested, that is, show that it was executed by the party in the presence of a witness or witnesses: in most cases this is rather for preserving the evidence, than for constituting the essence, of the deed, but attestation is essential for the validity of bills of sale (Bills of Sale Act 1878, and Bills of Sale Act (1878) Amendment Act 1882), and for deeds executing powers of appointment (Law of Property Act 1925, s. 159), and in a few other cases.

2. **Will.** Every will must now, by the Wills Act 1837, be made in the presence of two or more witnesses present at the same time, such witnesses *attesting* and subscribing the will in the presence of the testator, though not necessarily in the presence of each other. Before this Act three witnesses were necessary for a will of real property, but none for a will of personal property.

ATTESTATION CLAUSE. The clause wherein a witness to a deed, will, or other document certifies to its genuineness. It is not legally essential, even for a will (Wills Act 1837, s. 8), but is the simplest evidence of due execution and is universally included. [ATTESTATION.]

ATTESTED COPY. A copy of a document verified as correct.

ATTORN. 1. In feudal times a lord could not alien or transfer the fealty he claimed from a vassal without the consent of the latter. In giving this consent, the vassal was said to *attorn* (or *turn* over his fealty to the new lord), and the proceeding was called an *attornment*. This doctrine of attornment was extended to all lessees for life or years, and became very troublesome, until, by an Act of Queen Anne, attornments were made no longer necessary. By s. 151 of the Law of Property Act 1925 the conveyance of a reversion is valid without any attornment of the lessee, and an attornment by the lessee, if made without the consent of the lessor, is void, except in certain cases.

2. To *turn over* or intrust business to another; hence the word *attorney* is used to signify a person intrusted with the transaction of another's business. [POWER OF ATTORNEY.]

ATTORNEY. One appointed by another man to do something in his stead.

[ATTORN; ATTORNEY-AT-LAW; POWER OF ATTORNEY.]

ATTORNEY-AT-LAW is one who is put in the place, stead or *turn* of another, to manage his matters of law. Formerly every suitor was obliged to appear in person, but later it was permitted in general that attorneys might be made to prosecute or defend any action in the absence of the parties to the suit. Attorneys were officers of the Superior Court of Law at Westminster, and corresponded to the solicitors of the Court of Chancery and the proctors of the Admiralty and Ecclesiastical Courts. Since the Judicature Act 1873 (s. 87) (now repealed), all are styled solicitors of the Supreme Court. [SOLICITOR.]

ATTORNEY-GENERAL. The principal law officer of the Crown, and the head of the bar of England. It is his duty, among other things, to prosecute on behalf of the Crown, and to file, *ex officio*, informations in the name of the Crown. [INFORMATION.]

AUCTIONEER, a licensed agent, to sell property and conduct sales or auctions. He is deemed the agent of both parties, and can bind both by his memorandum of sale under the Law of Property Act 1925, s. 40 (replacing part of s. 4 of Statute of Frauds). The excise duty of £10 annually on auctioneers, formerly leviable under the Auctioneers Act 1845, was abolished by s. 14 of the Finance Act 1949.

AUDI ALTERAM PARTEM (hear the other side). Both sides should be heard before a decision is given.

AUDIENCE COURT (*Curia audientiæ Cantuariensis*) is a court belonging to the Archbishop of Canterbury, of equal authority with the Arches Court, though inferior both in dignity and antiquity. The Archbishop of York has also an audience court. But these courts, as separate courts, have long since been disused.

AUDIENDO ET TERMINANDO. A writ or commission formerly directed to certain persons when any riotous assembly, insurrection, or heinous misdemeanour or trespass was committed, for the appeasing and punishment thereof. [OYER AND TERMINER.]

AUDITA QUERELA. A writ that lay for the defendant against whom judgment was given, and who was therefore in danger

AUDITA QUERELA—*continued.*

of execution, or was perhaps actually in execution; but who was entitled to be relieved upon some matter of discharge which had happened since the judgment. Obsolete.

AUDITOR was defined by an old Act of Henry VIII to be an officer of the king, or some other great person, who, by yearly examining the accounts of all under-officers accountable, made up a general book that showed the difference between their receipts or charges and their payments or allowances.

The name has in modern times been assumed by persons employed to check the accounts of corporations, companies and partnerships. As to the duties of auditors of companies, see Companies Act 1948, ss. 159–162. Most accounts of local authorities are audited by district auditors. See ss. 156 *et seq.* of the Local Government Act 1972.

Trustees may have the trust accounts audited by an independent accountant (not more than once in three years, except for special reasons) and pay the costs of the audit out of income or capital. Trustee Act 1925, s. 22 (4).

AUTHENTIC ACT. An act or document certified by a notary or public authority.

AUTHENTICATION. A certificate of an act being in due form of law, given by proper authority.

AUTHOR. The maker of an original book, writing, photograph, etc. Authors' copyright is protected under the provisions of the Copyright Act 1956.

AUTHORISED CAPITAL. The total amount of capital which a company is authorised by its memorandum of association to offer to subscribers, as distinguished from its *issued* capital, or capital actually taken up by such subscribers, often on a lesser offer being made.

AUTHORITY. (1) Power given by one person to another enabling the latter to do some act. [AGENT.] As to authority given by trustees to solicitors or bankers, see Trustee Act 1925, s. 23; (2) a governing body, *e.g.*, county council or local authority [LOCAL AUTHORITY]; (3) grounds for some

legal proposition, *e.g.*, judicial decisions, or opinions of authors of standing.

AUTRE DROIT, IN. In right of another. A person may hold property in his own right or in right of another,*e.g.*, trustee in right of *cestui que trust*, or an executor or administrator in right of the deceased and his legatees, devisees, or the persons entitled on his intestacy.

AUTRE VIE. The life of another; thus an estate *pur autre vie* is an estate for the life of another.

AUTREFOIS ACQUIT (beforetime acquitted). By this plea a prisoner charged with an offence pleads that he has been tried before and acquitted of the same offence. The plea, however, is only good in reference to a verdict of *acquittal* by a *jury* or upon a final determination by a court of summary jurisdiction; and, therefore, if a man be committed for trial and the jury having him in charge be discharged by the judge before verdict, he is still liable to be indicted for the same crime. The first indictment must have been such that he could have been lawfully convicted upon it, and the true test whether such a plea is a sufficient bar in any particular case is, whether the evidence necessary to support the second indictment would have been sufficient to procure a legal conviction on the first: Criminal Procedure Act 1851, s. 28, and Evidence Act 1851, s. 13.

AUTREFOIS ATTAINT. A plea by an accused person that he had formerly been attainted for the same crime. Before the Criminal Law Act 1827 this plea might have been pleaded where a man, after being attainted of one felony, was afterwards indicted for *another* offence: for, the prisoner being dead in law by the first attainder, it was deemed superfluous to endeavour to attaint him a second time. But, by s. 4 of that statute, no plea setting forth any attainder might be pleaded in bar of any indictment, unless the attainder was for the same offence as that charged in the indictment. [ATTAINDER.]

Attainders were abolished, save in cases of outlawry, by the Forfeiture Act 1870, and the former plea is superseded by that of *autrefois convict (q.v.).*

AUTREFOIS CONVICT. A plea by an accused person that he has been previously convicted of the same crime of which he is accused. This plea is a good plea in bar to an indictment. It depends upon the same principle, and is governed by the same rules as *autrefois acquit* (*q.v.*). As to the form of the plea, see Criminal Procedure Act 1851, s. 28.

AVERAGE. 1. That service which the tenant owed the lord, to be done by the beasts of the tenant.

2. Stubble or short standing straw in cornfields after harvest.

3. *General Average* is the contribution which the proprietors, in general, of a ship, cargo, and freight, make towards the loss sustained by any individual of their number, whose property has been sacrificed for the common safety. The proportion which the value of the property so sacrificed bears to the entire value of the whole ship, cargo, and freight, including what has been sacrificed, is first ascertained; and then the property of each owner contributes in the proportion so found. Under the usual maritime policies the underwriters are liable for these payments made by the assured. See the Marine Insurance Act 1906.

4. *Particular Average*, as distinguished from general average, is a loss upon the ship, cargo, or freight, severally, to be borne by the owner of the particular property on which it happens; and, in cases where the loss is not total, it is called *average* or *partial* loss. In every case of partial loss the underwriter is liable to pay such proportion of the sum he has subscribed as the damage sustained by the subject of insurance bears to the whole value at the time of insurance. See the Marine Insurance Act 1906.

5. *Petty Average* consists of small charges paid by the master for the benefit of the ship and cargo, such as pilotage, towage, etc.

6. A small duty which merchants who send goods in another man's ship pay the master for his care, over and above the freight. [*Cf.* PRIMAGE.]

AVERMENT (Lat. *Verificatio*) has different meanings. 1. A positive statement of facts as opposed to an argumentative or inferential one. 2. The offer of a defendant to make good or justify his plea, either a *general* averment or a *particular* one, where a special method of verification was mentioned. 3. The technical name (in pleading)

for allegations, such as occur in declarations on contracts, of the due performance of all the conditions precedent, which the form and effect of each contract show to be necessary. For rules of pleading, see now R.S.C. 1965, Ord. 18.

AVOIDANCE. 1. A vacancy; especially of the vacancy of a living by the death of the incumbent.

2. Making void or null; especially of a plea by a defendant in *confession and avoidance* of the plaintiff's declaration. [CONFESSION AND AVOIDANCE.]

3. Destroying the effect of a written instrument, or of any disposition therein.

4. Avoidance of tax, which is permissible if done legally: as opposed to *evasion* of tax.

AVOWRY. [ADVOW; REPLEVIN.]

AVOWTRY. Adultery.

AVULSION. The sudden removal of soil from the land of one man, and its deposit upon the land of another, by the action of water. The soil in such case belongs to the owner from whose land it is removed.

AWARD. The decision of an arbitrator. [ARBITRATION.]

AWAY-GOING CROP. A crop sown during the last year of a tenancy, but not ripe till after its expiration. The out-going tenant is generally entitled to compensation either by the express terms of his contract or by the custom of the country or in accordance with s. 47 of the Agricultural Holdings Act 1948. [EMBLEMENTS.]

B

BACKADATION or **BACKWARDATION.** A premium given to obtain the loan of stock against its value in money, when stock is more in demand than money.

BACK-BOND. A deed which qualifies or attaches a condition to an absolute disposition and in conjunction with it constitutes a trust.

BACKING A WARRANT. The indorsement by a justice of the peace, in one county or jurisdiction, of a warrant issued in another. Now unnecessary. Backing of an English warrant is still necessary if it is

BACKING A WARRANT
—*continued.*

to be executed in Scotland, Northern Ireland or the Channel Islands. A warrant is often "backed for bail" which means that the police, having arrested the person accused, may release him on bail.

BACKSIDE. Formerly used to denote a yard at the back of a house, and belonging thereto.

BAD (in substance). The technical word for an unsound plea.

BADGER. (1) One who bought corn or victuals in one place and took them to another to sell; formerly required a licence. (2) A wild animal protected under the Badgers Act 1973. [CONSERVATION.]

BAIL (Fr. *Bailler*, to deliver). The freeing or setting at liberty one arrested or imprisoned, upon others becoming sureties by recognizance for his appearance at a day and place certainly assigned, he also entering into his own recognizance. The party is delivered (or *bailed*) into the hands of the sureties, and is accounted by law to be in their custody; they may, if they will, surrender him to the court before the date assigned and free themselves from further responsibility. Under the Magistrates' Courts Act 1952, justices are empowered to grant bail with or without sureties. See also the Criminal Justice Act 1948, s. 37. [COMMON BAIL; SPECIAL BAIL.]

BAIL BOND. A bond taken by a sheriff after arrest for the appearance of a defendant, generally with two sureties. Also used in Admiralty proceedings; see Admiralty Court Act 1861, s. 33, and R.S.C. 1965, Ord. 75.

BAIL COURT. A former branch of the Court of Queen's Bench, sometimes called the Practice Court, which sat for the purpose of taking new bail in addition to, or substitution for, existing bail, and for ascertaining the sufficiency of persons offering themselves as bail, and otherwise disposing of applications of ordinary occurrence in practice, and for other purposes.

BAIL HOSTEL. Premises for the accommodation of persons remanded on bail (Powers of Criminal Courts Act 1973, s. 57 (1)).

BAILABLE OFFENCE. An offence for which justices may or are bound to take bail. *Stone.*

BAILEE. A person to whom goods are entrusted by way of bailment. [BAILMENT.]

BAILIE, or **BAILLIE,** in Scotch law signifies a magistrate of a borough.

BAILIFF (Lat. *Ballivus*). A subordinate officer, appointed to execute writs and processes, and do other ministerial acts. Thus, there are *bound* (or bum) bailiffs, employed by the sheriffs, and *bound* annually to the sheriff, with sureties, for the due execution of their office; *special* bailiffs, bailiffs of manors, hundreds, liberties, and bailiffs of county and inferior courts.

BAILIFF-ERRANT. A bailiff's deputy.

BAILIWICK. The county or area over which a sheriff exercises jurisdiction; also that liberty which was exempted from the sheriff of the county, over which the lord of the liberty appointed a bailiff, with such powers within his precinct as the under-sheriff exercises under the sheriff of the county.

BAILMENT. A delivery of goods from one person, called the *bailor*, to another person, called the *bailee*, for some purpose, upon a contract, express or implied, that, after the purpose has been fulfilled, they shall be re-delivered to the bailor, or otherwise dealt with according to his directions, or kept till he reclaims them.

Bailments are of six kinds:—

1. *Depositum*, or the bare deposit of goods with another, for the exclusive use of the bailor.

2. *Commodatum*, the lending of goods for the use or convenience of the bailee.

3. *Locatio et conductio*, the placing of the goods with the bailee on hire.

4. *Vadium*, goods pawned or pledged.

5. *Locatio operis faciendi*, the delivery of goods to a carrier or to a person who is to carry out some services in respect of them for payment.

6. *Mandatum*, similar to the last, but where the carriage or services are to be gratuitous.

BAILPIECE. The slip of parchment on which the recognizance entered into by parties becoming bail is transmitted to the court.

BAIRMAN. A bankrupt or debtor left bare or naked.

BALANCE ORDER. A special order served upon a contributory to a company, after default made, to pay within four days the balance of a call due from him.

BALIVO AMOVENDO. A writ to remove a bailiff out of his office for want of sufficient living in his bailiwick. *Cowel.*

BALLASTAGE. A toll paid for the privilege of taking ballast from the bottom of a port or harbour.

BALLOT, VOTE BY. A method of secret voting, so called from the fact that originally voting for or against was made by placing a white or black "ball" in a box. This method of voting was introduced at parliamentary and municipal elections in 1872, and is now regulated by the Representation of the People Acts. See, *e.g.,* the provisions as to ballot papers, ballot boxes, etc., in Sch. II to the Act of 1949.

BANC, or BANCO, SITTINGS IN. Formerly sittings of one of the superior courts of Westminster, for the purposes of determining matters of law and transacting judicial business other than the trial of actions. Sittings *in banc* were opposed to sittings at *nisi prius*, in which a judge sat to try a case, with or without a jury. The business of the courts sitting *in banco* was transferred to divisional courts of the High Court of Justice in 1873. See now s. 63 of the Judicature Act 1925. [DIVISIONAL COURTS.]

BANDIT. A man outlawed, put under the ban of the law.

BANERET. [BANNERET.]

BANISHMENT. Expulsion from the realm; only permissible under special Acts of Parliament. [TRANSPORTATION.]

BANK-CREDIT. Accommodation allowed to a person on security given to a bank to draw upon the bank up to a certain amount agreed upon.

BANK HOLIDAYS. Days made holidays by statute for banks, customs, inland revenue offices, bonding warehouses, docks, and most Government offices, *viz.,* in England and Wales, Easter Monday; the *last* Monday in May; the *last* Monday in August; 26th December, if not a Sunday; and 27th December in a year in which the 25th or 26th December is on a Sunday (Banking and Financial Dealings Act 1971). From 1974, New Year's Day has been appointed a bank holiday by pro-

clamation in the *London Gazette*, under s. 1 (3) of the Act of 1971.

In Scotland the bank holidays are New Year's Day and the following day (if either falls on a Sunday, then January 3rd); Good Friday; the *first* Monday in May; the *first* Monday in August, and Christmas Day (if on a Sunday, 26th December (Act of 1971)).

See also R.S.C. 1965, Ord. 3, as to exclusion of such holidays in reckoning time.

BANK-NOTE. A promissory note issued by a bank, undertaking to pay to bearer on demand the amount of the note.

BANK RATE. [MINIMUM LENDING RATE.]

BANKER'S BOOKS. The Bankers' Books Evidence Act 1879 makes a copy of an entry in a banker's book *prima facie* evidence of such entry upon proof that the copy has been checked by comparison with the original entry.

BANKRUPTCY. A debtor, who by reason of some act or circumstance indicating a failure to meet his liabilities, and called an "act of bankruptcy", may be adjudicated a "bankrupt" by the High Court of Justice or by a county court exercising bankruptcy jurisdiction. With a few exceptions, any one, whether in trade or not, may be made a bankrupt, and proceedings are commenced by a petition for a receiving order either by a creditor or by the debtor himself, and upon such order the whole of the debtor's property, with a few minor exceptions, vests in an official receiver, and subsequently, if appointed, in a trustee, and becomes distributable among all the creditors in proportion to their debts, subject to certain preferential payments for rates, taxes, wages, etc. On obtaining his discharge from the court the debtor is (with a few exceptions) freed from all debts existing at the time of his bankruptcy. Bankruptcy Act 1914, Bankruptcy (Amendment) Act 1926, and Bankruptcy Rules 1952.

A criminal bankruptcy order may be made against a person convicted by the Crown Court, where as a result of the offence loss or damage of over £15,000 has been suffered by identifiable persons. A criminal bankruptcy petition may then be presented to the High Court and a trustee

BANKRUPTCY—*continued.*

of the criminal bankrupt's property may be appointed. See the Powers of Criminal Courts Act 1973, ss. 39–41, Sch. 2. [ACT OF BANKRUPTCY; ADJUDICATION.]

BANKRUPTCY NOTICE. A notice which is served by a judgment creditor on a debtor requiring him within a limited time to pay the debt or to secure or compound for the same. Non-compliance therewith constitutes an act of bankruptcy.

BANNERET, or **KNIGHT BANNERET** (Lat. *Miles vexillarius*). A knight made in the field, with the ceremony of cutting off the point of his standard, and making it, as it were, a banner; and accounted so honourable that if created in the king's presence he ranked next to a baron and before a baronet.

BANNIMUS. The form of expulsion of any member from the University of Oxford, by affixing the sentence in some public place, as a denunciation or promulgation of it.

BANNITUS. An outlaw, a banished man.

BANNS. The publishing of matrimonial contracts in church before marriage. They must be published on three Sundays before the solemnization of the wedding, in the parish (or each of the parishes) where the parties to be married reside. They must be published in an audible manner and in accordance with the form prescribed in the rubric prefixed to the office of matrimony in the Book of Common Prayer. Seven days notice should be given to the clergyman asked to publish banns. Banns may also be published by the chaplain or captain or commanding officer of one of Her Majesty's ships at sea. See more fully the Marriage Act 1949, ss. 6–14.

BANNUM, or **BANLEUGA.** The utmost bounds of a manor or town.

BAR. A term used in several senses.

1. Of the place where prisoners stand to be tried; hence the expression "prisoner at the bar".

2. Of the place where barristers stand in court to speak for their clients; hence the term *barristers*.

3. Of the profession of a barrister, and the person who practises it.

4. Of an impediment; thus one formerly spoke of uses or limitations in a deed "in bar of dower", because they were intended to prevent a wife becoming entitled to dower out of the lands comprised in the deed. [DOWER.] Also of "barring", or destroying, an entail.

5. Of *pleas in bar*, which are pleas which go to the root of the plaintiff's action, and, if allowed, destroy it entirely.

6. A trial at bar is a trial by jury before two or more judges of the Supreme Court for matters of great importance, or where the Crown is concerned.

7. A "bar" of licensed premises includes any place exclusively or mainly used for the sale and consumption of intoxicating liquor: Licensing Act 1964, s. 201.

BAR COUNCIL. A committee of barristers established in 1894 to supersede the old Bar Committee. The members are partly elected and partly co-opted. The duty of the Council is to protect the interests and etiquette of the Bar.

BAR FEE. A fee of twenty pence which every prisoner acquitted of felony anciently paid to the gaoler.

BAR OF THE HOUSE. The place at which witnesses before either house of parliament are examined, and to which persons guilty of a breach of privilege are brought to receive judgment. *May.*

BARE TRUSTEE is a trustee who has no duty to perform other than, on request, to convey the estate to his *cestui que trust* or according to the latter's direction.

BARGAIN AND SALE was properly a contract for sale of lands or goods, transferring the property from the bargainor to the bargainee, but it was used specially to prescribe a form of conveyance of lands. Prior to the Statute of Uses (now repealed by the Law of Property Act 1925) the effect of a bargain and sale was, that the bargainor stood seised of the land to the use of the bargainee, to the extent to which it was affected by the transaction: *i.e.*, though the bargainor's estate was still good *at law*, yet a court of *equity* considered the estate as belonging to the bargainee, who had paid the money. But the Statute of Uses had the effect of transferring the bargainee's interest into a *legal estate*. To secure publicity in the transfer of legal estates it was provided by a statute of Henry VIII that a bargain or sale of freehold estate must be by deed indented, sealed and enrolled, either in the county where the lands lay, or in one of the king's courts of record at Westminster, within six months after the date of the deed. The Law of Property Act 1925, s. 51, abolished the old forms of conveyance, including bargain and sale.

BARLEYCORN. (1) The third of an inch; (2) a nominal rent or consideration.

BARMOTE, BERGHMOTH, or **BERGHMOTE COURTS** are two courts, called the Great and Small Barmote Courts, having jurisdiction under s. 16 of the High Peak Mining Customs and Mineral Courts Act 1851, over the parts of the hundred of High Peak in Derbyshire, in which the Queen in right of the Duchy of Lancaster is entitled to the mineral duties. They are presided over by a judge, called "the steward", the executive officer being called the barmaster or berghmaster.

BARON has the following meanings:—
1. A degree of nobility next to a viscount. Barons hold (*a*) by prescription, (*b*) by patent. Includes a life peer under the Life Peerages Act 1958.
2. A judge of the Court of Exchequer. These judges were superseded by justices of the Queen's Bench Division of the High Court, under the Judicature Acts.
3. Baron is the word used formerly of a husband in relation to his wife.
4. The chief magistrates of London were also anciently called barons before they had a lord mayor, as appears by several ancient charters.

BARONET (Lat. *Baronettus*) is a dignity or degree of honour created by letters patent and descendible to issue male, with precedency before bannerets, knights of the bath, and knights bachelors, excepting only such bannerets as are made *sub vexillis regis in aperto bello, et ipso rege personaliter præsente.* [BANNERET.]

This order was created by King James I in 1611.

BARONY. The honour and territory that give title to a baron. Also a tract of land in Ireland.

BARRATOR, or **BARRETOR.** 1. A deceiver, a vile knave or unthrift.
2. A person guilty of barratry. [BARRATRY.]

BARRATRY. 1. Any wilfully wrongful or fraudulent act committed by the master of a ship or the mariners, causing damage to the ship or cargo, to which the owner is not a consenting party.
2. *Common barratry* was the offence of *frequently* inciting and stirring up suits and quarrels between Her Majesty's subjects, either at law or otherwise. Abolished by the Criminal Law Act 1967.
3. In Scotland the offence committed by a judge who is induced by a bribe to pronounce judgment.
4. It is also applied to the simony of clergymen going abroad to purchase benefices from the see of Rome.

BARRISTER. A person called to the bar by the benchers of the Inns of Court, giving exclusive right of audience in the Supreme Court except in bankruptcy (in certain cases, solicitors now also have a right of audience in the Crown Court). A barrister cannot sue for fees, but is not liable for negligence.

BARTON, BERTON, or **BURTON,** is a term used in Devonshire and other parts for the demesne lands of a manor; sometimes for the manor-house itself; and in some places for outhouses and fold-yards.

BAS CHEVALIERS. Low or inferior knights holding by base tenure: simple knights are called knights bachelors.

BASE COURT. An inferior court, not of record, as the court baron.

BASE ESTATE. The estate which base tenants had in their land; base tenants being those who held at the will of their lord. Pure copyholders were reckoned among base tenants. Copyholds were abolished by Part V of the Law of Property Act 1922, taking effect from 1st January, 1926.

BASE FEE. 1. The estate created by a tenant in tail, not in possession, who barred the entail without the consent of the protector of the settlement. He thus barred his own issue but not any remainder or reversion, and created a base fee determinable on the failure of his issue in tail. After 1925 the estate so created is not a base fee but an equitable interest equivalent to a base fee—see s. 130 of the Law of Property Act 1925. As to the powers to dispose by will of such an estate (in certain cases), see s. 176 of the Law of Property Act 1925.

BASE FEE—*continued.*
2. An estate descendible to heirs general, but terminable on an uncertain event. So long, however, as it lasted, it differed in nothing from a fee simple.

Thus if land were granted to the use of A and his heirs until B returned from Rome, and then to the use of B and his heirs, A's estate, so long as it lasted, was a base fee.

3. An estate formerly held at the will of the lord.

BASILICA. A body of law framed in A.D. 880 by the Emperor Basilius.

BASKET TENURE. Lands held by the service of making the king's baskets.

BASTARD, in English law, is one that is born of parents not legally married. As to the power of a bastard to dispose of real estate by will, see s. 178 of the Law of Property Act 1925. By the Legitimacy Act 1926 a person born a bastard may be legitimated by the subsequent marriage of the parents, and the Legitimacy Act 1959 provides that this may be done even where the child was born in adultery. By s. 9 of the Act of 1926 (repealed by the Family Law Reform Act 1969) a bastard was entitled, in certain circumstances, to succeed to the property of the mother on intestacy.

BASTARD EIGNÉ. When a man had a bastard son and after married the mother, and by her had a legitimate son, the eldest son was *bastard eigné* (*eigné* being from the French *aisné* or *ainé*), and the younger son was *mulier puisne*. [LEGITIMATION.]

BASTARDY ORDER. [AFFILIATION.]

BATH, KNIGHT OF THE. [KNIGHT, 3.]

BATTEL. [WAGER OF BATTEL.]

BATTERY. A violent striking or beating of any man: in law this includes any touching or laying hold of another, however slight. [ASSAULT.]

BAWDY HOUSE. [BROTHEL.]

BEACONAGE (*Beaconagium*). Money paid towards the maintenance of a beacon.

BEADLE. [BEDEL.]

BEAR, on the Stock Exchange, is a seller of stock which he cannot deliver; *i.e.,* one who speculates for the fall in price of stock which he does not possess, thus enabling him to buy it subsequently for less than he has previously sold it for. [BULL, 2.]

BEARER. 1. One who bears down or oppresses others. [MAINTENANCE.]

2. Money payable under a cheque or security may be expressed to be payable to a certain person or bearer, in which case anyone who presents the security may claim payment, and in case of transfer endorsement will not be necessary.

BEDEL (Fr. *Bedeau*) signifies a messenger or apparator of a court that cites men to appear and answer; also an inferior officer of a parish or liberty, to give notice of vestry meetings, etc.

BEDFORD LEVEL REGISTRY. An office for the registration of conveyances of lands forming part of the great level of the fens, in order that the grantees might obtain the privileges conferred by a statute of Charles II, and subsequent Acts thereon. Now abolished.

BEERHOUSE. A house licensed for the sale of beer for consumption either on or off the premises, as opposed to beershop for sale off only.

BEGIN, RIGHT TO. [RIGHT TO BEGIN.]

BEGUM. A lady, a princess, woman of high rank.

BENCH. A word often used with reference to judges and magistrates; thus "judges on the bench", "the judicial bench", "a bench of magistrates". Also the bishops of the Episcopal bench.

BENCH WARRANT. A warrant issued by the presiding judicial officer of a court for the apprehension of an offender; so called in opposition to a justice's warrant, issued by an ordinary justice of the peace or police magistrate.

BENCHERS. Principal officers of each inn of court, in whom the government of the inn is vested.

BENEFICE. An ecclesiastical living or cure of souls of a parish: see Benefices Act 1898. Anciently used of the interest of a grantee of lands under a feudal grant; a feud.

BENEFICIAL INTEREST. This expression is used to indicate a right of substantial enjoyment or equitable interest, in opposition to merely nominal ownership or legal interest. If A holds lands in trust for B, A is said to have the legal estate, and B is said to have the beneficial interest, or to be the beneficiary or *cestui que trust*.

BENEFICIAL OCCUPATION. Occupation of land which is to the benefit of the occupier. The word "beneficial" does not connote pecuniary profit, but means to the advantage of.

BENEFICIARY. 1. The person in possession of a benefice (*q.v.*).
2. One who has the beneficial interest.

BENEFIT BUILDING SOCIETY. [BUILDING SOCIETY.]

BENEFIT OF CLERGY (Lat. *Privilegium clericale*), or, as it was more shortly expressed, "clergy", originally consisted in the privilege allowed to a clerk in orders, when prosecuted in the temporal court, of being discharged from thence, and handed over to the Court Christian in order to make canonical purgation, that is to clear himself on his oath and that of twelve persons as his compurgators. In England this was extended to all who could read, and so were capable of becoming clerks, and ultimately it was allowed by a statute of Anne (1706), without reference to the ability to read. The privilege of benefit of clergy was entirely abolished by the Criminal Law Act 1827.

Benefit of clergy had no application except in capital felonies; and from several of these it had been taken away by various statutes, constituting the offences to which they respectively applied "felony without benefit of clergy".

BENELUX. [EUROPEAN ECONOMIC COMMUNITY.]

BENERTH. An ancient service rendered by an agricultural tenant to his lord with plough and cart.

BENEVOLENCE. Nominally a voluntary gratuity given by subjects to the king, but which was in reality a forced loan or tax. It was made an article in the Petition of Right 1627 that no man should be compelled to yield any gift, loan or benevolence, tax, or such-like charge, without common consent by Act of Parliament.

BENEVOLENT SOCIETY. [FRIENDLY SOCIETY.]

BEQUEATH. To dispose of personal property by will. In reference to real property the word "devise" is generally used.

BEQUEST. A disposition by will of personal property; a legacy.

BESTIALITY. The crime of men having carnal intercourse with beasts.

BET. A wager, under which money or money's worth is made payable on the result of some future uncertain event. Irrecoverable by s. 18 of the Gaming Act 1845. See the Betting, Gaming and Lotteries Acts 1963 to 1971. [BETTING OFFICE.]

BETACHES. Laymen using glebe lands.

BETTER EQUITY. Where A has, in the contemplation of a court of equity, a superior claim to land or other property than B has, he is said to have a *better equity*. Thus a second mortgagee, advancing his money without knowledge of a prior mortgage, has a better equity than the first mortgagee who has not secured for himself the possession of the title deeds, or has parted with them, so as to enable the mortgagor to secure the second advance as upon an unencumbered estate. After 1925 the priority of all mortgages depends upon registration except where the mortgage is protected by a deposit of title deeds, in which case the mortgage has the priority given by the old law: Law of Property Act 1925, s. 97.

BETTING OFFICE. The former law prohibiting the keeping of betting houses was done away with when the Betting Act 1853 was repealed by the Betting and Gaming Act 1960, itself subsequently repealed by the Betting, Gaming and Lotteries Act 1963.

Under the 1963 Act, betting office licences may be granted to the holders of bookmaker's permits, and such betting offices may be established. The offices are subject to the rules as to conduct contained in s. 10 of the Act, and Sch. 4 thereto.

BEYOND THE SEAS. An expression to indicate that a person is outside of the United Kingdom, the Channel Islands, and the Isle of Man. The Limitation Act 1939 abolished the old procedure whereby a defendant's absence beyond the seas suspended the operation of the Statutes of Limitation.

BID. To offer a price for a thing which is being sold. May be withdrawn before acceptance except where under seal.

BIGAMY (*Bigamia*). The offence of marrying a second time, by one who has a former husband or wife still living and not divorced. See s. 57 of the Offences Against the Person Act 1861.

BILATERAL CONTRACT. One in which the parties are under obligation reciprocally towards each other, *e.g.*, sale, where one becomes bound to deliver the thing sold and the other to pay the price.

BILBOES. A former punishment at sea, answering to the stocks.

BILINGUIS (two-tongued). In a legal sense is used for a jury *de medietate linguæ*, of which part were Englishmen and part strangers.

BILL. This word has several significations:—

1. An account delivered by a creditor to his debtor in respect of goods supplied or work done. Thus, a *bill of costs* is a bill furnished by a solicitor to his client, as to which see the Solicitors Act 1974.

2. A bill in equity or chancery was the written statement whereby the plaintiff in a chancery suit complained of the wrong upon which the suit was based, and sought the appropriate redress. Its place has been taken by a writ and statement of claim since the Judicature Acts.

3. A bill of indictment against a prisoner was the presentment charging his offence, and submitted to the grand jury, and to this they either returned "a true bill" or "ignore the bill". The grand jury is now obsolete.

4. Bill in parliament. A measure submitted to either house of parliament for the purpose of being passed into law. When a measure has been actually passed into law, it is called an "Act".

Bills are divided into public and private bills. It may be laid down generally (though not without exception) that bills for the particular interest or benefit of any person or persons, of a public company or corporation, a parish, a city, a county, or other locality, are treated as *private bills*, to be distinguished from measures of public policy in which the whole community are interested, which are called *public bills*.

A public bill must be introduced by a member of the House. *May.* See also the Parliament Acts 1911 and 1949.

BILL OBLIGATORY. [BILL OF DEBT.]

BILL OF ADVENTURE. [ADVENTURE, BILL OF.]

BILL OF ATTAINDER. A bill brought into parliament for attainting any person or persons. [ATTAINDER.]

BILL OF COMPLAINT. [BILL, 2.]

BILL OF CONFORMITY. A bill filed by an executor or administrator when the affairs of the testator or intestate were so much involved that he could not safely administer the estate except under the direction of the Court of Chancery. Now superseded by action or summons for administration. See R.S.C. 1965, Ord. 85.

BILL OF COSTS. [BILL, 1.]

BILL OF CREDIT. [LETTER OF CREDIT.]

BILL OF DEBT, or **BILL OBLIGATORY.** A written acknowledgment of a debt by a merchant, setting out the amount, the date, and the place of payment. It may be under seal or not.

BILL OF ENTRY. An account of the goods entered at the custom house both inwards and outwards. It must state the name of the merchant, the quantity and species of the goods, etc.

BILL OF EXCEPTIONS. If, during a civil trial, a judge, in his directions to the jury, or his decision, mistook the law, counsel on either side might require him publicly to seal a *bill of exceptions*, which was a statement in writing of the point wherein he was supposed to err, so that the point might be settled by a court of error. Bills of exceptions were abolished by the Judicature Acts and Rules, and the present mode of proceeding is by motion for a new trial.

BILL OF EXCHANGE. Defined by the Bills of Exchange Act 1882 as an unconditional order in writing, addressed by one person (the drawer) to another (the drawee, and afterwards acceptor), signed by the person giving it, requiring the person to whom it is addressed to pay on demand, or at a fixed or determinable future time, a sum certain in money to, or to the order of, a specified person, or to bearer (the payee).

BILL OF HEALTH. A certificate, signed by a consul and given to the ship's master on leaving a port, showing the sanitary condition of the port at the time the ship sailed. It may be clean, suspected (or touched), or foul.

BILL OF INDEMNITY. An Act of Parliament passed every session (until rendered unnecessary by the passing of the Promissory Oaths Act 1868) for the relief of those who had neglected to take the necessary oaths, etc., required for the purpose of qualifying them to hold their respective offices.

BILL OF LADING. A mode of authenticating the transfer of property in goods sent by ship. It is, in form, a receipt from the captain to the shipper or consignor, undertaking to deliver the goods, on payment of freight, to some person whose name is therein expressed, or endorsed thereon by the consignor. The delivery of this instrument will transfer to the party so named (usually called the consignee), or to any other person whose name he may think fit to endorse thereon, the property in such goods. It is thus used both as a contract for carriage and a document of title. See the Carriage of Goods by Sea Act 1924.

BILL OF MIDDLESEX was a fictitious mode of giving the Court of King's Bench jurisdiction in personal actions by arresting a defendant for a supposed trespass. Abolished in 1832. Since the Judgments Act 1838 all personal actions in the superior courts are commenced by writ of summons. [LATITAT.]

BILL OF PAINS AND PENALTIES. A bill introduced into parliament, for affecting any person or persons with pains and penalties short of death without the usual criminal proceedings.

BILL OF PARCELS. An invoice (*q.v.*).

BILL OF PARTICULARS. A specific statement by a plaintiff to a defendant of what he seeks to recover by his action, or of a defendant's set-off. [PARTICULARS OF CLAIM OR DEFENCE.]

BILL OF REVIEW. [REVIEW, BILL OF; REVIVOR.]

BILL OF RIGHTS. A declaration delivered by the Lords and Commons to the Prince and Princess of Orange, 13th February, 1688, and afterwards enacted in parliament, when they became king and queen. It declared illegal certain acts of the late king, and insisted on the rights and liberties asserted therein as being the "true, ancient, and indubitable rights of the people of this kingdom." *May.*

BILL OF SALE. An assignment under seal of chattels personal. Provision was first made by the Bills of Sale Act 1854 (repealed) for the registration of bills of sale within twenty-one days from the making thereof. The Act of 1878 applies now only to absolute bills of sale, *i.e.*, given otherwise than by way of mortgage, *e.g.*, a gift where donor remains in possession. The Act of 1882 applies to every bill of sale by way of mortgage. Both classes must be registered within seven days and re-registered every five years, and those under the Act of 1882 must set forth the consideration for which made, and must not be for less than £30 or they will be void. The Act of 1882 also makes void every bill of sale unless it be made in a form scheduled to the Act. See also the Bills of Sale Acts 1890, 1891; also the Law of Property Act 1925, s. 189 (1), which provides that a power of distress given by way of indemnity against a rent payable in respect of any land, or against the breach of any covenant or condition in relation to land, is not a bill of sale within the meaning of the above Acts.

BILL OF SIGHT. A document furnished to the customs officer by an importer of goods, who, being ignorant of their precise quality and quantity, describes the same to the best of his knowledge and information. Customs and Excise Act 1952, s. 29.

BILL OF STORE. A certified extract from the official customs records that certain goods have been exported.

BILL OF SUFFERANCE. A licence granted at the custom-house to a merchant, to suffer him to trade from one English port to another without paying custom.

BILLA VERA. A true bill found by a grand jury. [BILL, 3; GRAND JURY.]

BILLETING. The quartering of members of Her Majesty's forces in inns, hotels and other dwellings. Statutory provision for billeting in times of emergency is made in Part IV of the Army Act 1955, the relevant sections dealing, among other matters, with the provision of billets, payment for accommodation, appeals against billeting, etc.

BILLIARDS. Every house where a public billiard table is kept (other than a house licensed for the sale of intoxicating liquors for consumption on the premises) must be licensed by justices of the peace: Gaming Act 1845, ss. 10–14.

BILLS OF MORTALITY were returns of the deaths which occurred within a particular district. The cities of London and Westminster, the borough of South-wark, and thirty-four out-parishes in Middlesex and Surrey, used to be said to be "within the bills of mortality". The system from which the phrase was derived is now superseded by the system of civil registration of deaths provided for in Part II of the Births and Deaths Registration Act 1953.

BIND OVER. To order a person to enter into a recognisance, binding himself under a penalty to do some particular act, as *e.g.*, on being granted bail, to appear and stand his trial at a later date; or to abstain from committing some offence, *e.g.*, causing a breach of the peace. See ss. 5, 91, of the Magistrates' Courts Act 1952; and as to orders for conditional discharge, see s. 7 of the Powers of Criminal Courts Act 1973.

BIOLOGICAL STANDARDS. [NATIONAL BIOLOGICAL STANDARDS BOARD.]

BI-PARTITE. Of two parts.

BIRETTUM. The cap or coif of a judge or, formerly, a serjeant-at-law.

BISHOP. The principal officer of the Church in each diocese. He was elected by the sovereign's *congé d'élire* (*q.v.*) though in future all Church of England bishops are to be chosen by a Crown Appointments Commission, which will make nominations for presentation to the prime minister and appointment by the Queen. A *suffragan* bishop is a deputy or assistant bishop in spiritual matters, a *coadjutor* in temporal matters. 1 *Bl.*

BISHOP'S COURT. The consistory court in each diocese, held under the authority of the bishop, by his chancellor.

BISSEXTILE, vulgarly called Leap-year, every fourth year. It is called bissextile because formerly, in each such year, the *sixth* day before the calends of March was *twice* reckoned, *viz.*, on the 24th and 25th of February. By a statute of Henry III these days were, in each leap-year, to be accounted but one day, and the supernumerary day in leap-year is now added to the end of February and called the 29th.

BLACK CAP. The full head-dress of a judge, which was formerly worn when sentence of death was passed upon an offender.

BLACKMAIL denoted, in the northern counties, a certain rate of money, or other consideration, paid to persons near the borders, allied with robbers, for protection and safety from the danger of such. These robbers were called moss-troopers. Also rents paid in grain or baser money were called *reditus nigri*, or *black mail*, as opposed to *reditus albi*, or *white rents*, which were payable in silver. [ALBA FIRMA.]

The term blackmail is now used to signify the attempt to extract money by threatening letters or threats to accuse of crime. It is defined by s. 21 (1) of the Theft Act 1968 as follows: "A person is guilty of blackmail if, with a view to gain for himself or another or with intent to cause loss to another, he makes any unwarranted demand with menaces; and for this purpose a demand with menaces is unwarranted unless the person making it does so in the belief (*a*) that he has reasonable grounds for making the demand; and (*b*) that the use of the menaces is a proper means of reinforcing the demand."

BLACK ROD is the usher belonging to the most noble order of the Garter; so called because of the black rod he carries in his hand. He is also usher of the House of Lords. He is also called the *gentleman usher*, as opposed to his deputy, who is called the *yeoman usher*. He is appointed by letters patent from the Crown. He executes the orders of the house, for the commitment of parties guilty of breaches of privilege and of contempt, and assists at the introduction of peers, and other ceremonies. *May.*

BLACKSTONE, SIR WILLIAM (1723–1780). English jurist and judge. First Vinerian professor of law at Oxford, and author of famous *Commentaries on the Laws of England*.

BLANK ACCEPTANCE. An acceptance written on blank stamped paper, and acting as a *prima facie* authority by the acceptor to complete the bill for any amount the stamp will cover. See s. 20 of the Bills of Exchange Act 1882.

BLANK BAR (also called *common bar*) was a plea which a defendant sometimes pleaded in an action of trespass, when he wished the plaintiff to point out with greater particularity the place where the trespass was committed.

BLANK INDORSEMENT. [INDORSEMENT.]

BLANKS. A kind of white money coined by Henry V for his French possessions; forbidden to be current in this realm by a statute of 1423.

BLASPHEMY. Formerly the offence, punishable with fine and imprisonment, of denying in some scandalous way the being or providence of the Almighty, or contumelious reproaches of our Saviour Christ; also all profane scoffing at the Holy Scripture, or exposing it to contempt and ridicule. The Blasphemy Act 1697 was passed for the suppression of blasphemy and profanity. Under it, prosecution had to be on information laid within four days of the offence, and had to be within three months. The Act was repealed by the Criminal Law Act 1967.

BLENDED FUND. [MIXED FUND.]

BLOCKADE. An operation of war by which one of the belligerents is able so to apply his force to one of the enemy's ports or coast lines as to render it dangerous to attempt to enter or leave. A blockade to be binding must be effective; and a party violating it must be proved to have been aware of its existence. Any attempt on the part of a neutral ship to enter or leave a blockaded place with goods or forbidden information is deemed a breach of blockade, and exposes the vessel to seizure and confiscation. [DECLARATION OF PARIS.]

BLOOD. That relationship without which (before 1926) none could claim to succeed as heir by descent to the purchaser. Now it signifies that relationship by virtue of which a person is enabled to take by descent on intestacy. [HALF-BLOOD; WHOLE-BLOOD.]

BLOODWIT. An amerciament for blood shed.

BOARD. A body of persons having delegated to them certain powers of the central government, as the National Enterprise Board (*q.v.*); or set up for the purposes of local government, usually for the purpose of administering a service within the area of two or more local authorities; or elected as directors by the shareholders in public companies.

BOARD OF AGRICULTURE AND FISHERIES. By Act of 1889 the Board of Agriculture was constituted to take over the powers and duties of the Inclosures commissioners, Land commissioners, Copyhold commissioners, and certain others. By the Board of Agriculture and Fisheries Act 1903 there were transferred to the Board of Agriculture certain powers and duties relating to the industry of fishing and the Act of 1889 was annulled. By the Ministry of Agriculture and Fisheries Act 1919 the "Ministry of Agriculture and Fisheries" was substituted for the Board. The name of the Ministry is now the Ministry of Agriculture, Fisheries and Food (S.I. 1955 No. 554); the powers of the Minister are exercised jointly with the Secretary of State for Wales (S.I. 1969 No. 388).

BOARD OF GREEN CLOTH. A board composed of the Lord Steward and Treasurer of the Royal Household, Comptroller and other officers, having the management of the Royal Household; so called from the green cloth on the table.

BOARD OF TRADE. A committee of the Privy Council, charged with the consideration of matters relating to trade and industry which were not dealt with by other departments and other matters of a miscellaneous character. In practice the Board never met and was an administrative Government department presided over by a President.

As to the present exercise of the functions of the Board of Trade, see the Industrial Expansion Act 1968, s. 14 (1) and the Secretary of State for Trade and Industry Order 1970.

BODY OF AN INSTRUMENT signifies the main and operative part, as opposed to the recitals, etc., in a deed, to the title and jurat in an affidavit.

BOMB. [AMMUNITION.]

‾ **BONA.** In the civil law includes all sorts of property, movable and immovable.

BONA FIDES. Good faith, without fraud or deceit. *Bona fide* holder of a bill of exchange or other security—one without knowledge of any defect in title. See the Bills of Exchange Act 1882, s. 29.

BONA NOTABILIA are such goods as a party dying had in another diocese than that wherein he died, amounting to £5 at least. The will of such a person had to be proved before the archbishop of the province. Now that the granting of probates and letters of administration has been transferred to the Chancery Division of the High Court, the law as to *bona notabilia* has become obsolete.

BONA VACANTIA. 1. Goods found without any apparent owner. They belong to the first occupant or finder, unless they be royal fish, shipwrecks, treasure trove, waifs and estrays, which belong to the Crown.

2. Under the rules for the division of real and personal estate on intestacy which are contained in the Administration of Estates Act 1925, the residuary estate belongs (in default of certain relatives specified in the Act) as *bona vacantia* to the Crown or to the Duchy of Lancaster or the Duke of Cornwall (as the case may be).

3. Under s. 354 of the Companies Act 1948, certain property of dissolved companies.

BONA WAVIATA. Such goods stolen as are waived (or thrown away) by a thief in his flight, for fear of being apprehended. [WAIFS.]

BOND. An instrument under seal, whereby a person binds himself to do or not to do certain things; this is a *single* bond. The person so binding himself is called the *obligor*; the person to whom he is bound, who is entitled to enforce the bond, is called the *obligee*. In some cases the obligor binds himself to pay a certain sum, called a *penal sum* or *penalty*, to which a condition is added, that, if he does or does not do a particular act (that is, if he complies with the conditions which the bond is intended to secure), the bond shall be void, otherwise it is to be of full force and effect. This is a *double* bond. The obligee, however, cannot recover the whole penalty, but only the actual loss proved to have been suffered.

Bonds are frequently issued by governments and companies as security for money borrowed by them.

BOND CREDITOR. A creditor whose debt is secured by a bond.

BOND TENANTS. A name sometimes formerly given to copyholders and customary tenants.

BONDED GOODS. Imported goods deposited in a government warehouse until duty is paid.

BONDSMAN. A surety.

BONIS ASPORTATIS. Writ of trespass in respect of goods wrongfully taken otherwise than under distress.

BONUS. Premium or advantage; an occasional extra dividend paid by a company either out of profits or capital.

BOOK OF COMMON PRAYER. The book prescribed by the Act of Uniformity 1662, constituting the standard of faith, worship and discipline in the Church of England.

Although the General Synod of the Church of England is empowered to sanction alternative forms of service, the forms of service contained in the Book of Common Prayer *must* continue to be available for use in church. See the Church of England (Worship and Doctrine) Measure 1974, s. 1 (1).

BOOKMAKER. Any person who, whether on his own account or as servant or agent to any other person, carries on, whether occasionally or regularly, the business of receiving or negotiating bets or conducting pool betting operations. See further the full definition in s. 55 of the Betting, Gaming and Lotteries Act 1963.

Under the 1963 Act bookmakers are required to hold permits, and the Act also restricts street bookmaking whilst allowing betting offices. As to licensing of bookmakers at dog-race meetings, see the Betting and Gaming Duties Act 1972.

BOOTY OF WAR. Prize of war on land, as opposed to prize at sea. It belongs by right to the Crown, but was at one time usually given to the captors. Jurisdiction on matters of booty of war is in the Queen's Bench Division.

BORDER WARRANT, in Scotch law, is a warrant granted by a judge ordinary on the border between England and Scotland, on the application of a creditor, for arresting the person or effects of a debtor residing on the English side, until he finds security *judicio sisti.*

BOROUGH. As used in the Reform Act 1832 the term "borough" meant a town entitled to send a member to parliament, or "parliamentary borough", and in the Municipal Corporations Act 1882 a town incorporated for the purposes of internal government, or "municipal borough". A town or city which was granted a charter of incorporation became known as a borough, the corporation consisting of a mayor, aldermen and councillors. Under the reorganisation of local government areas, boroughs existing before 1st April 1974 ceased to exist (though the London boroughs were maintained): see s. 20 (6) of the Local Government Act 1972. Their rights and privileges were preserved, however, by Part XII of the Act of 1972, under which the status of borough may also be conferred on certain districts.

BOROUGH COURT. The Court of record for a borough, generally presided over by the recorder. Over 140 borough civil courts, including such courts as the Beccles Fen Court, the Buckingham Three Weeks Court, the Oxford Court of Husting and the Stockport Court of Portemanimote, were abolished by the Local Government Act 1972.

BOROUGH ENGLISH. A customary descent of lands or tenements, of Saxon origin, whereby, in all places where the custom held, lands and tenements descended to the youngest son; or, if the owner of the land had no issue, then to the youngest brother. Abolished as respects enfranchised land by the Law of Property Act 1922; and generally in regard to land by the Administration of Estates Act 1925.

BORSTAL INSTITUTION. A place in which offenders not less than sixteen but under twenty-one years of age may be detained and given such training and instruction as will conduce to their reformation and the prevention of crime: Prison Act 1952, s. 43.

BOTE. Compensation. Thus manbote, that is, compensation or amends for a man slain. It is also synonymous with *estovers* (*q.v.*). Thus house-bote is wood for repairs or burning in the house; plough-bote, wood for making and repairing instruments of husbandry.

BOTTOMRY, BOTTOMRY BOND, or **BUMMAREE.** A maritime bond in the nature of a mortgage of a ship, when the owner borrows money to enable him to carry on his voyage, and pledges the keel or bottom of the ship as a security for the repayment. In which case it is understood that, if the ship be lost, the lender loses his whole money; but, if it returns in safety, then he shall receive back his principal, and also the premium or interest agreed upon. [RESPONDENTIA.]

BOUGHT AND SOLD NOTES are copies of entries and memoranda made by brokers of their transactions in buying and selling stock, or shares, or other personal property, and delivered to the vendors and purchasers for whom they act. The copy of any such entry, delivered to the purchaser, is called the *bought* note; the copy delivered to the vendor is called the *sold* note.

BOUND BAILIFF. [BAILIFF.]

BOUNTY. A premium paid by Government to producers, exporters or importers in order to encourage certain industries.

BRACTON. A famous lawyer of the reign of Henry III, renowned for his knowledge both of the common and civil laws. He wrote a celebrated book, *De Legibus et Consuetudinibus Angliæ* (Concerning the Laws and Customs of England).

BRAWLING. Quarrelling or chiding, or creating a disturbance, in a church or churchyard.

There were two Brawling Acts, of 1551 and 1553, which were passed in the reigns of Edward VI and Mary respectively. The first made it an offence to quarrel, chide or brawl in any church or churchyard, and also to smite or lay violent hands upon any other person in church. Originally, the punishment was excommunication. The second Act was for preserving the peace during divine service, and provided for the punishment of persons disturbing preachers, contemptuously dealing with the Sacrament, defacing or breaking down crucifixes or crosses, etc.

The Act of 1551 was repealed by the Ecclesiastical Jurisdiction Measure 1963; that of 1553 by the Criminal Law Act 1967.

BREACH. An invasion of a right or violation of a duty. The word is specially used in the following expressions:—

1. *Breach of Close.* Unlawfully entering upon another person's land.

2. *Breach of Covenant or Contract.* A non-fulfilment of a covenant or contract, whether by commission or omission.

3. *Breach of the Peace.* A disturbance of the public peace.

4. *Breach of Pound.* Taking by force, out of a pound, things lawfully impounded.

5. *Breach of Prison.* The escape from arrest of a person lawfully arrested for a crime.

6. *Breach of Privilege.* An act or default in violation of the privilege of either House of parliament, as, for instance, by false swearing before a committee of the House, or by resisting the officers thereof in the execution of their duty. *May.*

7. *Breach of Promise.* A phrase used especially with reference to the non-fulfilment of a promise to marry. This formerly gave rise to a cause of action, but engagements to marry are no longer enforceable at law: Law Reform (Miscellaneous Provisions) Act 1970, s. 1.

8. *Breach of Trust.* A violation by a trustee of the duty imposed upon him by the instrument creating the trust.

BREAKDOWN OF MARRIAGE. The sole ground for a petition for divorce is no longer that of a specific matrimonial offence, as *e.g.* adultery, but is that of the irretrievable breakdown of the marriage. Breakdown may be *proved* by evidence of adultery, desertion, unreasonable behaviour, or the fact that the parties have lived apart for a number of years. See s. 1 of the Matrimonial Causes Act 1973. [DIVORCE.]

BREAKING A CLOSE. An unlawful entry on another's land. [BREACH, 1.]

BREATH TEST. A test for the purpose of obtaining an indication of the proportion of alcohol in a person's blood. See s. 12 (1) of the Road Traffic Act 1972.

BREWSTER SESSIONS. The general annual licensing meeting of the licensing justices of a particular district. The meeting must extend over at least two days, the first of which must be in the first fortnight of February. Business consists of renewals of licences, applications for new licences, removals and transfers. See the Licensing Act, 1964, s. 2.

BRIBERY. The taking or giving of money for the performance or non-performance of a public duty.

By s. 99 of the Representation of the People Act 1949 a person is guilty of bribery if he gives money or procures any office in order to induce a voter to vote or refrain from voting, etc. Bribery is a corrupt practice under the Act.

See also the Prevention of Corruption Acts 1889 to 1916; the Extradition Act 1906, under which bribery is made an extradition crime; and the Honours (Prevention of Abuses) Act 1925, under which any person who attempts to obtain a grant of honours by the provision of gifts or money is guilty of a misdemeanour.

BRIDEWELL. A house of correction. See s. 109 (2) of the Magistrates' Courts Act 1952.

BRIDLE PATH. A right of way over which it is lawful to ride or lead a horse, as opposed to a mere footpath.

BRIEF. A statement of a client's case written out by the solicitor for the instruction of counsel in a civil or criminal proceeding.

BRIGBOTE, or **BRUGBOTE.** Contribution to the repair of bridges. It signified also freedom from giving aid to the repair of bridges.

BRITISH LIBRARY. A library formed by bringing together four eminent libraries: (1) the British Museum Library (including the National Reference Library for Science and Invention); (2) the National Central Library; (3) the National Lending Library for Science and Technology; and (4) the British National Bibliography. See the British Library Act 1972.

BRITISH AIRPORTS AUTHORITY. A body corporate which manages the aerodromes at Heathrow, Gatwick, Stansted, Prestwick, etc. Airports Authority Act 1975.

BRITISH NATIONAL OIL CORPORATION. Established under the Petroleum and Submarine Pipe-Lines Act 1975, to exercise governmental rights in activities connected with petroleum. Mainly concerned with the production of oil and gas from the North Sea and other United Kingdom waters.

BRITISH STANDARD TIME. [SUMMER TIME.]

BRITISH SUBJECT. The status conferred upon every person who is a citizen of the United Kingdom and Commonwealth, of Canada, Australia, New Zealand, India, Pakistan, etc. The term "Commonwealth citizen" has the same meaning. British Nationality Acts 1948 to 1965.

BRITANNIA. A description of silver of a standard of fineness of 958.4 parts per 1000: see Hallmarking Act 1973, Sch. 2.

BRITTON. A famous treatise of the reign of Edward I, at whose command it was apparently written; founded on Bracton and Fleta.

BROAD ARROW. The mark on government stores, indicating that they belong to the Crown.

BROADCASTING. Communication by wireless telegraphy, whether by sound alone or by sound and vision. Provisions as to copyright in broadcast programmes are contained in s. 40 of the Copyright Act 1956. By s. 1 of the Defamation Act 1952 a broadcast programme is considered to be publication in a permanent form.

The functions of the Independent Broadcasting Authority (formerly called the Independent Television Authority) were extended to include the service of sound broadcasting by the Sound Broadcasting Act 1972, now consolidated in the Independent Broadcasting Authority Act 1973.

The British Broadcasting Corporation was incorporated by Royal Charter in 1926 and operates under a licence from the Secretary of State.

BROCAGE, or **BROKERAGE.** The wages or hire of a *broker*. Brokerage for procuring a marriage is contrary to public policy, and not recoverable.

BROKER (from the French word *Broieur*). A grinder or breaker into small pieces; because he that is of that trade draws the bargain into particulars. Now usually an agent between the contracting parties in mercantile transactions, paid by a commission, or brokerage. [FACTOR.] The term is also applied to a bailiff employed to distrain. [BAILIFF.]

BROTHEL. A place resorted to by persons of both sexes for prostitution, not a house occupied by one woman where she receives a number of men. By s. 33 of the Sexual Offences Act 1956 it is an offence for a person to keep or to manage or to assist in managing a brothel. Sections 34, 35 of the Act also make it an offence for a landlord to let premises for use as a brothel, or for a tenant to permit such use.

BUDGET. The financial statement of the national revenue and expenditure for each year, submitted to parliament by the Chancellor of the Exchequer. *May.*

BUILDING LEASE. A lease of land for a long term, usually ninety-nine years, at a rent called a ground rent, the lessee covenanting to build thereon.

By s. 99 of the Law of Property Act 1925 either a mortgagor or mortgagee in possession can (in case of mortgage made after 1925) make a valid building lease for 999 years. Under s. 41 of the Settled Land Act 1925 a tenant for life may make a building lease for 999 years; and see also ss. 44 and 46 of that Act.

BUILDING SOCIETY. A society established to raise funds by the subscriptions of its members, by advances from which funds members are enabled to build or purchase dwelling houses, or to purchase land, such advances being secured to the society by mortgages.

BULK SALE. (*Canada.*) A sale by a merchant of his stock-in-trade. Provincial laws require specified procedures to be carried out for the protection of creditors.

BULL. 1. An instrument granted by the Pope of Rome, and sealed with a seal of lead, containing in it his decrees, commandments or other acts, according to the nature of the instrument.

2. A *bull*, on the Stock Exchange, is one who *buys* stock for settlement at a future date, without intending to take delivery, but with a view to gain by a rise in price in the interval. [BEAR.]

BULLION. The ore or metal whereof gold is made. It signifies gold or silver in mass or billet.

BUM-BAILIFF. [BAILIFF.]

BURDEN OF PROOF (or *onus probandi*). The duty of proving one's case. It is a rule of evidence that the point in issue is to be proved by the party who asserts the affirmative, according to the maxim, *ei incumbit probatio qui dicit, non qui negat.*

BURDEN OF PROOF—*continued.*

Thus, in general, the burden of proof lies upon the plaintiff or prosecutor; but he may adduce evidence sufficient to establish a *prima facie* case, and the burden of proof is then said to be *shifted* on to the other side. In criminal cases it is exceptional for the burden to rest on the defence; even when it does the burden is lighter than that which rests on the prosecution.

BURG, or BURGH. [BOROUGH.]

BURGAGE TENURE. A tenure whereby burgesses, citizens, or townsmen held their lands or tenements of the king or other lord, for a certain yearly rent. It was a species of free socage. Borough English was the most important burgage custom. Abolished as regards enfranchised land by the Law of Property Act 1922, Sched. XII, para. 1 (*d*); and generally in regard to land by the Administration of Estates Act 1925, s. 45 (1) (*a*).

BURGAGE-HOLDING. A tenure by which lands in royal boroughs in Scotland are held of the sovereign.

BURGBOTE. A tribute or contribution towards the building or repairing of castles or walls of a borough or city. [BOTE.]

BURGESSES were once said to be the inhabitants of a borough or town, driving a trade there (*Cowel*). The term has now no local government significance.

BURGHMOTE. In former times, the court of a borough or city.

BURGLARY. Once the crime of house-breaking by night, *i.e.*, between 9 p.m. and 6 a.m., it consisted either (1) in breaking and entering a dwelling-house by night, with intent to commit a felony; or (2) in breaking out of a dwelling-house by night, after having committed a felony therein, or after having entered with intent to commit a felony.

The law as to burglary was entirely changed by the Theft Act 1968, which eliminated the element of "breaking" in or out and also abolished the distinction between a night-time and a daytime offence.

Section 9 of the Act of 1968 provides that a person is guilty of *burglary* if he enters any building or part of a building as a trespasser with intent to commit certain offences (*e.g.* stealing, inflicting grievous bodily harm, etc.); or having so entered, commits or attempts to commit such offences. Penalty: imprisonment for up to fourteen years.

Furthermore, by s. 10 of the Act, a person is guilty of *aggravated burglary* if he commits any burglary and at the time has with him any firearm or imitation firearm, any weapon of offence, or any explosive. Penalty: liability to imprisonment for life.

BURIAL in some part of the parish churchyard is a common law right of all parishioners (and a moral right of strangers, *Kempe* v. *Wickes* (1809), 3 Phil. 265, 274), and will be enforced by *mandamus.*

Since 1st April 1974 burial authorities are the councils of districts, London boroughs, parishes, the Common Council of the City of London, and the parish meetings of parishes having no parish council. See s. 214 of the Local Government Act 1972.

BUTLERAGE OF WINES. [PRISAGE.]

BY-LAWS, or BYELAWS. Laws made by councils, boards, corporations, and companies, under powers conferred by Acts of Parliament, for the government of their members and the management of their business. And, independently of statutory powers, byelaws made by a corporation aggregate are binding on its members, unless contrary to the laws of the land, or contrary to and inconsistent with their charter, or manifestly unreasonable.

The council of a district or of a London borough may make byelaws for the good rule and government of the whole or any part of the district or borough, and for the prevention and suppression of nuisances. See ss. 235–238 of the Local Government Act 1972.

C

C. A. V. [CUR. ADV. VULT.]

C. I. F. Cost, insurance, and freight. A price quoted "c.i.f." at a certain place usually includes everything up to delivery at port or place of destination. [*Cf.* F.O.B.]

CA. SA. [CAPIAS AD SATISFACIENDUM.]

CABINET. Those Privy Councillors who, under the name of cabinet ministers or cabinet council, actually transact the immediate business of the government, and assemble for that purpose from time to time as the public exigencies require. The cabinet is a body known only recently to the law; it was first established by Charles I.

CADIT QUAESTIO. There's an end to the argument.

CADUCIARY RIGHT, in Scotch law, is the Crown's right of escheat to the estate of a deceased person on failure of heirs; *caduca* in Roman law meaning the lapse of a testamentary disposition.

CÆSARIAN OPERATION. The delivery of a child by surgical operation. If, before 1926, a child was saved in this way after the mother's death the husband could not take as tenant by the curtesy.

CÆTERORUM. Administration *cæterorum* is administration granted as to the residue of an estate, after a *limited* power of administration, already given as to part of the estate, has been exhausted.

CALENDAR. 1. A list of prisoners' names at the former quarter sessions or assizes.

2. [MONTH.]

CALL. 1. Instalments whereby the capital in public companies is gradually paid up by the shareholders. See the Companies Act 1948, Sched. I, Table A, Articles 15–21.

2. The conferring on students of the degree of barrister-at-law.

3. The right to demand the allotment or transfer of shares at or before a given date at a given price.

CALL OF THE HOUSE. The calling over the names of members in either House of parliament, pursuant to a resolution of the House ordering the attendance of the members thereof, which order may be enforced by fine and imprisonment. *May.*

CALLING THE JURY. This consists in successively drawing out of a box, into which they have been previously put, the names of the jurors on the panels annexed to the *nisi prius* record, and calling them over in the order in which they are so drawn; and the twelve persons whose names are first called, and who appear, are sworn as the jury; unless some just cause of challenge or excuse, with respect to any of them, shall be brought forward. [CHALLENGE.]

CALLING THE PLAINTIFF. The old method of non-suiting a plaintiff who did not appear when called by the crier. [NON-SUIT.]

CALLING UPON A PRISONER. When a prisoner has been found guilty upon an indictment, the clerk of the court calls upon him to say why judgment should not be passed upon him.

CALLS ON CONTRIBUTORIES. Demands made by a joint stock company, or its official liquidator, upon persons liable to contribute to its assets.

CAMBIST. A person skilled in cambistry, or exchanges; a trader or dealer in promissory notes and bills of exchange.

CAMERA. The judge's private room behind the court. [SITTINGS IN CAMERA.]

CAMERA STELLATA. The Star-Chamber. [STAR-CHAMBER.]

CAMPBELL'S ACTS. [LORD CAMPBELL'S ACTS.]

CANCELLATION. The striking out or revocation of the contents of an instrument by drawing lines (*cancelli*) across it. Mere cancellation does not now revoke a will.

CANCELLI. Lattice-work placed before a window, a doorway, the tribunal of a judge, or any other place.

CANDLEMAS DAY. The feast of the Purification of the Blessed Virgin Mary (February 2), so called from the custom of blessing and distributing candles, of 11th-century origin. A quarter day in Scotland.

CANNABIS. The flowering or fruiting tops of a plant officially classed as a dangerous drug. Defined in s. 37 of the Misuse of Drugs Act 1971.

CANON. 1. A cathedral dignitary, appointed sometimes by the Crown and sometimes by the bishop. The benefice attached to it is called a *canonry*. [CHAPTER.]

2. A law or ordinance of the Church.

3. In civil law a rule, *e.g.*, the canons of inheritance.

CANON LAW. A body of Roman ecclesiastical law, compiled in the twelfth, thirteenth, and fourteenth centuries, from the opinions of the ancient Latin fathers, the decrees of General Councils, and the decretal epistles and bulls of the Holy See, and first codified by Gratianus in 1139.

CANON LAW—*continued.*

In the year 1603 certain canons were enacted by the clergy under James I. But, as they were never confirmed in parliament, it has been held that, where they are not merely declaratory of the ancient canon law, but are introductory of new regulations they do not bind the laity; whatever regard the clergy may think proper to pay them. They were revised again in 1865.

CAP OF MAINTENANCE. One of the regalia or ornaments of state belonging to the sovereign; also once used by the mayors of several cities in England.

CAPAX DOLI. [DOLI CAPAX.]

CAPE. A judicial writ formerly used in the old real actions for the recovery of land. It was of two kinds, the *cape magnum*, or *grand cape*, and the *cape parvum*, or *petit cape*.

Cape magnum was a writ which issued where the tenant or defendant made default at the day appointed for his appearance.

Cape parvum was a writ of the same kind, which issued when the tenant or defendant, *having appeared* at the day assigned, *afterwards* made default.

The proceedings in real actions were abolished by Acts of 1833 and 1860.

CAPE AD VALENTIAM. A species of *cape magnum*. [CAPE.]

CAPIAS. A writ, usually addressed to the sheriff, by which process is issued against an accused person after indictment found, where the accused is not in custody, in cases not otherwise provided for by statute. For other kinds of *capias*, see the following titles and *mesne process*. [MESNE.]

CAPIAS AD AUDIENDUM JUDICIUM. A writ issued in cases where a defendant has, in his absence, been found guilty of misdemeanour, to bring him in to receive judgment.

CAPIAS AD RESPONDENDUM. 1. A writ under which an absconding defendant in a civil action was formerly arrested or obliged to give special bail.

2. A writ issued against a defendant in misdemeanour against whom an indictment has been found to compel him to appear for arraignment.

CAPIAS AD SATISFACIENDUM (generally called a *ca. sa.*). A writ by which on a judgment for an amount exceeding £20, execution might issue against the person of the debtor, who might be arrested and imprisoned thereunder. This writ was practically abolished by s. 4 of the Debtors Act 1869.

CAPITA, DISTRIBUTION PER. A distribution of an intestate's estate, wherein each claimant has a share in his own right as in equal degree of kindred to the deceased, and not as representing another person, *i.e.*, distribution *per stirpes*. [STIRPES, DISTRIBUTION PER.]

CAPITAL. The net amount of property belonging to a merchant, after deducting the debts he is owing. This term, however, is more strictly applied, either to the sum of money which he has embarked in his business at first, or to the available sum he may afterwards have at command for carrying it on.

CAPITAL GAINS TAX. Tax charged in respect of capital gains, that is, chargeable gains accruing to a person on the disposal of assets. Certain kinds of property are exempt. Imposed by the Finance Act 1965.

CAPITAL PUNISHMENT. Death by hanging. Abolished as a punishment for murder by the Murder (Abolition of Death Penalty) Act 1965, but it can still be awarded for treason, piracy with violence, or setting fire to H.M. ships. [MURDER.]

CAPITAL TRANSFER TAX. A tax introduced to the United Kingdom by the Finance Act 1975. The tax, which replaced estate duty, charges tax, at progressive rates, on cumulative lifetime transfers and on death. Transfers between spouses are exempt, as are certain other transfers, *e.g.* gifts to charity, and annual transfers up to a total of £2,000.

CAPITATION TAX, FEE, GRANT, etc., is one raised or paid on each individual or according to the *heads*, *e.g.*, for each child in a school.

CAPITE. Tenants *in capite* were those who held land *immediately* from the sovereign either in right of his Crown or of some honour or manor. [FEUDAL SYSTEM.]

CAPITULARY. A code of laws.

CAPTION. That part of a legal instrument, *e.g.*, of an indictment, which shows where, when, and by what authority it is taken, found, or executed.

CAPTURE. A seizure; a word especially used of the seizure of a ship or cargo, etc., at sea by a belligerent in time of war.

CAR TAX. A tax on cars, chargeable in addition to value added tax under s. 52 of the Finance Act 1972.

CARAT. A description indicating that an article, or the metal in an article, is of so many carats is to be presumed to be an indication that the article or metal is of gold, and that its fineness is that specified in the following table for that number of carats (not applicable if, as in a case where the article is a precious stone, the word "carat" is used as a measure of weight for precious stones, and not as a measure of fineness).

TABLE

Number of carats	Indicates gold of a standard of fineness of	
9	375	parts per thousand
12	500	parts per thousand
14	585	parts per thousand
15	625	parts per thousand
18	750	parts per thousand
22	916·6	parts per thousand

and so in proportion for any other number of carats (Hallmarking Act 1973, Sch. 1, Part III, para. 2). [ASSAY; HALLMARK.]

CARAVAN. Any structure designed or adapted for human habitation which is capable of being moved from one place to another and any motor vehicle so designed or adapted, but not railway rolling stock, and not any tent. See the Caravan Sites and Control of Development Act 1960, s. 29 (1); also the Mobile Homes Act 1975.

CARCEL-AGE. Prison fees.

CARE ORDER. An order which may be made by a juvenile court where it is satisfied that a child or young person is being neglected, is exposed to moral danger, etc. See s. 1 of The Children and Young Persons Act 1969, and Part III of the Children Act 1975.

CARELESS DRIVING. Driving a motor vehicle on a road without due care and attention, or without reasonable consideration for other persons using the road. See s. 3 of the Road Traffic Act 1972. As to careless cycling see *ibid.*, s. 18.

CARGO. Goods and merchandise shipped for carriage by water.

CAROOME. A licence by the Lord Mayor of London to keep a cart.

CARRIER. A person who carries goods for another for hire.

A *common carrier* is one who exercises the business of carrying as a public employment, and undertakes to carry goods for all persons indiscriminately. The law casts upon the common carrier a duty (1) to carry for everyone who offers to pay his hire, which no one else is bound to do, except upon agreement; (2) to answer for all things carried as insurers; this liability, however, is restricted by the Carriers Acts, 1830 and 1865.

CARRY COSTS. A verdict is said to "carry costs" in those cases where by law it *prima facie* involves the payment of costs by the unsuccessful party to the party in whose favour the verdict is given. Costs are now within the discretion of the court. See R.S.C., 1965, Ord. 62.

CARRY OVER. A term used on the Stock Exchange signifying the postponement of completion of a contract to buy or sell shares. [CONTANGO.]

CARTE BLANCHE. A white sheet of paper; a phrase used especially to signify a paper given by one man to another with nothing on it but the signature of the former, so that the latter may fill it up at his discretion. Hence the figurative expression, "to give any one *carte blanche*", that is, unlimited authority.

CARTEL, or **CHARTEL.** An instrument executed between two belligerent powers for settling the exchange of prisoners of war and other like matters. Also a challenge to a duel to decide legal controversy.

The word cartel is also used to mean a combination of companies or businesses with the object of eliminating competition and so maintaining high prices for goods. Legislation against cartel agreements, overriding the laws of member states, is a feature of European Economic Community legislation.

CARTEL SHIP. A ship employed in effecting the exchange of prisoners of war.

CASE. A form of action which formerly lay for damages for wrongs or injuries not accompanied with immediate violence, *i.e.*, where *covenant* or *trespass* did not apply. [TRESPASS, 4.]

CASE, SPECIAL. [SPECIAL CASE.]

CASE STATED. A statement of facts prepared by one court for the opinion of another on a point of law. Thus it was formerly the practice of the Court of Chancery to refer difficult questions of law, which might arise in the course of a suit, to one of the common law courts, in the form of a "case stated" for the opinion of the common law court. 3 *Bl*. This was abolished in 1852. Now by the British Law Ascertainment Act 1859, a case may be stated by an English court for the opinion of a Scotch court, in a matter involving Scotch law, etc.

A person who was a party to any proceeding before a magistrates' court or is aggrieved by a conviction, etc., of the court may question the proceeding of the court on the ground that it is wrong in law or is in excess of jurisdiction by applying to the justices comprising the court to state a case for the opinion of the High Court on the question of law or jurisdiction involved: Magistrates' Court Act 1952, s. 87.

A counsel who opens a case before a jury is also said to "state the case" to the jury.

CASTING VOTE. The vote given by the chairman of a deliberative assembly, where the votes are equally divided.

CASTLE WARD, or **GUARD,** or **GARD.** An imposition laid upon such of the king's subjects as dwelt within a certain compass of any castle, towards the maintenance of such as might watch and ward the castle.

CASU PROVISO and **CASU CONSIMILI.** The first was a writ of entry given by the Statute of Gloucester (1278) to a reversioner of land which a dowress (or tenant in dowe) of the land had disposed of in fee, or for other greater estate than that which she held in the land. It could be brought in the lifetime of the dowress, and in this respect it differed from the writ *ad communem legem*. The writ *casu consimili* was given a like case where a tenant for life

or limited owner other than a dowress had disposed of the land. Abolished in 1833.

CASUAL EJECTOR. The fictitious tenant (generally called Richard Roe), nominal defendant in the old action of ejectment. [EJECTMENT.]

CASUS BELLI. An occurrence giving rise to or justifying or giving a pretext for war.

CASUS FŒDERIS. A case stipulated by treaty, or which comes within the terms of a contract.

CASUS OMISSUS. A case inadvertently left unprovided for by statute.

CATALLA. Chattels. [CHATTELS.]

CATCHING BARGAIN. A purchase from an expectant heir, for an inadequate consideration. By the Law of Property Act 1925, s. 174, no acquisition made in good faith, without fraud or unfair dealing, of any reversionary interest in real or personal property, for money or money's worth, shall be liable to be opened or set aside merely on the ground of under value. Equity, however, retains its right to relieve an heir or reversioner from a "catching bargain" in cases where the transaction is unconscionable.

CATCHLAND. Land in Norfolk, so called because it was not known to what parish it belonged, and the minister who first seized the tithes of it enjoyed them for that year.

CATCHPOLE. A name formerly given to a sheriff's deputy, or to a constable, or other officer whose duty it was to arrest persons.

CATHEDRAL. The principal church of a diocese.

CATTLE. [LIVESTOCK.]

CATTLEGATE. Common for one beast.

CAUSA CAUSANS. The immediate cause, the *causa proxima*, the last link in the chain of causation.

CAUSA MORTIS. [DONATIO MORTIS CAUSA.]

CAUSA PROXIMA ET NON REMOTA SPECTATUR. The immediate and not the remote cause is to be looked at.

CAUSE. 1. A suit or action at law.
2. That which produces or effects a result.

CAUSE OF ACTION. The ground on which an action can be maintained; but often extended to any claim on which a given action is in fact grounded, whether or not legally maintainable.

CAUSE-LIST. The printed list of causes made out for each day during the sittings of the courts; the causes being tried in the order of their entry.

CAUTION. 1. In ecclesiastical, admiralty, and Scotch law, signifies *surety* or *security*. It is also called *cautionary*.

2. Under the Land Registration Acts 1925 to 1966 a person interested can place on the register a caution preventing the proprietor from dealing with the land without notice to the cautioner.

3. A warning to an accused person that any statement made by him may be used in evidence against him.

CAVEAT (let him beware). An intimation made to the proper officer of a court of justice to prevent the taking of any step without intimation to the party interested (caveator) to appear. See the Judicature Act 1925, s. 154, as to caveats against grants of probate or administration.

CAVEAT EMPTOR (let the buyer beware). A maxim implying that the buyer must be cautious, as the risk is his and not that of the seller. The rule of law as to the sale of goods is, that if a person sells them as his own, and the price be paid, and the *title* prove deficient, the seller may be compelled to refund the money. But as to the *soundness* of the wares, the vendor is not usually bound to answer; but there are several exceptions now embodied in the Sale of Goods Act 1893, ss. 13–15, as amended by the Supply of Goods (Implied Terms) Act 1973.

CAVERS. Persons stealing ore from mines in Derbyshire, punishable in the Miners' Court; also officers of the mines.

CEAP. A bargain, anything for sale; chattel; also cattle as being the usual medium of barter (ceap-gild).

CEDE. To assign or transfer.

CEDENT (Sc.). An assignor.

CENSURE. 1. A custom in certain manors in Devon and Cornwall, where all persons above the age of 16 years were cited to swear fealty to the lord, to pay 11d. per poll and 1d. ever after (censores).

2. A condemnatory judgment, or, more particularly, a reprimand from a superior.

CENSUS. A numbering of the people. First taken in 1801 in England, and now taken every ten years. For particulars now required to be given, see the Census Act 1920.

CENTRAL CRIMINAL COURT. The court originally established by the Central Criminal Court Act 1834 (repealed) for trial of offences committed in London, Middlesex, and certain parts of Essex, Kent and Surrey.

The Courts Act 1971 provides that when the Crown Court sits in the City of London it shall continue to be known as the Central Criminal Court. The former courthouse and accommodation also continue to be known by that name, or, colloquially, as the "Old Bailey".

CENTRAL OFFICE OF THE SUPREME COURT. Established by the Judicature Act 1879 (repealed) to consolidate the offices of the Masters of the divisions of the High Court. See ss. 104, 105 of the Judicature Act 1925.

The central Office consists of the following departments: (1) the Masters' Secretary's and Queen's Remembrancer's Department; (2) the Action Department; (3) the Filing and Record Department; (4) the Crown Office and Associates' Department; and (5) the Supreme Court Taxing Office.

CEPI CORPUS (I have taken the body). The sheriff's return to a *capias* or other writ requiring him to seize the body of a party, indicating that he has complied with the writ. [CAPIAS.]

CERTIFICATE is used for a writing made in any court, to give notice to another court of anything done therein. *Cowel.*

CERTIFICATE, LAND. A certificate drawn up by the Land Registry and containing particulars of registered land, and delivered to the registered proprietor or deposited in the Registry as the proprietor may prefer. See the Land Registration Acts 1925 to 1966.

CERTIFICATE OF CONFORMITY. A certificate formerly granted to a bankrupt, indicating that he had conformed in

CERTIFICATE OF CONFORMITY
—*continued*.

all points to the directions of the law. An order of discharge is now substituted for the certificate of conformity.

CERTIFICATE OF MASTER. The written statement of a master in Chancery, embodying the result of enquiries and accounts in a chancery action taken before the master in accordance with the judgment or order made by the judge. [CHIEF CLERK.]

CERTIFICATE OF SHARES. A document declaring its owner entitled to shares or stock in a joint stock company.

CERTIFICATE, TRIAL BY. A form of trial in which the evidence of the person certifying was the only proper criterion of the point in dispute. Now practically obsolete.

CERTIFICATION. A writ formerly granted for a review or re-trial of a matter decided in an action; now entirely superseded by the remedy afforded by means of a new trial.

CERTIFIED CHEQUE. [CHEQUE.]

CERTIFIED COPY. One signed and certified as true by the official in whose custody the original is.

CERTIORARI (to be more fully informed of). An order commanding proceedings to be removed from an inferior court into a superior court for review. Thus an indictment might formerly be removed from an inferior court to the High Court by writ of *certiorari*.

The writ of *certiorari* was abolished by s. 7 of the Administration of Justice (Miscellaneous Provisions) Act 1938, which substituted therefor the present order of *certiorari*.

In many cases of summary conviction the right to *certiorari* has been taken away by statute.

CERT-MONEY. Head money formerly paid yearly by the residents of several manors to the lords thereof for the certain keeping of the leet: called *certum letae*.

CERTUM EST QUOD CERTUM REDDI POTEST (that is certain which can be rendered certain). It is a rule that rent must be certain, in order to support a distress. If, however, it is definitely ascertainable, that is enough to satisfy the rule.

CESS, or **CESSE.** An assessment or tax.

CESSER. 1. The ceasing or termination.

2. *Proviso for Cesser.* Where terms for years were raised by settlements it was usual to introduce a proviso that they should cease when the trusts were at an end. Now, by s. 5 of the Law of Property Act 1925, every such term ceases when the purposes for which it was created are satisfied, without the need for such a proviso.

CESSIO BONORUM (the yielding up of goods). The cession, or yielding up, by a debtor, of his goods to his creditors. Under the Roman law this only operated to discharge the debtor *pro tanto*, but exonerated him from imprisonment. This was the foundation of the modern law of bankruptcy, and the French and Scottish law conforms to the Roman in its leading outlines.

CESSIO IN JURE. (Roman law.) A fictitious suit in which the person who was to acquire the thing claimed it as his own, and the person who was to transfer it acknowledged the justice of the claim, and the magistrate thereupon pronounced it to be the property of the claimant.

CESSION was the name given where a vacancy was created by an incumbent of a living in taking another benefice, whereby the first was adjudged void according to the Pluralities Act, 1838. See now, as to procedure for the union of benefices, the Pastoral Measure, 1968.

CESSOR. A tenant of land who neglects the duties to which he is bound by his tenure. *Cowel.*

CESTUI QUE TRUST. The person for whose benefit a trust is created; the person entitled to the equitable, as opposed to the legal, estate. Thus, if land be granted to A in trust for B, B is *cestui que trust*, A is trustee.

CESTUI QUE USE. The person for whose benefit a use was created. His rights were the same as those of *cestui que trust*, the latter expression not being employed till after the Statute of Uses, 1535 (repealed by the Law of Property Act, 1925).

CESTUI QUE VIE. He for whose life any land or tenement is granted. Thus, if A be tenant of lands for the life of B, B is called the *cestui que vie*.

CHAFEWAX, or **CHAFFWAX.** An officer in Chancery who fixed the wax for the sealing of the writs, and such other instruments as were there to be made out. Abolished in 1852.

CHAIRMAN. The person elected by the directors of a company to be chairman of their meetings, including a person who, though not so elected, holds any office carrying similar functions; Companies Act 1967, s. 6. Generally, any person elected to take charge of and control meetings, as *e.g.* of a local council. He may have a casting vote.

CHALLENGE. An objection taken against jurors.

Challenges to a jury are of two kinds. (A) For cause, *viz.*:—

1. *Challenges to the array,* by which a party excepts to the whole panel of the jurors, by reason of the partiality of the Lord Chancellor or his officer who arrayed the panel: either *principal,* in case of direct partiality, or *for favour,* inferred partiality. This is unusual.

2. *Challenges to the separate polls,* by which a party excepts to individual jurors. These might formerly be made (1) *propter honoris respectum* (by reason of honour), as if a lord of parliament be empanelled on a jury; (2) *propter defectum*: as if a man have not estate sufficient to qualify him for being a juror (as to qualification for jury service, see s. 1 of the Juries Act 1974); (3) *propter affectum,* for suspicion of bias or partiality; (4) *propter delictum,* for some crime or misdemeanour that affects the juror's credit and renders him infamous.

There is no limit to the number of challenges for cause. See generally s. 12 of the Juries Act 1974.

(B) Peremptory. Challenges to the number of seven may be made by a prisoner without assigning cause: Juries Act 1974, s. 12 (1). The Crown may also challenge jurors in the first instance without assigning cause, until all the panel is gone through and it is found that there cannot be a full jury without the persons so challenged.

CHALLENGE TO FIGHT. Sending or bearing by word or letter is a misdemeanour punishable by fine and imprisonment.

CHAMBERLAIN. This word is variously used in our chronicles, laws, and statutes, as—

1. The Lord Great Chamberlain of England, to whose office belongs the government of the palace at Westminster and of the House of Lords during session.

2. The Lord Chamberlain of the Queen's House, the Queen's Chamberlain, to whose office it especially appertains to look to the Queen's furniture, pictures and plate, and to govern the under-servants belonging to the same. He formerly had authority to license theatres within the metropolis, and within those places where the sovereign usually resides; but these functions were abolished by the Theatres Act 1968.

CHAMBERS. The offices of a judge in which a large part of the business of the Superior Courts is transacted by a judge or a master. Applications by way of summons, and inquiries incidental to a suit, are made in chambers.

CHAMBERS OF THE KING (*Regiæ cameræ*). The havens or ports of the kingdom are so called in our ancient records. *Cowel.*

CHAMPARTY, or **CHAMPERTY** (Lat. *Campi partitio,* a dividing of the land). A maintenance of any man in an action or suit, upon condition to have part of the things (be it lands or goods) when recovered. *Cowel.* It was an offence against public justice. Abolished by the Criminal Law Act 1967.

CHANCEL. That part of a church where the communion table stands. The rector or impropriator is bound to repair it.

CHANCELLOR. A word used in several senses.

1. The Lord High Chancellor, who is the highest judicial functionary in the kingdom, and prolocutor or Speaker of the House of Lords by prescription. He is a privy councillor and cabinet minister by virtue of his office, and usually (though not necessarily) a peer of the realm. He goes out of office with the ministry. He may not be a Roman Catholic.

2. The Chancellor of the Duchy of Lancaster, an official of the Crown as owner of the Duchy of Lancaster. The duties are now little more than nominal.

3. The Chancellor of the Exchequer is an officer who formerly sat in the Court of Exchequer, but he is now the minister who

CHANCELLOR—*continued.*

has control over the national revenue and expenditure.

4. The Chancellor of a University, who is the principal officer of the university. His office is for the most part honorary. The Chancellor's Court of Oxford has a jurisdiction over the members of the university, and the judge of the court is the vice-chancellor or his deputy. A similar privilege formerly enjoyed by the University of Cambridge has been abolished.

5. The Chancellor of a Diocese is the officer appointed to assist a bishop in matters of law, and to hold his consistory courts for him.

6. The Chancellor of the Order of the Garter and other military orders is an officer who seals the commissions and keeps a register of proceedings, etc.

CHANCE-MEDLEY (*chaude melée*), was a phrase properly applied to such killing as happens in self-defence when, after two persons have become involved in a fight, one stops fighting and the other does not and the former kills the latter. Now obsolete.

CHANCERY COURT OF YORK. The court of the Archbishop of York, for ecclesiastical matters in the province. Therefrom, faculty appeals lie to the Judicial Committee of the Privy Council.

CHANCERY DIVISION. One of the three divisions of the High Court of Justice, superseding the former High Court of Chancery. The causes and matters assigned to the division include the administration of estates, partnership actions, actions relating to mortgages, portions and charges on land, trusts, etc. Bankruptcy business has also been assigned to the division.

Equity was at one time administered in the chancellor's, or Chancery, court; but by s. 36 of the Supreme Court of Judicature Act 1925 both law and equity are to be administered in all divisions of the High Court equally.

The division consists of the Lord Chancellor, who is president, and not less than five puisne judges, one of whom may be nominated as Vice-Chancellor.

CHANGING OF SOLICITOR. Formerly no solicitor in an action could be changed without the order of a judge, but by R.S.C. 1965, Ord. 67, it may be done by filing a notice.

CHAPEL is of two sorts, either adjoining to a church as a parcel of the same (as in the case of a lady chapel), or else separate from the mother church, where the parish is wide, and commonly called a chapel of ease, because it is built for the ease of one or more parishioners that dwell too far from the church. *Cowel.*

CHAPERON. A hood or bonnet anciently worn by Knights of the Garter; in heraldry, a little escutcheon fixed in the forehead of the horses that draw a hearse. *Cowel.*

CHAPTER (*Capitulum*). A body of dignitaries called canons, appointed sometimes by the Crown, sometimes by the bishop and sometimes by each other, attached to a cathedral church and presided over by a dean. This body constitutes the council of the bishop in both spiritual and temporal affairs of the see.

CHARGE. A word used in various senses.

1. Of the address delivered by the presiding judicial officer to the jury instructing them in their duties.

2. Of the bishop's address to his clergy at a visitation.

3. Of a criminal accusation against any one.

4. Of an incumbrance on land or on a fund, *e.g.*, by way of equitable mortgage, for duty, for improvements. As to the only charges on land which are capable of subsisting at law, see Law of Property Act 1925, s. 1 (2), and as to mortgages, see Law of Property Act 1925, Part III, and Sch. 1, Parts VII and VIII.

5. A commission.

6. Expenses or costs.

CHARGE BY WAY OF LEGAL MORTGAGE. A mortgage created by charge. One of the only two ways in which a legal mortgage can now be created. The mortgagee, under such a charge, does not get any legal term, but the effect of such a charge is to give him the same protection, powers and remedies as if a mortgage term by demise or sub-demise were vested in him. See s. 87 of the Law of Property Act 1925, and Form No. 1 in Sch. V to the Act.

CHARGÉ D'AFFAIRES. A resident minister of an inferior grade accredited by the government of one state to the minister of foreign affairs of another. He may be either originally sent and accredited by his government, or merely temporarily substituted in the place of the public minister of his nation during his absence.

CHARGE SHEET. The paper on which are entered the charges intended to be brought before a magistrate.

CHARGING ORDER. An order obtained by a judgment creditor who has obtained a judgment for a sum of money in a suit or action against another, under the Judgments Act 1838, that the property of the judgment debtor in government stock, or in the stock of any public company in England, shall stand *charged* with the payment of the amount for which judgment shall have been recovered, with interest. See R.C.S. 1965, Ord. 45, rr. 1, 13.

CHARITABLE TRUSTS. Trusts for the maintenance of schools, hospitals, etc. An enumeration of such trusts was given in the preamble of a statute of Elizabeth I, passed in 1601. Powers exercisable with respect to charities and gifts to charity are now governed by the provisions of the Charities Act 1960. [MORTMAIN.]

CHARITY. Any institution, corporate or not, which is established for charitable purposes and is subject to the control of the High Court in the exercise of the court's jurisdiction with respect to charities: Charities Act 1960, s. 45.

CHARITY COMMISSIONERS. A body of commissioners for England and Wales, appointed by the Secretary of State under s. 1 of, and Sched. I to, the Charities Act 1960. There is a Chief Charity Commissioner and two other commissioners; at least two of the three must be barristers or solicitors. One or two additional commissioners may be appointed if necessary. The commissioners have the general function of promoting the effective use of charitable resources by encouraging the development of better methods of administration, by giving information and advice, and by investigating and checking abuses.

CHARTA. A charter, for the holding an estate; also a statute.

CHARTA, MAGNA. [MAGNA CHARTA.]

CHARTER is taken in law for written evidence of things done between man and man.

1. Royal charters either to persons, *e.g.*, letters patent for title, or to corporations, *e.g.*, to a company, giving sovereign rights, as to the former British North Borneo Company, British South Africa Company.

2. Charters of private persons are deeds and instruments under seal for the conveyance of lands, etc.

CHARTERER. 1. One who "charters" or hires a ship under a charter-party; also called "freighter". [CHARTER-PARTY.]

2. An owner of freehold land in Cheshire.

CHARTER-LAND. Land held by deed under certain rents and free services; in effect free-socage lands. Otherwise called bookland.

CHARTER-PARTY (Lat. *Charta partita*, a writing divided). A mercantile instrument, by which one who would export goods from this country or import them from abroad, engages for hire usually an *entire* vessel for the purpose, at a freight or reward thereby agreed for. [BILL OF LADING.]

CHASE signifies—

1. The driving of cattle to or from any place. Also droveway.

2. A place for receiving deer, etc. It was commonly less than a forest, and larger and better stored with keepers and game than a park. Also a chase differs from a park in not being enclosed.

3. A right of keeping and hunting beasts of chase, or royal game, either in one's own ground, or in that of another.

CHASTISEMENT. The common law right of a parent, teacher, or other person having the lawful control or charge of a child or young person to administer punishment was saved by s. 1 (7) of the Children and Young Persons Act 1933.

CHATTEL MORTGAGE (*Canada.*) A mortgage upon chattels. Provision is made in the statutes of the provinces of Canada requiring registration of chattel mortgages.

CHATTELS (Lat. *Catalla*). The name given to things which in law are deemed personal property. Chattels are divided into *chattels real* and *chattels personal*; chattels real being interests less than free-

CHATTELS—*continued.*

hold in land which devolved after the manner of personal estate, as leaseholds. As opposed to freeholds, they are regarded as personal estate. But as being interests in real estate, they are called *chattels real* to distinguish them from movables, which are called *chattels personal.* The rules as to the devolution of estates on intestacy apply equally to real and personal estate.

The Administration of Estates Act 1925, s. 55 (1) (x) defines "personal chattels" as meaning carriages, horses, stable furniture and effects (not used for business purposes), motor cars and accessories (not used for business purposes), garden effects, domestic animals, plate, plated articles, linen, china, glass, books, pictures, prints, furniture, jewellery, articles of household or personal use or ornament, musical and scientific instruments and apparatus, wines, liquors and consumable stores.

CHEAT. To defraud another of his rights or property by means of some deceitful practice, *e.g.*, using false weights and measures, or dishonestly obtaining by deception property belonging to another (see ss. 15, 25 (5) of the Theft Act 1968).

Cheating at play is punishable in like manner as obtaining money under false pretences. See the Gaming Act 1845, s. 17.

CHEATOR. [ESCHEATOR.]

CHECK-WEIGH. To check-weigh, in relation to a vehicle, means to weigh it with its load, and then to weigh it again after unloading. See s. 58 of the Weights and Measures Act 1963.

CHEQUE. A written order addressed by a person (the drawer) to a banker to pay money, generally to some third party (the payee); it is defined by s. 73 of the Bills of Exchange Act 1882, as a bill of exchange drawn on a banker payable on demand.

A cheque may be drawn in favour of a specified person, or payable to his order, in which case it requires endorsement for transfer, or payable to bearer, when it is transferable by mere delivery. The law of cheques is codified in the above-mentioned Act, and in the Cheques Act 1957, both of which are to be construed as one.

A *certified* cheque (*Canada*) is a cheque which the bank upon which it is drawn has certified that it will accept and pay upon presentation.

A *crossed* cheque is a cheque crossed with two lines, between which may be *either* the name of a bank *or* the words "and company" in full or abbreviated. In the former case the banker on whom it is drawn must not pay the money for the cheque to any other than the banker named; in the latter case he must not pay it to any other than a banker.

CHIEF BARON. The title given to the judge who presided in the Court of Exchequer. Now superseded by Lord Chief Justice of England.

CHIEF CLERK. The officers formerly called chief clerks are now called Masters. They are officers of the Chancery Division. They are attached to the chambers of the judges of that division. They hear summonses and dispose of the less important matters thereon, and prepare others for the judge. They also take accounts and institute inquiries under judgment or order of court, and embody the result in a "certificate" to be dealt with by the judge on the "further consideration" of the action. [CERTIFICATE OF MASTER; FURTHER CONSIDERATION; MASTERS IN CHANCERY.]

CHIEF CONSTABLE. 1. Used by Sir Edward Coke as synonymous with *high constable.*

2. Now a person at the head of a constabulary force. [CONSTABLE.]

CHIEF, EXAMINATION IN, is the examination of a witness by the party who produces him.

CHIEF JUSTICE. The title formerly given to the heads of the Courts of King's Bench and Common Pleas. Now superseded by the Lord Chief Justice of England, who is President of the Queen's Bench Division (*q.v.*).

CHIEF, TENANTS IN. Those who held land immediately of the king; otherwise called tenants *in capite.* [CAPITE.]

CHIEF-RENTS. 1. Rents fixed by custom payable to the lord of a manor by the freeholders thereof. For mode in which they were made extinguishable, see Part VI of the Law of Property Act 1922.

2. A rent-charge payable by the purchaser of land to the seller as consideration for the sale.

CHILD. In general one who has not attained the age of fourteen years, though the meaning varies in different statutes. For example in Part 1 of the Children Act, 1958, "child" means a person under the age of eighteen; while in the Education Act, 1944, "child" means a person who is not over compulsory school age (now sixteen).

CHILD BENEFIT. Cash benefit payable for every child in a family. See the Child Benefit Act 1975, under which the former family allowances are abolished. Tax relief for children is also progressively replaced by the Act.

CHILD DESTRUCTION. Wilfully causing the death of a child capable of being born alive before it has an existence independent of its mother. See the Infant Life (Preservation) Act 1929, s. 1. But see also the Abortion Act 1967, which legalises abortion under certain circumstances.

CHILTERN HUNDREDS. Her Majesty's hundreds of Stoke, Desborough and Burnham. The office of steward or bailiff of these hundreds is ordinarily given by the Treasury to any member of the House of Commons who wishes to retire from the House; it being a settled principle of parliamentary law that a member, after he is duly chosen, cannot relinquish his seat; and in order to evade this restriction, a member who wishes to retire accepts an office under the Crown which legally vacates his seat, and obliges the house to order a new writ. See s. 4 of the House of Commons Disqualification Act 1975. [NORTHSTEAD, MANOR OF.]

CHIMNEY MONEY was a tax formerly payable upon every chimney in a house. It was abolished in 1688.

CHIVALRY (*Servitium militare*), from French *chevalier*; in our common law a tenure of land by knight-service. *Cowel*; 2 *Bl.* [COURT OF CHIVALRY; KNIGHT-SERVICE.]

CHOSE. A thing. *Choses* are of two kinds—*choses in action*, and *choses in possession*. A *chose in action* is a thing of which a man has not the present enjoyment, but merely a right to recover it (if withheld) by action. Thus money at a bank, or money due on a bond, is a *chose in action*. This may now be assigned by writing, signed by the assignor, absolute in terms, and notice in writing being given to the debtor. Law of Property Act 1925, s. 136 (1). A *chose in possession* is a thing of which the owner is in the actual enjoyment.

CHOSE LOCAL and **CHOSE TRANSITORY.** A *chose in possession* might be a *chose local*, annexed to a place, as a mill; or a *chose transitory*, which was movable, and might be carried from place to place. These expressions are now obsolete.

CHURCH. Apart from its architectural meaning (a *building* for religious worship) the expression "church" has two distinct meanings: (1) the aggregate of the individual members of a church; or (2) the quasi-corporate institution which carries on the religious work of the denomination whose name it bears, *e.g.* Church of England, Catholic Church, etc. (*Hals. Laws*). [GUILD CHURCH.]

CHURCH COMMISSIONERS were set up by the Church Commissioners Measure 1947 for the purpose of uniting Queen Anne's Bounty with the Ecclesiastical Commissioners, both of which bodies were dissolved and their functions, etc., transferred to the new Commissioners.

CHURCH-RATES. The rates by which the expenses of the church were defrayed. Since the Compulsory Church Rate Abolition Act 1868 they were not compulsory on the persons rated, and the only consequence of refusing to pay them was a disqualification from interfering with the monies arising from the rate. [EASTER DUES AND OFFERINGS.]

CHURCHESSET. Corn paid to the church.

CHURCHWARDENS, or **CHURCH REVES.** The guardians or keepers of the church, and representatives of the body of the parish. In general the minister chooses one, and the parishioners another. They are chosen yearly in or about Easter week. They have the care and management of the goods belonging to the church, such as the organ, Bible, and parish books.

CINEMATOGRAPH EXHIBITION. An exhibition of moving pictures produced on a screen by means which include the projection of light; see s. 9 of the Cinematograph Act 1952.

CINEMATOGRAPH FILM. Any sequence of visual images recorded on material of any description (whether translucent or not) so as to be capable of

CINEMATOGRAPH FILM
—continued.

being shown as a moving picture, or of being recorded on other material. See s. 13 of the Copyright Act 1956.

It is also defined by the Dramatic and Musical Performers' Protection Act 1958, s. 8, as any print, negative, tape, or other article on which a performance of a dramatic or musical work or part thereof is recorded for the purposes of visual reproduction.

CINQUE PORTS. The five ports of Hastings, Romney, Hythe, Dover, and Sandwich; to which Winchelsea and Rye have since been added. They have an especial governor or keeper, called by his office the Lord Warden of the Cinque Ports, and divers privileges granted upon them. The jurisdiction of the Lord Warden in civil suits was taken away in 1855, but he still possesses a peculiar maritime jurisdiction.

CIRCUIT. The Supreme Court and the county courts are administered by the Lord Chancellor, through a unified court service, which is organised on a circuit basis. England and Wales are divided into six circuits, *viz.* (1) the Midland and Oxford Circuit; (2) the North Eastern Circuit; (3) the Northern Circuit; (4) the South Eastern Circuit; (5) the Wales and Chester Circuit; and (6) the Western Circuit. A circuit administrator is responsible to the Lord Chancellor for the administration of the courts in each circuit.

The Lord Chief Justice appoints, for each circuit, two judges of the High Court to be presiding judges. They have overall responsibility for the conduct of judicial business and matters generally affecting the judiciary.

The Crown appoints additional circuit judges to serve in the Crown Court and county courts. They must be qualified persons (*e.g.* barristers of at least ten years standing, or recorders who have held office for at least five years). Deputy circuit judges may also be appointed (*Hals. Laws*). [CROWN COURT; JUDGE.]

CIRCUITY OF ACTION is a longer course of proceeding than is necessary to effect any result.

Now all counter-claims may be raised in the defence to an action to avoid circuity.

See Judicature Act 1925, s. 39. [COUNTER-CLAIM.]

CIRCULAR NOTES are instruments in the nature of letters of credit, drawn by bankers upon their foreign correspondents in favour of persons travelling abroad. [LETTER OF CREDIT.]

CIRCUMSPECTE AGATIS (that ye act circumspectly) was the title of a statute of Edward I, (1285) relating to prohibitions and other church matters. Repealed by the Ecclesiastical Jurisdiction Measure 1963.

CIRCUMSTANTIAL EVIDENCE. Proof of circumstances from which, according to the ordinary course of human affairs, the existence of some fact may reasonably be presumed. It is thus opposed to direct or positive evidence of the fact itself.

CIRCUMSTANTIBUS. By-standers. [TALES.]

CITATION. A summons to a party to appear; applied particularly to process in the Scotch courts, and in the ecclesiastical courts; also to the commencement of probate proceedings.

The word is also applied to the quoting of legal cases and authorities in courts of law.

CITIZEN OF THE UNITED KINGDOM AND COLONIES. One who is a British subject but whose rights as a citizen do not extend to the Dominions unless Dominion legislation expressly so provides. British Nationality Act, 1948.

CITY is defined by Cowel as being such a town-corporate as has a bishop and a cathedral church; by Blackstone, as a town incorporated, which is or has been the see of a bishop.

CITY OF LONDON COURT. A court in the City of London, formerly called the Sheriff's Court, later amalgamated with the Mayor's Court. [MAYOR'S AND CITY OF LONDON COURT.]

CITY OF LONDON POLICE. [CONSTABLE, 3.]

CIVIL stands for the opposite of criminal, of ecclesiastical, of military, or of political.

CIVIL BILL COURTS. The local courts of civil jurisdiction in Ireland, analogous to English county courts.

CIVIL COMMOTION. An insurrection of the people for general purposes, though not amounting to rebellion. The elements of turbulence or tumult are essential. A stage intermediate between a riot and civil war (*Hals. Laws*).

CIVIL DEATH. This expression was formerly used to indicate—

1. That a man had entered a monastery, and being *professed* in religion, became *dead* in law.

2. That a man had become outlawed.

3. That a man had become attainted of treason or felony.

The old doctrine of civil death is now obsolete; but a person who has been absent and not heard of for a period of seven years is, for many purposes, presumed to be dead.

CIVIL LAW is defined in Justinian's Institutes as "that law which every people has established for itself"; in other words, the law of any given state. But this law is now distinguished by the term *municipal law*; the term *civil law* being applied to the Roman civil law. [CORPUS JURIS CIVILIS.]

(*Canada.*) In Canada the term is usually used with reference to the Civil Code of Quebec.

CIVIL LIST. An annual sum granted by parliament to the Crown at the commencement of each reign in lieu of hereditary revenues, for the expense of the royal household and establishment, as distinguished from the general exigencies of the state. The Civil List Act 1972 fixed the sum at £980,000. This may be supplemented under the Civil List Act 1975.

CIVIL REMEDY. A remedy available to a private person by action, as opposed to a criminal prosecution.

CIVIL RESPONSIBILITY. To be *civilly* responsible for any act or omission means to be liable in an action or other proceeding at the suit of a private person or corporation, or (in certain cases) at the suit of the Crown suing as for a private wrong. This is opposed to criminal responsibility, which means liability to answer in a criminal court. The action, etc., is styled civil remedy, in opposition to prosecution, which is brought by the Crown.

CIVIL SERVICE. This term includes all servants of the Crown, other than holders of political or judicial offices, who are employed in a civil capacity and whose remuneration is paid wholly and directly out of monies voted by Parliament.

CIVIL SIDE. The side of a court devoted to civil causes.

CLAIM (Lat. *Clamare*). A challenge of interest in anything that is in the possession of another, or at least out of the possession of the claimant. *Cowel*. [STATEMENT OF CLAIM.]

CLAIM OF LIBERTY. A suit or petition to the sovereign in the former Court of Exchequer to have liberties and franchises confirmed there by the Attorney-General.

CLARENDON, CONSTITUTIONS OF. Enacted A.D. 1164. Confirmed A.D. 1176. Their object was to limit the pretensions of the clergy within the realm.

CLAUSUM FREGIT ("he broke the close," that is, committed an unwarrantable entry upon another's soil). These words were generally used in reference to an action of trespass in entering another's land. [BREACH, 1.]

CLAVES INSULÆ. The House of Keys of the Isle of Man. [KEYS.]

CLAYTON'S CASE. [APPROPRIATION, 2.]

CLEAN HANDS are required from a plaintiff in equity, *i.e.*, he must be free from reproach, or taint of fraud, etc., in his conduct *in respect of the subject-matter of his claim*. [EQUITY.]

CLEAR DAYS. A phrase used to indicate the calculations of days from one day to another excluding both the first and last day.

CLEARANCE. A certificate given by the collector of a port, that a ship has paid dues and been cleared at the customs house and may sail; and *clearance* has therefore been properly defined as *a permission to sail*.

CLEARANCE ORDER. An order made by a local authority, which must be confirmed by the Minister of Health, for the clearance of houses unfit for human habitation.

CLEARING HOUSE. The place where the operation termed "clearing" is carried on; "clearing" being a method adopted by London banks for exchanging

CLEARING HOUSE—*continued.*
the drafts of each other's houses and settling the difference.

CLERGY, besides its ordinary sense, once signified "benefit of clergy". [BENEFIT OF CLERGY.] In its ordinary sense it refers to clerks in Holy Orders of the Church of England. See s. 78 of the Marriage Act 1949.

CLERICAL WORK. Includes writing, book-keeping, sorting papers, filing, typing, duplicating, punching cards in tapes, machine calculating, drawing and the editorial preparation of matter for publication. See s. 32 of the General Rate Act 1967.

CLERK OF THE CROWN IN CHANCERY. A public officer whose duty it is to issue writs for elections on receiving the Lord Chancellor's warrant; and to deliver to the Clerk of the House of Commons the list of members returned to serve in parliament; to certify the election of representative peers for Scotland and Ireland, etc. Provision was made by the Lord Chancellor's Pension Act 1832 for the abolition of this office when it should become vacant. The office has, however, been continued, and the duties and salary of the Clerk are now regulated by s. 8 of the Great Seal (Offices) Act 1874. The duties formerly performed by the Keeper or Clerk of His Majesty's Hanaper are now performed by the Clerk of the Crown in Chancery. *May.* [HANAPER OFFICE.]

CLERK OF THE HOUSE OF COMMONS. One of the officers of the House of Commons, appointed by the Crown for life, by letters patent, in which he is styled "Under Clerk of the Parliaments, to attend upon the Commons." *May.*

CLERK OF THE PARLIAMENTS. The chief officer of the House of Lords, appointed by the Crown, by letters patent. *May.*

CLERKS OF RECORDS AND WRITS. Officers of the Court of Chancery. Their duties were transferred to the Masters of the Supreme Court and their office abolished. See the Judicature Act 1925, Part V.

CLIENT. A person who consults a solicitor. A solicitor, also, in reference to the counsel he instructs is spoken of as a client. The word is also used in reference to other professions.

CLOGGING EQUITY OF REDEMPTION. In a mortgage, no clog or fetter may be imposed upon the equity of redemption (*q.v.*). The maxim is "Once a mortgage, always a mortgage," and any stipulation contained in a mortgage transaction, the object of which is either to deprive the debtor of his right to redeem, or to prevent him from getting his property back in substantially the same state as at the beginning of the transaction, is void as being repugnant to the nature of a mere security.

CLOSE. A word most frequently used for a person's land. [CLAUSUM FREGIT.]

CLOSE COMPANY. With some exceptions, a company that is under the control of five or fewer participators, or of participators who are directors. See s. 282 of the Income and Corporation Taxes Act 1970, as amended by the Finance Act 1972.

CLOSE COPY. The copy of a document made by a solicitor acting as agent for the use of his solicitor client.

CLOSE ROLLS, or **CLAUSE ROLLS.** [CLOSE WRITS.]

CLOSE SEASON. A season in which hunting or fishing is prohibited. See, *e.g.* the Salmon and Freshwater Fisheries Act 1975, Sch. 1, for close seasons for salmon and trout. The close seasons for various types of game are laid down in s. 3 of the Game Act 1831, *e.g.* partridges, from 1st February to 1st September in any year; pheasants, 1st February to 1st October; grouse, 10th December to 12th August, etc. Hares and leverets are preserved during March to July by the Hares Preservation Act 1892. (*Canada.*) The periods of the year, similarly, when hunting certain birds or other animals or taking certain kinds of fish is prohibited by provincial laws. [OPEN SEASON.]

CLOSE WRITS. Grants of the Queen, sealed with her great seal, but directed to particular persons, and for particular purposes—and which, therefore, not being proper for public inspection, are closed up and sealed on the outside—are called writs close, *literæ clausæ*, or *letters close*, and are recorded in the *close rolls*; in the same manner as letters patent, *literæ patentes* are in the *patent rolls*.

CLOSING ORDER. (1) An order made by a local authority for the closing of that part of a building which is unfit for human habitation: Housing Act 1957. (2) An order by a local authority fixing the hours on which shops shall be closed: Shops Act 1950.

CLOSURE. The procedure whereby a debate is brought to a close. In parliamentary debates, if the motion "that the question be now put" is voted upon and carried (provided that not less than one hundred members vote in favour) the debate must cease.

CLUB. A voluntary association, for social or other purposes, of a number of persons who subscribe a certain sum either to a common fund for the benefit of the members or to a particular individual; in the former case it is a "members" club and in the latter a "proprietary" club. In a proprietary club the expense and risk are borne by a contractor who takes all profits. A members club is usually managed by a steward under the superintendence of a committee, and the members, merely as such, are not liable for debts incurred by the committee or for goods supplied to the club. A club as a body has no position recognised in law: it is not a partnership, nor a company, nor a society subject to statutory rules, except under the Licensing Acts. As to sale of intoxicating liquor in clubs, see the Licensing Act 1964, ss. 39 *et seq.*

COADJUTOR BISHOP. A bishop appointed in aid of a bishop incapacitated by permanent mental infirmity from the due performance of his episcopal duties. [SUFFRAGAN.]

COAST. The land which bounds the sea; the limit of land jurisdiction. The limit varies according to the state of the tide. When the tide is in, and covers the land, it is sea; when the tide is out it is land as far as low-water mark (*R.* v. *Forty Nine Casks of Brandy* (1836), 3 Hag. Adm. 257).

COAST GUARD. A body of officers and men formerly raised and equipped by the Commissioners of the Admiralty, for the defence of the coasts of the realm, and for the more ready manning of the navy in case of war or sudden emergency, as well as for the protection of the revenue against smugglers.

By the Coastguard Act 1925 the coastguard was transferred from the Admiralty to the Board of Trade, to be employed as a coast-watching force; and provision was made for the transfer of land held by the Admiralty in connection with the coastguard service to the Ministry of Works.

As to the functions of the Board of Trade, see now the Secretary of State (New Departments) Order 1974 (S.I. 1974 No. 692).

COCKPIT. A name which used to be given to the Judicial Committee of the Privy Council, the room where it sat being built on the site of the old cockpit in Whitehall Place.

CODE. A system or collection of laws.

CODE NAPOLÉON, otherwise called the *Code Civil,* is a code composed of thirty-six laws, the first of which was passed in 1803 and the last in 1804, which were united in one body under the name of *Code Civil des Français.*

Sometimes, however, the name is extended to the whole of Napoleon's legislation.

CODICIL. A schedule or supplement to a will, when the testator desires to add, explain, alter, or retract anything; it must be executed with the same formalities as a will under the Wills Act 1837.

COERCION. The threat of taking away from another something that he possesses, or of preventing him from obtaining an advantage he would otherwise have obtained, by influence or duress. See *Ellis* v. *Barker* (1871), 40 L.J. Ch. 603. "'Coercion' involves something in the nature of negation of choice": *Hodges* v. *Webb,* [1920] 2 Ch. 70. Formerly, at common law, there was a rebuttable presumption that an offence (other than homicide) committed by a wife in the presence of her husband was committed under his coercion. The *presumption* was abolished by s. 47 of the Criminal Justice Act 1925, but it is still a good defence to a wife if she can *prove* such coercion.

COGNATI. Relations on the mother's side. [AGNATES.]

COGNITION AND SALE. A process before the Court of Sessions for obtaining a warrant to sell a ward's estate.

COGNIZANCE (*Judicial*). Knowledge upon which a judge is bound to act without having it proved in evidence; as the public statutes of the realm, the several

COGNIZANCE—*continued.*

seals of the sovereign, etc. A judge is not bound to take cognizance of current events, however notorious, nor of the law of other countries. [JUDICIAL NOTICE.]

COGNOVIT ACTIONEM. An instrument in writing whereby a defendant in an action confessed a plaintiff's demand to be just. Former statutory provisions requiring registration, etc., of cognovits, were repealed by s. 16 of the Administration of Justice Act 1956.

COHABITATION. Living together as husband and wife, whether or not legally married.

CO-HEIR. Formerly one of several to whom an inheritance descended.

COIF. A title given to sergeants-at-law, who were called sergeants of the coif, from the coif they wore on their heads.

COIN. The coining of money is in all states the prerogative of the sovereign power. The Coinage (Offences) Act 1936 makes it felony to counterfeit coin. See also the Coinage Act 1971 and the Decimal Currency Acts 1967 and 1969.

COKE, SIR EDWARD. Lord Chief Justice of the King's Bench in the time of James I. He compiled reports, and was the author of four volumes of "Institutes" on the subject of the common law, and of an edition of Littleton's Treatise on Tenures.

COLIBERTS. Tenants in socage.

COLLATE. To bestow a living by *collation.* [ADVOWSON; COLLATION TO A BENEFICE.]

COLLATERAL. That which hangeth by the side. An assurance collateral to a deed is one which is made over and besides the deed itself. Thus if a man covenant with another, and enter into a bond for the performance of his covenant, the bond is called a collateral assurance. *Cowel.*

COLLATERAL CONSANGUINITY. The relationship between persons who descend from a common ancestor, but neither of whom descends from the other. 2 *Bl.*

COLLATERAL ISSUE on a criminal charge is an issue arising out of a plea which does not bear on the guilt or innocence of the accused. 4 *Bl.*

COLLATERAL SECURITY. An ad-

ditional security, for the better safety of a mortgagee.

COLLATIO BONORUM, in the Roman law, was where a portion advanced by a parent in his lifetime to a son or daughter was upon his death reckoned as part of his estate, or, as English lawyers would say, "brought into hotchpot" (*q.v.*).

COLLATION. The comparison of a copy with the original document, in order to ascertain its correctness.

COLLATION TO A BENEFICE. When the ordinary is also the patron, and *confers* the living, the presentation and institution are one and the same act, and are called a collation to a benefice.

COLLATIVE ADVOWSON. [ADVOWSON; COLLATION TO A BENEFICE.]

COLLECTIVE AGREEMENT. An agreement or arrangement made by or on behalf of one or more trade unions and one or more employers or employers' associations in relation to terms and conditions of employment, matters of discipline, membership or non-membership of trade unions, etc. See s. 30 (1) of the Trade Union and Labour Pelations Act 1974.

COLLEGE OF ARMS. [HERALDS' COLLEGE.]

COLLEGIATE CHURCH. A church consisting of a body corporate of dean and canons, such as Westminster, Windsor, etc., independently of any cathedral.

COLLIGENDUM BONA DEFUNCTI (LETTERS AD). Letters granted by the Chancery Division, to such discreet person as the court shall think fit, authorising him to keep the goods of a deceased person in his safe custody, and to do other acts for the benefit of such as are entitled to the property of the deceased. These letters differ from letters of administration in so far as they do not make the grantee the legal representative of the deceased. They are granted in the event of the person who is legally entitled to take out probate or letters of administration refusing to do so. 2 *Bl.*

COLLISION. Where damage is caused by collision at sea, liability is apportioned between the vessels in accordance with the degree in which each vessel was at fault. See the Maritime Conventions Act 1911.

COLLUSION. A deceitful agreement between two or more persons, to defraud another person or other persons of their right, or to frustrate some rule of public policy. The word is generally, though not necessarily, used with reference to collusive legal proceedings, and specially divorce. Collusion was formerly an absolute bar to a decree of dissolution of marriage, but is so no longer. The provisions of the Matrimonial Causes Act 1965, relating to collusion, were repealed by the Divorce Reform Act 1969, itself repealed and replaced by the Matrimonial Causes Act 1973.

COLONIES. Possessions or dependencies of the British Crown in certain parts of the world. Colonies are no part of the mother country, but distinct, though dependent territories. In general they were either gained from other states by conquest or treaty, or else were acquired by right of occupancy only.

Most of the former British colonies have now been given their independence.

COLONUS. A husbandman or villager, who was bound to pay yearly a certain tribute, or at certain times in the year to plough some part of the lord's land; and from hence comes the word *clown*. *Cowel*.

COLOUR, in pleading, signified an *apparent* or *prima facie* right; and the meaning of the old rule that pleadings in *confession and avoidance* [CONFESSION AND AVOIDANCE] should give colour was, that they should *confess* the matter adversely alleged, to such an extent at least as to admit some apparent right in the opposite party, which required to be encountered and *avoided* by the allegation of new matter. Colour was either express, *i.e.*, inserted in the pleading, or implied.

Abolished in 1852.

COLOURABLE. Not real, the reverse of *bona fide*, *e.g.*, an alteration made only for the purpose of evading the law of copyright.

COMBAT. [WAGER OF BATTEL.]

COMBINATION, UNLAWFUL. An assembly of workmen or others met to perpetrate unlawful acts. See the Conspiracy and Protection of Property Act, 1875.

COMES. A count or sheriff or superior officer of a county or comitatus.

COMITATUS. A county.

COMITY OF NATIONS. This expression is generally used to indicate the practice adopted by the courts of justice in one country of giving effect (within certain limits) to the laws of another country, and the judgments given by its courts.

COMMERCIAL COURT. A court constituted as part of the Queen's Bench Division, to take causes and matters entered in the commercial list: Administration of Justice Act 1970, s. 3 (1).

The judges of the court are such of the puisne judges of the High Court as the Lord Chancellor may from time to time nominate to be commercial judges.

COMMISSARY. One who is sent to execute some office or duty for a superior. In ecclesiastical law, an officer of the bishop who exercises spiritual jurisdiction in distant parts of the diocese.

COMMISSION. The warrant, or letters patent, that all men exercising jurisdiction, either ordinary or extraordinary, have for their power to hear and determine any cause or action. *Cowel*.

The word is also used in numerous other ways. It is used of the bailment called *mandatum*; of instructions given to an agent; of a broker's remuneration, etc. For certain special instances of its use, see the following titles.

COMMISSION, ASSENT TO BILLS BY. Under the Royal Assent by Commission Act 1541, the sovereign usually signified the royal assent by a commission of peers appointed by letters patent under the Great Seal. The Act of 1541 was repealed by the Royal Assent Act 1967, under which an additional method of signifying the royal assent was introduced. This is by pronouncing, in both Houses of Parliament, the fact of the Queen's assent by letters Patent under the Great Seal. The necessity for the Commons to come to the Upper House to hear royal assents has been abolished.

COMMISSION DEL CREDERE. [DEL CREDERE COMMISSION.]

COMMISSION OF DELEGATES. A commission under the great seal to certain persons, usually lords, bishops and judges of the law, to sit upon an appeal in the Court of Chancery in ecclesiastical and

COMMISSION OF DELEGATES
—*continued.*
admiralty suits. Abolished by the Privy Councils Appeal Act 1832, its functions being transferred to the Judicial Committee of the Privy Council.

COMMISSION OF GAOL DE-LIVERY. The former judges of assize sat by virtue of four several authorities, one of which, the commission of gaol delivery, required them to try every prisoner in gaol, for whatever offence he might be there. The jurisdiction of the assize courts was transferred to the Crown Court by the Courts Act 1971.

COMMISSION OF LUNACY. A commission formerly granted by the Lord Chancellor to inquire into the state of mind of an alleged lunatic. Persons suffering from mental disorder are now submitted to hospital on the recommendations of two medical practitioners, with the right of application to mental health review tribunals. See the Mental Health Act 1959.

COMMISSION OF NISI PRIUS. One of four separate authorities by which the former judges of assize sat. It empowered them to try, by jury, all civil causes in which issue had been joined in one of the divisions of the High Court of Justice. The jurisdiction of the assize courts was transferred to the Crown Court by the Courts Act 1971.

COMMISSION OF OYER AND TERMINER. One of the four separate authorities under which the former judges of assize sat. It gave them power to *hear and determine* all treasons, murders and other crimes. The jurisdiction of the assize courts was transferred to the Crown Court by the Courts Act 1971.

COMMISSION OF THE PEACE. A commission under the great seal, constituting one or more persons justice or justices of the peace within a particular district. A separate commission is issued for each county and for the City of London. See s. 1 of the Administration of Justice Act 1973. [JUSTICE OF THE PEACE.]

COMMISSION TO EXAMINE WITNESSES. By this is meant a commission issued to a foreign country, or other place out of the jurisdiction of a court in which a suit is instituted, for the purpose of obtaining such evidence of witnesses residing in such foreign country or other place, as may be material to the question before the court.

Modern procedure is now generally regulated either by conventions entered into between certain countries, to provide for the taking of evidence; or by the presentation of Letters of Request, through diplomatic channels, asking the government concerned that the required evidence be taken. See R.S.C. 1965 Ord. 39.

COMMISSIONERS, ECCLESIASTICAL. [ECCLESIASTICAL COMMISSIONERS.]

COMMISSIONERS FOR OATHS are solicitors appointed by the Lord Chancellor to administer oaths to persons making affidavits to be used in law suits, etc.

COMMISSIONERS OF SEWERS. [COURT OF COMMISSIONERS OF SEWERS.]

COMMITMENT. The sending of a person to prison. The word is also used of the document or warrant by which a commitment is directed.

COMMITTAL FOR TRIAL. The sending for trial before a jury of a person charged before the examining justices with an indictable offence.

COMMITTEE, JUDICIAL. [JUDICIAL COMMITTEE OF THE PRIVY COUNCIL.]

COMMITTEE OF INSPECTION. A committee appointed by the general body of creditors of a bankrupt for the purpose of superintending the administration by the trustee of the bankrupt's property. See the Bankruptcy Act 1914, s. 20, and Bankruptcy Rules 1952, rr. 349, 350.

COMMITTEE OF LUNATIC. A person to whom the maintenance of a person of unsound mind, or the management of his estate, was formerly committed. Guardianship, and the management of the property and affairs, of mentally disordered persons are now regulated by the Mental Health Act, 1959.

COMMITTEE OF SUPPLY. A committee into which the House of Commons resolves itself for considering the amount of supply to be granted to Her Majesty. *May.*

COMMITTEE OF THE WHOLE HOUSE. A parliamentary committee composed of every member of the house. To form it in the Commons, the Speaker quits the chair, another member being appointed chairman. In the Lords, the chair is taken by the chairman of committees. In these committees a bill is debated clause by clause, amendments made, blanks filled up, and sometimes the bill is entirely re-modelled. *May*.

COMMITTEE OF WAYS AND MEANS. A committee into which the House of Commons resolves itself, for the purpose of considering the ways and means of raising a supply. *May*.

COMMODATUM. A gratuitous loan of a specific chattel. It is a species of bailment. [BAILMENT.]

COMMON, or RIGHT OF COMMON, is a profit which a man has in the land of another, as to pasture beasts therein, to catch fish, to dig turf, to cut wood, or the like. It is chiefly of five kinds: common of *pasture*, of *piscary*, of *turbary*, of *estovers*, and *in the soil*.

(1) Common of *pasture* is the right of feeding one's beasts on another's land. This kind of common is either *appendant*, *appurtenant*, *because of vicinage*, or *in gross*.

(a) *Common appendant* is a right belonging to the owners or occupiers of arable land, under the lord of a manor, to put commonable beasts upon the lord's waste, and upon the lands of other persons within the same manor. Commonable beasts are either beasts of the plough, or such as manure the ground.

(b) *Common appurtenant* arises from no connection of tenure, but may be annexed to lands in other lordships; or may extend to such beasts as hogs, goats, or the like, which neither plough nor manure the ground. This kind of common can be claimed only by special grant or prescription.

It should be noted with regard to common appendant and appurtenant that the wholesale enfranchisement effected by s. 128 of the Law of Property Act 1922 does not affect rights of common enjoyed by the owners of the tenements (see Sch. XII (4) to the Act) and these continue to attach to their enfranchised tenements.

(c) *Common because of vicinage* is where the inhabitants of two townships, which lie contiguous to each other, have usually intercommoned with one another; the beasts of the one straying mutually into the other's fields, without any molestation from either. This is only a permissive right; and therefore either township may inclose and bar out the other, though they have intercommoned time out of mind.

(d) *Common in gross*, or at large, is such as is neither appendant nor appurtenant to the land, but is annexed to a man's person, being granted to him and his heirs by deed, or claimed by prescriptive right.

(2) Common of *piscary* is a liberty of fishing in another man's water.

(3) Common of *turbary* is a liberty of digging turf upon another's ground.

(4) Common of *estovers* or *estouviers*—that is, necessaries; from *estoffer*, to furnish—is a liberty of taking necessary wood, for the use of furniture of a house or farm, from off another's estate.

(5) Common *in the soil* consists of the right of digging for coals, minerals, stones, and the like.

The inclosure of commons is regulated now by the Inclosure Acts and by the various Commons Acts from 1285 to 1908. See also the Commons Registration Act 1965. By the Law of Property Act 1925 members of the public are given rights of access for air and exercise to certain wastes and commons, and restrictions are imposed on the inclosure of commons. See ss. 193 and 194 of the Act of 1925, as amended by the Local Government Act 1972, and the Countryside Act 1968.

COMMON ASSAULT. As assault unaccompanied with circumstances of aggravation.

COMMON ASSURANCES. [ASSURANCE, 1.]

COMMON BAIL. Especially applied to the two former fictitious persons John Doe and Richard Roe, in their capacity as sureties put in by the defendant in an action, upon entering an appearance, for his future attendance and obedience. [BAIL.]

COMMON BAR. [BLANK BAR.]

COMMON BENCH. A name sometimes given to the former Court of Common Pleas.

COMMON CARRIER. [Carrier.]

COMMON COUNTS. Counts in a plaintiff's declaration which stated the most ordinary causes of action, as for money lent; money received by the defendant for the use of the plaintiff; work and labour; goods sold and delivered, etc. As technical forms of pleading they were superseded by the Judicature Acts 1873 and 1875.

COMMON EMPLOYMENT. Under the doctrine of common employment a master was not liable at common law for injury to a workman resulting from the negligence of a fellow servant. The defence was abolished by the Law Reform (Personal Injuries) Act 1948.

COMMON FINE. A small sum of money, otherwise called *head silver*, which the persons resident within the jurisdiction of certain courts-leet paid to the lord.

COMMON FORM. Non-contentious or "common form" probate business means the business of obtaining probate and administration where there is no contention as to the right thereto. Non-contentious probate business was assigned to the Family Division by the Administration of Justice Act 1970.

. COMMON INFORMER. An informer who sued on a penal statute which entitled anyone to sue to recover the penalty imposed. The common informer procedure was abolished by the Common Informers Act 1951, which repealed the relevant provisions of the various statutes providing for such actions, the earliest of which had been on the statute book since the 12th century.

COMMON INTENDMENT, or **COMMON INTENT.** Ordinary meaning.

COMMON JURY. A jury consisting of persons who possessed only the ordinary qualification of property. [Jury.]

COMMON LAW. The ancient unwritten law of this kingdom. 1 *Bl.*

The term "Common Law" is used in various ways:—

1. Of the ancient law above mentioned embodied in judicial decisions as opposed to statute law, or the law enacted by parliament.

2. Of the original and proper law of England, formerly administered in the Common Law Courts, that is, the superior courts of Westminster, and the Nisi Prius Courts, as opposed to the system called *Equity*, which was administered in the Court of Chancery. Since the Judicature Act 1873 all courts administer law and equity concurrently.

3. Of the municipal law of England as opposed to the Roman civil law, or other foreign law.

COMMON LODGING HOUSE. A house provided for the purpose of accommodating by night poor persons, not being members of the same family, who resort thereto and are allowed to occupy one common room for the purpose of sleeping or eating. See s. 235 of the Public Health Act 1936.

COMMON MARKET. [European Economic Community.]

COMMON PLEAS. [Court of Common Pleas.]

COMMON PRAYER. [Book of Common Prayer.]

COMMON PROSTITUTE. [Prostitution.]

COMMON RECOVERY. [Recovery.]

COMMON SCOLD (Lat. *Communis rixatrix*). [Scold.]

COMMON SEAL. An expression used of the seal of a corporation.

COMMON SERJEANT OF LONDON. A judicial officer of the City of London, next to the recorder. Any person appointed to be Common Serjeant is, by virtue of that appointment, a circuit judge: Courts Act 1971.

COMMON, TENANCY IN. A tenancy in common is where two or more hold the *same* land (1) under different titles; or (2) accruing under the same title, other than *descent*, but at different periods; or (3) under the same written instrument, but by words importing that the grantees are to take in distinct shares. This tenancy therefore happens where there is a unity of possession merely; but there may be an entire disunion of interest, of title, and of time. By the provisions of the Law of

Property Act 1925 tenancy in common at law was abolished. The Act created a trust for sale n cases where such tenancy existed on 1st January, 1926, and prevented the creation of a legal tenancy in common in future. Such a tenancy is possible only in equity, the land being vested in trustees for sale. See ss. 34–39 and Sched. I, Part IV to the Act (as amended by the Law of Property (Amendment) Act 1926). [COPARCENARY; JOINT TENANCY.]

Tenancy in common may exist in movable property.

COMMON VOUCHEE. The person who was commonly "vouched to warranty" in the former fictitious proceeding called a *common recovery*. The crier of the court was generally employed for this purpose. [RECOVERY; VOUCHER, 1.]

COMMONABLE. 1. Held in common.
2. Allowed to pasture on common land. Commonable beasts are either beasts of the plough or such as manure the ground. *Bl.*

COMMONALTY. Persons who are not the nobility or peerage.

COMMONWEALTH. A word which properly signifies the common weal or public policy; sometimes it is used to designate a republican form of government: and especially the period of English history from the execution of Charles I in 1649 to the restoration of the monarchy under Charles II in 1660. Now used to describe the United Kingdom and the self-governing dominions.

COMMONWEALTH CITIZEN. Synonymous with British subject. See the British Nationality Act, 1948.

COMMORIENTES. Persons dying by the same accident or on the same occasion. In English law there was no presumption of survivorship. Under the provisions of s. 184 of the Law of Property Act 1925 the younger is deemed to have survived the elder.

COMMUNIS ERROR FACIT JUS. Common error sometimes passes current as law.

COMMUNITY. In Wales, the equivalent of a parish. Part II of the Local Government Act 1972 provides for community meetings and community councils.

COMMUNITY HOME. [APPROVED SCHOOL.]

COMMUNITY LAND. Land acquired for development by local or new town authorities under the provisions of the Community Land Act 1975.

COMMUNITY SERVICE ORDER. Where a person of or over seventeen years of age is convicted of an offence punishable with imprisonment, the court by which he is convicted may instead make a community service order, requiring him to perform unpaid work for a specified number of hours: Powers of Criminal Courts Act 1973, s. 14 (1).

COMMUTATION OF TITHES. This was the substitution of a rent-charge adjusted according to the average price of corn, for the payment of tithes in kind. [TITHES.]

COMMUTATIVE CONTRACT. One in which each of the contracting parties gives and receives an equivalent.

COMPANY. A body of persons associated together for the purposes of trade or business. Companies are formed (1) by charter, (2) by special Act of Parliament, (3) by registration at Somerset House.

Companies are regulated chiefly by the Companies Acts 1948 and 1967.

The liability of members of companies is usually limited, either by the charter, Act of Parliament, or memorandum of association. [CLOSE COMPANY; LIMITED COMPANY; PRIVATE COMPANY.]

COMPASSING. Contriving or imagining.

COMPENSATION. 1. An allowance for the apprehension of criminals.
2. The money paid by an authority taking land under an Act of Parliament, for the purchase of the interest in the land of the parties entitled thereto.
3. Money paid for damage caused by any wrong or breach of contract, or, under the Forfeiture Act 1870, to persons defrauded or injured by any criminal offence.
4. A set-off (Scotland). [SERVANT; SET-OFF.]

COMPENSATION ORDER. A court by or before which a person is convicted of an offence may, in addition to dealing with him in any other way, make an order requiring him to pay compensation for any personal injury, loss or damage resulting

COMPENSATION ORDER
—continued.

from that offence. See s. 35 of the Powers of Criminal Courts Act 1973.

COMPLAINT. The act by which civil proceedings are set in motion in the magistrates' courts, as distinguished from an *information* in respect of a criminal offence. See ss. 42, 43 of the Magistrates' Courts Act 1952.

COMPLAINANT. One who commences a prosecution against another.

COMPLETION. The finalisation of a contract, especially one for the sale of land. The vendor delivers up the land contracted to be sold with a good title; the purchaser pays the price and takes possession. Completion normally takes place at the office of the vendor's solicitors at an agreed period after the exchange of contracts. See the Statutory Form of Conditions of Sale (S.R. & O. 1925, No. 779), made under s. 46 of the Law of Property Act 1925.

COMPOS MENTIS. Of sound mind.

COMPOSITION. 1. A *real composition.* This was when an agreement was made between the owner of lands and the incumbent, with the consent of the ordinary and the patron, that the lands should, for the future, be discharged from payment of tithes, by reason of some land or other *real* recompense given in lieu and satisfaction thereof.

2. A sum of money agreed to be accepted by the creditors of a debtor in satisfaction of the debts due to them from the debtor. A composition may be a private one effected by deed and registered under the Deeds of Arrangement Act 1914, when only creditors assenting to it will be found; or a composition in bankruptcy proceedings under the Bankruptcy Act 1914, when, if passed by the requisite majority of creditors and approved by the court, it will find all creditors entitled to prove, and of course no registration under the Deeds of Arrangement Act 1914 is necessary.

Deeds of arrangement affecting land may be registered under s. 7 of the Land Charges Act 1972, in the name of the debtor. [ARRANGEMENTS.]

COMPOUND SETTLEMENT.
Where land is settled by a series of separate deeds, the deeds together form one settlement which is called a "compound settlement." The commonest example of this occurs in the case of a re-settlement, which requires several deeds. The fee simple is first settled on the father for life with remainder to his eldest son in tail; the entailed interest is barred by the son with the consent of his father as protector; and, finally, the land is resettled, roughly, on the father for life, then on the son for life, with remainder to the son's eldest son in tail. In this case the three deeds may be read as one, being together called a "compound settlement," and the Settled Land Act 1925, s. 1 (1), proviso, provides that the word "settlement" shall be construed as referring to such compound settlement, where it exists.

COMPOUNDING. 1. Arranging, coming to terms.

2. Compounding a felony was where a party robbed or otherwise injured by a felony took a reward from the felon, or in case of theft took back the stolen goods upon agreement not to prosecute; this was called *theftbote*, and was punishable with fine and imprisonment. It was no offence to compound a misdemeanour unless the offence was virtually an offence against the public. The distinction between felony and misdemeanour has been abolished. [FELONY.]

COMPRINT. A surreptitious printing by a man of another's books. [COPYRIGHT.]

COMPROMISE. An adjustment of claims in dispute by natural concession, either without resort to legal proceedings, or on the condition of abandoning such proceedings if already commenced.

COMPTROLLER. 1. One who observes and examines the accounts of the collectors of public money.

2. The *comptroller in bankruptcy* was an officer formerly appointed under the bankruptcy laws, the modern equivalent being the official receiver: see Bankruptcy Act 1914, ss. 70–75.

3. An officer of the royal household.

4. The *comptroller of the hanaper* was an officer of the Court of Chancery, whose office was abolished in 1842. So called because certain Chancery writs were kept in a hamper, or *in hanaperio*.

5. As to Comptroller-General of

Patents, Designs, and Trade Marks, see Patents and Designs Acts 1949 to 1961.

COMPULSORY PILOT. [PILOTAGE AUTHORITIES.]

COMPULSORY PURCHASE ORDER. An order, usually made by a local authority and confirmed by a minister, for the compulsory acquisition of land. Provisions as to compensation for compulsory purchase of land, or for injurious affection where part of a person's land is taken for the purpose of works, are now largely combined in the Land Compensation Act 1973.

COMPURGATORS. The twelve persons who, when a person was tried and made oath of his own innocence, were called upon to swear that they believed he spoke the truth. Supposed to be the origin of trial by jury. [BENEFIT OF CLERGY.]

COMPUTER. Any device for storing and processing information. See the Civil Evidence Act 1968, s. 5 (6).

COMPUTO. An ancient writ to compel a bailiff, receiver or accountant to yield up his accounts. Also lay against guardians.

CONCEALERS. Persons who were used to find out lands which were kept privily from the king by persons having no title thereto.

CONCEALMENT. (1) *Suppressio veri* to the injury or prejudice of another; if active and fraudulent it is ground for rescinding a contract. (2) Of birth is a misdemeanour. See the Offences against the Person Act 1861, s. 60. (3) Of documents, with a view to gain for himself or another or with intent to cause loss to another. See Theft Act 1968, s. 20; see also Law of Property Act 1925, s. 183.

CONCESSIT SOLVERE (he granted and agreed to pay). An action of debt upon a simple contract. It lay by custom in the Mayor's Court, London (later amalgamated with the City of London Court), and the Bristol City Court.

CONCILIATION. A settling of disputes without litigation. [ADVISORY, CONCILIATION AND ARBITRATION SERVICE.]

CONCLUDED is often used in the same sense as *estopped*. [CONCLUSION; ESTOPPEL.]

CONCLUSION is when a man, by his own act upon record, has charged himself with a duty, or other thing. In this sense it is tantamount to *estoppel*. [ESTOPPEL.] And this word *conclusion* is taken in another sense, as for the end or later part of any declaration, plea in bar, replication, conveyance, etc. *Cowel.*

CONCORD. 1. Part of the process by which a fine of lands was levied, prior to the abolition of fines by the Fines and Recoveries Act 1833. It was the agreement by which the pretended defendant acknowledged that the lands in question were the right of the complainant. [FINE, 1.]

2. A compromise.

CONCURRENT JURISDICTIONS. The jurisdiction of several different tribunals authorised to deal with the same subject-matter at the choice of the suitor.

CONCURRENT WRITS. Duplicate originals, or several writs running at the same time for the same purpose, for service on a person, when it is not known where he is to be found; or for service on several persons as when there are several defendants in an action. See R.S.C. 1965. Ord. 6.

CONDEMNATION. The adjudging of a captured vessel to be lawful prize.

CONDITION. A restraint annexed to a thing so that by the non-performance the party to it shall receive prejudice and loss, and by the performance commodity or advantage: it is also defined to be what is referred to an uncertain chance which may or may not happen. The following are the most important kinds of condition: (1) a condition in a deed, or express: a condition in law, or implied. (2) Precedent or subsequent.

CONDITIONAL FEE, otherwise called a fee simple conditional, properly comprises every estate in fee simple granted upon condition; but the term is usually understood to refer to that particular species called a "conditional fee" at the common law, which is an estate restrained in its form of donation to *some particular heirs* (exclusive of others): as, to the heirs of a man's body, or to the heirs male of his body; which the judges of former days construed, not as an estate descendible to some particular heirs, but an estate upon condition that the land was to revert to the

CONDITIONAL FEE—*continued.*

donor, if the donee had no heirs of his body. This construction of gifts of lands was put a stop to by c. 1 of the Statute of Westminster the Second (1285) commonly called the statute *De donis conditionalibus*, which provided that henceforth the will of the donor should be observed *secundum formam in carta doni expressam* (according to the form expressed in the charter of gift). Under the Law of Property Act 1925 legal estates tail are converted into equitable estates tail, and such last-mentioned estates may be created in any property, real or personal: ss. 1 (1) and (3), 130, and Sch. I, Part I. 2 *Bl.* [DE DONIS; ESTATE.]

CONDITIONAL LEGACY. A bequest whose operation depends upon the happening or not happening of some uncertain event, upon which it is either to take effect or to be defeated.

CONDITIONAL LIMITATION is a phrase used specially in the two following ways:—

1. Of an estate or interest in land so expressly defined and limited by the words of its creation that it cannot endure for any longer time than till a particular contingency happens. That is, a *present* interest, to be divested on a *future* contingency.

2. Of a future use or interest limited to take effect upon a given contingency, in derogation of a preceding estate or interest. This is likewise called a *shifting* or *secondary* use, and also an *executory interest*. It is a future estate to come into possession upon a given contingency. [ESTATE; EXECUTORY INTEREST.]

Thus, if land be granted to the use of A and his heirs until B returns from Rome, and then to the use of B and his heirs, A's estate is a conditional limitation of the first sort, and B's estate is a conditional limitation of the second sort above mentioned. Under the provisions of the Law of Property Act 1925 any such limitations can only take effect as equitable interests. See s. 1 and Sch. I, Part I of the Act. And a limitation which would (before 1926) have taken effect as a shifting or springing use will take effect now as a shifting or springing trust—see s. 4 (1) of the Act.

CONDITIONAL SALE AGREEMENT. "Conditional sale agreement"

means an agreement for the sale of goods under which the purchase price or part of it is payable by instalments, and the property in the goods is to remain in the seller (notwithstanding that the buyer is to be in possession of the goods) until such conditions as to the payment of instalments or otherwise as may be specified in the agreement are fulfilled. See the definition in s. 189 of the Consumer Credit Act 1974.

(*Canada.*) A sale of a chattel under a contract whereby possession passes to the purchaser but the seller retains the property in the chattel until the price is entirely paid, usually by stated instalments. [HIRE PURCHASE.]

CONDITIONS OF SALE. The terms stated in writing, upon which an estate or interest is to be sold by public auction. The Law of Property Act 1925, s. 45, applies certain conditions of sale to all contracts, unless otherwise expressly stated. And in exercise of his powers under s. 46 of the Act, the Lord Chancellor has prescribed a Statutory Form of Conditions of Sale which also apply to contracts by correspondence, unless excluded or modified thereby.

CONDITIONS PRECEDENT AND SUBSEQUENT. A condition *precedent*, in a conveyance or disposition of an estate, is a condition which must happen or be performed before the estate or interest can vest. A condition *subsequent* is a condition on the failure or non-performance of which an estate already vested may be defeated.

CONDOMINIUM (*Canada.*) A way of owning houses or suites in apartment houses whereby an individual owns the house or apartment but everything outside it, *e.g.* front lawn or apartment building corridor, are owned by a corporation the members of which are the owners of the houses and apartments. That which is common to all is maintained by the corporation.

CONDONATION. A pardoning, or remission, especially of a conjugal offence. The immediate effect of *condonation* was to bar the party condoning of his or her remedy for the offence in question. Condonation is no longer a statutory bar to divorce, but it may still be material in magistrates' courts.

CONDUCT MONEY. Money for the payment of the reasonable expenses of a witness at a trial.

CONDUCTIO. (Roman law.) A hiring (*q.v.*).

CONEY. A rabbit. [GAME.]

CONFEDERACY. A combination of two or more persons to commit some unlawful act or to do some damage or injury to another. [CONSPIRACY.]

CONFERENCE. 1. In parliamentary practice, is a mode of communicating important matters by one House of parliament to the other by means of deputations of their own members. *May.*

2. A meeting between a counsel and solicitor to advise on the client's cause. [CONSULTATION.]

CONFESSING ERROR. The consent by a party in whose favour judgment had been given that such judgment should be reversed, on allegation by the opposite party of "error" in fact or in law. [ERROR.]

CONFESSION by a criminal may be in open court when called upon to plead to the indictment or elsewhere. [VOLUNTARY CONFESSION.]

CONFESSION AND AVOIDANCE is a plea in bar whereby a party *confesses* the facts as stated by his adversary, but alleges some new matter by way of *avoiding* the legal effect claimed for them. As, if a man be sued for an assault, he may admit the assault, but plead that he committed it in self-defence.

CONFESSION, JUDGMENT BY. [COGNOVIT ACTIONEM.]

CONFESSION OF DEFENCE. Where any defendant alleged a ground of defence arising since the commencement of the action, the plaintiff might deliver confession of such defence and sign judgment for his costs up to the time of such pleading unless otherwise ordered. Obsolete.

CONFESSION OF PLEA. Same as confession of defence (*q.v.*).

CONFIDENTIAL COMMUNICATION. [PRIVILEGED COMMUNICATION.]

CONFIRMATIO CHARTARUM (confirmation of the charters). A statute enacted in the reign of Edward I (1297), confirming and making some additions to Magna Charta (*q.v.*).

CONFIRMATION. 1. A conveyance of an estate or right, whereby a voidable estate is made sure and unavoidable or a particular estate is increased.

2. The ratification by the archbishop of the election of a bishop by dean and chapter.

3. Confirmation is also the Scotch term corresponding to *probate* and *letters of administration* in England.

CONFISCATE. To appropriate to the revenue of the Crown.

CONFLICT OF LAWS. The discordance between the laws of one country and another, as applied to the same subject-matter; as, for instance, in the case of a contract made in one country and intended to be executed in another.

CONFORMITY, BILL OF. A bill filed by an executor or administrator against the creditors of the deceased, for the adjustment of their claims, where the affairs of the testator or intestate were found to be so much involved that it would not be safe to administer the estate, except under the direction of the Court of Chancery: a final decree was then issued by the court, to which all parties were bound to *conform*.

CONFUSION. A word in Scotch and French law, signifying the merger or extinguishment of a debt by the debtor succeeding to the property of his creditor, or *vice versa.*

CONFUSION OF GOODS is where the goods of two persons are so intermixed that the several portions can be no longer distinguished; as if the money, corn or hay of one man be intermixed with that of another. If the intermixture be by consent, it is supposed the proprietors have an interest in common in proportion to their shares, but if one man wilfully intermixes his property with another's without his consent, the law gives the entire property to him whose right is invaded and endeavoured to be rendered uncertain without his consent. 2 *Bl.*

CONGÉ D'ACCORDER signified leave to accord or agree for the purpose of levying a fine: prescribed by a statute of uncertain date of the reign of Edward II (*circa* 1325). *Cowel*; 2 *Bl.* [CONCORD; FINE, 1.]

CONGÉ D'ÉLIRE. The Queen's permission to a dean and chapter to choose a bishop. The dean and chapter are bound to elect such person as the Crown shall recommend, whose name is given in the letter missive which accompanies the *congé d'élire.*

CONGEABLE. A thing lawfully done, or done with leave. *Cowel.*

CONJOINTS. Persons married to each other.

CONJUGAL RIGHTS, SUIT FOR RESTITUTION OF, was a suit by a husband to compel his wife to live with him, or by a wife to compel the husband to take her back. A petition for restitution might be presented by either husband or wife, and the court, if satisfied that the allegations in the petition were true and that there was no legal ground why a decree for restitution should not be granted, might make the decree accordingly. Abolished by the Matrimonial Proceedings and Property Act 1970, itself now largely repealed by the Matrimonial Causes Act 1973.

CONJURATION. A plot or compact made by men to do any public harm. In the common law it was specially used for such as had personal conference with the devil, or evil spirits, to know any secret, or to effect any purpose. The laws against conjuration and witchcraft were repealed by the Witchcraft Act 1735, which made it an offence, however, to pretend to exercise witchcraft, sorcery, inchantment or conjuration, or to undertake fortunes, etc., such pretence to be punishable by imprisonment for a year. The Act of 1735 was repealed by the Fraudulent Mediums Act 1951.

CONNIVANCE signifies shutting of the eye. It was used especially with reference to a husband tacitly encouraging his wife to commit adultery, in order that he might obtain a divorce. Such connivance, if established, formerly deprived the husband of his remedy. Since the Divorce Reform Act 1969 (repealed and replaced by the Matrimonial Causes Act 1973) connivance is no longer a statutory bar to divorce.

CONSANGUINEUS FRATER. A brother by the father's side, in contradistinction to *frater uterinus,* the son of the same mother.

CONSANGUINITY. Relationship by blood, as opposed to *affinity,* which is relationship by marriage. [AFFINITY.]

CONSCIENCE, COURTS OF. Former local courts for the recovery of small debts, now superseded by the County Courts.

CONSENT presupposes a physical power, a mental power and a free and serious use of them, and if it be obtained by any fraud or undue influence it is not binding.

A girl or boy under the age of sixteen cannot in law give any consent which would prevent an act from being an indecent assault under ss. 14, 15 of the Sexual Offences Act 1956, otherwise consent, validly given, would be a good defence. See also *R.* v. *Woolaston* (1872), 26 L.T. 403.

CONSEQUENTIAL DAMAGE OR INJURY is damage or injury arising by *consequence* or *collaterally* to one man, from the culpable act or omission of another.

CONSERVATION. As to animals and plants, see the Conservation of Wild Creatures and Wild Plants Act 1975. Wild creatures protected by the Act include the greater horse-shoe bat, the natterjack toad and the large blue butterfly. Protected plants include the lady's slipper, the monkey orchid and the Snowdon lily.

See also the Protection of Birds Act 1954 and the Badgers Act 1973. [NATURE CONSERVANCY COUNCIL.]

CONSERVATOR OF THE PEACE is one who has an especial charge, by virtue of his office, to see the Queen's peace kept. Some conservators of the peace are so *virtute officii,* some are specially appointed, and are now called justices of the peace.

CONSIDERATION. A compensation, matter of inducement, or *quid pro quo,* for something promised or done. Valuable consideration is necessary to make binding every contract not under seal. It need not be adequate but must be of some value in the eye of the law and must be legal: it must also be present or future, it must not be past.

There is also a consideration called the consideration of "blood"; that is, natural love and affection for a near relation. This is, for some purposes, deemed a *good* consideration; but it is not held to be a *valuable* consideration, so as to support an action on a simple contract. It is sometimes called *meritorious* consideration.

CONSIGNMENT. The act of delivering goods; also the goods themselves so delivered. He who consigns the goods is called the consignor, and the person to whom they are sent is called the consignee.

CONSISTORY COURTS. Courts held by diocesan bishops within their several cathedrals, for the trial of ecclesiastical causes arising within their respective dioceses. The bishop's chancellor, or his commissary, is the judge; and from his sentence an appeal lies to the archbishop.

CONSOLATO DEL MARE. An ancient collection of the customs of the sea, including points relating to maritime warfare. It was probably compiled in the latter part of the fourteenth century, and seems to have been first published at Barcelona.

CONSOLIDATED FUND. A fund formed by the union, in 1787, of three public funds, then known as the *Aggregate* Fund, the *General* Fund, and the *South Sea* Fund. This Consolidated Fund of Great Britain was combined with that of Ireland by s. 1 of the Consolidated Fund Act 1816, Act the *Consolidated Fund of the United Kingdom.* The United Kingdom now means Great Britain and Northern Ireland only.

The Consolidated Fund constitutes almost the whole of the orinary public income of the United Kingdom, and is pledged for the payment of the whole of the interest of the National Debt, and is also liable to several specific charges imposed upon it from time to time by Act of Parliament.

CONSOLIDATION. The uniting of two benefices into one. *Cowel.*

CONSOLIDATION ACT. An Act of Parliament which repeals and re-enacts, if and where necessary, a number of previous enactments. Statutory provision is made for making corrections and minor improvements in consolidation by the Consolidation of Enactments (Procedure) Act 1949.

CONSOLIDATION OF ACTIONS. Two or more actions pending in the same Division between the same parties for the same cause of action may be consolidated, or put together for hearing as one action, by order of the court or a judge. See R.S.C. 1965, Ord. 4, r. 10; and C.C.R. 1936, Order 17, r. 1. [CONSOLIDATION ORDER.]

CONSOLIDATION OF MORTGAGES. A mortgagee, whether original or by assignment, who held more than one mortgage by the same mortgagor, had a right in equity to compel the mortgagor to redeem all the mortgages if he sought to redeem one of them. See as to consolidation of mortgages, the Law of Property Act 1925, s. 93.

CONSOLIDATION ORDER. A rule for consolidating actions, invented by Lord Mansfield, the effect of which is to bind the plaintiffs or defendants in several actions by the verdict in one, where the questions in dispute, and the evidence to be adduced, are the same in all. The application for such a rule is most frequently made in actions against underwriters upon policies of insurance. [CONSOLIDATION OF ACTIONS.]

CONSOLS. Funds formed by the consolidation of Government annuities. [CONSOLIDATED FUND.]

CONSORTIUM. The right of husband or wife to the affection, companionship and assistance of the other. Enticement of a spouse formerly entitled the other to an action for damages for loss of consortium (*Place* v. *Searle*, [1932] 2 K.B. 497). The action was abolished by the Law Reform (Miscellaneous Provisions) Act 1970.

CONSPIRACY. A combination or agreement between two or more persons to carry into effect a purpose hurtful to some individual, or to particular classes of the community, or to the public at large. See *e.g.* the Conspiracy and Protection of Property Act 1875.

CONSTABLE. An inferior officer to whom the service of maintaining the peace, and bringing to justice those by whom it is infringed, is more immediately committed.
1. *High and Petty Constables.*

High constables were appointed at the courts leet of the franchise or hundred over which they presided, or, in default of that, by the justices at their special sessions. The proper duty of the high constable seems to have been to keep the peace within the

CONSTABLE—*continued.*

hundred, as the petty constable did within the *parish* or *township*.

Petty constables were inferior officers in every town and parish, subordinate to the high constable. Their principal duty was the preservation of the peace, though they also had other particular duties assigned to them by Act of Parliament, particularly the service of the summonses and the execution of the warrants of the justices of the peace, relative to the apprehension and commitment of offenders. The various regional police forces have now superseded them, and they have not been appointed since 24th of March, 1873.

2. *Metropolitan Police.*

The Metropolitan Police Force is a body of men originally established by the Metropolitan Police Act 1829, and is under the immediate orders of an officer called the Commissioner of Police of the Metropolis, and two assistant commissioners.

The Metropolitan Police District does not include the City of London, but otherwise it extends to a radius of about fifteen miles from Charing Cross.

The Metropolitan Police Force is under the general control of the Home Secretary. See now the Police Act 1964.

3. *The City of London Police.*

The City of London Police Force was established by the City of London Police Act 1839. The management of the City Police is also in the hands of a Commissioner, appointed by the Lord Mayor, aldermen, and commons of the City, with the approval of the Queen. The police authority is the Common Council of the City of London.

4. *Police Areas.*

Outside London, the police force is divided into police areas, under Chief Constables. Police Committees, and Watch Committees have been abolished.

Various local forces have been amalgamated into larger divisions, *e.g.* Thames Valley Division.

5. *The River Tyne.*

This has its own police force under the authority of the Tyne Improvement Commissioners.

6. *Special Constables.*

These are appointed by the magistrates to execute warrants on particular occasions, or to act in aid of the preservation of the peace on special emergencies. This office, in the absence of volunteers, is compulsory.

CONSTABLEWICK. The place within which lie the duties of a constable.

CONSTAT. A certificate of what appears (*constat*) upon the record touching the matter in question. An exemplification of the enrolment of letters patent under the great seal is called a *constat*.

CONSTITUENCY. An area having separate representation in the House of Commons. See s. 4 of the House of Commons (Redistribution of Seats) Act 1949.

CONSTITUENT. 1. One who appoints an agent.
2. One who by his vote constitutes or elects a member of parliament.

CONSTITUTION is a word generally used to indicate the form of the supreme government in a state. Where this is established by a written instrument, as in the United States, the written instrument is called the Constitution. The word is also used of the enactments of the Roman emperors.

In countries having a written consituation, such as Switzerland and the United States, the word *constitutional* means "in conformity with the constitution", and the word *unconstitutional* means "in violation of the constitution"; the constitution, in all such countries, being the supreme law of the state. But, as applied to the legislation of the British parliament, the words in question are words of vague and indefinite import; they are often used as signifying merely approval or aversion, as the case may be. Sometimes they are used with greater precision, to indicate conformity with, or variation from, some traditional maxim of legislation, especially in reference to the *constitution* of the supreme legislative body.

CONSTRUCTION. Interpretation.

CONSTRUCTIVE is an adjective nearly synonymous with "implied"; meaning that the act or thing to which it refers does not exist, though it is convenient, for certain legal purposes, to assume that it does. See the following titles.

CONSTRUCTIVE DESERTION. In divorce proceedings, the doctrine of constructive desertion places the act of desertion upon one spouse although it is the other spouse who has left the matrimonial home, *e.g.* where the conduct of a husband or wife has forced the other to leave. *Rayden.*

CONSTRUCTIVE MALICE was formerly held to be present where a person in the course of committing some crime involving violence, the natural and probable consequence of which was not to cause the death of a human being, did in fact cause such a death.

It was also implied where a killing was caused while the person killed had been legally arresting or imprisoning the accused or executing other process of law in a legal manner.

The doctrine of constructive malice was abolished by s. 1 of the Homicide Act 1957, which provides that where a person kills another in the course or furtherance of some other offence, the killing shall not amount to murder unless done with malice aforethought.

CONSTRUCTIVE NOTICE. Notice imputed by construction of law. Whatever is sufficient to put any person of ordinary prudence on inquiry is constructive notice of everything to which that inquiry might have led. See the Law of Property Act 1925, s. 199, which provides that a purchaser shall not be prejudicially affected by any instrument, matter, fact, or thing unless it is within his own knowledge, or would have come to his knowledge if such inquiries and inspections had been made as ought reasonably to have been made by him.

CONSTRUCTIVE TOTAL LOSS. [TOTAL LOSS.]

CONSTRUCTIVE TREASON. An act raised by forced and arbitrary construction to the crime of treason; as the accroaching or attempting to exercise royal power was, in 1347, held to be treason in a knight of Hertfordshire, who forcibly assaulted and detained one of the king's subjects until he paid him £90.

CONSTRUCTIVE TRUST is a trust which is raised by construction of a court of equity, in order to satisfy the demands of justice, *without reference to the presumable intention of any party.* Thus, for instance, a constructive trust may arise where a person, who is only joint owner, permanently benefits an estate by repairs or improvements; for a lien or trust may arise in his favour in respect of the sum he has expended in such repairs or improvements. And it thus differs from an *implied* trust, which arises from the *implied* or presumed intention of a party.

CONSUETUDINARIUS. A ritual or book, containing the rites and forms of divine offices, or the customs of abbeys and monasteries. *Cowel.*

CONSUL. An agent appointed by a state to reside in a city belonging to another state, for the purpose of watching over the commercial interests of the subjects of the state from which he has received his commission. He is not clothed with the diplomatic character. His appointment is communicated to the government of the state wherein he is appointed to reside, and its permission is required to enable him to enter upon his functions. This permission is given by an instrument called an *exequatur.*

CONSULTARY RESPONSE. The opinion of a court of law upon a special case.

CONSULTATION. 1. An old writ whereby a cause, being removed by prohibition from the Ecclesiastical Court, could be returned there. *Cowel.* Analagous to a writ of *procedendo.* [PROCEDENDO.]

2. A meeting of two or more counsel and the solicitor instructing them for deliberating or advising. [CONFERENCE.]

CONSUMER SALE. A sale of goods (other than a sale by auction or by competitive tender) by a seller in the course of a business where the goods (*a*) are of a type ordinarily bought for private use or consumption; and (*b*) are sold to a person who does not buy or hold himself out as buying them in the course of a business. In the case of such sales, it is impossible to exclude by agreement any of the terms imported into a contract by the Sale of Goods Act 1893. See the Supply of Goods (Implied Terms) Act 1973.

CONSUMMATE TENANT BY CURTESY. The estate or interest of a

CONSUMMATE TENANT BY CURTESY—*continued.*

husband as tenant by the curtesy was said to be *consummate* on the death of his wife, as opposed to the *initiate* tenancy which arose on the birth of a child capable of inheriting the estate. Tenure by curtesy was abolished by the Administration of Estates Act 1925, s. 45. [CURTESY OF ENGLAND.]

CONSUMMATION. The completion of a thing, especially of a marriage by complete sexual intercourse.

CONTAGIOUS DISEASE. A disease passed from one person to another by contact, as contrasted with a disease that is infectious. The former Contagious Diseases Acts of 1866 and 1869, which were aimed at the prevention of venereal disease, were repealed in 1886. For "notifiable diseases" see the Health Services and Public Health Act 1968, s. 47 (cholera, plague, relapsing fever, smallpox and typhus). As to diseases of animals, see the Diseases of Animals Acts 1950 and 1975.

CONTANGO. The sum paid per share or per cent. on a settling day of the Stock Exchange, for continuing a "Bull" account to the next settlement. [BULL.]

CONTEMPT OF COURT. Anything which plainly tends to create a disregard of the authority of courts of justice; as the open insult or resistance to the judges who preside there, or disobedience to their orders. Contempt of court is punishable by the immediate imprisonment of the offender.

CONTEMPT OF PARLIAMENT. Anything which is a breach of the privileges of either House of parliament, according to the law and usage of parliament, is a contempt of the High Court of Parliament, and punishable by the House by committal. *May.*

CONTENTIOUS BUSINESS. Legal business where there is a contest, as opposed to non-contentious business where there is no such contest: the term is most frequently used in connection with obtaining probate or administration. Now assigned to the Chancery Division.

CONTENTIOUS JURISDICTION. That part of the jurisdiction of a court which is over matters in dispute, as opposed to its *voluntary* jurisdiction, which is merely concerned in doing what no one opposes. 3 *Bl.*

CONTESTATION OF SUIT (CONTESTATIO LITIS). The plea and joinder of issue in ecclesiastical suits.

CONTINGENCY WITH DOUBLE ASPECT. An expression sometimes used to denote the express limitation of one contingent remainder in substitution for another contingent remainder. As if land be given to A for life, and if he have a son, then to that son in fee; and if he have no son, then to B in fee. [CONTINGENT REMAINDER.]

CONTINGENT LEGACY. One bequeathed on a contingency; *e.g.*, if the legatee shall attain the age of 21 years.

CONTINGENT REMAINDER is an estate in remainder upon a prior estate, *limited* (*i.e.*, marked out in a deed or other written instrument) to take effect, either to a dubious and uncertain person, or upon a dubious and uncertain event.

Thus, if land be given A, a bachelor, for life, and after his death to his eldest son; this remainder to the eldest son of A is *contingent*, as it is not certain whether A will have any son. So, if land be given to A for life, and after his death to B, in case C shall then have returned from Rome; B's interest during A's life, until C shall have returned from Rome, is a contingent remainder.

A contingent remainder was defined by Fearne, in a work first published in 1772, as a remainder limited to depend on an event or condition, which might never happen or be performed, or which might not happen or be performed till after the determination of the preceding estate.

A contingent remainder (1) cannot take effect until the "prior particular estates" (*i.e.*, the interests for life, or otherwise, appointed to take effect before it) have come to an end; also (2) it cannot take effect unless the requisite contingency has happened. In the former respect it resembles a *vested remainder*, and differs from an *executory interest*. In the latter, it differs from a *vested remainder*, and resembles an *executory interest*. It has the weakness of both these estates, and the strength of neither. Under the Law of Property Act 1925, remainders (whether vested or contingent) can only subsist as equitable interests. See ss. 1, 4, and also Sch. I, Part I. [EXECUTORY INTEREST; REMAINDER; VESTED REMAINDER.]

CONTINUANCE. An adjournment of the proceedings in an action; or, more strictly, the entry on the record expressing the ground of the adjournment, and appointing the parties to reappear at a given date. Hence, a plea *puis darrein continuance* signified an allegation of a new matter of defence which has arisen *since the last adjournment* or *continuance*. Continuances are not now entered on the record or otherwise.

CONTINUANCE, NOTICE OF. Where a plaintiff could not be ready for trial on a day for which notice had been given, he might give notice of *continuance* and *continue* his notice to any future sitting. It is now obsolete; notice of trial not being given now for any particular sittings.

CONTINUANDO. In actions for trespasses of a permanent nature, where the injury was continually renewed, the plaintiff's declaration might allege the injury to have been committed *by continuation* from one given day to another, which was called laying the action with a *continuando*, and the plaintiff would not be ·compelled to bring separate actions for every day's separate offence.

CONTRA BONOS MORES. Against good morals.

CONTRA PACEM. "Against the peace of our lord the King, his crown and dignity"; a form formerly necessary in indictments for offences against the common law. Obsolete. See now, as to the form of indictment, the Indictment Rules 1971, S.I. 1971 No. 1253.

CONTRABAND, in its primary sense, denotes something prohibited by *ban* or *edict*, and indicates a prohibited trade.

But the most usual application of the term is to such articles as are contraband of war; that is, munitions and such other articles of merchandise carried in a neutral vessel in time of war as may be made directly available for hostile purposes by one belligerent against the other.

The latter belligerent is entitled to seize such articles *in transitu*, and in certain cases even to confiscate the ship in which they are carried. All belligerents have the right of visitation and search to prevent the conveyance of contraband goods to an enemy.

The definition of contraband articles has varied at different times, and on several occasions has been settled by treaties between states.

CONTRACT. A *contract* has been variously defined. Thus it is said to be "an agreement between competent persons, upon a legal consideration, to do or abstain from doing some act"; or more shortly as "an agreement enforceable at law." The agreement may be by *parol*, that is, by word of mouth, or writing not under seal; or it may be by specialty (*i.e.*, by writing under seal), in which case it is more properly termed a *covenant*. And where a contract is not by specialty, it is called a *parol* or *simple contract*, to distinguish it from a contract by specialty. A simple contract may be either *written* or *verbal*. A simple contract must be made upon a *consideration*, in order that an action may be founded upon it. [CONSIDERATION.]

An action of contract, or *ex contractu*, is an action in which the wrong complained of is a *breach of contract*, and is opposed to an action of *tort*, which is brought for a wrong *independent of contract*.

CONTRACTING OUT. Persons for whose benefit a statute has been passed may usually contract with others in such a manner as to deprive themselves of the benefit of the statute. In the case of certain statutes such "contracting out" is forbidden, *e.g.*, the Agricultural Holdings Act 1948, ss. 2, 65. The term is also applied to the rule whereby a member of a trade union may elect not to contribute towards political objects.

CONTRACT-NOTE. The note sent by a broker or agent to his principal advising him of the sale or purchase of any stock or marketable security.

CONTRIBUTION, SUIT FOR. A suit in equity, brought by one of several parties who has discharged a liability common to all, to compel the others to contribute thereto proportionably. See next title. Since the Law Reform (Married Women and Tortfeasors) Act 1935, there may be contribution by several persons who have jointly committed a tort in favour of one who has discharged the joint liability. See R.S.C. 1965, Ord. 16.

CONTRIBUTORY. A person liable to contribute to the assets of a company which is being wound up, as being a member or (in some cases) a past member thereof. Two lists of contributories are made out. The "A" list contains the names of those who were shareholders at the time of the winding-up order, who are primarily liable. The "B" list contains the names of those who have ceased to be shareholders within the 12 months preceding. These latter are liable in a secondary degree. See the Companies Act 1948, ss. 212–216.

CONTRIBUTORY MORTGAGE. One in respect of which the money secured is advanced by two or more lenders in separate amounts. In the absence of express power trustees may not lend money on such a mortgage.

CONTRIBUTORY NEGLIGENCE. Culpable negligence, by which a man contributes to the happening of an accident to himself, for which others are partially, or even mainly responsible. It was formerly a complete defence to an action for damages to prove that the plaintiff's own negligence was the cause of the accident. Now, the injured person will not be entitled to recover full damages for the injury if it can be shown that, but for his negligence, the accident would not have happened. Damages are apportioned in accordance with the Law Reform (Contributory Negligence) Act 1945.

CONTROLLER. [COMPTROLLER.]

CONVENTION. 1. The name of an old writ that lay for the breach of a covenant.

2. A name given to such meetings of the Houses of Lords and Commons as take place by their own authority, without being summoned by the Sovereign. This can only take place during great national crises. Thus, in the year 1660, the Convention Parliament met, which restored King Charles the Second; and in 1688, the Lords and Commons met to dispose of the crown and kingdom in favour of the Prince of Orange.

3. A treaty with a foreign power.

4. A term applied to constitutional rules which are observed although they have not the force of law.

• **CONVENTIONAL ESTATES** are *estates (i.e., interests in land) expressly created by the acts of parties, as opposed to* estates created by construction or operation of law.

CONVERSION. 1. The converting by a man to his own use of the goods of another. This will be a ground for an action by the latter (formerly known as an action for *trover* and *conversion*). In criminal law the modern term is "appropriation"; see s. 3 (1) of the Theft Act 1968. [APPROPRIATION.]

2. That change in the nature of property by which, for certain purposes, real estate is considered as personal, and personal estate as real, and transmissible and descendible as such. Thus money directed to be employed in the purchase of land, and land directed to be sold and turned into money, are to be considered as that species of property into which they are directed to be *converted*.

CONVEYANCE. 1. The transfer of the ownership of property, especially landed property, from one person to another; or the written instrument whereby such transfer is effected.

2. As used in the Law of Property Act 1925, conveyance includes a mortgage, charge, lease, assent, vesting declaration, vesting instrument, disclaimer, release, and every other assurance of property or of an interest therein by any instrument, except a will. "Convey" has a similar meaning. See s. 205 (1) (ii).

CONVEYANCER. One who draws conveyances; especially a barrister who confines himself to drawing conveyances, and other chamber practice.

CONVEYANCING. The practice of drawing conveyances and legal documents, which is a branch of the study and practice of the law.

CONVEYANCING COSTS. For scale of remuneration to solicitors in conveyancing matters see the Solicitors Remuneration Order 1883, and the Solicitors Remuneration (Registered Land) Order 1925, as amended from time to time, both of which have effect as if made under the Solicitors Act 1974.

CONVEYANCING COUNSEL, originally appointed under an Act of 1852, are counsel appointed for the purpose of assisting the court in the investigation of the title to any estate, and upon whose opinion the court or any judge thereof may act. By s. 217 of the Judicature Act 1925 (as amended by s. 14 of the Administration of Justice Act 1956) conveyancing counsel of the court are to be not more than six nor less than three in number, and shall be appointed by the Lord Chancellor. They must be conveyancing counsel in actual practice who have practised as such for ten years at least.

CONVICT is he that is found guilty of an offence by the verdict of a jury, or else appears and confesses. *Cowel.*

The term, however, was, by s. 6 of the Forfeiture Act 1870, restricted in that Act to mean any person against whom, after the passing of the Act, judgment of death, or of penal servitude, was pronounced or recorded by any court of competent jurisdiction in England, Wales or Ireland, upon any charge of treason or felony.

Section 6 of the Forfeiture Act 1870 was repealed by the Criminal Justice Act 1948; and both penal servitude and the death penalty have been abolished. The term convict is therefore now obsolete.

CONVICTION is where a man, being indicted for a crime, confesses it, or, having pleaded not guilty, is found guilty by the verdict of a jury. A summary conviction is where a man is found guilty of an offence on summary proceedings before a police magistrate or bench of justices.

CONVOCATION. A general assembly of the clergy, to consult on ecclesiastical matters.

There were two Convocations, one for the province of Canterbury, the other for that of York; and there were two distinct houses of either Convocation, of which the archbishop and bishops formed the upper house, and the lower consisted of deans, archdeacons, the proctors for (*i.e.*, representatives of) the chapters, and the proctors for the parochial clergy.

The former Church Assembly was renamed and reconstituted as the General Synod of the Church of England by the Synodical Government Measure 1969. By that Measure it was provided for the vesting of the functions, authority, rights and privileges of the Convocations of Canterbury and York in the General Synod.

CONVOY. A ship of war, or ships of war, appointed to protect merchantmen against hostile inspection and seizure.

COPARCENARY was where lands descended from an ancestor to two or more persons possessing an equal title to it. It arose by common law or particular custom. By common law, as where a landowner died intestate, leaving two daughters, who inherited equally: by particular custom, as where lands descended by the custom of gavelkind to all the males in equal degree.

An estate in *coparcenary* was distinguished from an estate held in *common* in that the former always arose from descent *ab intestato*: the latter arising from a deed or will, or the destruction of an estate in joint tenancy. Under the provisions of the Law of Property Act 1925 a trust for sale was created in respect of estates held in coparcenary and existing at the commencement of that Act. See Part IV of Sch. I to that Act. Since 1925 coparcenary does not arise (except in connection with entailed interests), as in the event of intestacy land vests in the personal representatives on trust for sale. See the Administration of Estates Act 1925, ss. 33 and 45.

COPE. 1. A mineral duty payable to the Crown out of the mines within the jurisdiction of the Barmote Courts. [BARMOTE COURTS.]

2. A hill.

3. The roof or covering of a house.

4. A church vestment.

COPYHOLD signified tenure by copy of court roll at the will of the lord of a manor according to the local custom. It was in *manors* only that copyholds were to be found; and it was by the immemorial *custom* of the particular manor that the copyholder's interest had to be regulated. Copyholders were originally villeins or slaves, permitted by the lord, as an act of grace or favour, to enjoy the lands at *his* pleasure; being in general bound to the performance of certain services. By the time of Edward III, the will of the lord came to be controlled by the custom of the manor. Under the provisions of the Law of Property Act 1922 copyholds were enfranchised and became freehold (or in certain cases leasehold).

COPYRIGHT. Copyright in relation to an original literary, dramatic or musical work is the exclusive right to do, or to

COPYRIGHT—*continued.*

authorise other persons to do, certain acts in relation to that work. Such acts include reproducing the work in any material form, publishing it, performing it in public, broadcasting it, or making any adaptation of it. This type of copyright, generally speaking, lasts during the lifetime of the author and for fifty years after his death.

Copyright similarly subsists in artistic works, sound recordings, cinematograph films, television and sound broadcasts.

See the Copyright Act 1956 and the Performers' Protection Acts 1958 to 1972, under which penalties are imposed for making records, cinematograph films, etc., without the consent of performers.

CO-RESPONDENT is any person made respondent to, or called upon to answer, a petition, or other proceeding, jointly with another. The word was used of a person charged by a husband, suing for a divorce, with adultery with the wife, and made jointly with her a respondent to the suit.

Adultery is no longer a **ground for** divorce, although evidence of adultery may be given in support of a divorce petition, for which the sole ground is now the irretrievable breakdown of marriage.

CORONATION OATH. The oath administered to every king or queen who succeeds to the imperial crown of these realms at his or her coronation, whereby he or she swears to govern the kingdom of England, and the dominions thereto belonging, according to the statutes in parliament agreed on, and the laws and customs of the same, and to maintain the Protestant reformed religion established by law. The form of the oath is prescribed by the Coronation Oath Act 1688.

CORONER. An ancient officer of the land, so called because he deals wholly for the Queen and Crown.

The coroner was formerly chosen by the freeholders, at a county court held for that purpose. For this purpose there was a writ *de coronatore eligendo.* The principal duty of a coroner is to inquire concerning the manner of the death of any person who is killed, or dies a violent or unnatural death or a sudden death the cause of which is unknown, or has died in prison. Under the Coroners (Amendment) Act 1926 a

coroner is empowered to hold an inquest without a jury, in certain cases; and is given certain other important powers. Another branch of his office used to be to inquire into shipwrecks, and to certify whether wreck or not, and who was in possession of the goods, but this jurisdiction was abolished by the Coroners Act 1887. Concerning treasure trove, he has to inquire who were the finders, and where it is. [TREASURE TROVE.] The coroner is also a conservator of the Queen's peace, and becomes a magistrate by virtue of his appointment.

He may be removed by the Lord Chancellor for extortion, neglect, inability, or misbehaviour in his office under the Coroners Act 1887, s. 8. As to remuneration, see the Coroners Act 1921; and the Coroners (Amendment) Act 1926, ss. 5–7.

Fees and allowances of witnesses and doctors attending coroners inquests are regulated under s. 1 of the Coroners Act 1954.

See further, as to the appointment of coroners, s. 220 of the Local Government Act 1972.

CORPORATION. A number of persons united and consolidated together so as to be considered as one person in law, possessing the character of perpetuity, its existence being constantly maintained by the succession of new individuals in the place of those who die, or are removed. Corporations are either *aggregate* or *sole.* Corporations aggregate consist of many persons, several of whom are contemporaneously members thereof, as the mayor and commonalty of a city, or the dean and chapter of a cathedral. Corporations sole are such as consist, at any given time, of one person only, as the king or queen, a bishop, a vicar, etc. A corporation must sue, or be sued, by its corporate name.

CORPOREAL HEREDITAMENTS. Things real, *e.g.,* land and houses.

CORPUS. The capital of a fund, as opposed to the income.

CORPUS JURIS CIVILIS. The body of the Roman civil law, published in the time of Justinian, containing: 1. The Institutes or Elements of Roman Law, in five books. 2. The Digest or Pandects, in fifty books, containing the opinions and writings of eminent lawyers. 3. A new Code, or collection of Imperial Constitutions, in twelve books. 4. The Novels, or New Constitutions, posterior in time to the other books, and amounting to a supplement to the Code.

CORROBORATION. Evidence in support of principal evidence. Required as to the evidence of an accomplice, in bastardy proceedings and some other cases.

CORRUPT PRACTICES. Treating, undue influence, bribery, and personation are corrupt practices at elections. See the Representation of the People Act 1949, particularly ss. 47, 99–101; and as to the appointment of commissioners to enquire into the existence of corrupt and illegal practices at elections, see the Election Commissioners Act 1949.

CORRUPTION. The corrupt acceptance of bribes by agents, the corrupt bribery of agents and other similar offences are punishable under the Prevention of Corruption Acts 1889 to 1916.

CORRUPTION OF BLOOD was one of the consequences of an attainder for treason or felony, whereby an attainted person could neither inherit lands or other hereditaments from his ancestors, nor retain those he was already in possession of, nor transmit them by descent to any heir; but the same escheated to the lord of the fee, subject to the king's superior right of forfeiture; and the person attainted also obstructed all descents to his posterity, whereon they were obliged to derive a title through him to a remoter ancestor. Abolished by s. 1 of the Forfeiture Act 1870.

COST-BOOK MINING COMPANIES. Partnerships for working mines. An agent, usually called a purser, was appointed by the partners. It was his duty to manage the affairs of the mine and to enter in a book, called the cost-book, the minutes of their proceedings, the names of all the partners or shareholders, and the number of shares held by each.

COSTS. The expenses incident to a suit or action, paid in general by the defeated party. Costs in actions at common law were first given to plaintiffs by the Statute of Gloucester, passed in the sixth year of Edward I, and by subsequent statutes of Henry VIII and James I the defendant was declared entitled to costs in all cases in which the plaintiff would have been entitled thereto had he succeeded.

Costs in equity were in the discretion of the judge, but were in general given to the successful party.

Rules as to costs in the High Court are now principally to be found in R.S.C. 1965, Ord. 62, the various rules of which deal with entitlement to costs, powers of taxing officers, procedure in taxation, assessment of costs, and application for review.

Costs in the County Court are according to scales set out in the Appendices to the County Court Rules 1936, which continue to have effect as if made under the County Courts Act 1959.

As to costs in criminal cases, see the Costs in Criminal Cases Act 1973.

COUCHANT. Lying down. [LEVANT AND COUCHANT.]

COUNSEL. A barrister-at-law. [BARRISTER; QUEEN'S COUNSEL.]

COUNTERCLAIM. By R.S.C. 1965, Ord. 15, r. 2, a defendant in an action may set off or set up by way of counterclaim any right or claim whether such set-off or counterclaim sound in damages or not, and such set-off or counterclaim has the same effect as a statement of claim in a cross action so as to enable the court to pronounce a final judgment in the same action both on the original and on the cross claim. But if in the opinion of the court such set-off or counterclaim cannot be conveniently disposed of in the same action or ought not to be allowed, the court may refuse permission to the defendant to avail himself of it. [SET-OFF.]

COUNTER-DEED. A secret writing, either before a notary or under a private seal which destroyed, invalidated, or altered a public one.

COUNTERFEIT. An imitation made without authority and with the object of defrauding. [COIN.]

COUNTERPART. When the several parts of an indenture are interchangeably executed by the parties thereto, that part or copy which is executed by the grantor is called *original*, and the rest are *counterparts*.

COUNTER-SECURITY. A security given to one who has entered into a bond or become surety for another.

COUNTER-SIGN. The signature of a secretary or other subordinate officer to

COUNTER-SIGN—*continued.*

vouch for the authenticity of a document signed by a superior.

COUNTY. A division of the kingdom, originally made up of an indefinite number of hundreds. The word is derived from *Comes*, the *Count* of the Franks; that is, the earl or *ealdorman* (as the Saxons called him) of a shire, to whom the government of it was entrusted.

Under the reorganisation of local government by the Local Government Act 1972, counties in England are classed as either metropolitan counties or non-metropolitan counties. The metropolitan counties are Greater Manchester, Merseyside, South Yorkshire, West Yorkshire, Tyne and Wear, and West Midlands. There are 39 non-metropolitan counties, which include most of the former well-known counties such as Kent, Surrey, etc., though generally with some boundary changes. A few new counties came into being (*e.g.* Avon, comprising Bath, Bristol, and parts of Gloucestershire and Somerset), whilst Rutland was swallowed up in Leicestershire.

Wales is divided into eight counties.

Each county is divided into districts, and each county and each district has its own council.

Greater London and the Isles of Scilly are excluded from the above provisions.

COUNTY BOROUGHS. The boroughs in England and Wales which were listed in Sch. I to the Local Government Act 1933, now repealed, and which were by that Act constituted county boroughs. They have been incorporated in the new local government areas under the Local Government Act 1972 [County.]

COUNTY CORPORATE. A city or town with more or less territory annexed to it, to which, out of special grace and favour, the kings of England granted the privilege to be counties of themselves, and not to be comprised in any other county; but to be governed by their own sheriffs and other magistrates. Such were London, York, Norwich, etc. By the Counties of Cities Act 1798, all causes of action arising, and offences committed, in a county corporate, might be tried in the next adjoining county at large.

COUNTY COUNCILS. The elective bodies established by ss. 2, 21 of the Local Government Act 1972. For every county (which may be metropolitan or non-metropolitan [County.]) there is a council consisting of a chairman and councillors. Elections are held every four years. Their functions, which include education, housing, town planning, etc., are listed in Part IX of the Act of 1972.

COUNTY COURT. The modern county courts, which form one of the three great judicial systems of England and Wales, were first established by the County Courts Act 1846. This Act and various amending Acts have been consolidated from time to time, the latest consolidation being that effected by the County Courts Act 1959.

There are at present about 320 county courts, all co-ordinated in a system covering the whole of England and Wales, though each is a distinct, self-contained and autonomous tribunal. The courts, which are local courts of record of civil jurisdiction, are normally presided over by circuit judges. They are among the most important of the inferior courts.

Jurisdiction is either *general, i.e.,* given by the Act of 1959, which is wholly concurrent with that of the High Court in common law, equity, admiralty, and probate but subject to specified limitations as to consent, class or amount; or *special, i.e.,* conferred by various statutes dealing with particular branches of law. This special jurisdiction may be exclusive to the county courts or may be exercised concurrently with the High Court or with magistrates courts or both.

Procedure in the county courts is regulated largely by the County Court Rules 1936, which still have effect as if made under the County Courts Act 1959. Appendix A to the Rules contains forms for use in the county courts, while Appendices B–E deal with scales of costs and allowances to witnesses. Fees payable on proceedings taken in the courts are regulated by the County Court Fees Order 1971.

COUNTY PALATINE. The counties Chester, Durham and Lancaster have for long been known as counties palatine. They were so called *a palatio*, because the owners thereof (the Earl of Chester, the Bishop of

Durham and the Duke of Lancaster) had formerly in those counties *jura regalia* (royal rights) as fully as the king had in his palace. They might pardon treasons, murders, and felonies; all writs and indictments ran in their names, as in other counties in the king's; and all offences were said to be done against *their peace*, and not, as in other places, *contra pacem domini regis* (against the peace of our lord the king). The Isle of Ely, according to Blackstone, was not a county palatine only but a royal franchise; the bishop having by grant of King Henry I *jura regalia* within the Isle of Ely, whereby he exercised a jurisdiction over all causes, as well criminal as civil.

These counties palatine have now been assimilated to the rest of England. By the Supreme Court of Judicature Act 1873, s. 16 (repealed and replaced by s. 18 of the Judicature Act 1925) the jurisdiction of the Court of Common Pleas at Lancaster and the Court of Pleas at Durham was transferred to the High Court of Justice. The jurisdiction of the Chancery Courts of Lancaster and Durham came to an end with the abolition of those courts by the Courts Act 1971.

COUNTY RATE. One levied on the occupiers of lands in a county for various local purposes. The present method of levying is for the county council to precept on the district councils who collect the rates from the occupiers. [RATE.]

COUPONS. Dividend and interest certificates. Generally attached to bonds or other certificates of loan; when the interest is payable they are cut off and presented for payment.

COURT (Lat. *Curia*) has various significations—
1. The house where the Queen remains with her retinue.
2. The place where justice is judicially administered.
3. The judges who sit to administer justice; and, in jury trials, the judge or presiding magistrate, as opposed to the jury.
4. A meeting of a corporation, or the principal members thereof; as in the term Court of Aldermen, Court of Directors, etc.

COURT BARON. A court formerly incident to every manor in the kingdom, held by the steward within the manor.

[MANOR.] This Court Baron was of two natures. (1) The one was a customary court appertaining entirely to the *copyholders*, in which their estates were transferred by surrender and admittance, and other matters transacted relative to their tenures only. (2) The other was a court of common law, not of record, held before the *freehold* tenants who owed suit and service to the lord of the manor; and of this court the steward of the manor was rather the registrar than the judge. The freeholders' court was anciently held every three weeks; and its most important business was to determine, in the real action called the *writ of right*, all controversies relating to lands within the manor. It might also hold plea (*i.e.*, assume jurisdiction of personal actions) where the debt or damages did not amount to 40s. This court, however, long ago fell into disuse, and its jurisdiction was abolished in 1867.

COURT, CONSISTORY. [CONSISTORY COURTS.]

COURT, COUNTY. [COUNTY COURT.]

COURT FOR CONSIDERATION OF CROWN CASES RESERVED. A court established in 1848 for the purpose of deciding any question of law reserved for its consideration by any judge or presiding magistrate in any court of oyer and terminer, gaol delivery, or quarter sessions, before which a prisoner had been found guilty by verdict. Superseded by the Court of Criminal Appeal, which in turn has been superseded by the criminal division of the Court of Appeal under the Criminal Appeal Acts 1966 and 1968.

COURT FOR DIVORCE AND MATRIMONIAL CAUSES. A court established in 1857 by the Matrimonial Causes Act of that year, and to which was transferred the matrimonial jurisdiction of the ecclesiastical courts, together with the power, previously exercised by private Acts of Parliament, to grant divorces *a vinculo* in certain cases, and to make declarations as to legitimacy.

Since 1873 this court has been merged in the Supreme Court of Judicature, and its business is now dealt with by the Family Division.

COURT, HUNDRED. [COURT BARON; HUNDRED COURT.]

COURT LANDS, *terræ curtiles*, otherwise called demesnes, *terræ· dominicales*. Domains kept in the lord's hands to serve his family: called court-lands as being appropriated to the house or court of the lord, and not let out to tenants.

COURT LEET. A court of record held once in the year and not oftener within a particular hundred, lordship, or manor, before the steward of the leet: being the king's court granted by charter to the lords of those hundreds or manors. Its office was to view the *frankpledges*, that is, the freemen within the liberty; to present by jury crimes happening within the jurisdiction; and to punish trivial misdemeanours.

COURT-MARTIAL. A court with jurisdiction to try and punish military offences.

By s. 84 of the Army Act 1955 courts-martial may be either general courts-martial, district courts-martial, or field general courts-martial. The powers of these different descriptions of courts-martial are defined in s. 85 of the Act.

Similar provisions are made in ss. 84, 85 of the Air Force Act 1955; and in ss. 48, 53–66, of the Naval Discipline Act 1957.

The Courts-Martial (Appeals) Act 1968 provides for the hearing of appeals against convictions by naval, army and air force courts-martial to the Courts-Martial Appeal Court, with a further appeal, on the certificate of the Attorney-General that a point of law of exceptional public importance is involved, to the House of Lords.

COURT OF ADMIRALTY. [ADMIRALTY.]

COURT OF APPEAL. A court of appellate jurisdiction originally established under s. 1 of the Supreme Court of Judicature (Consolidation) Act 1925, but which was reconstituted under the Criminal Appeal Act 1966. The Court of Appeal is now a superior court of record consisting of two divisions, the civil division and the criminal division. The civil division exercises the jurisdiction exercisable by the court prior to the Act of 1966; the criminal division exercises appellate jurisdiction under the Criminal Appeal Act 1968, the former Court of Criminal Appeal having been abolished.

The Court of Appeal consists of the Lord Chancellor (president of the court); ex-Lord Chancellors; any Lord of Appeal in Ordinary who, at the date of his appointment, would have been qualified to be appointed an ordinary judge of the Court of Appeal or who, at that date, was a judge of that court; the Lord Chief Justice; the Master of the Rolls; the President of the Family Division; and not less than eight nor more than fourteen ordinary members of the court, entitled Lords Justices of Appeal (*Hals. Laws*).

Generally speaking, appeals lie to the Court of Appeal from all orders and judgments of the High Court; although in certain circumstances an appeal may lie directly to the House of Lords from proceedings in the High Court under the Administration of Justice Act 1969.

As to appeals from the county court, see s. 108 of the County Courts Act 1959.

COURT OF ARCHDEACON. The most inferior court in the whole ecclesiastical polity, held before a judge appointed by the archdeacon himself, and called his *official*. Its jurisdiction comprises ecclesiastical causes in general arising within the archdeaconry. From the archdeacon's court an appeal generally lies to that of the bishop. Now virtually obsolete. [ARCHDEACON.]

COURT OF ARCHES. [ARCHES, COURT OF.]

COURT OF BANKRUPTCY. [BANKRUPTCY.]

COURT OF CHANCERY. [CHANCERY DIVISION.]

COURT OF CHIVALRY. A court held before the Earl Marshal of England, acting through his Surrogate, with jurisdiction relating to encroachments in the matter of coats of arms, etc. The court probably dates from the time of the Conquest.

After a lapse of some 200 years, during which the court had not sat, a citation was issued under the hand and seal of the Earl Marshal (the Duke of Norfolk) on Oct. 20, 1954, citing the defendants (a theatre company) to enter an appearance in the High Court of Chivalry to answer the complaint of the plaintiff corporation. In this way proceedings were commenced in *Manchester Corpn.* v. *Manchester Palace of Varieties, Ltd.*, [1955] 1 All E.R. 387. At the hearing, before the Earl Marshal and the Lord Chief Justice (Surrogate), it was **held** that the Court (despite Blackstone having regarded it as obsolete) still had jurisdiction to deal with complaints relating to the usurpation of armorial bearings.

COURT OF CLERK OF THE MARKET. A court incident to every fair and market in the kingdom, to punish misdemeanours therein, particularly offences in connection with weights and measures. Now obsolete.

COURT OF COMMISSIONERS OF SEWERS. These courts were erected by virtue of a commission under the great seal pursuant to the Statute of Sewers 1531. Their powers were confined to such county or particular place as their commission expressly named. Their jurisdiction was to overlook the repairs of the banks and walls of the sea coast and of navigable rivers, and to cleanse such rivers and the streams communicating therewith. They could also assess such rates or scots upon the owners of lands within their district as they judged necessary.

The Statute of 1531 was repealed by the Land Drainage Act 1930.

COURT OF COMMON PLEAS, or, as it was sometimes called, the Court of Common Bench, was one of the superior courts of common law. It took cognizance of all actions between subject and subject, without exception. It formerly had an exclusive jurisdiction over real actions, which excelled all others in importance. It was also entrusted with exclusive jurisdiction in appeals from the decisions of revising barristers, and in some other matters.

By s. 16 of the Supreme Court of Judicature Act 1873 the business of the Court of Common Pleas was transferred to the Common Pleas division of the High Court of Justice established under that Act, but by Order in Council of Dec. 16th, 1880, under s. 32 of the Act, that division was merged in the Queen's Bench Division.

COURT OF CONSCIENCE. [CONSCIENCE, COURTS OF; COURT OF REQUEST.]

COURT OF CRIMINAL APPEAL. A court formerly constituted under s. 1 of the Criminal Appeal Act 1907. Judges of the court were the Lord Chief Justice and all judges of the Queen's Bench Division.

Any person convicted on indictment had a right of appeal to the court (a) against his conviction on any ground of appeal which involved a question of law alone; (b) with the leave of the court itself, or upon the certificate of the judge who tried him, that it was a fit case for appeal upon a question of fact, or of mixed law and fact, or other sufficient ground; or (c) with the leave of the court itself against his sentence.

The Court of Criminal Appeal was abolished by the Criminal Appeal Act 1966, s. 1, its jurisdiction being transferred to the criminal division of the Court of Appeal. [COURT OF APPEAL.]

COURT OF EQUITY. [EQUITY.]

COURT OF ERROR. An expression formerly applied especially to the Court of Exchequer Chamber and the House of Lords, as taking cognizance of *error* brought. [ERROR.]

COURT OF EXCHEQUER, one of the superior courts of Westminster, was a very ancient court of record, intended principally to order the revenues of the Crown, and to recover the king's debts and duties. It was called the Exchequer, *scaccarium*, from the chequered cloth, resembling a chessboard, which covered the table there, and on which, when certain of the king's accounts were made up, the sums were marked and scored with counters. The Exchequer consisted of two divisions, the *receipt* of the Exchequer, which managed the royal revenue, and the *court*, or judicial part of it. This court was originally subdivided into a court of equity and a court of common law. But by an Act of 1841, all the equity jurisdiction of the Court of Exchequer was transferred to the Court of Chancery. The Court of Exchequer consisted, moreover, of a *revenue* side and of a common law or *plea* side. On the *revenue* side it ascertained and enforced the proprietary rights of the Crown against the subjects of the realm. On the *plea* side it administered redress between subject and subject in all actions personal.

By the Supreme Court of Judicature Act 1873 the business of the Court of Exchequer was transferred to the Exchequer Division of the High Court of Justice, and by Order in Council under s. 32 of that Act the Exchequer Division was in turn merged in the Queen's Bench Division.

COURT OF EXCHEQUER CHAMBER. An intermediate court of appeal between the superior courts of common

COURT OF EXCHEQUER CHAMBER—*continued.*

law and the House of Lords. When sitting as a court of appeal from any one of the three superior courts of common law, it was composed of judges of the other two courts. The powers of this court were, by s. 18 (4) of the Judicature Act 1873, transferred to the Court of Appeal established by that Act.

COURT OF FACULTIES. [FACULTY.]

COURT OF FOREST. [FOREST COURTS.]

COURT OF GREAT SESSIONS IN WALES. A court formerly held twice every year in each county in Wales by judges appointed by the Crown, from which writs of error lay to the Court of King's Bench at Westminster. The court was abolished in 1830, and the Welsh judicature entirely incorporated with that of England.

COURT OF HIGH COMMISSION. [HIGH COMMISSION COURT.]

COURT OF HUSTINGS. A court held within the City of London, before the Lord Mayor, Recorder, and Sheriffs. This court was the representative, within the City, of the ancient county court of the sheriff. It had exclusive jurisdiction in all real and mixed actions for the recovery of land within the city, except ejectment. But now that all real and mixed actions, except ejectment, are abolished, the jurisdiction of this court has fallen into desuetude.

Certain other boroughs formerly had courts of hustings, *e.g.* Lyme Regis, Oxford. In these two cases, the courts were abolished by the Local Government Act 1972, Sch. 28.

The word "husting" is derived from "house" and "thing", thus originally meaning a court in a house (*Hals. Laws*).

COURT OF KING'S (or QUEEN'S) BENCH. One of the superior courts of common law. It was so called because the sovereign used to sit there in person. This court might follow the sovereign's person wherever he went; and, after Edward I had conquered Scotland it actually sat at Roxburgh. The court kept all inferior jurisdictions within the bounds of their authority, and might either remove their proceedings to be determined before itself, or prohibit their progress below. It superintended all

civil corporations in the kingdom. It commanded magistrates and others to do what their duty required, in every case where there was no other specific remedy. It protected the remedy of the subject by speedy and summary interposition. It took cognizance both of criminal and civil causes; the former in what was called the *crown side* or *crown office*; the latter in the *plea side* of the court.

By s. 34 of the Judicature Act 1873 the jurisdiction of this court was assigned to the Queen's Bench Division of the High Court of Justice, and by Order in Council under s. 32 of the same Act the Common Pleas and Exchequer Divisions were merged in the Queen's Bench Division in February, 1881.

COURT OF LORD HIGH STEWARD OF GREAT BRITAIN. A court formerly instituted for the trial, during the recess of parliament, of peers or peeresses indicted for treason or felony, or for misprision of either. Into this court indictments against peers of parliament were removed by *certiorari*. The office was created *pro hac vice* only, whenever the occasion required it. During a session of parliament the trial was not properly in the court of the Lord High Steward but before the High Court of Parliament; a Lord High Steward was, however, always appointed to regulate the proceedings.

Privilege of peerage was abolished in criminal proceedings by s. 30 of the Criminal Justice Act 1948.

COURT OF LORD HIGH STEWARD OF THE QUEEN'S HOUSEHOLD. A court created by the Offences within the Court Act 1541, with jurisdiction to inquire of, hear, and determine all treasons, misprisions of treason, murders, and bloodshed committed within any of the Queen's houses or palaces. The Act was repealed so far as relating to certain offences by the Statute Law Revision Act 1948; but generally it remains in force and the jurisdiction of the court could still be evoked.

COURT OF MARSHALSEA. A court which held plea (*i.e.*, had jurisdiction) of all trespasses committed within the verge (*i.e.*, within twelve miles) of the king's court, where one of the parties was of the royal household; and of all debts and contracts,

when both parties were of that establishment. Abolished in 1849.

COURT OF PASSAGE. [LIVERPOOL COURT OF PASSAGE.]

COURT OF PECULIARS. A branch of the Court of Arches. The Court of Peculiars had jurisdiction over all those parishes, dispersed through the province of Canterbury, which were exempt from the ordinary's jurisdiction, and subject to the metropolitan only.

COURT OF PIEDPOUDRE (*Curia pedis pulverizati*, or *Court of powdered foot*). A court of record incident to every fair and market, of which the steward of him who owned the toll of the market was the judge. Its jurisdiction extended to all commercial injuries done in that fair or market, and not in any preceding one. From this court a writ of error lay in the nature of an appeal to the courts at Westminster. Various explanations have been given of the name. The jurisdiction of this court is now obsolete, the last to be abolished being the Pie Poudre Court of Bristol, by the Courts Act 1971.

COURT OF POLICIES OF ASSURANCE. A court first established in 1601, for the purpose of determining in a summary way all causes concerning policies of assurance in London, with an appeal by way of bill to the Court of Chancery. Abolished in 1863.

COURT OF PROBATE. A court established in 1857 under the Probate Act of that year. To this court was transferred, by that Act, the testamentary jurisdiction of the Ecclesiastical Courts.

Non-contentious probate business is now dealt with in the Family Division of the High Court; contentious business has been assigned to the Chancery Division.

COURT OF PROTECTION. The department of the High Court which dealt with the estates of persons incapable, by reason of mental disorder, of managing and administering their property and affairs.

Originally known as the Office of the Master in Lunacy, then as the Management and Administration Department, it is continued under its modern title by s. 100 of the Mental Health Act 1959.

COURT OF RECORD. A court whose acts and judicial proceedings are enrolled for a perpetual memorial and testimony; whose rolls are the *records* of the court. All courts of record are the Queen's courts, and no other court has authority to fine and imprison; so that the very erection of a new jurisdiction with the power of fine or imprisonment makes it instantly a court of record. Such common law courts as are *not* courts of record are of inferior dignity, and in a less proper sense the Queen's courts. And in these, the proceedings not being enrolled or recorded, as well their existence, as the truth of the matters therein contained, shall, if disputed, be tried and determined by a jury. A court not of record, says Blackstone, is the court of a private man, whom the law will not entrust with any discretionary power over the fortune or liberty of his fellow-subjects.

COURT OF REQUEST, otherwise called a *Court of Conscience*. These courts were for the recovery of small debts, established by Acts of Parliament in various parts of the kingdom, but now superseded by the county courts (*q.v.*). [CONSCIENCE, COURTS OF.]

COURT OF SESSION. The superior court, in Scotland, of law and equity, divorce and admiralty, having a universal civil jurisdiction.

COURT OF SHERIFF'S TOURN. [SHERIFF'S TOURN.]

COURT OF STANNARIES OF CORNWALL AND DEVON, established for the administration of justice among the tinners, was a court of record with a special jurisdiction, held before a judge called the vice-warden, with an appeal to the lord warden. All tinners and labourers in and about the stannaries (*i.e.*, the mines and works in Devon and Cornwall where tin metal was dug and purified) might sue and be sued in the court in all matters arising within the stannaries, excepting pleas of land, life, and member. By the Stannaries Court (Abolition) Act 1896 their jurisdiction was transferred to county courts.

COURT OF STAR-CHAMBER. [STAR-CHAMBER.]

COURT, PREROGATIVE. [PREROGATIVE COURT.]

COURT ROLLS. The rolls of a manor, whereon were entered all surrenders, wills, grants, admissions, and other acts relating

COURT ROLLS—*continued.*

to the manor. They were considered to belong to the lord of the manor, and were kept by the steward as his agent; but they were in the nature of public books for the benefit of the tenants as well as the lord, so that it was a matter of course for the courts of law to grant an inspection of the court rolls in a question between two tenants. Under the Law of Property Act 1922 copyholds became freeholds and manorial rights were extinquished subject to the provisions therein contained.

COVENANT. A clause of agreement contained in a deed whereby a party stipulates for the truth of certain facts, or binds himself to give something to another, or to do or not to do any act.

COVERTURE. The condition of a wife during her marriage, which before the Married Women's Property Acts and the Law Reform (Married Women and Tortfeasors) Act 1935, involved certain disabilities on the one hand, and certain protections or privileges on the other. A married woman now stands, with few exceptions, in the same legal position as a single woman.

CRAVEN. A word of disgrace and obloquy, pronounced by the vanquished champion in trial by battle. [WAGER OF BATTEL.] Trial by battle was formerly abolished by statute in 1819.

CREDITOR. One to whom another owes money.

CREDIT UNION (*Canada*). An association which receives money from its members and lends such money out to members.

CREMATION. The disposal of a dead body by burning instead of by burial. This is not illegal unless it be done so as to cause a nuisance, or with the intention of preventing a coroner's inquest. See the Cremation Acts 1902 and 1952, and s. 214 of the Local Government Act 1972.

CRIME. A crime, as opposed to a civil injury, is an act which is forbidden, or the omission to perform an act which is commanded by the common law, by statute or by regulations made by a subordinate authority; the remedy for which is the punishment of the offender at the instance of the State.

CRIMINAL BANKRUPTCY ORDER. [BANKRUPTCY.]

CRIMINAL CONVERSATION, sometimes abbreviated into *crim. con.*, was adulterous conversation, or living with the wife of another man. An action for criminal conversation was formerly allowed by law to the injured husband. The action was abolished in 1857.

CROSS APPEAL. If both parties to a judgment are dissatisfied by it, and each accordingly appeals, the appeal of each is called a cross appeal in relation to that of the other; it not being open to a respondent to an appeal, as such, to contend that the decision in the court below was not sufficiently favourable to him. But by R.S.C. 1965, Ord. 59, rr. 6, 7, a respondent will be allowed so to contend, if he has within due time given notice of his intention so to do to any parties who may be affected by such contention.

CROSS BILL. Was a bill brought by a defendant in a Chancery suit against a plaintiff or a co-defendant, praying relief in reference to the same subject-matter.

CROSS DEMAND. A counter-claim.

CROSS-EXAMINATION. The examination of a witness by the opposing counsel. Leading questions are allowed, which is not the case in examination in chief.

Also, an examination of a *hostile* witness on behalf of the party producing him is sometimes called cross-examination.

CROSS REMAINDER is where each of two grantees has reciprocally a remainder in the share of the other.

Thus, if an estate be granted, as to one half, to A for life, with remainder to his children in tail, with remainder to B in fee simple; and, as to the other half, to B for life, with remainder to his children in tail, with remainder to A in fee simple; these remainders are called cross remainders. They may be implied in a will, but must always be expressed in a deed, and should be expressly limited in a will. Under the Law of Property Act 1925 remainders can subsist only as equitable interests and not as legal interests. [REMAINDER.]

CROSSED CHEQUE. [CHEQUE.]

CROWN. A word often used for the king or queen as being the sovereign of these realms.

CROWN CASES RESERVED.
[COURT FOR CONSIDERATION OF CROWN CASES RESERVED.]

CROWN COURT. The Crown Court was established by the Courts Act 1971. It superseded the jurisdiction of the former assize courts and courts of quarter sessions. It is part of the Supreme Court, with jurisdiction throughout England and Wales, and is a superior court of record. Any High Court judge, circuit judge or recorder, sitting alone or with justices of the peace, may exercise its jurisdiction and powers. The Crown from time to time appoints circuit judges to serve in the Crown Court and county courts.

CROWN DEBTS. Debts due to the Crown. These were formerly recoverable by a summary process called an extent; but see now the Crown Proceedings Act 1947. [EXTENT.] By s. 28 (1) of the Bankruptcy Act 1914 a bankrupt's discharge is not to relieve him from such debts unless the Commissioners of the Treasury certify in writing their consent to his being discharged therefrom.

CROWN LANDS (Lat. *Térræ dominicales regis*, the desmesne lands of the Crown) include the share reserved to the Crown at the original distribution of landed property, and such as came to it afterwards by forfeitures or other means. In modern times the superintendence of the royal demesnes has been vested in the Commissioners of Woods, Forests, and Land Revenues, and it is now usual for the sovereign to surrender these lands at the commencement of his reign for its whole duration in consideration of the Civil List settled upon him. And see the Crown Lands Act 1927 (incorporating the Commissioners of Crown Lands) and the Crown Estate Act 1961.

CROWN LAW. The criminal law.

CROWN OFFICE. The *Crown side* of the former Court of King's Bench, on which it took cognizance of criminal causes, from high treason down to the most trivial misdemeanour or breach of the peace. Now the Crown Office and Associates' Department of the Central Office of the Supreme Court.

CROWN PAPER. A paper containing the list of cases which awaits decision on the Crown side of the Queen's Bench Division.

CROWN PROCEEDINGS. Any proceedings in contract or in tort which are brought by or against the Crown. Action may now be brought as of right. See the Crown Proceedings Act 1947.

CROWN SIDE. That jurisdiction of the Queen's Bench Division by which it takes cognizance of criminal causes, including many questions which are practically of a civil nature.

CROWN SOLICITOR. The Solicitor to the Treasury, formerly called the Public Prosecutor. Public prosecutions are now handled either by the Director of Public Prosecutions (*q.v.*) or by the police or by some public authority. In Scotland this duty is performed in every county by the Procurator-Fiscal, a subordinate of the Lord Advocate.

CRUELTY. Conduct on the part of husband or wife which entitled the other party to judicial separation or divorce.

The sole ground for divorce is now the irretrievable breakdown of a marriage. One of the grounds in proof of this is that the respondent has behaved in such a way that the petitioner cannot reasonably be expected to live with the respondent. Instances of cruelty may therefore be brought in evidence. Generally, as to divorce, see the Matrimonial Causes Act 1973.

Legal cruelty has been defined (*Russell* v. *Russell*, [1897] A.C. 525) as conduct of such a character as to have caused danger to life, limb, or health (bodily or mental), or as to give rise to a reasonable apprehension of danger. No hard and fast rules can, however, be laid down; and in determining what constitutes cruelty, regard must be had to the circumstances of each particular case, keeping always in view the physical and mental condition of the parties, and their character and social status. *Rayden.*

For summary proceedings for persistent cruelty see the Matrimonial Proceedings (Magistrates' Courts) Act 1960.

CRUELTY TO ANIMALS. The making of painful experiments on animals, and the practice of vivisection, are restricted by various statutes. See principally the Cruelty to Animals Act 1876, and the Protection of Animals Acts 1911 to 1964.

CRUELTY TO CHILDREN. For provisions for the prevention of cruelty to children see s. 1 of the Children and Young Persons Act 1933.

CUJUS EST SOLUM EJUS EST USQUE AD CŒLUM ET AD INFEROS. To whom belongs the soil, his it is, even to heaven, and to the middle of the earth. But note that by s. 40 of the Civil Aviation Act 1949 no action now lies in respect of trespass or nuisance by reason only of the flight of an aircraft over property at a reasonable height.

CUM TESTAMENTO ANNEXO. With the will annexed. [ADMINISTRATOR.]

CUMULATIVE LEGACY. A legacy which is to take effect *in addition* to another disposition whether by the same or another instrument, in favour of the same party, as opposed to a *substitutional* legacy, which is to take effect as a *substitute* for some other disposition.

CUMULATIVE SENTENCE. [ACCUMULATIVE JUDGMENT OR SENTENCE.]

CUR. ADV. VULT. [CURIA ADVISARI VULT.]

CURATE. Signifies literally one who has the cure of souls. The term is applied to one holding the lowest degree in the Church. He may be (a) *temporary* or *stipendiary* or (b) *perpetual*.

CURATOR. A person entrusted with the charge of an estate, or with the conduct of a minor past the age of pupillarity, or with the management of a lawsuit. Also used of the keeper of a museum.

CURE BY VERDICT. [AIDER BY VERDICT.]

CURFEW (Fr. *Couvre-feu*, coverfire). The ringing of a bell, by which the Conqueror willed every man to take warning for the raking up, or covering up of his fire, and the putting out of his light.

CURIA. A court of justice. It is sometimes, however, taken for the persons who, as feudatory and other customary tenants, did suit and service at the lord's court, and who were also called *pares curtis* or *pares curiæ*.

CURIA ADVISARI VULT. An expression often used in legal reports to indicate that the court wished to deliberate before pronouncing judgment.

CURIA REGIS. The king's court. A term formerly applied to any of the superior courts.

CURIALITY. The Scotch name for curtesy. [CURTESY OF ENGLAND.]

CURTAIN CLAUSES. This phrase is used to describe those provisions of the Law of Property Act 1925 which relate to the modification of the equitable doctrine of notice. Their general principle is that the legal estate in land should be vested in some person or persons authorised to sell, exchange, partition or lease it, and in certain cases to mortgage it so as to over-ride all equities other than certain excepted ones. The over-ridden equities are transferred from the land itself to the purchase money, if sold, or to the land taken in exchange on a partition, or to the rents and profits of the land leased.

CURTESY OF ENGLAND was the life estate which a husband had in the lands of his deceased wife; which by the common law took effect where he had had issue by her born alive, and capable of inheriting the lands.

Thus, if a wife had lands in tail male, *i.e.*, descendible to her *male* issue only, the birth of a son would entitle the husband to curtesy, but the birth of a daughter would not. This estate was abolished by s. 45 of the Administration of Estates Act 1925.

CURTILAGE. A garden, yard or field, or other piece of ground lying near or belonging to a house or messuage.

CUSTODES LIBERTATIS ANGLIÆ AUTHORITATE PARLIAMENTI (guardians of the liberty of England by the authority of Parliament) was the style wherein writs and other judicial proceedings ran from the execution of King Charles I to the usurpation of Cromwell.

CUSTODIA LEGIS. [IN CUSTODIA LEGIS.]

CUSTODIAM, or **CUSTODIAM LEASE.** A lease from the Crown, under the seal of the Exchequer, whereby the custody of lands, seized into the king's lands, was demised or committed to some person as custodee or lessee thereof.

CUSTODIAN TRUSTEE. A trustee appointed to have the custody as distinguished from the management of the trust property. As to those eligible to be appointed and their powers, see the Public Trustee Act 1906, s. 4. And see r. 30 of the Public Trustee Rules 1912, as amended.

CUSTODIANSHIP ORDER. Part II of the Children Act 1975 provides that as an alternative to adoption, relatives and others looking after children on a long-term basis can apply for and obtain the legal custody of the children. The courts are enabled to make custodianship orders, vesting the legal custody of a child in the applicant, who becomes known as the child's custodian. Application may be made by a relative or step-parent of the child, and certain other persons with whom the child has lived for a qualifying period.

CUSTOM. Unwritten law established by long use. Custom is of two kinds:—
1. General custom, or the common law properly so called. [COMMON LAW.]
2. Particular custom, that is to say, the customs which affect only the inhabitants of particular districts. These it is usual to designate by the word *customs*, to distinguish them from the common law just referred to.

These particular customs are probably the remains of local customs prevailing formerly over the whole of England, while it was broken into distinct dominions. Such was the custom of *gavelkind* in Kent; and the custom called *borough English* which prevailed in certain ancient boroughs; also the customs of the city of London. All are contrary to the general law of the land, and are good by special usage. The requisites to make a particular custom good are: It must have been (1) used so long that the memory of man runs not to the contrary, (2) continuous, (3) peaceable, (4) reasonable, (5) certain, (6) compulsory, (7) consistent with other customs. All special rules of descent by the custom of gavelkind or borough English or any other custom were abolished by the Administration of Estates Act 1925, s. 45.

CUSTOM HOUSE. A house in several cities and seaports, where the Queen's customs are received, and all business relating thereunto transacted. [CUSTOMS ON MERCHANDISE.]

CUSTOM OF LONDON. The customs peculiar to the city of London. Formerly principally with reference (1) to the law of intestate succession; (2) to the law of foreign attachment. The custom of London in respect to intestate succession was abolished in 1856. That with regard to foreign attachment has been extended to the whole of England and Wales [GARNISHEE.]

CUSTOM OF MERCHANTS (*Lex Mercatoria*). The branch of law which comprises the rules relating to bills of exchange, partnership and other mercantile matters. In mercantile custom, universality is of far greater importance than immemorial antiquity. [LAW MERCHANT.]

CUSTOM OF THE COUNTRY means, in agriculture, the usage which, unless expressly excluded, formerly governed the relations of agricultural landlords and tenants. Now becoming obsolete. See the Agricultural Holdings Act 1948.

CUSTOMARY TENANTS were such tenants as held by the customs of the manor. Thus copyholders were said to hold "at the wil of the lord, according to the custom of the manor"; the will being no longer arbitrary and precarious, but restrained so as to be exerted according to the custom of the manor. Under the Law of Property Act 1922 copyholds became freeholds and manorial rights were extinguished. [COPYHOLD.]

CUSTOMS ON MERCHANDISE. The duties, toll, tribute or tariff payable upon merchandise exported and imported. The law relating to custom and excise is now principally embodied in the Customs and Excise Act 1952.

CUSTOS ROTULORUM is he that has the custody of the rolls or records of the sessions of the peace. He is always a justice of the peace. By s. 5 of the Local Government (Clerks) Act 1931 the clerk of the peace is, subject to the power of the *custos rotulorum*, to have the actual custody of all county records and documents.

CY-PRÈS. When the intention of a donor or testator is incapable of being literally acted upon, or where its literal performance would be unreasonable, or in excess of what the law allows, the courts will often allow the intention to be carried into effect *cy-près*, that is, *as nearly as may be* practicable, or reasonable, or consistent with law; as (1) when a testator attempts to settle his property on future generations

CY-PRÈS—*continued.*

beyond the bounds allowed by law; or (2) where a sum of money is found to be too large for a charitable purpose to which it has been devoted, or for some other reason cannot be applied thereto. The *cy-près* doctrine, under wills, appears to be abolished. As to its application to charities, see ss. 13, 14 of the Charities Act 1960.

D

D.C.L. Doctor of Civil Law.

D.P.P. Director of Public Prosecutions.

DAIRY. Includes any farm, cowshed, milking house, milk store, milk shop, etc., from which milk is supplied on or for sale, or in which milk is kept or used for purposes of manufacture into butter, cheese, etc.; but not including a shop from which milk is only sold in closed and unopened vessels, or for consumption on the premises only. See s. 28 of the Food and Drugs Act 1955, which also defines "dairy farm",, "dairy farmer" and "dairyman". Dairies are controlled by the Milk and Dairies Regulations made under the provisions of s. 29 of the Act of 1955.

DAMAGE FEASANT. Doing hurt or damage (Fr. *faisant*); that is, when one man's beasts were in another man's ground without licence of the tenant of the ground, and there did seed, tread, and otherwise spoil the corn, grass, woods, and such-like. In this case the owner of the soil might distrain them (*i.e.*, take possession of them) until satisfaction was made him for the injury he had sustained.

The common law remedy of distress damage feasant as applicable to animals was replaced by s. 7 of the Animals Act 1971.

DAMAGES. The pecuniary satisfaction awarded by a judge or jury in a civil action for the wrong suffered by the plaintiff. [EXEMPLARY DAMAGES; NOMINAL DAMAGES.]

DAME. The proper legal title of the wife of a knight or baronet. The equivalent of a knighthood for a woman.

DAMNIFY. To injure, to damage, to cause loss to any person.

DAMNOSA HEREDITAS. A burdensome inheritance; that is to say, an inheritance of which the liabilities exceed the assets. In such case, in the Roman law, the heir, being liable to the full extent of the deceased's liabilities, was a loser by entering upon the inheritance.

DAMNUM ABSQUE INJURIA. A damage without injury, that is, effected without legal wrong. In such case, no action is maintainable. Thus, if I have a mill, and my neighbour builds another mill upon his own ground, whereby the profit of my mill is diminished, yet no action lies against him, for every one may lawfully erect a mill on his own ground.

DAMNUM FATALE. Fatal damage; that is, damage caused by a fortuitous event, or inevitable accident, and for which bailees are not liable.

DANEGELD or **DANEGELT,** was a tribute levied by the Anglo-Saxons, of twelve pence upon every hide of land, for the purpose of clearing the seas of Danish pirates.

DANGEROUS DRIVING. Driving a motor vehicle on a road recklessly, or at a speed or in a manner which is dangerous to the public, having regard to all the circumstances of the case, including the nature, use and condition of the road, and the amount of traffic which is actually at the time, or which might reasonably be expected to be, on the road. See ss. 1, 2 of the Road Traffic Act 1972. As to dangerous cycling, see *ibid.*, s. 17.

DARREIN CONTINUANCE. The plea *puis darrein continuance* alleged that "since the last continuance" new ground of defence had arisen. [CONTINUANCE.]

DARREIN PRESENTMENT. Last presentation. [ASSIZE OF DARREIN PRESENTMENT.]

DATIVE. A word derived from the Roman law, signifying "appointed by public authority". Thus, in Scotland, an executor-dative is an executor appointed by a court of justice, corresponding to an English *administrator*. [ADMINISTRATOR.]

DAY RULE. A certificate of permission given by the court to a prisoner to go beyond the "rules" of the old King's Bench prison for the purpose of transacting his business. Abolished in 1842.

DAY TRAINING CENTRE. In certain circumstances a court may require a person subject to a probation order to attend a day training centre where social education will be provided in conjunction with intensive probation supervision. See s. 4 of the Powers of Criminal Courts Act 1973.

DAY, YEAR AND WASTE. [YEAR, DAY AND WASTE.]

DAYS OF GRACE. 1. Three days of grace formerly allowed to a person summoned by writ, beyond the day named in the writ, in which to make his appearance.

2. Three days allowed for the payment of a bill of exchange or a promissory note after it has nominally become due. No such days of grace are allowed in the case of bills of exchange and promissory notes purporting to be payable on sight or on demand. See s. 14 of the Bills of Exchange Act 1882.

DAYSMAN. In some northern parts of England, any arbitrator, umpire, or elected judge is commonly termed a Deies-man, or Daysman.

DAYTIME. After sunrise, and before sunset. See *Tutton* v. *Darke* (1860), 5 H. & N. 647.

DE BENE ESSE may perhaps be translated "for what it is worth". To take or do a thing *de bene esse* is to allow or accept for the present, till it comes to be more fully examined, and then to stand or fall according to the merit of the thing in its own nature, so that *valeat quantum valere potest*. Thus, the taking evidence in a chancery action *de bene esse* is taking evidence out of the regular course, and is looked upon as a temporary and conditional examination, to be used only in case the witness cannot be afterwards examined in the suit in the regular way. See R.S.C. 1965, Ord. 39.

DE BONIS NON. [ADMINISTRATOR.]

DE DIE IN DIEM (from day to day); thus, a sitting *de die in diem* is a sitting until a case is concluded.

DE DONIS. The Statute of Westminster the Second (1285) *de donis conditionalibus*, which provided that, in grants to a man and the heirs of his body or the heirs male of his body, the will of the donor should be observed according to the form expressed in the deed of gift; and that the tenements so given should go, after the death of the grantee, to his issue (or issue male, as the case might be), if there were any; and, if there were none, should revert to the donor. This statute gave rise to the estate in fee tail, or *feudum talliatum*, generally called an estate tail or entail.

No legal estate tail can exist or be created after 1925. Equitable estates tail may be created after 1925 in any property real or personal. See the Law of Property Act 1925, ss. 1, 130.

DE FACTO. An expression indicating the actual state of circumstances, independently of any remote question of right or title; thus, a king *de facto* is a person acknowledged and acting as king, independently of the question whether some one else has a better title to the crown.

By the Treason Act 1495 subjects obeying a king *de facto* are excused thereby from any penalties of treason to a king *de jure*. [DE JURE.]

DE JURE. Sometimes used of a supposed right in contradistinction to actual fact; thus a government *de jure* is a so-called government which is not a government, but which, according to the speaker or writer, ought to be a government. [DE FACTO.]

DE MINIMIS NON CURAT LEX. The law takes no account of very trifling matters.

DE NOVO. Anew. Thus, to begin *de novo* is to begin again from the beginning.

DE PRÆROGATIVA REGIS. A statute of uncertain date, but attributed to the reign of Edward II, *circa* 1323, and now largely repealed. A provision that the Queen should have the custody of the lands of natural fools was repealed by the Mental Health Act 1959.

The remaining unrepealed provisions relate to advowsons, etc., belonging to the Queen; and enact that the Queen shall have whales and sturgeons taken within the realm. *Hals. Stat.*

DE SON TORT. [EXECUTOR DE SON TORT.]

DE SON TORT DEMESNE. Of his own wrong. Lat. *De injuria sua propria*.

DE TALLAGIO NON CONCEDENDO. A statute of Edward I (1297), by which it was declared that no tallage or aid should be taken or levied without the

DE TALLAGIO NON CONCEDENDO—*continued.*
goodwill and assent of the archbishops, bishops, earls, barons, knights, burgesses, and other freemen of the land.

DE VENTRE INSPICIENDO. [AD VENTREM INSPICIENDUM.]

DEACON. The lowest degree of holy orders in the Church of England.

DEAD FREIGHT. When a merchant has shipped only a part of a cargo, the freight payable for the part not shipped is called *dead freight.*

DEAD RENT. A rent payable on a mining lease in addition to a royalty, so called because it is payable although the mine may not be worked.

DEAN. The chief of the clergy appointed for the celebration of divine service in the bishop's cathedral.

DEAN OF THE ARCHES. The judge of the Arches Court, so called because he anciently held his court in the Church of St. Mary-le-Bow (*Sancta Maria de arcubus*). [ARCHES, COURT OF.]

DEATH-BED OR DYING DECLARATIONS. As an exception to the general rule against hearsay evidence, the statements of persons *in extremis* are admissible in evidence after their death as to cause thereof, *e.g.*, statements made by a person mortally wounded as to the identity of his assailant. Magistrates may take such depositions under the provisions of s. 41 of the Magistrates' Courts Act 1952.

DEATH DUTIES. Duties formerly payable on the passing of property on the death of the owner. They were abolished in respect of deaths after 12th March 1975, their place being taken by capital transfer tax (*q.v.*). See Part III of the Finance Act 1975.

DEBENTURE. 1. A custom-house certificate to the effect that an importer of goods is entitled to "drawback". [DRAWBACK.]
2. A charge in writing (usually under seal) of certain property with the repayment at a time fixed of the money lent at a given interest. Being for a fixed sum and time it was found to be inconvenient to lenders, and has been superseded in many cases by *debenture stock*, which is fre-

quently irredeemable and usually transferable in any amount. The issue of debenture stock in the case of companies incorporated by Act of Parliament is regulated either by their special Acts or by the Companies Clauses Act 1863. As to registration, see the Companies Act 1948, ss. 86, 87.

DEBT. A certain sum due from one person to another, either (1) by *record, e.g.*, judgment, (2) under *specialty*, or deed, or (3) under *simple* contract by writing or oral. With the exception of certain preferred debts, all debts are payable *pari passu* in bankruptcy. See the Bankruptcy Act 1914, ss. 30–36. In the administration of the estate of a deceased person the order is, (1) Crown debts, (2) rates, taxes, etc., (3) judgments, (4) recognizances and statutes, (5) specialty and simple debts, (6) voluntary debts, but when the estate is insolvent the order follows that of bankruptcy (Administration of Estates Act 1925, s. 34 (1), and Sch. I, Part I).

DEBTOR'S SUMMONS. A summons granted under the repealed Bankruptcy Act of 1869, against a debtor by a court having jurisdiction in bankruptcy, on the creditor proving that there was due to him from the debtor a liquidated sum of not less than £50, and that the creditor had failed to obtain payment of his debt after using reasonable efforts to do so. The Bankruptcy Act 1914 replaced this process by a "bankruptcy notice" which is applicable in the case of an unpaid *judgment* debt of *any* amount.

DECEIT. Fraud, craft, or collusion, employed for the purpose of gaining advantage over another. A false statement of fact made by a person knowingly or recklessly with intent that it shall be acted upon by another who does so act upon it and thereby suffers damage. There was an old writ called a "writ of deceit", which was brought in the Court of Common Pleas to reverse a judgment obtained in a real action by fraud and collusion between the parties. This writ was abolished in 1833. There was also an old action of deceit, to give damages in some particular cases of fraud. But the remedy in cases of fraud, whereby a man was injured, was in general by an action on the case for damages. [FRAUD.]

DECEPTION. By s. 15 (4) of the Theft

Act 1968 "deception" means any deception (whether deliberate or reckless) by words or conduct as to fact or as to law, including a deception as to the present intentions of the person using the deception or any other person. [CHEAT.]

DECLARANT. A person who makes a declaration.

DECLARATION. Formerly the first of the pleadings in an ordinary action, consisting of a written statement by the plaintiff of his ground of action. This declaration might be delivered at any time after an "appearance" had been entered on behalf of the defendant. A statement of claim now takes the place of the declaration. [STATE-MENT OF CLAIM.]

DECLARATION BY DEBTOR OF INABILITY TO PAY HIS DEBTS. To make such a declaration is an act of bankruptcy. See the Bankruptcy Act 1914, s. 1. [ACT OF BANKRUPTCY.]

DECLARATION IN LIEU OF OATH. Prior to 1835 a large number of oaths had to be taken in the course of business affairs, with the result that the taking of an oath came to be regarded as a pure formality. To check the abuse of the oath the Statutory Declarations Act 1835 was passed, providing for the substitution of a statutory declaration, in a form set out in a Schedule to the Act, except (a) in the case of an oath of allegiance and (b) in the case of an oath, affirmation or affidavit in a court of justice.

DECLARATION OF PARIS. This expression is generally used to denote a certain declaration respecting International Maritime Law, annexed to Protocol No. 23 of the Protocols drawn up at the Congress of Paris in April 1856, after the conclusion of the Crimean War. The articles of this declaration were as follows:—

1. Privateering is and remains abolished.

2. The neutral flag covers enemy's goods except contraband of war.

3. Neutral goods, except contraband of war, are not liable to confiscation under a hostile flag.

4. Blockades, to be binding, must be effective.

DECLARATION OF TRUST. A declaration whereby a person admits that he holds property upon trust for another. A declaration of trust of land, whether freehold or leasehold, must, by the Law of Property Act 1925, s. 53, be evidenced in writing, and signed by the party declaring the trust. But declarations of trust of money, or chattels personal, need not be so evidenced. For form of trust instrument on settlement of land, see the Settled Land Act 1925, Sch. I, Form No. 3.

DECLARATION, STATUTORY. [STATUTORY DECLARATION.]

DECLARATORY ACT. An Act of Parliament which professes to *declare* existing law, and not to enact new law. Legislative declaration, however, like judicial, is frequently deceptive, and enacts new law under the guise of expounding the old.

DECLARATION DECREE. One that declares the rights of parties, but does not order anything to be done.

DECLINATORY PLEA. A plea of sanctuary, or of benefit of clergy. Abolished in 1827. [BENEFIT OF CLERGY; SANCTUARY.]

DECREE. The sentence of the former Court of Chancery delivered on the hearing of a cause; corresponding to a judgment at law. Since the Judicature Acts the expression *judgment* is adopted in reference to the decisions of all the Divisions of the Supreme Court. The word is also used in Scotland to signify the final sentence of a court.

DECREE ABSOLUTE. Final decree in suits for dissolution or nullity of marriage. [DECREE NISI.]

DECREE ARBITRAL. The Scotch term for the award of an arbitrator.

DECREE NISI. Section 1 (5) of the Matrimonial Causes Act 1973 provides that every decree of divorce shall, in the first instance, be a *decree nisi*, not to be made absolute until after the expiration of a fixed time—at present six weeks (Matrimonial Causes (Decree Absolute) General Order 1972, which continues to have effect under the Act of 1973).

After the pronouncing of the *decree nisi*, and before it is made absolute, any person may show cause why the decree should not be made absolute. Failing any such intervention, the party who has obtained the

DECREE NISI—*continued.*
decree normally applies for, and is granted, a *decree absolute*, when the parties are finally divorced. *Rayden.*

DEDICATION OF WAY. The giving up a private road to the use of the public.

Where a way over any land has been actually enjoyed by the public as of right and without interruption for a full period of 20 years, the way is deemed to have been dedicated as a highway unless there is evidence that there was no intention to dedicate it. See more fully s. 34 of the Highways Act 1959. See also s. 33 (dedication of highway by agreement with parish council) and s. 71 (3) (dedication of land for the widening of highways) of the same Act.

DEED. A written instrument signed, sealed and delivered. [DELIVERY OF A DEED.] A deed is either a *deed poll* or a *deed indented.* If a deed be made by more parties than one, there ought to be regularly as many copies of it as there are parties; and the deed so made is called an indenture, because each part used formerly to be cut or *indented* in acute angles on the top or side, to tally or correspond one with the other. Such deeds were formerly called *syngrapha* by the canonists, and later *chirographa.* Now, by the Law of Property Act 1925, s. 56 (2), a deed between parties, to effect its objects, has the effect of an indenture though not indented or expressed to be an indenture.

A deed made by one party only is not and never was indented, but *polled* or shaved quite even, and therefore called a *deed poll*, or a single deed.

Deeds may be described as deeds, or as conveyances, trust instruments, settlements, mortgages, etc., according to their nature (Law of Property Act 1925, s. 57).

Execution of deeds (*e.g.*, sealing and delivery) must also include signatures, and in the case of a corporation, the affixing of the seal of the corporation (*ibid.*, ss. 73, 74). [DELIVERY OF A DEED.]

DEED OF ARRANGEMENT. [ARRANGEMENTS.]

DEED OF COMPOSITION. [COMPOSITION.]

DEED OF COVENANT. Covenants are often entered into by separate deed, *e.g.*, a deed of covenant for production of deeds

(now generally replaced by an acknowledgment).

DEED OF SEPARATION. [SEPARATION DEED.]

DEED-POLL. [DEED.]

DEEM. To consider something to be. See *R.* v. *Norfolk County Council* (1891), 60 L.J.Q.B. 379, in which Cave, J., said: "Generally speaking, when you talk of a thing being deemed to be something, you do not mean to say that it is that which it is deemed to be. It is rather an admission that it is not what it is deemed to be, and that, notwithstanding it is not that particular thing, nevertheless . . . it is to be deemed to be that thing". See also *St. Aubyn* v. *A.-G.* (No. 2), [1951] 2 All E.R. 473, *per* Lord Radcliffe, at p. 498.

DEEMSTERS. A kind of judges in the Isle of Man, who without process, writings, or any charge, decide all controversies there.

DEFAMATION. The general term for words either spoken or written, which tend to injure a person's reputation. [LIBEL; SLANDER.]

DEFAULT is an offence in omitting that which one ought to do; as in the expression "wilful neglect or default". It is often taken for non-appearance in court at a day assigned; and judgment given against a party by reason of such non-appearance, or other neglect to take any of the steps required of him within due time, is called *judgment by default.*

DEFAULT ACTION. A procedure in the county courts for the summary recovery of a debt or liquidated demand: Ord. 10 of the County Court Rules 1936, which continue in force as if made under the County Courts Act 1959.

DEFEASANCE. A collateral deed, made at the same time with a feoffment or other conveyance, containing certain conditions, upon the performance of which the estate then created may be defeated or totally undone. So, a defeasance on a bond or recognizance, or judgment recovered, is a condition which, when performed, defeats or undoes it. It is inserted in a separate deed in the same manner as the defeasance of an estate above mentioned.

DEFECTIVE. A "defective" is defined by s. 45 of the Sexual Offences Act 1956 (as substituted by s. 127 of the Mental Health Act 1959) as "a person suffering from severe subnormality" within the meaning of the Act of 1959. "Severe subnormality" is in turn defined (by s. 4 (2) of the Act of 1959) as a state of arrested or incomplete development of mind which includes subnormality of intelligence and is of such a nature or degree that the patient is incapable of living an independent life or of guarding himself against serious exploitation, or will be so incapable when of an age to do so.

DEFENCE. [STATEMENT OF DEFENCE.]

DEFENCE OF THE REALM ACTS. Gave power to the King in Council to make regulations for the defence of the realm during the First World War (1914–1918). They ceased to have effect on 31st August 1921.

DEFENCE REGULATIONS. Wide powers were conferred on the Government during the Second World War (1939–1945) by the Emergency Powers (Defence) Acts 1939 to 1945, and numerous defence regulations, general and particular, were made thereunder. The great majority of these regulations were revoked or repealed after the war, and the process was completed by the Emergency Laws (Repeal) Act 1959.

DEFENDANT. A person sued in an action or charged with a misdemeanour. A person who is charged with a criminal offence is called the *prisoner.*

DEFENDER OF THE FAITH. The title, Defender of the Faith (*fidei defensor*) was first given by Pope Leo X to Henry VIII in 1521, Henry having written against Martin Luther on behalf of the Catholic church. Despite the subsequent events of the Reformation the title has continued to be used by the Kings and Queens of England to the present day. The title (expressed F.D. or Fid. Def.) is still stamped on coins of the realm.

DEFERMENT OF SENTENCE. The Crown Court or a magistrates' court may defer passing sentence on an offender to enable the court to have regard to his future conduct or to any change in his circumstances. The offender must consent and deferment must be for not more than six months. See s. 1 of the Powers of Criminal Courts Act 1973.

DEFERRED SHARES OR STOCK. Stock or shares in a company, the holders of which have a right to participate in the net earnings of the company, but the right is *deferred* until the prior claims of preferred and ordinary stock or shareholders have been met.

DEFINITIVE SENTENCE. The final judgment of a spiritual court, as distinguished from an interlocutory or provisional judgment.

DEFORCE. To deprive another of lands.

DEGRADATION. 1. Of peers. Where a person who has been in the rank of peers has ceased to be such; as when a peeress, who is such only by marriage, is married to a commoner; or where a peer is deprived of his nobility by Act of Parliament.

2. Of ecclesiastics. As thus applied, the word signifies an ecclesiastical censure, whereby a clergyman is deprived of his holy orders.

DEGREE. A step; the distance between kindred.

DEL CREDERE COMMISSION is a commission for the sale of goods by an agent, who, for a higher reward than is usually given, becomes responsible to his principal for the solvency of the purchaser. In other words, the agent (who is then called a *del credere* agent) guarantees the due payment of the price of the goods sold.

DELEGATION. The assignment of a duty or power of action to another.

DELEGATUS NON POTEST DELEGARE. An agent cannot delegate his authority.

DELICTO, ACTION EX. A phrase occasionally used to designate an action of *tort*; that is, an action for a wrong which is such independently of contract, as for libel, assault, etc.

DELIVERY. The transferring of possession from one person to another. It may be *actual,* as when in fact goods change hands, or *constructive,* as *e.g.,* where a buyer is already in possession of goods before sale, and afterwards pays for them.

DELIVERY OF A DEED. This is held to be performed by the person who executes the deed placing his finger on the seal, and saying "I deliver this as my act and

DELIVERY OF A DEED—*continued.*
deed". A deed takes effect only from this tradition or delivery. A delivery may be either absolute, that is to the other party or grantee himself; or to a third person, to hold until some condition be performed by the grantee; in which latter case it is called an *escrow.* It was once a moot point whether in theory a deed must be signed as well as sealed. The Law of Property Act 1925, s. 73, provides that an individual executing a deed shall either sign or place his mark upon the same and sealing alone shall not be deemed sufficient. [DEED.]

DELIVERY ORDER. An order addressed by the owner of goods to a bailee requiring him to deliver the goods to a named person. Included in the term "document of title" as defined by s. 1 of the Factors Act 1889.

DEM., in such an expression as Doe dem. Smith, in the former action of ejectment, meant *demise* in the sense of lease; indicating that Doe as lessee of Smith was the nominal plaintiff. [EJECTMENT.]

DEMISE (Lat. *Demittere*). To lease. This word implies an absolute covenant on the part of the lessor for quiet enjoyment. This implied covenant may be, and usually is, qualified by an express covenant more limited in extent. The word was formerly applicable to the grant of a freehold estate, but it is not now so applied.

DEMISE OF THE CROWN. A phrase used to denote the death or abdication of the king or queen, because the kingdom is thereby transferred or *demised* to his successor.

DEMOLITION ORDER. Under the provisions of the Housing Act 1957 local authorities are empowered to make demolition or closing orders in respect of premises which they consider unfit for human habitation. The content of such demolition order is specified in s. 21 of the Act; it must require vacation within a period to be specified (not less than 28 days), and that thereafter the premises shall be demolished within six weeks. As to what matters are to be taken into account in determining the question of fitness for human habitation, see *ibid.*, s. 4.

DEMONSTRATIVE LEGACY. A gift by will of a certain sum to be paid out of a specific fund.

DEMPSTER. [DEEMSTERS.]

DEMURRAGE. The daily sum payable by a merchant, who, having hired a ship, detains it for a longer time than he is entitled to do by his contract. Sometimes the delay itself is called *demurrage.*

DEMURRER. A written formula, whereby a party objected to a bill or information, declaration, indictment, or other pleading of his adversary, on the ground that it was, on the face of it, insufficient in point of law. Obsolete.

DEMURRER BOOK. A book containing at length a transcript of the proceedings in cases where questions of law arose as to the sufficiency of matters alleged in the pleadings. Demurrers have been abolished and demurrer books are not made up, but any party who sets down an action for trial must deliver to the officer of the court two copies of the relevant documents, including the pleadings, one bundle of which is for the use of the judge at the trial. See R.S.C. 1965, Ord. 34, r. 3.

DENIZEN. An alien born who obtained *ex donatione regis* (from the gift of the king) letters patent to make him a British subject. A denizen was in a kind of middle state, between an alien and natural-born subject, and partook of them both. See now, as to the naturalisation of aliens, s. 10 of the British Nationality Act 1948.

DEODAND. Any personal chattel which was the immediate occasion of the death of any reasonable creature: which was formerly forfeited to the king, to be applied to pious uses, and distributed in alms by his high almoner, though in earlier times it was destined to a more superstitious purpose. Deodands were abolished in 1846.

DEPARTURE, in pleading, is the shifting of his ground by a party, or a variation from the title or defence which he has once insisted on. See R.S.C. 1965, Ord. 18, r. 10.

DEPENDANT. A person who to some extent depends on others for the provision of the ordinary necessities of life; a person to some extent maintained by another (*Re Ball, Hand* v. *Ball,* [1947] 1 Ch. 228).

DEPONENT. A person who gives evidence, whether orally or by affidavit.

DEPORTATION. Transportation, banishment.

DEPOSE. To make a deposition or statement on oath. [DEPOSITION.]

DEPOSIT. 1. The act of entrusting money to a bank is called a *deposit* in a bank; and the amount of the money deposited is also called the *deposit*.

2. A species of bailment by which a person entrusts another with a chattel to keep safely without reward. In this sense, the Latin form of the word, *depositum*, is more frequently adopted. [BAILMENT.]

3. Money paid as earnest or security for the performance of a contract, *e.g.*, the money paid by the purchaser on signature of a contract for sale.

4. Of litter. An offence under the Litter Acts 1958 and 1971.

DEPOSIT OF TITLE DEEDS. This is when the title deeds of an estate are deposited (generally with a bank) as a security for the repayment of money advanced. This operates as an equitable mortgage. The right to create equitable charges by deposit of deeds is preserved by ss. 2 (3) and 13 of the Law of Property Act 1925. [EQUITABLE MORTGAGE; MORTGAGE.]

DEPOSITION. A word used to indicate written evidence or oral evidence taken down in writing. This cannot be read at the trial except where the witness himself cannot be produced. See R.S.C. 1965, Ord. 39. Rules of Court make provision for the taking of evidence upon affidavit and the Evidence Act 1938 enables written evidence to be admitted under certain conditions. Depositions may be taken of persons dangerously ill and unlikely to recover under s. 41 of the Magistrates' Courts Act, 1952. The word is also used to signify the depriving a person of some dignity; and it seems to have been at one time taken to signify death. [EVIDENCE.]

DEPOSITUM. A species of bailment. [DEPOSIT, 2.]

DEPRIVATION. A depriving or taking away: as when a bishop, parson, vicar, etc., is deposed from his preferment.

DEPUTY. One who acts for another in some office. Judges of the Supreme Court cannot act by deputy, but deputy circuit judges may be appointed under s. 24 (2) of the Courts Act 1971. By the Sheriffs Act

1887 every sheriff must appoint a deputy having an office within a mile of the Inner Temple Hall for the receipt of writs, etc.

DEPUTY LIEUTENANT. The deputy of a lord lieutenant of a county, each of whom has several deputies. See s. 218 of the Local Government Act 1972.

DERELICT. A thing forsaken or thrown away by its owner, especially a vessel forsaken at sea.

DERELICTION is where the sea shrinks back below low water-mark, so that land is gained from the sea. If this gain is gradual, it goes to the owner of the land adjoining; but if it is sudden, the land gained belongs to the Crown. [ACCRETION.]

DERIVATIVE CONVEYANCE. A conveyance which presupposes some other conveyance precedent, and serves to enlarge, confirm, alter, restrain, restore, or transfer the interest granted by such original conveyance. [PRIMARY CONVEYANCES.]

DERIVATIVE SETTLEMENT. [SETTLEMENT.]

DEROGATE. To take away from or to evade. The maxim that "No man can derogate from his own grant" means that a man, having contracted *e.g.* to sell land, cannot afterwards prejudice the purchaser by obstructing the easements, etc., implied in the grant.

DESCENT. The title whereby a man, under the former law of inheritance, on the death of his ancestor intestate acquired his estate by right of representation as his heir-at-law. See now Part IV of the Administration of Estates Act 1925.

DESERTION. 1. The criminal offence of abandoning the naval, military or air force service without licence.

By s. 15 of the Naval Discipline Act 1957 a person is guilty of desertion if he leaves or fails to attend at his ship or place of duty with the intention of remaining permanently absent from duty without proper authority or if, having left or failed to attend at his ship or place of duty in any circumstances, he does any act with the like intention. Desertion is also dealt with under s. 37 of the Army Act 1955 and s. 37 of the Air Force Act 1955.

2. An abandonment of a wife or hus-

DESERTION—*continued.*

band, which is a matrimonial offence. Formerly a ground for divorce in High Court proceedings. Evidence of desertion may now be given on a petition for divorce on the ground of irretrievable breakdown of marriage. See s. 1 of the Matrimonial Causes Act 1973. Summary proceedings for desertion may also be taken under the provisions of the Matrimonial Proceedings (Magistrates' Courts) Act 1960.

DESIGNS, if registered, are protected by the provisions of the Registered Designs Acts 1949 to 1961. By s. 1 of the Act of 1949, "design" means features of shape, configuration, pattern or ornament applied to an article by any industrial process or means, being features which in the finished article appeal to and are judged solely by the eye. It does not include a method or principle of construction or feature of shape or configuration which is dictated solely by the function which the article has to perform.

DETAINER. The forcible detention of a man's person or property. [FORCIBLE DETAINER.]

DETENTION CENTRES. Centres first established under s. 18 of the Criminal Justice Act 1948, and now provided under s. 43 of the Prison Act 1952, where persons of not less than fourteen but under twenty-one years of age may be detained for a disciplinary period suitable to their age and description.

DETERMINABLE FREEHOLDS. Freeholds which are terminable on a given contingency, specified in the deed creating them. After 1925 they subsist only as equitable interests in land. See s. 1 and Sch. I, Part I, of the Law of Property Act 1925.

DETINUE. The form of action whereby a plaintiff seeks to recover a chattel personal unlawfully detained. It differs from *trover*, inasmuch as in *trover* the object is to obtain *damages* for a wrongful conversion of the property to the defendant's use: but in *detinue* the object is to recover the *chattel itself*, or failing that, its value, and damages. And now by R.S.C. 1965. Ord. 45, r. 4, the court may, upon the application of the plaintiff, order a writ of delivery to issue for the return of the chattel detained. See also the Sale of Goods Act

1893, s. 52, under which the court has power to order specific performance in any action for breach of contract to deliver specific or ascertained goods.

DEVASTAVIT. The waste or misapplication of the assets of a deceased person committed by an executor or administrator which makes him personally liable to those who have claims upon the deceased's assets, *e.g.* creditors, legatees, etc.

DEVELOPMENT. For the purposes of the Town and Country Planning Act 1971, development means, with certain exceptions, the carrying out of building, engineering, mining or other operations in, on, over or under land, or the making of any material change in the use of any buildings or other land. The latter includes the conversion of a single dwelling into two or more dwellings; the display of advertisements on buildings not normally so used; etc. Planning permission must be sought from the local planning authority before developments are carried out.

Local planning authorities themselves are required to carry out periodic surveys of their areas and to prepare "structure plans", outlining their policies and general proposals for development, for the approval of the Minister of Housing and Local Government. See the Town and Country Planning Act 1971, s. 7 (3).

DEVIATION. A departure from a plan conceived and agreed upon.

1. The word is used principally in reference to policies of marine insurance, as to which it is held that the slightest *deviation* from the voyage marked out in the policy, except under circumstances of absolute necessity, will render the insurance ineffectual. But deviation to save life or property is justified (Carriage of Goods by Sea Act 1924, Schedule, Article IV, 4.) Delay in commencing and prosecuting the voyage for purposes foreign to the adventure is also called *deviation.*

2. By a railway in course of construction, deviation is only allowed within certain limits. See the Railways Clauses Consolidation Act 1845, ss. 11 *et seq.*

DEVISE (Lat. *Divisa*). A bequest by a man of his lands and goods by his last will and testament in writing. The term "devise" is principally used with reference to landed property, and "bequeath" and "bequest" with reference to personalty. The giver is called the *devisor* and the recipient the *devisee*.

DICTUM. 1. Arbitrament.

2. A saying or opinion of a judge, during the hearing of a case. [OBITER DICTUM.]

DIE WITHOUT ISSUE. [DYING WITHOUT ISSUE.]

DIES FASTI ET NEFASTI. *Dies fasti* were the days in heathen Rome in which it was lawful to conduct litigation. *Dies nefasti* were days in which it was not lawful. *Ovid, Fasti, I.* 47, 48.

DIES JURIDICUS. An ordinary day in court, as opposed to Sundays and other holidays, upon which the courts do not sit.

DIES NON (*scil.* **JURIDICUS**). A day on which legal proceedings cannot be carried on, as Sundays, etc. [DIES JURIDICUS.]

DIET. A name sometimes given to a general assembly on the continent of Europe.

DIEU ET MON DROIT ("God and my right"). The motto of the royal arms, introduced by Richard I, indicating that the Queen holds her dominions of none but God.

DIGAMY. A second marriage after the death of the first wife.

DIGEST. 1. The Digest of the Emperor Justinian (otherwise called the Pandects) was a collection of extracts from the most eminent Roman jurists. In A.D. 530 Justinian authorised Tribonian, with the aid of sixteen commissioners, to prepare such a collection, and alowed ten years for the work. It was, however, completed in three years, and published under the title of Digest or Pandects, on the 16th of December, 533, and declared to have the force of law from the 30th of that month.

2. A Digest of Cases is a compilation of the head-notes or main points of decided cases, arranged in alphabetical order, according to the branches or subjects of law which they respectively illustrate.

DIGNITARY. A dean or provost of a cathedral church; an archdeacon, canon, prebendary, etc. See s. 12 of the Church Dignitaries (Retirement) Measure, 1949; and see also the Ecclesiastical Offices (Age Limit) Measure 1975.

DIGNITIES. A species of incorporeal hereditament in which a man may have a property or estate. They were originally annexed to the possession of certain estates in land, and are still classed under the head of real property.

DILAPIDATION. 1. The name for ecclesiastical waste committed by the incumbent of a living; which is either voluntary, by pulling down; or permissive, by suffering the chancel, parsonage-house, and other buildings thereunto belonging, to decay.

2. Also used to signify a want of repair for which a tenant is liable who has agreed to give up the premises in good repair.

DILATORY PLEA. A plea by a defendant in an action, founded on some matter of fact not connected with the merits of the case, but such as might exist without impeaching the right of action itself. They are now, for the most part, obsolete. A dilatory plea could be either—

1. A plea *to the jurisdiction*, showing that, by reason of some matter therein stated, the case was not within the jurisdiction of the court.

2. A plea *of suspension*, showing some matter of temporary incapacity to proceed with the suit.

3. A plea *in abatement*, showing some matter for *abating* the action. [ABATEMENT, 6.]

The effect of a dilatory plea, if established, was to defeat the particular action, leaving the plaintiff at liberty to commence another in a better form.

A dilatory plea was opposed to a peremptory plea, otherwise called a *plea in bar*, which was founded on some matter tending to impeach the right of action.

DILIGENCE, besides its ordinary meaning, has a special meaning in the law of Scotland, in which it signifies the warrants issued by the courts for the attendance of witnesses, or the production of writings; also the process whereby persons or effects are attached or seized on execution, or in security for debt.

DIMISSORY LETTERS. Letters sent by one bishop to another, requesting him to ordain a candidate for holy orders, who has a title in the diocese of the former bishop, but is anxious to be ordained by the latter.

DIOCESAN COURTS. The consistory courts of the bishops for the trial of ecclesiastical causes arising within their respective dioceses. [CONSISTORY COURTS.]

DIOCESE, or **DIOCESS.** The circuit of a bishop's jurisdiction.

DIPLOMA. 1. A royal charter or letters patent.

2. A certificate less in status than a degree.

DIPLOMACY. The conduct of negotiations between nations, by means of correspondence or by ambassadors or the like.

DIPLOMATIC PRIVILEGE. The privilege of immunity from process, etc., accorded to ambassadors and representatives of foreign powers and the Dominions, and to their servants. See the Diplomatic Privileges Act, 1964.

DIRECT EVIDENCE is evidence directly bearing upon the point at issue, and which, if believed, is conclusive in favour of the party adducing it; and is opposed to *circumstantial* evidence, from which the truth as to the point at issue can be only inferentially deduced. [CIRCUMSTANTIAL EVIDENCE.]

DIRECTION TO A JURY is where a judge instructs a jury on any point of law, in order that they may apply it to the facts in evidence before them. Misdirection may be a ground for a new trial if, in the opinion of the Court of Appeal, some substantial wrong or miscarriage has been thereby occasioned: R.S.C. 1965, Ord. 59, r. 11.

DIRECTIONS, SUMMONS FOR. A general summons which is issued in most actions at an early stage of the proceedings for directions as to discovery and inspection of documents, mode and place of trial, and the like. See R.S.C. 1965, Ord. 25.

DIRECTOR. A person who conducts the affairs of a company. Every company must have at least two directors. It is usual for directors to be required to hold qualification shares. The number of these is fixed by the company in general meeting, and provisions relating to such qualification are laid down in ss. 181, 182 of the Companies Act 1948. See also ss. 184 *et seq.* of the Act of 1948 for other matters relating to directors, as *e.g.* removal or retirement of directors, prohibition of tax-free payments or the making of loans to directors, etc.

DIRECTOR OF PUBLIC PROSECUTIONS. An official whose office was created by the Prosecution of Offences Act 1879, and whose duties include the instituting, undertaking or carrying on of criminal proceedings under the directions of the Attorney-General. He must be a barrister or solicitor of not less than ten years standing (Prosecution of Offences Act 1908, s. 1).

DIRECTORY STATUTE. A statute is said to be merely directory when it directs anything to be done or omitted, without invalidating acts or omissions in contravention of it.

DISABILITY. At the present day the word is generally used to indicate an incapacity for the full enjoyment of ordinary legal rights; thus persons under age and mentally disordered persons are under disability. It may be either *absolute* or *partial*.

Sometimes the term is used in a more limited sense, as when it signifies an impediment to marriage; or the restraints placed upon clergymen by reason of their spiritual avocations.

DISABLING STATUTE. A statute which disables or restrains any person or persons from doing that which formerly was lawful or permissible; as a statute of Elizabeth I (1558), which disabled archbishops and bishops from making leases for more than twenty-one years or three lives, or without receiving the usual rent.

DISBAR. To deprive a barrister of his privileges and status as such.

DISBENCH. To deprive a bencher of his privileges. [BENCHERS.]

DISCHARGE. A word used in various senses:— 1. Of the discharge of a bankrupt under s. 26 of the Bankruptcy Act 1914, by which he is freed of all debts and liabilities provable under the bankruptcy, with certain specified exceptions.

2. Of the discharge of a surety, whereby he is released from his liability as surety.

3. Of the release of a prisoner from confinement.

4. Of the payment of a debt whereby the debtor is freed from further liability.

5. Of the release of lands, or money in the funds, from an incumbrance, by payment of the amount to the incumbrancer, or otherwise by consent of the in-

cumbrancer. As to discharge of mortgage by means of indorsed receipt, see s. 115 of the Law of Property Act 1925, and Form No. 2 set out in Sch. III to that Act.

6. Of an order of a court of justice dismissing a jury on the grounds that they have performed their duties, or are unable to agree in a case before them.

7. Of the reversal of an order of a court of justice; thus it is said that an order was "discharged on appeal", etc.

8. A rule *nisi* is discharged where the court decides that it shall not be made absolute.

9. Of a jury, on the giving of a verdict, or on failure to agree to a verdict..

10. Of a person who is found guilty of an offence and, without further punishment, is discharged absolutely or conditionally. See s. 7 of the Powers of Criminal Courts Act 1973.

DISCLAIMER is a renunciation, denial, or refusal. It is (or was) used:—

1. Of an answer of a person made defendant to a bill in Chancery in respect of some interest he was supposed to claim, whereby he disclaimed all interest in the matters in question. Now obsolete.

2. Of any act whereby a person refuses to accept an estate which is attempted to be conveyed to him; as, for instance, where the land is conveyed to an intended trustee without his consent, and he refuses to accept it. This is called the disclaimer of an estate. Powers of disclaimer are given by s. 23 of the Administration of Estates Act 1925 to the personal representative of a tenant for life of the trust estate.

3. Of the refusal by the trustee in a bankruptcy to accept a burdensome lease or other onerous property of the bankrupt. Bankruptcy Act 1914, s. 54.

4. Of disclaimer of tenure; that was where a tenant, who held of any lord, neglected to render him the due services, and, upon an action brought to recover them, disclaimed to hold of the lord; which disclaimer of tenure in any court of record was a forfeiture of the lands to the lord.

5. Of disclaimer of a trade-mark under s. 14 of the Trade Marks Act 1938.

6. Of disclaimer of powers. Under s. 156 of the Law of Property Act 1925 a person to whom any power, whether coupled with an interest or not, is given may by deed disclaim the power.

DISCLOSURE. Every solicitor whose name is on a writ must on demand in writing by a defendant declare whether the writ was issued with his privity. R.S.C. 1965, Ord. 6, r. 5.

As to disclosure of partners' names, etc., where writ issued in the name of the firm, see *ibid.*, Ord. 81, r. 2.

DISCONTINUANCE OF ACTION. The breaking off of an action, *e.g.*, on withdrawal by consent. See generally R.S.C. 1965, Ord. 21.

DISCOUNT. 1. An allowance made to bankers or others for advancing money upon bills before they become due.

2. An allowance frequently made at the settlement of accounts, by way of deduction from the amount payable.

DISCOVERT. A word applied to a woman who is a widow or unmarried, formerly as not being under the disabilities of *coverture*. [COVERTURE.]

DISCOVERY. 1. Of *facts*, obtainable by either party to an action, in the form of answers on oath to questions known as interrogatories administered by the other after approval of the court, and on payment of deposit as security for the costs. The answers or any of them may be put in as evidence on the trial, and are obtained with the object of getting admissions or discovery of such material facts as relate to the case of the party interrogating.

(*Canada.*) The term usually refers to a *viva voce* examination on discovery.

2. Of *documents*, obtained as above. The party against whom an order for discovery of documents is made must file an affidavit setting out all the documents relating to the action which are or have been in his possession or power. See R.S.C. 1965, Ord. 26.

3. The word is also used in reference to the disclosure by a bankrupt of his property for the benefit of his creditors.

DISCREDIT. To show to be unworthy of credit. The term is employed chiefly in regard to witnesses in a court of justice. As a general rule, a party is not entitled to discredit his own witness.

DISCRETION STATEMENT. A statement formerly lodged by a petitioner for a divorce, praying that the court should exercise its discretion in granting a decree *nisi*, notwithstanding the petitioner's own adultery. The lodging of such a statement is not now necessary, as adultery is no longer a bar to relief.

DISCRETIONARY TRUST. A trust under which the trustees have absolute discretion to apply the income and capital of the trust as they will.

DISCRIMINATION. (1) Unlawful on grounds of race, colour, ethnic group or nationality: Race Relations Act 1968. (2) Sex discrimination is also made unlawful (subject to certain exceptions) by the Sex Discrimination Act 1975. Sections 1, 2, 3 and 4 of that Act relate respectively to sex discrimination against women; sex discrimination against men; discrimination against married persons in the employment field; and discrimination by way of victimisation. [EQUAL OPPORTUNITIES COMMISSION.]

DISENTAILING DEED. A deed executed by a tenant in tail under the Fines and Recoveries Act 1833. If the deed was duly enrolled within six months of its execution, the tenant in tail was enabled, by s. 15 of the Act, to alienate the land for an estate in fee simple or any less estate, and thereby to destroy the entail. Enrolment of disentailing deeds (whether in regard to real or personal estates) is not now necessary by virtue of s. 133 of the Law of Property Act 1925.

DISFRANCHISE. To take away from one his privilege or franchise.

At the present day it is used to signify the depriving an individual of his right of voting, or a constituency of its right of returning a member to parliament. *May.*

DISHONEST. It is enacted by s. 1 of the Theft Act 1968 that a person is guilty of theft if he "dishonestly" appropriates property belonging to another with the intention of permanently depriving the other of it. [THEFT.]

Section 2 of the Act elaborates on the question of what is, and what is not, dishonesty. For example, a person's appropriation of property belonging to another is not to be regarded as dishonest if he appropriates the property in the belief that he has a legal right to deprive the other of it; nor if he believes that the other would have given his consent had he known of the appropriation and the circumstances of it. On the other hand, a person's appropriation of property may be dishonest notwithstanding that he is willing to pay for it.

DISHONOUR is where the drawee of a bill of exchange refuses to accept it, or, having accepted it, fails to pay it according to the tenor of his acceptance. See the Bills of Exchange Act 1882, s. 47.

DISMES DECIMAE. Tithes; also the tenths of all spiritual livings formerly payable to the Pope, and afterwards to the Crown. [TITHES.]

DISMISSAL OF ACTION. This may take place upon default in delivery of statement of claim, non-appearance at trial, etc. See R.S.C. 1965, Ord. 19.

DISMISSAL OF BILL IN EQUITY signified a refusal by the court to make a decree as prayed by a plaintiff's bill. This might be (1) *on the merits of the case*, or (2) *for want of prosecution*, that is to say, of due diligence on the part of the plaintiff or his advisers in taking the steps required by the practice of the court. The dismissal on the merits might be partial or entire, according to circumstances.

DISORDERLY HOUSE. A bawdy house or brothel, the keeping of which was always an offence at common law. By the Disorderly Houses Act 1751, now largely repealed, provision was made for the prosecution of keepers of such houses, upon information. Further provisions for the suppression of brothels are contained in ss. 33–36 of the Sexual Offences Act 1956. [BROTHEL.]

DISPARAGEMENT. A word used to signify *inequality* or unsuitableness in marriage.

DISPENSATION. 1. An exemption from some law.

2. An ecclesiastical licence.

DISSEISIN was a wrongful putting out of him that was seised of the freehold. Formerly remedied by entry, if it could be peaceably effected, and otherwise by action commonly called ejectment. [ENTRY, WRIT OF; OUSTER.]

DISSENTERS. Persons who do not conform to the Established Church. The word is usually confined to Protestant seceders from their Established Church, and their descendants.

DISSOLUTION. The act of breaking up.

1. Of *parliament* is where a final period is put to the existence of a parliament by the sovereign's will, expressed either in person or by representation, or by lapse of time. Parliaments were formerly dissolved by the death of the sovereign, but this rule was abolished in 1867.

2. Of *partnership*, by proper notice, by effluxion of time as agreed in the articles of partnership, by order of a court, by death, insolvency, etc., of a partner.

3. Of *marriage*, by decree of divorce (*q.v.*).

4. Of *companies*, by winding up, etc. See the Companies Act 1948, ss. 274, 290 and 300.

DISTRAIN. To execute a distress. [DISTRESS.]

DISTRAINT. A distress. [DISTRESS.]

DISTRESS. The taking of a personal chattel out of the possession of a wrong-doer into the custody of the party injured, to procure satisfaction for the wrong committed. The word is most frequently (though not at all exclusively) used with reference to the taking by a landlord of goods for the non-payment of rent.

DISTRESS INFINITE. A distress that had no bounds with regard to its quantity, and might be repeated from time to time, until the stubbornness of the wrongdoer was overcome, *e.g.*, distress for fealty or suit of court, and for compelling jurors to attend.

DISTRIBUTION. A word used specially for the division of the personal estate of an intestate among the parties entitled thereto as next of kin.

The Administration of Estates Act 1925 contains a code of succession on intestacy, applying, in the case of deaths occuring after 1925, alike to real and personal estate.

DISTRICT AUDITOR. [AUDITOR.]

DISTRICT COUNCIL. Formerly these were either urban district councils or rural district councils; but this distinction was abolished by the Local Government Act 1972. Under that Act England and Wales are divided into local government areas known as counties [COUNTY] and those counties are sub-divided into local government areas known as districts, each with its district council consisting of a chairman and councillors. As to their functions, see Part IX of the Act of 1972.

DISTRICT REGISTRIES. District registries of the High Court of Justice are established by the Lord Chancellor by order. Writs and originating summonses in the Queens Bench Division and writs in chancery or admiralty actions may be issued in any district registry. In any action except a probate action the plaintiff may issue a writ of summons out of any district registry. There are at present 128 district registries: see the District Registries Order 1971. The practice of the Central Office must be followed, proceedings being regulated by R.S.C. 1965, Ord. 32 (*Hals. Laws*).

DISTRINGAS (that you distrain). 1. A writ formerly issuing against the goods and chattels of a defendant who did not appear.

2. *Distringas* against a sheriff for neglecting to execute a writ of *venditioni exponas*, or exposure of goods for sale; also *distringas nuper vice comitem*, against a sheriff who has gone out of office.

3. *Distringas notice.* A procedure, formerly by writ of *distringas*, to prevent the transfer of stock or shares in a company, now replaced by the filing of an affidavit and notice as to stock under R.S.C. 1965, Ord. 50, r. 15.

DISTURBANCE. A form of real injury done to some incorporeal hereditament, by hindering or disquieting the owners in their regular and lawful enjoyment of it. Blackstone enumerates five sorts of this injury:— (1) Disturbance of *franchises.* (2) Disturbance of *common.* (3) Disturbance of *ways.* (4) Disturbance of *tenure.* (5) Disturbance of *patronage.* It is also used in connection with a tenant who quits an agricultural holding.

DIVIDEND. 1. *Dividenda.* A word used in the Statute of Rutland, 1284, to signify one part of an indenture.

2. The periodical income arising from stocks, shares, etc.

3. The proportion of a creditor's debt payable to him on the division of a bankrupt's or insolvent's estate.

DIVINE RIGHT or **DIVINE RIGHT OF KINGS**, is the name generally given to the patriarchal theory of government, according to which the monarch and his legitimate heirs, being by *divine right* entitled to the sovereignty, cannot forfeit that right by any misconduct, however gross, or any period of dispossession, however long. It was by this right that the English sovereigns in the seventeenth century claimed to reign.

DIVINE SERVICE. A tenure by which the tenants were obliged to do some special divine services in certain; as to sing so many masses, to distribute such a sum in alms, and the like.

Tenure by *divine service* differed from tenure in *frankalmoign* in this: that in the case of the tenure by *divine service*, the lord of whom the lands were held might distrain for its non-performance, whereas in the case of *frankalmoign* the lord had no remedy by distraint for neglect of the service, but merely a right of complaint to the visitor to correct it. Abolished by the Law of Property Act 1922. [FRANKALMOIGN.]

DIVISIONAL COURTS. Courts originally established in 1873, and held under the provisions of s. 63 of the Judicature Act 1925. Such courts are normally constituted of two or three judges, and proceedings before them are regulated by R.S.C. 1965, Ord. 53.

The principal jurisdiction of the divisional courts of the Queen's Bench Division consists of appeals by case stated from magistrates' courts and the Crown Court, appeals from inferior courts in respect of orders or decisions relating to contempt of court, election petitions, and certain statutory appeals from inferior tribunals. To divisional courts of the Chancery Division come appeals from county courts in bankruptcy and land registration matters. Divisional courts of the Family Division deal with appeals by case stated from the Crown Court or a magistrates' court relating to affiliation proceedings or maintenance agreements, appeals from matrimonial orders made by magistrates' courts, etc. (*Hals. Laws*).

DIVISIONS OF THE HIGH COURT. The High Court at the present time is made up of three Divisions:

(i) The Chancery Division, consisting of the Lord Chancellor (president) and not less than five puisne judges, one of whom may be nominated as Vice-Chancellor;

(ii) The Queen's Bench Division, consisting of the Lord Chief Justice (president) and not less than seventeen puisne judges;

(iii) The Family Division, consisting of a president and not less than three puisne judges.

The maximum number of puisne judges of the High Court is seventy-five; see Administration of Justice Act 1968, s. 1. [PUISNE.]

Causes and matters are distributed among the several divisions as directed by rules of court: (see R.S.C. 1965, Ord. 4; nevertheless, all jurisdiction vested in the High Court belongs to all Divisions alike (s. 4 (4) of the Act of 1925).

Power to alter the number of Divisions by Order in Council is given by s. 5 of the Act of 1925.

DIVORCE. The termination of a marriage otherwise than by death or annulment.

A petition for divorce might formerly be presented to the High Court by a husband or wife on the ground of:— (*a*) adultery; (*b*) desertion for at least three years immediately preceding the presentation of the petition; (*c*) cruelty; (*d*) insanity, *i.e.*, that the respondent was incurably of unsound mind and had been continuously under care and treatment for a period of at least five years immediately preceding the presentation of the petition. The wife might also petition on the ground that the husband had, since the celebration of the marriage, been guilty of rape, sodomy, or bestiality.

Since 1st January 1971 the only ground on which a petition for divorce may be presented by either party to a marriage is that the marriage has broken down irretrievably: see now s. 1 of the Matrimonial Causes Act 1973.

Breakdown of the marriage is (by s. 1 (2) of the Act of 1973) proved by showing that (*a*) the respondent has committed adultery and the petitioner finds it intolerable to live with him/her; (*b*) the respondent has behaved in such a way that the petitioner cannot reasonably be expected to live with him/her; (c) the respondent has deserted the petitioner for a continuous period of at least two years before the presentation of the petition; (d) the parties to the marriage have lived apart for a continuous period of at least two years before presentation of the petition and the respondent consents to a decree being granted; or (e) that the parties to the marriage have lived apart for a continuous period of at least five years immediately preceding the presentation of the petition.

DIVORCE DIVISION. The Matrimonial Causes Act 1857 constituted a court of record called the Court for Divorce and Matrimonial Causes, to which was transferred all jurisdiction in matrimonial matters which was then exercisable by any ecclesiastical court in England; which jurisdiction s. 16 of the Judicature Act 1873 transferred to the High Court. S. 34 of the Act of 1873 assigned to the Probate, Divorce and Admiralty Division all matters which would have been within the exclusive cognisance of the Court for Divorce and Matrimonial Causes.

The Probate, Divorce and Admiralty Division was dissolved in 1971, admiralty business being transferred to the Queen's Bench Division and contentious probate business to the Chancery Division. Matrimonial causes (including divorce) and non-contentious probate business were assigned to the then newly-constituted Family Division (q.v.)

DOCK. The place in court where a prisoner is placed while on trial. He may, from the dock, instruct counsel without the intervention of a solicitor.

DOCK WARRANT. A document given to the owner of goods imported and warehoused in the docks, as a recognition of his title to the goods, on the bills of lading and other proofs of ownership being produced. Like a bill of lading, it passes by indorsement and delivery, and transfers the absolute right to the goods described in it.

DOCTORS' COMMONS. A college of Doctors of Laws established near St. Paul's Churchyard. The Ecclesiastical and Admiralty Courts used to be held here until the institution was dissolved under ss. 116, 117 of the Court of Probate Act 1857.

DOCUMENT. A written paper or something similar which may be put forward as evidence. By s. 6 (1) of the Evidence Act 1938 (repealed) "documents" included books, maps, plans, drawings and photographs; and by the Civil Evidence Act 1968 it may also include graphs, discs, tapes, sound tracks, films, etc. The Iron and Steel Act 1967, Sched. 2, went further: any device by which information is recorded or stored.

DOCUMENT OF TITLE. A document enabling the possessor to deal with the property described therein as if he were the owner, as e.g., a bill of lading. S. 46 of the Larceny Act 1916 (repealed) defined "document of title to goods" as including (inter alia) any "document used in the ordinary course of business as proof of the possession or control of goods," etc.; and "document of title to lands" as including any deed, map, roll, register, paper, or parchment, etc., being or containing evidence of title to any real estate or interest in real estate.

DOE, JOHN. Generally the name of the fictitious plaintiff in the old action of ejectment. [EJECTMENT.]

DOG. Includes any bitch, sapling, or puppy: Protection of Animals Act 1911, s. 15. Liability for damage done by dogs, including damage to livestock, is governed by the Animals Act 1971. Establishments for the breeding of dogs must be licensed under the Breeding of Dogs Act 1973. By the Guard Dogs Act 1975 guard dogs may not be used to guard premises unless under the control of a handler or properly secured.

DOG RACE. A race in which an object resembling a hare, propelled by mechanical means is pursued by dogs: Betting, Gaming and Lotteries Act 1963, s. 55.

DOLI CAPAX (capable of crime). An expression used to indicate that in any given case a child between the ages of eight and fourteen has, contrary to the ordinary presumption in such cases, sufficient understanding to discern between good and evil, so as to be criminally responsible for his actions. This is otherwise expressed by the maxim, *Malitia supplet ætatem* (malice supplies the want of age).

DOLI INCAPAX. Incapable of crime. There is a conclusive presumption that children under eight years of age are *doli*

DOLI INCAPAX—*continued.*

incapax. Nothing, therefore, that they do can make them liable to be punished by a criminal court.

DOM. PROC. An abbreviation for *Domus Procerum*, the House of Lords.

DOME, or **DOOM.** A judgment, sentence, or decree. There are several words that end in *dom*, as kingdom, earldom, etc., so that it may seem to signify the jurisdiction of a lord or a king.

DOME-BOOK (Lat. *Liber judicialis*). Probably a book of statutes proper to the English Saxons, wherein perhaps the laws of former Saxon kings were contained.

This book is said to have been compiled by Alfred, and to have been extant so late as the reign of Edward IV, but it is now lost.

DOMESDAY-BOOK (Lat. *Liber judiciarius*). An ancient record made in the reign of William the Conqueror, containing a survey of the lands in England. It was begun by five justices assigned for that purpose in each county in the year 1081, and was finished in 1086.

DOMESMEN. Judges or men appointed to doom, and determine suits or controversies.

DOMESTIC SERVANTS. Servants whose main or general purpose is to be about their employers' persons or establishments, residential or quasi-residential, for the purpose of ministering to their employers' needs or wants, or to the needs or wants of those who are members of such establishments, including guests. See *Re Junior Carlton Club*, [1922] 1 K.B. 166, per ROCHE, J.

DOMICELLUS. An old appelation given as an addition to the king's illegitimate sons in France. John of Gaunt's illegitimate sons were called *domicelli* in the charter of legitimation. *Domicellus* also signified a private gentleman; also a better sort of servant.

DOMICILE. The place in which a man has his fixed and permanent home, and to which, whenever he is absent, he has the intention of returning. It is of three sorts: (1) by birth; (2) by choice; (3) by operation of law. Upon domicile depend questions of personal status and the devolution of movable property.

Formerly, the common law ruled that a woman acquired her husband's domicile on marriage. This rule was abolished by the Domicile and Matrimonial Proceedings Act 1973, which provides for a married woman's domicile to be ascertained independently.

DOMINA. A title given to honourable women, who anciently in their own right of inheritance held a barony.

DOMINANT TENEMENT. A tenement in favour of which a service or "servitude" is constituted. Thus an estate, the owner of which has, by virtue of his ownership, a right of way over another man's land is called the *dominant tenement* in respect thereof; and the land over which the right of way exists is called the *servient tenement*. These terms are derived from the Roman civil law.

DOMINION. Those former dependencies of the United Kingdom which had obtained complete self government. First legally defined in the Statute of Westminster 1931 to include Canada, Australia, New Zealand, South Africa, Eire and Newfoundland. Of these Eire and South Africa left the Commonwealth and Newfoundland became a province of Canada. The term "dominion", having come to be thought of as conveying a misleading impression of the constitutional and international status of the countries concerned, has now ceased to be used for official purposes.

DOMINIUM. A term in the Roman law, used to signify *ownership of a thing*, as opposed (1) to a mere life interest or usufruct; (2) to an equitable or "praetorian" right; (3) to a merely possessory right; (4) to a right *against a person*, such as a covenantee has against a covenanter.

DOMINUS. This word prefixed to a man's name usually denoted him a knight or a clergyman; sometimes the lord of a manor.

DOMINUS LITIS. The controller of a suit or litigation.

DOMITAE NATURAE (of a tame disposition). An expression applied to animals of a nature tame and domestic, as horses, kine, sheep, poultry, and the like. In these a man may have as absolute a property as in any inanimate thing. [ANIMALS.]

DOMO REPARANDA (for repairing a house). An ancient writ that lay for a man against his neighbour, by the anticipated fall of whose house he feared damage to his own. The writ directed the neighbour to put his house in a proper state of repair.

DONATIO MORTIS CAUSA (a gift by 'reason of death) is a gift of personal property made by one who apprehends that he is in peril of death, and evidenced by a manual delivery by him, or by another person in his presence and by his direction, to the donee or to some one else for the donee, of the means of obtaining possession of the same, or of the writings whereby the ownership thereof was created, and conditioned to take effect absolutely in the event of his not recovering from his existing disorder, and not revoking the gift before his death.

A *donatio mortis causa* differs from a legacy mainly in its being wholly independent of the donor's last will and testament, and it therefore requires no assent on the part of his executor or administrator to give full effect to it. It is liable to the donor's debts in case of insufficiency of assets, and is subject to capital transfer tax.

DONEE. [DONOR.]

DONIS, DE. [DE DONIS.]

DONOR is he who makes a gift to another; and he to whom the gift is made is called the *donee.*

DOOM. [DOME.]

DORMANT PARTNER. One who takes no active part in the partnership affairs, and is not known to the world as a partner, but who receives profits of the partnership.

DOUBLE COMPLAINT. [DUPLEX QUERELA.]

DOUBLE COSTS OR TREBLE COSTS, given in various cases by Act of Parliament. All such provisions as were enacted for this purpose before the year 1842 were repealed by the Limitations of Actions and Costs Acts 1842.

DOUBLE ENTRY. A system of mercantile bookkeeping in which the entries are made so as to show the debit and credit of eevery transaction.

DOUBLE INSURANCE is where a person, being fully insured by one policy, effects another with some other insurer or insurers, the risk and interest being the same in both. He may recover the amount of his actual loss from either insurer, but not both, as the contract is one of indemnity only. The insurer who pays is entitled to contribution from the other.

DOUBLE QUARREL. [DUPLEX QUERELA.]

DOUBLE RENT is payable by a tenant who continues in possession after the time for which he has given notice to quit, until the time of his quitting possession. Distress for Rent Act 1737, s. 18.

DOUBLE VALUE. Double the yearly value of lands payable by a tenant who wilfully "holds over" (*i.e.,* continues in possession) after the expiration of his term, and after notice by the landlord requiring him to leave. Landlord and Tenant Act 1730, s. 1. [VALOR MARITAGII.]

DOUBLE WASTE. When a tenant bound to repair suffers a house to be wasted, and then unlawfully fells timber to repair it, he is said to commit double waste.

DOWAGER. A queen dowager is the widow of a king. So, a duchess dowager, countess dowager, etc., is the widow of a duke, earl, etc.

DOWER. 1. By the Roman law *dower* is that which a wife brings to her husband in marriage. It is sometimes spoken of as *dowry.*

2. By the law of England, *dower* was a portion which a widow had of the lands of her husband. This extended by the common law to the third part of the freehold lands and tenements whereof the husband was solely seised for an estate of inheritance during the marriage; and might be enjoyed for the life of the widow. But in order to entitle a widow to dower out of the land, the husband's estate or interest therein had to be such that their common issue might have inherited it. If, therefore, a man had lands to himself and the heirs of his body by his wife A, a second wife B would not be entitled to dower out of such lands. By the Dower Act of 1833 (repealed), the dower of women married on or after the 1st of January, 1834, was placed entirely in the power of their husbands, as it was barred by the lands being disposed of by the husband during his life or by will, or by his giving the

DOWER—*continued.*

wife *any* lands out of which dower might have been claimed, or by declaration to bar dower either in the deed conveying the lands to the husband, or in any separate deed or by his will. Thus where the Act applied, dower could only be claimed where the husband died intestate and there was no declaration by deed barring dower.

As to copyholds, see FREEBENCH, to which the Dower Act did not apply. Dower and freebench were abolished by s. 45 of the Administration of Estates Act 1925.

DOWER, WRIT OF RIGHT OF. The remedy of a widow who had been deforced of part of her dower. Abolished in 1860.

DOWRESS. A widow entitled to dower, otherwise called a "tenant in dower".

DOWRY. That which the wife brings her husband in marriage. [DOWER, 1.] Not to be confounded with the *dower* of the English law. [DOWER, 2.]

DRAFT signifies a cheque or bill of exchange, or other negotiable instrument; also the rough copy of a legal document before it has been engrossed.

DRAMATIC WORK. By s. 48 of the Copyright Act 1956 "dramatic work" includes a choreographic work or entertainment in dumb show if reduced to writing in the form in which the work or entertainment is to be presented. It does not include a cinematograph film *as distinct from* a scenario or script for a cinematograph film.

DRAWBACK. The repayment of duties or taxes previously charged on commodities, from which they are relieved on exportation.

DRAWEE. A person on whom a bill of exchange is *drawn*, as one who may be expected to "accept" it. [BILL OF EXCHANGE.]

DRAWER. A person who draws a bill of exchange.

DRAW-LATCHES were thieves and robbers.

DROIT. A French word, answering to the Latin *jus*, and signifying either (1) a right; or (2) law, as used in such phrases as "the law of nations", etc.

DROITS OF ADMIRALTY. A word applied to ships and property of the enemy

taken by a subject in time of war without commission from the Crown. Any such prize would, by the effect of the prerogative, become an admiralty *droit*, or a right of the admiralty. The rights of the admiralty were relinquished in favour of the captors. [PRIZE.]

DROITURAL ACTIONS include the "writ of right", and all actions in the nature of a writ of right, as opposed to *possessory* actions. [WRIT OF RIGHT.]

DRUGS. 1. By s. 135 of the Food and Drugs Act 1955 the term "drugs" includes medicine for internal or external use.

2. "Dangerous drugs" were defined in the Dangerous Drugs Acts 1965 and 1967 (both repealed; see now the Misuse of Drugs Act 1971). These drugs are cannabis, cannabis resin, coca leaves, opium (medicinal, prepared or raw) and poppy-straw.

3. "Drug addict" is defined by the Matrimonial Proceedings (Magistrates' Courts) Act 1960 (amended by the Misuse of Drugs Act 1971) as a person who, by reason of the habitual taking or using of any controlled drug (within the meaning of the Act of 1971), is at times dangerous to himself or to others, or incapable of managing himself or his affairs; or who so conducts himself that it would not be reasonable to expect a spouse of ordinary sensibilities to continue to cohabit with him.

Controlled drugs are listed in Sch. 2 to the Act of 1971.

DRUNKENNESS. Intoxication with alcoholic liquor. Habitual drunkenness is regulated by the Habitual Drunkards Act 1879 and the Inebriates Acts 1888 and 1898, under which Acts drunkards may, in certain circumstances, be confined in inebriate reformatories. See also ss. 6, 19 of the Road Traffic Act 1972, as to driving with blood-alcohol concentration above a prescribed limit, and as to cycling whilst under the influence of drink or drugs. [HABITUAL DRUNKARD.]

DRY RENT. Rent-seck. [RENT.]

DUBITANTE (doubting). A word used in legal reports to signify that a judge cannot make up his mind as to the decision he should give.

DUCES TECUM (bring with thee). A subpoena commanding a person to appear at a certain day in court, and to *bring with* *him* some writings, evidences, or other things, which the court would view.

DUCES TECUM LICET LAN-GUIDUS. A writ formerly directed to a sheriff, upon a return (*i.e.*, upon his having made a statement endorsed on a previous writ) that he could not bring his prisoner without danger of death, commanding him to bring him nevertheless. Obsolete.

DUCHY COURT OF LANCASTER. A special jurisdiction held before the Chancellor of the Duchy or his deputy concerning equitable interests in lands held of the Crown in right of the Duchy of Lancaster. Although it has not been abolished, the court last sat in 1835. [CHANCELLOR, 2.]

DUEL is where two persons engage in a fight with intent to murder the other. If either of them is killed the other and the seconds are guilty of murder. It is a misdemeanour to challenge another to fight or to provoke another to send a challenge.

DUKE. 1. An ancient elective officer among the Germans, having an independent power over the military state.

2. The first title of nobility next to the royal family. No subject was honoured with this title till the time of Edward III, who, in the eleventh year of his reign, created his son, Edward the Black Prince, Duke of Cornwall.

At the present time there are 4 royal dukes and 27 dukes, including those of Scotland.

DUM BENE SE GESSERIT (so long as he shall behave himself well). Words used to signify that the tenure of an office is to be held during good behaviour, and not at the pleasure of the Crown or the appointer.

DUM CASTA VIXERIT (so long as she shall live chaste). Deeds of separation between husband and wife often provide that the allowance to the wife is to be paid only so long as she lives a chaste life and may be inserted on a decree for dissolution or orders for maintenance. The clause to this effect is called the "*dum casta* clause".

DUM SOLA (while single). An expression used to indicate the period of a woman being unmarried or a widow. [COVERTURE.]

DUMPING. To dump means to unload, to tip out rubbish. The word is used legally in two connections: (*a*) permanently depositing substances and articles in the sea from a vehicle, ship, aircraft, etc. (Dumping at Sea Act 1974); (*b*) exporting goods at a price lower than the comparable prevailing price in the country of origin (European Economic Community Council Regulations).

DUPLEX QUERELA (double complaint or quarrel). A complaint in the nature of an appeal from the ordinary to his next immediate superior, as from a bishop to an archbishop. This complaint is available to a clergyman who, having been presented to a living, is refused institution by the ordinary.

DUPLICATE. 1. Second letters patent granted by the Lord Chancellor in a case wherein he had formerly done the same, when the first were void.

2. A copy or transcript of a deed or writing.

3. The ticket given by the pawnbroker to the pawner.

DUPLICATE WILL. A will executed in duplicate; the intention usually being that the testator shall keep one copy himself, and that the other shall be deposited with someone else. Upon probate both copies must be deposited at the Probate Registry.

DURANTE ABSENTIA. [ADMINISTRATOR.]

DURANTE LITE, or **PENDENTE LITE.** During the continuance of a suit. [ADMINISTRATOR.]

DURANTE MINORE AETATE. During minority. [ADMINISTRATOR.]

DURANTE VIDUITATE (during widowhood). Words used with reference to an estate granted to a widow until she marries again.

DURESS (Lat. *Durities*). A constraint. Of this there are two kinds.

1. Actual imprisonment,, where a man actually loses his liberty.

2. Duress *per minas* (by threats), where the hardship is only threatened and impending. A contract made under duress is voidable at the option of the person upon whom it is practised, but the person who has employed the force cannot avail of it as a defence if the contract be insisted upon by the other party.

DURHAM. Formerly one of the counties palatine, in which the Bishop of Durham had *jura regalia* as fully as the king in his palace. [COUNTY PALATINE.] But the palatinate jurisdiction of the Bishop of Durham was taken away by the Durham (County Palatine) Act 1836 and vested as a franchise or royalty in the Crown; and the jurisdiction of the Court of Pleas at Durham, the relic of the palatinate jurisdiction, is now vested in the High Court; see s. 18 (2) (vi) of the Judicature Act 1925. The Palatine Court of Durham (*i.e.*, the Chancery Court) was abolished by the Courts Act 1971.

DUTCH AUCTION. In this so-called "auction" the property is set up for sale at a price beyond its value, and the price is gradually lowered until some person takes it.

DWELLING. A building or part of a building occupied or intended to be occupied as a separate dwelling, together with any yard, garden, out-houses and appurtenances belonging to or usually enjoyed with that building or part. It implies a building used or capable of being used as a residence by one or more families and provided with all necessary parts and appliances such as floors, staircases, windows, etc.

"DYING WITHOUT ISSUE." These words, in a will executed since 1st Jan. 1838, are held, under s. 29 of the Wills Act 1837, to refer only to the case of a person dying and leaving no issue behind him *at the date of his death.* Prior to that time the words were held to refer to the case of death and *subsequent failure of issue* at an indefinite time afterwards, however remote; by which interpretation many dispositions were held void for remoteness, and testator's intentions defeated in many ways.

DYKE-REED or **DYKE-REVE.** The officer having oversight of the dykes and drains in a fen country.

E

E. CONVERSO. Conversely, contrariwise.

E.O.E. [ERRORS EXCEPTED.]

E.R. An abbreviation for Elizabeth Regina.

EALDERMAN, or **EALDORMAN,** among the Saxons, was as much as earl among the Danes. It is as much as an elder or statesman, called by the Romans *senator.* [ALDERMAN.]

EARL. An ancient title of nobility, equivalent to *ealdorman* among the Saxons. Earls were also called *schiremen,* because they had each the civil government of a several division or shire. The word is now a title of nobility ranking between a marquis and a viscount.

EARL MARSHAL. The officer who (formerly jointly with the Lord High Constable) presides over the Court of Chivalry. Under him is the Herald's Office or College of Arms. The office is of great antiquity and has been for several centuries hereditary in the family of the Howards. [COURT OF CHIVALRY.]

EARLDOM. The *status* of an earl; but originally the jurisdiction of an earl. [DOME.]

EARMARK. A mark for the purpose of identifying anything which is a subject of property.

EARNED INCOME. Income arising in respect of remuneration from any office or employment of profit, etc., or from a trade, profession or vocation. See now the Income and Corporation Taxes Act 1970.

EARNEST. The evidence of a contract of sale; money paid as part of a larger sum, or goods delivered as part of a larger quantity; or anything given as security to bind a bargain.

EASEMENT. A right enjoyed by a man over his neighbour's property; such as a right of way, or a right of passage for water; called in the Roman law a *servitude.* Generally (and, according to some authorities, necessarily) it belongs to a man as being the owner of some specific house or land, which is then called the *dominant tenement.* Under the Law of Property Act 1925 an easement at law must be for an interest equivalent to an estate in fee simple absolute in possession or a term of years absolute. After 1925, all other easements are equitable only. See s. 1 of the Law of Property Act 1925. [DOMINANT TENEMENT; SERVITUDES.]

EAST INDIA COMPANY. A body of persons originally incorporated for purposes purely commercial, who gradually acquired immense territorial dominions by which they became effectively (though subject to the undoubted supremacy of the British Crown) the sovereigns of India. Their exclusive right of trading to India was abolished in 1833 and they were debarred from engaging, in the future, in commercial transactions. In 1858 the political powers and rights of the East India Company were transferred to the Crown; and on 1st June, 1874, the Company was finally dissolved.

EASTER DUES AND OFFERINGS were payments made by parishioners to their clergy at Easter as a composition for personal tithes or the tithes for personal labour.

EAT INDE SINE DIE. A form of words indicating that a defendant may be dismissed from an action, and "go without day", that is, without any future day appointed for his reappearance.

EAVES-DROPPERS were such as listened under walls or windows, or the eaves of a house, to hearken after discourse, and thereupon to frame slanderous and mischievous tales.

ECCLESIA. A church or place set apart for the service of God. Sometimes it means a parsonage.

ECCLESIASTICAL COMMISSIONERS. A body of commissioners appointed to consider the state of the several dioceses, with references to the amount of their revenues, and the more equal distribution of episcopal duties; also the best means of providing for the cure of souls in parishes. The first commissioners for this purpose were Royal Commissioners, appointed in 1835; the statute incorporating the Ecclesiastical Commissioners was the Ecclesiastical Commissioners Act 1836.

As a body the Ecclesiastical Commissioners have now been dissolved, and their functions, rights, property, etc., have vested in the Church Commissioners. See the Church Commissioners Measure 1947.

ECCLESIASTICAL CORPORATION. A corporation of which the members are entirely spiritual persons, such as bishops, parsons, deans and chapters, archdeacons, etc. The visitor of an ecclesiastical corporation is the ordinary.

ECCLESIASTICAL COURTS are the Archdeacon's Court (now practically obsolete) the Consistory Courts, the Provincial Courts (*i.e.* the Court of Arches of Canterbury and the Chancery Court of York), and the Court of Faculties. These are the ecclesiastical courts proper; but there is also the Court of Final Appeal, which used to be the Court of Delegates, but is now the Judicial Committee of the Privy Council. [JUDICIAL COMMITTEE OF THE PRIVY COUNCIL; SUPREME COURT OF JUDICATURE.]

EDICT. A proclamation, prohibition or command. A law promulgated.

EDUCATION. [SCHOOL.]

EFFECTS. Goods and chattels; a man's property.

EFFLUENT. [TRADE EFFLUENT.]

EGYPTIANS. [GIPSIES.]

EI QUI AFFIRMAT, NON EI QUI NEGAT, INCUMBIT PROBATIO. The burden of proof lies upon him who affirms and not upon him who denies.

EIGNE (Fr. *Aisné* or *Aîné*). The eldest. [BASTARD EIGNE.]

EIRE. A journey. [EYRE.]

EJECTMENT. An action to try the title to land. The old action, which was very elaborate in procedure, was abolished in 1852. The action is now called one for the recovery of land.

EJUSDEM GENERIS (of the same kind or nature). Where in a statute, etc., particular classes are specified by name, followed by general words, the meaning of the general words is generally cut down by reference to the particular words, and the general words are taken to apply to those *ejusdem generis* with the particular classes.

ELDER BRETHREN. The masters of The Trinity House, by whom the affairs of the corporation are managed. [TRINITY HOUSE.]

ELECTION is when a man is left to his own free will to take or do one thing or another, which he pleases. But it is more frequently applied to the choosing between two rights by a person who derives one of them under an instrument in which an intention appears (or is implied by a court of law or equity) that he should not enjoy both. *E.g.*, where A gives B property but by

ELECTION—*continued.*

the same instrument gives to C property which really belongs to B, B would have to elect between retaining his own property and to that extent abandoning what A gave him, or taking what A gave him and allowing his (B's) property to go to C.

The word is also commonly applied to the choosing of officers or representatives; especially the choosing, by a constituency, of some person or persons to represent it in parliament.

ELECTION AGENT. The representative of a candidate at a parliamentary or local government election under s. 55 of the Representation of the People Act 1949. As to his duties with regard to election expenses, etc., see *ibid.*, ss. 60 *et seq.*

ELECTION COMMISSIONERS. Commissioners formerly appointed to enquire into the existence of corrupt and illegal practices at parliamentary elections.

ELECTION JUDGES. Judges of the High Court selected in pursuance of the Parliamentary Elections Act 1868, s. 11, and the Judicature Act 1925, s. 67, for the trial of election petitions. Such judges are selected each year from the puisne judges of the Queen's Bench Division, to be placed on a rota for the trial of petitions for the ensuing year.

ELECTION PETITION. A petition complaining of an undue return of a member to serve in parliament. Such petition, in a prescribed form, must be presented in the Queen's Bench Division to be tried by two judges on the rota [ELECTION JUDGES]. See ss. 107 *et seq.* of the Representation of the People Act 1949. Local elections may similarly be questioned under *ibid.*, ss. 112 *et seq.*

ELEEMOSYNÆ. The possessions belonging to churches.

ELEEMOSYNARY CORPORA-TION. A corporation constituted for the perpetual distribution of the free alms or bounty of the founder, to such persons as he has directed. Of this kind are hospitals and colleges.

ELEGIT. A former writ, once the usual method of execution against land under a judgment or order for the payment of money. Under the writ, the lands of the judgment debtor were delivered to the judgment creditor to be held by him until the satisfaction of the debt. Abolished by s. 34 of the Administration of Justice Act 1956.

EMANCIPATION. A word which, in the Roman law, originally signified selling out of one's possession by the form of *mancipation.* By a law of the Twelve Tables, a father was not allowed to sell his son more than three times; and if a son was manumitted after being three times sold by his father, he became free. Afterwards, a threefold sale became a matter of form for giving freedom to a son; and hence the modern use of the word *emancipation.*

EMBARGO ON SHIPS. A prohibition issued by the Crown upon ships, forbidding them to go out of any port.

The term "embargo" is borrowed from the Spanish law procedure, and signifies *arrest* or *sequestration*; and it is applied to the seizure or detention of persons or property which happen to be within the territory of the nation at the time of seizure. The seizure of ships and cargoes under the authority of municipal law is spoken of as a *civil* embargo. An *international* embargo, on the other hand, is an act not of civil procedure, but of hostile detention. It may be made for the same object as *reprisals* are made upon the high seas, namely, for the satisfaction of a debt or the redress of an injury; and it may also be made by way of prelude to war.

EMBEZZLEMENT. A clerk or servant or anyone employed in that capacity who fraudulently intercepted money or goods before they came into his master's legal possession, and converted them to his own use, was guilty of the offence of embezzlement. This was a separate statutory offence under s. 17 of the Larceny Act 1916, but is no longer so since the repeal of that Act by the Theft Act 1968. [THEFT.]

EMBLEMENTS. The profits of a crop which has been sown, *i.e.*, any products created by *annual industry, e.g.*, corn as opposed to grass, *fructus industriales* not *fructus naturales.* The general rule as to emblements sown by an out-going tenant, whose estate ended before harvest time, was, that the out-going tenant or his representatives should have the crop if the termination of the estate arose from the act of God or the will of the landlord, but not if the termination of the estate was due to effluxion of time, or any act of forfeiture committed by the tenant. See s. 4 of the Agricultural Holdings Act 1948, which provides for an extension of tenancy in lieu of claims to emblements.

EMBRACEOR. A person guilty of embracery. [EMBRACERY.]

EMBRACERY. An offence which consisted of an attempt to influence a jury corruptly. Abolished by the Criminal Law Act 1967.

EMINENT DOMAIN (Lat. *Dominium eminens*) is the right which every state or sovereign power has to the use of property of its citizens for the common welfare. This right is the true foundation of the right of taxation.

EMPANEL. [IMPANELLING A JURY.]

EMPHYTEUSIS may be described as a perpetual lease. It was a right known in the Roman law, by which the perpetual use of land was given to a person for the payment of rent.

EMPLOYMENT. Includes any trade, business, profession, office or vocation: Social Security Act 1975, Sch. 20.

EMPLOYMENT AGENCY. A business providing services for the purpose of finding workers employment with employers or of supplying employers with workers. Such agencies must be licensed under the provisions of the Employment Agencies Act 1973.

EMPLOYMENT APPEAL TRIBUNAL. A body established under the Employment Protection Act 1975 to hear appeals from industrial tribunals on various matters relating to employment.

EMPTOR. A buyer. [CAVEAT EMPTOR.]

EN AUTER DROIT, or **EN AUTRE DROIT** (in another person's right); as, for instance, an executor holds property and brings actions in right of those entitled to his testator's estate.

EN VENTRE SA MERE. In his mother's womb. Of an unborn child.

ENABLING STATUTE. A statute enabling persons or corporations to do that which, before it was passed, they could not do, as contrasted with a prohibiting statute, under which acts are forbidden.

ENCROACHMENT. An unlawful gaining upon the possession of another.

ENDORSEMENT. [INDORSEMENT.]

ENDOWMENT signifies:—

1. The giving or assigning dower to a woman. [DOWER.]

2. The setting or severing of a sufficient portion for a vicar towards his perpetual maintenance.

3. Also any permanent provision for the maintenance of schools is called an *endowment*.

4. The word is now generally used of a permanent provision for any institution or person.

ENDOWMENT POLICY. [INSURANCE.]

ENEMY. Persons engaged in armed operations against any of Her Majesty's forces, including armed mutineers, armed rebels, armed rioters, and pirates: Army Act 1955, s. 225.

ENEMY GOODS, ENEMY SHIP. A maxim which would imply that goods of an enemy carried on board a neutral ship render the ship liable to confiscation as enemy's property. Such a doctrine was contended for by France in the 16th and 17th centuries, but never received general acceptance.

ENEMY SHIP, ENEMY GOODS. A maxim which would imply that the fact of goods being in an enemy's ship renders them liable to confiscation as enemy's goods. The doctrine was sanctioned by various treaties between the years 1640 and 1780, but it has never been regarded as part of the general law of nations. It was repudiated by the Declaration of Paris of 1856, by which it is declared that neutral goods, other than contraband of war, are exempt from capture in enemy's ships. [DECLARATION OF PARIS.]

ENFRANCHISE. To make free, to incorporate a man into a society or body politic.

Enfranchisement is a word which is now used principally in three different senses:—

1. Of conferring a right to vote at a parliamentary election. [FRANCHISE.]

2. Of giving to a borough or other constituency a right to return a member or members to parliament.

3. Of the conversion of leasehold into freehold. [ENLARGE.]

ENGAGEMENT. A betrothal, or mutual promise of marriage. Engagements to marry are not enforceable at law: Law Reform (Miscellaneous Provisions) Act 1970, s. 1. The gift of an engagement ring is, however, presumed to be an absolute gift, unless the presumption is rebutted by proof that the ring was given on condition that it should be returned if the marriage did not take place.

ENGLESCHERIE. The name given in the times of Canute and of William the Conqueror to the presentment of the fact that a person slain was an Englishman. This fact, if established, excused the neighbourhood from the fine they would have been liable to, had a Dane or a Norman been slain.

ENGLISH INFORMATION. A proceeding in the former Court of Exchequer in revenue matters.

ENGROSSING. 1. The getting into one's possession, or buying up, in gross or wholesale, large quantities of corn, or other dead victuals, with intent to sell them again.

2. The fair copying of a deed or other legal instrument.

ENLARGE. To *enlarge* frequently means to put off or extend the time for doing anything. Thus, enlarging a rule signifies extending the time for doing that which by a rule of court is required to be done.

To *enlarge an estate* is to increase a person's interest in land; as for instance, where there is an estate in A for life, with remainder to B and his heirs, and B releases his estate to A, A's estate is said to be *enlarged* into a fee simple. As to enlargement of the residue of long terms into fee simple, see s. 153 of the Law of Property Act 1925.

ENQUEST. An inquisition by jurors. [INQUEST.]

ENQUIRY, WRIT OF. [WRIT OF INQUIRY.]

ENROLMENT was the registering, recording, or entering of any lawful act. Thus, for instance, bargains and sales of freeholds were, under the Statute of Enrolment 1535, required to be enrolled; so, by the Charitable Uses Act 1735, were conveyances to corporations; and so were disentailing deeds by the Fines and Recoveries Act

1833. The necessity for enrolment of such deeds, however, was abolished by the Law of Property Act 1925, s. 133.

Decrees in Chancery were formerly enrolled at the Enrolment Office, now merged in the Central Office.

ENTAIL, in legal treatises, was used to signify an estate tail, especially with reference to the restraint which such an estate imposed upon its owner, or, in other words, the points wherein sch an estate differed from an estate in fee simple. [DISENTAILING DEED; ESTATE, 1; FINE, 1; RECOVERY.] And this was often its popular sense; but sometimes it was, in popular language, used differently, so as to signify a succession of life estates, as when it was said that "an entail ends with A B," meaning that A B was the first person who was entitled to bar or cut off the entail, being in law the first tenant in tail. No legal estate tail can exist or be created after 1925. An equitable estate tail may be created after 1925 in real or personal property (Law of Property Act 1925, s. 130).

ENTERING APPEARANCE. [APPEARANCE.]

ENTERING BILLS SHORT. This is when a banker, having received an undue bill from a customer, does not carry the amount to the credit of the latter, but notes down the receipt of the bill in the customer's account, with the amount and the time when due. Whether, however, any given bill is to be regarded as "a short bill" (that is, not to be treated as cash) must depend not so much upon whether it has been "entered short" as upon the surrounding circumstances, and the general mode of dealing between the parties.

ENTERPLEADER. [INTERPLEADER.]

ENTICEMENT. [CONSORTIUM.]

ENTIRE CONTRACT. A contract wherein everything to be done on one side is the consideration for everything to be done on the other. This is opposed to a severable or apportionable contract.

ENTIRE TENANCY signifies a sole possession in one man, in contradistinction to a several tenancy, which implies a tenancy jointly or in common with others.

ENTIRETIES, TENANCY BY. Where an estate was devised or conveyed to husband and wife during coverture, they were formerly said to be *tenants by entireties, i.e.,* each was seised of the whole estate and neither of a part. They were seised *per tout,* and not *per my et per tout.*

Tenancies by entireties were abolished by Sch. I, Part VI, to the Law of Property Act 1925, under which those still existing were converted into joint tenancies.

ENTIRETY. Denotes the whole, as contradistinguished from a moiety, etc.

ENTRY signifies:—
1. Putting down a mercantile transaction in a book of account.
2. The taking possession of lands or tenements. See the following titles.

ENTRY, FORCIBLE. [FORCIBLE ENTRY.]

ENTRY OF JUDGMENT. The setting down of judgment by a registrar of the Chancery Division, or in the Action Department (Queen's Bench Division), in a book kept for the purpose. See R.S.C. 1965, Ord. 42.

ENTRY, RIGHT OF. A right to enter and take possession of lands or tenements without bringing an action to recover the same; a remedy allowed in various cases by common or statute law, or the deed by which an estate (*i.e.,* a person's interest in land) is marked out and limited.

ENTRY, WRIT OF. A writ by which a party claiming the right of possession to lands disproved the title of the tenant or possessor, by showing the unlawful means by which he entered or continued possession, by *intrusion,* or *disseisin,* or the like.

A writ of entry was called a writ of entry *sur disseisin, sur intrusion, sur alienation,* etc., according to the circumstances of the case.

Writs of entry were abolished in 1833.

ENUMERATORS. Persons appointed to take the census.

ENURE. To take effect, operate, result, or be available. When it is said that a transaction enures to the benefit of A B, it is meant that A B gets the benefit of it.

ENVIRONMENTAL LAW (*Canada.*) The body of statutory laws enacted in recent years to protect the environment and provide, so far as possible, for clean water and clean air.

ENVOY. A diplomatic agent despatched by one state to another.

EO NOMINE. In that name; on that account.

EPISCOPALIA. Synodals and other customary payments from the clergy to their bishop or diocesan, which dues were formerly collected by the rural deans, and by them transmitted to the bishop.

EQUAL OPPORTUNITIES COMMISSION. A body set up under the Sex Discrimination Act 1975. Its duties are to work towards the elimination of discrimination and to promote equality of opportunity between men and women generally. It consists of 8–15 commissioners, one of whom is to be appointed chairman.

EQUITABLE ASSETS. Assets of a deceased person, which could not be made available to a creditor of the deceased through the medium of a court of equity. See now s. 32 of the Administration of Estates Act 1925. [ASSET.]

EQUITABLE DEFENCE AT COMMON LAW. A defence to an action at common law on *equitable* grounds; that is, on grounds which, prior to the passing of the Common Law Procedure Act 1854, would have been cognizable only in a court of equity.

Now, by s. 36 of the Judicature Act 1925, law and equity are to be concurrently administered in the High Court and the Court of Appeal; and where the rules of common law and equity conflict, equity is to prevail.

EQUITABLE ESTATE. An estate in land formerly not fully recognised as such except in a court of *equity.* Now, any estate, interest or charge in or over land which is not a legal estate takes effect as an equitable interest; Law of Property Act 1925, s. 1 (3).

EQUITABLE LIEN. [LIEN.]

EQUITABLE MORTGAGE. A mortgage originally recognised in a court of equity only. An equitable mortgage may be effected either by a written instrument or by a deposit of title deeds with or without writing. The right to effect such an equitable mortgage is preserved by the Law of Property Act 1925. (See ss. 2 (3), 13.)

EQUITABLE WASTE. An unconscientious or unreasonable use of settled

EQUITABLE WASTE—*continued.*

property, as by a tenant for life pulling down a mansion-house, or felling timber standing for ornament, or doing other permanent injury to the inheritance. This kind of waste is forbidden, even to a tenant for life who holds *without impeachment of waste.*

S. 135 of the Law of Property Act 1925 provides that an equitable interest for life without impeachment of waste does not confer upon the tenant for life any right to commit equitable waste, unless an intention to confer such a right appears in the instrument creating the equitable interest.

EQUITY is described by *Cowel* as being of two sorts, and these of contrary effects; for the one abridges and takes from the letter of the law, the other enlarges and adds thereto. And the instance of the first kind he gives is that of a person acquitted of a capital crime on the ground of insanity or infancy. The instance he gives of the latter is that of the application of a statute to *administrators*, which in its terms applies to *executors* only.

Equity, in the sense in which it is distinguished from the common law, consisted originally in a body of rules and procedure which grew up separately from the common law and which were administered in different courts. The common law courts might provide no remedy for a plaintiff, and it became customary for suitors to apply to the Chancellor, who as "keeper of the King's conscience" would give equitable relief. From the time of Edward II, or earlier, the Chancellor and his officials, later the Court of Chancery, issued writs and exercised jurisdiction which did not, however, override the common law, but which was intended to remedy its imperfections.

The Court of Chancery has now become the Chancery Division of the High Court, and for convenience certain matters of equitable jurisdiction are still assigned to it; but by s. 36 of the Judicature Act 1925 both law and equity are to be administered in all divisions of the High Court and in the Court of Appeal. But where there is any conflict between the rules of common law and the rules of equity, the latter are to prevail.

A few of the "maxims" of equity may be briefly stated, as follows:—

(1) "Equity acts *in personam*," *i.e.*, against a specific person rather than against property, and so compels performance of contracts, trusts, etc.

(2) "Equity follows the law," that is, does not depart *unnecessarily* from common law principles.

(3) "Equity delights in equality," *i.e.*, attempts to adjudicate fairly or equally between the parties.

(4) "He who seeks equity must do equity," or a plaintiff must himself be prepared to see justice done. Similarly

(5) "He who comes into equity must come with clean hands," and not have been guilty of improper conduct in regard to the subject matter of litigation.

EQUITY OF A STATUTE. The sound interpretation of a statute, the words of which may be too general, too special, or otherwise inaccurate and defective.

EQUITY OF REDEMPTION. The right which a mortgagor has, on payment of the mortgage debt, with interest and costs, to *redeem* the mortgaged estate, even after the right of redemption is gone at law.

EQUITY TO A SETTLEMENT was the right which a wife had in equity to have a portion of her equitable property settled upon herself and her children. This right was originally granted to the wife when the husband sued in a court of equity for the purpose of reducing the property into his possession, on the principle that he who seeks equity must do equity.

Since the Married Women's Property Act 1882 all a wife's property, both real and personal, vests in her as her separate estate and by the Law Reform (Married Women and Tortfeasors) Act 1935 a married woman is put in the same position with regard to her property as an unmarried woman.

ERRANT (Lat. *Itinerans, journeying*) is a word attributed to justices that go on circuit, and to bailiffs travelling from place to place to execute process.

ERROR signifies especially an error in pleading, or in the process; and the writ formerly brought for remedy of this oversight was called a writ of error, or, in Latin, *breve de errore corrigendo* (a writ for correcting an error).

Proceedings in error in civil cases were abolished by the Judicature Act 1875, and in criminal cases by the Criminal Appeal Act 1907.

ERRORS EXCEPTED. A phrase appended to an account stated, to excuse slight mistakes or oversights. Sometimes "Errors and omissions excepted."—E.O.E.

ESCAPE. At common law, every person is guilty of an escape who (1) being a prisoner, *without force*, escapes from custody or prison; (2) being an officer, intentionally or negligently allows a prisoner to escape from his custody; or (3) being a private person, and having a person in his lawful custody, permits him to escape. A prisoner escaping *by force* is guilty of breach of prison.

By s. 39 of the Prison Act 1952 it is a felony to aid any prisoner in escaping or attempting to escape from a prison.

ESCAPE-WARRANT. A warrant addressed to all sheriffs, etc., throughout England, to re-take an escaped prisoner and to commit him to gaol when taken.

ESCHEAT. An obstruction of the course of descent, by which land naturally resulted back by a kind of a reversion to the original grantor or lord of the fee.

Escheats were divided by Blackstone into escheats *propter defectum sanguinis*, and escheats *propter delictum tenentis*; the one sort, if a tenant died without heirs; and the other, if his blood were attainted. This latter form differed from a forfeiture of goods and chattels in that a forfeiture always went to the Crown, but an escheat to the immediate lord (who might or might not be the king).

Escheat was abolished by s. 45 of the Administration of Estates Act 1925.

ESCHEATOR. An officer, formerly existing in every county, appointed by the Lord Treasurer to hold inquests with a view to enforcing right of escheat, etc. [ESCHEAT.]

ESCROW (Lat. *Scriptum*). A scroll or writing sealed and delivered to a person not a party thereto, to be held by him till some condition or conditions be performed by the party intended to be benefited thereby; and, on the fulfilment of those conditions, to be delivered to such party, and to take effect as a deed to all intents and purposes.

ESCUAGE (Lat. *Scutagium*) in law signified a kind of knight's-service, called *service of the shield*, whereby the tenant was bound to follow his lord into the Scotch or Welsh wars at his own charge. But the above form of *escuage*, which was *uncertain* in its burdens, was changed in process of time into an *escuage certain*, whereby a yearly rent was paid in lieu of all services; which latter was *escuage* merely in name. Knight's-service, with other military tenures, was abolished by the Tenures Abolition Act 1660. [KNIGHT-SERVICE.]

ESKIMO (*Canada*.) A member of the race of aboriginal people who live along the shores of the Arctic ocean. Their own name for themselves is Inuit, which is now coming into more general use.

ESQUIRE, or **ESQUIER** (Lat. *Armiger*; Fr. *Escuier*, a word derived from the Latin *Scutiger*, shield-bearer), was originally one who attended a knight in time of war, and carried his shield.

There are several sorts of esquires:—

1. The eldest sons of knights, and their eldest sons.

2. The younger sons of peers, and their eldest sons.

3. Esquires created by the king's letters patent, or other investiture, and their eldest sons.

4. Esquires by virtue of their offices; as justices of the peace, and others who bear any office of trust under the Crown, and are named "esquires" by the Crown in their commission or appointment.

5. Esquires of Knights of the bath, each of whom constitutes three at his installation.

6. Foreign peers.

7. The chiefs of ancient families are so by prescription.

ESSENCE OF A CONTRACT. In contracts certain stipulations, *e.g.*, as to time, are sometimes stated to be *of the essence of the contract*. This means that such stipulations must under all circumstances be strictly complied with.

ESTATE. An interest in land.

Prior to 1926 estates might be variously classified:—

I. According to the *quantity* of interest. The primary division of estates was into such as were *freehold* and such as were *not freehold*.

ESTATE—*continued*.

The principal freehold estates were:—

1. Estates in fee simple.
2. Estates in fee tail, otherwise called estates tail.
3. Estates for life.

An *estate in fee simple* was, and still is, an absolute and unqualified estate of inheritance. It is the most extensive estate of inheritance that a man can possess; it is the entire property in the land, and to it is attached the right of alienation to the full extent of the interest which is vested in the tenant himself, or for any smaller estate. At common law, in order to create such an estate it was essential that the word "heirs" should be used; *e.g.*, "To A and his heirs". Now, however, no words of limitation are necessary: Law of Property Act 1925, s. 60.

An *estate in fee tail* was that which a man had to hold to him and the heirs of his body, or to him and particular heirs of his body. By the statute *De Donis conditionalibus*, passed in 1285, an estate so limited devolved, at the death of the donee, on his issue; and, on the failure of issue, reverted to the donor and his heirs. In the construction of this statute the judges held that the donee had an estate which they called a *fee tail*. This estate thus assumed the form of a perpetual entail until the reign of Edward IV, when, in a celebrated case called *Taltarum's case*, it was held by the judges that an estate tail might be *barred* by the collusive and fictitious proceeding called a *common recovery* [RECOVERY], and thus turned into an estate in fee simple. And, in the reign of Henry VIII, the process called a *fine* was made effectual to enable a tenant in tail to bar his issue, but not the remainderman or reversioner. [FINE, 1.] Fines and recoveries were abolished by the Fines and Recoveries Act 1833, under which Act an estate tail might in general be barred by a simple disentailing deed to be enrolled in Chancery within six months, in cases where it could, previously to the Act, have been barred by fine or recovery.

But estates tail of which the reversion was in the Crown could not be barred so far as regarded the reversion; and estates tail created by Act of Parliament could not in general be barred. So, a tenant in tail after possibility of issue extinct could not bar his estate.

An estate tail can now only take effect as an equitable interest, called an entailed interest, which can be created in any property, real or personal: Law of Property Act 1925, s. 130. The necessity for enrolment of a disentailing deed is abolished by *ibid.*, s. 133.

An *estate for life* was in general an estate to one for his own life. But an estate during widowhood was also reckoned among estates for life.

In addition to these three kinds of estate were the following kinds, which were less than freehold:—

4. An estate for years.
5. An estate at will.
6. An estate at sufferance.

An *estate for years* was, and is, often spoken of as "a term of years." The instrument by which it is created is called a *lease* or *demise*, and the estate itself is called a *leasehold interest*. It is generally made subject to covenants and conditions.

An *estate at will* was where lands and tenements were let by one man to another to have and to hold at the will of the lessor, and the tenant by force of this lease obtained possession. Such an estate might also arise by implication of law.

An *estate at sufferance* was where one came into possession under a lawful demise, and, after such demise was ended, wrongfully continued the possession.

Besides these several divisions of estates there was another species, called an *estate upon condition*; which was an estate whose existence depended upon the happening or not happening of some event. Under these were included:—

7. Estates held upon condition *implied*.
8. Estates held upon condition *expressed*.

Under these last might have been included:—

9. Estates held in mortgage. [MORTGAGE.]
10. Estates by statute merchant or statute staple. [STATUTE, 2.]
11. Estates held by elegit. [ELEGIT.]

II. Estates might also have been divided with regard to the *time* at which the quantity of interest was to be enjoyed. Thus, an estate might be:—

1. An estate in possession.
2. An estate in expectancy.

An estate in *possession* implied a right of present possession, involving a right of entry; that is, the right of entering upon and taking possession of the land withheld, where that could be done without breach of the peace. [POSSESSION.]

An estate in *expectancy* was of two kinds—an estate in *reversion* and an estate in *remainder*; the distinction between the two being as follows:—

1. When a person granted an estate for life, or other estate of limited interest to another, such estate was called a *particular estate*; and the residue remaining in the grantor was called his *reversion*.

2. When a person granted an estate for life, or other *particular estate* to one man, and the residue to another, the interest of the latter was called a *remainder*, though it was often popularly spoken of as a *reversion*.

III. Estates might further be divided, with respect to the number and connection of their owners, into:—

1. Estates in severalty. [SEVERALTY.]
2. Estates in joint-tenancy. [JOINT-TENANCY.]
3. Estates in coparcenary. [COPARCENARY.]
4. Estates in common. [COMMON, TENANCY IN.]

The whole law as to the different kinds of estate was altered by the Law of Property Act 1925, by s. 1 of which, as from 1st January, 1926, the only estates in land which are capable of subsisting or of being conveyed or created at law are:—

(*a*) An estate in fee simple absolute in possession;

(*b*) A term of years absolute.

Similarly, the only interests or charges in or over land which are capable of subsisting or being conveyed or created at law are:—

(*a*) An easement, right or privilege in or over land for an interest equivalent to an estate in fee simple absolute in possession or a term of years absolute;

(*b*) A rentcharge in possession issuing out of or charged on land being either perpetual or for a term of years absolute;

(*c*) A charge by way of legal mortgage;

(*d*) Land tax and any other similar charge on land which is not created by an instrument;

(*e*) Right of entry exercisable over or in respect of a legal term of years absolute, or annexed, for any purpose, to a legal rent charge.

All other estates, interests, and charges in or over land take effect only as equitable interests.

ESTATE AGENT. A person who, by way of profession or trade, provides services for the purpose of finding premises for persons seeking to acquire them or assisting in the disposal of premises. So defined in, perhaps rather unexpectedly, the Sex Discrimination Act 1975.

ESTATE CLAUSE. An *express* clause formerly added in conveyances to the description of the parcels, passing all the estate, etc., of the grantor in the property conveyed. No such clause is now necessary, the conveyance itself being effectual to pass the estate without it. See s. 63 of the Law of Property Act 1925.

ESTATE CONTRACT. A contract by an estate owner to convey or create a legal estate, *e.g.*, contract for sale of a legal estate. See the Land Charges Act 1972.

ESTATE DUTY. A duty formerly levied upon the principal value of all property, real or personal, settled or not settled, which passed or was deemed to pass on death. The rate of duty was graduated according to the total value of the estate. The duty was abolished in respect of deaths occurring after 12th March 1975, being replaced by capital transfer tax under the provisions of the Finance Act 1975.

ESTATE OWNER. The owner of a legal estate as defined by ss. 1 (4) and 205 (1) (v) of the Law of Property Act 1925. An infant cannot be an estate owner. [ESTATE.]

ESTATES OF THE REALM are, according to *Blackstone* and *Hallam*:—

1. The lords spiritual.
2. The lords temporal—who sit together with the lords spiritual in one House of parliament.
3. The commons—who sit by themselves in the other.

Some writers, however, have argued, from the want of a separate assembly and separate negative of the prelates, that the lords spiritual and temporal are now in reality only one estate; which is unquestionably true in every effectual sense, though the ancient distinction between them still nominally continues.

ESTOP, TO. [ESTOPPEL.]

ESTOPPEL. The law in some cases estops or prevents a person from alleging certain facts, which then cannot be proved by him. "An estoppel," says *Blackstone*, "happens where a man hath done some act or executed some deed which estops or precludes him from averring anything to the contrary."

Estoppels may conveniently be divided into four kinds:—

1. Estoppel by Record. The rule that a person may not deny the fact of a judgment of a court which has previously been decided against him, appears to be based on two maxims—*Interest reipublicae ut sit finis litium* and *Nemo debet bis vexari pro eadem causa*. It applies generally to judgments of all civil and criminal Courts.

2. Estoppel by Deed. The rule that a party to a deed is not permitted to deny facts stated therein affords an illustration of the importance of a seal in English law. There is no such estoppel in the case of ordinary signed documents, unless it comes within the definition of estoppel by conduct.

3. Estoppel by Conduct. A person who, by his words or conduct, wilfully causes another person to believe in the existence of a certain state of things, and induces him to act on that belief, so as to alter his position for the worse, is estopped from setting up against the latter person a different state of things as existing at the time in question.

4. Estoppel *in pais*. A tenant of land is estopped from disputing the title of the landlord by whom he was let into possession, or whom he has acknowledged by payment of rent.

ESTOVERS. Common of estovers, that is necessaries, is a liberty of taking necessary wood for the use or furniture of a house or farm, from off another's estate. This right is generally appurtenant to a house, though of course it may be attached to land for the purpose of repairing fences. Tenants for life and tenants for years are entitled to take estovers from the land. This right is limited by immediate necessity: a tenant cannot cut or store wood with a view to future requirements.

ESTRAYS are such valuable animals as are found wandering in any manor or lordship, and no man knows the owner of them, in which case the law gives them to the king as the general owner and lord paramount of the soil.

ESTREAT (Lat. *Extractum*). 1. A true copy, or duplicate, of an original writing. 2. The *estreat of a recognizance* means the *extracting*, or taking out from among the other records, of a recognizance or obligation which has become forfeited, and sending it to be enforced; or, in some cases, directing it to be levied by the sheriff, and returned by the clerk of the peace to the Lords of the Treasury. No recognizance removed into the Queen's Bench Division may be estreated without the order of a judge. If it appears to the judge that default has been made in performing the conditions of the recognizance he may order it to be estreated.

ESTREPE (Fr. *Estropier*, to maim). To commit waste.

ESTUARY. The tidal part of a river.

ET SEQ. *Et sequentes*: "and those which follow."

EURATOM. [EUROPEAN ATOMIC ENERGY COMMUNITY.]

EUROPEAN ATOMIC ENERGY COMMUNITY. An association of European states for the pooling of atomic knowledge and resources, established on 25th March 1957, and of which the United Kingdom became a member on 1st January 1973. Referred to as "Euratom": see the European Communities Act 1972, Sch. 1.

EUROPEAN COAL AND STEEL COMMUNITY. An association of European states for pooling resources of iron, coal and steel. It was established by the Treaty of Paris on 18th April 1951, and the United Kingdom became a member on 1st January 1973. Its principal functions are to supervise the formation of prices, to control investment, and to eliminate intra-zone tariffs. The Treaty provides for free and equal access of all users to the sources of production; antitrust legislation and control of monopolies; and the financing of technical research.

EUROPEAN COURT. The Court of Justice of the European Communities. Each of the European Treaties is accompanied by a protocol supplying the basic structure for the court and its daily operation. The decisions of the court are published in each of the official languages of the

Community and the most important of them are published monthly in the Common Market Law Reports.

EUROPEAN ECONOMIC COMMUNITY. This association of European states, often referred to as "the Common Market," was established by the Treaty of Rome on 25th March 1957. Following the successful customs union of the Benelux countries (Belgium, Holland and Luxembourg) immediately following the war, the Treaty of Rome admitted France, Germany and Italy to membership with those countries. The United Kingdom became a member on 1st January 1973.

The purpose is economic, with the aim of creating one big market area. The prime means of achieving this are the abolition of customs barriers and quantitative restrictions, the free movement and establishment of members of the Community, and the provision of services to facilitate trade. There is a common agricultural policy, cartels and monopolies are controlled, and there is co-ordination of policies in the spheres of commerce and finance. An eventual aim is to establish a common currency.

EVICTION. Dispossession; also a recovery of land by form of law.

EVIDENCE. That which, in a court of justice, makes clear, or ascertains the truth of, the very fact or point in issue, either on the one side or on the other.

Any matter, lawfully deposed to on oath or affirmation, which contributes (however slightly) to the elucidation of any question at issue in a court of justice, is said to be *evidence*.

Evidence is either *written* or *parol*; *written evidence* consists of records, deeds, affidavits, or other writings: *parol* or *oral evidence* consists of witnesses personally appearing in court, and in general sworn to the truth of what they depose. Evidence may also be primary, *i.e.*, best evidence, or secondary; direct, circumstantial, or hearsay; real or extrinsic. [CIRCUMSTANTIAL EVIDENCE; DIRECT EVIDENCE; HEARSAY EVIDENCE.]

The Evidence Act 1938 provides that in any court proceedings where direct oral evidence of a fact would be admissible, any statement made by a person in a document and tending to establish that fact shall, on production of the original document, be admissible as evidence of that fact, if the maker of the statement either (*a*) had personal knowledge of the matters dealt with by the statement; or (*b*) where the document is, or forms part of, a continuous record made by anyone whose duty it was to record information supplied to him by a person who had personal knowledge of the matters recorded. The document must be identifiable by handwriting, initials or signature. The maker of the statement must be called as a witness in the proceedings, but if he is dead, or unfit, or overseas, and if it is not reasonably practicable to secure his attendance, this condition need not be satisfied. To save undue delay or expense, the court may in any civil proceedings admit such a statement in evidence even though (*a*) the maker is available but is not called as a witness or (*b*) the original document is not produced.

See also the Civil Evidence Acts of 1968 and 1972.

EX ABUNDANTI CAUTELA. From excessive caution.

EX CATHEDRA. With the weight of one in authority; originally applied to the decisions of the Popes from their *cathedra* or chair.

EX CONTRACTU. Actions *ex contractu* are actions arising out of breaches of contract, expressed or implied.

EX DEBITO JUSTITIÆ. As a matter of right; in opposition to a matter for the favour or discretion of the court. Thus the improper rejection of evidence in an action is ground for a new trial as a matter of right, or *ex debito justitiæ*.

EX DELICTO, or **EX MALEFICIO.** Actions *ex delicto*, or *ex maleficio*, are actions founded on some wrong other than a breach of contract, express or implied.

EX DOLO MALO NON ORITUR ACTIO. No right of action arises out of a fraud.

EX FACTO JUS ORITUR. The law arises out of the fact.

EX GRATIA. As a matter of favour.

EX MERO MOTU. Words formerly used in the king's charters and letters patent, to signify that he granted them on his own mere motion, without petition or suggestion from any other. [EX PROPRIO MOTU.]

EX NUDO PACTO NON ORITUR ACTIO. No action arises from a bare pact, *i.e.*, one made without consideration. This applies to simple contracts, not to specialty, which are dependent upon sealing and delivery.

EX OFFICIO. By virtue of an office. Any prerogative or jurisdiction which a person in office has, by virtue of that office, he is said to exercise *ex officio*.

EX OFFICIO INFORMATION. 1. A criminal information filed by the Attorney-General *ex officio* on behalf of the Crown in the Queen's Bench Division. This kind of information was specifically saved by s. 12 of the Administration of Justice (Miscellaneous Provisions) Act 1938, under which other criminal informations were abolished.

2. The expression is also applied, though not very frequently, to information filed by the Attorney-General in the Chancery Division to have a charity properly established. [INFORMATION.]

EX PACTO ILLICITO NON ORITUR ACTIO. No action arises on an illegal agreement.

EX PARTE. 1. Of the one part, one-sided. Thus, an *ex parte* statement is a statement of one side only. So, an injunction granted *ex parte* is an injunction granted after hearing one side only.

2. The phrase "*ex parte*" preceding a name in the heading of a reported case indicates that the party whose name follows is the party on whose application the case is heard.

EX POST FACTO signifies something done so as to affect another thing that was committed before. An *ex post facto* law is one having a retrospective application.

EX PROPRIO MOTU. Of his own mere motion, spontaneously; as when a judge, without application from any party, orders a witness to be prosecuted for perjury, or commits him for trial. [EX MERO MOTU.]

EX TURPI CAUSA NON ORITUR ACTIO (no right of action arises from a base cause), *e.g.*, on a contract founded on an immoral consideration.

EXACTION. A wrong done by an officer, or one pretending to have authority, in taking a reward or fee for that with the law does not allow. [EXTORTION.]

EXAMINATION. 1. The interrogation of witnesses. The *examination-in-chief* of a witness is the interrogation of a witness, in the first instance, by the counsel of the party producing him. His examination by the opposing counsel is called his *cross-examination*; and his further examination by his own side, on points arising out of the cross-examination, is called his *re-examination*.

2. The examination of a bankrupt is the interrogation of a bankrupt, by a court having jurisdiction in bankruptcy, as to the state of his property.

3. The examination of a prisoner is the inquiry into the charge made against him by a police magistrate or justice of the peace, preparatory to his being committed for trial, in case there should appear to be a *prima facie* case against him.

EXAMINERS OF THE COURT. Barristers of not less than three years' standing appointed by the Lord Chancellor to examine witnesses out of court. See R.S.C. 1965, Ord. 39.

EXAMINING JUSTICES. [EXAMINATION, 3.]

EXCEPTION signifies:—

1. An objection. Thus, for instance, an exception to a defendant's answer in Chancery was an objection taken to it for some cause allowed by the practice of the court, as insufficiency, or scandal and impertinence.

2. A saving clause in a deed, preventing certain things passing which would otherwise pass thereby.

3. In the Roman law, and in the Scotch law, the word means a defence.

EXCEPTIONS, BILL OF. [BILL OF EXCEPTIONS.]

EXCERPTA or **EXCERPTS.** Extracts.

EXCHANGE. 1. The place appointed for the exchange of bullion, gold, silver, plate, etc., with the Queen's coin.

2. An exchange of land is a mutual grant of equal interest in lands or tenements, the one in consideration of the other.

EXCHANGE, BILL OF. [BILL OF EXCHANGE.]

EXCHEQUER. The department of state having the management of the royal revenue. It consisted formerly of two divisions, the first being the office of the receipt of the Exchequer, for collection of the royal revenue; the second being a court for the administration of justice. [CHANCELLOR; COURT OF EXCHEQUER.]

EXCHEQUER BILLS AND BONDS. Bills of credit issued by the Exchequer, under the authority, for the most part, of Acts of Parliament passed for the purpose; and containing an engagement, on the part of the Government, for the repayment of the principal sums advanced, with interest in the meantime.

EXCHEQUER CHAMBER. [COURT OF EXCHEQUER CHAMBER.]

EXCISE was a name formerly confined to the imposition upon beer, ale, cider, and other commodities manufactured within the realm, being charged sometimes upon the consumption of the commodity, but more frequently upon the retail sale of it.

Under recent Acts of Parliament, however, many other imposts have been classed under excise. Such is the case with regard to the licence which must be taken out by every one who keeps a dog, uses a gun, or deals in game. See particularly the Customs and Excise Act 1952.

EXCLUSAGIUM. A payment due to the lord for the benefit of a sluice.

EXCOMMUNICATION, or **EX-COMMENGEMENT.** A spiritual censure for offences falling under ecclesiastical cognizance. It is described in the books as twofold: (1) The *lesser* excommunication, which is an ecclesiastical censure, excluding the party from the sacraments. (2) The *greater*, which excluded him from the company of all Chrisians, and rendered him incapable of any legal act.

EXCUSABLE HOMICIDE is of two sorts:—

1. Where one kills another *per infortunium, i.e.,* by misadventure, in doing a lawful act; or

2. *Se defendendo,* in defending one's self upon a sudden affray or chance-medley. [*q.v.*]

EXEAT. Leave to depart. [NE EXEAT REGNO.]

EXECUTE. [EXECUTION.]

EXECUTED and **EXECUTORY.** These words are used in law in a sense very nearly equivalent to *past* (or *present*) and *future* respectively. Thus,

1. A contract may be either *executed,* as if A and B agree to exchange horses, and they do it immediately; here the possession and the right are transferred together; or *executory,* as if they agree to exchange next week; here the *right* only vests, and their reciprocal *property* in each other's horse is not in *possession* but in *action;* for a contract executed, which differs nothing from a grant, conveys a *chose in possession;* a contract executory conveys only a *chose in action.* [CHOSE.]

2. So, a *consideration* for a promise may be *executed* or *executory,* according as the consideration precedes the promise or not; and its character in this respect is determined by the relation which it bears in point of time to the promise, as being prior or subsequent. [CONSIDERATION.]

3. A *use* was also executed or executory. Thus, on a conveyance to A to the use of B, the use in B was said to be *executed* by the Statute of Uses. But a use in land, limited *in futuro,* on a condition independent of any preceding estate or interest in the land, was an *executory* use, because it was not *executed* by the Statute of Uses till the fulfilment of the condition on which it was to take effect. Such a use was also called a *springing* use. [EXECUTORY INTEREST; SPRINGING USE; USE.]

4. So, a *devise (i.e.,* a disposition of land by will), by which a future estate is allowed to be limited contrary to the rules of the old common law, is called an *executory devise.* [EXECUTORY INTEREST.]

5. Also, an estate in possession, whereby a present interest passes to the tenant, is sometimes called an *executed* estate, as opposed to the *executory* class of estates depending on some *subsequent* circumstances or contingency.

6. A trust may also be *executed* or *executory.* An *executed* trust is one where the trust estate is completely defined in the first instance, no future instrument of conveyance being contemplated. An *executory* trust is a trust where the party whose benefit is designed is to take through the medium of a future instrument of conveyance to be executed for the purpose. The importance of the distinction lies in this, that an *executed* trust is construed strictly according to the technical meaning of the terms used; an *executory* trust is construed according to the apparent meaning of the

EXECUTED and EXECUTORY
—continued.

author of the trust, as gathered from the instrument by which it is created.

This is one of the most technical and difficult distinctions in English law. It might at first be supposed that an executed trust was a trust fully administered by the final distribution, on the part of the trustee, of the trust property among the parties entitled thereto; and that an executory trust was a trust not yet fully administered. As Lord St. Leonards said in the case of the *Earl of Egerton* v. *Brownlow* (4 House of Lords Cases, 210): "All trusts are in a sense executory, because a trust cannot be executed except by conveyance, and therefore there is always something to be done. *But that is not the sense which a court of equity puts upon the term executory trust*." And his lordship went on to distinguish the two in this way:—An *executory* trust is where the author of the trust has left it to the court to make out from *general expressions* what his intention is. An executed trust is where "you have nothing to do but to take the limitations he has given you, and convert them into legal estates." Or, perhaps, we may express it in this way:—An *executory* trust is one of which the author indicates, either by the vagueness and generality of the words he has used, or by his intention expressed in the instrument creating the trust, that some further conveyance should be executed for expressing the trusts in proper legal form. Whereas, an *executed* trust is a trust itself expressed in proper legal form. An executory trust thus bears to an executed trust the same relation which the heads of a settlement bear to the settlement itself. This use of the term "executed" may, perhaps, be illustrated by such expressions as "the execution of a will," "execution of a deed."

EXECUTION. 1. The putting in force the sentence of the law in a judicial proceeding. It is styled *final process*, and is regulated by R.S.C. 1965, Ord. 46. [For the various writs of execution, see under their several titles.]

2. The signing of a deed or will, or other written instrument, in such manner as to make it (so far as regards form) legally valid. See ss. 73, 74 of the Law of Property Act 1925.

3. The carrying out of a trust.

4. The carrying out of the sentence of death, as formerly regulated by the Capital Punishment Amendment Act 1868 and the Homicide Act 1957.

EXECUTIVE. That branch of government which is entrusted with carrying the laws into effect. The supreme executive power in this kingdom is vested in the king or queen for the time being who by convention acts on ministerial advice.

EXECUTOR. One to whom another, by his last will and testament, commits the execution of the directions and dispositions thereof. His duties are:—

1. To bury the deceased in a manner suitable to the estate which he leaves behind him.

2. To prove the will of the deceased.

3. To make an inventory of the goods and chattels of the deceased, and to collect the goods so inventoried; and for this purpose, if necessary, to take proceedings against debtors to his testator's estate.

4. To pay, *first*, the debts of his testator, and *then* the legacies bequeathed by his will; and to distribute the residue, in default of any residuary disposition, among the persons entitled thereto on an intestacy.

An executor is the legal personal representative of his testator, and the testator's rights and liabilities devolve for the most part upon him. A person appointed executor is not on that account bound to accept the office. See, generally, the Administration of Estates Act 1925 and the Judicature Act 1925, Part VI.

EXECUTOR DE SON TORT. One who, without any just authority, intermeddles with the goods of a deceased person, as if he had been duly appointed executor. An *executor de son tort* is liable to the trouble of an executorship without its advantages. He cannot bring an action himself in right of the deceased, but actions may be brought against him. See ss. 28, 29 of the Administration of Estates Act 1925.

EXECUTORY INTEREST. In one sense any future estate in land is an executory estate or interest. [EXECUTED and EXECUTORY.] But the term "executory interest" is especially applied to such an interest in real estate as is "limited" to commence at a future time, upon some contingency not depending on the determination of a prior estate. As, if land be limited by deed to A and his heirs in trust for B and his heirs until C shall return from Rome, and then in trust for D and his heirs, D's interest is called an *executory interest*. Before 1925, such interests could be created as springing or shifting uses. After 1925 such an interest will only subsist as an equitable interest. See Part I of the Law of Property Act 1925. [EXECUTED and EXECUTORY, 3, 4, 5.]

EXECUTRIX. Feminine of executor.

EXEMPLARY DAMAGES. Damages on an unsparing scale, given mainly in respect of tortious acts, committed through malice or other circumstances of aggravation.

EXEMPLI GRATIA (abbrv. *ex. gr.* or *e.g.*). For the sake of example.

EXEMPLIFICATION. 1. A copy.

2. A certified transcript under the seal of a court.

EXEQUATUR. A rescript or order given by the foreign department of a state to which a consul is accredited, authorising the functionaries of the home department to recognise the official character of the consul. [CONSUL.] It may be revoked at any time at the discretion of the government wherein he is established.

EXHIBIT. A document or other thing shown to a witness while giving evidence and sworn by him.

Usually applied to a document referred to in an affidavit and shown to the deponent when being sworn. The exhibit is marked by the commissioner or other person before whom it is sworn.

EXHIBITION, in the law of Scotland, signifies the production of deeds; and an *action of exhibition* is an action for compelling production of the same.

EXITUS. 1. Issue, child or children, offspring.

2. The rents or profits of land.

3. The conclusion of the pleadings.

EXONERATION generally signifies relieving part of the estate of a deceased person, charged with a debt, by the payment of the debt out of another part thereof. This may be by law, or by the special direction of the deceased in his will.

EXPATRIATION. The forsaking one's own country and renouncing allegiance, with the intention of becoming a permanent resident and citizen in another country. See s. 19 of the British Nationality Act 1948, under which, upon registration of renunciation of citizenship, a person ceases to be a citizen of the United Kingdom and Colonies.

EXPECTANCY, ESTATES IN, are interests in land which are limited or appointed to take effect in possession at some future time. [ESTATE.]

EXPECTANT HEIR. One who has a prospect of coming into property on the death of another person.

Such persons have always been peculiarly under the protection of courts of equity, who have relieved them from unconscionable bargains. See s. 174 of the Law of Property Act 1925, which provides that no acquisition made in good faith, without fraud or unfair dealing, of any reversionary interest in real or personal property (including an "expectancy") for money or money's worth, shall be liable to be opened or set aside merely on the ground of under-value. [CATCHING BARGAIN.]

EXPECTATION OF LIFE. In matters of life insurance, and the granting of annuities, this expression is used to signify the length of time that any specified person may expect, according to the table of averages, to live.

EXPEDIMENT. The whole of a person's goods and chattels.

EXPERT. A skilled witness called to give evidence on the art or mystery with which he is specially conversant. As to the rules of court relating to, and the admissibility of, expert opinion, see ss. 2, 3 of the Civil Evidence Act 1972. [SKILLED WITNESS.]

EXPILATION. Robbery.

EXPIRING LAWS CONTINUANCE ACT. An Act passed each year for the purpose of continuing—usually for one full year more—temporary Acts which would otherwise expire.

EXPLOSIVES. Defined by the Explosives Act 1875 as including gunpowder, nitro-glycerine, dynamite, gun cotton, blasting powders, fulminate of mercury or of other metals, coloured powders, etc., also including fog-signals, fireworks, cartridges and ammunition. By the Theft Act 1968, s.

EXPLOSIVES—*continued*.

10, it means any article manufactured for the purpose of producing a practical effect by explosion.

The Criminal Jurisdiction Act 1975 amends the Explosive Substances Act 1883 so as to make it an offence under United Kingdom law to cause an explosion likely to endanger life or to cause serious injury to property in the Republic of Ireland or in the United Kingdom.

EXPLEES (*Expletiae*). Rents or profits of land, otherwise called *esplees*.

EXPORT GUARANTEES. Guarantees given by the Secretary of State for Trade and Industry to persons carrying on business in the United Kingdom in connection with the export, manufacture, etc. of goods. There is an Export Guarantees Advisory Council. See the Export Guarantees Act 1975.

EXPOSING. A term used for various purposes:—

1. Exposing food for sale: an offence under the Food and Drugs Act 1955, if it contains substances injurious to health or is unfit for human consumption.

2. Exposing a child: an offence under s. 27 of the Offences Against the Person Act 1861, and under s. 1 of the Children and Young Persons Act 1933.

3. Exposing the person. [INDECENT EXPOSURE.]

EXPRESS. That which is not left to implication: as express promise or covenant.

EXPRESS COLOUR. [COLOUR.]

EXPRESS CONTRACT OR CONVENTION. A contract or convention expressed in words, or by signs which custom or usage has made equivalent to words.

EXPRESS TRUST. A trust which is clearly expressed by the authors thereof, or may fairly be collected from a written document.

EXPRESSIO UNIUS EST EXCLUSIO ALTERIUS. The mention of one is the exclusion of another.

EXPRESSUM FACIT CESSARE TACITUM (what is expressed makes what is implied to cease). *E.g.*, an express covenant in a lease destroys that which would otherwise be implied by the use of the word "demise".

EXPROMISSOR. A surety—Roman law.

EXPROPRIATION. The surrender of a claim to exclusive property.

(*Canada*.) The compulsory taking of land by a public authority, with compensation to be fixed by a board or court.

EXTEND. To value the lands or tenements of a judgment debtor, or one whose recognizance was forfeited, so that by the yearly rent the creditor might in time be paid his debt. [EXTENT.]

EXTENDI FACIAS was a writ formerly called a writ of extent. [EXTENT.]

EXTENT. A writ or commission to the sheriff for the *valuing* of lands and tenements and goods and chattels of a judgment-debtor.

Extents were of several kinds, as follows:—

1. A process of execution under the laws relating to statute staple and statutes merchant, by which the lands and goods of a person whose recognizance had been forfeited, or whose debt had been acknowledged on statute staple or statute merchant, might be appraised and delivered to the creditor.

2. An *extent in chief*, a writ issuing out of the Court of Exchequer, for the recovery of debts of record due to the Crown; by which the sheriff was directed to cause the lands, goods and chattels of the debtor to be appraised at their full value, and to be seised into the hands of the sovereign.

3. An *extent in aid*, issued at the suit or instance of a *Crown debtor* against a person indebted to the Crown debtor himself.

4. A special writ of extent directing the sheriff to seize the lands and goods of a *deceased* Crown debtor. This writ was called *diem clausit extremum*.

These proceedings were abolished by the Crown Proceedings Act 1947.

EXTERRITORIALITY. A term used in international law to denote the condition of persons who are considered to be outside the territory of the State in which they reside and so are not amenable to its laws. An example is that of an ambassador and the persons belonging to his suite, whose residence is exterritorial and protected by diplomatic privilege.

EXTINGUISHMENT signifies an effect of consolidation. Thus, if a man purchases lands out of which he has a rent, then the property and the rent are consolidated, and the rent is said to be extinguished. So, if a lessee or tenant for life purchases the reversion, his estate for years or life may be *extinguished*, being merged in the reversion unless there is a contrary intention; Law of Property Act 1925, s. 185. So, an extinguishment of copyhold was effected by enfranchisement. Similarly an extinguishment of right of way is effected by the purchase, on the part of the owner of the right of way, of the land wherein the way lies.

Also, a parol contract is said to be *extinguished* by a contract *under seal* between the same parties to the same effect.

EXTORTION. An unlawful or violent wringing of money or money's worth from any man. The word is used especially as follows:—

1. In reference to demanding money or other property by threats, and menaces of various kinds. [BLACKMAIL.]

2. In reference to the unlawful taking by an officer, under colour of his office, of money not due to him, or more than was due. This offence was abolished by s. 32 of the Theft Act 1968.

EXTRA COSTS. [AFFIDAVIT OF INCREASE.]

EXTRA VIRES. [ULTRA VIRES.]

EXTRADITION. The surrender of a person by one state to another. The word is generally applied to the surrender of a person charged with an offence to the state having jurisdiction to try that offence. The law of England with regard to extradition depends entirely upon statute. There is no doubt of the right of the executive power to remove from the country, upon such grounds as may seem to it sufficient, any persons who are subjects of another state. This right is exercised in Great Britain by proceedings which are authorised and regulated by the Extradition Acts 1870 and 1873. The Acts may also be extended to British possessions by Order in Council.

EXTRAJUDICIAL. Any act done or word spoken by a judge, outside the authority and jurisdiction which for the time being he is exercising, is called *extrajudicial*. [OBITER DICTUM.]

EXTRAORDINARY RESOLUTION. [RESOLUTION.]

EXTRAPAROCHIAL PLACES. Places not united to, or forming part of, any parish.

EXTRA-TERRITORIALITY. [EX-TERRITORIALITY.]

EYE-WITNESS. One who gives evidence as to facts seen by himself.

EYRE. The justices in eyre, or justices *in itinere*, were regularly established by the parliament of Northampton, A.D. 1176, with a delegated power from the king's court or *aula regia*, being looked upon as members thereof; and they afterwards made their circuit round the kingdom once in seven years for trying causes. They were afterwards directed by *Magna Charta*, 1215, to be sent into every county once a year to take or receive the verdict of jurors or "recognitors" in certain actions, then called *recognitions* or *assizes*, the most difficult of which they were directed to adjourn into the Court of Common Pleas, to be there determined. [ASSIZE, WRIT OF.] The itinerant justices were sometimes mere justices of assize, or of dower, or of gaol delivery, and the like; but they sometimes had a more general commission, being constituted *justitiarii ad omnia placita*. These were superseded by the justices of assize and *nisi prius*, established in 1280 by the Statute of Westminster the Second. They, in turn, have been replaced by the circuit judges of the Crown Court, the assize courts having been abolished by the Courts Act 1971.

F

F.C.S. Free of capture and seizure, a term exempting marine underwriters from liability for the acts of the Queen's enemies, pirates, etc.

F.O.B. (free on board). A term often inserted in contracts for sale of goods to be shipped. It signifies that the cost of shipping, *i.e.*, putting on board at port or place of shipment, is to be paid by the vendor.

FABRIC LANDS. Lands given to the rebuilding, repair, or maintenance of the fabrics of cathedrals or other churches.

FAC SIMILE PROBATE. This is where the probate copy of a will is a *fac simile* of the original will. It is allowed in cases where the construction of the will

FAC SIMILE PROBATE—*continued.* may be affected by the appearance of the original paper.

FACIO UT DES. I do that you may give; as when I agree to perform anything for a price. This is one of the considerations for contracts mentioned in the Roman law.

FACIO UT FACIAS. I do that you may do; as when I agree with a man to do his work for him, if he will do mine for me. Roman law.

FACTOR. An agent remunerated by a commission, who is entrusted with the possession of goods to sell in his own name, as apparent owner. The Factors Acts were amended and consolidated by the Factors Act 1889.

FACTORAGE, also called "commission", is an allowance given to factors by a merchant.

FACTORY. 1. A place where a considerable number of *factors* reside, in order to negotiate for their masters or employers.

2. Any premises in which persons are employed in manual labour in any process for or incidental to (*a*) the making of any article or of part of any article, or (*b*) the altering, repairing, ornamenting, finishing, cleaning or washing or breaking up or demolition of any article, or (*c*) the adapting for sale of any article, or (*d*) the slaughtering of cattle, etc., or (*e*) the confinement of such animals in certain premises whilst awaiting slaughter, being premises in which the work is carried on by way of trade or for purposes of gain, and over which the employer has the right of access or control. See the Factories Act 1961, s. 175, which also specifies a number of classes of premises, as *e.g.*, ship yards, dry docks, laundries, etc., which are to be included in the expression "factory".

FACTUM. An act or deed.

FACULTY. 1. A privilege of special dispensation, granted to a man by favour and indulgence to do that which by the common law he could not do, *e.g.*, to marry without banns, or erect a monument in a church, etc. For the granting of these there is a special court of the Archbishop of Canterbury called the Court of the Faculties, with a chief officer called the Master of the Faculties (Lat. *Magister ad Facultates*), whose power was given by the Ecclesiasti-

cal Licences Act 1533. Faculties are also granted by the ordinary Consistory Courts.

2. A department of a university.

3. In Scotch Law, "faculty" means a power which any person is at liberty to exercise.

FACULTY OF ADVOCATES. The college of advocates in Scotland, *i.e.*, the barristers entitled to practise in the Supreme Court.

FAILING OF RECORD is where a defendant, having pleaded any matter of record, fails to prove it, or brings in such a one as is no bar to the action.

FAINT ACTION, or **FEIGNED ACTION.** An action in which the words of the writ are true, yet for certain causes the party bringing it has no title to recover thereby. Whereas in a *false action* the words of the writ are false.

FAINT PLEADER, or **FAINT PLEADING.** A false, covinous, or collusory manner of pleading, to the deceit of a third party.

FAIR. A solemn or greater sort of market granted to any town by privilege, for the more speedy and commodious provision of such things as the subject needs. *Cowel.* Fairs are controlled by various statutes, one of the earliest being the Statute of Northampton (1328) which required that fairs should be held according to charter and for the time limited thereby. A number of fairs have been abolished by the Home Secretary under powers conferred by s. 3 of the Fairs Act 1871, and other old fairs are held annually as, *e.g.*, at Oxford, Banbury, Warwick, etc., under charters granted several centuries ago.

A "pleasure fair" used for providing certain entertainments, including circuses, the exhibition of human beings or performing animals, merry-go-rounds, coconut shies, hoop-las, and so forth. See s. 75 of the Public Health Act 1961 and the Betting, Gaming and Lotteries Act 1963.

FAIR COMMENT. It is a defence to an action for libel or slander that the words complained of were fair comment on a matter of public interest, provided that they were not published maliciously. The defence must be substantially true: see s. 6 of the Defamation Act 1952.

FAIR TRADING, DIRECTOR GENERAL OF. [MONOPOLY.]

FAIT. A deed.

FALDSTOOL, or **FOLDSTOOL.** A place at the south side of the altar, where the sovereign kneels during the coronation ceremony.

FALLOW-LAND. Land ploughed but not sown, and after summer's crops left uncultivated for a time.

FALSA DEMONSTRATIO NON NOCET. A false demonstration does not injure. [FALSE DEMONSTRATION.]

FALSA GRAMMATICA NON VITIAT CHARTAM. Bad grammar does not nullify the deed.

FALSE ACTION. [FAINT ACTION.]

FALSE DEMONSTRATION. An erroneous description of a person or thing in a written instrument. The import of the maxim that "a false demonstration does not injure", is this—that where there is an adequate naming or definition, with a convenient certainty, of any person or thing in a written instrument, a subsequent erroneous addition will not vitiate it.

FALSE IMPRISONMENT is a trespass committed against a man by imprisoning him without lawful cause. Every confinement of the person is an imprisonment, whether it be in a common prison, or in the stocks, or even by forcibly detaining one in the public streets. False imprisonment is usually made the subject of a civil action, but is also indictable at the suit of the Crown.

FALSE JUDGMENT, WRIT OF. A writ which lay to amend errors in the proceedings of an inferior court, *not being a court of record.*

FALSE PERSONATION. The offence of personating another for the purpose of fraud. This is a misdemeanour at common law, and has been made highly penal in many cases under various statutes.

The False Personation Act 1874 made it felony, punishable with imprisonment for life, to personate any person, or the heir, executor, etc., of any person, with intent fraudulently to obtain any land, estate, chattel, money, valuable security or property. Personation of a voter is an offence under s. 47 of the Representation of the People Act 1949; personation of a master for the purpose of giving a false character to a servant is a misdemeanour by s. 1 of the Servants' Characters Act 1792; and impersonation of a husband in order to commit rape is an offence under s. 1 of the Sexual Offences Act 1956.

FALSE PLEA. [SHAM PLEA.]

FALSE PRETENCE. Any false statement of fact whereby a person, knowing it to be false, obtained from another, for himself or for his own benefit, any chattel, money, or valuable security, with intent to cheat or defraud any person. It was formerly punishable by fine and imprisonment but the equivalent offence under s. 15 of the Theft Act 1968 is that of "obtaining property by deception".

FALSE-RETURN by a sheriff, etc., to a writ, renders him liable to an action for damages.

FALSE SIGNALS, or **LIGHTS.** Exhibiting such signals with intent to bring ships into danger was an offence under s. 47 of the Malicious Damage Act 1861, now largely repealed by the Criminal Damage Act 1971.

FALSE TRADE DESCRIPTION. A trade description which is false to a material degree, or which is misleading. See s. 3 of the Trade Descriptions Act 1968.

FALSE VERDICT formerly rendered a jury liable to be prosecuted by writ of attaint at the instance of the injured party. Such writs of attaint were abolished in 1825.

FALSI CRIMEN. Fraudulent subornation or concealment.

FALSIFY signifies, 1. To prove a thing to be false.
2. To tamper with any document, whether of record or not, by interlineation, obliteration, or otherwise. Such falsifying of the records of any court is an offence under s. 28 of the Forgery Act 1861, and so is the falsifying of dividend warrants, registers of births, marriages, burials, etc., under other sections of the same Act. See also the Forgery Act 1913.
3. To represent facts falsely, as for instance to state a pedigree falsely. Law of Property Act 1925, s. 183.

FAMILIA signified all the servants belonging to a particular master; but in another sense it was taken for a portion of land sufficient to maintain one family. Sometimes it was taken for a *hide* of land,

FAMILIA—*continued.*

which was also called a *manse*; sometimes for *carucata*, or *plough-land* containing as much as one plough with oxen could till in one year.

FAMILY. A word with various meanings, according to the context in which it is found. Thus in one sense it may mean a whole household, including servants and perhaps lodgers. In another it means all persons descended from a common stock, *i.e.* all blood relations. In a third, the word includes children only; thus when a man speaks of his wife and family, he means his wife and children (*Re Makein*, [1955] 1 All E.R. 57).

A recent statute defines "family" as consisting of the following members of a household: (*a*) one man or single woman engaged, and normally engaged, in remunerative full-time work; and (*b*) if that person is a man, a woman to whom he is married and who lives with him as his wife; and (*c*) the child or children whose requirements are provided for, in whole or in part, by that or those persons (Family Income Supplements Act 1970).

FAMILY ALLOWANCE. A small allowance payable by the state in respect of children (other than the first child) of up to school-leaving age under the former Family Allowances Acts 1965 to 1968. Abolished by the Child Benefit Act 1975. [CHILD BENEFIT.]

FAMILY DIVISION. One of the three divisions of the High Court of Justice. So named on the reorganisation of the courts in 1971 (see the Administration of Justice Act 1970 and the Courts Act 1971). To it was assigned the High Court's matrimonial and domestic business (previously dealt with by the Probate, Divorce and Admiralty Division), as well as non-contentious or common form probate business. The division consists of a President and not less than three puisne judges (Act of 1970, s. 1). There are at present sixteen puisne judges.

FAMILY PROVISION. Provision for dependants which the courts are empowered to make out of the estate of a deceased person under the Inheritance (Provision for Family and Dependants) Act 1975. Applicants for such provision include a surviving spouse, a former spouse who has not remarried, any child of the deceased, any person who though not a child of the deceased had been treated as a child of the family, and any person (even if not related) who was being wholly or partly maintained by the deceased at the time of his death.

FARDEL OF LAND (*Fardella terræ*) is, according to some authors, the fourth part of a yard-land; yet Noy, in his "Compleat Lawyer", page 57, will have two fardels make a *nook*, and four *nooks* make a yard-land.

FARE. Money paid for a passage by land or water.

Under railway bye-laws travelling without prepayment, and with intent to defraud, is punishable.

FARM, FERM, or **FEORME** (Fr. *Ferme*) is said by Blackstone to be an old Saxon word signifying *provisions*; and he says that it came to be used of rent or render, because anciently the greater part of rents were reserved in provisions, till the use of money became more frequent. So that a farmer, *firmarius*, was one who held his lands upon payment of a rent or *feorme*; though at present, by a gradual departure from the original sense, the word "farm" is brought to signify the very estate so held upon farm or rent. "To farm let" are usual, though not necessary, words of operation in a lease.

FARO, or **PHAROAH.** A game of chance, at one time unlawful, which attracts gaming licence duty under the Betting and Gaming Duties Act 1972. [GAMING.]

FARRIERY. Any work in connection with the preparation or treatment of a horse's foot for shoeing: the fitting of a shoe to a horse's foot, and incidental work. See the Farriers (Registration) Act 1975, which created a Farriers Registration Council, and otherwise legislated to prevent unnecessary suffering by horses through shoeing by untrained persons.

FARYNDON INN. The old name for Serjeants' Inn. [INNS OF CHANCERY.]

FAST-DAY. A day of abstinence appointed by the Church.

Days of general fast may also be appointed by royal proclamation. Although such appointment is very rare, such a day would be a day on which no legal business would be transacted (R.S.C. 1965, Ord. 64, r. 7).

A fast day appointed by royal proclamation would similarly be a "non-business day" for the purposes of computing time under the Bills of Exchange Act 1882.

FEALTY. Faith, fidelity. An oath, taken at the admittance of every tenant, to be true to the lord of whom he holds his land. In the usual oath of fealty there was frequently an exception of the faith due to a superior lord; but when the acknowledgment was made to the superior himself, who was vassal to no man, it was no longer called the oath of fealty, but the oath of allegiance.

The term *fealty* is applied not only to the oath, but to the actual tie which binds the vassal to his lord.

FEDERAL GOVERNMENT. A government formed by the aggregation of several states, previously independent, in such manner that the sovereignty over each of the states resides thenceforth in the aggregate of the whole, while each of the states, though losing its individual sovereignty, retains nevertheless important political powers within its own territory, and shares the sovereignty of the entire federation with the other states, and (in general) with a new legislative or executive body having a limited jurisdiction over the entire area of the federation, and called "the general government". If the individual states retain severally their sovereign character, the federation is called a *permanent confederacy of supreme governments.*

FEE. 1. The true meaning of this word is the same with that of *feud* or *fief.* In the northern languages it signified a conditional stipend or reward. These feuds, fiefs, or fees, were large districts or parcels of lands allotted by the conquering general to the superior officers of the army, and by them dealt out again in smaller parcels to the inferior officers and deserving soldiers. The condition annexed to them was that the possessor should do service faithfully, both at home and in the wars, to him by whom they were given. A fee or feud is therefore defined as being the right which the vassal or tenant has in land, to use the same and take the profits thereof to him and his heirs, rendering to the lord his due services.

2. Hence the word *fee* is used to signify an estate of inheritance, being the highest and most extensive interest which a man can have in a feud; and when the term is used simply, without any adjunct, or has the adjunct of *simple* annexed to it, it is used in contradistinction to a fee conditional at the common law, or a fee tail under the *Statute de Donis,* importing an absolute inheritance descendible to heirs general, and liable to alienation at the pleasure of the owner, whether by will or deed, to the full extent of his interest, or for a smaller estate. Since 1925 the words "heirs" or "successors" or the words "in fee simple" are not necessary, even in a deed, in order to pass an estate in fee simple. See s. 60 of the Law of Property Act 1925. [CONDITIONAL FEE; DE DONIS; ESTATE.]

FEE BASE. [BASE FEE.]

FEE CONDITIONAL. [CONDITIONAL FEE.]

FEE FARM is when a tenant holds of his lord in fee simple, paying to him the value of half or other proportion of the land by the year.

FEE FARM RENT is where an estate in fee is granted subject to a rent in fee of at least one-fourth of the value of the land at the time of its reservation. It can be distrained for. See the Law of Property Act 1925, ss. 121, 205 (1) (xxiii).

FEE SIMPLE. An estate limited to a man and his heirs; the most absolute interest which a subject can possess in land. A "fee simple absolute in possession" is one of the two legal estates in land which are now capable of subsisting under s. 1 (1) of the Law of Property Act 1925; and by s. 60 of the same Act, a conveyance of freehold land without words of limitation passes the fee simple, unless a contrary intention appears. [ESTATE.]

FEE SIMPLE CONDITIONAL. [CONDITIONAL FEE.]

FEE TAIL. An estate limited to a man and the heirs of his body, generally called an *estate tail.* [ESTATE.]

FEIGNED ACTION. [FAINT ACTION; FEIGNED ISSUE.]

FEIGNED ISSUE. An issue formerly directed in the same form as if an action had been commenced at common law upon a

FEIGNED ISSUE—*continued.*

bet or *wager* involving the fact in dispute; the issue joined thereon was referred to a jury. Now obsolete.

FELO DE SE. Self-murder, or suicide. [SUICIDE.]

FELON. A person who formerly committed felony. [FELONY.]

FELONY, in the general acceptation of our English law, comprised every species of crime which at common law occasioned a forfeiture of lands and goods. Treason, therefore, was a species of felony. At the time when Blackstone wrote, an Act of Parliament making an offence felony without benefit of clergy meant that the offender, if convicted, was to suffer death, and incur a forfeiture of his lands and goods. But, as capital punishment never entered into the true idea of felony, so it had long ceased to have any necessary connection with it in practice. By s. 1 of the Forfeiture Act 1870 forfeiture for treason and felony was abolished; so that the essence of the distinction between felony and misdemeanour was already lost before that distinction was finally abolished by s. 1 (1) of the Criminal Law Act 1967.

FEME (Fr. *Femme*). A woman.

FEME COVERT (Lat. *Femina viro co-operta*). A married woman; opposed to *feme sole*, which means a single woman.

FEME SOLE. A single woman, including those who have been married, but whose marriage has been dissolved by death or divorce, and (for most purposes) those women who are judicially separated from their husbands.

FENCE-MONTH, or **DEFENCE-MONTH.** A forest word, signifying a *close time* during the space of thirty-one days in the year, that is to say, fifteen days before Midsummer, and fifteen days after, in which time it was forbidden for any man to hunt in the forest, or to go into it to disturb the beasts. The reason was because the female deer were then fawning.

FEOFFEE. A person to whom a feoffment is made. [FEOFFMENT.]

FEOFFEE TO USES. A person to whom a feoffment of lands was made to the use of some other person. Prior to the Statute of Uses (1536) the feoffee to uses had

the *legal estate* in the lands so conveyed by feoffment; the claim of the person to whose *use* they were conveyed being enforceable by the Court of Chancery. But by that statute, uses were turned into legal estates, and the feoffee to uses had no longer even a legal estate in the land; he had only what is called a *scintilla juris.* The Statute of Uses was repealed by the Law of Property Act 1925. [FEOFFMENT; LEGAL ESTATE; SCINTILLA JURIS; USE.]

FEOFFMENT (Lat. *Feoffamentum*) was properly *donatio feudi,* the gift of the fee; and it might (says Blackstone) be defined as the gift of any corporeal hereditament to another. [CORPOREAL PROPERTY.]

But in practice the word was never used in this possession sense; for by a *feoffment* was always meant the feudal mode of transferring estates of freehold in possession called *feoffment with livery of seisin.* This "livery of seisin" was the pure feudal investiture. It was either "in deed" or "in law".

Feoffments, having long been disused, were practically abolished in 1845.

FEOFFOR. A person who makes a *feoffment.* [FEOFFMENT.]

FEORME. The same as farm. [FARM.]

FERAE NATURAE. Of a wild disposition; an expression applied to animals which are generally found at liberty, though it may happen that they are sometimes tamed and confined by the art and industry of man. Regarded as property but not capable of being stolen unless first reduced into possession. See s. 4 (4) of the Theft Act 1968.

FERRY. A liberty or franchise by prescription, or by the Queen's grant or Act of Parliament, to have a boat for passage upon a great stream for the carriage of persons, etc., for reasonable toll. This right, where it exists, involves a right of action on the part of the owner of the ferry against those who set up a new one so near as to diminish his custom. On the other hand, the existence of the right implies also a duty, on the part of the grantee, to keep up a boat over the stream, if not otherwise fordable, for the convenience of the public: and neglect of this duty will render him liable to a criminal prosecution.

FEU, or **FEW.** The prevailing tenure of land in Scotland, where the vassal, in place of military service, makes a return in grain or in money. A form of landholding, *e.g.* as in the case of building land granted in perpetuity (with no reversion), the landlord receiving a perpetual annual payment or feu-duty. It is in the nature of a perpetual lease.

FEUD. The same as fee. [FEE.]

Also it signifies implacable hatred, not to be satisfied but with the death of the enemy; and especially a combination of the kindred of a murdered man to avenge his death upon the slayer and all his race.

FEUDAL-SYSTEM. The system of military tenures, perfected in this country by William the Conqueror. The main incidents of the feudal system continued until the abolition of military tenures by the Tenures Abolition Act 1660.

FI. FA. [FIERI FACIAS.]

FIAT. A short order or warrant of a judge for making out and allowing certain processes; or an indorsement by the Lord Chancellor or Attorney-General, on behalf of the Crown, upon a petition for any purpose for which the consent of the Crown is necessary.

FIAT JUSTITIA RUAT COELUM. Let justice be done though the heavens should fall.

FICTION OF LAW (Lat. *Fictio juris*) is defined as a supposition of law that a thing is true, without inquiring whether it be so or not, that it may have the effect of truth so far as is consistent with justice. There are many instances of fictions used in English law, *e.g.*, *Ejectment*, *Fine*, *Trover*, etc. (*q.v.*).

The phrase "implied by law" is frequently used to cover a legal fiction. For instance, when it is said that a contract of request is "implied by law", it is frequently meant that no such contract or request has ever been made, but that, for certain legal purposes, it must be held to have been made. But the phrase is applied equally to the most rational and obvious inferences of fact. [IMPLIED.]

FIDEI DEFENSOR. [DEFENDER OF THE FAITH.]

FIDEJUSSORES. Sponsors, sureties; a word derived from the Roman law.

FIDUCIARY ESTATE. The estate or interest of a trustee in lands or money, as opposed to the beneficial interest or enjoyment thereof.

FIELD MONUMENT. [ANCIENT MONUMENTS.]

FIEF. [FEE, 1.]

FIERI FACIAS, or **FI. FA.** A writ of execution for him that has recovered in an action of debt or damages, addressed to the sheriff to command him to levy the debt or damages from the goods of the party against whom judgment is recovered. The effect and manner of its execution is governed by R.S.C. 1965, Ord. 47.

FIERI FACIAS DE BONIS ECCLESIASTICIS. A writ of execution issued when a judgment debtor is a clerk in holy orders, and the sheriff returns (*i.e.*, endorses on the writ) that the debtor has no lay fee within his county. See R.S.C. 1965, Ord. 47, rr. 3 and 5.

FIERI FECI. A return to the writ of *fieri facias*, denoting that the sheriff or other officer to whom it is directed has levied the sum named in the writ, either wholly or as to that part to which the return is applicable. [RETURN.]

FILING BILL IN EQUITY signified placing a copy of the bill on the files of the court. This was done by one of the clerks of records and writs. [CLERK OF RECORDS AND WRITS.] The filing of the bill was the commencement of the formal proceedings in a Chancery suit. Obsolete.

FILIUS NULLIUS. FILIUS POPULI. (Son of no man. Son of the people.) Expressions used of a bastard.

FILUM AQUAE MEDIUM. The thread or middle part of a stream which divides the jurisdictions or properties. Riparian owners possess the bed of a river *usque ad medium filum*.

FINAL JUDGMENT is a judgment awarded at the *end* of an action, as opposed to an *interlocutory judgment*. If the defendant does not enter an appearance within the period named in the writ, the plaintiff is, as a rule, entitled to judgment in default of appearance. Where the writ claims a liquidated, that is an ascertained,

FINAL JUDGMENT—*continued.*

sum of money and the defendant does not appear, the plaintiff may enter final judgment for the full amount claimed on the writ, interest and costs. See R.S.C. 1965, Ord. 13. [INTERLOCUTORY JUDGMENT.]

FINAL PROCESS. The expression used to denote execution on final judgment. [FINAL JUDGMENT; PROCESS.]

FINDER OF GOODS has a special property in them, good against everyone but the true owner. [TREASURE TROVE.]

FINDING OF A JURY. The verdict of a jury. The expression was also applied to the presentment of the former grand jury; it used to be said that a true bill was *found* against such a party.

FINE. 1. Fine of lands and tenements.

This was sometimes called a *feoffment of record*; though it might with more accuracy be called an *acknowledgment of a feoffment on record.* [FEOFFMENT.] It was an amicable composition or agreement of a suit, either actual or fictitious, by leave of the king or his justices, whereby lands in question became, or were acknowledged to be, the right of one of the parties. In its origin it was founded on an actual suit commenced at law for recovery of possession of lands. It was called a *fine*, because it put an *end*, not only to the suit thus commenced, but also to all other suits and controversies concerning the same matter.

2. Fine on alienation.

This was a sum of money paid in ancient times to the lord by a tenant whenever he had occasion to make over his land to another; and so, even until 1926, fines were payable by the custom of most manors, to the lord, upon every descent or alienation of a copyhold tenement. Copyholds, however, became extinct under the provisions of the Law of Property Act 1922.

3. Fine for endowment.

This was a fine anciently payable to the lord by the widow of a tenant, without which she could not be endowed of her husband's lands. It was abolished under Henry I, and afterwards by *Magna Charta*. 2 *Bl.*

4. A sum of money payable by a lessee on a renewal of the lease.

5. Any pecuniary penalty or pecuniary forfeiture or pecuniary compensation payable under a conviction. See s. 126 of the Magistrates' Courts Act 1952.

FIRE INSURANCE. [INSURANCE.]

FIRE ORDEAL. An ancient form of ordeal confined to persons of high rank. [ORDEAL.]

FIREARM. A lethal barrelled weapon of any description from which any shot, bullet or other missile can be discharged. It also includes certain "prohibited" weapons such as machine guns and gas guns. It is also an offence in certain circumstances, to carry an imitation firearm, *i.e.* anything which has the appearance of being a firearm, whether or not it is capable of discharging any shot, bullet or other missile. See s. 57 of the Firearms Act, 1968.

Firearm also includes air gun or air pistol: see s. 10 of the Theft Act 1968.

FIREARMS CERTIFICATE. Under Part II of the Firearms Act 1968, an application for the grant of a firearm or shot gun certificate must be made in prescribed form to the chief officer of police for the area in which the applicant resides. If granted, such certificate continues in force for three years, and is renewable for further periods of three years. The fee for a firearm certificate is £7 (£4·50 on renewal); for a shot gun certificate (grant or renewal) the fee is £2.

(*Canada.*) A "firearm", within the meaning of the Criminal Code of Canada, means any barrelled weapon from which any shot, bullet or other missile can be discharged and that is capable of causing serious bodily injury or death to the person, and includes anything which can be adapted for use as a firearm.

FIREBOTE, otherwise called housebote, signifies a sufficient allowance of wood to burn in a house.

FIRM. The name or style under which a house of trade is carried on; also the collective name of the partners. See the Partnership Act 1890, s. 4. As to suing partners in the name of the firm, see R.S.C. 1965, Ord. 81. As to registration of names of firms, see the Registration of Business Names Act 1916.

FIRMA NOCTIS. A customary tribute formerly paid towards the entertainment of the king for one night.

FIRST CLASS MISDEMEANANT. A former category of prisoner. Separate divisions of prisons were abolished by s. 1 of the Criminal Justice Act 1948.

FIRST FRUITS, or ANNATES. The first year's whole profits of every spiritual living in one year, given in ancient times to the Pope throughout all Christendom. These payments were restrained by various Acts of Parliament, but they were made notwithstanding, until they were annexed to the Crown by a statute of Henry VIII (1535). In the year 1704 they were restored to the church by Queen Anne under the name of Queen Anne's Bounty (*q.v.*). By the First Fruits and Tenths Measure 1926, these payments, with a few exceptions, were extinguished or provision made for their redemption.

FIRST IMPRESSION. A case of *first impression* (Lat. *primae impressionis*) is a case for which there is no precedent applicable in all respects.

FIRST INSTANCE, COURT OF. That before which an action is first tried. Thus distinguished from a court of appeal.

FIRST OFFENDER. A magistrates' court may not pass sentence of imprisonment on a person of 21 or over unless it is of opinion that no other method of dealing with him is appropriate. See s. 14 of the Criminal Justice Act 1972.

FISC, or FISCUS. The treasury of a state.

FISCAL. Belonging to the exchequer or revenue.

FISH ROYAL. Whale and sturgeon which, when thrown ashore, or caught near the coast, are the property of the sovereign.

FISHERIES. [BOARD OF AGRICULTURE AND FISHERIES.]

FISHERY is a word often used to denote a right of fishing. The right is of three kinds: (1) A free fishery. (2) A several fishery. (3) A common of piscary. A *free fishery* is an exclusive right of fishing in a public river. A *free fishery* differs from a *several* fishery, because he that has a *several* fishery must be the owner of the soil, which in a free fishery is not requisite. It differs also from a *common of piscary* in that a *free fishery* is an exclusive right, and a *common of piscary* (the right of fishing in another's waters) is not so.

FIVE MILE ACT was a name given to a statute of Elizabeth I (1592), whereby popish recusants convicted for not going to church were compelled to repair to their usual place of abode and not to remove above five miles from thence under certain penalties. Repealed in 1844.

FIXTURES. Things of an accessory character, annexed to houses or lands; including not only such things as grates in a house, or steam engines in a colliery, but also windows and palings. To be a fixture, a thing must not constitute part of the principal subject, as in the case of the walls or floors of a house; but on the other hand, it must be in actual union or connection with it, and not merely brought into contact with it, as in the case of a picture suspended on hooks against a wall. As a general rule the property, by being annexed to the land, immediately belongs to the freeholder, but there are three exceptions to the rule. (*a*) In favour of trade fixtures. (*b*) For agricultural purposes. See the Agricultural Holdings Act 1948, s. 13. (*c*) For ornament and convenience.

FLAGRANTE DELICTO. An expression applied to the apprehension of a man red-handed in the act of committing a crime.

FLAT. A separate and self-contained set of premises, whether or not on the same floor, constructed for use for the purposes of a dwelling and forming part of a building from some other part of which it is divided horizontally.

FLEET. 1. A place where the tide flows—a creek, hence Northfleet, etc.

2. A famous prison in London, so called from a river or ditch that was formerly there, and on the site whereof it stood. It was principally a debtors' prison. It was closed down under an Act of 1842, and demolished three years later.

FLEET-BOOKS contain the entries of marriages solemnised in the Fleet Prison from 1686 to 1754. They are now deposited in the Registrar-General's office under the provisions of the Non-parochial Registers Act 1840.

FLETA. A feigned name of a learned lawyer, who lived in the time of Edward I. He wrote a book of the common law of England, as it existed in his time. The work is entitled "Fleta, seu Commentarius Juris

FLETA—*continued*.

Anglicani". He is supposed to have been confined in the Fleet Prison, hence the name.

FLIGHT. [HIJACKING.]

FLOATING CAPITAL. Capital retained for the purpose of meeting current expenditure.

FLOATING CHARGE is a charge created by a company in a debenture on its assets for the time being. It gives the debenture-holders no immediate right *in rem* over the assets that it affects; but leaves the company free power of disposition over the whole of its property. [DEBENTURE.]

"A floating charge is ambulatory and hovers over the property until some event occurs which causes it to settle and crystallise into a specific charge" (*Barker* v. *Eynon*, [1974] 1 All E.R. 900).

FLOOR OF THE COURT. That part between the judge and the first row of counsel. Parties who appear in person stand there.

FLOTSAM, or **FLOATSAM,** signifies any goods that by shipwreck be lost, and lie *floating* or swimming upon the top of the water. The expression is included in the definition of "wreck" in s. 510 of the Merchant Shipping Act 1894. Flotsam, with other wreck, belongs to the Crown if no owner appears to claim it within a year. [WRECK.]

FOENUS NAUTICUM. The extraordinary rate of interest, proportioned to the risk, demanded by a person lending money on a ship, or on *bottomry* as it is termed. The agreement for such a rate of interest is also called *fœnus nauticum*. [BOTTOMRY.]

FOLIO signifies generally seventy-two words of a legal document. But for some purposes ninety words are reckoned to the folio.

FOLKLAND, in the times of the Saxons, was land held in villenage, being distributed among the common *folk*, or people, at the pleasure of the lord of the manor, and resumed at his discretion. Not being held by any assurance in writing, it was opposed to *book* land, or *charter* land, which was held by deed.

FOLKMOTE. A word which, in its meaning, included two kinds of courts; the

old county court and the sheriff's tourn. Some think that it was a common council of all the inhabitants of a city, town, or borough, convened by sound of bell to the mote-hall or house.

FOOT OF A FINE. The conclusion of a fine. [FINE, 1.]

FOOTPATH. A highway over which the public have a right of way on foot only, not being a footway: Highway Act 1959, s. 295.

FOOTWAY. A way comprised in a highway which also comprises a carriageway, being a way over which the public have a right of way on foot only: Highways Act 1959, s. 295.

FORCE generally means unlawful violence.

FORCE AND ARMS (Lat. *Vi et armis*). Words formerly inserted in indictments, and in declarations for trespass, but now no longer necessary.

FORCE MAJEURE. Irresistible compulsion or coercion.

FORCIBLE DETAINER. A forcible holding possession of any lands or tenements, whereby the lawful entry of justices, or others having a right to enter, is barred or hindered.

FORCIBLE ENTRY. The violent entering and taking possession of lands or tenements with menaces, force, and arms, which is both a civil and a criminal injury.

FORECLOSURE. The forfeiture by a mortgagor of his equity of redemption, by reason of his default in payment of the principal or interest of the mortgage debt within a reasonable time. Foreclosure may be enforced in equity by a proceeding called a *foreclosure action*, and now on originating summons. And see now the Law of Property Act 1925, s. 88 (2), which provides that where a mortgagee obtains an order for foreclosure absolute, the order shall operate to vest the fee simple in him.

FOREGIFT. A payment in advance; a word generally applied to a premium, or money paid down, in consideration of a lease, by the intending lessee. Forbidden by s. 30 of the Ecclesiastical Leasing Act 1842.

FOREHAND RENT. Rent payable in advance.

FOREIGN. Any country (*e.g.*, Scotland) which has a separate jurisdiction and law of its own.

FOREIGN ATTACHMENT. A process by which a debt due to a judgment debtor from a person not a party to the action or suit is made available for satisfying the claim of the judgment creditor. Such a process has been immemorially used in London, Bristol and other cities. [CUSTOM OF LONDON; GARNISHEE.]

FOREIGN BILL OF EXCHANGE is any bill of exchange which is not an inland bill. See the Bills of Exchange Act 1882, s. 4. [INLAND BILL OF EXCHANGE.]

FOREIGN ENLISTMENT ACTS are statutes for preventing British subjects serving foreign states in war. The Foreign Enlistment Act of 1870 provides that if any British subject shall, without the licence of Her Majesty, accept any commission in the military or naval service of any foreign state at war with any friendly state (*i.e.*, a state at peace with Her Majesty) he shall be punishable by fine or imprisonment to the extent of two years, or both. And any person who, without licence from the Crown, shall build or equip any ship for the service of a foreign state at war with a friendly state, is punishable in like manner.

FOREIGN LAW is a question of fact which must be proved by the evidence of expert witnesses; Foreign Law Ascertainment Act 1861. See also s. 102 of the Judicature Act 1925; s. 97 of the County Courts Act 1959, whereby questions of foreign law are to be decided by the judge alone and not by a jury; and s. 4 of the Civil Evidence Act 1972.

FOREIGN PLEA. A plea objecting to the judge on the ground that the matter in hand is not within his jurisdiction.

FOREJUDGER (Lat. *Forisjudicatio*). A judgment whereby a man is deprived of a thing in question. To be forejudged the court is when an officer or attorney of any court is expelled from the same for some offence.

FOREMAN. The presiding member of a jury.

FORENSIC MEDICINE. The science of medical jurisprudence, comprising those matters which may be considered as common ground to both medical and legal practitioners; as, for instance, inquiries relating to suspected murder or doubtful sanity.

FORESHORE. That part of the shore which is covered by an ordinary tide. It *prima facie* belongs to the Crown.

FOREST. As a legal right, it was defined as the right of keeping, for the purpose of hunting, the wild beasts and fowls of forest, chase, park, and warren, in the safe protection of the king, in a territory or precinct of woody ground or pasture set apart for the purpose (*Manwood's Forest Laws*, 1598). Courts known as forest courts were formerly held for the government of the king's forests in different parts of the kingdom. Such courts are now obsolete.

Most of the ancient forest laws, the earliest still on the statute book being a charter of 1297, were repealed by the Wild Creatures and Forest Laws Act 1971. The statute abolished any franchises of forest, free chase, park or free warren, and abrogated the forest law except in so far as it relates to the appointment and functions of verderers.

FORESTALLING. [ENGROSSING, 1.]

FORFEITURE is defined by Blackstone as a punishment annexed by law to some illegal act or negligence, in the owner of lands, tenements, or hereditaments, whereby he loses all his interest therein, and they go to the party injured, as a recompense for the wrong which either he alone, or the public together with himself, has sustained. *E.g.*, alienation in mortmain, disclaimer by tenant of lord's title, breach of copyhold customs, breach of covenants in a lease. Relief against forfeiture is provided for by the Law of Property Act 1925, s. 146, and by s. 18 (2) of the Landlord and Tenant Act 1927.

Many of the grounds of forfeiture which formerly existed are now obsolete. And, especially, forfeitures to the Crown for treason and felony were abolished by s. 1 of the Forfeiture Act 1870.

FORFEITURE OF MARRIAGE (Lat. *Forisfactura maritagii*). A writ which lay against him who, holding by knight's service, and being under age and unmarried, refused her whom the lord offered him without disparagement, and married another. *Cowel.* [DISPARAGEMENT; VALOR MARITAGII.]

FORGERY. The making of a false document in order that it may be used as genuine, or the counterfeiting of certain seals and dies. See s. 1 of the Forgery Act 1913, under which Act the law relating to forgery and kindred offences was consolidated.

FORMA PAUPERIS (in the character of a pauper). Any person might formerly be admitted to take or defend or be a party to any legal proceedings in the High Court of Justice as a poor person on proof that he had reasonable grounds for taking or defending or being a party to such proceedings and that he was not worth £50, or in special circumstances £100 (excluding his wearing apparel, tools of trade, and the subject-matter of such proceedings), and had an income of less than £4 per week.

This procedure has now been superseded by legal aid under the Legal Aid and Advice Act 1974. [LEGAL AID.]

FORSPEAKER. An attorney or advocate in a cause.

FORTHWITH. When a defendant is ordered to plead *forthwith* he must plead within twenty-four hours. In a statute the word means within a reasonable time.

FORTUNA is sometimes used for *treasure trove*. [TREASURE TROVE.]

FORTUNE-TELLER. A person pretending or professing to tell fortunes, or using any subtle craft, means, or device, by palmistry or otherwise, to deceive and impose on any of Her Majesty's subjects. Such a person may be punishable as a rogue and vagabond under s. 4 of the Vagrancy Act 1824. Note however that persons who, with intent to deceive or by using any fraudulent device, purport to act as spiritualistic mediums or to exercise powers of clairvoyance, etc., are punishable under s. 1 of the Fraudulent Mediums Act 1951.

FORUM. A word frequently used to signify the place where jurisdiction is exercised in a given case. Thus, if a person be sued in England, on a contract made in France, England in the given case is the *forum*, and the law of England is, accordingly, the *lex fori*.

FORUM ORIGINIS. The court of the country of a man's domicile by birth.

FORWARDING MERCHANT. One who receives and forwards goods taking upon himself the expenses of transportation, for which he receives a compensation from the owners, having no concern in the vessels or wagons by which they are transported, and no interest in the freight, and not being deemed a common carrier, but a mere warehouseman and agent.

FOSTER-LAND. Land given for finding food or victuals for any person or persons, as for monks in a monastery.

FOSTER-LEAN (Sax.). A nuptial gift; the jointure or stipend for the maintenance of a wife; the remuneration fixed for the rearing of a foster-child.

FOUR CORNERS of an instrument; that which is contained on the face of a deed (without any aid from the knowledge of the circumstances under which it was made) is said to be within its four corners, because every deed is supposed to be written on one entire skin.

FOUR SEAS. The seas surrounding England; divided into the western, including the Scotch and Irish; the northern; the eastern or North Sea; and the English Channel. [BEYOND THE SEAS.]

FOWL. Includes any cock, hen, chicken, capon, turkey, goose, gander, duck, drake, guinea-fowl, peacock, pea-hen, swan or pigeon: Protection of Animals Act 1911, s. 15.

FRACTION OF A DAY, the law does not recognise, except in cases of necessity and for the purposes of justice. When therefore a thing is to be done on a certain day, all that day is allowed for doing it.

FRANCHISE. A royal privilege, or branch of the Queen's prerogative, vested in the hands of a subject. It arises either from royal grant or from prescription which presupposes a grant. It is an incorporeal hereditament and is synonymous with liberty. There are many kinds, *e.g.*, bodies corporate, the right to hold fairs, markets, ferries, fisheries. At the present day, the word is most frequently used to denote the right of voting for a member to serve in parliament, which is called the parliamentary franchise; or the right of voting for a county or district councillor, which is called the local government franchise.

(*Canada*.) In Canada, the term is frequently used with reference to a contract whereby a business man is permitted to use a well-known business name, and receives advice and assistance, in return for money and/or purchasing stock-in-trade from, or at the direction of, the other party to the contract.

FRANK. To *frank* a letter means to send it post-free, so that the person who receives it shall have nothing to pay. This is now done in the ordinary way by prepaying the postage. Formerly members of parliament, peers, etc., had the privilege of franking their letters by autograph. This right was abolished on the establishment of the penny postage in 1840.

FRANK BANK. The same as *freebench.* [FREEBENCH.]

FRANKALMOIGN. Tenure in *frankalmoign,* or free alms, was a spiritual tenure, whereby religious corporations held lands of the donors to them and their successors for ever. They were free of all other but religious services, and the *trinoda necessitas.* This tenure was expressly excepted by s. 7 of the Tenures Abolition Act 1660, and therefore still subsisted until it was virtually abolished by the Administration of Estates Act 1925 Sch. II, Part I. It differed from *tenure by divine service,* in which the tenants were obliged to do some special divine service for neglect of which the lord might distrain, without any complaint to the visitor.

FRANK-FEE. A tenure in which no service is required. This is sometimes called an *improper feud,* because free from all services, but not from homage.

FRANK-FOLD. [FALDAGE.]

FRANKLIN. A steward; a bailiff of land.

FRANK-MARRIAGE, or **FREE MARRIAGE.** A tenure in tail special, which arises when a man seised of land in fee simple gives it to another man and his wife, who is the daughter or sister or otherwise of kin to the donor, *in free marriage* (*in liberum maritagium*), by virtue of which words they have an estate in special tail, and hold the land of the donor quit of all manner of services, except fealty, till the fourth degree of consanguinity be past between the issues of the donor and past between the issues of the donor and

donee. This tenure has now grown out of use, but is still capable of subsisting. Under the Law of Property Act 1925 entailed estates exist only in respect of equitable interests.

FRANK-PLEDGE. A pledge of surety to the sovereign for the collective good behaviour of a group. [COURT LEET.]

FRANK-TENEMENT (Lat. *Liberum tenementum*). The same as freehold; used in old time in opposition to *villenage.* [FREEHOLD.]

FRATER CONSANGUINEUS, in a narrow sense, indicates a brother by the father's side, as opposed to *frater uterinus,* a brother by the mother's.

FRATER NUTRICIUS. An expression used in ancient deeds for a bastard brother.

FRATER UTERINUS. A brother by the mother's side.

FRAUD. The modes of fraud are infinite, and it has been said that the courts have never laid down what shall constitute fraud, or any general rule, beyond which they will not go in giving equitable relief on the ground of fraud. Fraud is, however, usually divided into two large classes, actual fraud and constructive fraud.

An actual fraud may be defined to be something said, done or omitted by a person with the design of perpetrating what he must have known to be a positive fraud.

Constructive frauds are acts, statements or omissions which operate as virtual frauds on individuals or which, if generally permitted, would be prejudicial to the public welfare, and yet may have been unconnected with any selfish or evil design; as, for instance, bonds and agreements entered into as a reward for using influence over another, to induce him to make a will for the benefit of the obligor. For such contracts encourage a spirit of artifice and scheming and tend to deceive and injure others.

"To amount to fraud, conduct must be deliberately dishonest": *R.* v. *Sinclair,* [1968] 3 All E.R. 241.

FRAUD ON A POWER is such an exercise of a power of appointment as defeats the intention of the person creating it. As to the protection afforded to purchasers in good faith, see s. 157 of the Law of Property Act 1925.

FRAUDS, STATUTE OF. A statute passed in 1677 for the prevention of frauds and perjuries. The statute is now largely repealed. S. 4, as amended, provides that unless there is an agreement, or some memorandum or note thereof, in writing, signed by the party to be charged therewith or some other person lawfully authorised by him, no action may be brought upon any promise to answer for the debt, default or miscarriage of another.

FRAUDULENT CONVERSION. Formerly, the fraudulent appropriation to his own use of property entrusted to a person by another. Such an act is now theft under the Theft Act 1968.

FRAUDULENT CONVEYANCE. A conveyance of property made with intent to defraud creditors. Such a conveyance is voidable under s. 172 of the Law of Property Act 1925, unless it has been made for valuable consideration (or upon good consideration) and in good faith to a person without notice of the intent to defraud.

FRAUDULENT MEDIUM. [MEDIUM.]

FRAUDULENT PREFERENCE. [PREFERENCE (FRAUDULENT).]

FREE CHAPEL. Places of worship of royal foundation exempted from the jurisdiction of the ordinary, or founded by private persons to whom the Crown has thought fit to grant the same privilege.

FREE FISHERY. [FISHERY.]

FREE SERVICES were such as were not unbecoming the character of a soldier or a *freeman* to perform; as to serve under his lord in the wars, to pay a sum of money, and the like. [FREEHOLD.]

FREE SHIPS, FREE GOODS. A maxim implying that, in time of war, neutral vessels are to impart a neutral character to the goods of belligerents carried therein, so as to exempt them from capture. This doctrine, except so far as relates to contraband of war, is recognised in the document generally known as the Declaration of Paris (1856). [DECLARATION OF PARIS.]

FREE WARREN. A franchise or royalty derived from the Crown, empowering the grantees to take and kill beasts and fowls of warren; also for the preservation and custody thereof. [WARREN.]

FREEBENCH (*Francus bancus*). The right which a widow had in her husband's copyhold lands, corresponding to dower in the case of freeholds. The extent of the right to freebench, and the conditions under which it was to be enjoyed, varied according to the custom of the manor. Abolished in 1925.

FREEDOM. [FREEMAN.]

FREEHOLD, or **FRANK-TENEMENT** (Lat. *Liberum tenementum*), is that land or tenement which a man holds in fee, fee tail, or at the least for term of life. It is said that freehold is of two sorts, freehold *in deed* and freehold *in law*. Freehold *in deed* is the real possession of land or tenements in fee, fee tail, or for life; and freehold *in law* is the right that a man has to such tenements before entry. It has likewise been extended to those offices which a man holds either in fee or for term of life. A less estate than an estate for life was not deemed worthy of the acceptance of a free man. But an estate which may come to an end by the voluntary act of the tenant in his lifetime may nevertheless be a freehold. Thus an estate during widowhood is regarded as a freehold.

The term freehold is used at present in opposition to leasehold, *i.e.*, to indicate *estate*; formerly it was also used in opposition to copyhold, *i.e.*, to indicate *tenure*.

A leasehold interest, being an estate for a term of years, is but a chattel interest, and in law is less than an estate of freehold, however long the term may be.

A copyhold interest (now abolished) was originally an estate *at the will of the lord of the manor*, and it remained so in name though not in fact; and an estate at will is the smallest estate known to the law. And in their origin copyholds were deemed worthy the acceptance only of villeins and slaves.

A freehold is sometimes spoken of as if it were such an estate as a man is *free* to do what he likes with. This is probably owing to the comparative absence in freeholds of those restrictions and liabilities which, in the case of copyholds, were imposed by custom, and, in the case of leaseholds, by covenants in the lease. But the notion of rights of property in land, without corresponding duties, is abhorrent to the general spirit of our old common law. The distinguishing marks of a freehold were—

(1) that it should last for life (unless sooner put an end to by the voluntary act, neglect, or default of the tenant); (2) that the duties or services should be *free*, that is, worthy the acceptance of a free man. To fulfil this latter condition, it was necessary that the services by which the land was held, and by the non-performance of which it would be forfeited, should be *honourable* (*i.e.*, not servile) in respect of their quality, and *certain* in respect both of their quality and quantity. [COPYHOLD; ESTATE; TENURE.]

FREEMAN. An allodial proprietor, one born or made free to enjoy certain municipal immunities and privileges.

By former local government legislation, persons of distinction, or who had rendered eminent services, might be admitted to be honorary freemen of a borough. Under s. 20 (6) of the Local Government Act 1972 the former boroughs (save for the London boroughs) ceased to exist. Section 248 of that Act, however, provides for the retention of the status and rights of the freemen of the former boroughs, and also for the admission, in the future, of persons to the freedom of cities and towns. The roll of freemen of any such city or town is to be kept by an officer of the relevant district council.

FREEMAN OF LONDON. The freedom of the City of London can be obtained in three different methods: (1) By *patrimony*, that is, as the son of a freeman born after the father has acquired his freedom; (2) *servitude*, that is, by serving an apprenticeship to a freeman; and (3) *redemption*, that is, by purchase.

As to the second method, apprenticeship is to a member of one of the City livery companies, *e.g.* The Merchant Taylors' Company. Upon completion of his apprenticeship (in the case of the above-mentioned Company, seven years) the former pupil is entitled not only to membership of the Company, but also to the freedom of the City.

The last method includes the case where the freedom of the city is obtained by honorary gift, as a mark of distinction for public services.

FREIGHT. The sum payable for the hire of a vessel, or for the carriage of goods therein. It may also, in a policy of marine insurance, include the benefit which a shipowner expects to derive from carrying his goods in his own vessel. As to shipowner's lien for freight, see ss. 494, 495 of the Merchant Shipping Act 1894.

FREIGHTER. The hirer of a vessel.

FRESH PURSUIT, or FRESH SUIT (Lat. *Recens persecutio*). Instant and immediate following with intent to recapture a thing lost, as a bird or beast escaped, or goods stolen, etc. In this latter case the party pursuing them had back his stolen goods, which otherwise were forfeited to the Crown.

FRIARS. The name of an order of religious persons, of which there were four principal branches; (1) Minors, Grey Friars, or Franciscans; (2) Augustines; (3) Dominicans, or Black Friars; (4) White Friars, or Carmelites.

FRIENDLESS MAN was the Saxon word for an outlaw.

FRIENDLY SOCIETY. An association for the purpose of affording relief to the members in sickness, and assistance to their widows and children at their deaths. See the Friendly Societies Act 1974.

FRIENDLY SUIT. A suit brought not in a hostile manner, the object being to settle some point of law, or do some act which cannot safely be done except with the sanction of a court of justice.

FROM. Generally excludes the day from which the time is to be reckoned.

FRONTAGER. One who owns property which fronts or abuts on a street, etc.

FRUCTUS INDUSTRIALES. [EMBLEMENTS.]

FRUSTRATION. The prevention of the carrying out of a contract, *e.g.*, by reason of the destruction of the subject-matter. "The premature determination of an agreement between parties, lawfully entered into and in course of operation at the time of its premature determination, owing to the occurrence of an intervening event or change of circumstances so fundamental as to be regarded by the law both as striking at the root of the agreement, and as entirely beyond what was contemplated by the parties when they entered into the agreement": *Cricklewood Property* v. *Leighton's Trust*, [1945] A.C. 221, H.L., *per* Lord Simon, L.C., at p. 228.

FUGITIVE OFFENDER. The Fugitive Offenders Act 1967 provides for the apprehension and sending back of persons accused of any offence to which the Act applies to that part of the Crown's dominions where the offence is alleged to have been committed.

FULL AGE. The age of majority was reduced to eighteen as from 1st January 1970 by s. 1 of the Family Law Reform Act 1969. In the case of the heir apparent or heir presumptive to the throne the age majority is also eighteen: see s. 12 of the Regency Act 1953.

FULL COURT. A court composed of all the judges, members thereof, *e.g.*, the full court in divorce and matrimonial causes consisted of the judge ordinary and at least two other members of the court. Its jurisdiction was transferred to the Court of Appeal by the Judicature Act 1881.

FUNCTUS OFFICIO. A person who has discharged his duty, or whose office or authority has come to an end, is said to be *functus officio*.

FUND, CONSOLIDATED. [CONSOLIDATED FUND.]

FUNERAL EXPENSES. It is the first duty of an executor or administrator to bury the testator in a manner suitable to the estate he has left, and the expenses will form a first charge on the estate; if, however, he is extravagant he commits a *devastavit*, for which he is answerable to the creditors or legatees.

FUNGIBLES. Movable goods which may be estimated by weight, number or measure, as grain or coin. They are opposed to jewels, paintings, etc.

FURANDI ANIMUS. The intention of stealing; that is, the intention, in one who takes goods, of unlawfully depriving the right owner of his property therein. [THEFT.]

FURTHER ADVANCE or CHARGE. A second or subsequent loan of money to a mortgagor by a mortgagee, either on the same or on an additional security.

FURTHER ASSURANCE. Covenant for further assurance, in a deed of conveyance, means a covenant to make to the purchaser any additional "assurance" which may be necessary to complete his title. It is *implied* on use of appropriate words, *e.g.*, "as beneficial owner", in conveyances made on and after 1st January, 1882, by virtue of the Conveyancing Act 1881. See now, as to implied covenants for title, s. 76 of, and Sch. II to, the Law of Property Act 1925. [ASSURANCE, 1.]

FURTHER CONSIDERATION. It frequently happens that a judgment in the Chancery Division directs accounts and inquiries to be taken before the master, and reserves the further consideration. The hearing on the master's certificate is called a hearing on *further consideration*.

FUTURE ESTATE. An estate to take effect in possession at a future time. The expression is most frequently applied to contingent remainders and executory interests; but it would seem to be also applicable to vested remainders and reversions. [CONTINGENT REMAINDER; EXECUTORY INTEREST; VESTED REMAINDER.]

G

GAGE (*Vadium*). A pawn or pledge.

GAGE, ESTATES IN. Estates held in pledge; such pledge being of two kinds: *vivum vadium*, living pledge, or *vifgage* (a phrase now obsolete); and *mortuum vadium*, dead pledge, or *mortgage*. [MORTGAGE.]

GALE. The payment of a rent or annuity [GAVAL].

GALE DAY. The day on which rent is payable.

GAME. A name used to denote animals and birds that are objects of the chase, *feræ naturæ*.

This word is defined under the Game Acts as including hares, pheasants, partridges, grouse, heath or moor game, black game, and bustards; though some of the provisions of these Acts are directed to deer, woodcock, snipe, quail, landrails, and rabbits.

At common law game belongs to a tenant and not to a landlord, but the right to game is frequently reserved to the landlord in the lease.

A game licence must be taken out by anyone killing or taking game. As to the right of an occupier to kill hares and rabbits, see the Ground Game Act 1880 and the Ground Game (Amendment) Act 1906. See also the Agricultural Holdings Act 1948, s. 14.

GAMING, or GAMBLING. "Gaming" means the playing of a game of chance for winnings in money or money's worth, whether any person playing the game is at risk of losing any money or money's worth or not; a "game of chance" includes a game of chance and skill combined, but not any athletic game or sport. See s. 52 of the Gaming Act 1968.

A gaming machine is a machine constructed or adapted for playing a game of chance by means of the machine, and which has a slot or other aperture for the insertion of money or money's worth in the form of cash or tokens (*ibid.*, s. 26).

Gaming licence duty is now payable under Part II of the Betting and Gaming Duties Act 1972, in respect of the following games: baccarat, punto banco, big six, blackjack, boule, chemin-de-fer, chuck-a-luck, craps, crown and anchor, faro, faro bank, hazard, poker dice, pontoon, French roulette, American roulette, trent-et-quarante, vingt-et-un, and wheel of fortune. A special duty is imposed on the game of bingo, but gaming carried on both in a private dwelling and on a domestic occasion do not require a licence. Dominoes and cribbage may be played in public houses.

GANANCIAL. A species of community in property enjoyed by husband and wife, the property being divisible equally between them on a dissolution of the marriage.

GAOL DELIVERY, COMMISSION OF. A commission which empowered the judges and others to whom it was directed to try every prisoner who should be in the gaol when they arrived at the circuit town.

GARNISHEE. A person who is *garnished* or warned. The word is especially applied in law to a debtor who is *warned* by the order of a court to pay his debt, not to his immediate creditor, but to a person who has obtained a final judgment against such creditor. The order is called a *garnishee order*. See R.S.C. 1965, Ord. 49 as to garnishee proceedings generally. [ARREST-MENT; CUSTOM OF LONDON.]

GARNISHMENT. Warning, notice, or instruction; as, a warning or notice given to a person to furnish the court with information material to a case before it; or to interplead with the plaintiff. [IN-TERPLEADER.] But the term is now generally used in connection with the attachment of debts in the hands of a third party. See preceding title.

GARROTTING. The criminal choking or strangling of a person, with intent to commit an indictable offence. It was formerly punishable by whipping under the Garrotters Act 1863; but that Act was repealed by the Criminal Justice Act 1948 on the abolition of the sentence of whipping.

GARTER. The honourable ensign of a great and noble society of knights, called Knights of the Order of St. George, or of the Garter. This order was first instituted by Edward III, upon good success in a skirmish, wherein the king's garter, it is said, was used as a token. The Order of the Garter is the first dignity after the nobility.

GARTH. A little backside or close in the north of England; an enclosure about a house or church; also a dam or weir in a river, for the catching of fish, vulgarly called a fishgarth.

GAVAL signifies tribute, toll, custom, annual rent or revenue, of which there were of old several sorts.

GAVELKIND. A tenure which before 1926 obtained by custom in the county of Kent, almost the whole of which was subject to it. It was also to be found in some other parts of the kingdom, and is supposed to have been the general custom of the realm in Saxon times. It was said to be a species of socage tenure, modified by the custom of the county. The principal characteristics of this tenure were these:—

1. The tenant was of age sufficient to alien his estate by feoffment at the age of fifteen. [FEOFFMENT.]

2. The estate never escheated in case of an attainder for felony; the maxim being "the father to the bough, the son to the plough." [ATTAINDER; ESCHEAT; FELONY.]

3. The tenant always enjoyed the power of disposing by will of the lands and tenements so held.

4. The lands descended on an intestacy,

GAVELKIND—*continued.*

not to the eldest son, but to all the sons together.

5. The widow was endowed of half the lands of which her husband died seised, and the husband was tenant by curtesy of the half, although he had no issue by his wife; but the estate of the husband and wife ceased by a second marriage.

Gavelkind was abolished by the Law of Property Act 1922 as respects enfranchised land; and by the Administration of Estates Act 1925, s. 45 as regards land generally. [CURTESY OF ENGLAND; DOWER.]

GAZETTE. The official publication of the Government, also called the *London Gazette.* It is evidence of acts of state, and of everything done by the Queen in her political capacity. Orders of adjudication in bankruptcy are required to be published therein; and the production of a copy of the *Gazette,* containing a copy of the order of adjudication, is conclusive evidence of the fact, and of the date thereof.

GELD, among the Saxons, signified money or tribute; also the compensation for a crime; also a fine or amerciament.

GEMOTE. A Saxon word, signifying an assembly or court.

GENERAL AGENT. An agent empowered to act *generally* in the affairs of his principal, or at least to act for him *generally* in some particular capacity; as opposed to one authorised to act for him in a particular manner.

GENERAL ANNUAL LICENSING MEETING. Sometimes called Brewster Sessions, this is a meeting of a committee of the justices for a petty sessional division, held annually in February for the purpose of granting and reviewing licences for the sale of intoxicating liquor.

GENERAL AVERAGE. [AVERAGE, 3.]

GENERAL DEMURRER. A demurrer not setting forth any special cause of demurrer. A general demurrer admitted all the facts as alleged to be true, and referred the case to the judgment of the court upon the substantial merits. Obsolete. [DEMURRER; SPECIAL DEMURRER.]

GENERAL EQUITABLE CHARGE. Any charge in the nature of a mortgage which is not secured by a deposit of documents relating to the legal estate affected, and does not arise, or affect an interest arising, under a trust for sale or a settlement. See Land Charges Act 1972, s. 2 (4), Class C (iii).

GENERAL ISSUE, PLEA OF. A plea which traversed, thwarted, and denied *generally* the whole of the declaration, information, or indictment, without offering any special matter whereby to evade it. Such was the plea of *not guilty* in an action of tort or on indictment for a criminal offence; a plea of *never indebted* in an action of debt, etc. Such pleas were called the general issue, because, by importing an absolute and general denial of what was alleged in the declaration, they amounted at once to an issue, *i.e.,* a fact affirmed on one side and denied on the other.

Since the Judicature Acts, the plea of the general issue is not admissible in ordinary civil actions, except in cases where it is expressly sanctioned by statute. See R.S.C. 1965, Ord. 18, r. 8, as to matters which must be specifically pleaded.

In criminal proceedings the general issue is "not guilty," which is pleaded *viva voce* by the prisoner at the bar. [NOT GUILTY.]

GENERAL LIEN. The right of a bailee to detain a chattel from its owner until payment be made, not only in respect of that particular article, but of any balance that may be due, on a general account between the bailor and bailee in the same line of business. [BAILMENT.]

GENERAL MEDICAL COUNCIL. A body established by s. 1 of the Medical Act 1956. The Council consists of eight members nominated by the Queen; twenty-seven members appointed by various bodies named in s. 3 of the Act (*e.g.,* the universities of Oxford, Cambridge, Durham, etc., the Royal Colleges of Physicians of London, Edinburgh, and so on); and eleven members elected by registered medical practitioners.

GENERAL SHIP. A merchant ship which is open *generally* to the conveyance of goods belonging to different owners; as opposed to a ship *chartered* or *freighted,* that is, a ship which is hired entirely by a single individual. [CHARTER-PARTY.]

GENERAL SYNOD. [SYNOD.]

GENERAL TAIL. [TAIL GENERAL.]

GENERAL VERDICT. A verdict which, in a civil suit, is absolutely for the plaintiff or for the defendant, or, in a criminal case, is a verdict of guilty or not guilty; opposed in either case to a special verdict, in which the naked facts are stated, and the inference of law left to be determined by the court.

GENERAL WORDS. These used generally to be added in conveyances, to convey the easements and rights subsisting in the grantor. They are now implied by s. 62 of the Law of Property Act 1925.

GENERALIA SPECIALIBUS NON DEROGANT. Generalities do not derogate from particular provisions.

GENERALIA VERBA SUNT GENERALITER INTELLIGENDA. General words are to be understood generally.

GENOCIDE. Acts committed with the intention of destroying, wholly or in part, a national, ethnical, racial or religious group. A Convention on the Prevention and Punishment of the Crime of Genocide (approved by the General Assembly of the United Nations) was entered into by the United Kingdom by the Genocide Act 1969.

GENTLEMAN. Under this name is comprised all above the rank of yeomen. [YEOMAN.]

GENTLEMAN USHER OF THE BLACK ROD. [BLACK ROD.].

GIFT. A conveyance which passes either land or goods. As to things immovable, when strictly taken, it was said to be applicable only to lands and tenements given in tail. This limitation of the word is, however, quite obsolete. Blackstone distinguishes a *gift* from a *grant* in that a gift is always gratuitous, without binding considerations, and therefore void in certain cases, whereas a grant is made upon some consideration or equivalent. [DONATIO MORTIS CAUSA; GRANT.]

GILD. A voluntary association or fraternity. [GUILD.] Also used as synonymous with *geld*, in such compounds as *weregild*. [GELD.]

GILDA MERCATORIA. A mercantile meeting or assembly, by the grant of which from the Crown to any set of men they become an incorporated society.

GIPSIES. An early definition under a statute of Henry VIII (1530) described "Egyptians" as wandering impostors and jugglers, using no craft nor feat of merchandise, pretending to tell men's and women's fortunes, and by craft and subtlety defrauding the people of their money.

This description would probably be most offensive to a true Romany, who would claim to be strictly honest and the preserver of various old country crafts. Nevertheless the colloquial meaning of gipsies is that of "persons without fixed abode who lead a nomadic life, dwelling in tents or other shelters, or in caravans or other vehicles" (*Mills* v. *Cooper*, [1967] 2 All E.R. 100).

By s. 16 of the Caravan Sites Act 1968, "gipsies" means persons of nomadic habit of life, whatever their race or origin, but does not include members of an organised group of travelling showmen, or of persons engaged in travelling circuses.

GIST OF ACTION. The cause for which an action lies, without which it is not maintainable.

GLANVILLE. The author of a book, written about 1181, entitled *Tractatus de legibus et consuetudinibus regni Angliae*, probably the first work of the kind in England.

GLEBE signifies the land of which a rector or vicar is seised in right of the church. The Tithe Act 1842 provided that the Tithe Commissioners (now the Minister of Agriculture, Fisheries and Food) should have power to ascertain and define the boundaries of the glebe lands of any benefice. As to sale of glebe see the Glebe Lands Act 1888, and rules made thereunder.

GLEBÆ ADSCRIPTITII. Villeinsocmen who could not be removed from the soil so long as they performed the services due from them.

GOD-BOTE. A church or ecclesiastical fine paid for offences committed against God.

GOD'S ACRE. A churchyard.

GOD'S PENNY. Earnest money given to a servant when hired.

GOLD. Where English law is the proper law of a contract under which a debt is payable, any reference in the contract

GOLD—*continued.*

to gold or gold coin will *prima facie* be construed as an indication of the means by which the amount of the debt is to be measured, and not as a requirement to make actual payment in gold. The word "gold" generally means gold coin or gold bullion.

As to hallmarking of gold and silver, see the Hallmarking Act 1973. [ASSAY ; CARAT ; HALLMARK.]

GOOD ABEARING (Lat. *Bonus gestus*). See next title.

GOOD BEHAVIOUR. Under ss. 91, 92 of the Magistrates' Courts Act 1952 magistrates have power to order any person to enter into a recognisance, with or without sureties, to keep the peace or to be of good behaviour. Such a person, if failing to comply with the order, may be committed to prison.

GOOD CONSIDERATION. A consideration founded on relationship or natural love and affection. This is not a *valuable* consideration, and will not "sustain a promise"; that is, that whereas in certain cases a "consideration" is necessary to give legal validity to a promise, so that an action may be brought for breach of the same, a merely "good" consideration will not be sufficient for this purpose. [CONSIDERATION ; CONTRACT.]

GOOD FAITH. A thing is deemed to be done in good faith where it is in fact done honestly, whether it is done negligently or not: Bills of Exchange Act 1882, s. 90. [BONA FIDES.]

GOOD HUSBANDRY. [HUSBANDRY.]

GOOD LEASEHOLD TITLE. Under the Land Registration Act 1925 leaseholds may sometimes be registered with a good leasehold title, which is intermediate between absolute and possessory title (*q.v.*). The effect of first registration with a good leasehold title is the same as registration with an absolute title, save that such registration does not affect or prejudice the enforcement of any estate, right or interest affecting or in derogation of the title of the lessor to grant the lease (s. 10).

GOODS AND CHATTELS, in the fullest sense, include any kind of property which, regard being had either to the subject-matter, or to the quantity of interest therein, is not freehold. But in practice the expression is most frequently limited to things movable, especially things movable in possession.

GOODWILL. The *goodwill* of a trade or business comprises every advantage which has been acquired by carrying on the business, whether connected with the premises in which the business has been carried on, or with the name of the firm by whom it has been conducted. "Probability that the old customers will resort to the old place" (Lord Eldon in *Cruttwell* v. *Lye* (1810), 17 Ves. 346).

Formerly a tenant could claim compensation for loss of goodwill, where the landlord would not renew the tenancy of business premises. This consideration must now be disregarded in the granting of a new tenancy by order of the court under s. 34 of the Landlord and Tenant Act 1954.

GOVERNMENT. This word is most frequently used to denote the principal executive officer or officers of a state or territory. Thus, when we in England speak of "the government," we generally understand the ministers of the Crown for the time being. But sometimes the word is used differently, so as to indicate the supreme legislative power in a state, or the legislature in a dependent, or semi-independent territory. The word is also used to indicate the art or science of government.

GRACE, ACT OF. [ACT OF GRACE.]

GRACE, DAYS OF. [DAYS OF GRACE.]

GRAND ASSISE. A peculiar species of trial by jury, introduced by King Henry II with consent of parliament, as an alternative open to the tenant or defendant, in the action called a *writ of right*, which he might demand in lieu of trial by battel, which up to that time had been the only means of deciding upon writs of right. Abolished in 1833. [WAGER OF BATTEL ; WRIT OF RIGHT.]

GRAND CAPE. [CAPE.]

GRAND COUSTUMIER OF NORMANDY. An ancient book containing the ducal customs of Normandy, by which the Channel Islands are for the most part governed.

GRAND DISTRESS. A more extensive kind of distress than ordinary, extending to all the goods and chattels of the party distrained within the county; it lay in those cases when the tenant or defendant was attached, and appeared not, but made default; and also when the other party made default after appearance.

It was thus more extensive than the writs of *grand* and *petit cape*. Obsolete. [CAPE.]

GRAND JURY. Until 1933 a bill of indictment (*q.v.*) had to be laid before a grand jury of from twelve to twenty-three persons. If the grand jury found a true bill, the bill became an indictment and was presented to the petty jury. The origin of the grand jury can be found in the Assize of Clarendon, 1166.

The Administration of Justice (Miscellaneous Provisions) Act 1933 abolished grand juries except those for the Counties of London and Middlesex for the purpose, in particular, of trials of offences by officials, such as colonial governors and others, committed abroad. The Criminal Justice Act 1948, abolished the grand jury altogether.

GRAND LARCENY. The name formerly given to the offence of stealing goods above the value of twelve pence. Abolished in 1827.

GRAND SERJEANTY. A tenure whereby the tenant was bound, instead of serving the king *generally* in the wars, to do some *special* honorary service to the king in person, as to carry his banner, his sword, or the like; or to be his butler, champion, or other officer at his coronation. It was in most other respects like knight-service. The services incident to grand and petty serjeanty were expressly retained by s. 136 of the Law of Property Act 1922. [PETIT SERJEANTY.]

GRANT (Lat. *Concessio*). 1. A grant may be defined generally as the transfer of property by an instrument in writing without the delivery of the possession of any subject-matter thereof. This may happen (1) where there is no subject-matter capable of delivery, as in the case of an advowson, patent right, or title of honour; (2) where the subject-matter is not capable of *immediate* delivery, as in the case of a reversion or remainder; (3) where, by reason of the subject-matter of the property being in the custody of another, or for any other cause, it is impracticable or undesir-

able to transfer the immediate possession. The person making the grant is called the *grantor*; the person to whom it is made the *grantee*. Where the grantor transfers his whole interest in any subject-matter, the grant is generally called an *assignment*.

A grant has always been the regular method of transferring incorporeal hereditaments, as an advowson, etc., and estates in expectancy, because no "livery", that is, physical delivery, could be made of such estates. For this reason they were said to *lie in grant*; while corporeal hereditaments in possession were formerly said to *lie in livery*. The word "grant" formerly implied a warranty of title, unless followed by a covenant imposing on the grantor a less liability. By s. 59 of the Law of Property Act 1925 the word "grant" is not to imply any covenant in law save where otherwise provided by statute. Nor is the word "grant" necessary to convey land or to create any interest therein. Nevertheless all lands and all interests therein lie "in grant" and are no longer capable of being conveyed by livery (*ibid.*, s. 51).

According to Blackstone, a *grant* is distinguished from a *gift* as being made upon some consideration or equivalent, whereas a gift is gratuitous. [GIFT.]

2. The word *grant* is also frequently used in reference to public money devoted by parliament for special purposes. *May.*

GRANT TO USES. This was the usual mode of transferring realty. It was a grant with uses superadded. Under the Law of Property Act 1925 the Statute of Uses was repealed and any provision in any statute or other instrument requiring land to be conveyed to uses now takes effect as a direction to convey the land upon the requisite trusts (s. 1 (9)).

GRASSON. A fine formerly paid on the transfer of a copyhold estate.

GRATUITOUS. Made without consideration or equivalent.

GRAVAMEN. 1. The *gravamen* of a charge or accusation is that part of it which weighs most heavily against the accused.

2. The word is applied specially to grievances alleged by the clergy, and made by them a subject of complaint to the archbishop and bishops in Convocation.

GRAY'S INN. One of the Inns of Court. [INNS OF COURT.]

GREAT CHARTER. [MAGNA CHARTA.]

GREAT SEAL. A seal by virtue of which a great part of the royal authority is exercised. The office of the Lord Chancellor, or Lord Keeper, is created by the delivery of the Great Seal into his custody. By art. 24 of the Union between England and Scotland it was provided that there should be one Great Seal for Great Britain, for sealing writs to summon parliaments, for sealing treaties with foreign states, and all public acts of state which concern the United Kingdom.

GREAT TITHES were generally held to include tithes of corn, hay and wood, otherwise called *praedial* tithes. In *appropriated* livings, they were for the most part reserved to the appropriators. No clear line of demarcation was drawn between *great* and *small* tithes. [APPROPRIATION; TITHES; VICAR.]

GREEN. A town or village green is land which has been allotted for the exercise or recreation of the inhabitants of any locality or on which such inhabitants have a customary right to indulge in lawful sports or pastimes. See s. 22 of the Commons Registration Act 1965.

GREEN CLOTH. The counting house of the royal household; so called from the green cloth on the table. [BOARD OF GREEN CLOTH.]

GREEN WAX signified originally the wax in which the seal of the Court of Exchequer was affixed to the estreats (*i.e.*, the extracted and authorised copies) of fines and amerciaments which the sheriff was directed to levy. Hence the expression "green wax" is applied to the estreats themselves. Now abolished.

GREGORIAN EPOCH. The time from which the Gregorian calendar or computation dates, *i.e.*, from the year 1582. So called after Pope Gregory XIII, who ordained that ten days in that year should be suppressed, in order to adjust the incorrect Julian calendar to the solar year. The Gregorian calendar was adopted by most countries in Europe, though not by England until the passing of the Calendar (New Style) Act 1750.

GRETNA GREEN MARRIAGES. An expression formerly applied to marriages contracted in Scotland by parties who had gone there for the purpose of being married without the delay and formalities required by the law of England. They were usually celebrated at Gretna Green in Dumfriesshire, as being the nearest and most convenient place for the purpose. The Marriage (Scotland) Act 1939, which came into operation on 1st July 1940, provided that such irregular marriages by declaration *de presenti* or by promise *subsequente copula* are invalid. The Act provided that any two persons who desired to be married in Scotland might contract to do so in the office of an authorised registrar, or, if certain conditions were complied with, by a sheriffs' licence.

GROGGING. Extracting spirits absorbed in the wood of casks. Prohibited by s. 114 of the Customs and Excise Act 1952.

GROSS. A word indicating independent ownership of incorporeal property. A right *in gross* is one which does *not* belong to the party invested with it *as being the owner or occupier of specifically-determined land* (*i.e.*, which is not *appendant* or *appurtenant* to another thing), but is annexed to, or inheres in, his person; being quite unconnected with anything corporeal, and existing as a separate subject of transfer; thus we speak of a common *in gross*, an advowson *in gross*, etc.

GROSS ADVENTURE. A loan on bottomry, that is, on mortgage of a ship. [BOTTOMRY.]

GROUND GAME. [GAME.]

GROUND RENT. A rent payable on a building lease.

GROUNDAGE. A former tribute paid for the ground on which a ship stood in port.

GUARANTEE, in the strict sense, is where one man contracts as surety on behalf of another an obligation to which the latter is also liable as the proper and primary party. A promise to answer for the debt, default or miscarriage of another, which to be enforceable must be evidenced in writing under s. 4 of the Statute of Frauds 1677.

GUARD DOG. [DOG.]

GUARDIAN. One who has the charge or custody of any person or thing; but commonly he who has the custody and education of such persons as are not of sufficient discretion to manage their own affairs.

I. GUARDIAN AND WARD.

The disabilities of a minor and his legal incapacity to manage his own affairs render it necessary that for the protection of his interests and for the management of his property he should have a guardian of his person and property, to whom he stands in the relation of ward. A person may be the guardian of a minor in various ways:—

1. *By Parental Right.* A father or mother has by parental right the guardianship of the person of a minor up to the age of eighteen as his natural guardian in the wider sense of the term.

2. *By Custom.* In some cities and boroughs there have been special customs as to the guardianship of a minor whose father is dead. In the City of London the Lord Mayor and Aldermen, in the Court of Orphans, had the right to the custody of the person and estate of a minor whose father was a freeman of the City and died within its limits.

3. *By Parental Appointment.* Both the father and the mother have power to appoint persons to act as guardians of a minor after their respective deaths, if the child is then a minor. No special words are necessary in making the appointment, which may be made by deed or will. See the Guardianship of Minors Acts 1971 and 1973.

4. *By Appointment of the Court.* The Family Division of the High Court of Justice in the exercise of its general jurisdiction over minors may, if it is for the minor's benefit so to do, appoint a guardian either where the minor has no guardian or where he has testamentary guardians or even if the minor's father is living, and can also, in the interests of the minor, remove an existing guardian and appoint another. The appointment by the court of a guardian of a minor who has no guardian constitutes the minor a ward of court. In appointing a guardian, the court must regard the welfare of the minor as the first and paramount consideration. See the Guardianship of Minors Acts 1971 and 1973.

Proceedings for the appointment of a minor's estate alone continue to be assigned to the Chancery Division.

II. GUARDIAN AD LITEM.

A minor defends all proceedings by a guardian *ad litem*, and a person to fill that office must be named before appearance is entered. Where he is assigned by the court, he must be a person within the jurisdiction. It is a matter of course for the guardian of the minor's person to be his guardian *ad litem*, but the office may be assigned to the official solicitor of the Court. See R.S.C. 1965, Ord. 80. For the practice of the County Courts as to the guardian *ad litem* see C.C.R., 1936, Ord. 5, rr. 11–18.

III. GUARDIAN OF MENTAL PATIENT.

An application for guardianship of a patient may be made under s. 33 of the Mental Health Act, 1959, on the grounds that such patient (*a*) is suffering from mental disorder, that is, mental illness or severe subnormality (or in the case of a patient under twenty-one years, psychopathic disorder or subnormality) and (*b*) that it is necessary (because his condition warrants it) that he should be so received into guardianship. The person named as guardian in the guardianship application must either be a local social services authority, or a person acceptable to the local social services authority. Regulations as to guardianship, correspondence with patients, visits and medical examinations, leave of absence from hospital, etc., while under guardianship are all dealt with in ss. 35 *et seq.* of the Act.

IV. GUARDIAN OF THE PEACE.

A person entrusted with the keeping of the peace as conservator thereof. [CONSERVATOR OF THE PEACE.]

V. GUARDIANS OF THE POOR.

Persons who formerly had the management of parish workhouses and unions. The National Assistance Act 1948 abolished the existing poor law and set up the National Assistance Board whose duty it became to assist persons who were without resources to meet their requirements.

GUILD. A voluntary association or fraternity, usually for some commercial purpose.

GUILD HALL means the place of meeting of a guild. [GUILD.]

GUILD CHURCH. Certain churches have been established in the City of London as guild churches, with the primary purpose of serving the non-resident daytime population of the City. Such churches

GUILD CHURCH—*continued.*
are free from the normal jurisdiction and control of incumbent, churchwardens and parochial church council, and their free-holds vest in the Bishop of London. See more fully the City of London (Guild Churches) Acts 1952 and 1960.

GUILD MERCHANT. A mercantile meeting of a guild. 1 *Bl.* [GUILD.]

GUILDHALL SITTINGS. Sittings held in the Guildhall of the City of London for City of London causes.

GULE OF AUGUST. The first of August, being the day of *St. Peter ad Vincula.*

GUN LICENCE. [FIREARMS CERTIFICATE.]

GYPSIES. [GIPSIES.]

H

HABEAS CORPORA JURATORUM. The name given to a compulsive process issuing out of the Court of Common Pleas for the bringing in of a jury, or of so many of them as refused to come upon a *venire facias,* upon the trial of a cause brought to issue. Abolished in 1852.

The corresponding process in the Court of King's (or Queen's) Bench was called a *distringas.* [DISTRINGAS.]

HABEAS CORPUS. This is the most celebrated writ in the English law, being the great remedy which that law has provided for the violation of personal liberty.

The most important species of *habeas corpus* is that of *habeas corpus ad subjiciendum,* which is the remedy used for deliverance from illegal confinement. This is directed to any person who detains another in custody, and commands him to produce the body, with the day and cause of his caption and detention, *ad faciendum, subjiciendum et recipiendum*—to do, submit to, and receive whatsoever the judge or court awarding such writ shall direct. This writ existed at common law, though it has been improved by statute. By the Habeas Corpus Act 1862, no writ of *habeas corpus* shall issue out of England, by authority of any judge or court therein, into any colony or foreign dominion of the Crown, where Her Majesty has a lawfully-established court with power to grant and issue such

writ, and with power to ensure its due execution throughout such colony or dominion. It has been held that this statute does not extend to the Isle of Man.

There are also other kinds of *habeas corpus* mentioned in the books.

1. *Ad respondendum*; which was to bring up a prisoner confined by the process of an inferior court to charge him with a fresh action in the court above.

2. *Ad satisfaciendum,* with a similar object when *judgment* in an inferior court has been obtained against the prisoner.

3. *Ad faciendum et recipiendum* (otherwise called a *habeas corpus cum causa*). This writ was applied for when, in an action in an inferior court, the defendant had been arrested; and it had for its object to remove the proceedings and bring up the body of the defendant to the court above, "to do and receive what the king's court shall deliver in that behalf."

4. *Ad prosequendum, testificandum, deliberandum,* etc., which was issued for bringing up a prisoner to bear testimony in any court, or to be tried in the proper jurisdiction.

But the present law of arrest for debt has lessened the importance of all these species except the last; and, with regard to the last, the occasions for its use have diminished now that, by various recent enactments, its objects can be attained by order of a judge or of a secretary of state.

HABENDUM. That clause of a deed which determines the estate or interest granted by the deed.

HABERE FACIAS POSSESSIONEM. A writ of execution to recover possession of a chattel interest in real estate. Now, by R.S.C. 1965, Ord. 45, r. 3, a judgment that a party recover possession of land may be enforced by writ of possession.

HABIT AND REPUTE. By Scottish law marriage may be established by habit and repute when the parties cohabit and are at the same time held and reputed as man and wife.

HABITUAL CRIMINAL. Under the Prevention of Crime Act 1908 a person who had, since attaining the age of sixteen, been convicted at least three times of a crime, and was leading a dishonest life, could be convicted of being an habitual criminal. The Prevention of Crime Act was repealed by the Criminal Justice Act 1948, under which the term "habitual criminal" was replaced by the term "persistent offender". As to the power of courts to deal with persistent offenders, see now ss. 28, 29 of the Powers of Criminal Courts Act 1973.

HABITUAL DRUNKARD. A person who, not being a mentally disordered person within the meaning of the Mental Health Act 1959, is notwithstanding, by reason of habitual intemperate drinking of intoxicating liquor, at times dangerous to himself or to others, or incapable of managing himself or his affairs; or who so conducts himself that it would not be reasonable to expect a spouse of ordinary sensibilities to continue to cohabit with him. See the Habitual Drunkards Act 1879, which establishes retreats, etc.; and the Matrimonial Proceedings (Magistrates' Courts) Act 1960, under which relief is made available to either husband or wife on the grounds of the habitual drunkenness of the other.

HÆREDITAS NUNQUAM ASCENDIT. The right of inheritance never lineally ascends. This is no longer true, since by s. 6 of the Inheritance Act 1833 every lineal ancestor is capable of being heir to any of his issue.

HÆRETICO COMBURENDO. The writ known as *breve de hæretico comburendo* formerly lay for burning him who, having once been convicted of heresy by his bishop, afterwards fell again into the same or some other heresy, and was thereupon delivered over to the secular power. It was abolished in the reign of Charles II by the Ecclesiastical Jurisdiction Act 1677.

HALF-BLOOD. The relationship between two persons who have but one *nearest* common ancestor, and not a pair of *nearest* common ancestors.

In the succession to personal property, the law made no difference between relationship by the half-blood and that by the whole blood; but in the succession to land the rule was that the kinsman of the half-blood succeeded next after the kinsman in the same degree of the whole blood when the common ancestor was a male, and next after the common ancestor when the common ancestor was a female: see s. 9 of the Inheritance Act 1833. Under s. 46 of the Administration of Estates Act 1925, which relates equally to real and personal estate, relatives of the whole blood take priority over relatives of the half-blood, *i.e.*, the half-blood relatives take immediately after the whole blood relatives of the same degree.

HALLMARK. A stamp authorised to be impressed on gold or silver articles. The law as to hallmarking was revised by the Hallmarking Act 1973. Hallmarks must be stamped by assay offices.

Approved hallmarks for articles comprised of a single precious metal made in the United Kingdom are, for the respective assay offices: London, a leopard's head; Edinburgh, a castle; Birmingham, an anchor; Sheffield, a rose. For articles other than those made in the United Kingdom, the approved marks are: London, the sign of the constellation Leo; Edinburgh, St. Andrew's Cross; Birmingham, an equilateral triangle; Sheffield, the sign of the constellation Libra. In addition, articles of gold made in the United Kingdom must be marked with a crown, and those of silver with a lion passant (Edinburgh, a lion rampant) and those of platinum with an orb surmounted by a cross. All articles must also be marked with a standard of fineness. [ASSAY; CARAT.]

HALLMOTE, or **HALIMOTE.** The meeting of tenants of one hall or manor. A Saxon court answering to our court-baron.

HALYMOTE. A holy or ecclesiastical court. Also the same as hallmote. [HALLMOTE.]

HAM. A house; also a village or little town.

HAMESECKEN, or **HAMSOKEN.** The ancient word for burglary or housebreaking.

HAMLET. The diminutive of *ham.* [HAM.]

HANAPER OFFICE. A former office in the Court of Chancery on its *common law side* (*i.e.*, within what was formerly called the "ordinary jurisdiction" of the court). [CHANCERY.] Of the writs issuing out of this "common law side", those having exclusive reference to the affairs of the *subject* were formerly kept in a *hamper* (*in hanaperio*); while those relating to matters in which the Crown was mediately or immediately concerned were kept in a little

HANAPER OFFICE—*continued.*

sack or bag (*in parva baga*). Hence the *hanaper office* signified the office on the common law side of the Court of Chancery devoted to business relating to the affairs of the subject. Abolished by incorporation in the Central Office under the Judicature Acts.

HANDLING of stolen goods, the modern expression for the offence formerly known as *receiving* stolen goods. See s. 22 of the Theft Act 1968.

HAND-SALE. A sale made by shaking of hands.

HARBOURING. An offence under various enactments; *e.g.*, it was an offence to harbour thieves or reputed thieves, by ss. 10, 11 of the Prevention of Crimes Act 1871 (though these sections have now been repealed as obsolete or redundant by the Theft Act 1968); and to harbour common prostitutes and reputed thieves in refreshment places, by s. 35 of the Town Police Clauses Act 1847, etc.

Harbouring of a spouse or child was also formerly an offence, but actions for harbouring were abolished by the Law Reform (Miscellaneous Provisions) Act 1970.

HARD LABOUR. A punishment most usually inflicted in company with imprisonment, first introduced in 1706 and abolished by the Criminal Justice Act, 1948. Section 1 (2) of that Act provided that every enactment conferring power on a court to pass a sentence of imprisonment with hard labour should be construed as conferring power to pass a sentence of imprisonment.

HARE. A beast of warren. It is "game" within s. 2 of the Game Act 1831. By s. 1 of the Hares Act 1848 owners and occupiers and persons authorised by them may kill hares without a game certificate. A close season for hares is imposed by the Hares Preservation Act 1892, which prevents them from being *sold* from March to July. See also the Ground Game Act 1880, and the Ground Game (Amendment) Act 1906.

HARIOT. The same as heriot. [Heriot.]

HAWKER. Any person who travelled with a horse or other beast bearing or drawing burden, and who went from place to place or to other men's houses carrying to sell or exposing for sale any goods, wares or merchandise, including any person who travelled by any means of locomotion to any place in which he did not usually reside or carry on business, and there sold or exposed for sale any goods, etc., in or at any house, shop, room, booth, stall, etc.; Hawkers Act 1888, repealed by the Local Government Act 1966. Hawkers no longer require excise licences.

HAYBOTE, or **HEDGEBOTE.** Necessary stuff to make and repair hedges, or to make rakes and forks, and suchlike instruments; or a permission, expressed or implied, to take the same.

HEADBOROUGH, or **HEADBOROW,** signified him that was chief of the frankpledge, tithing, or decennary, appointed to preside over the rest, being supposed the discreetest man in the borough, town or tithing. [FRANKPLEDGE; TITHING.] The office of headborough was united with that of petty constable, on the institution of the latter office, about the reign of Edward III. [CONSTABLE, 1.]

HEARING. The trial of an action. In general, all cases, both civil and criminal, must be heard in open court, but in certain exceptional cases, where the administration of justice would be rendered impracticable by the presence of the public, the court may sit in camera, *e.g.* where it is necessary for the public safety, or in proceedings for an offence against morality or decency when evidence is given by children or young persons (*Hals. Laws*). [SITTINGS IN CAMERA.]

HEARSAY EVIDENCE. Evidence of a fact not actually perceived by a witness with one of his own senses, but proved by him to have been stated by another person. Hearsay evidence is in general not admissible, but the law has from early times allowed several exceptions. The instances of admissible hearsay evidence may be stated as follows:—

(1) Admissions in civil cases.
(2) Voluntary confessions in criminal cases.
(3) Declarations in course of duty.
(4) Declarations against interest.
(5) Declarations as to pedigree.
(6) Declarations as to public and general rights.

(7) Declarations as to bodily or mental conditions.
(8) Dying declarations where murder or manslaughter is the subject of the charge.
(9) Declarations as to contents of wills.
(10) Evidence given in former proceedings.
(11) Statements in public documents.

The other branch of exceptions to the rule excluding hearsay consists of those arising out of the Evidence Act 1938.

In any civil proceedings a statement other than one made by a person while giving oral evidence in those proceedings is admissible only by virtue of the Civil Evidence Act 1968, or other statutory provision or by agreement. See generally the Civil Evidence Acts 1968 and 1972.

HEARTH MONEY. [CHIMNEY MONEY.]

HEIR. 1. At common law, an heir was he that succeeded by right of blood to any man's lands and tenements in fee; that is, he upon whom, by right of blood, the law cast the real estate of a deceased person intestate. Part IV of the Administration of Estates Act 1925 abolished heirship in this sense and made new provisions as to intestacy, applying equally to real and personal estate. Under s. 132 of the Law of Property Act 1925 a limitation of real or personal property in favour of the heir, either general or special, which would, before the Act, have conferred on the heir an estate, operates to confer a corresponding equitable interest on the person who would have answered to the description of heir if the Act had not been passed.

2. The term heirs was used in conveyances of estates in which it was intended that the fee-simple should pass: thus, a conveyance before 1926 to "A and his heirs" gave A an estate in fee-simple. The word as thus used was called a word of *limitation* and not of *purchase*, because the heirs of A took nothing *directly* under the grant, but the word was used to *limit* or *mark out* the estate taken by A. [RULE IN SHELLEY'S CASE.] This so-called Rule in Shelley's Case has been abolished but an exception is made by s. 130 of the Law of Property Act 1925, which expressly provides that an interest in tail or in tail male or in tail female or in tail special may be created by the same words as before 1926 so

that "to A and the heirs of his body" are words of limitation conferring an entailed interest on A while apparently the words "to A and his heirs" confer a mere life interest upon A.

HEIR APPARENT and **HEIR PRESUMPTIVE.** It is a rule in law, that no one is the heir of a living person (*nemo est hæres viventis*). The heir is called into existence by the death of his ancestor, for no man in his lifetime can have an heir.

The *heir apparent* is the person who, if he survives the ancestor, must certainly be his heir, as the eldest son in the lifetime of his father.

The *heir presumptive* is the person who would be the heir in case of the ancestor's immediate decease. Thus, an only daughter there being no sons, is the heiress presumptive of her father: for if he were now to die, she would at once be his heir; but he may have a son who would supplant her. For the present rules as to intestacy, see the Administration of Estates Act 1925.

HEIR AT LAW. The person who, before 1926, succeeded as heir by right of blood, according to the disposition of the law. [HEIR.]

HEIR BY CUSTOM. One upon whom a local custom cast the inheritance of a deceased ancestor, *e.g.*, gavelkind.

HEIR IN TAIL. The person selected by law to succeed to the estate tail of an ancestor dying intestate. After 1925, if an entailed interest is not devised or barred, it still descends to an heir in the same manner as it did before 1926. See s. 130 (4) of the Law of Property Act 1925, and s. 45 (2) of the Administration of Estates Act 1925.

HEIRESS. A female heir. Sometimes the word is used in a more extended sense, as in the expression *fraudulent abduction of heiress*; an offence formerly punishable by imprisonment for fourteen years under s. 18 of the Sexual Offences Act 1956 (repealed by the Family Law Reform Act 1969). The meaning of "heiress" in the section was a girl under the age of twenty-one, who was taken or detained out of the possession of her parent or guardian against *his* (the parent or guardian's) will, if she had property or expectations of property, and was so taken or detained by fraud and with the intention that she should marry or have unlawful sexual intercourse.

HEIRLOOM signifies, strictly, a *limb* or member of the inheritance. By *heirlooms* are generally meant implements or ornaments of a household, or other personal chattels, which accrued to the heir with the house itself by custom; or else such chattels, *e.g.*, furniture, pictures, etc., as are directed by will or settlement to follow the limitations thereby made of some family mansion or estate.

HELL. A colloquial name for a debtor's prison, *e.g.*, that under the Exchequer Chamber in which the king's debtors were once confined.

HERALDS' COLLEGE. The College of Arms, or Heralds' College, is an ancient royal corporation instituted by Richard III in 1483. At its head is the Earl Marshal, a hereditary title held by the Dukes of Norfolk. He is assisted by thirteen officers of the College, as follows: Garter King-at-Arms, Clarenceux King-at-Arms, Norroy King-at-Arms; the Richmond, Windsor, Somerset, Lancaster, York and Chester Heralds; and four Poursuivants, or messengers, with the titles Rouge Dragon, Rouge Croix, Bluemantle, and Portcullis.

The Heralds' office is still empowered to make grants of arms and to permit changes of name. Their books are good evidence of pedigrees. The Earl Marshal also presides over the Court of Chivalry (*q.v.*) which exercises jurisdiction in questions of precedence and the use of armorial bearings.

HERBAGE. The fruit of the earth, produced by nature for the bite and food of cattle. But it is also used for a liberty that a man has to feed his cattle in another man's ground.

HERBAGIUM ANTERIUS. The first crop of grass or hay, in opposition to *aftermath*, or second cutting. [AFTERMATH.]

HEREDITAMENT means any real property which on an intestacy occurring before 1926 might have devolved upon an heir. See the Law of Property Act, 1925, s. 205 (1) (ix). The word includes everything which might have descended to the heir. [CORPOREAL PROPERTY; HEIR; HEIRLOOM; INCORPOREAL HEREDITAMENT; REAL AND PERSONAL PROPERTY.]

HERESY. An offence which consisted not in a total denial of Christianity, but of some of its essential doctrines, publicly and obstinately avowed. [HÆRETICO COMBURENDO.] Heresy was subject to ecclesiastical correction, by virtue of the Ecclesiastical Jurisdiction Act 1677, repealed by the Ecclesiastical Jurisdiction Act 1963.

HERETIC. [HÆRETICO COMBURENDO; HERESY.]

HERIOT. The best beast or other chattel of a tenant, seized on his death by the lord. The heriot of a military tenant was his arms and habiliments of war, which belonged to the lord for the purpose of equipping his successor. Heriots from freeholders were rare; but heriots from copyholders remained until recently, in many manors, a badge of ancient servility of the tenure. But the right of the lord, in this as in other respects, was controlled by the custom of the manor. In some cases the heriot consisted merely of a money-payment. The above kind of heriot was called *heriot custom*; but there was another kind, called *heriot service*, which was due upon a special reservation in a grant or lease of lands; but this kind of heriot scarcely ever existed except where it formed part of the service by which a particular tenement had been held from time immemorial. Under the provisions of the Law of Property Act 1922 copyholds and manorial incidents (including heriots) became extinct. Pending extinguishment of the right, however, it was provided by s. 128 (2) of the Act that the lord was not entitled, as formerly, to seize the best beast or chattel, but that a sum equal to its value was payable to him.

HERRING SILVER. A composition in money for the custom of supplying herrings for the provision of a religious house.

HIDAGE. An extraordinary tax paid for every hide of land.

HIDE OF LAND. A certain quantity of land, such as might be ploughed with one plough in a year. According to some it was sixty acres; others say eighty, and others a hundred. The quantity probably was always determined by local usage.

HIGH BAILIFFS. Officers formerly appointed to sit in county courts, and whose duty it was to serve all summonses and orders, and to execute all the warrants, precepts and writs issued out of the court. The last high bailiff retired in 1958 and the office is now held by the registrar (*q.v.*) *virtute officii*. References to a high bailiff in any enactment, etc., are accordingly to be construed as references to a registrar: County Courts Act 1959, s. 207.

HIGH COMMISSION COURT. A court of ecclesiastical jurisdiction, erected and united to the regal power by the Act of Supremacy 1588. It was intended to vindicate the peace of the church by reforming, ordering, and correcting the ecclesiastical state and persons, and all manner of errors, heresies, schisms, abuses, offences, contempts, and enormities. Under the shelter of these very general words the High Commission Court exercised extraordinary and despotic powers of fine and imprisonment. Nor did it confine its jurisdiction altogether to cases of spiritual cognizance. For these reasons the court was abolished in 1640. James II afterwards attempted to revive it, but it was finally declared illegal by the Bill of Rights 1688.

HIGH CONSTABLE. [CONSTABLE.]

HIGH COURT OF CHANCERY. [CHANCERY, COURT OF.]

HIGH COURT OF JUSTICE. [SUPREME COURT OF JUDICATURE.]

HIGH SEAS. That part of the sea which is more than three miles distant from the coast. The territorial jurisdiction of a country does not extend beyond the three-mile limit. Offences committed on board a British ship on the high seas are punishable by English law as if committed on British soil, such a ship being in law part of the territory of the United Kingdom.

HIGH STEWARD. An expression used:—

1. Of the Lord High Steward, who held a court appointed, *pro hac vice*, during a recess of parliament, for the trial of a peer indicted for treason or felony, or for misprision of either. The privilege of peerage in relation to criminal proceedings was abolished in 1948. [COURT OF LORD HIGH STEWARD OF GREAT BRITAIN.]

2. Of the Lord High Steward of the Royal Household. [COURT OF LORD HIGH STEWARD OF THE QUEEN'S HOUSEHOLD.]

3. Of the Lord High Steward of the University of Oxford, an officer of the University appointed to preside at the trial of any scholar or privileged person of the University, or any indictment for treason or felony, of which the Vice-Chancellor of the University may have claimed and been allowed cognizance. Before the office of the High Steward is called into action he must have been approved by the Lord High Chancellor of England. [UNIVERSITY COURTS.]

HIGH TREASON. [TREASON.]

HIGH-WATER MARK. That part of the sea shore which the waters usually reach when the tide is highest.

HIGHWAY. A public road which all the subjects of the realm have a right to use for the purposes of passing and repassing. Highways exist by prescription, by Act of Parliament, or by dedication to the public on the part of individuals. The law relating to the creation, maintenance, improvement, etc., of highways is consolidated in the Highways Acts 1959 to 1971. [DEDICATION OF WAY; PRESCRIPTION.]

HIGHWAY CODE. A code compiled by the Secretary of State for the Environment, containing directions for the guidance of persons using the roads. See s. 37 of the Road Traffic Act 1972. Failure to observe a provision of the Code does not of itself render a person liable to criminal proceedings, but such failure may be relied upon by any party to proceedings as tending to establish a negative liability.

HIJACKING. An offence committed by any person who, on board an aircraft in flight, by the use of force or by threats of any kind, seizes or exercises control of the aircraft. The offence was created by the Hijacking Act 1971, which enabled the United Kingdom to ratify the Convention for the Suppression of Unlawful Seizure of Aircraft (1970).

"Flight", for the purpose of this enactment, is deemed to include any period from the moment an aircraft's external doors are closed following embarkation until the moment when any such door is opened for disembarkation and, in the case of a forced landing, any period until the competent authorities take over responsibility for the aircraft and for persons and property on board.

It is also an offence to hijack a vehicle or a ship in Northern Ireland or the Republic of Ireland: see s. 2 of the Criminal Jurisdiction Act 1975.

HIRE-PURCHASE SYSTEM. Under this system the person who hires the goods becomes, upon payment of the last instalment of the amount fixed, the owner of them. The hirer is given certain rights although he defaults in his payments. The Hire-Purchase Acts are now largely repealed by the Consumer Credit Act 1974, which controls the extension of credit to individuals, including "consumer hire agreements".

HIRING (Roman law, *locatio conductio*) is a contract which differs from borrowing only in this, that hiring is always for a price, stipend, or additional recompense; whereas borrowing is merely gratuitous. It is a bailment for reward whereby the possession of goods, with a transient property therein, is transferred for a particular time or use, on condition to restore the goods so hired as soon as the time is expired or use performed. It is of four kinds. The hiring (1) of a thing for use (*locatio rei*); (2) of work and labour (*locatio operis faciendi*); (3) of services to be performed on the thing delivered (*locatio custodiæ*); (4) of the carriage of goods (*locatio operis mercium vehendarum*). [BAILMENT.]

HISTORIC BUILDING. [ANCIENT MONUMENT.]

HISTORIC WRECK. [WRECK.]

HOLDER. A payee or indorsee in possession of a bill of exchange or a promissory note.

HOLDER IN DUE COURSE. One who has taken a bill of exchange, cheque or note, complete and regular on the face of it, and who became the holder of it before it was overdue and without notice of previous dishonour and who took it in good faith and for value without notice of any defect in the title of the person who negotiated it. See s. 29 of the Bills of Exchange Act 1882.

HOLDING, in the Agricultural Holdings Act 1948, means the aggregate of the agricultural land comprised in a contract of tenancy.

HOLDING OUT. Inducing other persons to believe in the existence of an authority which does not exist in fact. The party so holding out may afterwards be estopped from denying the supposed authority. As to holding one's self out as a partner, see s. 3 of the Partnership Act 1890.

HOLDING OVER is where a man, having come into possession of land under a lawful title, continues possession after the title has expired; as if a man takes a lease for a year, and after the year is expired continues to hold the premises without any fresh lease from the owner of the estate. [DOUBLE RENT; DOUBLE VALUE.]

HOLOGRAPH is a deed or writing written entirely by the "grantor's" own hand. On account of the difficulty with which the forgery of such a document can be accomplished it is held by the Scotch law valid without witnesses. So, a holograph will is a will written in the testator's own hand.

HOLY ORDERS in the English Church are the orders of bishops (including archbishops), priests and deacons.

HOMAGE. A ceremony performed by a vassal or tenant upon investiture, in which, openly and humbly kneeling, being ungirt, uncovered and holding up his hands both together between those of his lord, who sat before him, he professed that "he did become his *man*, from that day forth, of life and limb and earthly honour"; and then he received a kiss from his lord. The ceremony was denominated *homagium* or *manhood* by the feudists, from the stated form of words, *devenio vester homo*.

Homage auncestral was where a man and his ancestors had immemorially holden land of another or his ancestors by the service of homage.

The word *homage* is also used to signify the tenants of a major present at the lord's court, and a jury consisting of such tenants was called a *homage jury*.

HOMAGER. One that does, or is bound to do, homage to another.

HOMESTEAD (*Canada*). A term used in Western Canada with respect to exemption from seizure under execution, and to right similar to dower. It means a dwelling house occupied by the owner as his home.

HOMICIDE. The killing of a human being by a human being. It is usually divided into three kinds—*justifiable*, *excusable*, and *felonious*.

1. *Justifiable homicide* is of three kinds:—

(1) The putting a man to death pursuant to a legal sentence, as *e.g.*, for treason.

(2) The killing, by an officer of justice, of a person who assaults or resists him, and cannot otherwise be taken.

(3) The killing of persons for the dispersion of riots or rebellious assemblies, or the prevention of atrocious crimes, such as murder and rape.

2. *Excusable homicide* is of two sorts: either—

(1) *Per infortunium,* by misadventure.

(2) *Se defendendo,* in self-defence.

This kind of self-defence is to be distinguished from that included under the head of justifiable homicide, to hinder the perpetration of a capital crime, by the fact that, in the case now supposed, the person killing has himself to blame (though ever so slightly) for the circumstances which have led to the killing. There is now no practical difference between justifiable and excusable homicide.

3. *Criminal homicide.* This is any killing not included in the two previous categories and is divided into three kinds, *manslaughter, murder* and *infanticide* which will be found discussed under their respective titles.

HONEST. [DISHONEST.]

HONORARIUM. A gratuity given for professional services.

HONORARY FEUDS. Titles of nobility, which were not of a divisible nature, but could be inherited only by the eldest son; whereas, originally, the *military* feuds descended to all the sons alike. [FEUDAL SYSTEM.]

HONORARY SERVICES were such as were incident to grand-serjeanty. They were commonly annexed to some *honour.* [HONOUR.]

HONOUR, besides its general signification is a word used more especially—

1. For the nobler sort of seigniories, whereupon other inferior lordships and manors depended. It seems that originally none were "honours" but such as belonged to the king, though afterwards given in fee to noblemen.

2. The word is also used in reference to the acceptance *for honour* of a bill of exchange. [ACCEPTANCE SUPRA PROTEST.]

3. It is also used generally in regard to bills of exchange. To honour a bill is to pay it.

HONOUR COURTS were courts held within *honours.* [HONOUR, 1.]

HOSTILE WITNESS. If a witness under examination in chief shows himself "hostile" to the party who called him, he may by leave of the judge be cross-examined by the party who called him, as though he had been called by the opposite party. See s. 3 of the Criminal Procedure Act 1865.

HOTCHPOT literally signifies a pudding mixed with divers ingredients; but, by a metaphor, it signifies a commixture or putting together of lands of several tenures, for the equal division of them. The word is frequently applied in reference to settlements which give a power to a parent of appointing a fund among his or her children, wherein it is provided that no child, taking a share of the fund under any appointment, shall be entitled to any share in the unappointed part without bringing his or her share into "hotchpot" and accounting for the same accordingly. The effect of such a clause would be to prevent a child who takes under an appointment from claiming his full share in the unappointed part, in addition to his appointed share. See also s. 47 of the Administration of Estates Act 1925.

HOTEL. An establishment held out by the proprietor as offering food, drink and, if so required, sleeping accommodation, without special contract, to any traveller presenting himself who appears able and willing to pay a reasonable sum for the services and facilities provided and who is in a fit state to be received: Hotel Proprietors Act 1956, s. 1 (3). [INN.]

HOUSE OF COMMONS. The lower House of Parliament, consisting of the representatives of the nation at large, exclusive of the peerage and the prelates. *May.* Although the House of Commons together with the House of Lords forms the High Court of Parliament it is not strictly speaking a judicial body. Its jurisdiction is confined to bills of attainder and of pains and penalties. In addition the House has jurisdiction over persons for committing any breach of the privileges of the House or of any of its members (*Hals. Laws*).

HOUSE OF KEYS. [KEYS.]

HOUSE OF LORDS. The upper House of the legislature, consisting of the

HOUSE OF LORDS—*continued.*

lords spiritual and the lords temporal. The lords spiritual consist of the archbishops of Canterbury and York; of the bishops of London, Durham, and Winchester; and of twenty-one other bishops. The lords temporal are the hereditary peers of England, Scotland, Great Britain and the United Kingdom who have not disclaimed their peerages under the Peerages Act 1963; life peers created under the Life Peerages Act 1958; and Lords of Appeal in Ordinary created under the Appellate Jurisdiction Act 1876. A certain number of peers are elected, under the Act of Union with Scotland, to represent in the House of Lords the body of the Scottish nobility; but it was held in *Petition of the Earl of Antrim*, [1967] 1 A.C. 691, that the right to elect Irish representative peers no longer exists. The aggregate number of the Lords temporal is indefinite, and may be increased at will by the Crown. The House of Lords is also the court of final appeal in all civil causes except from certain Commonwealth courts, appeals from which are heard by the Judicial Committee of the Privy Council as a court of final appeal. *May*. In addition to its appellate jurisdiction the House of Lords has jurisdiction in impeachment and over peerage claims, and also over any breach of its privileges.

HOUSEBOTE signifies estovers, or an allowance of necessary timber out of the lord's wood, for the repair and support of a house or tenement, and for fuel. This belongs, of common right, to a lessee for years or for life.

HOUSEBREAKING was the offence of breaking and entering a house, building, shop, etc., and committing a felony therein, or with the intention of committing a felony therein; or, after committing a felony therein, breaking out of the same. It differed from burglary in that burglary was formerly committed by night, and only in respect of a dwelling-house; whereas house-breaking might be by day and in respect of other buildings.

The law was radically altered by the Theft Act 1968, under which housebreaking is no longer a separate offence, although the offence of possessing "house-breaking implements" remains. Burglary is no longer a night-time offence. The distinction between felony and misdemeanour was abolished by s. 1 of the Criminal Law Act 1967. [BURGLARY; FELONY; THEFT.]

HOUSE-BURNING. [ARSON.]

HOUSE-DUTY. A tax on inhabited houses imposed in 1851 in lieu of window-duty. Abolished by the Finance Act 1924.

HUE AND CRY (Lat. *Hutesium et clamor*) is the old common law process of pursuing, with horn and with voice, all felons, and such as have dangerously wounded another. If a man wantonly and maliciously raises a hue and cry without cause he is liable to fine and imprisonment, and also to an action at the suit of the party injured. See s. 8 of the Sheriffs Act 1887.

HUNDRED was part of a county or shire, probably so called because at first it contained ten tithings, composed each of ten families; or else because the king found therein a hundred able men of his wars. The hundred was originally governed by a high constable or bailiff; and formerly there was regularly held in it the hundred court for the trial of causes. [CONSTABLE, 1; HUNDRED COURT.]

HUNDRED COURT. A larger Court Baron, being held for all the inhabitants of a particular hundred instead of a manor. The free suitors were here also the judges, and the steward the registrar, as in the case of the Court Baron. Causes might be removed from it, and its decisions reviewed by a writ of false judgment. [FALSE JUDGMENT, WRIT OF.] It had been long obsolete when its jurisdiction was practically abolished by s. 28 of the County Courts Act 1867 (repealed) by which it was enacted that no action which could be brought in a county court should thenceforth be maintainable in any hundred or other inferior court not being a court of record.

HUNDREDERS, or **HUNDREDORS,** were men empanelled, or fit to be empanelled, as jurors upon a controversy, dwelling in the hundred where the land in question lay, or the cause of action arose, or accusation was tried. It was formerly necessary that there should be a competent number of hundreders on every panel. They were also liable for damage done by rioters, until such liability was transferred to police districts in 1886.

HUSBAND AND WIFE. At common law they were for the most part treated as one person. The property of a wife became, with few exceptions, that of the husband. At common law a husband could not make a conveyance directly to his wife. This could be effected, however, through the medium of a use or trust, or by will. The *property* distinction between a married woman and an unmarried woman has been almost entirely removed by statute. See the Married Women's Property Acts, the Law of Property Act 1925, and the Law Reform (Married Women and Tortfeasors) Act 1935, which latter act also abolished the husband's liability for his wife's torts and ante-nuptial contracts, etc.

HUSH-MONEY. A bribe to hinder the giving of information.

HUSTINGS. A *house* of *things* or causes from *hus*, house, and *thing*, cause. A platform from which parliamentary candidates formerly addressed the electors. [COURT OF HUSTINGS.]

HUTESIUM ET CLAMOR. Hue and cry. [HUE AND CRY.]

HYPNOTISM. Includes mesmerism, and any similar act or process which produces or is intended to produce in any person any form of induced sleep or trance, in which the susceptibility of the mind of that person to suggestion or direction is increased or intended to be increased. Demonstrations of hypnotism at places of entertainment and other places are controlled by the Hypnotism Act 1952.

HYPOTHECA, HYPOTHEC, or **HYPOTHEK.** A security for a debt which remains in the possession of the debtor; differing thus from a *pledge*, which is handed over to the creditor:—

1. Thus, a mortgage of land, where the mortgagee does not take possession, is in the nature of a *hypotheca*. 2 *Bl*.

2. So, to mortgage a ship for necessaries is called *hypothecation*. 2 *Bl*.

HYPOTHECATION. See previous title.

I

I O U (I owe you) is a written acknowledgment of a debt. It operates merely as evidence of a debt due by virtue of some antecedent contract. It does not require to be stamped.

IBIDEM, IBID., ID. In the same place or case.

ID CERTUM, ETC. [CERTUM, ETC.]

IDEM SONANS (sounding alike). The courts will not set aside proceedings on account of misspelling of names, provided the variance is so slight as not to mislead, or the name as spelt be *idem sonans, e.g.,* Lawrance for Lawrence.

IDENTITY OF PERSON. A phrase applied especially to those cases in which the issue before the jury is, whether a man be the same person with one previously convicted or attainted.

IDES. A division of time among the Romans. In the Roman calendar the Ides of March, May, July and October were on the 15th of the month; of the remaining months on the 13th.

IDIOT. A natural fool, or one who from his birth was *non compos mentis*; formerly distinguished from a *lunatic*, who was one that had had understanding, but by disease, grief, or other cause had lost the use of his reason.

The former classes of mentally deficient persons have now been reclassified under the Mental Health Act 1959, and the term "idiot" is no longer in use.

IDLE AND DISORDERLY PERSON. [VAGRANT.]

IGNIS JUDICIUM. The ordeal of fire. [ORDEAL.]

IGNORAMUS. A word formerly written by the grand jury on the back of a bill preferred to them, when they considered the evidence too defective or too weak to support an indictment. [BILL, 3; INDICTMENT.]

IGNORANTIA EORUM QUÆ QUIS SCIRE TENETUR NON EXCUSAT. Ignorance of those things which one ought to know is no excuse.

IGNORANTIA JURIS (or LEGIS) NEMINEM EXCUSAT. Ignorance of the law excuses no man.

IGNORE means properly to be ignorant of. The word was used especially with reference to the throwing out of a bill of indictment, by a grand jury. [IGNORAMUS.]

ILLEGAL PRACTICES. Offences committed during the course of parliamentary or local government elections. They include voting offences, failure to make returns and declarations of expenses, incurring unauthorised expense, causing disturbances at meetings, etc. Persons may be prosecuted for illegal practices under s. 147 of the Representation of the People Act 1949.

ILLEGITIMACY. [BASTARD.]

ILLUSORY APPOINTMENT was where a person having power to appoint any real or personal property among a limited class of persons, appointed to any one of them a merely nominal share (as one shilling) of the property subject to the power of appointment. This in equity made the exercise of the power bad. This was altered by an Act of 1830, and by a further Act passed in 1874 it was provided that under a power to appoint among certain persons, appointments may be made wholly excluding one or more of the objects of the power. See now the Law of Property Act 1925, s. 158, which reproduces the provisions of the earlier Acts, but extends the principle there laid down to appointments whenever made. [POWER.]

IMBARGO. A stop or stay put upon ships by public authority. [EMBARGO ON SHIPS.]

IMBASING OF MONEY is mixing the species with an alloy below the standard of sterling.

IMBECILE. Under the former law relating to mental deficiency, an imbecile was a person who, while not being an idiot (*q.v.*), was yet mentally defective to such a degree as to be incapable of managing himself or his affairs. The term is no longer in use since the reclassification of mentally disordered persons under the Mental Health Act 1959.

IMMEMORIAL USAGE. A practice which has existed from before the time of legal memory.

IMMORAL CONTRACTS. Those founded upon immoral considerations (*contra bonos mores*) are void. *Ex turpi causa non oritur actio* (*q.v.*).

IMMOVABLE means a thing which can be touched but which cannot be moved and includes a chattel real. The general rule

as to the law governing immovables is that all rights over, or in relation thereto, are governed by the law of the country where the immovable is situate (the *lex situs*).

IMPANELLING A JURY signifies the writing and entering into a parchment schedule, by the sheriff, of the names of a jury. [PANEL, 1.]

IMPARL. To confer with [IMPARLANCE.]

IMPARLANCE (Lat. *Licentia loquendi*) was a licence formerly given to a defendant for a respite until some further day to put in his answer, to see if he could end the matter amicably without further suit, by talking with the plaintiff.

IMPEACHMENT. A prosecution of an offender before the House of Lords by the Commons of Great Britain in parliament. The articles of impeachment are a kind of indictment found by the House of Commons, and afterwards tried by the House of Lords.

It has always been settled law that a peer could be impeached for any crime.

As regards commoners, however, Blackstone lays it down that a commoner cannot be impeached before the lords for any capital offence, but only for committing high misdemeanours. The contrary doctrine, however, was laid down when Chief Justice Scroggs, a commoner, was impeached of high treason. And when, on 26th June 1689, Sir Adam Blair and four other commoners were impeached of high treason, the lords resolved that the impeachment should proceed.

This form of prosecution has rarely been called into action in modern times; the last memorable cases are those of Warren Hastings in 1788 and Lord Melville in 1806. *May.*

IMPEACHMENT OF WASTE. A restraint from committing waste upon lands and tenements. The phrase is intended to denote the ordinary legal liability incurred by a tenant for life or other limited interest, in committing waste on the property. [WASTE; WITHOUT IMPEACHMENT OF WASTE.]

IMPERFECT OBLIGATIONS. Moral duties not enforceable at law, such as charity, gratitude, or the like.

IMPERFECT TRUST. An executory trust (*q.v.*). [Executed and Executory, 6.]

IMPERSONATION. [False Personation.]

IMPERTINENCE. Irrelevancy in pleading or evidence, by the allegation of matters not pertinent to the question at issue. Any unnecessary or scandalous, frivolous or vexatious pleading may be struck out by order of the court. See R.S.C. 1965, Ord. 18, r. 19.

IMPLEAD. To sue, arrest or prosecute by course of law.

IMPLICATION. A legal inference of something not directly declared.

IMPLIED. This term can only be properly used to signify "established by indirect or circumstantial evidence" or, which comes to the same thing, "presumed under certain circumstances to exist, in the absence of evidence to the contrary", especially with reference to inward intentions or motives as inferred from overt acts.

Thus an *implied trust* has been defined as "a trust which is founded in an unexpressed but presumable intention", as contrasted with a *constructive trust*, which is one raised by construction of a court of equity without reference to the presumable intention of any party; in this it differs both from an *implied* trust and from an express trust.

But the general use of the word "implied" by legal text-writers is more indiscriminate. The phrase "implied contract" is often applied to all those events which in law are treated as contracts, whether they arise from a presumed mutual consent or not, provided only they be not express contracts.

Thus the phrase is used to signify *sometimes* a genuine consensual contract not expressed in words, or in signs which usage has rendered equivalent to words; *sometimes* an event to which, though not a genuine consensual contract, the law annexes most or all of the incidents of a genuine contract as against any person or persons.

The implied but genuine contract is frequently spoken of as a *tacit* contract. It may be defined, in opposition to an express contract, as "a contract not expressed in words, or in signs which usage had rendered equivalent to words". As if I order a coat from a tailor, without saying anything as to the price or quality. He, in undertaking the order, tacitly promises me that the coat shall be reasonably fit for wear. I tacitly promise him to pay a reasonable price for it. In implied contracts of this class there is no agreement as to precise terms and conditions, but there *is* an agreement, though of a vague and general character.

The implied contract which is such by fiction of law is frequently called a *quasi*-contract. Thus a person saves my goods on board a ship which is being wrecked, and claims from me "salvage-money" for doing so. This claim is said to arise "*quasi ex contractu*" (*as if* from a contract). It is totally independent of any consent on the part of the owner to pay for the saving of his goods. In implied contracts of this class there is no agreement at all; the supposed agreement being a pure fiction of law, adopted for the purposes of what is called "substantial justice".

The expression "implied request" is used in a manner analogous to "implied contract". A request is said to be "implied by law" sometimes when it has been in fact made, though not in express words: sometimes when it has never been made at all, but, by a fiction of law, is supposed or imagined to have been made.

IMPLIED TERMS AND CONDITIONS. Where it appears from the nature of the contract and the surrounding circumstances that the parties have contracted on the basis that some specified thing without which the contract cannot be fulfilled, will continue to exist, or that a future event which forms the foundation of the contract will take place; the contract, though in terms absolute, is to be construed as being subject to an implied condition, that if before breach performance becomes impossible without default of either party, and owing to circumstances which were not contemplated when the contract was made, the parties are to be excused from further performance. In the case of commercial contracts this principle is commonly spoken of as "the frustration of the adventure".

In the case of consumer sales (*q.v.*) the freedom of parties to exclude by agreement the statutory warranties and conditions in contracts of sale of goods is limited by the

IMPLIED TERMS AND CONDITIONS—*continued.*

Supply of Goods (Implied Terms) Act 1973.

IMPLIED MALICE. [MALICE.]

IMPOSSIBILITY OF PERFORMANCE. Impossibility of performance does not as a rule discharge the liability under a contract, but in certain cases the promisor is excused from performing his promise if it is shown that performance is impossible without any default on his part. A promise which is manifestly incapable of performance either in fact or in law at the time when it was made cannot form a binding contract, because there is no real consideration; and where the subject-matter of the contract has without the knowledge of either party ceased to exist before the contract was made, the contract is void on the ground of mistake. Impossibility, as an excuse for non-performance, must as a general rule be a physical or legal impossibility and not merely an impossibility with reference to the ability and circumstances of the promisor. See the Law Reform (Frustrated Contracts) Act 1943.

IMPOSSIBILIUM NULLA OBLIGATIO EST. An impossible consideration carries no obligation.

IMPOST. (Lat. *imponere*, to lay on), any tax or tribute imposed by authority; particularly a tax or duty on goods imported.

IMPOSTER. One who impersonates another. [FALSE PERSONATION.]

IMPOTENCE. Physical inability of a man or woman to perform the act of sexual intercourse. A marriage is void if at the time of the celebration either party is incurably impotent, and may be declared void by a decree in a suit of nullity of marriage. *Rayden.*

IMPOTENTIA EXCUSAT LEGEM. Inability avoids the law.

IMPOUND. To place in a pound goods or cattle distrained. [POUND.]

Also, to retain in the custody of the law: which is ordered when a forged or otherwise suspicious document is produced at a trial, so that the document may be produced in case criminal proceedings should be subsequently taken.

IMPRESSMENT. The arresting and retaining mariners for the king's service.

IMPRIMATUR. A licence to print or publish.

IMPRISONMENT. [FALSE IMPRISONMENT; PRISON.]

IMPROPER FEUD. A feud held otherwise than by military service.

IMPROPRIATION. [ADVOWSON; APPROPRIATION.]

IN ACTION. [CHOSE.]

IN ALIENO SOLO. In another's ground.

IN ARTICULO MORTIS. In a dying state.

IN AUTER (or **AUTRE**) **DROIT** (in another's right). As where an executor sues for a debt in right of his testator.

IN BANCO. [BANC.]

IN CAMERA. [CAMERA.]

IN CAPITE. Tenants who held their land *immediately* of the king were said to hold it *in capite*, or *in chief.*

In theory, all the land in the country is held originally of the Crown. The immediate tenants of the Crown under the feudal system frequently granted out portions of their lands to inferior persons, and those inferior persons became tenants to them, as they were of the king; and it was in contradistinction to such inferior tenants that those who held immediately of the king were called tenants *in capite.* [FEUDAL SYSTEM; SUBINFEUDATION.]

IN CHIEF. A phrase used variously. [CHIEF, TENANTS IN; EXAMINATION, 1; IN CAPITE.]

IN CUSTODIA LEGIS (in the custody of the law). An expression used with regard to goods which, on account of having been already seized by the sheriff under an execution, are exempt from distress for rent.

IN ESSE. In being, as opposed to a thing *in posse*, which may be, but is not. Thus a child, before he is born, is said to be *in posse*; but after he is born, and for many purposes after he is conceived, he is said to be *in esse*, or in actual being.

IN EXTENSO. In full; a copy of a document made *verbatim.*

IN EXTREMIS. On the point of death.

IN FORMA PAUPERIS. [FORMA PAUPERIS.]

IN GROSS is that which belongs to the person of a lord or other owner, and not to any manor, lands, etc. The phrase, applied to an incorporeal interest in land, signifies that the incorporeal interest in question is not appendant or appurtenant to any corporeal thing, but is enjoyed by its owner as an independent subject of property. [APPENDANT; APPURTENANCES; GROSS.]

IN INVITUM. Against a person's will.

IN JURE, NON REMOTA CAUSA SED PROXIMA SPECTATUR. In law the immediate, not the remote, cause of any event is regarded.

IN LIMINE (on the threshold). An objection *in limine* is a preliminary objection.

IN LOCO PARENTIS. In the place of a parent.

IN ODIUM SPOLIATORIS OMNIA PRÆSUMUNTUR. Every presumption is made against a wrong-doer.

IN PAIS. Done without legal proceedings. [ESTOPPEL.]

IN PARI CAUSA POSSESSOR POTIOR HABERI DEBET. Other things being equal the possessor is in the stronger position.

IN PARI DELICTO MELIOR EST CONDITIO DEFENDENTIS (or **POSSIDENTIS**). Where both parties are equally in the wrong, the position of the defendant (or possessor) is the more favourable.

IN PARI MATERIA. In an analogous case.

IN PERSONAM. A proceeding *in personam* is one in which relief is sought against, or punishment sought to be inflicted upon, a specific person.

IN RE (in the matter of). These words used at the beginning of a lawyer's letter indicate the subject of the letter. And, in headings to legal reports, they are applied especially (though by no means exclusively) to estates or companies which are being wound up, or to the owners of such estates.

IN REM. A proceeding *in rem* is one in which relief is not sought against, or punishment sought to be inflicted upon, any person. Actions *in rem* are generally instituted to try claims to some property or title or status; as, for instance, where it is sought to condemn a ship in the Court of Admiralty, or to recover land in an action of ejectment, etc.

IN TERROREM (for the purpose of intimidation). A condition which the law will not enforce is so called.

IN TRANSITU (in passage from one place to another). Generally it is used of goods in their passge from the vendor to the purchaser. [STOPPAGE IN TRANSITU.]

INADEQUACY OF CONSIDERATION does not affect the validity of a contract. [CONSIDERATION.]

INALIENABLE. Not transferable.

INCEST. Sexual intercourse between a man and his grand-daughter, daughter, sister or mother; or between a woman of the age of sixteen or over and her grandfather, father, brother or son, by her consent. See ss. 10, 11 of the Sexual Offences Act 1956. Attempted incest with a girl under thirteen years of age is punishable with up to seven years imprisonment under the Indecency with Children Act 1960.

INCHOATE. Begun but not completed. *E.g.*, the expression is used of bills of exchange by the Bills of Exchange Act 1882, s. 20 (marginal note).

INCIDENT. A thing appertaining to or following upon another as principal, and passing by a general grant thereof.

Thus, rent may be made incident to a reversion; and, when so incident, it passes by a general grant of the reversion. Formerly the rent so incident was destroyed when the reversion was destroyed by surrender or merger; but this doctrine, so far as regards cases of surrender or merger, was abolished in 1845. See now the Law of Property Act 1925, s. 139.

INCITEMENT. To incite another person to commit a crime is a misdemeanour at common law, and if a crime is actually committed the person inciting becomes an accessory before the fact, or in case of a misdemeanour is equally guilty with the other party.

INCLOSURE. 1. The extinction of commonable rights in fields and waste lands. For restrictions on inclosure of commons, see s. 194 of the Law of Property Act 1925.

2. Land inclosed.

INCOME TAX. A tax of so much in the pound on income. It is levied under various Schedules in respect of interest on government securities and other profits arising from public revenue dividends; professional or trade earnings or profits and from interest and other annual profits or gains; official and other salaries. The law relating to income tax which was formerly consolidated in the Income Tax Act 1952, was reconsolidated in the Income and Corporation Taxes Act 1970.

INCORPORATE. 1. To declare that one document shall be taken as part of the document in which the declaration is made as much as if it were set out at length therein.

2. To establish as a corporation by grant from the Crown or Act of Parliament.

INCORPOREAL CHATTELS are personal rights and interests which are not of a tangible nature—such as personal annuities, stocks and shares, patents and copyrights.

INCORPOREAL HEREDITAMENT is any possession or subject of property which, before 1926, was capable of being transmitted to heirs, and is not the object of the bodily senses. It is in general a right annexed to, or issuing out of, or exercisable within, a corporeal hereditament; as a right of common of pasture, a right of way over land, or an annuity payable out of land. The provisions of Part I of the Law of Property Act 1925 relating to freehold land apply also to incorporeal hereditaments. See s. 201 of the Act.

INCREASE. [AFFIDAVIT OF INCREASE.]

INCUMBENT. A clergyman in possession of an ecclesiastical benefice.

INCUMBER. To charge with an incumbrance. [INCUMBRANCE.]

INCUMBRANCE. A charge or mortgage upon real or personal estate.

INCUMBRANCER. A person entitled to enforce a charge or mortgage upon real or personal estate.

INDEBITATUS ASSUMPSIT. An action alleging that the defendant, being indebted to the plaintiff, undertook or promised to pay, but failed, whereupon the plaintiff claimed damages for the non-performance by the defendant of his undertaking. Obsolete since the Judicature Acts. [ASSUMPSIT.]

INDECENT ASSAULT. An assault accompanied by circumstances of indecency. It is an offence to commit such an assault on a woman, or on a man, by ss. 14, 15 of the Sexual Offences Act 1956. Consent, which would prevent an indecent act from being an assault, cannot be given by persons under sixteen. In the case of a girl under the age of thirteen, a sentence of up to five years may be imposed under the Indecency with Children Act 1960.

INDECENT CONDUCT. Acts of gross indecency with or towards children under the age of fourteen, or inciting children to such acts. Punishable by fine or imprisonment or both under the Indecency with Children Act 1960.

INDECENT EXPOSURE is an indictable offence at common law, and an offender is also punishable as a rogue and vagabond under s. 4 of the Vagrancy Act 1824.

INDECENT PRINTS OR BOOKS. It is an offence under the Obscene Publications Acts 1959 and 1964 to publish any obscene article (containing or embodying matter to be read or looked at or both) the effect of which is such as to tend to deprave or corrupt. [OBSCENITY.]

INDEFEASIBLE. That cannot be made void.

INDEFINITE PAYMENT is where a debtor owes several debts to the same creditor, and makes a payment without specifying to which of the debts the payment is to be applied.

INDEMNITY. Compensation for wrong done, or trouble, expense, or loss incurred. An undertaking, usually by deed, to indemnify another. See also next title.

INDEMNITY ACT. An Act of Parliament formerly passed every year to relieve from forfeiture persons who had accepted office without taking certain oaths then required by law. Rendered unnecessary by the Promissory Oaths Act 1868. Also any act for pardon or oblivion of past offences against the law, e.g., the Indemnity Act 1920, which restricted the taking of legal proceedings in respect of certain acts done during the first World War.

INDENTURE. A deed made by more parties than one; so called because there ought regularly to be as many copies of it as there are parties; and formerly each was cut or indented like the teeth of a saw, or in a waving line, to tally or correspond with the other. By the Law of Property Act 1925, s. 56 (2), a deed purporting to be an indenture has the effect of an indenture, though not actually indented. By s. 57 of the same Act, any deed, whether or not being an indenture, may be described as a deed simply or as a conveyance, mortgage, or otherwise according to the nature of the transaction. [DEED.]

INDIAN (*Canada*). Indians are, together with the Eskimos, the aborigines of North America. In the Indian Act, R.S.C. 1970, c. I–6, however, the meaning is restricted to persons who, under the Act, are registered as Indians or are entitled to be registered as such. The provisions for registrability are complicated but speaking in a general way includes persons who have been entitled to live on a reserve or any male person who is a direct descendant in the male line of a male person entitled to live on a reserve, or the wife or widow of any male person who is so entitled.

INDIAN RESERVE (*Canada*). By the Indian Act of Canada, a "reserve" is defined as a tract of land, the legal title to which is vested in Her Majesty, that has been set apart by Her Majesty for the use and benefit of a band. Probably most reserves were tracts of land reserved from lands surrendered to the Crown.

INDICAVIT. A writ or prohibition that formerly lay for a patron of a church, when the clergyman presented by him to a benefice was made defendant in an action of tithes commenced in the ecclesiastical court by another clergyman, where the tithes in question extended to the fourth part of the benefice; for in this case the suit belonged to the king's court (*i.e.*, the common law court) by the Statute of Westminster II, 1285.

The person sued might also avail himself of this writ.

INDICTMENT. A written accusation that one or more persons have committed a certain crime. As to the form of indictment, see now the Indictment Rules 1971, S.I. 1971 No. 1253.

INDIRECT EVIDENCE. The same as circumstantial evidence. [CIRCUMSTANTIAL EVIDENCE; EVIDENCE.]

INDORSEE. [INDORSEMENT.]

INDORSEMENT. A writing on the back of a document. Thus, one speaks of an indorsement on a deed, on a bill of exchange, on a writ, etc.

An *indorsement in blank* is where a person, to whom a bill or note is payable, writes his name on the back simply. The effect of such an indorsement is that the right to sue upon the bill will be transferred to any person to whom the bill is delivered.

A *special* indorsement, or indorsement in full, is an indorsement directing payment of the bill to a specified person or his order; such person is thereupon called the *indorsee*. In this case the bill or note, in order to become transferable, must be again indorsed by the indorsee. For the requisites of a valid indorsement, see Bills of Exchange Act 1882, s. 32. [SANS RECOURS.]

Special indorsement may be made on a writ of summons in an action.

INDORSEMENT OF ADDRESS. By R.S.C. 1965, Ord. 6, r. 5, it is provided that the solicitor of a plaintiff suing by a solicitor shall indorse upon every writ of summons the address of the plaintiff, and also his own name or firm and place of business within the jurisdiction which shall be an *address for service*.

INDORSEMENT OF CLAIM. By R.S.C. 1965, Ord. 6, r. 2, every writ of summons in the High Court must be indorsed with a statement of claim or with a concise statement of the nature of the claim made, or of the relief or remedy required; such indorsement must be made on the writ before it is issued.

INDORSEMENT OF SERVICE. By R.S.C. 1965, Ord. 10, r. 1, the date of service and other particulars must be indorsed upon every writ within three days of such service.

INDORSER. A person who indorses any document. [INDORSEMENT.]

INDOWMENT. [ENDOWMENT.]

INDUCEMENT. 1. The motive or incitement to any act.

2. Inducement, in pleading, is matter brought forward by way of explanatory introduction to the main allegations of the pleading.

INDUCTION. A ceremony performed after a clergyman has been instituted to a benefice, by a mandate from the bishop to the archdeacon. It is done by giving the clergyman corporal possession of the church. This is the investiture of the temporal part of the benefice, as *institution* is of the spiritual.

INDUSTRIAL AND PROVIDENT SOCIETY. A society for carrying on any industries, businesses or trades specified in or authorised by its rules, whether wholesale or retail, and including dealings of any description with land. Such societies are regulated by the Industrial and Provident Societies Acts 1965 to 1975.

INDUSTRIAL DISEASES. In the Workmen's Compensation Act 1925 certain diseases due to the nature of the employment were scheduled, and were for the purposes of compensation to be deemed personal injury by accident. This Act was repealed in 1946. See now the Social Security Act 1975, ss. 76–78.

INDUSTRIAL SCHOOLS. Later known as approved schools. See s. 79 of the Children and Young Persons Act 1933. Provision is made for the discontinuance of approved schools on the establishment of *community homes* under the Children and Young Persons Act 1969.

INDUSTRIAM, PER. *Per industriam* is a phrase applied to the reclaiming animals *feræ naturæ*, and making them tame by art, industry, and education; or else by confining them so that they cannot escape and use their natural liberty. [ANIMALS.]

INEVITABLE ACCIDENT. An accident that cannot be avoided by the use of ordinary care, caution and skill. Where such inevitable accident is due, directly and exclusively and without human intervention, to natural causes against which no human foresight could provide, it is termed an Act of God. Inevitable accident can be a defence to an action of negligence.

INFAMOUS CONDUCT. Dishonourable or disgraceful conduct in a medical practitioner or dentist, which may be dealt with by the General Medical Council (*q.v.*) under s. 33 of the Medical Act 1956, or under the Dentists Acts 1957 and 1973.

INFAMY. Public disgrace, upon conviction for perjury, forgery, etc. Formerly a person who had incurred infamy was incompetent to give evidence, but this disqualification was removed by the Evidence Act 1843.

INFANT, in law, was a person under the age of twenty-one years; an age at which persons were considered competent for all that the law required them to do, and which was therefore designated as *full age.* The age of majority was reduced to eighteen (with some exceptions) by the Family Law Reform Act 1969, which also provides that any person not of full age may be described as a *minor* instead of as an infant. [GUARDIAN.]

INFANTICIDE. S. 1 of the Infanticide Act 1938 provides that where a woman by any wilful act or omission causes the death of her child, being a child under the age of twelve months, the balance of her mind being disturbed at the time by the aftereffects of the child's birth, etc., her offence shall amount to infanticide and not to murder. A woman convicted of infanticide may be punished as if she had been guilty of manslaughter.

INFERIOR COURTS. The origin of the inferior courts, of which there are many varieties, may be traced back to the principle that justice should be taken to every man's door by constituting as many courts as there were manors in the kingdom. They were primarily the court baron, which was incident to every manor, the hundred court, and the common law county courts, now practically extinct. To these were added numerous borough and other local courts which have been almost totally abolished, a variety of courts held for special purposes (*e.g.* the sheriffs' courts) and the modern county courts. They derived their general title of inferior courts because they were and are, in the great majority of cases, subject to the control and supervision of the Court of King's Bench or Queen's Bench Division as a superior court. This means that they can be stopped from exceeding their jurisdiction by order of prohibition (*Hals. Laws*).

INFEUDATION OF TITHES. The granting of tithes to laymen.

INFORMATION. A proceeding on

behalf of the Crown against a subject otherwise than by indictment.

Informations are (or were) of various kinds:—

1. An information in Chancery, which differed from a bill only by the fact that it was instituted in the name of the Attorney-General on behalf of the Crown, or of those who partook of its prerogative, or whose rights were under its particular protection; whereas a bill was filed on behalf of a subject merely. It often happened, however, that the proceeding by way of information was prosecuted in the name of the Attorney-General by some private person, interested in the maintenance of the public right which it was intended to enforce. Such private person was then called the *relator*, and was responsible for the conduct of the suit and for the costs. This species of information was superseded by action in the High Court of Justice.

2. Proceedings on the Revenue Side of the Queen's Bench Division were abolished by the Crown Proceedings Act 1947.

3. Informations in the nature of *quo warranto* were abolished by the Administration of Justice (Miscellaneous Provisions) Act 1938, s. 9 (1).

4. An information on a penal statute. Formerly this often gave the informer a right to a share in the penalty, but such common informer actions were abolished by s. 1 of the Common Informers Act 1951.

5. A criminal information in the Queen's Bench Division. This may be by the Attorney-General *ex officio*, or by a private prosecutor in the name of the Crown. But in the latter case the information cannot be filed except by the express direction of the Court itself.

6. A statement by which a magistrate is informed of the offence for which a summons or warrant is required. See generally the Magistrates' Courts Act 1952.

Of these six classes, the first two were civil in their nature, and differed from ordinary suits and actions by the fact of their being instituted on behalf of the Crown. The third class was in its origin a criminal proceeding, but even in Blackstone's time it had assumed the character of a civil proceeding for the purpose of trying a right. The fourth class was partly a civil, partly a criminal proceeding. In its form it partook more of the civil character;

but its object was a penal one, and not the redress of any private wrong. The last two classes of informations are purely criminal in their nature.

INFORMATION IN REM. An information *in rem* was a proceeding in the Queen's Bench Division, claiming property on behalf of the Crown. [INFORMATION, 2.]

INFORMER. Any one who informs or prosecutes in any of the courts of law those that offend against any law or penal statute. Especially of one who informed for the purpose of sharing in the money to be paid by way of penalty on conviction; a procedure now abolished by the Common Informers Act 1951. [COMMON INFORMER; INFORMATION, 4.]

INFORTUNIUM. Misadventure or mischance. [HOMICIDE.]

INFRINGEMENT. A violation of another's right; a word used principally with reference to the violation of another's patent or copyright.

INGRESS, EGRESS and **REGRESS.** Free entry into, going forth of, and returning from a place.

INGROSSING. [ENGROSSING.]

INHERITANCE. A perpetuity in lands or tenements to a man and his heirs. The word is mostly confined to the title to lands and tenements by *descent*. [DESCENT; ESTATE, 1.]

INHIBITION signifies a writ to *inhibit* or forbid a judge from farther proceeding in a cause depending before him; an ancient synonym for *prohibition*. In ecclesiastical law it signifies a command from a bishop or ecclesiastical judge that a clergyman shall cease from taking any duty.

With regard to registered land an inhibition is an entry on the register prohibiting for a time or until the occurrence of an event named therein, or generally until further order, any or some specified dealing with the land. See ss. 57, 61 of the Land Registration Act 1925.

INJUNCTION. A writ issuing, prior to the Judicature Acts, only out of Chancery, in the nature of a prohibition, by which the party enjoined or prohibited was commanded not to do, or to cease from doing, some act not amounting to a crime. Injunctions may now be granted by all Divisions of the High Court and by the

INJUNCTION—*continued.*
Court of Appeal. They are either (1) *interlocutory, i.e.*, provisional or temporary until the hearing of the cause, or (2) *perpetual.* By s. 41 of the Judicature Act 1925 no cause or proceeding at any time pending in the High Court of Justice, or before the Court of Appeal, shall be restrained by prohibition or injunction. By s. 45 of the same Act, an injunction may be granted by an interlocutory order of the court in all cases in which it appears just or convenient. See R.S.C. 1965, Ord. 29.

INJURIA. An actionable wrong.

INJURIA NON EXCUSAT INJURIAM. An injury received is no excuse for doing an injury.

INJURIOUS AFFECTION. A physical interference with the public or private property rights of others, by the construction of works on adjoining or nearby land. Compensation for injurious affection are awardable under the Compulsory Purchase Act 1963 and the Land Compensation Act 1973.

INJURY. A violation of another's right; or a violation of legal duty to the prejudice of another.

INLAGARY, or **INLAGATION.** Formerly a restitution of one outlawed to the king's protection, and to the benefit or estate of a subject.

INLAND BILL OF EXCHANGE. "A bill which on the face of it purports to be (*a*) both drawn and payable within the British Islands; or (*b*) drawn within the British Islands upon some person resident therein." Any other is a foreign bill, but unless the contrary appears on the face of the bill the holder may treat it as an inland bill. Bills of Exchange Act 1882, s. 4.

INLAND REVENUE. The revenue of the United Kingdom collected or imposed as stamp duties and taxes, and placed under the care and management of the Commissioners of Inland Revenue.

INN. An inn at common law is a house, the owner of which holds out that he will receive all travellers and sojourners who are willing to pay a price adequate to the sort of accommodation provided, and who come in a condition in which they are fit to be received. He is bound to accommodate and entertain all properly conducted persons provided there is room in the house. A similar definition has now been applied to the word "hotel" (*q.v.*) by s. 1 (3) of the Hotel Proprietors Act 1956, s. 1 (1) of which provides that a hotel within the meaning of the Act shall be deemed to be an inn. The rights and obligations of innkeepers are defined in the Act, *e.g.*, as regards property belonging to guests, etc.

An innkeeper may dispose of goods left with him, if unclaimed and unpaid for, after six weeks: Innkeepers Act 1878, s. 1.

INNER TEMPLE. One of the Inns of Court. [INNS OF COURT.]

INNINGS. Lands recovered from the sea in Romney Marsh by draining. When they are rendered profitable they are termed *gainage* lands.

INNKEEPERS. [INN.]

INNOCENT CONVEYANCE. A conveyance which could not operate by wrong. Thus, a lease and release, and a bargain and sale, and a covenant to stand seised were called *innocent conveyances*, because they could not, like a feoffment, have a tortious operation.

INNOTESCIMUS. Letters patent so called, being always of a charter or feoffment, or other instrument not of record; so called from the words of the conclusion, *innotescimus per præsentes.*

INNOVATION. [NOVATION.]

INNS OF CHANCERY were Clifford's Inn, Clement's Inn, New Inn, Staple Inn, Barnard's Inn, Furnival's Inn, the Strand Inn, Lyon's Inn, and Thavie's Inn. There was also Serjeants' Inn, which consisted of serjeants only. The Inns of Chancery and the Inns of Court were originally two sorts of collegiate houses in the same juridical university, the Inns of Chancery being those in which the younger students of the law were usually placed. The Inns of Chancery have now sunk into insignificance, and an admission to them is no longer of any avail to a student in his progress to the bar. [INNS OF COURT.]

INNS OF COURT are Lincoln's Inn, the Inner Temple, the Middle Temple, and Gray's Inn. They enjoy the exclusive privilege of conferring the rank or degree of barrister-at-law, the possession of which constitutes an indispensable qualification for practising as an advocate or counsel in the superior courts. The Inns of Court are governed by officers called "benchers", to whom application is made by students desirous to be called to the bar. The benchers have also authority to deprive a bencher or a barrister of his *status*, which proceedings are called respectively "disbenching" and "disbarring". An appeal from decisions of the benchers lies to the judges in their capacity of visitors. Full information as to the regulations, examinations, fees, etc., imposed previous to call to the bar can be obtained by application to the treasurer of any of the Inns.

INNUENDO (from *innuo*, to beck or nod with his head) is a word the office of which is only to declare and ascertain the person or thing which was named or left doubtful before; as to say, he (*innuendo*, the plaintiff) is a thief, where there was mention before of another person. The word *innuendo* is most frequently applied to signify, in a proceeding for libel, the averment of a particular meaning in a passage *prima facie* innocent, which, if proved, would establish its libellous character.

INOFFICIOUS TESTAMENT. A will made contrary to the natural duty of the testator and without proper regard to the claims of kindred.

INQUEST. An inquisition or inquiry.

1. The inquest of office was an inquiry formerly made by the king's officer, his sheriff, coroner, or escheator, either *virtute officii*, or by writ to them sent for that purpose, or by commissioners specially appointed, concerning any matter that entitled the king to the possession of lands or tenements, goods or chattels. This was done by a jury of no determinate number, being either twelve, or less, or more. Now obsolete.

2. A coroner's inquest is an inquiry into the manner of the death of any one who has been slain, or has died suddenly, or in prison. It must be held before a jury which consists of not less than seven nor more than eleven jurors. See s. 3 of the Coroners Act 1887. Under s. 13 of the Coroners (Amendment) Act 1926 a coroner is, however, empowered to hold an inquest without a jury in certain cases. See generally the Coroners Acts 1887 to 1954 and s. 220 of the Local Government Act 1972.

3. Similarly, coroners have jurisdiction, under s. 39 of the Coroners Act 1887 to hold inquests on treasure trove (*q.v.*).

4. Under the former lunacy law, inquisitions were held to decide whether an alleged lunatic was of unsound mind. This procedure has been abolished and such questions are now determined by Mental Health Review Tribunals under the Mental Health Act 1959.

INQUIRY, COURT OF. 1. A court directed under military law to inquire into the conduct of officers, losses of materials, etc., with a view to further proceedings by court-martial or otherwise.

2. Also a court for hearing the complaints of private soldiers.

INQUIRY, WRIT OF. [WRIT OF INQUIRY.]

INQUISITION. [INQUEST.]

INQUISITORS are sheriffs, coroners, or the like, who have power to inquire in certain cases.

INROLMENT. [ENROLMENT.]

INSANITY. [MENTAL DISORDER.]

INSOLVENCY. Inability to pay debts. Prior to the year 1861, there was a distinction between bankruptcy and insolvency; an insolvent debtor was a person, *not a trader*, who was unable to meet his liabilities, whereas only *traders* could be made bankrupt. And the term "insolvency" was frequently applied to the means of getting rid of pecuniary engagements, afforded by Acts of Parliament passed for the relief of insolvent debtors.

All the Acts relating to insolvent debtors were repealed in 1861. See now the Bankruptcy Act 1914 and the Deeds of Arrangement Act 1914. [ACT OF BANKRUPTCY: BANKRUPT.]

INSOLVENT DEBTOR. [INSOLVENCY.]

INSPECTION. A mode of trial formerly in use for the greater expedition of a cause, in which the point at issue was one capable of being easily settled by the use of the bodily senses.

INSPECTION, COMMITTEE OF. [COMMITTEE OF INSPECTION.]

INSPECTION OF DOCUMENTS. The right of a party in an action or suit to inspect and take copies of documents material to his case, which may be in the

INSPECTION OF DOCUMENTS
—continued.

possession of the opposite party. Either party is, as a rule, entitled (after notice) to inspect documents referred to in the pleadings or affidavits of the other. With regard to other documents, the party desiring to inspect takes out a summons requiring his opponent to state what documents he has in his possession, and to make an affidavit in a prescribed form for that purpose. See R.S.C. 1965, Ord. 24.

INSPECTION OF PROPERTY. The judge by whom any cause or matter is tried may inspect any place or thing with respect to which any question arises in the cause or matter. He may also authorise a jury to inspect such property. See R.S.C. 1965, Ord. 35, r. 8.

INSPECTORSHIP DEED. A deed by which inspectors are appointed to watch a debtor's affairs on behalf of the creditors, the creditors undertaking not to sue the debtor, and the debtor agreeing to pay the creditors a composition of so much in the pound. [COMPOSITION.]

INSTALLATION. The ceremony of inducting or investing with any charge, office, or rank, *e.g.*, the installation of a bishop, of a dean, of a knight.

INSTALMENT. 1. The ceremony by which possession is given of an ecclesiastical dignity.
2. A sum of money less than the whole sum due, paid by a debtor in partial liquidation of the debt.

INSTANCE COURT OF ADMIRALTY. The court in which the judge of the Admiralty formerly at by virtue of a commission from the Great Seal which enumerated the objects of his jurisdiction, but which had no jurisdiction in matters of prize. Now part of the High Court.

INSTANTER. Immediately, without delay.

INSTITUTES. 1. Justinian's Institutes. An elementary treatise on Roman law, written by command of the emperor Justinian and published in A.D. 533. [CORPUS JURIS CIVILIS.]
2. Sir Edward Coke's Institutes. This work was published by Sir Edward Coke in the year 1628. They have little of the

institutional method to warrant such a title. The first volume is an extensive comment upon a treatise of tenures, compiled by Judge Littleton in the reign of Edward IV. The second volume is a comment upon many old Acts of Parliament without any systematic order; the third, a more methodical treatise of the pleas of the Crown; and the fourth an account of the several species of courts. [COKE, SIR EDWARD.]

INSTITUTION. The ceremony by which a clergyman presented to a living is invested with the spiritual part of his benefice. Before institution, the clergyman must renew the declaration of assent to the Book of Common Prayer, as required by the Clerical Subscription Act 1865; he must also subscribe the declaration against simony, and must take the oath of allegiance to the Queen before the archbishop or bishop, or their commissary, and he must also take the oath of canonical obedience to the bishop. Prior notice of institution must be given to the churchwardens under s. 2 of the Benefices Act 1898.

INSTRUCT. To convey information, as a client to a solicitor, or as a solicitor to counsel; to authorise one to appear as advocate.

INSTRUMENT. A deed, will, or other formal legal document in writing.

INSUFFICIENCY, prior to the Judicature Acts, was where a defendant's answer in Chancery did not fairly answer the interrogatories of the plaintiff. Where this was the case, the plaintiff might *except* to it for insufficiency.
By R.S.C. 1965, Ord. 26, r. 1, interrogatories are to be answered by affidavit; and if the party interrogated answers insufficiently, the party interrogating may apply to the court or a judge, by motion or summons, for an order requiring him to answer further.

INSURANCE, or ASSURANCE, is a contract by which one party, in consideration of a premium, engages to pay money on a given event, *e.g.*, death, or indemnify another against a contingent loss. The party who pays the premium is called the *insured* or *assured*; the party giving the security is termed the *underwriter* and the instrument is called a policy of insurance.

Insurances are mainly of four kinds:—

1. Marine insurances, which are insurances of ship, goods, and freight, against the perils of the sea, and other dangers therein mentioned.

2. Fire insurances, which are insurances of a house or other property against loss by fire, not exceeding a sum mentioned in the policy. Losses to property by theft, flood, etc., are of the same kind.

3. Life insurances, which are engagements to pay to the representatives of the assured, within a limited period from the date of his death, a specified sum of money, or to pay any such sum to the assured or his representatives, within a limited period of the death of some other person specified in the policy of assurance, or to pay to the assured on his attaining a certain age or to his representatives if he die earlier (endowment policy). Though a life policy is not a contract of indemnity (as fire and marine policies are), a person can only insure a life in which he has an interest, *viz.*, his own, his debtors', trustees', or a wife her husband's. See s. 11 of the Married Women's Property Act 1882. A husband also has an insurable interest in the life of his wife.

4. Accident insurances, which are those against personal injuries caused by accidents of all kinds whether to the insured himself or to an employee.

INTAKERS. Receivers of stolen goods. [HANDLING.]

INTENDMENT. The understanding, intention, and true meaning of any document. Thus, intendment of law is the intention and true meaning of law. [INTENTION, 1.]

INTENTION. 1. In reference to the construction of wills and other documents:

The *intention* of a document is the sense and meaning of it as gathered from the words used therein. Parol evidence is not ordinarily admissible to explain it; the main exceptions to the rule being in the case of a latent ambiguity [AMBIGUITY], and in the case of a word or expression having acquired by local custom a sense different from the ordinary sense.

2. In reference to civil and criminal responsibility:

Where a person contemplates any result as not unlikely to follow from a deliberate act of his own, he may be said to *intend* that result, whether he desire it or not. Thus, if a man should, for a wager, discharge a gun among a multitude of people, and any should be killed, he would be deemed guilty of *intending* the death of such person; for every man is presumed to *intend* the natural consequence of his own actions.

Intention is often confounded with *motive*, as when we speak of a man's "good intentions".

INTER ALIA. Amongst other things.

INTER VIVOS. Between living persons; from one living person to another, as in the case of a gift. Contrasted with *donatio mortis causa (q.v.)*, a gift made in anticipation of death.

INTERCOMMONING is where the commons of two manors lie together, and the inhabitants of both have, time out of mind, depastured their cattle promiscuously in each.

INTERDICT. In the Roman Law this was equivalent to our injunction.

INTERDICTION. An ecclesiastical censure prohibiting the administration of divine service.

INTERESSE TERMINI. The right of entry on lands demised which the demise gave to the lessee, before he had entered upon the lands. The doctrine of *interesse termini* was abolished by s. 149 of the Law of Property Act 1925. Leases are to take effect from the date fixed for commencement of the term, without actual entry.

INTEREST. 1. A right or title to, or estate in, any real or personal property.

2. The income of a fund invested; or the annual profit or recompense on a loan of money.

3. Such a personal advantage derivable from his judgment as disqualifies a judge by virtue of the rule "*Nemo debet judex esse in causa sua propria*", as where a judge is a shareholder in a company which is plaintiff or defendant in an action.

4. Interest does not now exclude a witness from giving evidence. See s. 1 of the Evidence Act 1843.

INTEREST SUIT. An action in the Chancery Division to determine which paty is entitled to a grant of letters of administration of the estate of a deceased person.

INTERIM DIVIDEND. A dividend paid by a company during the course of the financial year, as distinguished from a *final* dividend, which is paid after the completion of the financial year and when the results of that year's trading have been finally assessed.

INTERIM ORDER. An order to take effect provisionally, or until further directions. The expression is used especially with reference to orders given pending an appeal.

INTERLINEATION. Writing between the lines in a deed, will, or other document. A deed may be avoided by interlineation, unless a memorandum be made thereof at the time of the execution or attestation. As to interlineation in affidavits, see R.S.C. 1965, Ord. 41, r. 7.

INTERLOCUTORY. Intermediate, with especial reference to a suit or action.

INTERLOCUTORY DECREE or **ORDER** is a decree or order which does not conclude a cause, *e.g.*, an order for inspection of documents.

INTERLOCUTORY INJUNCTION is an injunction granted for the purpose of keeping matters *in statu quo* until a decision is given on the merits of the case. [INJUNCTION.]

INTERLOCUTORY JUDGMENT is a judgment in an action at law, given upon some defence, proceeding, or default, which is only intermediate and does not finally determine or complete the action. The phrase is most frequently applied to those judgments whereby the *right* of the plaintiff to recover in the action is established, but the *quantum* of damages sustained by him is not ascertained.

INTERNATIONAL LAW (Lat. *Jus inter gentes*).

International law is divided into two branches:—

1. Public international law, which comprises the rights and duties of sovereign states towards each other.

2. Private international law, which comprises the rights and duties of the *citizens* of different states towards each other, and is mainly conversant with questions as to the particular law governing doubtful cases. This is otherwise called the "conflict of laws". [CONFLICT OF LAWS.]

INTERPLEADER. Interpleader is a proceeding for relief from adverse claims. It sometimes happens that a man finds himself exposed to the adverse claims of two opposite parties, each requiring him to pay a certain sum of money or to deliver certain goods, and that he is unable to comply safely with the requisition of either, because a reasonable doubt exists as to which of them is the rightful claimant. Interpleader, in such cases, can be of two types: (1) *Stakeholder's interpleader*, where the person seeking relief is under any liability for any debt, money, goods, or chattels for or in respect of which he is, or expects to be, sued by two or more parties making adverse claims; or (2) *Sheriff's interpleader*, where the applicant is a sheriff or other officer charged with the execution of process, etc., and claim is made to goods, etc., by a person other than the person to whom the process is issued.

For procedure, see R.S.C. 1965, Ord. 17.

INTERPRETATION CLAUSE. A clause frequently inserted in Acts of Parliament, declaring the sense in which certain words used therein are to be understood.

INTERREGNUM. In kingdoms where the monarch is elected, the time during which the throne is vacant is called an interregnum. Where sovereignty is hereditary, no interregnum can occur.

INTERROGATORIES. 1. Questions in writing administered by a plaintiff to a defendant, or by a defendant to a plaintiff, on points material to the suit or action. Discovery by interrogatories is made under R.S.C. 1965, Ord. 26. [DISCOVERY.]

2. Questions administered to a person suspected of, or charged with, contempt of court, now probably obsolete.

INTERVENER. A person who intervenes in a suit, either on his own behalf or on behalf of the public. Section 49 (5) of the Matrimonial Causes Act 1973 allows intervention by a person not already a party in a divorce suit where adultery with any party to the suit is alleged against that person. Further, the Queen's Proctor may intervene where collusion is suspected. [QUEEN'S PROCTOR.]

INTERVENTION BOARD. The Intervention Board for Agricultural Produce was set up by the European Communities

Act 1972, to carry out the European Economic Community's common agricultural policy in the United Kingdom, including the collection of the Community's agricultural levies. See s. 6 of the Act.

INTESTATE. Without making a will, or without fully disposing of property by will. Administration of the estates of persons so dying is governed by the provisions of the Administration of Estates Act 1925.

INTIMIDATION. The using of violence, threats, etc., to compel a person to do or abstain from doing that which he has a legal right to do or abstain from doing. Such intimidation is a misdemeanour under s. 7 of the Conspiracy and Protection of Property Act 1875; and it is an offence under s. 2 of the Sexual Offences Act 1956 to procure a woman to have unlawful intercourse by threats or intimidation.

INTOXICATING LIQUOR. Spirits, beer, cider, wine and British wine: Customs and Excise Act 1952, s. 307. [SPIRITS.] See also s. 201 of the Licensing Act 1964.

INTOXICATION. [DRUNKENNESS.]

INTRA VIRES (within its powers). The converse of *ultra vires* (*q.v.*).

INTRUSION. A species of injury to freehold, which happens when a tenancy for life, or other "particular estate of freehold", has come to an end, and a stranger enters, before the person entitled in remainder or reversion. There was formerly a writ of *entry sur intrusion*, which was abolished in 1833.

INUENDO. [INNUENDO.]

INURE. To take effect. [ENURE.]

INVENTION, TITLE BY. [PATENT; COPYRIGHT.]

INVENTORY. 1. A description or list made by an executor or administrator of all the goods and chattels of the deceased, which he is bound to deliver to the court if and when thereunto lawfully required. See s. 25 of the Administration of Estates Act 1925.

2. Any account of goods sold, or exhibited for the purpose of sale.

INVESTITURE. The giving possession or seisin. [HOMAGE.]

The word is also often applied to a ceremonial introduction to some office or dignity. [INDUCTION; INSTITUTION; LAY INVESTITURE OF BISHOPS.]

INVESTMENT. Securities in which trustees are authorised by law to invest moneys. In the absence of express powers given in a settlement or will, such investments must be made in accordance with the provisions of the Trustee Act 1925.

INVITEE. At common law, an invitee is a person who enters on premises by the permission of the occupier granted in a matter in which the occupier has himself some pecuniary or material interest. Such person receives permission from the occupier as a matter of business and not as a matter of grace. A licensee (*q.v.*), on the other hand, is one who is merely licensed to enter premises.

The duty owed by an occupier of premises to his visitors is now regulated by the Occupiers Liability Act 1957, and the distinction which formerly existed between the duty owed to invitees and the duty owed to licensees has been abolished. The common law rules continue to determine who is an occupier and to whom the duty of care is owed.

INVOICE. A list of goods that have been sold by one person to another, stating the particulars and prices. The invoice is sent by the seller to the buyer, either along with the goods or separately by post.

IPSE DIXIT. He himself said; words used to denote an assertion resting on the authority of an individual.

IPSO FACTO. By the very act. These words are often applied to forfeitures, indicating that when any forfeiture is incurred, it shall not be necessary to declare such forfeiture in a court of law, but that the penalty shall be incurred by the doing of the act prohibited. And so, when it is enacted that any proceeding shall be *ipso facto* void, it means that such a proceeding is to have not even *prima facie* validity, but may be treated as void for all purposes *ab initio*. [VOID AND VOIDABLE.]

IRREGULARITY. A departure from rule, or neglect of legal formalities. In practice the term is most frequently (though not exclusively) applied to such departure, neglect, or informality as does not affect the validity of the act done. Thus an *irregular distress* is not now vitiated, so

IRREGULARITY—*continued.*

as to make the distrainer a trespasser *ab initio*, and so to render all his proceedings illegal from the first; but where distress is made for rent justly due, subsequent irregularity will do no more than give an action for damages to the party grieved, and not even that, if tender of amends is made before action brought. See s. 19 of the Distress for Rent Act 1737. As to irregularity in proceedings see R.S.C. 1965, Ord. 2, r. 2. [AB INITIO; DISTRESS.]

IRREPLEVIABLE, or IRREPLEVISABLE. That which cannot be replevied or set at large upon sureties. [REPLEVIN.]

IRREVOCABLE. That cannot be revoked. Powers of appointment are sometimes executed so as to be irrevocable. A will is never irrevocable.

ISSUABLE PLEA. A plea which raises a defence on the merits of the case, so that the plaintiff may take issue thereon, and go to trial. [ISSUE, 5.]

ISSUE has various meanings in law:—
1. The children begotten between a man and his wife.
2. Descendants generally: see s. 33 of the Wills Act 1837.
3. The profits growing from amerciaments and fines.
4. The profits of lands and tenements.
5. The point or matter issuing out of the allegations and pleas of the plaintiff and defendant in a cause, whereupon the parties join, and put their cause upon trial. See *e.g.* R.S.C. 1965, *Ord.* 18, *r.* 14.
6. *The putting out of banknotes and other paper money for public circulation.*

ITINERANT. Travelling or taking a journey; and those were anciently called justices *itinerant*, or justices *in eyre* (*in itinere*), who were sent into divers counties with commission to hear causes. [EYRE.]

J

J.P. Justice of the peace.

JACTITATION. Boasting of something which is challenged by another. Specially with reference to *jactitation of marriage*, where one of two parties has falsely boasted or given out that he or she was married to the other, whereby a common reputation of their matrimony might ensue, and the other sues for an order enjoining perpetual silence on that head. Jurisdiction was given to the High Court to hear such causes by s. 21 of the Judicature Act 1925.

JACTUS, or JACTURA MERCIUM. [JETTISON.]

JAVELIN-MEN. Yeomen retained by the sheriff to escort the judge of assize.

JEOFAIL (from the old French *j'ay faille*, I have failed), in a legal sense, denotes an oversight in pleading. Various statutes, called statutes of amendment and jeofails, allowed a pleader to amend any slip which he might have made in the form of his pleadings. Formerly, the most trifling objection in point of form might be alleged in arrest of judgment. [AMENDMENT.]

JETSAM. Goods thrown overboard by a ship in danger, to lighten her, the vessel subsequently sinking. [JETTISON; WRECK.]

JETTISON, or JACTUS, or JACTURA MERCIUM. The act of throwing goods overboard for the purpose of lightening a ship in danger of wreck. Such goods are styled jetsam.

JOBBER. [STOCKBROKER.]

JOHN DOE. The name generally given to the fictitious plaintiff in the old action of ejectment. [EJECTMENT.]

JOINDER IN PLEADING. [ISSUE, 5.]

JOINDER OF CAUSES OF ACTION. Joining in one action several causes of action. By R.S.C. 1965, Ord. 15, the plaintiff may in certain circumstances, claim in one action relief against the same defendant in respect of more than one cause of action.

JOINDER OF PARTIES. Two or more persons may be joined together in one action, either as plaintiffs or as defendants. See R.S.C. 1965, Ord. 15, r. 4.

JOINT ACCOUNT. Where two or more persons advance money and take a mortgage to themselves jointly, the rule in equity is that they are tenants in common, and therefore the survivor is a trustee for the personal representatives of the deceased mortgagees. To avoid this it became usual, where trustees lend money on mortgage, to insert what is known as a joint account clause in the mortgage deed declaring that upon the death of one of the mortgagees the receipt of the survivor shall be a sufficient discharge for the money, and that the survivor shall be able to re-convey the land without the concurrence of the personal representatives of the deceased trustee. The Law of Property Act 1925, s. 111, provides that where the sum advanced on mortgage is expressly stated to be lent on a joint account or the mortgage is made to the mortgagees jointly, the money lent shall be deemed to belong to the mortgagees on a joint account, and the survivor shall be able to give a complete discharge for the money.

JOINT AND SEVERAL. When two or more persons declare themselves jointly and severally bound, this means that they render themselves liable to a joint action against all, as well as to a separate action against each, in case the conditions of the bond or agreement be not complied with. And the party to whom they are so jointly and severally bound is called a joint and several creditor.

JOINT STOCK BANK. The ordinary name given to banking companies other than the Bank of England.

JOINT TENANCY is where an estate is acquired by two or more persons in the same land, by the same title, not being a title by descent, and at the same period; and (if created by a written instrument) without any words importing that the parties are to take in distinct shares. The principal feature of this tenancy is that on the death of one of the parties his share accrues to the others by survivorship. Joint tenants are said to be seised *per my et per tout.* In joint tenancy there are four unities, *viz.,* of possession, interest, title and time. By the Law of Property Act 1925, s. 36, it is provided that where a legal estate (not being settled land) is beneficially limited to or held in trust for any persons as joint tenants, the same shall be held on trust for sale, but not so as to sever their joint tenancy in equity. And see Part IV of Sched. I to that Act.

A joint tenancy is distinguished from a tenancy in common. [COMMON, TENANCY IN; COPARCENARY.]

The phrase is also applied to the holding of personal property under the like conditions.

JOINTRESS. A woman entitled to jointure. [JOINTURE, 2.]

JOINTURE. 1. A name sometimes given to an estate in joint tenancy.

2. Formerly, under the repealed Statute of Uses (1535) an estate settled upon a husband and wife before marriage, as a full satisfaction and bar of the woman's dower.

JOURNALS OF THE HOUSES OF PARLIAMENT. The daily records of the proceedings of the Houses. They are evidence in courts of law of the proceedings in parliament, but are not conclusive of facts alleged by either House unless they be within their immediate jurisdiction. *May.*

JUDGE. One invested with authority to decide questions in dispute between parties, and to award the proper punishment to offenders.

The judges of the High Court of Justice are the Lord Chancellor, the Lord Chief Justice, the President of the Family Division, and not more than seventy-five puisne judges, who are attached to the several divisions by the Lord Chancellor. They are appointed by the Crown by letters patent, and to qualify they must be barristers of at least ten years standing. A judge holds his office during good behaviour, subject to a power of removal by the Crown. No High Court judge may sit in the House of Commons.

The Crown may also from time to time appoint *circuit* judges to serve in the Crown Court and the county courts and to carry out such other judicial functions as may be conferred on them under the Courts Act 1971 or any other enactment. The qualification is again to be a barrister of at least ten years standing, or a recorder of five years standing. Deputy circuit judges may also be appointed.

By virtue of his office every circuit judge is capable of sitting as a judge for any county court district in England and Wales. In practice they are assigned to different districts by the Lord Chancellor. [CIRCUIT; COUNTY COURT; CROWN COURT.]

No action lies against a judge for anything said or done in his judicial capacity, but if he act without jurisdiction, he may be made answerable for the consequences. [INTEREST, 3.]

JUDGE ORDINARY. The judge of the former Court of Probate.

JUDGE-ADVOCATE-GENERAL. An officer appointed to advise the Crown in reference to courts-martial and other matters of military law except the preparation of prosecutions which are dealt with by departmental staffs.

JUDGE'S ORDER. An order made on summons by a judge at chambers. [CHAMBERS; SUMMONS.]

JUDGMENT. The sentence or order of the court in a civil or criminal proceeding. [FINAL JUDGMENT; INTERLOCUTORY JUDGMENT.]

JUDGMENT CREDITOR. A creditor who claims to be such by virtue of a judgment; that is, a party entitled to enforce execution under a judgment.

JUDGMENT DEBT. A debt due under a judgment.

JUDGMENT DEBTOR. A person against whom a judgment ordering him to pay a sum of money stands unsatisfied, and who is liable therefore to have his property taken in execution under the judgment.

JUDGMENT SUMMONS. A summons issued under the Debtors Act 1869, and the rules framed in pursuance thereof, on the application of a plaintiff who has obtained a judgment or order in a county court for the payment of any sum or sums of money, but has not succeeded in obtaining payment from the defendant of the sum or sums so ordered to be paid. The judgment summons cites the defendant to appear personally in court, and be examined on oath touching the means he has, or has had since the date of the judgment, to pay the sum in question, and also to show cause why he should not be committed to prison for his default.

Imprisonment for debt under s. 5 of the Act of 1869 is now restricted to a limited number of instances by the Administration of Justice Act 1970.

JUDICATURE ACTS. [SUPREME COURT OF JUDICATURE.]

JUDICIAL ACT. An act by a judicial officer which is not merely ministerial. By numerous statutes summary power is given to justices of the peace, and it is declared that certain acts shall only be valid if done by two magistrates. If such acts are merely ministerial it is not requisite that the two magistrates should be together at the time of doing the act; if it be judicial they must.

JUDICIAL COMMITTEE OF THE PRIVY COUNCIL. A council consisting of the Lord President of the Council, the Lord Chancellor, former Lords President, the Lords of Appeal in Ordinary, and such other members of the Privy Council as shall from time to time hold or have held high judicial office. See the Judicial Committee Act 1833, as extended by the Appellate Jurisdiction Acts of 1876 and 1887. Membership has also been extended to Privy Councillors who are, or have been, chief justice or a judge of the Supreme Court of Canada, a chief judge or a justice of the High Court of Australia, and some other judges of superior courts in Canada, Australia, New Zealand, Rhodesia, etc.

The jurisdiction of the Judicial Committee extends principally to appeals from certain parts of the Commonwealth, and some Admiralty and ecclesiastical appeals.

JUDICIAL NOTICE. Of many things as *e.g.* the course of nature, the rule of the road, the normal period of gestation, etc., the court takes judicial notice, and formal proof is not required.

JUDICIAL PROCEEDINGS (REGULATION OF REPORTS) ACT 1926, regulates the publication of reports of judicial proceedings in such manner as to prevent injury to public morals.

JUDICIAL SEPARATION. A separation of man and wife by the High Court or the county court, which has the effect, so long as it lasts, of making the wife a single woman for all legal purposes, except that she cannot marry again; and similarly the husband, though separated from his wife, is not by a judicial separation empowered to marry again.

Petitions for judicial separation are founded upon s. 17 of the Matrimonial Causes Act 1973. Any such petition may be presented by a husband or wife on the ground that there exists any fact which (on a petition for divorce) would satisfy the court of the irretrievable breakdown of the marriage, as, *e.g.*, that the respondent has committed adultery and the petitioner finds it intolerable to live with him.

Orders may also be made by magistrates in cases of assault, desertion, persistent cruelty, etc., under the Matrimonial Proceedings (Magistrates' Courts) Act 1960.

JUDICIAL TRUSTEE. A trustee appointed by, and to act under the control of, the court. See the Judicial Trustees Act 1896, and rules made thereunder.

JUDICIAL WRIT. [WRIT.]

JUSTICIARY, HIGH COURT OF. (*Scotland*). The highest criminal court in Scotland, consisting of the Lord Justice-General, the Lord Justice-Clerk and other judges of the Court of Session.

JUDICIUM DEI. The judgment of God; a term applied by our ancestors to the trial by ordeal. [ORDEAL.]

JUNIOR BARRISTER. A barrister under the rank of Queen's counsel. Also, the junior of two counsel employed on the same side in any judicial proceeding.

JURA REGALIA. Royal rights, or rights in the nature of royal rights; especially civil and criminal jurisdiction. [COUNTY PALATINE.]

JURAT. 1. A short statement at the foot of an affidavit, *when, where,* and *before whom* it was sworn. See R.S.C. 1965, Ord. 41, r. 1.

2. An officer in the island of Jersey.

3. Officers in the nature of aldermen in some corporations in Kent and Sussex.

JURIDICAL. Acting in the administration of justice. *Juridical days* are those days on which the court sits to administer justice.

JURIS ET DE JURE (of law and from law). A presumption which may not be rebutted is so called.

JURISDICTION. A dignity which a man has by a power to do justice in causes of complaint made before him (*Termes de la Ley*). The authority which a court has to decide matters that are litigated before it or to take cognisance of matters presented in a formal way for its decision. The limits of this authority are imposed by the statute, charter or commission under which the court is constituted, and may be extended or restricted by similar means. If no restriction or limit is imposed the jurisdiction is said to be unlimited (*Hals. Laws*).

JURISPRUDENCE. 1. The science of law.

2. Sometimes used of a body of law.

JURIST. A civil lawyer.

JUROR. A member of a jury.

JUROR'S BOOK. A book formerly made out in each county of persons therein qualified to serve as jurors. From this book the sheriff took the names of the jurors to be summoned. The electoral register is now the basis of juror selection: see s. 26 of the Criminal Justice Act 1972. [JURY.]

JURY signifies a body of persons sworn to inquire of a matter of fact and to declare the truth upon such evidence as is before them. In criminal cases, juries were formerly of two kinds; grand juries, which have been abolished, inquired whether there was a *prima facie* ground for an indictment, while the petty jury was the judge of fact at the trial. There was no equivalent to the grand jury in civil cases. On the other hand, in civil cases the jury, which nowadays is rare, might be either special or common. Special juries, for which a higher property qualification was required, have been abolished except in commercial cases in the City of London. The Juries Act 1974 consolidates previous Acts relating to juries, jurors and jury service.

JURY BOX. The place in which jurors sit for the trial of matters submitted to them.

JURY OF MATRONS. A jury of twelve matrons formerly appointed to inquire whether a woman, who pleaded pregnancy in bar of execution, was quick with child. [AD VENTREM INSPICIENDUM, 2.]

JURY PROCESS, now abolished, consisted of two writs for the summoning of juries. A jury is now summoned by precept.

JUS. Law or right. In the Roman law, the whole of civil procedure was expressed by the two words *jus* and *judicium*, of which the former comprehended all that took place before the prætor or other magistrate (*in jure*) and the latter all that took place before the judex (*in judicio*): the judex being a juryman appointed to try disputed facts. In many cases a single judex was considered sufficient: in others, several were appointed, and they seem to have been called *recuperatores*, as opposed to the single judex. For other meanings of *jus* see the following titles.

JUS ACCRESCENDI. The right of survivorship between joint tenants. [JOINT TENANCY.]

JUS AD REM. An inchoate and imperfect right; such, for instance, as a clergyman presented to a living acquires, before induction, by presentation and institution.

Jus ad rem is merely an abridged expression for *jus ad rem acquirendam*; and it properly denotes a right to the *acquisition* of a thing.

JUS CIVILE. The civil law. It is defined by Justinian as the law which each state has established for itself; but the term is now almost exclusively appropriated to the Roman civil law. [CORPUS JURIS CIVILIS.]

JUS DISPONENDI. The right of disposing of property.

JUS EX INJURIA NON ORITUR. No right can arise in favour of a person out of an injury committed by him.

JUS GENTIUM. The law of nations, which is thus described in the opening passages of Justinian's Institutes:—"Quod vero naturalis ratio inter omnes homines constituit, id apud omnes populos peræque custoditur, vocaturque jus gentium, quasi quo jure omnes gentes utuntur" (that law which natural reason has established among men is maintained equally by all nations, and is called the law of nations, as being the law which all nations adopt).

JUS HABENDI ET RETINENDI. The right to have and retain the profits, tithes, and offerings of a rectory or parsonage.

JUS HONORARIUM. The body of Roman law made up of the edicts of the supreme magistrates, particularly of the prætors.

JUS IN PERSONAM. A right availing against a determinate person or persons, as opposed to a right *in rem*, which avails against all the world.

JUS IN RE. Full and complete right, accompanied by corporal possession.

JUS IN REM. A right availing against all the world. Thus the phrase denotes the *compass* and not the *subject* of the right.

JUS LIBERORUM. A privilege granted in ancient Rome to such persons as had three children, whereby they were exempted from various troublesome offices.

JUS MARITI. The right acquired by a husband in the movable estate of his wife, by virtue of the marriage prior to the passing of the Married Women's Property Act 1882.

JUS PATRONATUS. 1. The right of patronage or presentation to a benefice.

2. A commission from the bishop awarded when two rival presentations are made to him upon the same avoidance of a living. This commission is directed to the bishop's chancellor, and others of competent learning, who are to summon a jury of six clergymen and six laymen to inquire who is the rightful patron.

JUS POSTLIMINII. [POSTLIMINIUM.]

JUS TERTII. The right of a third party. If A, who *prima facie* is liable to restore property to B, alleges that C has a paramount title, A is said to set up the *jus tertii*. This may not be done by an agent as against his principal.

JUSTICE OF THE PEACE. A subordinate magistrate appointed to keep the peace within a given jurisdiction, and to inquire of crimes and misdemeanours; with a statutory jurisdiction to decide summarily in many cases, and in some cases to adjudicate upon claims of a civil nature.

Justices of the peace for counties are appointed by the Lord Chancellor under the Administration of Justice Act 1973. There is a separate commission of the peace for each county. See also s. 217 of the Local Government Act 1972. [CONSERVATOR OF THE PEACE; CUSTOS ROTULORUM; QUORUM.]

JUSTICES. Officers deputed by the Crown to administer justice, and do right by way of judgment. The puisne judges of the High Court are called "Justices of the High Court" (see s. 2 (4) of the Judicature Act 1925), but the word is usually applied to justices of the peace. [JUSTICE OF THE PEACE.]

JUSTICES IN EYRE. Justices who formerly made a circuit every seven years round the kingdom to try causes. [CIRCUIT; EYRE; ITINERANT.]

JUSTICIARY (or **JUSTICIAR), CHIEF.** The old name of judge, before the *Aula Regia* was divided.

JUSTICIES. A special writ empowering the sheriff, for the sake of despatch, to do the same justice in his county court as might otherwise be had at Westminster.

The jurisdiction of the sheriff's county court is now almost wholly superseded. [COUNTY COURT.]

JUSTIFIABLE HOMICIDE. [HOMICIDE.]

JUSTIFICATION is the showing of a sufficient reason, by a defendant, why he did what he is called upon to answer, particularly in an action of libel, *e.g.*, damages cannot be recovered for the publication of a defamatory statement if the defendant pleads and proves that it is true. In a criminal prosecution for libel the truth of a matter is no defence unless the accused proves also that its publication was for the public benefit, or in an action of assault showing the violence to have been necessary. By s. 5 of the Defamation Act 1952 it is provided that in an action for libel or slander in respect of words containing two or more distinct charges against the plaintiff, a defence of justification shall not fail by reason only that the truth of every charge is not proved, if the words not proved to be true do not materially injure the plaintiffs' reputation, having regard to the truth of the remaining charges.

JUSTIFICATORS. [COMPURGATORS.]

JUSTIFYING BAIL. Showing the sufficiency of persons tendering themselves as bail.

JUSTINIAN. [INSTITUTES.]

JUVENILE COURTS. Courts for the trial of charges against children and young persons, now governed by ss. 45–49 of the Children and Young Persons Act 1933. The general public is excluded from hearings before such courts. *Bona fide* representatives of the press may be present but there are restrictions on newspaper reports of proceedings. As to care proceedings in juvenile courts, see s. 1 of the Children and Young Persons Act 1969.

K

K.B. King's Bench.

K.B.D. King's (now Queen's) Bench Division.

K.C. King's (now Queen's) Counsel.

KEELAGE. A custom to pay money for ships resting in a port or harbour.

KEEPER OF THE GREAT SEAL is, since the Lord Keeper Act 1562, the Lord Chancellor.

KEEPER OF THE PRIVY SEAL, now called the Lord Privy Seal. [LORD PRIVY SEAL.]

KEEPER OF THE TOUCH. In the Mint, the master of the assay.

KEEPING HOUSE, as an act of bankruptcy, is when a man absents himself from his place of business and retires to his private residence, so as to evade the importunity of creditors. The usual evidence of "keeping house" is denial to a creditor who has called for money. See the Bankruptcy Act 1914, s. 1 (1) (*d*). [ACT OF BANKRUPTCY.]

KEEPING TERM, by a student of law, consists in eating a sufficient number of dinners in hall to make the term count for the purpose of being called to the bar.

KEEPING THE PEACE. Avoiding a breach of the peace; or persuading or compelling others to refrain from breaking the peace.

Magistrates have power to bind over any person to keep the peace or be of good behaviour. The person concerned enters into a recognizance (*q.v.*), with or without sureties, and for failure to comply with the order he may be committed to prison. See s. 91 of the Magistrates' Courts Act 1952; also s. 92, dealing with discharge from recognizances.

KEYS, in the Isle of Man, are the twenty-four chief commoners, who form the local legislature.

KIDNAPPING. The forcible abduction or taking away of a man, woman, or child from their own country, and sending them into another. As to children, see s. 56 of the Offences against the Person Act 1861, which makes child-stealing an offence.

The Pacific Islanders Protection Act 1872, which made it an offence to decoy away a native of the islands, etc., was formerly known as the Kidnapping Act 1872.

Abduction of a woman by force for the sake of her property is an offence under s. 17 of the Sexual Offences Act 1956, and other cases of abduction are dealt with by ss. 19–21 of that Act.

KIN. Legal relationship.

KINDRED AND AFFINITY. [AFFINITY.]

KING. The King or Queen is the person in whom the supreme executive power of this kingdom is vested. In domestic affairs the sovereign is a constituent part of the supreme legislative power, and may in theory negative all new laws, and is bound by no statute unless specially named therein. The sovereign is also considered as the general of the kingdom, and as such may raise armies, fleets, etc. The sovereign is also the fountain of justice and general conservator of the peace, and may erect courts, prosecute offenders, pardon crimes, etc. The sovereign is also head of the Church of England and as such appoints bishops, etc., and receives appeals in ecclesiastical causes. [CIVIL LIST; QUEEN.]

As the statutes of the realm and the older law cases and other records are often referred to as being of such a year of such a reign, a list is appended of the kings and queens of England, with the dates of their accessions and deaths, from the Conqueror to the present time.

King or Queen	Accession	Reigned until
William I (the Conqueror)	1066	1087
William II (William Rufus, son of William I).. ...	1087	1100
Henry I (youngest son of William I)..	1100	1135
Stephen	1135	1154
Henry II	1154	1189
Richard I (otherwise called Richard Coeur de Lion)..	1189	1199
John	1199	1216
Henry III	1216	1272
Edward I	1272	1307
Edward II	1307	1327
Edward III	1327	1377
Richard II	1377	1399
Henry IV	1399	1413
Henry V	1413	1422
Henry VI	1422	1461
Edward IV	1461	1483
Edward V	1483	1483
Richard III	1483	1485
Henry VII	1485	1509
Henry VIII	1509	1547
Edward VI	1547	1553

King or Queen	Accession	Reigned until
Mary (married in 1554 to Philip of Spain; hence the subsequent statutes of her reign are referred to as those of Philip and Mary)	1553	1558
Elizabeth I	1558	1603
James I	1603	1625
Charles I	1625	1649
Commonwealth declared ...	1649	
Oliver Cromwell, Protector.	1653	1658
Richard Cromwell, Protector	1658	1659
Charles II	1660	1685

The statutes of the reign of Charles II are dated as if from the year 1649, when his father was beheaded, on the assumption that, as heir to the Crown, he began to reign immediately on his father's death. Thus the Tenures Abolition Act, 1660, is known by the regnal year and chapter number 12 Car. 2, c. 24; the Act of Uniformity, 1662, as 14 Car. 2, c. 4; etc.

King or Queen	Accession	Reigned until
James II	1685	1688
William III	1689	1702
and Mary..	1689	1694
Anne..	1702	1714
George I	1714	1727
George II	1727	1760
George III	1760	1820
George IV	1820	1830
William IV	1830	1837
Victoria	1837	1901
Edward VII	1901	1910
George V ·	1910	1936
Edward VIII	1936	1936
George VI	1936	1952
Elizabeth II	1952	

KING'S BENCH. [COURT OF KING'S (OR QUEEN'S) BENCH; QUEEN'S BENCH DIVISION.]

KING'S BOOKS. Books formerly containing the valuation of ecclesiastical benefices and preferments, pursuant to Acts of 1534 and 1558, both now repealed.

KING'S SILVER. A name given to the money formerly payable to the king in the Court of Common Pleas, for the licence there granted to any man to pass a fine. [FINE, 1.]

KING'S WIDOW. A widow of the king's tenant in chief, who could not marry without the king's leave. [In Capite.]

KINGS-AT-ARMS. The principal heralds. There are three existing in England: Garter, Clarenceux, and Norroy. *Lyon* King-at-Arms is the chief in Scotland, and *Ulster* in Ireland. [Herald's College.]

KLEPTOMANIA. A species of mental disorder in the form of an irresistible mania for thieving.

KNIGHT. A commoner of rank, originally one that bore arms, who for his martial powers was raised above the ordinary rank of gentleman. The following are different degrees of knights:—

1. Knight of the Order of St. George, or of the Garter: first instituted by Edward III, probably about the year 1345.

2. Knight Banneret. A knight formerly created on the field of battle by the ceremony of cutting off the points of his *pennon* (triangular or swallow-tailed flag carried on the lance), thus converting it into a *banner*. [Banneret.]

3. Knight of the Order of the Bath. So called from the ceremony, formerly observed, of bathing the night before their creation.

4. Knight Bachelor; the most ancient, though the lowest title of dignity among us. King Alfred is said to have conferred this order on his son Ethelstan.

5. Knight of the Order of St. Michael and St. George: an order instituted on the 27th of April, 1818, for the reward of public service in the Ionian Islands and Malta, and now conferred on persons for distinguished service in any of the colonies and dependencies of the British Empire.

6. Knight of the Thistle: an order instituted by King Achias, of Scotland, and re-established by Queen Anne on the 31st of December, 1703.

7. Knight of the Royal Victorian Order: instituted by Queen Victoria, 21st April, 1896.

8. Knight of the Most Excellent Order of the British Empire: instituted in June, 1917, and extended December, 1918.

KNIGHT OF THE BATH. [Knight, 3.]

KNIGHT OF THE CHAMBER. A knight bachelor, so made in time of peace. [Knight, 4.]

KNIGHT OF THE SHIRE. A gentleman of worth chosen by the free holders of a county to represent it in parliament.

KNIGHTHOOD. The dignity of a knight.

KNIGHT-SERVICE (Lat. *Servitium militare*). The most universal and most honourable species of tenure under the feudal system. It was entirely military. To make a tenure by knight-service, a determinate quantity of land was necessary, which was called a knight's fee. [Knight's Fee.] And he who held this proportion of land by knight-service was bound to attend his lord to the wars for forty days in every year, if called upon. There were other burdens attached to this tenure, under the name of aids, reliefs, primer seisins, etc.

Knight-service was abolished, with other military tenures, by the Tenures Abolition Act 1660. [Aid; Act Seisin; Relief.]

KNIGHT'S FEE (Lat. *Feudum militare*). A quantity of land sufficient to maintain a knight with convenient revenue. In the reign of Henry III it was £15 per annum. In the reign of Edward I it was estimated at twelve ploughlands, and its value in that and the following reign was stated at £20 per annum. But there are many different opinions as to its extent and value at various times.

Also, the rent that a knight paid to his lord of whom he held. [Knight-Service.]

KNOCK-OUT. This is an agreement among prospective bidders at an auction sale that certain of them shall refrain from bidding, so that the actual bidder may get the goods at a price lower than he might otherwise have done. By the Auctions (Bidding Agreements) Act 1927, such an arrangement is made illegal in certain circumstances.

KNOT (nautical term). A division of the log-line equal to 120th part of a mile. The knots are counted per half minute. Thus, if a ship is going 10 miles per hour it is said to be travelling at 10 knots.

KNOW-HOW. In tax law the expression is used to mean any industrial information and techniques likely to assist in the manufacture or processing of goods or materials, or in the working of a mine,

KNOW-HOW—*continued.*

oilwell, etc., or in the carrying out of any agricultural, forestry or fishing operations. See s. 386 of the Income and Corporation Taxes Act 1970.

L

L.C.J. Lord Chief Justice.

L.J. Lord Justice of Appeal.

L.S. [LOCUS SIGILLI.]

LA REYNE LE VEULT. "The Queen wills it so to be." The form of words by which the Queen assents to a public bill which has passed through both houses of Parliament. The form of assent to a private bill is in the words "soit fait comme il est désiré," and to a money bill or grant of supply "La Reyne remercie ses bons sujets, accepte leur benevolence, et ainsi le veult." The royal assent was normally given by Commissioners under powers granted in the reign of Henry VIII. The last time it was given in person was by Queen Victoria in 1854.

An alternative mode of signifying royal assent was prescribed by the Royal Assent Act 1967, which makes it unnecessary for the Commons to attend the Lords, the royal assent being duly given by the Queen signing letters patent under the Great Seal.

LA REYNE S'AVISERA. "The Queen will consider." The form by which the Queen would refuse the royal assent to a bill passed by both houses of Parliament. Such power has not been exercised since 1707, when Queen Anne refused her assent to a bill for settling the militia in Scotland.

LACHES. Slackness or negligence. In general it signifies neglect in a person to assert his rights, or long and unreasonable acquiescence in the assertion of adverse rights. This neglect or acquiescence will often have the effect of barring a man of the remedy which he might have had if he had resorted to it in proper time. Thus, under the Limitation Acts 1939 to 1975, the time is specified within which various classes of actions respectively therein mentioned may be brought. Independently of these statutes, a court of equity will often refuse relief to a plaintiff who has been guilty of unreasonable delay in seeking it. [LIMITATIONS, STATUTES OF.]

LACUNA. *Lit.* a ditch. A blank in writing.

LADA. 1. Purgation, exculpation.

2. A form of tenant's service which consisted in supplying beasts of burden.

3. An inferior court of justice.

4. A course of water.

LADY-COURT. The court of a lady of the manor.

LADY-DAY. 1. The 25th March, so called because it is the Feast of the Annunciation of the Blessed Virgin Mary. A quarter-day for the payment of rent.

2. Sometimes also, *e.g.*, in Ireland, the 15th August, from the Catholic festival of the Assumption of the Blessed Virgin.

LÆSÆ MAJESTATIS CRIMEN. The name in Roman law for high treason; called also *majestas*.

LÆSIONE FIDEI. Suits *pro læsione fidei* were suits for nonpayment of debts or breaches of civil contracts, which, in the reign of Stephen, were brought in the ecclesiastical courts. This attempt to turn the ecclesiastical courts into courts of equity, on the ground that such acts were offences against conscience, was checked by the Constitutions of Clarendon, A.D. 1164, which provided that such matters should be within the jurisdiction of the king's court.

LAGAN or **LAGON.** [LIGAN.]

LAMBETH DEGREES. Degrees conferred by the Archbishop of Canterbury.

LAMMAS DAY. The first of August. On that day the tenants that held land of York Cathedral were bound by their tenure to bring a living lamb into the church at high mass.

LAMMAS LANDS. Lands over which there is a right of pasturage, from about Lammas or reaping time until sowing time, by persons other than the owner of the land.

LANCASTER COUNTY PALATINE was erected into a county palatine in the fiftieth year of Edward III (1377), and granted to his son John for life, that he should have *jura regalia*, and a kinglike power therein. [COUNTY PALATINE; DUCHY COURT OF LANCASTER; JURA REGALIA.]

LAND signifies generally not only arable ground, meadow, pasture, woods, moors, waters, etc., but also messuages and houses; comprehending everything of a permanent and substantial nature. Thus an action to recover possession of a pool must be brought for so much land covered with water, etc. The word "land" is used in a wide sense in the Law of Property Act 1925. It includes "land of any tenure, and mines and minerals, whether or not held apart from the surface, buildings or parts of buildings (whether the division is horizontal, vertical or made in any other way) and other corporeal hereditaments; also a manor, an advowson, and a rent and other incorporeal hereditaments and an easement, right, privilege, or benefit in, over, or derived from land; but not an undivided share in land." See s. 205 (1) (ix).

LAND CERTIFICATE. [CERTIFICATE, LAND.]

LAND CHARGES. This term is comprehensive, and includes a number of different rights and interests affecting land. They comprise, *inter alia*, restrictive covenants, estate contracts, general equitable charges, and equitable easements. The Land Charges Act 1972 consolidated previous legislation on the subject, dealing with the registration in the land charges register of various charges in unregistered land. The Local Land Charges Act 1975 repealed earlier legislation relating to local land charges.

LAND COMMISSIONERS, formerly called the Copyhold Inclosure and Tithe Commissioners. Their duties were transferred to the Board (since 1919, the Ministry) of Agriculture and Fisheries in 1889.

LAND COMPENSATION. [COMPULSORY PURCHASE.]

LAND REGISTRATION. See the Land Registration Acts 1925 to 1966, which provide for the compulsory extension of the registration system originally established by the repealed Land Transfer Acts of 1875 and 1897.

LAND TAX. A tax upon land, the origin of which may be traced, Blackstone says, to our military tenures. The personal attendance required of tenants of knights' fees growing troublesome, the tenants found means of compounding for it, first, by sending others in their stead, and in process of time by making a pecuniary satisfaction to the Crown in lieu of it. This pecuniary satisfaction at last came to be levied by assessments under the name of *escuage* or *scutage*. [ESCUAGE.]

In the year 1692 there was a new assessment or valuation of estates throughout the kingdom, according to which land tax was imposed and for long continued a permanent charge on land. Part V of the Finance Act 1949 provided for the ultimate extinction of the tax, by exonerating certain properties and by providing for the compulsory redemption of the tax on others, and it was finally abolished by s. 68 of the Finance Act 1963.

LAND TITLES (*Canada*). A system of registration of titles to land which involves a guarantee of title.

LANDLORD. He of whom lands and tenements are held; who has a right to distrain for rent in arrear, etc., the *tenant* being the person holding the lands.

LANDS TRIBUNAL. A tribunal with powers to determine questions relating to the compulsory acquisition of land, etc. Constituted under the Lands Tribunals Act 1949.

LANDWAITER. An officer of the Custom house.

LAPSE. 1. A species of forfeiture whereby the right of presentation to a benefice accrues to the ordinary, by neglect of the patron to present; to the archbishop, by neglect of the ordinary; and to the Crown, by neglect of the archbishop. It is in the nature of a spiritual escheat.

2. The failure of a testamentary disposition in favour of any person, by reason of the death of the intended beneficiary in the lifetime of the testator.

In two cases, however, of the intended beneficiary dying in the testator's lifetime, there is now no lapse. The first case is that of a devise of real estate to any person for an *estate tail*, where any issue who would inherit under such entail are living at the testator's death. The second case is that of a devise or bequest to a *child* or *other issue* of the testator, leaving issue, any of whom are living at the testator's death. See ss. 32, 33 of the Wills Act 1837.

LARCENY. The unlawful taking and carrying away of things personal, with intent to deprive the right owner of the same. The taking had to be *animo furandi* (*i.e.*, with the intention of stealing), in order to constitute larceny. There had also to be an "asportation," that is, a "carrying away"; but for this purpose the smallest removal was sufficient.

Larceny, as a statutory offence, was replaced by a new statutory conception of "theft", the Larceny Acts of 1861 and 1916 being repealed by the Theft Act 1968, [BURGLARY; ROBBERY; THEFT.]

LAST COURT. A court held by the twenty-four jurats in the marshes of Kent, and summoned by the bailiffs. [JURAT, 3.]

LAST HEIR (Lat. *Ultimus hæres*). He to whom land formerly came by escheat, for want of lawful heirs; in some cases, the lord of whom they were held; in others, the king. [ESCHEAT.]

LAST RESORT. A court from which there is no appeal is called a court of last resort.

LASTAGE. 1. A custom exacted in some fairs and markets, to carry things bought where one will.

2. The ballast of a ship.

3. Stowage room for goods in a vessel.

4. A custom paid for wares sold by the last.

LATENT AMBIGUITY. [AMBIGUITY; INTENTION, 1.]

LATITAT. A writ sued out on a supposed bill of Middlesex, when the defendant did not reside in Middlesex, alleging that the defendant *latitat et discurrit* (lurks and runs about) in the county in which he really resided. [BILL OF MIDDLESEX.]

LAUDIBUS LEGUM ANGLIÆ. The treatise *De Laudibus Legum Angliæ* was a panegyric on the laws of England written by Sir John Fortescue in the reign of Henry VI.

LAW was defined by Blackstone as a rule of action prescribed or dictated by some superior, which an inferior was bound to obey.

Austin described a law as being a *command* to *a course of conduct*; a *command* being the expression of a wish or desire conceived by a rational being that another rational being should do or forbear, coupled with the expression of an intention in the former to inflict some evil upon the latter, in case he did not comply. But besides laws properly so called, Austin alluded to laws improper, imposed by public opinion; also laws metaphorical or figurative, such as the laws regulating the movements of inanimate bodies, or the growth or decay of vegetables; or that uniformity in the sequence of things or events which often goes by the name of *law*. Law was sometimes used as opposed to equity; now, however, by the Judicature Act 1925, full effect is given to all equitable rights in all branches of the Supreme Court and in inferior courts.

LAW AGENT. Any person entitled to practice as an agent (solicitor) for another in a court of law in Scotland.

LAW DAY signified a day for holding a leet or sheriff's tourn. [COURT LEET; HUNDRED; SHERIFF'S TOURN.]

LAW LIST. An annual publication of a quasi-official character containing a list of barristers, solicitors, and other legal practitioners. It is *prima facie* evidence that the persons therein named as solicitors or certified conveyancers are such. See the Solicitors Act 1974.

LAW LORDS are peers who hold or have held high judicial office, *i.e.*, a puisne judgeship of the High Court or higher office.

LAW MARTIAL. The martial law.

LAW MERCHANT (*Lex mercatoria*). The general body of European usage in matters relative to commerce, comprising rules relative to bills of exchange, partnership, and other mercantile matters, incorporated into the law of England.

LAW OF MARQUE. A law of reprisal, by which persons who have received wrong, and cannot get ordinary justice within the precincts of the wrongdoers, take their ships and goods. [LETTERS OF MARQUE AND REPRISAL.]

LAW OF NATIONS (Lat. *Jus gentium*). [INTERNATIONAL LAW; JUS GENTIUM.]

LAW OF THE STAPLE. The same as law merchant. [LAW MERCHANT.]

LAW OFFICERS OF THE CROWN. The Attorney-General (*q.v.*) and the Solicitor-General (*q.v.*), the Attorney-General for Northern Ireland, and, in Scotland, the Lord Advocate.

LAW REPORTS are the authorised monthly reports of decided cases commencing from 1866 inclusive. They are published under the direction of a body called the Incorporated Council of Law Reporting. [REPORTS.]

LAW SOCIETY. A society of solicitors, whose function it is to carry out the Acts of Parliament and orders of court with reference to the examinations of articled clerks; to provide for legal education; to keep an alphabetical roll of solicitors; to issue certificates to persons duly admitted and enrolled; also to exercise a general control over the conduct of solicitors in practice, and to deal with cases of misconduct. Disciplinary powers are conferred upon a separate disciplinary committee. See generally the Solicitors Act 1974.

LAW SPIRITUAL. The ecclesiastical law, according to which the ordinary, and other ecclesiastical judges, do proceed in causes within their cognizance. *Cowel.*

LAWS OF OLERON. [OLERON, LAWS OF.]

LAWSUIT. This is not a legal expression, but it is generally used to denote a case before the courts of law or equity in which there is a controversy between two parties.

LAY. A word opposed to *professional*. It is generally, but not necessarily, used in opposition to *clerical*.

LAY CORPORATIONS. Corporations not composed wholly of spiritual persons, nor subject to the jurisdiction of the ecclesiastical courts. Lay corporations are either *civil* or *eleemosynary*. Eleemosynary corporations are such as are constituted for the perpetual distribution of the free alms or bounty of the founder of them, to such purpose as he had directed. All other lay corporations are civil corporations. [CORPORATION.]

LAY DAYS. The days ordinarily allowed to the charterer of a vessel for loading and unloading the cargo. Also called *running* days. [DEMURRAGE.]

LAY FEE. Lands held in fee of a lay lord, involving services of a temporal character, as opposed to *frankalmoign*, which is a tenure of a spiritual character. [FEE; FRANKALMOIGN.]

LAY IMPROPRIATORS. [APPROPRIATING.]

LAY INVESTITURE OF BISHOPS. The formal act whereby the Crown invested a bishop with the temporalities of his office.

LAZARET or **LAZARETTO.** Places where quarantine is to be performed by persons coming from infected countries.

LE ROY LE VEULT. "The king wills it so to be." The form of words by which a king assented to a public bill which had passed through both Houses of Parliament. [LA REYNE LE VEULT.]

LE ROY S'AVISERA. "The king will consider." The form in which a king could refuse the royal assent to a bill passed by both Houses of Parliament. [LA REYNE S'AVISERA.]

LEADER. The leading counsel in a case as opposed to a *junior*.

LEADING CASES are the cases which have had the most influence in settling the law.

LEADING QUESTIONS. Questions which suggest the answer which is expected: as "Did you not see this?" or "Did you not hear that?" Such questions are not allowed except in cross-examination. [HOSTILE WITNESS.]

LEAP YEAR. [BISSEXTILE.]

LEASE. A demise or letting of lands or tenements, rights of common, rent, or any hereditament, by one person, called the *lessor*, to another called the *lessee*, for a term of years or life, or at will, usually for a rent reserved. The interest created by the lease must be *less* than the lessor has in the premises, or it is not a *lease* but an *assignment*. By ss. 53, 54 of the Law of Property Act 1925 all leases except those not exceeding three years and with a rent of not less than two-thirds of the improved annual value must be by deed. [INTERESSE TERMINI.]

LEASE AND RELEASE. 1. At common law consisted of first a lease to a proposed alienee, which demise, if perfected by entry, conferred on him a complete

LEASE AND RELEASE—*continued.*
estate of leasehold, and then, being tenant of the "particular estate" on which the reversion was expectant, he became capable of receiving a *release* of the reversion, which was accordingly executed to him and his heirs. [PARTICULAR ESTATE.]

2. The conveyance of the same name under the Statute of Uses is much better known. It consisted of:—First, a bargain and sale; secondly, a common law conveyance of release. The bargain and sale would not have been sufficient under the Statute of Enrolments (1535) to transfer the *freehold* unless the same were by deed indented, and enrolled within six months after its date. [BARGAIN AND SALE.] The practitioners of that day, being anxious to effect secret conveyances, made the conveying party execute a bargain and sale for some *leasehold* interest, generally for a year, which passed the legal estate for a year to the bargainee (the Statute of Enrolments not extending to leaseholds), and the estate so transferred was complete without entry. The transferee, therefore, was capable of receiving a release of the feeehold and reversion; which release was accordingly granted to him on the next day. This form of conveying a freehold estate soon became so generally established as to supersede every other. In 1841 the release was made effectual without the previous lease; and in 1845 it was provided that corporeal hereditaments should, as regards the conveyance of the immediate freehold thereof, be deemed to *lie in grant* as well as *in livery*, and so become transferable by deed of grant, which is now the ordinary method of transferring such estates. By s. 51 of the Law of Property Act 1925 all lands and all interests therein now lie in grant only. [ENROLMENT; GRANT, 1; LIE IN GRANT; LIE IN LIVERY; USE.]

LEASEHOLD. Any interest in land less than freehold might be so called ; but in practice the word is generally applied to an estate for a fixed term of years.

LEAVE AND LICENCE. A defence to an action for trespass, setting up the consent of the plaintiff to the trespass complained of.

LEAVE TO DEFEND. By R.S.C. 1965, Ord. 14, a plaintiff may, in certain circumstances, apply to the court for summary judgment on the ground that the defendant has no defence to a claim included in the writ, or to a particular part of such a claim, except as to the amount of damages claimed. Such application cannot be made in actions for libel, slander, malicious prosecution, false imprisonment, seduction, breach of promise of marriage, or those based on allegations of fraud.

By r. 4 of Ord. 14, a defendant may be given *leave to defend* such action either unconditionally or on terms as to security for costs, etc.

LEET. A court of local jurisdiction. [COURT LEET.]

LEGACY. A bequest or gift of goods and chattels by testament.

A legacy may be either specific, demonstrative, or general.

1. A *specific legacy* is a bequest of a specific part of the testator's personal estate.

2. A *demonstrative legacy* is a gift by will of a certain sum directed to be paid out of a specific fund.

3. A *general legacy* is one payable out of the general assets of the testator. [ADEMPTION OF A LEGACY.]

LEGACY DUTY. A duty formerly payable by an executor out of the legacies bequeathed by his testator or by administrator on share passing on intestacy. The proportion of legacy duty varied, according to the relationship which the legatee or beneficiary bore to the testator or intestate. Abolished by s. 27 of the Finance Act 1949. [ESTATE DUTY.]

LEGAL AID. Under the Legal Aid and Advice Act 1974, legal aid is available for any person whose disposable income does not exceed £24.50 a week. His expenses are then wholly or in part payable from a legal aid fund, to which, however, he may be required to contribute, according to the amount of his disposable income or capital.

LEGAL ASSETS. Assets of a deceased person available in a court of law to satisfy the claims of creditors. [ASSET.]

LEGAL ESTATE. An estate in land, fully recognised as such in a court of common law, has been hitherto called the "legal estate." For the different estates and interests in land (subsisting or created at law) which are by the Law of Property Act 1925 authorised to subsist or to be created at law and which are referred to in that Act as legal estates, see title ESTATE. [EQUITABLE ESTATE.]

LEGAL MEMORY. The time of "legal memory" runs back to the commencement of the reign of Richard I.

LEGAL POWERS. The term is used in the Law of Property Act 1925 to mean the powers vested in a chargee by way of legal mortgage or in an estate owner under which a legal estate can be transferred or created.

LEGAL TENDER is a tender in payment of a debt which will be held valid and sufficient. Gold coin was always a legal tender, so far as a debt admits of being paid in gold, and still is so; the following are also legal tender: (i) coins of cupro-nickel or silver of denominations of more than ten new pence, for payment of any amount not exceeding £10; (ii) coins of cupro-nickel or silver of denominations of not more than ten new pence, for payment of any amount not exceeding £5; (iii) coins of bronze, for payment of any amount not exceeding twenty pence. See s. 2 of the Coinage Act 1971.

LEGITIMACY DECLARATION. By s. 45 of the Matrimonial Causes Act 1973 a British subject may apply to the court for a declaration that he is legitimate and that the marriage of his parents or grandparents was valid, or that his own marriage was valid, or for a decree declaring his right to be deemed a British subject, that he is a natural-born subject of the Queen.

He may also petition for a decree that he or his parent or any remoter ancestor became or has become a legitimated person.

LEGITIMATION *per subsequens matrimonium.* A legitimation of children by the subsequent marriage of their parents. This may be done according to the civil and canon law, and the systems founded thereon, including the law of Scotland. The right was not recognised in England until 1927 when the Legitimacy Act of 1926 came into operation. Under that Act an illegitimate child could be rendered legitimate by the subsequent marriage of his parents, and by the Legitimacy Act 1959 this was so even where the child was born in adultery.

The Children Act 1975, s. 8 (9) and Sch. 1,

sets out provisions relating to the status of legitimated persons.

LEONINA SOCIETAS. A partnership in which one partner has all the loss, and another all the gain. It is so called, because the lucky partner has the "lion's share" of the profits.

LESSEE. A person to whom a lease is made. As used in the Law of Property Act 1925 the term includes the persons deriving title under him: see s. 205 (1) (xxiii). [LEASE.]

LESSOR. A person by whom a lease is made. As used in the Law of Property Act 1925 the word includes an underlessor and a person deriving title under a lessor or underlessor: see s. 205 (1) (xxiii).

LETHAL WEAPON. A weapon capable of killing, as, *e.g.*, a firearm (*q.v.*). [OFFENSIVE WEAPON.]

LETTER MISSIVE. A letter from the Queen to a dean and chapter, containing the name of the person whom she would have them elect as bishop. [BISHOP; CONGÉ D'ELIRE.]

2. A letter sent by the Lord Chancellor to a peer, who was made a defendant to a bill in Chancery, to request his appearance.

LETTER OF ATTORNEY. [POWER OF ATTORNEY.]

LETTER OF CREDIT. A letter written by one man (usually a merchant or banker) to another, requesting him to advance money, or entrust goods to the bearer, or to a particular person by name, and for which the writer's credit is pledged. It may be either *general*, addressed to all merchants or other persons, or *special*, addressed to a particular person by name. It is not negotiable.

LETTER OF LICENCE was an instrument or writing made by creditors to a man that had failed in his trade, allowing him longer time for the payment of his debts, and protecting him from arrests in going about his affairs.

LETTERS OF ADMINISTRATION. [ADMINISTRATION; ADMINISTRATOR.]

LETTERS OF MARQUE AND REPRISAL. These words, *marque* and *reprisal*, were used as synonymous; *reprisal* signifying a *taking in return*, and *marque* the passing over the *marches* or frontiers in order to do so. Letters of marque and

LETTERS OF MARQUE AND REPRISAL—continued.

reprisal were granted by the law of nations whenever the subjects of one State were oppressed and injured by those of another, and justice was denied by that State to which the oppressor belonged.

The term was applied to commissions granted in time of war to merchants and others to fit out *privateers* or armed ships, authorising them to take the ships of the enemy, and directing that the prizes captured by them should be divided between the owners, the captains and the crew.

Letters of marque and reprisal have fallen into disuse since the Declaration of Paris in 1856. Prize taken by any ship, not being one of Her Majesty's ships, belongs to the Crown as a droit of the Admiralty. [DECLARATION OF PARIS.]

LETTERS OF REQUEST. 1. Letters formerly granted by the Lord Privy Seal preparatory to granting letters of marque. [LETTERS OF MARQUE AND REPRISAL.]

2. Letters whereby a bishop, within whose jurisdiction an ecclesiastical cause has arisen, and who is desirous to waive such jurisdiction, requests the Dean of the Arches to take cognizance of the matter. The acceptance of such letters on the part of the Dean of Arches is not optional.

LETTERS OF SAFE CONDUCT. [SAFE CONDUCT.]

LETTERS PATENT (Lat. *Literæ patentes*) are writings sealed with the Great Seal of England, whereby a man is authorised to do or to enjoy anything that otherwise of himself he could not. They are so termed by reason of their form, because they are open (*patentes*) with the seal affixed, ready to be shown for confirmation of the authority given by them. [PATENT.]

LEVANT AND COUCHANT (Lat. *Levantes et cubantes*).

1. When land to which a right of common pasture is annexed can maintain a certain number of cattle during the winter by its produce, or requires a certain number of cattle to plough and manure it, those cattle are said to be levant and couchant on the land.

2. If cattle escape from A's land into B's land by default of B (as for want of his keeping a sufficient fence) they cannot be distrained for rent by B's landlord until they have been levant and couchant on the land, that is, until they have been at least one night there. If they escape by default of A, they may be distrained immediately.

LEVARI FACIAS. A writ of execution directed to the sheriff, for the levying a sum of money upon the lands and tenements of the judgment debtor. Abolished in 1883. [FIERI FACIAS; SEQUESTRARI FACIAS.]

LEVITICAL DEGREES. Degrees of kindred within which persons were prohibited to marry, set forth in the eighteenth chapter of Leviticus. They were referred to in an Act of 1540 (Henry VIII), now repealed. As to prohibited degrees of marriage, see now Sched. I to the Marriage Act 1949, as amended by the Marriage (Enabling) Act 1960.

LEX DOMICILII. The law of the place of a man's domicile. [DOMICILE.]

LEX FORI. The law of the *forum*, that is, the law of the place in which any given case is tried. [FORUM; LEX LOCI CONTRACTUS.]

LEX LOCI ACTUS. The law where a legal act takes place. Thus, if X, a British subject domiciled in England, makes a will in Scotland, the *lex loci actus* is the law of Scotland.

LEX LOCI CONTRACTUS. The law of the place in which a contract was made. Thus, if an action were brought in England upon a contract made in France, the law of England would, as regards such action, be the *lex fori*, and the law of France the *lex loci contractus*.

LEX LOCI REI SITÆ, or **LEX SITUS.** The law of the place in which a thing in question happens to be. Thus it is said that the descent of immovable property is regulated according to the *lex loci rei sitæ*; that is, according to the law of the place where it is situated.

LEX LOCI SOLUTIONIS. The law of the country where a contract is to be performed. Thus, if X contracts in London to deliver goods to A in Italy, the *lex loci solutionis* is the law of Italy.

LEX MERCATORIA signifies the law or custom of merchants. [CUSTOM; LAW MERCHANT.]

LEX NON SCRIPTA. The unwritten or common law which includes general and particular customs. [CUSTOM.]

LEX POSTERIOR DEROGAT PRIORI. The latter law abrogates the earlier.

LEX SCRIPTA. The written (or statute) law.

LEZE-MAJESTY (*Læsæ Majestatis Crimen*). An offence against sovereign power; treason, rebellion.

LIABILITY. The being under an obligation; an obligation.

LIBEL (Lat. *Libellus*). A little book. Hence it signifies:—

1. The original declaration of an action in the civil law.

2. Articles drawn out in a formal allegation in the Ecclesiastical Court, setting forth the complainant's ground of complaint.

3. The charge on which, in Scotland, a civil or criminal prosecution takes place.

4. An obscene, blasphemous, or seditious publication, whether by printing, writing, signs, or pictures. [OBSCENITY.]

5. A defamatory publication upon a person by writings, pictures, or the like. All contumacious matter that tends to degrade a man in the opinion of his neighbours, or to make him ridiculous, will, if published, amount to libel. Thus libel differs from slander, in that slander consists in oral defamation only, whereas a libel must consist of matter published in permanent form; also the scope of the offence of libel is more extensive than that of slander. Libel may be punished criminally, whereas a person guilty of slander can only be proceeded against civilly, unless an immediate breach of the peace is to be expected. Various statutes have been passed to correct injustices arising from the development of case law and to give relief to newspapers from the overstrict application of the common law. In particular, the Defamation Act 1952 provides that broadcast statements are to be treated as publication in permanent form; that offering and making amends shall avoid proceedings in cases of unintentional defamation; that certain newspaper statements shall have qualified privilege, etc.

LIBERTIES, or FRANCHISES. 1. At common law, a franchise is a royal privilege or branch of the Crown's prerogative, subsisting in the hands of a subject, either by grant or by prescription. Liberties or franchises are of two classes—(i) those which originally formed part of the Crown's prerogative; such as the franchises of waifs, estrays, wrecks, royal fish, forests, etc.; (ii) those which can only be created by granting them to a subject: such as fairs, markets, tolls, etc.

2. Franchise also means the locality subject to a franchise.

3. In ancient times, among other franchises usually granted by the Crown to a new borough on its incorporation, was the right of sending burgesses to Parliament; and hence franchise came to mean the right to elect members of parliament, whether in boroughs or counties.

LIBRARY. [BRITISH LIBRARY.]

LICENCE. 1. A power or authority to do some act which, without such authority, could not lawfully be done.

2. In real property law, a licence is an authority to do an act which would otherwise be a trespass. A licence passes no interest, and therefore if A grants to B the right to fasten boats to moorings in a river, this does not amount to a demise, nor does it give the licensee an exclusive right to the use of the moorings.

LICENCE TO MARRY. [MARRIAGE LICENCE.]

LICENSEE. A "licensee" is a person who enters on premises by the permission of the occupier, granted gratuitously in a matter in which the occupier has himself no interest. This is in contradistinction to an invitee, who at common law is a person who enters on business in which the occupier himself has some pecuniary or material interest.

There was formerly a distinction between the duty owed by an occupier to a licensee and an invitee respectively, but this distinction was abolished by the Occupiers Liability Act 1957. [INVITEE.]

LICENSING ACTS. 1. Acts of Parliament for the restraint of printing, except by licence; or any Act of Parliament passed for the purpose of requiring a licence for doing any act whatever.

2. The Acts regulating the sale of intoxicating liquors, now principally the Licensing Acts 1964 to 1967.

LIE. An action is said to *lie*, if it is legally maintainable.

LIE IN FRANCHISE. Waifs, wrecks, estrays, and the like, which the persons entitled thereto may seize without the aid of a court, are said to *lie in franchise.*

LIE IN GRANT. To *lie in grant,* when said of property, means to be capable of passing by deed of grant, as opposed to the passing of property by physical delivery. [FEOFFMENT; GRANT, 1; LEASE AND RELEASE, 2; LIE IN LIVERY.]

LIE IN LIVERY. To *lie in livery* is to be capable of passing by physical delivery. [CORPOREAL PROPERTY; FEOFFMENT; LIE IN GRANT.]

LIEGE, bound by some feudal tenure. [ALLEGIANCE.]

LIEN. 1. As applied to personalty, a lien is understood to be the right of a bailee to retain the possession of a chattel entrusted to him until his claim upon it be satisfied. [BAILMENT; GENERAL LIEN; MARITIME LIEN; PARTICULAR LIEN.]

2. As applied to realty, a *vendor's lien* for unpaid purchase-money is his right to enforce his claim upon the land sold; a right which is recognised in a court of equity, subject to the doctrines of that court for the protection of *bona fide* purchasers for valuable consideration without notice.

LIEUTENANCY, COMMISSION OF. A commission for mustering the inhabitants of a district for the defence of the country. These commissions of lieutenancy were introduced by the Tudors, and superseded the old commissions of array.

LIFE ANNUITY. [ANNUITY.]

LIFE ASSURANCE. A transaction whereby in consideration of a single or periodical payment of premium a sum of money is secured to be paid upon the death of the person whose life is assured. [INSURANCE.]

LIFE ESTATE. [ESTATE.]

LIFE PEERAGE. Letters patent, conferring the dignity of baron for life only, formerly did not enable the grantee to sit and vote in the House of Lords. A new class of life peers, having such rights and ranking as barons, was created by the Life Peerages Act 1958. [LORDS OF APPEAL IN ORDINARY.]

LIGAN. Goods sunk in the sea, but tied to a buoy, in order to be found again. [JETTISON.]

LIGEANCE, LIGEANCY. The same as *allegiance.* [ALLEGIANCE.]

LIGHTS. The right which a man has to have the access of the sun's rays to his windows free from any obstruction on the part of his neighbours. It is a species of easement. [EASEMENT.] This is sometimes spoken of as "the right to light and air"; sometimes as "ancient lights," because the possessor must have enjoyed them for a certain time before the right is indefeasible. This period under the Prescription Act 1832 was twenty years, though this was temporarily extended to twenty-seven years by s. 1 of the Rights of Light Act 1959 (repealed).

LIMITATION OF ACTIONS. [LIMITATIONS, STATUTES OF.]

LIMITATION OF ESTATES. The "limitation" of an estate is the marking out, in a deed or other instrument in writing, of the estate or interest which a person is intended to hold in any property comprised therein. Thus when it was said, with reference to a conveyance to A and his heirs, that the word *heirs* in a deed was a word of *limitation* and not of *purchase,* it meant that the word *heirs* marked out the nature of the estate taken by A, which was an estate in fee simple; and that the *heirs* of A took nothing *directly* (*i.e.,* took nothing "by purchase") under such a "limitation." In relation to instruments coming into operation after 1925 the rule in *Shelley's Case* has been abolished and the word "heirs" operates in equity as a word of purchase, not of limitation. See the Law of Property Act 1925, s. 131. [RULE IN SHELLEY'S CASE.]

LIMITATION OF LIABILITY. 1. The limitation of liability of members of a company according to their shareholdings, etc. [COMPANY.]

2. The liability of shipowners for loss or injury to goods or passengers carried in their ships is limited by s. 503 of the Merchant Shipping Act 1894, as amended by the Merchant Shipping (Liability of Shipowners and Others) Act 1958.

LIMITATION, WORDS OF. [LIMITATION OF ESTATES.]

LIMITATIONS, STATUTES OF. A statute of limitation is one which provides that no English Court shall entertain proceedings for the enforcement of certain rights if such proceedings were set on foot after the lapse of a definite period of time, reckoned as a rule from the date of the violation of the right. Various statutes have been passed with this object; they were consolidated with amendments by the Limitation Act 1939. That Act provided *inter alia* that actions founded on simple contract and tort should not be brought after the expiration of six years from the date on which the cause of action accrued; that an action upon a specialty (*q.v.*) should not be brought after the expiration of twelve years; that in general no action should be brought to recover land after the expiration of twelve years from the date when the right of action accrued. The Law Reform (Limitation of Actions, etc.) Act 1954 reduced to three years the period of limitation for actions for negligence, nuisance or breach of duty in respect of personal injuries; the Act also repealed the special periods of limitation and other privileges formerly accorded to public authorities.

The Limitation Act 1963 provided for an extension of the time limit in certain cases of actions for negligence, nuisance or breach of duty where damages for personal injuries or in respect of a person's death were claimed.

Further changes were made by the Limitation Act 1975. New time limits were introduced for commencing actions for personal injuries; the courts are empowered to override the time limits provided by the Act of 1939; and the rule was abolished whereby, previously, time ran against a person under disability if he was in the custody of a parent.

LIMITED ADMINISTRATION means an administration of certain specific effects of a deceased person, the rest being committed to others. [ADMINISTRATION.]

LIMITED COMPANY. A company in which the liability of each shareholder is limited by the number of shares he has taken or by guarantee, so that he cannot be called on to contribute beyond the amount of his shares or guarantee. See generally the Companies Acts 1948 and 1967. [COMPANY.]

LIMITED EXECUTOR. An executor of a deceased person for certain limited purposes, or for a certain limited time. [EXECUTOR.]

LIMITED LIABILITY. [LIMITED COMPANY.]

LIMITED OWNER. A tenant for life, in tail or by courtesy, or other person not having a fee simple in his absolute disposition. See the Settled Land Act 1925, s. 20. [SETTLED LAND.]

LIMITED PARTNERSHIP. A partnership consisting of one or more persons called general partners, who are liable for all the debts and obligations of the firm, and one or more persons called limited partners, who at the time of entering into the partnership contribute a stated amount of capital, and are not liable for the obligations of the firm beyond that amount. See the Limited Partnerships Act 1907.

LINCOLN'S INN. One of the Inns of Court. [INNS OF COURT.]

LINEAL CONSANGUINITY. The relationship between ascendants and descendants; as between father and son, grandfather and grandson, etc.

LINEAL DESCENT. Direct genealogical descent.

LIQUIDATED DAMAGES. The ascertained amount, expressed in pounds and pence, which an injured party has sustained, or is taken to have sustained. The term is used in contradistinction to a penalty.

LIQUIDATION. 1. A method by which, under the former bankruptcy law, an insolvent debtor's affairs were liquidated under the supervision of a trustee. The procedure was abolished by the Bankruptcy Act 1914.
2. The winding up of a company. [LIQUIDATOR.]

LIQUIDATOR. An officer appointed to conduct the winding-up of a company; to bring and defend actions and suits in its name, and to do all necessary acts on behalf of the company. He may be appointed either by resolution of the shareholders in a voluntary winding-up, or by the court in a compulsory winding-up. See Part V of the Companies Act 1948. [OFFICIAL LIQUIDATOR.]

LIS MOTA. A lawsuit put in motion.

LIS PENDENS. A pending suit; an expression used especially of pending suits relating to land, as affecting the title to the land in question. By s. 5 of the Land Charges Act 1972 a pending action may be registered in the register of pending actions.

LITE PENDENTE. While a suit is pending. [LIS PENDENS.]

LITERARY WORK. Includes any written table or compilation: see s. 48 of the Copyright Act 1956. The expression also covers work which is expressed in print or writing, irrespective of whether the quality or style is high: *University of London Press Ltd.* v. *University Tutorial Press Ltd.* [1916] 2 Ch. 601.

LITIGIOUS. A church is said to be *litigious* when two rival presentations are offered to the bishop upon the same avoidance of the living. [AVOIDANCE; JUS PATRONATUS.]

LITIS CONTESTATIO. 1. In Ecclesiastical Courts, the issue of an action.

2. In Roman law, the submission to the decision of a judge.

LITTLETON. A judge in the reign of Edward IV, who wrote a treatise of tenures upon which Chief Justice Coke has written an extensive comment.

LIVERPOOL COURT OF PASSAGE. An ancient court of record in Liverpool, originally called the Mayor's Court of Pays Sage, but afterwards called the Court of Passage of the City of Liverpool. It had jurisdiction in causes of action arising within the city, and also in Admiralty matters. Abolished by the Courts Act 1971.

LIVERY (Lat. *Liberatura*). 1. A delivery of possession to tenants who held of the king *in capite*, or by knight-service. [IN CAPITE; KNIGHT-SERVICE.]

2. A writ which lay for the heir to obtain the possession or seisin of land at the king's hands. [FEOFFMENT; LIVERY OF SEISIN.]

3. The members of a company of the City of London chosen out of the freemen. [LIVERYMAN.]

LIVERY OF SEISIN. A delivery of feudal possession, part of the ceremony called a *feoffment*. [FEOFFMENT.]

LIVERYMAN. A member of a company in the City of London, chosen out of the freemen, to assist the master and wardens in the government of the company.

LIVESTOCK. Cattle (bulls, cows, oxen, heifers or calves), sheep, goats, swine, horses (including asses and mules), or poultry (domestic fowls, turkeys, geese or ducks). See Dogs (Protection of Livestock) Act 1953, s. 3. In Part 1 of the Agriculture Act 1967, the term is limited to cattle, sheep and pigs; whereas under the Agriculture Act 1947, s. 109, it includes any creature kept for the production of food, wool, skins or furs, or for the purpose of its use in the farming of land.

By s. 11 of the Animals Act 1971 the word "livestock" means cattle, horses, asses, mules, hinnies, sheep, pigs, goats and poultry and also deer not in the wild state, and, in cases where dogs cause injury or death to them, pheasants, partridges and grouse in captivity.

LLOYD'S. An association in the City of London, the members of which underwrite each other's policies. [UNDERWRITER.]

LOAD-LINE. This word indicates the depth to which a ship is loaded so as to sink in salt water, and beyond which it may not be loaded. See the Merchant Shipping (Safety and Load Line Conventions) Act 1932.

LOAN SOCIETIES. Those established for advancing money on loan to the industrial classes. See the Loan Societies Act 1840.

LOCAL ACTION. An action founded on such a cause as refers necessarily to some particular locality, as in the case of trespasses to land, and in which the venue must as a rule have been laid in the county where the cause of action arose. [VENUE.]

LOCAL ALLEGIANCE. Such as is due from an alien or stranger born so long as he continues within the sovereign's dominions and protection and in certain circumstances even after he has left.

LOCAL AND PERSONAL ACTS. This expression is applied to the second category of Acts of Parliament as classified for publication. These Acts when passed are to be judicially noticed as public Acts. See the Interpretation Act 1889, s. 9.

LOCAL AUTHORITY. Local authorities were reorganised by the Local

Government Act 1972. The expression now means a county council, the Greater London Council, a district council, a London borough council or a parish or community council (*ibid.*, s. 270 (1)).

LOCAL COURTS are courts whose jurisdiction is confined to certain districts, as the county courts, police courts, etc.

LOCAL GOVERNMENT BOARD. A department of the Government, established by the Local Government Board Act 1871. To this department were transferred all the powers and duties of the Poor Law Board, which then ceased to exist, as well as certain powers that had been exercised by the Home Secretary, or in the Privy Council, under certain Acts of Parliament specified in the schedule to the Act. The powers of the Board were transferred to the Ministry of Health in 1919, and in 1943 to the Minister of Housing and Local Government.

LOCATIO. The contract of letting and hiring, also called *locatio-conductio*; *locatio* expressing the letting out to hire, and *conductio* the hiring. This contract is a species of bailment. [BAILMENT.]

LOCATIO OPERIS FACIENDI. The letting to hire of work to be done; a species of bailment, which consists in one man delivering to another any article of property for the latter to expend work and labour upon it; or, in other words, *let his work to hire*; as when one gives a tailor a coat to be repaired. [BAILMENT.]

LOCATIO OPERIS MERCIUM VEHENDARUM. The hire of a person's labour for the purpose of carrying goods or merchandise from one place to another.

LOCATIO REI. The letting of anything to hire for temporary use. This also is a species of bailment. [BAILMENT.]

LOCUM TENENS. A deputy or substitute.

LOCUS IN QUO. The place in which anything is alleged to be done.

LOCUS PŒNITENTIÆ. A place or chance of repentance; a phrase generally applied to a power of drawing back from a bargain before anything has been done to confirm it in law.

LOCUS REGIT ACTUM. The place governs the act, *i.e.*, the act is governed by the law of the place where it is done.

LOCUS SIGILLI. The place of the seal; the initials (L.S.) are also used in a copy of a document, to indicate the place where the seal was in the original document.

LOCUS STANDI (a place of standing) signifies a right of appearance in a court of justice, or before parliament, on any given question. In other words, it signifies a right *to be heard*, as opposed to a right *to succeed on the merits*.

LODGER. A tenant having exclusive possession of a part of a house, the general dominion over which remains in the landlord or his agent. A lodger's goods are protected against distraint by the superior landlord by the Law of Distress Amendment Act 1908.

LOG, or **LOG-BOOK,** is a journal kept by the chief mate or first officer of a ship in which the situation of the ship from time to time, the winds, weather, courses, and distances, the misconduct or desertion of any of the crew, and everything of importance, are carefully noted down.

An *official log-book* is a book required by law to be kept in every ship (except those employed exclusively in the coasting trade of the United Kingdom) in a form sanctioned by the Board of Trade, either in connection with, or distinct from, the ordinary log-books. Merchant Shipping Act 1894, ss. 239–243.

LOITERING. Travelling indolently, with frequent pauses, lingering. See *Williamson* v. *Wright*, [1924] S.C. (J.) 57. Loitering or soliciting for purposes of prostitution is an offence under the Street Offences Act 1959.

LONDON GAZETTE. [GAZETTE.]

LONG VACATION. The Long Vacation begins on 1st August, and ends on 30th September. See generally, as to vacations, R.S.C. 1965, Ord. 64.

LORD ADVOCATE. The principal Crown lawyer in Scotland. [*cf.* ATTORNEY-GENERAL.]

LORD CAMPBELL'S ACTS. 1. The Libel Act 1843 for amending the law respecting defamatory words and libel, by allowing a defendant in pleading to an *indictment* or *information* for defamatory libel to allege the truth of the matters charged and that their publication was for the public benefit.

LORD CAMPBELL'S ACTS
—continued.

2. The Fatal Accidents Act 1846 for enabling the executors or administrators of persons killed by negligence to bring actions for the benefit of the wife, husband, parent or children of the deceased, against the parties guilty of negligence.

3. The Obscene Publications Act 1857 authorising magistrates to issue warrants for the seizure of obscene books, papers, writings, or representations kept in some place for the purpose of being sold, distributed, lent on hire, or otherwise published for gain. Repealed and replaced by the Obscene Publications Acts 1959 and 1964.

LORD CHAMBERLAIN. [CHAMBERLAIN.]

LORD CHANCELLOR. [CHANCELLOR.]

LORD CHIEF JUSTICE OF ENGLAND. The presiding judge of the Queen's Bench Division, and, in the absence of the Lord Chancellor, President of the High Court. He is also an *ex-officio* judge of the Court of Appeal. [CHIEF JUSTICE.]

LORD HIGH ADMIRAL. [ADMIRAL.]

LORD HIGH STEWARD. [HIGH STEWARD.]   **LORD JUSTICE.** [LORDS JUSTICES OF APPEAL.]

LORD JUSTICE-CLERK. (*Scotland.*) A judge of the High Court of Justiciary (*q.v.*); also senior judge of the second division of the Court of Session.

LORD JUSTICE-GENERAL. [LORD PRESIDENT.]

LORD KEEPER. [KEEPER OF THE GREAT SEAL.]

LORD LIEUTENANT. 1. Formerly the Viceroy of the Crown in Ireland.

2. One of the principal honorary officers of a county, originally appointed for the purpose of mustering the inhabitants for the defence of the country. The Lord Lieutenant of a county was in general to be appointed president of the County Territorial Association. It is at his recommendation that magistrates are appointed.

LORD MAYOR'S COURT. [MAYOR'S AND CITY OF LONDON COURT.]

LORD OF A MANOR. [COPYHOLD; MANOR.]

LORD PARAMOUNT. [PARAMOUNT.]

LORD PRESIDENT. (*Scotland.*) The president of the first division of the Court of Session, the office being united with that of Lord Justice-General in the criminal courts.

LORD PRIVY SEAL. Usually one of the members of the Cabinet, through whose hands all charters, etc., passed before they came to the Great Seal. The Great Seal Act Act 1884, s. 3, provided that it should not be necessary in future that any instrument be passed under the Privy Seal. The Lord Privy Seal has really no duties as such.

LORD TENTERDEN'S ACT. [TENTERDEN'S ACT.]

LORD TREASURER, otherwise called the Lord High Treasurer of England, was a high officer of State, who had the charge and government of the king's wealth contained in the Exchequer. The office of Lord Treasurer has now for a long time been entrusted to commissioners, who are called the Lords Commissioners of the Treasury. The chief of the commissioners is called the First Lord, and the Chancellor of the Exchequer is the second, and there are five others, who usually act as "Whips" for the political party in power.

LORD WARDEN OF THE CINQUE PORTS. The principal officer of the Cinque Ports having the custody thereof, and formerly having a civil jurisdiction therein. [CINQUE PORTS.]

LORDS COMMISSIONERS. When a high public office in the State, formerly executed by an individual, is put into commission, the persons charged with the commission are called Lords Commissioners, or sometimes Lords or Commissioners simply. At the present time the places of the Lord Treasurer and Lord High Admiral of former times are taken by the Lords Commissioners of the Treasury, and the Lords Commissioners of the Admiralty; and whenever the Great Seal is put into commission, the persons charged with it are called Commissioners or Lords Commissioners of the Great Seal.

LORDS, HOUSE OF. [HOUSE OF LORDS.]

LORDS JUSTICES OF APPEAL. The ordinary judges of the Court of Appeal. That court is constituted by *ex-officio* judges and not more than fourteen ordinary judges. See s. 6 of the Judicature Act 1925.

LORDS OF APPEAL IN ORDINARY. Persons having held high judicial office for two years or practised at the bar for not less than fifteen years, to aid the House of Lords and the Judicial Committee of the Privy Council in hearing appeals. They rank as barons for life, but sit and vote in the House of Lords during the time of their office only. See the Appellate Jurisdiction Acts 1876 to 1947.

The maximum number of Lords of Appeal in Ordinary is eleven, two of whom are normally appointed from the Scottish bench or bar.

LORDS SPIRITUAL. Those bishops who have seats in the House of Lords: being the Archbishops of Canterbury and York, the Bishops of London, Durham, and Winchester, and twenty-one other bishops.

LORDS TEMPORAL. The peers of the realm who have seats in the House of Lords, other than the bishops.

LOSS. Includes a loss by not getting what one might get, as well as a loss by parting with what one has. See s. 34 of the Theft Act 1968.

LOSS, TOTAL. [TOTAL LOSS.]

LOST OR NOT LOST. These words are often inserted in a policy of marine insurance. They enable the insurer to recover although, unknown to both parties, the vessel was lost at the time of effecting the insurance.

LOTTERY. A game of chance, or a distribution of money or prizes by chance, without the application of choice or skill. Illegal unless falling within the provisions of the Betting, Gaming and Lotteries Act 1963 and the Lotteries Act 1975, which permit certain lotteries for sporting or other purposes.

LUCID INTERVAL. A period of sanity which intervenes between two attacks of insanity. Acts done during such an interval are valid.

LUCRI CAUSA. For the sake of gain.

LUNATIC. [MENTAL DISORDER.]

LYING BY. Neglecting to assert rights, or allowing persons to deal with land or other property as if one had no interest in it; as when a mortgagee allows his mortgagor retain the title deeds and raise money upon a fresh mortgage of the land, without notice to the new mortgagee of the prior mortgage. [LACHES.]

LYING IN FRANCHISE. [LIE IN FRANCHISE.]

LYING IN GRANT. [GRANT; INCORPOREAL HEREDITAMENT; LIE IN GRANT.]

LYING IN LIVERY. [LIE IN LIVERY.]

LYNCH LAW. The execution of summary justice by a mob without reference to the process of ordinary municipal law.

LYON KING AT ARMS. An officer who takes his title from the armorial bearing of the Scotch king, the lion rampant. [KINGS-AT-ARMS.]

LYON'S INN. [INNS OF CHANCERY.]

LYTTLETON. [LITTLETON.]

M

M.R. Master of the Rolls.

MAGISTRATE. A person entrusted with the commission of the peace for any county, city or other jurisdiction. [CONSERVATOR OF THE PEACE; JUSTICE OF THE PEACE; STIPENDIARY MAGISTRATES.]

MAGNA CHARTA was a charter granted by King John in the year 1215, at Runnymead, and confirmed in Parliament in the 9th year of Henry III, A.D. 1225, and again by the *Confirmatio Chartarum*, in the 25th year of Edward I, A.D. 1297. [CONFIRMATIO CHARTARUM.]

This Great Charter is based substantially on the Saxon common law and contains thirty-eight chapters on various subjects, especially with reference to landed estates and their tenures. Many of its provisions are now repealed.

MAIDEN ASSIZE. One at which there were no prisoners to be tried.

MAIHEM or **MAYHEM.** The violently depriving another of the use of a member proper for his defence in fight.

MAIL. Every conveyance by which postal packets are carried, whether it be a ship, aircraft, vehicle, horse, or any other

MAIL—*continued.*
conveyance; also a person employed in conveying or delivering postal packets.

MAIMING. [MAIHEM.]

MAINPERNABLE. Under a statute of Edward III (Statute of Westminster I, 1275) this signified that which might be held to bail.

MAINPRISE (Lat. *Manucaptio*). A writ directed to the sheriff, commanding him to take sureties for a prisoner's appearance, usually called *mainpernors*, and to set him at large. As opposed to bailing him or giving him into custody. Obsolete.

MAINTAINORS. Persons guilty of *maintaining* a lawsuit. [MAINTENANCE, 1.]

MAINTENANCE. 1. An officious intermeddling in a suit that in no way belonged to one, by maintaining or assisting either party, with money or otherwise, to prosecute or defend it. The offence was abolished by s. 13 of the Criminal Law Act 1967.

2. Providing children, or other persons in a position of dependence, with food, clothing, and other necessaries.

3. A maintenance order is one which magistrates may make in favour of a wife whose husband neglects to maintain her.

MAINTENANCE AGREEMENT. An agreement in writing made between the parties to a marriage, being either (*a*) an agreement containing financial arrangements, whether made during the continuance or after the dissolution or annulment of the marriage; or (*b*) a separation agreement which contains no financial arrangements in a case where no other agreement in writing between the parties contains such arrangements: Matrimonial Causes Act 1973, s. 34. Such agreements may be altered by the court. Application for an order making such alteration is generally to a magistrates' court or by originating application in a divorce county court.

MAINTENANCE AND EDUCATION CLAUSES, in a deed or will wherein property is conveyed or bequeathed upon trust, are clauses empowering the trustee or trustees to expend the income of the trust property in the maintenance and education of the children who are to participate in the property when they come of age. This power was given to all trustees of settled property in 1881, but the present provisions as to the maintenance and education of children are contained in s. 31 of the Trustee Act 1925.

MAINTENANCE PENDING SUIT. An order requiring either party to the marriage to make to the other such periodical payments for his or her maintenance, and for such term as the court thinks reasonable. Such order may be made on a petition for divorce, nullity of marriage or judicial separation: Matrimonial Causes Act 1973, s. 22.

MAJORA REGALIA. The Queen's dignity, power, and royal prerogative; as opposed to her *revenue*, which is comprised in the *minora regalia.*

MAJORITY. Full age, formerly twenty-one, but reduced to eighteen by the Family Law Reform Act 1969.

MAKER, of a promissory note, is he who signs it. By so doing, he engages to pay it according to its tenor. See s. 88 of the Bills of Exchange Act 1882.

MAL. A prefix meaning bad, wrong, fraudulent.

MALA FIDES. Bad faith.

MALA GRAMMATICA NON VITIAT CHARTAM. Bad grammar does not vitiate a deed.

MALA IN SE. Acts which are wrong in themselves, such as murder, whether prohibited by human laws or not, as distinguished from *mala prohibita*, which are indifferent in themselves, but are wrong by reason of being expressly prohibited by human laws, *e.g.*, playing at unlawful games.

MALA PRAXIS is improper or unskilful management of a case by a surgeon, physician, or apothecary, whereby a patient is injured; whether it be by neglect, or for curiosity and experiment.

MALA PROHIBITA. [MALA IN SE.]

MALESWORN. Forsworn. *Cowel.*

MALFEASANCE. The commission of some act which is in itself unlawful, as opposed to *nonfeasance*, which is the omission of an act which a man is bound by law to do; and to *misfeasance*, which is the improper performance of some lawful act.

MALICE. 1. The wicked and mischievous purpose which is of the essence of the crime of murder. Also called "malice aforethought", "malice and forethought", "malice prepense". It exists where any one contemplates the death of any person or persons as a probable consequence of an act done by himself without lawful justification or excuse, or of some unlawful omission, and is implied where he does any act the natural or probable consequence of which is to cause the death of a person.

Formerly, under the doctrine of "constructive malice", malice was implied in cases where killing had been caused in the cause or furtherance of some other felony involving an act of violence or an act dangerous to life, or where the person killed was legally arresting or imprisoning the accused or executing other process of law in a legal manner. This doctrine was abolished by s. 1 of the Homicide Act 1957. There must now be actual intent to kill, or knowledge that the act in question will probably cause death or grievous harm, for a killing to be murder.

2. As regards malicious injuries to persons or property, especially the latter, a "malicious act" has been defined as a wrongful act, intentionally done without just cause or excuse. See *Bromage* v. *Prosser* (1825), 4 B. & C. 247, 255. Under the Malicious Damage Act 1861 it must be understood in a more restricted sense than the malice which is of the essence of murder. An act lawful in itself is not converted by malice into an actionable wrong (*Allen* v. *Flood*, [1898] A.C.1).

MALICE AFORETHOUGHT. "The distinction between murder and manslaughter, both felonies at common law, appears to derive from the statutes of Henry VIII and Edward VI by which benefit of clergy was withdrawn from murder committed *ex malitia præcogitata*, which in the form 'malice prepense' or 'prepensed' and 'malice aforethought' has continued in common use in legal circles to the present date. The precise value of this phrase is open to doubt. As long ago as 1883 Stephen [History of the Criminal Law] described it as 'a phrase which is never used except to mislead or to be explained away' and advised its abolition as a term of art and the substitution for it of a 'definite enumeration of the states of mind intended to be taken as constituent elements of murder'. In the present case Cairns, L.J., in delivering the judgment now appealed from, said: 'There is no doubt that murder is killing "with malice aforethought", and there is no doubt that neither the word "malice" nor the word "aforethought" is to be construed in any ordinary sense.' I agree with this latter observation, and would myself think that the sooner the phrase is consigned to the limbo of legal history the better for precision and lucidity in the interpretation of our criminal law." *Hyam* v. *Director of Public Prosecutions*, [1974] 2 All E.R. 41, H.L., *per* Lord Hailsham of St. Marylebone.

MALICIOUS PROSECUTION. A prosecution undertaken against a person without reasonable or probable cause. In an action for malicious prosecution, the burden lies upon the plaintiff to show that no probable cause existed.

MALINGERING. Falsely pretending to be suffering from sickness or disability. Used principally of members of the forces so doing to escape duty. Punishable under s. 27 of the Naval Discipline Act 1957, and under s. 42 of the Army Act 1955, and s. 42 of the Air Force Act 1955.

MALVERSATION. Misbehaviour in an office, commission, or employment.

MANAGER. [RECEIVER.]

MANDAMUS. The order in lieu of the prerogative writ of mandamus. This is, in its form, a command issuing in the Queen's name, and directed to any person, corporation, or inferior court of judicature, requiring them to do some particular thing which appertains to their office and duty. In its application, it may be considered as confined to cases where relief is required in respect of the infringement of some *public* right or duty, and where no effectual relief can be obtained in the ordinary course of an action. For the rules of procedure, see R.S.C. 1965, Ord. 53.

MANDATE. 1. A command of the Queen, or her justices, to have anything done for despatch of justice.

2. A contract by which one man employs another gratuitously in the management of his affairs. [BAILMENT.]

MANDATED TERRITORY. The method adopted at the end of the First

MANDATED TERRITORY
—continued.

World War (1914–1918) for dealing with the colonies and territories of Germany and Turkey, which it was decided to detach from them, was known as the mandate system, and was embodied in Article 22 of the Covenant of the League of Nations. Under this system, those detached territories were not in the ownership of any State, but were entrusted to certain States called "Mandatory States" to administer on behalf of the League upon the conditions laid down in written agreements, called "mandates", between the League and each mandatory. This system was a novelty in international law. It has been replaced by trusteeship under the United Nations.

MANDATORY or **MANDATARY.** 1. He to whom a charge or commandment is given.

2. He that obtains a benefice by *mandamus.*

MANDATUM. [BAILMENT.]

MANDAVI BALLIVO. A return to a writ whereby a sheriff states that he has committed its execution to the bailiff.

MANIFEST. A document signed by the master of a ship giving a description of the ship, of the goods laden in her, etc.

MANOR was originally a district of ground held by a lord or great personage, who kept to himself such parts of it as were necessary for his own use, which were called *terræ dominicales* or *demesne lands,* and distributed the rest to freehold tenants. Of the demesne lands, again, part was retained in the actual occupation of the lord, and other portions were held in villenage; and there was also a portion which, being uncultivated, was called the lord's waste, and served for public roads and for common of pasture to the lord and his tenants. Manors were also called baronies, as they still are lordships, and each baron or lord was empowered to hold a domestic court called the *court baron,* for redressing misdemeanours and nuisances within the manor, and for settling disputes of property among the tenants. In most manors we find that species of tenants called *copyholders,* whose lands, though substantially their own property, are nominally part of the lord's demesnes. But a manor, in its proper and perfect state, also comprises land occupied by *freehold tenants* holding of the manor in perpetuity. The essence of a manor seems to consist in the jurisdiction exercised by the lord in his court; and it was formerly said that if the number of suitors should so fall as not to leave sufficient to make a jury or homage, that is, two tenants at least to attend in the court, the manor itself would be lost. But by an Act of 1841, this attendance was made unnecessary.

The civil and criminal jurisdiction of these local courts is now obsolete, but many other rights, *e.g.,* mineral rights, sporting rights, etc., still remain in the hands of the lord of a manor. [COMMON; COPYHOLD; COURT BARON; FREEHOLD; VILLENAGE.]

MANPOWER SERVICES COMMISSION. A Commission established by the Employment and Training Act 1973, to make such arrangements as it considers appropriate for the purpose of assisting persons to select, train for, obtain and retain employment.

MANSION or **MANSION-HOUSE.** The lord's chief dwelling-house within his fee, otherwise called the *capital messuage* or manor-place.

Under the Settled Land Act 1925 the principal mansion-house (unless it is usually occupied as a farm house, or its park, etc., does not exceed twenty-five acres in extent) may not be sold, exchanged, or leased by a tenant for life without the consent of the trustees of the settlement or the order of the Chancery Division. In regard to a settlement made or coming into operation after 1925 this restriction will only apply if the settlement expressly so provides. See s. 65 of the Settled Land Act 1925.

MANSLAUGHTER is defined as the unlawful killing of another without malice express or implied: which may be either voluntarily, upon a sudden heat, or involuntarily, but in the commission of some unlawful or negligent act.

The absence of such malice as would constitute the act murder may be inferred under the following circumstances:—

1. Where the person charged was provoked to lose his self-control, whether by things done or by things said or by both together: see s. 3 of the Homicide Act 1957.

2. Where there is a time to consider the probable consequences of an unlawful act wilfully done, and yet the death of any person is by no means a natural or probable consequence of such unlawful act; as if two parties fight without deadly weapons; or where there is a high degree of negligence, provided that the negligence in question be not such as to indicate a wanton and palpable disregard of human life, in which case it will amount to murder. [MURDER.] This definition would imply that the difference between murder and manslaughter is often one of degree which is in fact the case.

3. Persons suffering from diminished responsibility, *i.e.*, mental abnormality of mind, must not be convicted of murder but of manslaughter: see s. 2 of the Homicide Act 1957.

MAN-TRAPS, to catch trespassers, are unlawful except in a dwelling-house for defence between sunset and sunrise. See s. 31 of the Offences against the Person Act 1861.

MANUMISSION. The freeing of a villein or slave out of his bondage.

MANUSCRIPT. The original document embodying a work, whether written by hand or not. See s. 48 of the Copyright Act 1956.

MARCHERS. [MARQUIS.]

MARCHES. Boundaries or frontiers.

The boundaries and limits between England and Wales, or between England and Scotland; or generally the borders of the dominions of the Crown.

MARE CLAUSUM. A celebrated treatise by Selden (1584–1654) written in answer to the treatise called *Mare Liberum* (*q.v.*).

MARE LIBERUM. A famous treatise by Grotius (1583–1645) to prove that all nations have an equal right to use the sea.

MARINE INSURANCE. [INSURANCE.]

MARITAL. Pertaining to a husband, or of the nature of marriage.

MARITIME COURTS. Courts having jurisdiction in maritime causes, formerly the Court of Admiralty, and the Judicial Committee of the Privy Council on appeal therefrom. By the Judicature Act 1875 this jurisdiction was vested in the Probate, Divorce, and Admiralty Division of the High Court, with an appeal to the Court of Appeal. The Probate, Divorce and Admiralty Division was abolished in 1970, Admiralty business being transferred to the Queen's Bench Division.

MARITIME LAW. The law relating to harbours, ships, and seamen.

MARITIME LIEN. A claim which attaches to the *res, i.e.,* the ship, cargo, or freight. It arises either *ex delicto, e.g.,* in respect of compensation for damage by collision, or *ex contractu,* in respect of services rendered to the *res.*

MARK. [TRADE MARK.]

MARKET. An emporium of commerce or place of buying and selling; or the liberty to set up such a place, which any person or body corporate may have by Act of Parliament, grant, or prescription. Generally, as to the provision and regulation of markets, see ss. 49–61 of the Food and Drugs Act 1955.

MARKET OVERT. Open market; an expression applied to the open sale of goods as opposed to a clandestine or irregular sale. Market overt, in the country, is held only on the special days provided for particular towns; but in the City of London every day, except Sunday, is market-day. Also in the country the market-place is the only market overt; but in London every shop in which goods are exposed publicly for sale is market overt for the sale by the occupier of such things as he professes to trade in. See also s. 22 of the Sale of Goods Act 1893.

The effect of a sale in market overt is that it will in general give the purchaser a secure title to the goods which he has bought, though the vendor has had no property therein. To this rule, however, there are some exceptions; as, if the goods be Crown property; or if the goods be stolen, and the owner has prosecuted the thief to conviction.

MARKET TOWNS are towns entitled to hold markets.

MARKSMAN. A person who cannot write, and therefore, instead of signing his name, makes his mark, generally a cross. In practice it is desirable that the mark should be attested by a witness.

MARLBRIDGE, STATUTE OF. A statute made at Marlbridge, Marleberge, or Marlborough, in the reign of Henry III (1267), directed chiefly against excessive distress.

MARQUE. [LETTERS OF MARQUE AND REPRISAL.]

MARQUIS, or **MARQUESS,** is a title of honour next before an earl, and next after a duke. It first came up in the time of Richard II, when it was applied to those lords who had the charge and custody of *marches* or limits, and who before that time were called *marchers* or *lords marchers*.

MARRIAGE. The ceremony or process by which the legal relationship of husband and wife is constituted.

The law of marriage is consolidated in the Marriage Acts 1949 to 1970. The Act of 1949 is divided into six parts. Part 1 sets out the various restrictions on marriage, such as the prohibited degrees of kindred and affinity, age, and the hours in which marriage may be solemnized. Part II regulates marriage according to the rites of the Church of England, whether after the publication of banns of matrimony, or on the authority of a special licence, a common licence, or the certificate of a superintendent registrar. Part III makes provision for marriage under a superintendent registrar's certificate, *e.g.*, marriages in a registry office, Quaker marriages, Jewish marriages, etc. Part IV deals with the registration of marriages, Part V with marriage in naval, military and air force chapels, and Part VI with miscellaneous and general matters.

MARRIAGE ARTICLES. Heads of an agreement for a marriage settlement.

MARRIAGE BROKAGE CONTRACTS are agreements whereby a party engages to give another a remuneration if he will negotiate a marriage for him. Such agreements are void, as tending to introduce marriage not based on mutual affection, and therefore contrary to public policy.

MARRIAGE BY CERTIFICATE. A person may be married by superintendent registrar's certificate without licence. In order to obtain this certificate, notice in prescribed form must be given to the superintendent registrar of the district or districts in which both the parties have dwelt for not less than 7 days. After 21 days the certificate is issued. See ss. 27, 31 of the Marriage Act 1949.

MARRIAGE LICENCE is of the following kinds:—

1. A common licence, granted by the ordinary or his surrogate.

2. A special licence from the Archbishop of Canterbury or any other person by virtue of the Ecclesiastical Licences Act 1533.

3. A licence from the superintendent registrar of the district.

A licence obtained in either of the forms (1) or (2) will enable the parties to marry without banns, according to the forms of the Church of England; and a licence obtained in form (3) will enable the parties to marry in any other lawful manner. In this case the presence of the registrar was formerly necessary. His presence is now dispensed with in many cases. See the Marriage Act 1949.

MARRIAGE SETTLEMENT. A settlement of property between an intended husband and wife, made in consideration of their marriage.

MARRIED WOMEN'S PROPERTY. [HUSBAND AND WIFE.]

MARROW. Author of a famous book, written in the reign of Henry VII, on the office of a justice of the peace.

MARSHAL. 1. An officer (paid by the Treasury) who formerly attended on each judge of assize, and whose duty it was to swear in the grand jury, and, on the civil side, to receive records and enter causes.

2. The marshal of the Queen's Bench, who had the custody of the Queen's Bench Prison. An officer called the Keeper of the Queen's Prison was substituted by an Act of 1842, now repealed.

3. An official of the Admiralty Court, having duties very similar to a sheriff at common law.

MARSHALLING OF ASSETS. An adjustment of the assets of a deceased person so as to pay as many claims upon his estate as possible. Thus if A has a claim on funds X and Y, and B only upon X; and A goes against X and thus disappoints B of his fund, B under this doctrine may go against Y fund to the extent that A had drawn upon X funds.

MARSHALSEA COURT. [COURT OF MARSHALSEA.]

MARTIAL COURTS. [COURT-MARTIAL.]

MARTIAL LAW. A state of war in which a military commander is in full control. It is not law in the ordinary sense.

MARTINMAS. The 11th of November, the feast of St. Martin of Tours. In Scotland, a quarter-day.

MASTER AND SERVANT. [SERVANT.]

MASTER IN LUNACY. The former title of the Master of the Court of Protection (q.v.).

MASTER OF A SHIP. A chief officer of a merchant ship, having a certificate from the Ministry of Transport, which is either a certificate of competency obtained in an examination, or a certificate of service obtained by his having attained a certain rank in the service of Her Majesty.

MASTER OF THE COURT OF PROTECTION. The Court of Protection is an office of the Supreme Court, whose task is the protection and management of the property of mentally disordered persons. The Master and Deputy Master are appointable by the Lord Chancellor under s. 100 of the Mental Health Act 1959.

MASTER OF THE CROWN OFFICE. The coroner and attorney of the sovereign, whose duty it was to file criminal informations in the Court of Queen's Bench under the direction of the court, upon the complaint or relation of a private person. He is now an officer of the Supreme Court.

MASTER OF THE FACULTIES. An officer under the Archbishop of Canterbury, appointed to grant licences, dispensations, etc. [FACULTY.]

MASTER OF THE MINT is an officer whose duty it is to receive in the silver and bullion from the goldsmiths to be coined, and to pay them for it, and to superintend everything belonging to the Mint. By s. 14 of the Coinage Act 1870 (repealed by the Coinage Act 1971) the Chancellor of the Exchequer for the time being was made Master of the Mint.

MASTER OF THE ROLLS was one of the judges of the Court of Chancery, and keeper of the rolls of all patents and grants that pass the Great Seal, and of all records of the Court of Chancery. He was formerly one of the Masters in Chancery, and his earliest judicial attendances seem to have been merely as assessor to the Chancellor, with the other Masters. His character as an independent judge was fully established in the reign of George II. He is an *ex-officio* judge of the Court of Appeal. See s. 6 (2) of the Judicature Act 1925. [ROLLS COURT.]

MASTERS IN CHANCERY. Masters of the High Court of Chancery, who assisted the Lord Chancellor. Their office was abolished in 1852, and their duties relegated to Chief Clerks. Since 1897 the officials previously called Chief Clerks have been called "Masters". [CHIEF CLERK.]

MASTERS OF THE COURTS OF COMMON LAW were the most important officers of the respective courts, appointed to record the proceedings of the court to which they belonged, to superintend the issue of writs, and the formal proceedings in an action; to receive and account for the fees charged on legal proceedings, and moneys paid into court. There were five to each court. They were originally appointed in 1837. These officers became, under the Judicature Acts, officers of the Supreme Court, and may, with certain exceptions, transact all such business as may be done by a judge at chambers. See R.S.C. 1965, Ord. 32, r. 11. [CHANCERY MASTERS; QUEENS BENCH MASTERS; TAXING MASTERS.]

MATE. The deputy of the master in a merchant ship. There are sometimes one, sometimes two, three or four.

MATERNITY PAY FUND. A fund established under Part II of the Employment Protection Act 1975, to be financed by employers' contributions under the Social Security Act 1975. An employee who is absent from work because of pregnancy or confinement is entitled to maternity pay, and an employer who has paid this may claim a rebate of an equivalent sum from the fund. Failure to permit the return of a woman who has been absent through pregnancy is to be treated as unfair dismissal.

MATRICIDE. The killing of a mother.

MATRIMONIAL CAUSES are causes respecting the rights of marriage, which

MATRIMONIAL CAUSES—*continued.*
were formerly a branch of the ecclesiastical jurisdiction, but which were placed by the Matrimonial Causes Act 1857, under the cognisance of the Court for Divorce and Matrimonial Causes, and now assigned to the Family Division by the Administration of Justice Act 1970. The chief are either for—

(1) Judicial separation.
(2) Dissolution of marriage.
(3) Nullity of marriage.

See the Matrimonial Causes Act 1973.

MATRIMONIAL HOME. The Matrimonial Homes Act 1967 gives no rights to a wife who already has a proprietary, contractual or statutory right to occupy the home, but an innocent wife who is joint owner of the matrimonial home has: (*a*) if in occupation, a right not to be evicted or excluded from the dwelling-house or any part thereof by the other spouse, except by court order; (*b*) if not in occupation, a right, by court order, to enter into and occupy the dwelling-house (*Gurasz* v. *Gurasz*, [1969] 3 All E.R. 822).

(*Canada.*) In actions for divorce or other actions in which a husband and wife, or former husband and wife, are litigating the division of property, the house in which the parties formerly jointly made their home, and which one or the other, or both, own, is frequently referred to as the matrimonial home.

MATRIMONIUM signifies—

1. Marriage.
2. Inheritance descending to a man from his mother or her relatives.

MATRONS, JURY OF. [JURY OF MATRONS.]

MATTER. 1. *Matter in Deed* is a truth to be proved by some deed or "specialty", *i.e.*, writing under seal.

2. *Matter in Pais*, strictly speaking a thing done in the country, is matter to be proved by witnesses, and tried by a jury of the country. This is otherwise called *nude matter*. The expression, however, is also used so as to include *matter in deed*. [ESTOPPEL.]

3. *Matter of Record* is matter which may be proved by some record, as having been done in some court of record.

MATURITY. A bill or note is said to be at *maturity* when the time arrives at which it is payable.

MAYHEM. [MAIHEM.]

MAYOR. The Queen, on a petition presented to her by the council of a district praying for the grant of a charter, may confer on that district the status of a borough, and therefore the chairman and vice-chairman of the council will be entitled to the style of mayor and deputy mayor of the borough: Local Government Act 1972, s. 245 (1).

The council of a parish or community which is not grouped with any other parish or community may resolve that the parish or community shall have the status of a town, and thereupon the chairman and vice-chairman of the council shall respectively be entitled to the style of town mayor and deputy town mayor: *ibid.*, s. 245 (6).

MAYORS AND CITY OF LONDON COURT. An amalgamation of two former courts, the Mayor's Court of London and the City of London Court. It was abolished by the Courts Act 1971 and the City of London became a county court district. Nevertheless the county court for the district of the City continues to be known as the Mayor's and City of London Court, and the judge assigned to it as the judge of the Mayor's and City of London Court (*Hals. Laws*).

MEASURE. An enactment of the Church Assembly, with the effect of a statute. [SYNOD.]

MEASURE OF DAMAGE. The rule by which the *amount* of damage in any given case is to be determined.

MEASUREMENT. Generally, for the definition of length, area, volume, capacity, weight and electricity, see Sched. 1 to the Weights and Measures Act 1963.

MECHANICS' LIENS. (*Canada.*) Under provincial legislation, a person working on the construction of a building has a lien on the property which may be realized upon by taking the steps provided for in the statutes of the various provinces.

MEDICAL COUNCIL. [GENERAL MEDICAL COUNCIL.]

MEDICAL JURISPRUDENCE. [FORENSIC MEDICINE.]

MEDICAL OFFICER OF HEALTH. An officer appointed by a local authority to supervise matters relating to public health. [PUBLIC HEALTH ACTS.]

MEDICAL PRACTITIONER. [PRACTITIONER.]

MEDIUM. A person who professes to communicate with spirits, or through whom persons in the next world communicate with those remaining in this; a spiritualist, a clairvoyant. Persons fraudulently purporting to act as spiritualistic mediums or to exercise powers of telepathy, etc., are punishable under the Fraudulent Mediums Act 1951. [WITCHCRAFT.]

MEETING. A gathering or assembly of persons, convened for the conducting of business *e.g.*, of a company, or relating to the affairs of a bankrupt.

Provisions as to meetings of companies are contained in ss. 130 *et seq.* of the Companies Act 1948. Such meetings include (*a*) *The statutory meeting*, a general meeting of the members of a company which must be called not less than one month nor more than three months from the date at which the company is entitled to commence business. At this meeting the directors are to report on the total allotment of shares, cash received, etc. (*b*) *Annual general meeting*, which must be held each year and at an interval of not more than fifteen months after the preceding annual general meeting. (*c*) *Extraordinary general meeting*, which may be convened on the requisition of members holding not less than one-tenth of the paid-up capital of the company.

MELIOR EST CONDITIO POSSIDENTIS ET REI QUAM ACTORIS. The position of the defendant in possession is better than that of the plaintiff.

MELIUS INQUIRENDO, or **MELIUS INQUIRENDUM,** was a writ that lay for a *second* inquiry as to what lands and tenements a man died seised of, where partial dealing was suspected upon the writ of *diem clausit extremum*, or where the facts were insufficiently specified in the inquisition upon such writ. Obsolete.

MEMORANDUM OF ASSOCIATION. A document to be subscribed by seven or more persons (or, in the case of a private company, by two or more persons) associated for a lawful purpose, by subscribing which, and otherwise complying with the requisitions of the Companies Act in respect of registration, they may form themselves into an incorporated company, with or without limited liability. It must give name, particulars of capital, objects, etc., and cannot be varied even by the whole body of shareholders except under the special provisions of the Companies Act 1948, ss. 4, 5.

MEMORIAL. A document containing particulars of a deed, etc., for purposes of registration.

MEMORY, TIME OF LEGAL. [LEGAL MEMORY.]

MENACES. [BLACKMAIL.]

MENIALS (from Lat. *Maenia*, the walls of a house) are household servants, that is, such as live within the walls of their master's house. *T.L.; Cowel; 1 Bl.*

MENS REA. A guilty mind or intent; usually one of the essentials of a crime. [MALICE; MISTAKE.]

MENSURA, in a legal sense, is taken for a bushel, as *mensura bladi*, a bushel of corn. *Cowel.*

MENTAL DISORDER. "Persons suffering from mental disorder" is the phrase used in the Mental Health Act 1959 to describe those persons once known as lunatics and later as persons of unsound mind.

Mental disorder, by s. 4 of the Act, means mental illness, arrested or incomplete development of mind, psychopathic disorder, and any other disorder or disability of the mind.

The Act repealed the former Lunacy and Mental Treatment Acts 1890 to 1930, and the Mental Deficiency Acts 1913 to 1938, and provided a new code of treatment for mentally disordered persons and persons suffering from subnormality or psychopathic disorder.

MERCEN-LAGE. The Mercian laws. A system of law observed in many of the midland counties, and those bordering on Wales, about the beginning of the eleventh century. This was one of the three systems of laws out of which the Conqueror framed our common law; the other two systems being the West Saxon-Lage and the Dane-Lage.

MERE RIGHT signifies a right of property without possession.

MERGER. The sinking or drowning of a less estate in a greater, by reason that they both coincide and meet in one and the same person. Thus, if there be a tenant for years, and the reversion in fee simple descends to or is purchased by him, the term of years may be *merged* in the inheritance and shall never exist any more.

S. 185 of the Law of Property Act 1925 provides that there shall no longer be any merger by operation of law only of any estate the beneficial interest in which would not be deemed to be merged or extinguished in equity.

MERITORIOUS CONSIDERA- TION. [CONSIDERATION.]

MERITS. The substantial question at issue in an action or other proceeding.

MERITS, AFFIDAVIT OF. In cases where a defendant seeks to set aside a judgment obtained against him in consequence of his default, he must generally file an *affidavit of merits*, showing that he has a good defence.

MERTON, STATUTE OF. A statute of Henry III (1235), so called because passed at Merton, in Surrey.

MESNE. Middle, intermediate.

A *mesne lord* is a lord who has tenants holding under him, and yet himself holds of a superior lord.

Mesne process was a phrase applied to the writs issued in an action subsequently to the first or original writ, but prior to the writ of execution, that is, all such process as intervened between the beginning and end of a suit. 3 *Bl.*

Mesne profits are profits of land taken by a tenant in wrongful possession, from the time that the wrongful possession commenced to the time of the trial of an action of ejectment brought against him.

MESSUAGE. A house, comprising the outbuildings, the orchard, and curtilage or courtyard and, according to the better opinion, the garden also.

METAYER SYSTEM. A system of land tenure which prevails in some parts of Europe, under which ech farm is let to a single family, the landlord supplying the stock, and being paid in lieu of rent a fixed share of the produce.

METRIC SYSTEM. A decimal sub-division of weights and measures. See Sched. 1 to the Weights and Measures Act 1963. The metric system is gradually being introduced into the United Kingdom. As to coinage, see the Decimal Currency Acts 1967 and 1969 and the Coinage Act 1971.

METROPOLITAN BOARD OF WORKS. A board established in 1855 for the general local management of the metropolis. The powers, etc., of the Board were transferred to the London County Council by the Local Government Act 1888, and more recently to the Greater London Council by the London Government Act 1963.

METROPOLITAN COUNTY. [COUNTY.]

MICHAELMAS DAY. [QUARTER DAYS.]

MICHAELMAS SITTINGS. [SITTINGS.]

MICHAELMAS TERM. [SITTINGS.]

MICHEL GEMOTE. The Great Council of the English nation in the Saxon times; more frequently called *witena-gemote*. 1 *Bl.*

MIDDLE MAN. A person intermediate between two others; a word often used of a person who leases land (especially in Ireland) which he lets out again to tenants. The phrase is thus used as analogous to the "mesne lord" of feudal times. [MESNE.]

MIDDLESEX, BILL OF. [Bill of Middlesex.]

MIDDLESEX REGISTRY. A registry established in the reign of Queen Anne (1708) for the registration of deeds and wills affecting lands in the county of Middlesex. It was transferred to the Land Registry in 1891. The register is now closed for all purposes and accordingly no search may be made by the Chief Land Registrar or his officers or otherwise, and the Law of Property Act 1925, s. 197 (making registration actual notice), has ceased to have effect as respects the register (Middlesex Deeds Act 1940, s. 1 (1).)

MIDSUMMER DAY. [QUARTER DAYS.]

MIDWIFE. A woman who assists others at childbirth. Midwives are required to hold certificates, issuable by the Central Midwives Board, which body also keeps a roll of certified midwives. See generally the Midwives Act 1951 and rules made thereunder.

MILEAGE. Travelling expenses allowed according to scale.

MILITARY COURTS. 1. The Court of Chivalry, which is a court of honour. [COURT OF CHIVALRY.]

2. Courts-martial, having jurisdiction to try and to punish offences committed against naval, military and air force law. [COURT-MARTIAL.]

3. The courts which, under the name of courts-martial, are used for dealing with offenders where a state of war actually exists. [MARTIAL LAW.]

MILITARY FEUDS. [FEE; FEUDAL SYSTEM; KNIGHT-SERVICE.]

MILITARY TENURES. The tenures by:—1. Knight-service; 2. Grand serjeanty; 3. Cornage. [See under their respective titles.] These were all abolished by the Tenures Abolition Act 1660, except the honorary services of grand serjeanty. [FEE; FEUDAL SYSTEM.]

MILITARY TESTAMENT. A will made by a soldier on active service, without those forms which in ordinary cases are required by statute: Wills Act 1837, s. 11; see also the Wills (Soldiers and Sailors) Act 1918.

MILK. Includes cream and separated milk, but not dried or condensed milk, in the Food and Drugs Act 1955. See s. 135 of the Act. [DAIRY.]

MINERAL COURTS. [BARMOTE COURTS.]

MINIMENTS, otherwise called *muniments*, are the evidences or writings whereby a man is enabled to defend the title of his own estate.

MINISTER. 1. The holder of an office in the government of the country. He may be in the Cabinet, as *e.g.*, the Prime Minister, the Secretary of State for Foreign Affairs, etc., or not in the Cabinet, as *e.g.*, the Solicitor-General.

2. A clergyman with a cure of souls. The term is generally used of nonconformist clergy.

3. A foreign envoy, or minister plenipotentiary.

MINE. An excavation or system of excavations made for the purpose of, or in connection with, the getting, wholly or substantially by means involving the employment of persons below ground, of minerals (whether in their natural state or in solution or suspension) or products of minerals. See s. 180 of the Mines and Quarries Act 1954, which Act establishes a code of safety and working conditions for mines.

MINIMUM LENDING RATE. The minimum rate of discount charged for the time being by the Bank of England for discounting, *i.e.* cashing, before due, the bills of the first mercantile houses. The fluctuations in the rate are announced from time to time, the changes being made as part of governmental economic strategy. Formerly known as *bank rate.*

MINISTRI REGIS (servants of the king). Persons having ministerial offices under the Crown; also the judges of the realm. *Cowel.*

MINOR. A person under the age of eighteen years. See the Family Law Reform Act 1969. [GUARDIAN; INFANT.]

MINOR CANONS are officers of a cathedral appointed to conduct the cathedral services. Their appointment is vested in the chapter.

MINOR INTERESTS. This expression is defined by s. 3 of the Land Registration Act 1925 as "the interests not capable of being disposed of or created by registered dispositions and capable of being overridden (whether or not a purchaser has notice thereof) by the proprietors unless protected as provided by this Act, and all rights and interests which are not registered or protected on the register and are not overriding interests, and include:—

(a) in the case of land held on trust for sale, all interest and powers which are under the Law of Property Act 1925 capable of being overridden by the trustees for sale, whether or not such interests and powers are so protected; and

(b) in the case of settled land, all interests and powers which are under the Settled Land Act 1925, and the Law of Property Act 1925, or either of them, capable of being overridden by the

MINOR INTERESTS—*continued.*
tenant for life or statutory owner, whether or not such interests and powers are so protected as aforesaid."

MINORA REGALIA. The Queen's revenue, as opposed to her dignity and regal power.

MINT. 1. The place where money is coined, formerly near the Tower of London, now in Wales. The constitution of the Mint was remodelled in the year 1815, and again by the Coinage Act 1870, when the Chancellor of the Exchequer was made the Master of the Mint; the custody of the standard weights was committed to the Board of Trade; and the general superintendence of the Mint was entrusted to the Treasury.

2. Formerly a pretended place of privilege in Southwark.

MINUTES. 1. The record kept of a meeting.

2. *Of an order or judgment.* An outline of the order or judgment, drawn by one party and agreed to by the other party. Afterwards embodied in a formal order or judgment of the court.

MIRROR OF JUSTICE, generally spoken of as the Mirror, or Mirrour, is a work generally ascribed to the reign of Edward II. It is stated to have been written by one Andrew Horne.

MISADVENTURE. An unfortunate mischance arising out of a lawful act. It is a word generally used with reference to accidental homicide.

MISCARRIAGE. 1. A failure of justice.
2. Abortion (*q.v.*).

MISCHIEF. The object or purpose of a statute.

MISDEMEANOUR. An offence not amounting to felony. The word is generally confined to indictable offences.

The punishment of a misdemeanour at common law was by fine and imprisonment at the discretion of the court; and this is therefore the law at the present day in cases to which no statutory enactment applies. But the misdemeanours most frequently committed are punishable with imprisonment under various statutes, for terms specified in the Acts relating to them. The distinction between misdemeanour and felony was abolished by s. 1 of the Criminal Law Act 1967. [FELONY.]

MISDESCRIPTION. A description of the subject-matter of a contract which is incorrect or misleading in a material particular. Where substantial, such misdescription renders the contract voidable at the option of the party who is misled.

MISDIRECTION. The wrong direction of a judge to a jury on a matter of law. [NEW TRIAL.]

MISE. 1. A gift or customary present formerly made by the people of Wales to a new king or prince on his entrance into that principality.

2. A tax or tallage.
3. Costs and expenses.
4. A writ of right so called.
5. The issue in a writ of right.
6. Cast, or put upon.
7. For *mease*, a messuage or tenement.

MISFEASANCE. [MALFEASANCE.]

MISJOINDER OF PARTIES. The wrongful joining of parties in a cause. No action can now be defeated because of such misjoinder; see R.S.C. 1965, Ord. 15, r. 6.

MISNOMER. Calling a person by a wrong name in a declaration or other pleading. Any mistake of this kind may now be amended in civil proceedings under R.S.C. 1965, Ord. 20, and in criminal pleading by the Indictments Act 1915, s. 5.

MISPLEADING is the omission, in pleading, of anything essential to the action or defence. The word was especially applied to such an error in pleading as could not be *cured by verdict*. [AIDER BY VERDICT; AMENDMENT.]

MISPRISION (from the French *Mépris*). Contempt, neglect, or oversight. Thus, 1. Misprision of treason or felony is a neglect or light account shown of treason or felony by not revealing it to a judge or justice of the peace. 2. The word has been applied to coining foreign coin, the reason given being that the offence was at one time visited with the same punishment as misprision. 3. It has also been applied to the neglect of clerks in writing and keeping records.

MISREPRESENTATION, *i.e., suggestio falsi,* either by words or by conduct. To found an action for tort the misrepresentation must be a false statement of fact, and not a mere broken promise. The statement must also be wilfully false: mere negligence in the making of false statements is not actionable. See *Derry* v. *Peek*, (1889), 14 A.C. 337.

Innocent misrepresentation, *i.e.*, when the statement is not known to be false, is ground for relief against a contract if such statement furnished a material inducement to the plaintiff to enter into that contract. See *MacKenzie* v. *Royal Bank of Canada*, [1934] A.C., at p. 475. [DECEIT; FRAUD.]

MISTAKE. 1. In criminal law except in the cases where proof of *mens rea* is unnecessary, *bona fide* mistake or ignorance as to matters of fact is available as a defence. Ignorance of law cannot be set up as a defence even by a foreigner, although it may be a ground for the mitigation of sentence. In cases where a particular intent or state of mind is of the essence of an offence, a mistaken but *bona fide* belief by a defendant that he had a right to do a particular act may be a complete defence as showing that he had no criminal intent.

2. In civil cases at common law, mistake was admitted as a foundation of relief in three cases only, namely:—(i) In actions "for money had and received" to recover money paid under a mistake of fact; (ii) in actions of deceit to recover damages in respect of a mistake induced by fraudulent misrepresentation (*q.v.*); and (iii) as a defence in actions of contract where the mistake of fact was of such a nature as to preclude the formation of any contract in law, as, for example, where there was a mutual mistake as to the subject-matter of the contract, and therefore, no consensus *ad idem* by the parties, or where the mistake was made as to the identity of one of the parties where such identity was an inducement to the other to enter into the contract, or where the mistake related to the nature of the contract under such circumstances as would, if the contract were embodied in a deed, justify a plea of *non est factum* (*q.v.*).

3. In equity, mistake gives title to relief in a much wider range of cases than at common law, though it must be borne in mind that "mistake", as a legal term on which a right to relief may be founded, has a much narrower meaning than as a popular expression. The relationship between the parties to a transaction may impose a duty upon one party to inform the mind of the other part of all the material facts, and if, in such a case, the party owing such duty enters into a transaction with the party to whom the duty is owed, without informing him of all material facts, the latter is entitled to relief on the ground of breach of duty.

Clearly proved and obvious mistakes in written instruments, etc., will also be relieved against by the court. The rectification, setting aside, etc., of written instruments is part of the business assigned to the Chancery Division of the High Court. See s. 56 of the Judicature Act, 1925.

MISTRIAL. A false or erroneous trial.

MISUSER. Such use of an office or grant as is contrary to the express or implied condition upon which it may have been made, and which works a forfeiture of it.

MITIGATION. Abatement of anything penal, or of damages.

An address in mitigation is a speech made by the defendant or his counsel to the judge after verdict or plea of guilty, and which may be followed by a speech in *aggravation* from the opposing counsel.

MIXED ACTIONS. [ACTIONS MIXED.]

MIXED FUND. A fund consisting of the proceeds of both real and personal estate.

MIXED GOVERNMENT. A form of government which combines the three regular forms of government, *viz.*, monarchy, aristocracy, and democracy. The British Government is an instance.

MIXED POLICY is a policy of marine insurance in which not only the time is specified for which the risk is limited, but the voyage also is described by its local termini, *e.g.*, "at and from London to Cadiz for six months", as opposed to policies of insurance for a particular voyage without any limits as to time, and also to purely time policies in which there is no designation of local termini at all.

MIXED PROPERTY. 1. Property which, though falling under the definition of things real, is attended with some of the legal qualities of things personal, *e.g.*, *emblements*.

2. Property which, though falling under the definition of things personal, is attended with some of the legal qualities of things real, *e.g.*, heirlooms.

MIXED QUESTIONS OF LAW AND FACT. Cases in which a jury finds the facts, and the court decides, by the aid of established rules of law, what is the legal result of those facts.

MIXED TITHES were tithes consisting of natural products, but nurtured and preserved in part by the care of man; as tithes of cheese, milk, etc.

MOBILE HOME. [CARAVAN.]

MOBILIA SEQUUNTUR PERSONAM. Movables follow the person.

MODO ET FORMA. Words signifying that the defendant, in his pleading, denied having done the thing for which he was sued *in manner and form* as in the declaration alleged. This evasive kind of pleading was abolished under the Judicature Act 1875.

MOIETY. One-half.

MOLLITER MANUS IMPOSUIT (he laid hands on him gently). A plea by a defendant, who is sued in an action for an assault and battery, to the effect that he used no more violence upon the plaintiff than was necessary and justifiable under the circumstances.

MOLMUTIAN LAWS. The laws of Dunvallo Molmutius, sixteenth king of the Britons. These laws were famous in the land till the time of William the Conqueror.

MONEY BILL. A bill for granting aids and supplies to the Crown. It is defined in the Parliament Act 1911 as a public bill which in the opinion of the Speaker of the House of Commons contains only provisions dealing with finance and taxation.

MONEY COUNTS, otherwise called the *indebitatus* or "common counts", were the counts formerly used in a plaintiff's declaration expressing the most usual grounds of action; as (1) for money lent; (2) for money paid by the plaintiff for the defendant at his request; (3) for money received by the defendant for the use of the plaintiff; and (4) for money found to be due from the defendant to the plaintiff, upon an account stated between them.

MONEY LAND. A phrase sometimes used to signify money held upon trust to be laid out in the purchase of land.

MONEY, PAYMENT OF, INTO COURT. [PAYMENT OF MONEY INTO COURT.]

MONEY-LENDER. By the former Money-lenders Act 1900 a money-lender, for the purposes of the Act, was defined as "every person whose business is that of money-lending, or who advertises or announces himself or holds himself out in any way as carrying on that business". The term, however, did not apply to pawnbrokers, loan societies, banking or insurance companies, and some others. Money-lenders to whom the Act applied were placed under an obligation to be registered, and they were liable to have their contracts judicially varied. Under the former Moneylenders Act 1927, every money-lender had to be licensed in his own true name and at an authorised address. That Act also contained restrictions on money-lending advertisements, provisions with regard to excessive interest; and provided that an action by a money-lender had to be brought within twelve months from the date on which the cause of action accrued.

Both the above Acts were repealed by the Consumer Credit Act 1974, and replaced by ss. 137–140 of that Act (extortionate credit bargains).

MONITION. A warning; generally a warning to a defendant in an ecclesiastical court not to repeat an offence of which he has been convicted.

MONOPOLY. A licence or privilege allowed by the sovereign for the buying and selling, making, working, or using of anything, to be enjoyed exclusively by the grantee. Monopolies were, by the Statute of Monopolies 1623, declared to be illegal and void, subject to certain exceptions therein specified, including patents in favour of the authors of new inventions. For the present law relating to monopolies see the Fair Trading Act 1973. This Act creates a new office, the Director General of Fair Trading, transferring to him the functions of the former Registrar of Restrictive Trading Agreements and investing him with certain duties in connection with monopoly situations and mergers. The Act also re-establishes the former Monopolies Commission, now known as the Monopolies and Mergers Commission. [PATENT.]

MONSTER is one which has not the shape of mankind, but in any part evidently resembles the brute creation; it cannot inherit land.

MONSTRANS DE DROIT. Manifestation or plea of right; which was a claim made against the Crown when the Crown was in possession of a title the facts of which were already set forth upon record. This proceeding was extended by statutes of Edward III and Edward VI to almost all cases where a subject claimed against the right of the Crown founded on an inquisition of office. [INQUEST, 1; PETITION OR RIGHT.]

The judgment in a *monstrans de droit* or other proceeding against the Crown was called *amoveas manus*, or *ouster le main*. These proceedings were abolished by the Crown Proceedings Act 1947.

MONUMENTS. [ANCIENT MONUMENTS.]

MONTH is a space of time containing by the week twenty-eight days, and by the calendar twenty-eight, thirty, or thirty-one days. At common law the meaning of the term "month" is twenty-eight days, otherwise called a *lunar month*. But, in ecclesiastical and mercantile matters, a month is interpreted to mean a calendar month; also, by the Interpretation Act 1889, in an Act of Parliament it is henceforth to mean a calendar month; as also in the Rules of Court. See R.S.C. 1965, Ord. 3, r. 1. Also by s. 61 of the Law of Property Act 1925 the word "month" in all deeds, contracts, wills, orders, and other instruments executed, made, or coming into operation after 1925, means a calendar month, unless the context otherwise requires.

MOOT. 1. A court, plea, or convention.
2. An exercise, or arguing of cases, which was formerly practised by students in the Inns of Court, the better to enable them to defend their clients. The places where moot-cases were argued was anciently called a *moot-hall*; and those who argued the cases were called *moot-men*. Hence a *moot point* signifies a point open to argument and discussion.

MORE OR LESS. These words, appended to measurements in a conveyance of land, import a vagueness, within certain small limits, in the measurements of the land referred to: if there be a considerable deficiency the purchaser will be entitled to an abatement on the price.

MORGANATIC MARRIAGE. The marriage which a prince or nobleman contracts with a woman of humble birth, on the express condition that the ordinary civil effects shall not result therefrom, and that the wife and children shall be contented with certain specified advantages. The restrictions relate only to the rank of the parties and successions to property, and do not affect the nature or validity of the matrimonial engagement.

MORMON MARRIAGES. These marriages, under a system in which plurality of wives is allowed, are not recognised by our law nor by that of the United States.

MORTALITY. [Bills of Mortality.]

MORT D'ANCESTOR. A real action or assize available to a demandant who complained of an "abatement" to or entry upon his freehold, effected by a stranger on the death of the demandant's father or mother, brother or sister, uncle or aunt, nephew or niece. Abolished in 1833. [ABATEMENT, 5; ASSIZE, WRIT OF.]

MORTGAGE (Lat. *Mortuum vadium*, *i.e.*, dead pledge) is a conveyance, assignment, or demise of real or personal estate as security for the repayment of money borrowed.

If the conveyance, assignment, or demise be of land or any estate therein, the transaction is called a mortgage, notwithstanding that the creditor enters into possession; but the transfer of the possession of a movable chattel to secure the repayment of a debt is called not a *mortgage*, but a *pledge*. Mortgages are either (*a*) legal, including statutory, or (*b*) equitable.

The term "mortgage" is applied indifferently: (1) to the mortgage transaction; (2) to the mortgage deed; and (3) to the rights conferred thereby on the mortgagee. Before 1926 a mortgage of freehold land was usually effected by a conveyance of the land to the mortgagee. Now, by s. 85 of the Law of Property Act 1925, a mortgage of an estate in fee simple is only capable of being effected at law either by a demise for a term of years absolute, subject to a provision for cesser on redemption, or by a charge by deed expressed to be by way of legal mortgage. Any purported conveyance of an estate in fee simple by way of mortgage made after 1925 will operate as a demise to the mortgagee, in the case of a

MORTGAGE—*continued.*
first mortgage, for a term of 3,000 years; and in the case of a second or subsequent mortgage for a term one day longer than the term vested in the first or other mortgagee.

Under s. 86 a legal mortgage of leaseholds can now only be made by a subdemise for a term of years absolute, less by one day than the term vested in the mortgagor, or by a charge by deed expressed to be by way of legal mortgage. The right to create equitable charges by deposit of documents or otherwise is, however, preserved.

MORTGAGEE. The creditor to whom a mortgage is made. [MORTGAGE.]

MORTGAGOR. The debtor who makes a mortgage. [MORTGAGE.]

MORTIS CAUSA DONATIO. [DONATIO MORTIS CAUSA.]

MORTMAIN ACTS. The statutes whereby the rights of corporations to take lands by grant or devise were abridged. The Act formerly known as the "Mortmain" Act was the Charitable Uses Act 1735, later repealed and replaced by Acts of 1888 and 1891. At the time of the passing of the earliest Act, no devise of lands to a corporation was good, except for charitable uses.

The law of mortmain was abolished, and the Acts relating thereto were repealed, by the Charities Act 1960, which replaced the former laws with new and simplified provisions, *e.g.*, for the registration of charities, the keeping of indexes of local charities, the application of the *cy-près* doctrine, etc.

MORTUARY. 1. A mortuary was originally a gift left by a man at his death to his parish church, for the recompense of his personal tithes and offerings not duly paid in his lifetime. Also a kind of ecclesiastical heriot.

2. A place for the temporary reception of the dead.

MORTUUM VADIUM. Dead pledge or mortgage. [MORTGAGE.]

MOTE. A court; a plea; an assembly. [MOOT, 1.]

MOTION. An application made to a court or judge *viva voce* in open court. Its object is to obtain an order or rule, directing some act to be done in favour of the applicant.

A motion must in general be preceded by notice to any party intended to be affected

thereby. Sometimes, however, it may be made *ex parte*. See R.S.C. 1965, Ord. 8.

MOVABLES. Goods, furniture, etc., which may be moved from place to place.

MULCT. A fine or penalty.

MULIER PUISNE. The lawful issue preferred before an elder brother born out of matrimony. [BASTARD EIGNE.]

MULTIFARIOUSNESS, in a bill in equity, was the improperly joining distinct subjects in the same bill of complaint. [JOINDER OF CAUSES OF ACTION.]

MULTIPLICITY OF SUITS or **ACTIONS** is where several different suits or actions are brought upon the same issue. This was obviated sometimes by a proceeding in equity called a bill of peace; sometimes by a rule of a court of common law for the consolidation of different actions. See s. 43 of the Judicature Act 1925. [CONSOLIDATION ORDER.]

MULTURE. A toll paid to a miller for grinding corn; the grist or grinding; the corn ground.

MUNICIPAL CORPORATION. The corporation of borough, consisting of a mayor, aldermen and burgesses. By s. 1 (11) of the Local Government Act 1972 the municipal corporation of every borough outside Greater London ceased to exist on 1st April 1974 (see *ibid.*, s. 20 (6) as to Wales). Their functions were transferred from the former borough councils to county or district councils. London borough councils were retained.

MUNICIPAL LAW means strictly the law of a municipality. The expression is, however, generally used to denote the positive law of a particular state as opposed to the law of nations or international law.

MUNIMENTS OF TITLE. The deeds and other evidences which fortify or protect a man's title to his estates.

MURDER is unlawful homicide committed with "malice aforethought", express or implied. Express malice exists where the person killing does so with the *intention* of causing death or grievous bodily harm. Implied malice exists where the person killing does not actually intend to kill or do grievous bodily harm, yet intentionally does an act which to his knowledge is likely to cause such death, etc.

Formerly there was a doctrine of "constructive malice", by which malice was implied where a killing had been caused in the course or furtherance of some felony involving an act of violence, etc. This doctrine was abolished by s. 1 of the Homicide Act 1957.

The Act of 1957 also introduced, for a short period, a distinction between capital murder and non-capital murder.

Capital murders (that is to say, murders for which the death sentence might be given) were classified by s. 5 of the Act as follows:

(a) Any murder done in the course or furtherance of theft;

(b) Any murder by shooting or causing an explosion;

(c) Any murder done in the course of, or for the purpose of resisting or preventing or avoiding, a lawful arrest, or of effecting or assisting an escape or rescue from legal custody;

(d) Any murder of a police officer acting in the execution of his duty or of a person assisting a police officer so acting;

(e) In the case of a person who was a prisoner at the time when he did or was a party to the murder, any murder of a prison officer acting in the execution of his duty or of a person assisting a prison officer so acting.

The death penalty for murder was abolished for a trial period by the Murder (Abolition of Death Penalty) Act 1965, the Act finally being made permanent by affirmative resolutions of both Houses of Parliament in December 1969.

All murders are now punishable with imprisonment for life. [HOMICIDE; MANSLAUGHTER; PROVOCATION; SUICIDE.]

MURDRUM. The secret killing of another; or the fine or amerciament imposed by the Danish and Norman conquerors upon the town or hundred wherein the same was committed. [ENGLESCHERIE.]

MUSHROOM. By a provision of the Theft Act 1968 (s. 4 (3)) the picking of mushrooms growing wild on another person's land is not stealing, unless picked for sale. Wild flowers and fruit (as, e.g. blackberries) are included in the subsection. "Mushroom" includes any fungus.

MUTATIS MUTANDIS. With the necessary changes.

MUTE. Speechless, who refuses to speak; a word applied formerly to a prisoner who, being arraigned of treason or felony,

1. Made no answer at all; or
2. Answered foreign to the purpose; or
3. Having pleaded not guilty, refused to put himself upon his country.

Standing mute was, in high treason, in petty larceny, and in misdemeanours held to be equivalent to conviction. But in other felonies, and in petty treason, it exposed the prisoner to the *peine forte et dure*. [PEINE FORTE ET DURE.] Now the court may order the proper officer to enter a plea of "not guilty" on behalf of the prisoner so standing mute of malice. See s. 6 (1) (c) of the Criminal Law Act 1967.

MUTINY. A combination between two or more persons subject to service law to overthrow or resist lawful authority in Her Majesty's forces, etc. For full statutory definition see s. 31 of the Army Act 1955, s. 31 of the Air Force Act 1955, and s. 8 of the Naval Discipline Act 1957.

MUTUAL DEBTS. Debts due on both sides, as between two persons. [SET-OFF.]

MUTUAL PROMISES. Concurrent considerations which support one another, unless one or the other be void. In that case, as there is no consideration on one side, no contract can arise.

MUTUAL TESTAMENTS. Wills made by two persons who leave their effects reciprocally to the survivor.

MUTUALITY. Reciprocity of obligation, two persons being mutually bound.

MUTUUM. The contract of a loan to be repaid in kind; as, so much barley, wine, etc.

MYSTERY. An art, trade, or occupation.

N

N. L. [NON-LIQUET.]

NAAM or **NAM.** The taking another man's movable goods, either by lawful distress or otherwise.

NAMATION. Taking or impounding.

NAME. Either christian or surname. A man may change his surname and his christian name, but the latter strictly only

NAME—*continued.*
by Act of Parliament or upon confirmation by a bishop or by addition or adoption. See the review of the law in *Re Parrott*, [1946] Ch. 183. See also the Registration of Business Names Act 1916. By *a name and arms clause* in a settlement or will is meant one by which a gift is made conditionally on the donee assuming the name and arms of the donor.

NAME AND ARMS CLAUSE. A clause sometimes inserted in a settlement or a will which directs a person to assume the name and arms of the settlor or testator or else to forfeit the benefits that would otherwise be conferred on him. Many such clauses have been held to be void for uncertainty.

NAMIUM. A pledge or distress. [NAAM.]

NAMIUM VETITUM. [WITHERNAM.]

NARRATIO. A declaration or count. [DECLARATION.]

NATIONAL BIOLOGICAL STANDARDS BOARD. A body established under the Biological Standards Act 1975 to perform functions in relation to the establishment of standards for biological substances, *i.e.* substances whose purity or potency cannot be adequately tested by chemical means. Such substances may include vaccines, antibiotics, etc.

NATIONAL DEBT. The debt due by the nation to individual creditors, whether our own people or foreigners. This national debt is in part *funded* and in part *unfunded*; the former being that which is secured to the national creditor upon the public funds; the latter, that which is not so provided for. The unfunded debt is comparatively of small amount, and is generally secured by Exchequer bills and bonds. [CONSOLIDATED FUND; EXCHEQUER BILLS AND BONDS.]

NATIONAL ASSISTANCE. Assistance given to persons without resources to meet their requirements, or whose resources must be supplemented in order to meet their requirements. Such grants, etc., are made by the Ministry of Social Security, under the provisions of the National Assistance Acts 1948 to 1959.

NATIONAL ENTERPRISE BOARD. A public corporation established by the Industry Act 1975. Its purposes are to develop or assist the economy, to promote industrial efficiency and international competitiveness, and to provide, maintain or safe-guard productive employment in the United Kingdom. It consists of a chairman and from 8 to 16 members appointed by the Secretary of State for Industry.

NATIONAL HEALTH SERVICE. The health service first established under the National Health Service Act 1946. The service was at first free but charges have been imposed from time to time under various amending Acts. The service was reorganised by the National Health Service Reorganisation Act 1973.

NATIONAL INSURANCE. A system of insurance to which every person contributes a weekly amount (part being paid by employers) with corresponding benefits in the case of sickness, unemployment, retirement, etc. See the Social Security Act 1975.

NATIONAL LOANS FUND. A account kept by the Treasury at the Bank of England under the National Loans Act 1968, out of which funds may be advanced for government purposes.

NATIONAL TRUST. The National Trust for Places of Historic Interest or Natural Beauty, established under the National Trust Acts 1907 to 1971, for the general purposes of promoting the permanent preservation of lands and tenements of beauty or historic interest, their natural features, animal and plant life, etc.

NATIONS, LAW OF. [JUS GENTIUM; LAW OF NATIONS.]

NATIONS, LEAGUE OF. [LEAGUE OF NATIONS.]

NATURAL AFFECTION. Often used in deeds for the motive, or consideration for a gift arising from relationship. In many cases this consideration is not sufficient to "sustain a promise," *i.e.*, to give an action to the promisee against the promisor for its non-fulfilment.

NATURAL ALLEGIANCE. The perpetual allegiance due from natural-born subjects, as distinguished from *local* allegiance, which is temporary only. [ALLEGIANCE.]

NATURAL CHILD. The child of one's body, whether legitimate or illegitimate.

The word, however, in popular language, is usually applied only to an illegitimate child.

NATURAL LIFE. That which terminates by natural death, as opposed to civil death. [CIVIL DEATH.]

NATURAL PERSONS. Persons in the ordinary sense of the word, as opposed to *artificial* persons or corporations.

NATURAL-BORN SUBJECTS included by the common law:

1. All English, Scottish, Irish or Welsh persons born within the United Kingdom, or in the Commonwealth and dependencies, except such as were born of alien enemies in time of war.

2. The children of the sovereign, wherever born.

3. The children of our ambassadors born abroad.

The law relating to British nationality is now subject to the British Nationality Acts 1948 to 1965 and the Immigration Act 1971. [ALIEN; BRITISH SUBJECT; CITIZEN OF THE UNITED KINGDOM AND COLONIES.]

NATURALISATION. The giving to a foreigner the *status* of a natural-born citizen. This may be done by a certificate of the Secretary of State, on his taking the oath of allegiance. For conditions of such naturalisation see the British Nationality Act 1948. [ALIEN; ALLEGIANCE; NATURAL-BORN SUBJECTS.]

NATURE   CONSERVANCY COUNCIL. A body established under the Nature Conservancy Council Act 1973. Among its functions are the establishment and maintenance of nature reserves, and the provision of advice on conservation policies.

NAVAL DISCIPLINE ACT. The method of ordering seamen in the royal fleet, and keeping up a regular discipline there, was first directed by certain express rules, articles and orders, enacted by the authority of parliament soon after the Restoration. The Act at present in force is the Naval Discipline Act 1957, as amended by the Armed Forces Act 1971.

NAVIGATION LAWS. Acts of Parliament (now repealed) regulating the trading intercourse of foreign countries with the United Kingdom and the British possessions in general.

NAVY BILLS. Those drawn by officers of the Royal Navy for their pay, etc.

NE ADMITTAS (do not admit him). A prohibitory writ which lay for the plaintiff in a *quare impedit* to restrain the bishop from admitting the clerk of a rival patron until the contention be determined. Now practically obsolete. [QUARE IMPEDIT.]

NE EXEAT REGNO (that he leave not the kingdom). A prerogative writ whereby a person is prohibited from leaving the realm, even though his usual residence is in foreign parts. The writ is directed to the sheriff of the county in which the defendant is resident, commanding him to take bail from the defendant not to quit England without leave of the court. It is granted on motion, supported by affidavit showing that a sum of money is due from the defendant to the plaintiff, or will be due on taking accounts between them, and that the defendant intends to abscond.

The writ was formerly applied to great political purposes, but it is now applied in civil matters only, and is almost superseded by orders under the Debtors Act 1869, s. 6.

NEAT CATTLE. Oxen and heifers.

NECESSARIES, in the case of an infant, include meat, drink, apparel, physic, and likewise good teaching and instruction, whereby he may profit himself afterwards; now defined as "goods suitable to the condition in life of such infant, and to his actual requirements at the time of the sale and delivery" (Sale of Goods Act 1893, s. 2). For the supply of all such things an infant may bind himself by contract.

Formerly, a wife had power to pledge her husband's credit, as agent of necessity, in respect of either household necessaries or legal costs. This power was abolished by s. 41 of the Matrimonial Proceedings and Property Act 1970, itself since repealed by the Matrimonial Causes Act 1973. The authority which a wife has while running her husband's household is not affected.

NECESSITY is a constraint upon the will, whereby a man is urged to do that which his judgment disapproves, and is thereby excused from responsibility which might be otherwise incurred. It includes:—

1. The obligation of civil subjection.

2. In certain cases, the coercion of a wife by her husband.

3. In certain cases also *duress per minas*, which impels a man to act in a given way

NECESSITY—*continued.*

from fear of death or personal injury. [DURESS.]

4. Where a man is constrained to choose the lesser of two evils.

5. Agent of. [AGENT OF NECESSITY.]

NEGLIGENCE. A culpable omission of a positive duty. It differs from *heedlessness*, in that heedlessness is the doing of an act in violation of a *negative* duty, without adverting to its possible consequences. In both cases there is inadvertence, and there is breach of duty.

The question of negligence is one of fact for the jury, after the judge has decided that there is evidence from which negligence may be reasonably inferred. In criminal cases it is necessary to prove a higher degree of negligence than in civil. [CONTRIBUTORY NEGLIGENCE.]

NEGLIGENT ESCAPE is where a prisoner escapes without his keeper's knowledge or consent. It is thus opposed to a *voluntary* escape, which is an escape by consent or connivance of the officer. [ESCAPE.]

NEGOTIABLE INSTRUMENTS are instruments purporting to represent so much money, in which the property passes by mere delivery, such as bills of exchange, promissory notes, etc. See ss. 31, 32 of the Bills of Exchange Act 1882. Such instruments constitute an exception to the general rule that a man cannot give a better title than he himself.

NEGOTIATE. To transfer for value a negotiable instrument.

NEGOTIATION FEE. As to the remuneration of solicitors see the Solicitors Act 1974.

NEGOTIORUM GESTOR is a person who does an act to his own inconvenience for the advantage of another, but without the authority of the latter, or any promise to indemnify him for his trouble. The *negotiorum gestor* was entitled, by the Roman law, to recover compensation for his trouble; and this is so by the law of England in cases of salvage, and in some other cases.

NEMINE CONTRADICENTE (abbrev. *nem. con.*). No one contradicting; that is, unanimously; a phrase used with especial reference to votes and resolutions

of the House of Commons; *nemine dissentiente* being the corresponding expression as to unanimous votes of the House of Lords.

NEMO AGIT IN SEIPSUM. No one brings legal proceedings against himself.

NEMO DAT QUOD NON HABET. No one can give that which he has not (*i.e.*, no one can give a better title than he has). [NEGOTIABLE INSTRUMENTS.]

NEMO DE DOMO SUA EXTRAHI DEBET. No one can be forcibly taken from his own house.

NEMO EST HÆRES VIVENTIS. No one is the heir of a living man. [HEIR APPARENT.]

NEMO POTEST ESSE SIMUL ACTOR ET JUDEX. No one can be at the same time suitor and judge.

NEMO TENETUR AD IMPOSSIBILIA. No one can be held to an impossible contract.

NEMO TENETUR SEIPSUM ACCUSARE. No one is compelled to accuse himself.

NEPOS. A grandson.

NEPTIS. A granddaughter.

NEVER INDEBTED. A plea in actions of contract which denied the matters of fact from which the liability of the defendant arose; thus, in actions for goods bargained and sold, the plea operated as a denial of the bargain and sale.

Denials must now be specific, general denials being no longer admitted in pleading. See R.S.C. 1965, Ord. 18, r. 13.

NEW ASSIGNMENT. A reply by the plaintiff to a defendant's plea, by which the plaintiff alleged that he brought his action not for the cause supposed by the defendant, but for some other cause to which the plea pleaded was irrelevant. Everything which was formerly alleged by way of new assignment is now introduced by amendment.

NEW INN. One of the Inns of Chancery. [INNS OF CHANCERY.]

NEW STYLE. [OLD STYLE.]

NEW TRIAL has been held to be grantable in civil cases on motion, on any of the following among other grounds:—

1. That the judge misdirected the jury on a point of law.

2. That he admitted or rejected evidence improperly.

3. That he improperly discharged the jury.

4. That he refused to amend the record when an amendment ought to have been made.

5. That the defendant did not receive due notice of trial.

6. That the successful party misbehaved.

7. That the jury, or any of them, have misbehaved, as by drawing lots for the verdict.

8. That the damages are excessive.

9. That the damages are too slight.

10. That the verdict has been obtained by a surprise.

11. That the witnesses for the prevailing side are manifestly shown to have committed perjury.

12. That the verdict was against the weight of evidence.

13. That new and material facts have come to light since the trial.

14. Default or misconduct of officer of court.

15. Absence of counsel or solicitor.

16. That one of several issues was wrongfully decided.

17. Where there has been a previous new trial.

A new trial is not to be ordered on the ground of misdirection, or of the improper admission or rejection of evidence, or because the verdict of the jury was not taken upon a question which the judge at the trial was not asked to leave to them, unless in the opinion of the Court of Appeal some substantial wrong or miscarriage has been thereby occasioned: see R.S.C. 1965, Ord. 59, r. 11.

A new trial is not the same thing as a *venire de novo*, which is a much more ancient proceeding and is applicable where the proceedings in the lower court were a nullity. [VENIRE DE NOVO.]

NEXT FRIEND. An adult under whose protection an infant institutes an action or other legal proceeding, and who is responsible for the conduct and the costs of the same. See R.S.C. 1965, Ord. 80.

Mentally disordered persons also sue by their guardian or next friend, and defend by their guardian *ad litem*.

NEXT OF KIN. 1. An expression generally used for the persons who, by reason of kindred, were on the death of a person intestate, before 1926, entitled to his personal estate and effects under the Statute of Distributions. For the rules of succession on intestacy, see the Administration of Estates Act 1925.

2. Those who are, lineally or collaterally, related in the nearest degree to a given person.

NEXT PRESENTATION. The right to present to a living on the next vacancy. The purchase of the next presentation to a vacant benefice is illegal and void; so is the purchase by a clergyman, either in his own name or in another's, of the next presentation, simply with the view of presenting himself to the living, though the benefice be not vacant at the time of purchase. And see further restrictions under the Benefices Act 1898 and the Benefices Act 1898 (Amendment) Measure, 1923. [SIMONY.]

NIENT COMPRISE. An exception formerly sometimes taken to a petition as unjust, because the thing desired is not contained in the act or deed whereon the petition is granted.

NIENT CULPABLE. Not guilty.

NIENT DEDIRE. To suffer judgment by not denying or opposing it, that is, by default.

NIENT LE FAIT. Not his deed.

NIGHT. Night was anciently accounted to be the time from sunset to sunrise.

By s. 15 of the Night Poaching Act 1828 night is to be considered to commence at the expiration of one hour after sunset, and to conclude at the beginning of the last hour before sunrise.

In the Customs and Excise Act 1952 it is defined as the period between the hours of eleven o'clock at night and five o'clock in the morning (s. 307).

NIHIL (nothing). A return made by the sheriff in some cases. [NULLA BONA.]

NIHIL DEBET, or **NIL DEBET** (he owes nothing). The plea of the general issue in an action of debt. Abolished. [NEVER INDEBTED.]

NIHIL DICIT, or **NIL DICIT,** means a failure on the part of a defendant to put in his defence. [DEFAULT.]

NIHIL HABUIT, or **NIL HABUIT, IN TENEMENTIS.** A plea which could sometimes be pleaded by a lessee, when an action of debt was brought against him by a party claiming as landlord for rent due. The import of it was that the plaintiff had no title in the land demised, and that the defendant was not "estopped" by deed or otherwise from disputing the plaintiff's title. [ESTOPPEL.]

NISI PRIUS. A writ judicial, whereby the sheriff of a county was commanded to bring the men impanelled as jurors in any civil action to the court at Westminster on a certain day, unless before that day (*nisi prius*) the justices of assize came into the county, in which case, by the statute of Nisi Prius (1285) it became his duty to return the jury, not to the court at Westminster, but before the justices of assize. The *nisi prius* business was thus at first a mere adjunct to the *assizes*, or real actions. Although real actions were abolished, the name *assizes* was for some time retained; and the judges in civil cases at the assizes were said to sit at *nisi prius*. And a trial at *nisi prius* was generally understood to mean a trial, before a judge and jury, of a civil action, which had been brought in one of the superior courts. It was thus to be distinguished from (1) a trial at bar, (2) a criminal trial, (3) a trial in an inferior court.

The assize courts have now been abolished, their place being taken by the Crown Court. [CROWN COURT.]

NISI PRIUS RECORD. The parchment roll on which the issue in a civil action, consisting of a record of the pleadings which had taken place, was formerly transcribed for the purpose of being delivered to the proper officer of the court, for the use of the judge who was to try the case.

NOBILITY. The rank or dignity of peerage comprising—1. Dukes. 2. Marquesses. 3. Earls. 4. Viscounts. 5. Barons. 6. Life peers, who rank as barons.

NOLENS VOLENS. Whether willing or unwilling.

NOLLE PROSEQUI (to be unwilling to prosecute) was a formal averment by the plaintiff in an action, that he would not further prosecute his suit as to one or more of the defendants, or as to part of the claim or cause of action. Its effect was to with-draw the cause of action, in respect of which it was entered, from the record.

A *nolle prosequi* could only be entered in a criminal prosecution by leave of the Attorney-General.

NOMINAL DAMAGES. A trifling sum recovered by verdict in a case where, although the action is maintainable, it is nevertheless the opinion of the jury that the plaintiff has not suffered substantial damage.

NOMINAL PARTNER. [OSTENSIBLE PARTNER.]

NOMINATUM. By name.

NOMINATION. (1) Of candidates at an election. See the Representation of the People Act 1949, and Part III of the Local Government Act 1972. (2) By a member of a Friendly Society, of a person to whom his interest is to go at his death. See the Friendly Societies Act 1974.

NOMINATION TO A LIVING. A power that a man has by virtue of a manor, or otherwise, to appoint a clerk to a patron of a benefice, to be by him presented to the ordinary. Also called an advowson.

NON-ACCESS. [ACCESS.]

NON ASSUMPSIT (he did not promise). The plea of the general issue in an action of assumpsit, to the effect that the defendant did not promise as alleged in the plaintiff's declaration. [ASSUMPSIT; GENERAL ISSUE, PLEA OF.]

NON CEPIT. The plea of the general issue in the action of *replevin*; that the defendant did not take the goods as alleged by the plaintiff. [GENERAL ISSUE, PLEA OF; REPLEVIN.]

NON COMPOS MENTIS. Not of sound mind. A phrase sometimes used of mentally disordered persons, and less frequently of persons suffering from temporary loss of memory or drunkenness.

NON CONSTAT (it is not evident). This phrase is often used as importing that an alleged inference is not deducible from given premises. [NON SEQUITUR.]

NON-CONTENTIOUS BUSINESS. [COMMON FORM.]

NON CUL. Short for *non culpabilis*, not guilty. [NOT GUILTY.]

NON DAT QUI NON HABET. He cannot give who has not.

NON DETINET (he does not detain). The plea of the general issue in an action of detinue, which operates as a denial of the detention of the goods, but not of the plaintiff's property therein. [DETINUE; GENERAL ISSUE, PLEA OF.]

NON-DIRECTION. Omission on the part of a judge to enforce a necessary point of law upon a jury. [NEW TRIAL.]

NON EST FACTUM. The plea of the general issue in an action on a deed denying the *fact* of the deed having been executed. [GENERAL ISSUE, PLEA OF.]

NON EST INVENTUS (he has not been found). A return by the sheriff to a writ of *capias*, when he cannot find the defendant within his bailiwick.

NON INTROMITTANT CLAUSE. A clause in the charter of a borough by which it was exempted from the jurisdiction of the county justices.

NON-ISSUABLE PLEA. A plea which does not raise an issue on the merits of the case. [ISSUABLE PLEA.]

NON-JUROR. One who (in the belief that the Stuart family had been wrongly deposed) refused to swear allegiance to their successors on the Throne.

NON LIQUET (it is not clear). A verdict given by a jury when a matter was to be deferred to another day of trial.

NON-METROPOLITAN COUNTY. [COUNTY.]

NON OBSTANTE (notwithstanding). A clause by which the Crown occasionally attempted to give effect to grants and letters-patent, notwithstanding any statute to the contrary. The doctrine of *non obstante*, which set the prerogative above the laws, was abolished by the Bill of Rights at the Revolution.

NON OBSTANTE VEREDICTO (notwithstanding the verdict). A motion for judgment *non obstante veredicto* was a motion made on the part of a plaintiff for judgment in his favour after verdict found for the defendant, *e.g.*, where the jury had found for the defendant contrary to law. Disused.

NON OMITTAS PROPTER ALIQUAM LIBERTATEM. A clause now generally inserted in writs directed to a sheriff, by which he is commanded "not to omit, by reason of any liberty within his bailiwick," to execute the process which the writ enjoins, but to execute the same within liberties and privileged places as well as in the county at large. [BAILIWICK; LIBERTIES.]

NON PROS. or **NON PROSEQUITUR.** The delay or neglect by a plaintiff in proceeding with his action. So a judgment for the defendant by reason of such neglect in the plaintiff was called judgment of *non pros.* Now, by R.S.C. 1965, Ord. 19, the defendant may apply for an order to dismiss the action if the plaintiff makes default in pleading.

NON-RESIDENCE. The neglect by a clergyman to reside on his benefice. The cases in which non-residence is to be permitted to the clergy are now regulated by statute.

NON SEQUITUR (it does not follow). An expression used in argument to indicate that the premises do not warrant the inference drawn from them.

NON SUM INFORMATUS. I have no instructions.

NON TENURE. An exception to the plaintiff's count in a real action, to the effect that the defendant did not hold the land mentioned in the count. *Cowel.* [ACTIONS REAL AND PERSONAL.]

NON VIDENTUR QUI ERRANT CONSENTIRE. They are not considered to consent who act under a mistake.

NONAGE. The absence of full age, which is for most purposes eighteen years. [NONAGIUM.]

NONAGIUM, or **NONAGE.** The ninth part of movable goods formerly payable to the clergy on the death of persons in their parish.

NONCONFORMISTS. Dissenters from the Church of England; a word used more especially of the Protestant bodies who have seceded from the Church.

NONFEASANCE. [MALFEASANCE.]

NON-JOINDER. A plea in abatement by which it was alleged that the plaintiff had omitted to *join* in the action all the persons who should have been parties to it. Under R.S.C. 1965, Ord. 15, r. 6, no action is to be defeated by the misjoinder or non-joinder of parties. Pleas in abatement have been abolished in civil actions.

NON-SUIT. A renouncing of a suit by the plaintiff; most commonly upon the discovery of some error or defect, when the matter was so far proceeded with as that the jury was ready at the bar to deliver their verdict. So, if the plaintiff did not appear at all he was said to be non-suit or non-suited. A non-suit might, however, be entered by the court where the plaintiff failed to make out a legal cause of action.

A plaintiff cannot now elect to be non-suited and bring his action over again. [WITHDRAWING THE RECORD.]

NORTHSTEAD, MANOR OF. A manor the stewardship of which is treated as an office of profit under the Crown, and therefore disqualifies the holder from membership of the House of Commons. A member wishing to retire from the House may therefore apply for this stewardship, or for that of the Chiltern Hundreds. [CHILTERN HUNDREDS.] See s. 4 of the House of Commons Disqualification Act 1975.

NOSCITUR A SOCIIS. The meaning of a doubtful word may be ascertained by reference to the meaning of words associated with it.

NOT FOUND. [IGNORAMUS.]

NOT GUILTY. The plea of the general issue formerly used in actions of trespass (or trespass on the case), and still in criminal trials. But there is this difference between the two cases. In criminal cases special matter, as, for instance, matter by way of justification, may in general be given in evidence on a plea of not guilty; whereas in civil actions special matter had in general to be specially pleaded.

Under the present rules of pleading, it is not sufficient for a defendant in his defence to deny generally the facts alleged by the plaintiff's statement of claim, but he must deal specifically with each allegation of fact of which he does not admit the truth. R.S.C. 1965, Ord. 18.

NOT NEGOTIABLE. If a cheque is crossed with these words the person taking it has not and is not capable of giving a better title to the cheque than that which the person from whom he took it had. Bills of Exchange Act 1882, s. 81. [NEGOTIABLE INSTRUMENTS.]

NOT PROVEN. A verdict of a jury in a Scotch criminal trial, to the effect that the guilt of the accused is not made out, though his innocence is not clear. The legal effect of such a verdict is the same as that of a verdict of Not Guilty.

NOTARY, or **NOTARY PUBLIC.** (Lat. *Registrarius, Actuarius, Notarius*), is one who attests deeds or writings to make them authentic in another country. He is generally a solicitor.

It is the office of a notary, among other things, at the request of the holder of a bill of exchange of which acceptance or payment is refused, to *note* and *protest* the same. [NOTING A BILL.]

NOTE OF A FINE. An abstract which used to be made by the chirographer of the proceedings in a fine, before it was engrossed. Abolished in 1833. [FINE, 1.]

NOTE OF HAND is the same as a promissory note. [PROMISSORY NOTE.]

NOTICE is a word which sometimes means knowledge, either actual, or imputed by construction of law; sometimes a formal notification of some fact, or some intention of the party giving the notice; sometimes the expression of a demand or requisition. See the following titles. [CONSTRUCTIVE NOTICE.]

NOTICE OF DISHONOUR is a notice that a bill of exchange has been dishonoured. This notice the holder of a dishonoured bill is bound to give promptly to those to whom, as drawers or indorsers, he wishes to have recourse for payment of the bill. The rules as to notice of dishonour are contained in s. 49 of the Bills of Exchange Act 1882. [BILL OF EXCHANGE; DISHONOUR.]

NOTICE OF MOTION. [MOTION.]

NOTICE OF TITLE is where an intending mortgagee or purchaser has knowledge, by himself or his agent, of some right or title in the property adverse to that of his mortgagor or vendor. Thus we speak of a *bona fide* purchaser for valuable consideration *without notice*; meaning that the purchaser of the property has paid the price to those who, he believes, have the right to sell.

"Notice" does not of necessity imply actual knowledge. For whatever is sufficient to put a man of ordinary prudence on an inquiry is constructive notice of everything to which that inquiry might have led. Thus, negligence in investigating a title will not exempt a purchaser from responsibility for knowledge of facts stated in the deeds which are necessary to establish the title.

In reference to real property, the doctrine of notice is mainly important as between a prior owner or incumbrancer of an *equitable* interest in the land, and a subsequent purchaser of the *legal* estate. The subsequent purchaser will be preferred if, when he advanced his money, he had no notice of the equitable incumbrance; but not otherwise.

As between incumbrancers on a fund in the hands of trustees, it is notice to the trustees which regulates the respective priorities of the incumbrancers; so that a prior incumbrancer neglecting to give notice of his claim will be postponed to a subsequent incumbrancer who gives notice. The Law of Property Act 1925, s. 199, provides that a purchaser is not to be prejudicially affected by notice of rights capable of being registered under the Land Charges Act 1925, but not in fact registered. See also s. 44 (5) and (8) of the Law of Property Act 1925.

NOTICE OF TRIAL. A notice formerly given by a plaintiff to a defendant that he intended to bring on a cause for trial. Such notice is no longer necessary. A plaintiff must now set down an action for trial within the period fixed by the order for directions, failing which the defendant may himself set down the action or apply for its dismissal. See R.S.C. 1965, Ord. 34, r. 2.

NOTICE TO ADMIT is where one party in an action calls on another to admit a document or to admit specific facts. If the party so called on should neglect or refuse to make the admission, he will bear the cost of proving the same, unless the judge certify that such refusal was reasonable. See R.S.C. 1965, Ord. 27, r. 5.

NOTICE TO PRODUCE. A notice by one party in an action to the other to produce, at the trial, certain documents in his possession or power relating to any matter in question in the action. If, after receiving this notice, the party does not produce them, then secondary evidence of their contents may be given.

NOTICE TO QUIT. A notice often required to be given by landlord to tenant,

or by tenant to landlord, before the tenancy can be terminated. In cases of a tenancy from year to year, the notice required is generally a six months' notice. The length of notice may vary according to special agreement between the parties or by local custom, or by statute: for example, under the Agricultural Holdings Act 1948, which requires written notice of not less than one year nor more than two in cases where the Act applies. See also s. 69 of the Landlord and Tenant Act 1954.

NOTICE TO THIRD PARTY. [THIRD PARTY.]

NOTICE TO TREAT. A notice given under the Lands Clauses Consolidation Act 1845 by public bodies having compulsory powers of purchasing land, to the person interested in the land which they propose to purchase for the purposes of their undertaking. See ss. 18 *et seq.* of the Act.

NOTING A BILL. When a bill of exchange is not duly paid on presentation the holder applies to a notary-public, who again presents the bill; if not paid, he makes a memorandum of the non-payment, which is called *noting the bill.* Such memorandum by the officer consists of his initials, the month, day and year, and his charges for minuting; and is considered as the preparatory step to a protest. See the Bills of Exchange Acts 1882 to 1917. [PROTEST, 3.]

NOVA STATUTA (new statutes). An appellation sometimes given to the statutes passed since the beginning of the reign of Edward III.

NOVATIO NON PRÆSUMITUR. Novation is not presumed.

NOVATION. The substitution of a new obligation for an old one, or of a new debtor for an old one, with the consent of the creditor.

NOVEL DISSEISIN originally signified a disseisin committed since the last eyre or circuit of justices. [ASSIZE OF NOVEL DISSEISIN; DISSEISIN; EYRE.]

NOVELS (Lat. *Novellæ Constitutiones*) were Constitutions of the Emperor Justinian, published after the completion of the code. [CONSTITUTION; CORPUS JURIS CIVILIS.]

NOVUS ACTUS INTERVENIENS. A new act intervening. If the chain of

NOVUS ACTUS INTERVENIENS
—continued.

causation between a man's act and damage done is broken by the intervening act of a third person, he will not be liable for the damage unless it could be foreseen that it would necessarily follow from his original act.

NUDE CONTRACT, or NUDUM PACTUM. A bare promise of a thing without any "consideration" or equivalent. [CONSIDERATION.]

NUISANCE. Whatsoever unlawfully annoys or damages another. Nuisances are of two kinds: (1) public or common nuisances, which affect the public and are an annoyance to all, or at least to an indefinite number, of the Queen's subjects, *e.g.*, the obstructing of a highway; the remedy is usually by indictment; (2) private nuisances, which cause special damage to particular persons, or a limited and definite number of persons, and do not amount to trespasses, *e.g.*, where one man so uses his own property as to injure another: the remedy in this case is usually by action for an injunction and damages.

NULLA BONA (no goods). A return made by the sheriff to the writ of *fieri facias*, when there are no goods within the county on which to levy the distress. [RETURN.]

NULLITY OF MARRIAGE. A matrimonial suit instituted for the purpose of obtaining a decree declaring a supposed marriage null and void, *e.g.*, on the ground that one of the parties is impotent in which case the marriage is voidable, or on the ground that it is a bigamous marriage in which case it is void.

See the Matrimonial Causes Act 1973, ss. 11 and 12 of which respectively set out fully the grounds on which a marriage is either void, or voidable.

NULLIUS FILIUS (the son of no man). An expression sometimes applied to a bastard.

NULLUM TEMPUS OCCURRIT REGI. Time does not run against the Crown. This rule is modified by the Limitation Act 1939, s. 30 of which applies the Act (with some exceptions) to the Crown and the Duke of Cornwall.

NUNC PRO TUNC. Now instead of then; meaning that a judgment is entered, or document enrolled, so as to have the same legal force and effect as if it had been entered or enrolled on some earlier day.

NUNCUPATIVE WILL. A will declared by a testator before a sufficient number of witnesses, and afterwards reduced into writing. Nuncupative wills are not now allowed, except in the case of soldiers and sailors on actual service. See the Wills (Soldiers and Sailors) Act 1918.

NUNQUAM INDEBITATUS. [NEVER INDEBTED.]

NURSING HOME. Any premises used or intended to be used for the reception of, and the providing of nursing for, persons suffering from any sickness, injury or infirmity. It includes a maternity home. A mental nursing home is one used or intended to be used for the care of one or more mentally disordered patients. See ss. 1, 2 of the Nursing Homes Act 1975.

O

O.E.C.D. [ORGANISATION FOR ECONOMIC CO-OPERATION AND DEVELOPMENT.]

O. NI. (*Oneratur, nisi habet sufficientem exonerationem*—Let him be charged, unless he have sufficient excuse.) A mark formerly set against a sheriff when he had entered into his accounts in the Exchequer, to indicate that he thenceforth became the king's debtor for such accounts.

O YES. [OYEZ.]

OATH. An oath is required by law for many purposes. The Oaths Act 1888, in certain circumstances, allows an affirmation instead of an oath to be made in all places and for all purposes where an oath is or shall be required by law.

OATH EX OFFICIO was the oath by which a clergyman charged with a criminal offence was formerly allowed to swear himself to be innocent; also the oath by which the compurgators swore that they believed in his innocence. [COMPURGATORS.]

OATH OF ALLEGIANCE. An oath to bear true allegiance to the Sovereign, required from most officers of the Crown, and for persons granted a certificate of naturalization. [ALLEGIANCE; NATURALIZATION.]

OBITER DICTUM. A dictum of a judge on a point not directly relevant to the case before him.

OBJECTS OF A POWER. Where property is settled subject to a power given to any person or persons to appoint the same among a limited class, the members of the class are called the *objects of the power*. Thus, if a parent has a power to appoint a fund among his children, the children are called the objects of the power. [POWER.]

OBJURGATRIX. A common scold.

OBLATIONS. Offerings to the church, part of the revenues of the clergy.

OBLIGATION. 1. Legal or moral duty as opposed to physical compulsion.
2. A bond containing a penalty, with a condition annexed, for the payment of money, performance of covenants, or the like.

OBLIGOR. The person bound by an obligation to another person called the *obligee*, who is entitled to the benefit of the bond or obligation.

OBSCENITY. For the purposes of the Obscene Publications Acts 1959 and 1964 an article (book, record, film, picture, etc.) is deemed to be obscene if its effect is such as to tend to deprave or corrupt persons who are likely to read, see or hear the matter contained or embodied in it. Publication of any such article is an offence, punishable with a fine or imprisonment or both; such publication includes distributing, circulating, letting on hire, etc., or showing it, playing it, etc.

In proceedings under the Act it is made a defence that publication of the article in question is justified as being for the public good on the ground that it is in the interests of science, literature, art, or learning, or of other objects of general concern (*ibid.*, s. 4).

OBSTRUCTION. Obstruction of a highway may be a public nuisance at common law. See also s. 78 of the Highway Act 1835. When caused by a motor vehicle it is also an offence under the Motor Vehicles (Construction and Use) Regulations 1973.

OBVENTIONS. Offerings or tithes.

OCCUPANCY. The taking possession of those things which before belonged to nobody.

OCCUPANT. One who took property by occupancy. [OCCUPANCY.] Especially one who entered upon land on the death of the tenant *pur autre vie* during the life of the *cestui que vie*. That is, A having an estate during the life of B, and dying in B's lifetime, C entered; C was called an *occupant*. If C had no right prior to his entry, he was called a *general occupant*, and his occupancy was called *common occupancy*, but if he entered as A's heir under a grant to A and his heirs, he was called a *special occupant*. Common occupancy cannot now exist. See the Wills Act 1837, ss. 3, 6. Special occupancy is also abolished under the provisions of s. 45 of the Administration of Estates Act 1925. [ADMINISTRATOR; AUTRE VIE; CESTUI QUE VIE; CHATTELS; EXECUTOR.]

OCCUPATION. 1. The putting a man out of his freehold in time of war, corresponding to disseisin in time of peace.
2. The use, tenure, or possession of land.
3. An usurpation upon the sovereign, as when one uses liberties which one has not. [LIBERTIES.]

OCCUPIER. The person residing or having the right to reside in or upon any house, land or place. As to the liability of occupiers to third parties entering upon their premises, see the Occupiers' Liability Act 1957. [INVITEE.]

OFFENCE. An act or omission punishable under the criminal law. *Horsfield* v. *Brown*, [1932] K.B. 355, *per* Macnaghten, J., at p. 367.

OFFENSIVE WEAPON. Any article made or adapted for use for causing injury to the person, or intended by the person having it with him for such use by him. It is an offence under the Prevention of Crime Act 1953 to carry such a weapon without lawful authority or reasonable excuse. A similar definition is to be found in s. 10 of the Theft Act 1968.

(*Canada.*) Under the Criminal Code of Canada "offensive weapon" or "weapon" means anything that is designed to be used as a weapon or anything that a person uses or intends to use as a weapon, whether or not it is designed to be used as a weapon. The words include a firearm. [FIREARM.]

OFFER. An expression of readiness to do something (*e.g.*, to purchase or sell), which, if followed by the unconditional

OFFER—*continued.*

acceptance of another, results in a contract. As to the offer of shares or debentures in a company, see s. 45 of the Companies Act 1948.

OFF-GOING CROP. [AWAY-GOING CROP.]

OFFICE. A species of incorporeal hereditament, consisting in the right to exercise a public or private employment. But, in it more limited sense, it is a right which entitles a man to act in the affairs of others without their appointment or permission.

OFFICE COPY is a copy, made under the sanction of a public office, of any deed, record, or other instrument in writing deposited therein.

OFFICE FOUND is when, by an *inquest of office*, facts are found entitling the Crown to any real or personal property by forfeiture or otherwise. [INQUEST.]

OFFICE, INQUEST OF. [INQUEST.]

OFFICE OF A JUDGE. A criminal suit in an ecclesiastical court, not being directed to the reparation of a private injury, is regarded as a proceeding emanating from the *office of the judge*, and may be instituted by the mere motion of the judge. But in practice these suits are instituted by private individuals, with the permission of the judge or his surrogate; and the private prosecutor in any such case is, accordingly, said to *promote the office of the judge.*

OFFICE OF PROFIT. A paid office under the Crown. It was provided by s. 3 of the Act of Settlement 1700 that no person having an office or place of profit under the Crown could sit as a member of the House of Commons. The relevant part of s. 3 has been repealed, but certain offices still carry disqualification from sitting in the Commons. See s. 1 of, and Sch. I to, the House of Commons Disqualification Act 1957. [CHILTERN HUNDREDS.]

OFFICIAL, or **OFFICIAL PRINCIPAL,** in the ancient civil law, signified him who was the minister of, or attendant upon, a magistrate. In the canon law it is especially taken for him to whom any bishop generally commits the charge of his spiritual jurisdiction, and in this sense the chancellor of the diocese is called the official principal. The word official also includes the deputy of an archdeacon.

OFFICIAL ASSIGNEES. Officers of the bankruptcy courts formerly appointed by the Lord Chancellor under the Bankruptcy Acts for the purpose of acting, as occasion might require, with other assignees in the winding up of bankrupts' estates.

These officers have been abolished; but Official Receivers under the Bankruptcy Act 1914 resemble them.

OFFICIAL CUSTODIAN FOR CHARITIES. An officer appointed under s. 3 of the Charities Act 1960 to act as trustee for charities in the cases provided for by the Act.

OFFICIAL LIQUIDATOR. The Official Receiver, or one of the same nominated by the Board of Trade (whose functions are now exercised concurrently with the Secretary of State for Trade and Industry) in case of an order for the compulsory winding up of a company, is to bring and defend suits and actions in the name of the company, and generally to do all things necessary for the winding up the affairs of the company, until he or any other person shall on the application of the creditors or contributories be appointed by the court as liquidator. If *he* be appointed he is then called Official Receiver and Liquidator. See the Companies Act 1948, s. 239. [LIQUIDATOR.]

OFFICIAL LOG BOOK. [LOG.]

OFFICIAL PRINCIPAL. [OFFICIAL.]

OFFICIAL RECEIVERS. Officials appointed by the Board of Trade, who act as interim receivers and managers of bankrupts' estates. See the Bankruptcy Act 1914. The functions of the Board of Trade are now exercised concurrently with the Secretary of State for Trade and Industry.

OFFICIAL REFEREES are officers attached to the Supreme Court of Judicature, to whom the trial of any question arising in any civil proceeding before the High Court of Justice may be referred by the court. The law as to references was consolidated by the Arbitration Act 1950, s. 11 of which provides for reference to an official referee.

OFFICIAL SECRETS. Espionage, and the unauthorised obtaining or disclosure of official information, are offences under the Official Secrets Acts 1911 to

1939. The Acts have been extended by the European Communities Act 1972 to cover the communication of atomic secrets to unauthorised persons: *ibid.*, s. 11 (2).

OFFICIAL SOLICITOR. An officer of the Supreme Court who acts for persons suffering under disability, etc. See s. 129 of the Judicature Act 1925.

OIL. [BRITISH NATIONAL OIL CORPORATION.]

OLD BAILEY. [CENTRAL CRIMINAL COURT.]

OLD STYLE. The mode of reckoning time which prevailed in this country until the year 1752. This method (based on the Julian calendar, so-called from its introduction into the Roman empire by Julius Caesar) differed from the *New Style* at present in use in the following particulars:—

1. The year commenced on the 25th of March, instead of, as now, on the 1st of January.

2. The reckoning of days was based on the assumption that every fourth year was a leap-year, no exception being admitted; instead of, as now, but 97 leap-years in 400 years.

3. The rules for determining the feast of Easter were far less elaborate than at present.

The New Style was introduced into the British dominions by the Calendar (New Style) Act 1750. A similar calendar, the Gregorian, introduced by Pope Gregory XIII, had prevailed in the Roman Catholic countries of the Continent since the year 1582.

OLD TENURES. A treatise on tenures in the reign of Edward III, called "Old Tenures," to distinguish it from Littleton's book on the subject of tenures. [LITTLETON.]

OLERON, LAWS OF. A code of maritime laws compiled in the twelfth century by Richard I at the isle of Oleron in the bay of Aquitaine, on the coast of France, then part of the possessions of the Crown of England.

OMNIA PRÆSUMUNTUR CONTRA SPOLIATOREM. All things are presumed against a wrongdoer.

OMNIA PRÆSUMUNTUR SOLEMNITER (or RITE) ESSE ACTA.

All things are presumed to have been done rightly.

OMNIUM. A term used in the Stock Exchange, to express the aggregate value of the different stocks in which a loan is usually funded.

ONUS PROBANDI. The burden of proof. [BURDEN OF PROOF.]

OPEN CONTRACT. A contract of which not all the terms are expressly mentioned. The term is used especially of a contract for sale of land in which there is no express condition as to title and in which the law makes certain presumptions.

OPEN COURT. A court to which the public have access as of right.

OPEN POLICY. An *open policy* is one in which the value of the subject insured is not fixed or agreed upon in the policy, but is left to be estimated in case of loss. An *open policy* is opposed to a *valued policy*, in which the value of the subject insured is fixed for the purpose of the insurance, and expressed on the face of the policy. [INSURANCE; VALUED POLICY.]

OPEN SEASON (*Canada.*) The period of the year when hunting certain birds or other animals or taking certain kinds of fish is permitted by the game and fish laws of the provinces. [CLOSE SEASON.]

OPEN SPACE. Land laid out as a garden or for purposes of recreation. First defined in the Open Spaces Act 1906. See the Town and Country Planning Act 1971.

OPENING ACCOUNTS. The commencement of dealings in account. When an account has been settled and its correctness is afterwards impugned it is said to be reopened.

OPENING BIDDINGS is where an estate having been put up and sold by auction, it is again put up to competition. This practice long prevailed in sales under the authority of the Court of Chancery, if, after the sale, an intending purchaser offered a large increase over the price at which the estate had been actually knocked down; so that a *bona fide* purchaser was never sure of his bargain. The practice was abolished by s. 7 of the Sale of Land by Auction Act 1867; and the opening of biddings is now allowed only in cases of fraud or misconduct in the sale.

OPENING PLEADINGS is the statement, in a concise form, of the pleadings in a case by the junior counsel for the plaintiff, for the instruction of the jury.

OPERATIVE PART OF A DEED is that part whereby the object of the deed is effected, as opposed to the recitals, etc. [RECITAL.]

OPTION. 1. The archbishop had a customary prerogative, when a bishop was consecrated by him, to name a clerk or chaplain of his own to be provided for by such bishop; in lieu of which the bishop used to make over by deed to the archbishop, his executors and assigns, the next presentation of such dignity or benefice in the diocese within the bishop's disposal, as the archbishop himself should choose; which, therefore, was called his *option.* Disused.

2. The word is also used on the Stock Exchange to express a right to take or sell stock on a future day. [TIME BARGAIN.]

3. An option of purchase in a lease is the right given to the lessee to purchase, during the term, the reversion.

4. As to options to purchase land, and registration thereof, see ss. 2, 3 of the Land Charges Act 1972.

5. As to the powers of a tenant for life to grant options, see the Settled Land Act 1925, s. 51.

OPTIONAL WRIT. Original writs were either *optional* or *peremptory.* An optional writ, otherwise called a *præcipe,* was a writ commanding a defendant to do a thing required, or else to show the reason wherefore he had not done it; thus giving the defendant his choice, either to redress the injury, or to stand the suit. [ORIGINAL WRIT.]

ORAL PLEADINGS. Pleadings put in *viva voce* in court, which was formerly done in civil cases until the reign of Edward III.

ORATOR. A word formerly used in bills in Chancery to denote the plaintiff; *oratrix* being the word used to denote a female plaintiff.

ORDEAL, or **ORDEL.** The most ancient species of trial, called also *judicium Dei* (the judgment of God), and based generally on the notion that God would interpose miraculously to vindicate an earthly right. This was of four sorts: (1) fire ordeal, (2) hot water ordeal, (3) cold water ordeal, (4) ordeal by combat or battle.

ORDER. Any command of a superior to an inferior may be so called. But the word is frequently applied to those acts of courts of justice which do not dispose of the merits of any case before them, *e.g.*, in interlocutory proceedings.

Besides these orders, which are applicable merely in particular instances, there are what are called General Orders, which are framed by courts of justices, sometimes by virtue of their inherent jurisdiction, but now more frequently under the express authority of some statute; such are the revised "Rules of the Supreme Court 1965," which are divided into Orders and subdivided into rules.

Some Statutory Instruments are called Orders.

ORDER AND DISPOSITION is a phrase denoting the apparent possession, on the part of a bankrupt, of goods not his own, with the consent of the true owner. In such case the title of the trustee in the bankruptcy, as representing the creditors, will in general prevail over that of the person claiming the goods as owner. See s. 38 of the Bankruptcy Act 1914.

ORDER IN COUNCIL. An order made by Her Majesty in Council, that is, "by and with the advice of Her Privy Council." Such Order in Council is normally signed by the Clerk of Her Majesty's Privy Council.

Thus the Queen, in the exercise of the Royal Prerogative, may make decrees, *e.g.*, coinage proclamations, etc.; but she cannot, by Order in Council, not made in exercise of a statutory power, make decrees that alter the common law or the statute law of the realm (*The Zamora,* [1916] 2 A.C. 90).

ORDER OF COUNCIL. This type of order is similar to an Order in Council in all respects except that it is made in the exercise of Her Majesty's powers during her absence, illness, etc. See, however, the Regency Acts 1937 to 1953.

The term is also used to describe an instrument made under a statutory power conferred on Her Majesty's Privy Council to make orders or to confirm by order instruments made by another body, as *e.g.*, the instruments made under the Veterinary Surgeons Act 1966.

ORDER OF DISCHARGE. An order obtainable by a bankrupt after passing his public examination, made by a court of bankruptcy, which has the effect of releasing the bankrupt from his debts, except such as are due to the Crown, and such as have been incurred by fraud. See ss. 26, 28 of the Bankruptcy Act 1914.

ORDER, PAYABLE TO. A bill or note payable to order is a bill or note payable to a given person, or as he shall direct by any indorsement he may make thereon. Until he has so indorsed it, no one else can maintain an action upon it; and in this respect it differs from a bill or note *payable to bearer*.

ORDINANCE OF PARLIAMENT. In ancient times there seems to have been a distinction between the *statutes* and *ordinances* of parliament. A *statute* was drawn up with the advice and deliberation of the judges and other learned men, and was entered on a roll called the *statute roll*; whereas *ordinances* appear to have been answers of the king to the great men and commons in parliament entered upon the parliament roll. Ordinances were, in theory, merely declaratory of the existing law.

ORDINARY. 1. In the civil law, an *ordinary* signifies any judge who has authority to take cognisance of causes in his own right, and not by deputation.

2. In the common law, it is taken for him that has exempt and immediate jurisdiction in causes ecclesiastical, who is generally the bishop of the diocese.

ORDINATION. The admission by the bishop of any person to the order of priest or deacon.

ORDNANCE, BOARD OF, was a public department consisting of six officers, under the control of the Master General. It was the duty of the Master General and the Board to direct all matters relating to the Corps of Artillery and Engineers, and to superintend the construction and repair of fortifications, barracks, and military buildings in the United Kingdom and in the Colonies, and of the Colonial Government Buildings; also the supply of arms, ammunition, and military stores for the army and navy.

By the Ordnance Board Transfer Act 1855 these powers and duties were transferred to the Secretary of State for War.

ORDNANCE SURVEY. A survey of Great Britain and the Isle of Man, first authorised by the Ordnance Survey Act 1841, and which is subject to continual revision and improvement.

ORGANISATION FOR ECONOMIC CO-OPERATION AND DEVELOPMENT. An organisation established by a Convention signed in Paris in December 1960 between the United Kingdom and various foreign powers. A support fund, to assist members who are in balance of payments difficulties, became available to United Kingdom participation by the O.E.C.D. Support Fund Act 1975.

ORIGINAL AND DERIVATIVE ESTATES. An original estate is contrasted with a derivative estate; the latter is a particular interest carved out of a larger estate.

ORIGINAL WRIT was formerly the beginning or foundation of every action. When a person had received an injury for which he desired satisfaction at law, the first step in the process of obtaining redress was to sue out, or purchase, by paying the stated fees, an *original*, or *original writ*, from the Court of Chancery. This original writ was a mandatory letter from the king on parchment, sealed with his Great Seal, and directed to the sheriff of the county wherein the injury was supposed to have been committed, requiring him to command the wrong-doer or party accused either to do justice to the complainant, or else to appear in court and answer the accusation against him. Whatever the sheriff did in pursuance of the writ, he was bound to *return* or certify to the Court of Common Pleas, together with the writ itself, which was the foundation of the jurisdiction of that court, being the king's warrant for the judges to proceed to the determination of the causes. Various devices were in course of time resorted to by the connivance of the judges, in order to avoid the expense of an original writ, until, in 1832, an Act was passed by which a comparatively simple and uniform system was introduced into actions at common law. [WRIT.]

ORIGINATING SUMMONS. A summons whereby proceedings are commenced in the Chancery Division, and in

ORIGINATING SUMMONS
—*continued.*

some cases in the Queen's Bench Division, without the issue of a writ. Such summonses are used in a variety of matters, *e.g.*, to determine particular questions arising in the administration of a trust, where a general administration is not required. See, as to the form and issue of such summonses, R.S.C. 1965, Ord. 7; and for other matters of procedure in connection therewith, the subsequent rules of that Order.

OSTENSIBLE or **NOMINAL PARTNER** is a man who allows his credit to be pledged as a partner; as in the case where a man's name appears in a firm, or where he interferes in the management of the business, so as to produce in strangers a reasonable belief that he is a partner. The person so acting is answerable as a partner to all who deal with the firm without having notice at the time that he is a stranger to it in point of interest.

OSTIUM ECCLESIÆ. The door of the church. [AD OSTIUM ECCLESIÆ.]

OUSTER. The dispossession of a lawful tenant, whether of freehold or chattels real, giving remedy at law, in order to gain possession, with damages for the injury sustained.

OUSTER LE MAIN (out of the hand).
1. A delivery of lands out of the king's hands by judgment given in favour of the petitioner in a *monstrans de droit*. [MONSTRANS DE DROIT.]
2. A delivery of the ward's lands out of the hands of the guardian on the former arriving at the proper age, which was twenty-one in males, and sixteen in females. Abolished by the Tenures Abolition Act 1660.

OUT OF COURT. This is a colloquial phrase often applied to a litigant party, which may be otherwise expressed by saying that "he has not a leg to stand on." Thus, when the principal witness, who was expected to prove a party's case, breaks down, it is often said, "that puts him *out of court*."

OUTER BAR. A phrase applied to the junior barristers who plead "ouster" or outside the bar, as opposed to Queen's Counsel, who are admitted to plead within the bar.

OUTGOINGS. This is a term often found in connection with the sale of land. The liability to outgoings, *e.g.*, rates and taxes, is coterminous with the right to receive the rents and profits of the land, and, therefore, where a time for completion is fixed by the contract for sale, as from which the purchaser is to be let into possession, or into receipt of the rents and profits, it is presumed that the vendor is liable to outgoings up to that date only. Where no time for completion is fixed, then, in the absence of express stipulation, the outgoings must be borne by the vendor up to the time when the purchaser could prudently have taken possession of the premises sold. Usually, however, the conditions of sale provide that, upon completion, all rents, profits, rates, taxes and other outgoings shall be apportioned, if necessary, as from the date fixed for completion; so that where apportionable outgoings have been paid in advance by the vendor, as rates and taxes often are, he will require to be repaid the proportion due to be paid by the purchaser. As to apportionable outgoings not paid in advance, such as ground rent, the purchaser is allowed to deduct from the purchase-money the proportion payable by the vendor.
dor.

OUTLAWRY. Putting a man out of the protection of the law, so that he became incapable of bringing an action for redress of injuries, and forfeited all his goods and chattels to the king. Abolished, as regards civil proceedings, in 1879; and as regards criminal, by the Administration of Justice (Miscellaneous Provisions) Act 1938.

OUTSTANDING TERM. A term of years (that is, an interest for a definite period of time [TERM, 2]) in land, of which the legal estate was vested in some person other than the owner of the inheritance, in trust for such owner; such a term was said to *attend* or *protect* the inheritance, because it took priority of any charges which might have been made upon the inheritance, of which the owner had no notice when he took his conveyance and paid his purchase-money. [NOTICE OF TITLE.] But in such case, if the owner took an assignment of the term for himself, it would become merged and lost in the inheritance [MERGER]; and he would lose the benefit of its protection. The Satisfied Terms Act 1845 (repealed) provided that such terms should for the future cease and determine, on becoming attendant upon the inheritance. The Law of Property Act 1925, s. 5, extends the provisions of the Satisfied Terms Act to terms of years created or limited out of leasehold land. See also Sched. I, Part II, to the Act of 1925. [ATTENDANT TERM.]

OUTWORKER. A person to whom articles or materials are given out to be made up, cleaned, washed, altered, ornamented, finished or repaired or adapted for sale in his own home or on other premises not under the control or management of the person who gave out the materials or articles.

OVER. In conveyancing, a gift or limitation *over* signifies one which is to come into existence on the determination of a particular estate.

OVER INSURANCE is where the whole amount insured in different policies is greater than the whole value of the interest at risk.

OVERCROWDING. A dwelling house is deemed to be overcrowded at any time when the number of persons sleeping in the house either (*a*) is such that any two of those persons, being persons ten years old or more of opposite sexes and not being persons living together as husband and wife, must sleep in the same room; or (*b*) is, in relation to the number and floor area of the rooms of which the house consists, in excess of the permitted number. See s. 77 of the Housing Act 1957, and, as to the "permitted number," Sched. VI thereto.

As to abatement of overcrowding, and offences in relation to overcrowding, see ss. 76 *et seq.* of the Act.

OVERDUE BILL OR NOTE. A bill or note is said to be *overdue* so long as it remains unpaid after the time for payment is past.

OVER-REACHING CLAUSE. In a resettlement this is a clause which keeps alive the powers in the original settlement annexed to the estates of the tenants for life; the object being to enable such powers to be exercised so as to over-reach the trusts of the resettlement in the same manner as if the trusts of the latter had been contained in the original settlement.

OVERSEERS. Officers formerly ap-

pointed in each parish, under the Poor Relief Act 1601, to provide for the poor of the parish. The National Assistance Acts 1948 to 1959, and the Ministry of Social Security Act 1966, terminated the poor law and provided for the assistance of persons in need by the Minister of Social Security and by local authorities.

OVERT (Fr. *Ouvert*). Open: thus, an overt act is an open act, as opposed to an intention conceived in the mind, which can be judged only by overt acts. [MARKET OVERT; POUND.]

OWNERSHIP. The right to the exclusive enjoyment of a thing. It may be *absolute*, in which case the owner may freely use or dispose of his property, or *restricted*, as in the case of joint ownership. *Beneficial* ownership is the right of enjoyment of property, as distinguished from *legal* ownership.

OYER AND ꝑERMINER. To hear and determine; a commission issued to judges and others for hearing and determining cases upon indictments found at the old assizes, being the largest of the commissions by which judges of assize sat in their several circuits. The assize courts have been abolished and replaced by the Crown Court. [CROWN COURT.]

OYER OF DEEDS AND RECORDS. The hearing them read in court. Formerly, a party suing upon or pleading any deed was bound to make *profert* of the same, that is, to bring it into court (Lat. *profert in curiam*), and the opposite party was entitled to crave *oyer* of the same; that is, to have it read by the officer of the court. Abolished in 1852.

OYEZ (hear ye). Now generally pronounced O yes. It is used by criers in courts and elsewhere when they make proclamation of anything.

P

P.A.Y.E. [PAY-AS-YOU-EARN.]

P.C. Privy Council; Privy Councillor.

P.P. [PER PROCURATIONEM.]

PACKAGE. A duty formerly charged in the port of London on goods imported and exported by aliens.

PACT. A promise or contract.

PAINS AND PENALTIES, ACTS OF, for attainting particular persons of treason or felony, or for inflicting pains and penalties beyond or contrary to the common law. It is an incident of such bills that persons to be effected by them have, by custom, the right to be heard at the bar of the House in opposition to the bill.

PAIRING OFF. A kind of system of negative proxies, by which a member whose opinions would lead him to vote on one side of a question agrees with a member on the opposite side that they shall both be absent at the same time, so that a vote is neutralised on each side. This practice has been resorted to for many years in the House of Commons. Generally, members of opposite parties pair with each other, not only upon particular questions, but for a period. *May.*

PAIS, or **PAYS.** The country. A trial *per pais* is a trial by the country, that is, by a jury; and matter *in pais* is matter triable by the country; that is, an ordinary matter of fact. [MATTER, 2.] A conveyance of land *in pais* meant originally a conveyance on the spot to be transferred.

PALATINE. [COUNTY PALATINE.]

PANDECTS. A name given to the Digest of Roman Law, compiled by order of the Emperor Justinian. [CORPUS JURIS CIVILIS.]

PANEL. 1. A schedule or roll of parchment containing the names of jurors which the sheriff has returned to pass upon any trial.

2. Any list of persons for official purposes, *e.g.*, "Panel Doctors" under the former National Health Insurance Acts.

PANNAGE, or **PAWNAGE.** 1. The food which swine feed on in the woods, as mast of beech, acorns, etc.

2. Money taken by the *agisters* for the same. [AGIST.]

PANNEL. [PANEL.]

PAPER BLOCKADE. When a blockade is proclaimed in time of war, and the naval force on watch is not sufficient to repel attempts to enter or get out, the blockade is called a paper blockade as opposed to a *good* or *effective* blockade. [BLOCKADE.]

PAPER BOOKS. Copies of the demurrer-book formerly taken for the perusal of the judges.

PAPER OFFICE. 1. An ancient office within the palace of Whitehall, wherein State papers were kept.

2. An ancient office belonging to the Court of King's Bench, where the records of the court were kept.

PARAGE. Equality of name, blood or dignity; also of lands to be partitioned. Hence comes the word *disparagement*, which signifies inequality. [DISPARAGEMENT.]

PARAMOUNT. 1. The supreme lord of a fee. Thus, the Queen is lord paramount of all the lands in the kingdom.

2. The word was also frequently used in a *relative* sense, to denote a superior lord as opposed to a mesne lord holding under him.

PARAMOUNTCY. Formerly the relationship of the Emperor of India to the rulers of the native states of India. It was ended by the Indian Independence Act 1947.

PARAPHERNALIA. *Things besides dower*; the goods which a wife, besides her dower or jointure, was, after her husband's death, allowed to have, as furniture for her chamber, and wearing apparel.

PARAVAIL. The lowest tenant; being he who was supposed to make *avail* or profit of the land. It was thus the reverse of *paramount*. [PARAMOUNT.]

PARCEL (Lat. *Particula*). A small piece of land.

A description of *parcels*, in a deed, is a description of lands with reference to their boundaries and local extent.

A *bill of parcels* is an account of the items composing a parcel or package of goods, transmitted with them to a purchaser.

PARCENERS. The same as *coparceners*; those who hold an estate in coparcenary. [COPARCENARY.]

PARDON is either (1) by the Sovereign in virtue of the prerogative, or (2) by Act of Parliament.

(1) Must be pleaded specially and at a proper time; it cannot, however, be pleaded in bar of an impeachment by the Commons.

(2) Need not be pleaded, but the court is bound to take notice of it.

PARENS PATRIÆ (parent of his country). A title sometimes applied to the Queen (or king).

PARENTELA. Kindred. *De parentela se tollere* was to renounce one's kindred. This was done in open court before a judge, and in the presence of twelve men, who made oath that they believed it was done lawfully, and for a just cause. This renunciation incapacitated the person from inheriting from any of his kindred.

PARES. Peers, equals. Thus, the various tenants of the same manor were called *pares curtis* or *pares curiæ*, as being *equals* in attendance upon the lord's court. [PEERS.]

PARI PASSU. On an equal footing, or proportionately. A phrase used especially of the creditors of an insolvent estate, who (with certain exceptions) are entitled to payment of their debts in shares proportioned to their respective claims. [PREFERENTIAL PAYMENTS.]

PARISH. 1. A circuit of ground committed to the charge of one parson or vicar, or other minister having the cure of souls therein.
2. A division of a district for the purposes of the Local Government Act 1972.

PARISH APPRENTICES. The children of parents unable to maintain them could by law be *apprenticed*, by the guardians or overseers of their parish, to such persons as might be willing to receive them as apprentices. Such children were called *parish apprentices*. See now, as to the duties of local authorities in assuming care of orphans, deserted children, etc., the Children Acts 1948 and 1975.

PARISH CLERK. An officer of a church, generally appointed by the incumbent. By custom, however, he may be chosen by the inhabitants. Formerly, the parish clerk was very frequently in holy orders, and was appointed to officiate at the altar; but now his duty consists chiefly in making responses in church to the minister. By the common law he has a freehold in his office. The office seems now to be falling into desuetude.

PARISH COUNCILS. Established in 1894 for rural parishes with populations of 300 and upwards. Their principal duties are now set out in the Parish Councils Act 1957, as amended by the Local Government Act 1972. Under the latter Act, which created new structures for local government in England and Wales, parish councils retain their former functions, having powers, *e.g.*, relating to footpaths and bridleways, off-street parking, footway lighting, open spaces, etc. Each parish council consists of a chairman and parish councillors, the number of which (not less than five) is fixed from time to time by the district council.

PARISH MEETING. A meeting of the local government electors of a parish. Such a meeting must be held once a year, or at least twice a year where there is no parish council. See ss. 9–17 of the Local Government Act 1972.

PARK, in a legal sense, was a piece of ground enclosed, and stored with beasts of chase, which a man might have by prescription, or the king's grant. Now used either of national parks, being large tracts of country, or small areas set aside for recreation, or the land attached to a mansion.

PARLIAMENT. A solemn conference of all the estates of the kingdom, summoned together by the authority of the Crown, to treat of the weighty affairs of the realm. The constituent parts of the parliament are the sovereign and the three estates of the realm, namely, the lords spiritual and lords temporal, who sit together with the sovereign, in one House, and the commons, who sit by themselves, in another. *May*. [ESTATES OF THE REALM; HOUSE OF COMMONS; HOUSE OF LORDS; LORDS SPIRITUAL; LORDS TEMPORAL.]

PARLIAMENTARY AGENTS are agents (generally solicitors) who, in parliament, promote or oppose the passing of private bills, and conduct other proceedings for pecuniary reward. No member or officer of the House may act as an agent. *May*.

PARLIAMENTARY COMMITTEE. A committee appointed by either House for making inquiries, *e.g.*, in the case of private bills.

PAROL. Anything done by word of mouth.

PAROL AGREEMENT. An agreement by word of mouth. Sometimes,

PAROL AGREEMENT—*continued.*

however, the phrase is used to include writings not under seal; since at common law, prior to the Statute of Frauds, there was no difference between an agreement by word of mouth and one in writing without seal. [FRAUDS, STATUTE OF.]

PAROL ARREST. An arrest, ordered by a justice of the peace, of one who is guilty of a breach of the peace in his presence.

PAROL EVIDENCE, otherwise called *oral evidence,* is evidence given *viva voce* by witnesses, as opposed to that given by affidavit. As a general rule parol evidence cannot be given to contradict, alter, or vary a written instrument.

PAROLE (*Canada*). Authority granted under the Parole Act, R.S.C. 1970, c. P-2, to a prison inmate to be at large during his term of imprisonment. [TICKET OF LEAVE.]

PARRICIDE. He that kills his father; or the crime of killing a father.

PARS RATIONABILIS. A reasonable part.

PARSON (*Persona ecclesiæ*). The rector or incumbent of a parochial church, who has full possession of all the rights thereof. He is called parson, *persona,* because by his person the church, which is an invisible body, is represented; and he is himself a body corporate, in order to protect and defend the rights of the church, which he personates, by a perpetual succession. There are four requisites to his appointment: holy orders, presentation, institution, and induction.

PARSONAGE. A certain portion of lands, tithes, and offerings, established by law, for the maintenance of the minister who has the cure of souls. The word is generally used for the *house* set apart for the residence of the minister.

PART OWNERS. Persons who have a share in anything, especially those who have an interest in a ship. See s. 5 of the Merchant Shipping Act 1894.

PART PERFORMANCE. Certain contracts, *e.g.,* contracts for the sale or other disposition of land or any interest in land, are not enforceable unless they are evidenced in writing. See s. 40 (1) of the Law of Property Act 1925. Under the equitable doctrine of part performance, however, where there has been a sufficient act of part

performance by the plaintiff, the absence of a memorandum in writing will not in itself be permitted to vitiate the contract. *Ibid.,* s. 40 (2).

PARTIAL LOSS, in marine insurance, otherwise called an *average* loss, is one in which the damage done to the thing insured is not so complete as to amount to a *total loss,* either actual or constructive. In every such case the underwriter is liable to pay such proportion of the sum which would be payable on total loss, as the damage sustained by the subject of insurance bears to the whole value at the time of insurance. [TOTAL LOSS.]

PARTICEPS CRIMINIS. An accomplice or partaker in wrongdoing.

PARTICULAR AVERAGE. [AVERAGE, 4.]

PARTICULAR ESTATE is an estate in land which precedes an estate in remainder or reversion, so called because it is a *particula,* or small part, of the inheritance. [CONTINGENT REMAINDER; ESTATE; REMAINDER; REVERSION; VESTED REMAINDER.]

PARTICULAR LIEN, as opposed to a *general lien,* is a lien upon a particular article for the price due or the labour bestowed upon the article. [GENERAL LIEN; LIEN.]

PARTICULAR TENANT. The tenant of a particular estate. [PARTICULAR ESTATE.]

PARTICULARS OF CLAIM OR DEFENCE. By R.S.C. 1965, Ord. 18, r. 7, a plaintiff or defendant is required to give a statement in summary form of all material facts on which he relies for his claim or defence, and in cases in which particulars may be necessary they are to be stated in the pleading (*ibid.,* r. 12).

PARTICULARS OF SALE are the particulars of the property which is to be sold, an the terms and conditions on which the sale is to take place.

PARTIES. 1. Persons who voluntarily take part in anything, in person or by attorney; as the parties to a deed.

2. Persons required to take part in any proceedings, and bound thereby, whether they do so or not; as the defendants in a suit or action. The rules as to parties in actions will be found in R.S.C. 1965, Ord. 15.

PARTITION. A dividing of land held in joint tenancy, in coparcenary, or in common, between the parties entitled thereto; so that the estate in joint tenancy, coparcenary or common is destroyed, and each party has henceforth an undivided share. This may be done by agreement, by deed of partition, or compulsorily by an action in the Chancery Division. There was formerly a *writ* of partition, but that was abolished in 1833.

Under the Judicature Act 1925, s. 56 (1) (*b*) the partition of real estates was assigned to the Chancery Division of the High Court of Justice. By Sched. VII to the Act, elaborate provisions were made for the vesting of land held in undivided shares in trustees on trust for sale. See ss. 34–36; and also Sch. I, Part IV, para. 1 (ii) to the Act. By s. 28 (3) trustees for sale were given power to partition the land remaining unsold or any part thereof.

PARTNERSHIP, as defined by s. 1 of the Partnership Act 1890, is as follows: Partnership is the relation which subsists between persons carrying on a business in common with a view of profit.

The relation between members of any company or association which is (*a*) registered as a company under the Companies Act 1948 or any other Act of Parliament for the time being in force and relating to the registration of companies; or (*b*) formed or incorporated by or in pursuance of any other Act of Parliament or letters patent or royal charter; or (*c*) a company engaged in working mines within and subject to the jurisdiction of the Stannaries is not a partnership within the meaning of the Act.

A partnership is often constituted by a deed, the provisions of which are usually called *articles of partnership*. The law on the subject was codified by the Act of 1890. [LIMITED PARTNERSHIP.]

PARTY AND PARTY, COSTS AS BETWEEN. [COSTS.]

PARTY-WALL. A wall adjoining lands or houses belonging to two different owners. The common user of such a wall by the adjoining owners is *prima facie* evidence that it belongs to them in equal moieties as tenants in common. By s. 38 of the Law of Property Act 1925, and Sch. I, Part V, it is enacted that a wall which under the old law would have been held by tenants in common shall be regarded as severed vertically as between the respective owners, and that the owners of each part shall have such rights to support and user over the other part as he would have had as tenant in common under the old law. *Hill & Redman.*

PASSAGE COURT. [LIVERPOOL COURT OF PASSAGE.]

PASSING OFF. Selling goods or carrying on business in a manner calculated to mislead the public into believing that goods, business, etc., are those of another. An action for damages or for an injunction may be brought.

PASSIVE TRUST. A trust in which the trustee has no active duty to perform. [BARE TRUSTEE.]

PASSPORT means strictly a licence to *pass* a *port* or haven; that is, a licence for the safe passage of any man from one place to another.

PASTURE. Any place where cattle may feed; also feeding for cattle. [COMMON, 1.]

PATENT. Letters patent from the Crown. [LETTERS PATENT.] These are granted for various purposes; among other things, for conferring a peerage. But the term *patent*, or *patent right*, is usually restricted to mean a privilege granted by letters patent from the Crown to the first inventor of any new contrivance in manufacture, that he alone shall be entitled, during a limited period, to benefit by his own invention. This is one of the exceptions reserved in the Statute of Monopolies 1623, by which the granting of monopolies is in general forbidden. From this general prohibition are excepted all letters patent for the term of fourteen years or under, by which the privilege of sole working or making any new manufactures within this realm, which others at the time of granting the letters patent shall not use, shall be granted to the true and first inventor thereof; "so as they be not contrary to law, nor mischievous to the State, nor to the hurt of trade, nor generally inconvenient". The grant of a patent right is not *ex debito justitiæ*, but is an act of royal favour; though in a fit case it is never refused.

The mode in which a patent is to be obtained is prescribed by the Patents Acts

PATENT—*continued.*
1949 to 1961. The term is now 16 years, which may be extended.

PATENT OF PRECEDENCE. Letters patent formerly granted to such barristers as the Crown thought fit to honour with that mark of distinction, whereby they were entitled to such rank and pre-audience as were assigned in their respective patents, which was sometimes next after the Attorney-General, but more usually next after King's (Queen's) Counsel then being. These ranked promiscuously with the King's (Queen's) Counsel, but were not the sworn servants of the Crown. Now obsolete.

PATENT RIGHT. [PATENT.]

PATENTEE. A person to whom a patent is granted.

PATRICIDE. [PARRICIDE.]

PATRIMONY. An hereditary estate. The legal endowment of a church or religious house was called ecclesiastical patrimony.

PATRON. In the canon and common law, is the person who has the gift of a benefice.

PAUPER. 1. Formerly a person who, on account of his poverty, became chargeable to the parish.
2. A person who, on account of his poverty, was admitted to sue or defend *in forma pauperis.* [ASSISTED PERSON; FORMA PAUPERIS.]

PAWN. The transfer of a chattel as security for a debt. [PLEDGE.]

PAWNBROKER. One whose business it is to lend money, usually in small sums, upon pawn or pledge. Formerly defined by s. 5 of the Pawnbrokers' Act 1872 as a person who "carries on the business of taking goods and chattels in pawn". The Act of 1872 was repealed by the Consumer Credit Act 1974.

PAY-AS-YOU-EARN. The name popularly given to the system of tax collection under Schedule E to the Income and Corporation Taxes Act 1970, whereby the person chargeable has tax deducted by instalments from his salary by his employer, who is then accountable to the Commissioners of Inland Revenue for the payment of the sums so deducted. See Part VIII, Chapter III, and in particular s. 204, of the Act of 1970.

PAYEE. A person to whom, or to whose order, a bill of exchange, cheque, or promissory note is expressed to be payable.

PAYMASTER-GENERAL. A public officer whose duties consist in the payment of all the voted services for the army and navy, and all charges connected with the naval and military expenditure. The Paymaster-General likewise makes payments for the civil services in England, and for some in Scotland. The office of Accountant-General was abolished in 1872 and its duties transferred to that of the Paymaster-General. By s. 133 (6) of the Judicature Act 1925 the Paymaster-General was replaced by an Accountant-General as to the pay office of the Supreme Court. At the present day the personal duties of the holder of the office are nominal.

PAYMENT OF MONEY INTO COURT. In an action. This is when a defendant in an action for a debt or damages pays money into court in satisfaction of the cause of action, in order to save the expense of further proceedings.

The general effect of the rules as to payment into court (see R.S.C. 1965, Ord. 22) may be summarised as follows: (1) The defendant may pay into court one lump sum in respect of two or more causes of action. (2) Notice of payment in must specify the fact and the amount of payment, and whether any counter-claim has been taken into account. (3) Neither the fact nor the amount of the payment in must be disclosed in the pleadings except where tender is pleaded or under the Libel Act 1843. (4) Payment into court may be made or increased after the trial or hearing of an action has begun. (5) Costs are in the absolute discretion of the court.

As to lodgment of funds in court in the Chancery Division by a life insurance company, a trustee, etc., see R.S.C. 1965, Ord. 92.

PAYMENT OF MONEY OUT OF COURT. Pay office rules and practice are explained in ss. 6, 7 of the Administration of Justice Act 1965. See also Part VI of the Supreme Court Funds Rules 1975.

PEACE, CLERK OF. [CLERK OF THE PEACE.]

PEACE, COMMISSION OF. [COMMISSION OF THE PEACE.]

PEACE, JUSTICES OF. [JUSTICE OF THE PEACE.]

PEACE OF THE QUEEN. That peace and security, both for life and goods, which the Queen promises to all her subjects, or others taken under her protection.

PECULIAR. A particular parish or church exempt from the jurisdiction of the ordinary. All ecclesiastical causes arising within them are cognisable in the Court of Peculiars. [COURT OF PECULIARS.]

PEDLAR. (*Canada.*) A pedlar is a hawker (*q.v.*)

PEERAGE. The dignity of the lords or peers of the realm, whether hereditary peers or life peers under the Life Peerages Act 1958. The House of Lords exercises an original jurisdiction in regard to matters of peerage. Since the time of Charles II all doubtful or contested claims to peerage have been referred to the Lords by the Crown. The procedure is by way of petition to the Crown. For the most recent example see the *Ampthill Peerage Case*, [1976] 2 All E.R. 411. [PEERS, 2.]

PEERESS. A woman who has the dignity of peerage, either in her own right or by right of marriage. In the latter case she loses the dignity by a second marriage with a commoner.

PEERS (Lat. *Pares*). Equals. 1. Those who are impanelled in an inquest upon any man, for the convicting or clearing him of any offence for which he is called in question. "The co-vassals by whose verdict a vassal is condemned of felony."

2. Those that be of the nobility of the realm and lords of parliament. [ESTATES OF THE REALM; LORDS TEMPORAL; NOBILITY.]

PEINE FORTE ET DURE. This was the punishment for standing mute of malice on an indictment of felony. Before it was pronounced the prisoner had a threefold admonition (*trina admonitio*), and also a respite of a few hours; and the sentence was distinctly read to him that he might know his danger. The sentence was that he be remanded to prison and loaded with weights, etc., till he died or answered. It was abolished in 1772. [MUTE.]

PENAL ACTIONS. [ACTIONS CIVIL AND PENAL.]

PENAL LAWS. Laws imposing penalties or punishments for the doing of prohibited acts.

The question whether a given provision in an Act of Parliament is a penal one or not, is sometimes important. For instance, it is a rule that penal statutes must be construed *strictly* (that is, narrowly).

PENAL SERVITUDE. A punishment introduced in 1853 in lieu of transportation beyond seas. It ranged in duration from a minimum period of three years to the life of the convict. Abolished by the Criminal Justice Act 1948.

PENAL STATUTES. [PENAL LAWS.]

PENALTY. 1. Punishment; used of a pecuniary fine.

2. Money recoverable by virtue of a penal statute.

3. A sum named in a bond as the amount to be forfeited by the obligor in case he comply not with the condition of the bond. Notwithstanding that a sum may be so named, still, in an action on the bond, a jury is directed to inquire what damages the plaintiff has sustained by breach of the condition; and the plaintiff cannot take out execution for a larger amount than the jury shall so assess. See, *e.g.*, as to administration bonds, s. 167 of the Judicature Act 1925.

4. A sum agreed to be paid on breach of an agreement, or some stipulation in it. [LIQUIDATED DAMAGES.]

PENDENTE LITE. While a suit is pending. Thus letters of administration may be granted *pendente lite*, where a suit is commenced touching the validity of a will. See s. 163 of the Judicature Act 1925. [ADMINISTRATOR; MAINTENANCE PENDING SUIT.]

PENDING ACTION. [LIS PENDENS.]

PENSION. The payment of a sum of money; especially a periodical payment for past services.

PEPPERCORN RENT. A rent of a peppercorn, that is, a nominal rent.

PER AUTRE VIE. For another's life. [OCCUPANT; PUR AUTRE VIE.]

PER CAPITA. [CAPITA, DISTRIBUTION PER.]

PER CURIAM (by the court). An expression implying that such a decision

PER CURIAM—*continued.*

was arrived at by the court, consisting of one or more judges, as the case might be.

Similarly, the word *per*, preceding the name of a judge, signifies that a dictum which follows is quoted on the authority of the judge.

PER, IN THE. To come in the *per* was to claim by or through the person last entitled to an estate; to come in the *post* was to claim by a paramount and prior title, as, formerly, the lord by escheat. [ENTRY, WRIT OF.]

PER INCURIAM. Through want of care.

PER INFORTUNIUM. By mischance.

PER MY ET PER TOUT (by the half and by all). An expression applied to occupation in joint tenancy, indicating, according to some, that the joint-tenants had each of the entire possession as well of every parcel as of the whole; according to others, that the joint-tenants were all jointly seised of the whole, with the right to transfer in equal shares. See now s. 36 of, and Sch. I, Part IV to, the Law of Property Act 1925.

PER PAIS (Lat. *Per patriam*). By the country. A trial *per pais* is a trial by jury of the country.

PER PROCURATIONEM. By means of procuration or agency. The phrase is often used, either in full or abbreviated into "p.p." where one man signs a receipt or other written document as agent for another. But the phrase is especially applied to the acceptance, etc., of a bill of exchange by one man as agent for another.

The words "per procuration", attached to a signature on a bill of exchange, are held to be an express intimation of a special and limited authority; and a person who takes a bill so drawn, accepted, or indorsed, is bound to inquire into the extent of the authority. See ss. 25, 26 of the Bills of Exchange Act 1882.

PER QUÆ SERVITA (by which services). A writ judicial issuing from the note of a fine, which lay for the cognizee of a manor, seigniory, etc., to compel the tenant of the land to attorn unto him. Abolished in 1833. [ATTORN, 1.]

PER QUOD (by reason of which). A phrase indicating special damage sustained by the plaintiff by reason of the defendant's conduct. In most cases of slander, for instance, it is necessary for the plaintiff to aver special damage to have happened by reason of the alleged slander, which is called laying his action with a *per quod*.

PER QUOD CONSORTIUM or **SERVITIUM AMISIT.** An allegation by a husband or master that he had lost the benefit of his wife's society or of his servant's assistance; being the special damage shown by a husband or master who brought a separate action against a person for grossly maltreating the wife or servant, whereby he was deprived of her or his company or assistance.

The action for loss of consortium was abolished by the Law Reform (Miscellaneous Provisions) Act 1970. That for enticement of a servant apparently remains. [CONSORTIUM.]

PER SE. Of itself, taken alone.

PER STIRPES. [STIRPES, DISTRIBUTION PER.]

PER TOTAM CURIAM. By the whole court. [PER CURIAM.]

PERAMBULATION. A walking of boundaries.

PEREMPTORY signifies a final and determinate act, without hope of renewing or altering. See also the following titles.

PEREMPTORY CHALLENGE is where a party challenges a juror without showing cause. [CHALLENGE.]

PEREMPTORY MANDAMUS. A *mandamus* to do a thing at once, directed to a person to whom a previous writ of *mandamus* has issued to do the thing in question, and who has made some excuse, either insufficient in law, or false in fact, for not doing it. [MANDAMUS.]

PEREMPTORY PLEAS, more usually termed *pleas in bar*, were pleas by a defendant tending to impeach the plaintiff's right of action, as opposed to what were called *dilatory pleas*. [DILATORY PLEA.]

PEREMPTORY UNDERTAKING. An undertaking by a plaintiff to bring on a cause for trial at the next sittings.

PEREMPTORY WRIT. An original writ not optional. [OPTIONAL WRIT; ORIGINAL WRIT.]

PERFECT TRUST. An executed trust.

PERFECTING BAIL is a phrase used to signify the completion of the proceedings whereby persons tendering themselves as sureties for the appearance of a party in court on a day assigned are admitted in that capacity, when they have established their pecuniary sufficiency. [BAIL.]

PERFORMANCE. The doing wholly or in part of a thing agreed to be done. [SATISFACTION, 2; SPECIFIC PERFORMANCE.] In the Copyright Act 1956 the term includes delivery of lectures, addresses, speeches and sermons; visual and acoustic presentation by wireless, cinematograph film, etc. See s. 48 of the Act.

PERILS OF THE SEAS. Policies of marine insurance include all fortuitous occurrences which are incident to navigation: the law has extended the phrase considerably.

PERJURY is the swearing wilfully, absolutely, and falsely, in a judicial proceeding, in a matter material to the issue or cause in question. By many statutes, however, false oaths in certain cases, not of a judicial kind, are to be deemed to amount to perjury, and to be visited with the same penalties. The penalties of perjury also attach to wilful falsehood in an affirmation by a Quaker, Moravian, or Separatist, or any other witness, where such affirmation is in lieu of an oath, and would, if believed, have the same legal consequences. See the Perjury Act 1911.

PERMISSIVE WASTE. [WASTE.]

PERMIT. A licence or warrant for persons to pass with and sell goods, on having paid the duties of customs or excise for the same.

PERPETUAL CURATE. A permanent minister in holy orders of an "appropriated" church in which no vicar had been endowed, was, until the year 1868, called a *perpetual curate*. But by s. 2 of the Incumbets Act 1868 it was provided that every incumbent of a church (not being a rector), who is entitled to perform marriages, etc., and to claim the fees for his own use, shall, for the purpose of style and designation, be deemed and styled a *vicar*, and his benefice a vicarage. [APPROPRIATION, 1; VICAR.]

PERPETUAL INJUNCTION. An injunction which is not merely temporary or provisional, and which cannot be dissolved except by appeal, or some proceeding in the nature of an appeal. An interim injunction granted on motion is sometimes made *perpetual* by the decree. [INJUNCTION.]

PERPETUALLY RENEWABLE LEASE OR UNDERLEASE. As used in s. 190 of the Law of Property Act 1922, this meant a lease or underlease the holder of which was entitled to enforce (whether or not subject to the fulfilment of any condition) the perpetual renewal thereof and included a lease or underlease for a life or lives or for a term of years whether determinable with life or lives or not which was perpetually renewable. The Act abolished this form of tenure and provided for its conversion into a long term of fixed duration subject to determination.

PERPETUATING TESTIMONY. Proceedings in equity to enable a person to take evidence, otherwise in danger of being lost, where the facts likely to come into dispute cannot be immediately investigated by legal process; for instance, where the person filing it has merely a future interest. See R.S.C. 1965, Ord. 39.

PERPETUITY. 1. The settlement of an estate in tail so that it cannot be undone or made void. This is contrary to the policy of the law.

2. And generally, the attempt, by deed, will, or other instrument, to control the devolution of an estate beyond the period allowed by law, is spoken of as an attempt to create a *perpetuity*, and the disposition so attempted to be made is *void for remoteness*, though in some cases the courts will, by the operation of the *cy-près* doctrine, give effect to the disposition to the extent permitted by law. See also ss. 161, 162 of the Law of Property Act 1925, and the Perpetuities and Accumulations Act 1964. [CY-PRÈS.]

PERSISTENT OFFENDER. An extended sentence of imprisonment may be given where an offender has been convicted on indictment on at least three previous occasions since he attained the age of twenty-one, of offences punishable with

PERSISTENT OFFENDER
—continued.

imprisonment for two years or more. The court must be satisfied that it is expedient to protect the public from him for a substantial time. See ss. 28, 29 of the Powers of Criminal Courts Act 1973. [HABITUAL CRIMINAL.]

PERSON is used variously as follows:—

1. A human being capable of rights, also called a *natural* person.

2. A corporation or legal person, otherwise called an *artificial* person. See s. 19 of the Interpretation Act 1889.

PERSONA DESIGNATA. An individual as distinguished from a member of a class.

PERSONAL ACTION signifies:

1. An action which can be brought only by the person himself who is injured, and not by his representatives [ACTIONS PERSONAL.]

2. An action which is not an action for the recovery of land. [ACTIONS REAL AND PERSONAL.]

PERSONAL CHATTELS are things movable, as opposed to interests in land. [CHATTELS.]

PERSONAL PROPERTY. [REAL AND PERSONAL PROPERTY.]

PERSONAL REPRESENTATIVE. An executor or administrator, whose duty it is to settle the affairs and dispose of the property of a deceased person. [ADMINISTRATOR; EXECUTOR.]

PERSONAL RIGHTS. Rights of personal security, *i.e.*, those of life, limb, body, health, reputation and liberty.

PERSONAL TITHES. Tithes paid out of the fruits of personal labour, as of manual occupations, trades, fisheries, and the like. [TITHES.]

PERSONALTY. Personal property. Personalty is either *pure* or *mixed*. Pure personalty is personalty unconnected with land; mixed personalty is a personal interest in land, or connected therewith. [CHATTELS.]

PERSONATION. Pretending to be some other particular person. Thus, a man who induces a married woman to have sexual intercourse with him by impersonating her husband is guilty of rape: Sexual Offences Act 1956, s. 1.

Personation in order to obtain admittance to a prohibited place is also an offence under s. 1 (1) (*d*) of the Official Secrets Act 1920. [OFFICIAL SECRETS.]

Personation at a parliamentary or local government election is an offence punishable with up to two years imprisonment under s. 146 of the Representation of the People Act 1949. A person is deemed guilty of personation if he (*a*) votes in person or by post as some other person, whether as an elector or as proxy, and whether that other person is living or dead or is a fictitious person; or (*b*) votes in person or by post as proxy either for a person whom he knows or supposes is dead or fictitious, or when he knows or supposes that his proxy is no longer in force (*ibid.*, s. 47).

PERVERSE VERDICT. A verdict given by a jury who refuse to follow the direction of the judge on a point of law.

PETER-PENCE, or **PETER'S PENCE,** was a tribute formerly paid to the Pope through the papal legates: also called Romescot and Hearth-Penny.

PETIT JURY. [JURY; PETTY JURY.]

PETIT SERJEANTY. Holding lands of the Queen by the service of rendering to her annually some small implement of war, as a bow, a sword, a lance, an arrow or the like. The services of this tenure being free and certain, it is in all respects like free socage. The services incident to this tenure were expressly retained by the Law of Property Act 1922, s. 136.

PETIT TREASON. A lower kind of treason, which might formerly be committed:

1. By a servant killing his master.

2. By a wife killing her husband.

3. By an ecclesiastical person killing his superior, to whom he owed faith and obedience.

Any killing which formerly amounted to petit treason amounted to murder only under s. 8 of the Offences against the Person Act 1861, which section was repealed by the Criminal Law Act 1967.

PETITIO PRINCIPII. A begging of the question.

PETITION has a general signification for all kinds of supplications made by an inferior to a superior, especially one having jurisdiction and authority. Thus there are petitions to the Queen, petitions to parliament, etc. The subject has a right to petition the sovereign, or parliament, subject to certain restrictions.

A petition in Chancery is an application, addressed to a judge, stating the matters on which it is founded, put in the same manner as a bill, and concluding with a prayer for the specific order sought; or for such other order as the judge shall think right. See R.S.C. 1965, Ord. 9.

The word "petition" is variously used in English legal proceedings, as *e.g.*, a *petition* for a receiving order in bankruptcy, a *petition* for a divorce. Petitions against the election of members of parliament used formerly to be addressed to the House of Commons, but now they are tried by two judges.

PETITION DE DROIT. [PETITION OF RIGHT, 1.]

PETITION OF RIGHT. 1. A petition for obtaining possession or restitution of property, either real or personal, from the Crown, which suggested such a title as controverted the title of the Crown, grounded on facts disclosed in the petition itself, in which case the petitioner had to be careful to state truly the whole title of the Crown, otherwise the petition abated. As if a disseisor of lands died without heir, and the Crown entered, the disseisee had remedy by petition of right.

Since the Crown Proceedings Act 1947 came into force, there has been no need for a petition of right.

2. The Petition of Right 1627, being a parliamentary declaration of the liberties of the people, including personal liberty and immunity from arbitrary taxation, assented to by King Charles I in the beginning of his reign.

PETITIONING CREDITOR. A creditor who petitions that his debtor may be adjudicated bankrupt. The creditor's debt must be a liquidated one of not less than £50, and grounded on an act of bankruptcy within three months before the petition. See the Bankruptcy Act 1914, ss. 3 *et seq.*

PETROLEUM REVENUE TAX. A tax on profits from oil and natural gas produced in the United Kingdom, and in its territorial waters and its continental shelf. Imposed by the Oil Taxation Act 1975.

PETTY BAG OFFICE. The office belonging to the common law side of the Court of Chancery, out of which writs issued in matters wherein the Crown was mediately or immediately concerned; so called because the writs were kept originally in a little sack or bag, *in parva baga*. The Petty Bag Office was also formerly used for suits for and against officers of the Court of Chancery. When the common law jurisdiction of the Court of Chancery was transferred to the High Court of Justice the office of Clerk of the Petty Bag was abolished. [CHANCERY; HANAPER OFFICE.]

PETTY JURY. Twelve good and lawful men of a county impanelled by the sheriff for the trial of issues of fact in criminal cases; so called in opposition to the former grand jury. [GRAND JURY; JURY.]

PETTY LARCENY. Theft under the value of twelve pence, formerly distinguished from *grand* larceny, which was theft to a higher amount. This distinction is now abolished; and the Larceny Acts of 1861 and 1916 were repealed by the Theft Act 1968.

PETTY SERJEANTY. [PETIT SERJEANTY.]

PETTY SESSIONS. The sitting of two or more justices or a metropolitan or stipendiary magistrate or the Lord Mayor or an alderman of the City of London for trying offences in a summary way under various Acts of Parliament empowering them to do so; for making orders in bastardy, appeals, and other civil purposes. See also s. 13 (12) of the Interpretation Act 1889.

PETTY TREASON. [PETIT TREASON.]

PEW. An enclosed seat in a church. The right to sit in a particular pew in a church arises either from prescription, the pew being appurtenant to a messuage, or from a faculty or grant from the ordinary, who has the disposition of all pews which are not claimed by prescription.

PHOTOGRAPH. Photographs are included in the definition of "artistic works" in s. 3 of the Copyright Act 1956, irrespective of whether, in fact, they have any artistic quality. Copyright protection is given by the Act to the author of any photograph: "author" being the person

PHOTOGRAPH—*continued.*
who, at the time when the photograph is taken, is the owner of the material on which it is taken. "Photograph" means any product of photography or of any process akin to photography. Copyright in cinematograph films is separately dealt with under s. 13 of the 1956 Act.

PICCAGE, PICAGE, or **PICKAGE.** Money paid in fairs, for breaking the ground to set up booths or stalls.

PICKETING. The posting of persons outside a manufactory or place of business to molest or intimidate workmen.

By s. 15 of the Trade Union and Labour Relations Act 1974 it is enacted that it is lawful for one or more persons in contemplation or furtherance of a trade dispute to attend at or near (*a*) the place where another person works or carries on business; or (*b*) any other place where another person happens to be, not being a place where he resides, for the purpose only of peacefully obtaining or communicating information, or peacefully persuading any person to work or abstain from working.

In *Hubbard* v. *Pitt,* [1975] 3 All E.R. 1, Lord Denning said: "Picketing is not a nuisance in itself. . . . It does not become a nuisance unless it is associated with obstruction, violence, intimidation, molestation or threats. . . . Picketing is lawful so long as it is done merely to obtain or communicate information, or peacefully to persuade; and is not such as to submit any other person to any kind of constraint or restriction of his personal freedom."

PIE POUDRE COURT. [COURT OF PIEDPOUDRE.]

PIGNUS (Roman Law). A mortgage.

PILOT. He who has the government of a ship, under the master; any person not belonging to a ship who has the conduct thereof. See s. 742 of the Merchant Shipping Act 1894.

PILOTAGE AUTHORITIES are various bodies of persons in different parts of the kingdom, having powers and jurisdictions with regard to the appointment and regulation of pilots for the districts in which they respectively act. [TRINITY HOUSE.]
The Ministry of Transport constitutes the pilotage authority in districts where none already exists.

The employment of a properly qualified and licensed pilot is in general compulsory upon the masters of ships within the limits of the pilotage jurisdictions. Where such pilotage is compulsory the owner and master of the ship are not answerable for any damage caused by the fault or neglect of the compulsory pilot. See the Merchant Shipping Act 1894 and the Pilotage Act 1913.

PIN-MONEY. A sum payable by a husband to a wife for her separate use, in virtue of a particular arrangement, to be applied by the wife in attiring her person in a manner suitable to the rank of her husband, and in defraying other personal expenses.

PIRACY. 1. The crime of piracy consists in committing those acts of robbery and depredation upon the high seas which, if committed upon land, would amount to crime there.
Under the Piracy Acts, the following offences are also to be deemed piratical:—
The betrayal of his trust by a commander or other seafaring person (Piracy Act 1698, s. 8).
Endeavouring to make a revolt on board ship (*ibid.*).
Trading with known pirates, or fitting out a vessel for a piratical purpose, etc. (Piracy Act 1721, s. 1).
2. The infringement of a copyright.

PISCARY. A liberty of fishing in another man's waters. [COMMON, II; FISHERY.]

PIXING THE COIN signifies the ascertaining whether coin is of the proper standard. For this purpose, resort is had on stated occasions to an ancient mode of inquisition called the *trial of the pyx*, before a jury of members of the Goldsmith's Company. See now, as to coinage, the Coinage Act 1971.

PLACITA. Pleas or pleadings. Formerly it signified the public assemblies at which the king presided.

PLAINT. The written statement of an action in the county court, which is entered by the registrar in a book kept for the purpose. See County Court Rules 1936, Ord. 6, r. 3.

PLAINTIFF. By s. 225 of the Judicature Act 1925, "plaintiff" includes every person asking any relief (otherwise than by way of counterclaim as a defendant) against any other person by any form of proceeding, whether the same be taken by action, suit, petition, motion, summons, or otherwise.

PLANNING PERMISSION. Permission to carry out development to land. Such permission must be sought from the local planning authority under the provisions of the Town and Country Planning Act 1971.

PLEA. 1. The defendant's answer to the declaration of the plaintiff in an action at common law. The general division of pleas was into dilatory pleas and peremptory pleas, or, which is nearly the same thing, pleas in abatement and pleas in bar. Pleas in abatement in civil actions are now abolished.

2. A short statement, in answer to a bill in equity, of facts which, if inserted in the bill, would render it demurrable. It differed from an answer, in that an answer was a complete statement of the defendant's case, and contained answers to any interrogatories the plaintiff might have administered.

The pleas formerly used in civil proceedings in the Superior Courts are superseded by the "statement of defence" (q.v.). Pleas in civil causes were called common pleas and in criminal prosecution pleas of the Crown.

PLEADER. One who pleads or draws pleadings. [SPECIAL PLEADER.]

PLEADING is a word used: 1. Of drawing the written pleadings in a suit or action. 2. Of advocating a client's cause *viva voce* in court.

PLEADING OVER is where a party pleads without taking advantage, by demurrer or otherwise, of a defect in his adversary's pleading. Also where a defendant, having demurred or specially pleaded, has judgment given against him on such demurrer or special plea, and proceeds to plead the general issue, he is said to plead over. [DEMURRER; GENERAL ISSUE, PLEA OF; SPECIAL PLEA.]

PLEADINGS are the mutual formal altercations in writing or print between the parties in a suit or action, with a view to the development of the point in controversy between them, and include the proceedings from the statement of claim to issue joined. The general rules of pleading at present in use are contained in the R.S.C. 1965, Ord. 18.

PLEAS OF THE CROWN. [PLEA, 2.]

PLEDGE. 1. The transfer of a chattel by a debtor to his creditor to secure the repayment of the debt.

2. The chattel so transferred.

3. A surety. [FRANK-PLEDGE.]

PLENA PROBATIO. [SUPPLETORY OATH.]

PLENARTY. Fullness: a word indicating that an ecclesiastical benefice is occupied and not vacant.

PLENARY CAUSE. A phrase used in ecclesiastical law of those causes in which the prescribed order of proceedings must be exactly adhered to; as opposed to summary. Plenary causes now comprise only suits for dilapidations, church sittings and tithes.

PLENE ADMINISTRAVIT. A plea by an executor or administrator to an action brought against him as representing the deceased, on the ground that he has already fully administered the estate of the deceased, and that the assets come to his hands have been exhausted in the payment of debts.

PLENE ADMINISTRAVIT PRÆTER. A plea by an executor or administrator that he has fully administered the testator's estate, with the exception of certain assets acknowledged to be still in his hands. If the plea is good the plaintiff should enter judgment in respect of the assets acknowledged to be in the executor's hands and in respect of assets *in futuro* for the residue of his claim.

PLENIPOTENTIARY. A person who is fully empowered to do anything.

PLEVIN. A warrant or assurance.

PLIGHT. An old English word, signifying the estate held by any one in land; also the habit nd quality thereof.

PLIGHT AND CONDITION, AFFIDAVIT OF. In Probate practice this signifies an affidavit proving that a will is in the same condition as that in which it was found at the testator's death.

PLOUGH BOTE. Wood to be employed in repairing instruments of husbandry.

PLOUGH LAND, or carucate, was as much land as a team of oxen could plough in a season.

PLUNDERAGE. Embezzling goods on board ship.

PLURALITY. The having two, three or more benefices. The holder thereof is called a *pluralist.* The holding of benefices in plurality is strictly regulated but not uncommon. The Pluralities Act 1838 provided that benefices might be held in plurality if the distances between such benefices were not more than four miles, and the annual value of one of the benefices did not exceed £400. These limitations do not apply when a plurality is under the Pastoral Measure 1968.

PLURIES. A *pluries* writ is a writ that issues in third place, after two former writs have been disregarded.

POACHING. The unlawful destruction of game, especially by night; also trespassing by night on land in pursuit of game. See the Night Poaching Acts 1828 and 1844, and the Poaching Prevention Act 1862. As to the offences of poaching deer and fish, see the Theft Act 1968, Sch. 1.

POCKET JUDGMENT. A statute merchant, or bond, which was enforceable at any time after nonpayment o the day assigned without the necessity for further proceedings. [STATUTE, 2.]

POCKET SHERIFFS. Sheriffs appointed by the sole authority of the Crown, not having been previously nominated in the Exchequer. The practice of occasionally naming pocket sheriffs continued until the reign of George III. [PRICKING FOR SHERIFFS; SHERIFF.]

POLICE. A force for the due regulation and domestic order of the kingdom. Especially that part of it which is connected with the prevention and detection of crime. [CONSTABLE.]

POLICIES OF ASSURANCE, COURT OF. [COURT OF POLICIES OF ASSURANCE.]

POLICY OF ASSURANCE or **INSURANCE.** [INSURANCE.]

POLICYHOLDERS PROTECTION BOARD. A body set up under the Policyholders Protection Act 1975, to indemnify policyholders who have been prejudiced by the inability of insurance companies to meet their liabilities.

POLITICAL ASYLUM. [ASYLUM.]

POLL. The process of giving and counting votes at an election. [POLLING; POLLS.]

POLL, DEED. [DEED.]

POLL MONEY, POLL SILVER, or **POLL TAX.** A tax by which every person in the kingdom was assessed by the head or poll, according to his degree. It has been imposed at various periods in our history.

POLLING. Counting heads; especially used of counting voters at an election.

POLLS. Heads or individuals; also the place where polling takes place for the purpose of an election. [CHALLENGE, 2.]

POLLUTION. [TRADE EFFLUENT.]

POLYGAMY. The having more wives than one. The Matrimonial Proceedings (Polygamous Marriages) Act 1972 empowers the court to grant matrimonial relief and to make declarations concerning the validity of a marriage notwithstanding that the marriage in question was entered into under a law which permits polygamy.

PONDUS REGIS. The king's weight; signifying the original standard of weights and measures in the time of Richard I.

PONE. 1. A writ whereby a cause depending in an inferior court might be removed into the Court of Common Pleas. Obsolete.

2. *Pone per vadium et plegios* was a writ whereby the sheriff was commanded to take security of a man for his appearance at a day assigned. It generally issued when a defendant failed to appear. Obsolete.

PONTAGE. A toll or tax for the maintenance or repair of bridges.

POOR LAWS. Laws formerly relating to the relief of the poor, but which have been superseded by the National Assistance Acts, National Health Service Acts and the Social Security Acts.

POOR PERSON. [FORMA PAUPERIS.]

POOR RATE. The rate formerly levied by churchwardens and overseers for the relief of the poor.

POPULAR ACTION. [QUI TAM ACTIONS.]

PORT. A place where persons and merchandise are allowed to pass into and out of the realm. The duty of appointing ports and sub-ports, and declaring the limits thereof, is confided, by s. 13 of the Customs and Excise Act 1952 to the Commissioners of Customs and Excise. See also the Administration of Justice Act 1956, by s. 4 of which "port" means any port, harbour, river, estuary, haven, dock, canal or other place so long as a person or body of persons is empowered by or under an Act to make charges in respect of ships entering it or using the facilities therein.

PORTION. A part of a person's estate which is given or left to a child or person to whom another stands in *loco parentis*. The word is specially applied to payments made to younger children out of the funds comprised in their parents' marriage-settlement, and in pursuance of the trusts thereof. [ADVANCEMENT; SATISFACTION.]

POSITIVE LAW is properly synonymous with law properly so called. For every law is *put* or set by its author. But in practice the expression is confined to laws set by a sovereign to a person or persons in a state of subjection to their author; that is, to laws enacted by sovereign States, or by their authority, disobedience to which is *malum prohibitum*. [MALA IN SE.]

POSSE. A word signifying a possibility. A thing *in posse* means a thing which may be; as opposed to a thing *in esse*, or in being.

POSSE COMITATUS. The power of the county; that is, the people of the county whom the sheriff might command to attend him for keeping of the peace and pursuing felons; also for defending the country against the Queen's enemies. To this summons all persons, except peers, women, clergymen, persons decrepit, and infants under the age of fifteen, were bound to attend, under pain of fine and imprisonment. Now obsolete.

POSSESSIO FRATRIS FACIT SOROREM ESSE HEREDEM (the possession of the brother makes the sister heir). A maxim indicating that if a man, having a son and daughter by a first wife, and a son (with or without other children) by a second wife, died intestate, and his eldest son died after him without entering on the land; then the younger son would inherit as heir to their common father, who was the last person actually seised. But if the eldest brother, before his death, entered and took possession, and died seised of the land and intestate, that possession enabled the sister to succeed in exclusion of the brother; because the descent was traced from the person last seised. This maxim would not now apply; for, by s. 2 of the Inheritance Act 1833, the descent is to be traced from the *purchaser*; that is, the last person who acquired the land *otherwise than by descent*. So that, in the case above put, there could be no descent traced from the eldest son, as he himself succeeded to the land by descent; and the younger brother would inherit, as from the father, on the death of the elder brother intestate.

POSSESSION. 1. When a man actually enters into lands and tenements. This is called actual possession.

2. When lands and tenements descend to a man, and he has not yet entered into them. This is called possession in law. Thus there are estates in possession as opposed to estates in remainder or reversion. Into the former a man has a right to enter at once; of the latter the enjoyment is delayed.

3. The exercise of the right of ownership, whether rightfully or wrongfully. This has been defined as "physical detention, coupled with the intention to use the thing detained as one's own".

4. As used in the Law of Property Act 1925, possession includes receipt of rents and profits or the right to receive the same, if any. See s. 205 (1) (xix).

POSSESSION MONEY. The fee payable to the sheriff's officer for keeping possession of property under writ of execution.

POSSESSION, WRIT OF. A writ giving a person possession of land. A phrase used especially with reference to the fictitious plaintiff in the old action of ejectment. See R.S.C. 1965, Ord. 45.

POSSESSORY ACTION was an action brought for the purpose of regaining possession of land whereof the demandant or his ancestors had been unjustly deprived by the tenant or possessor of the freehold, or those under whom he claimed. Abolished in 1833. [ASSIZE, WRIT OF; ENTRY, WRIT OF.]

POSSESSORY TITLE. Under the Land Registration Act 1925 land may be registered with a possessory title, on the

POSSESSORY TITLE—*continued.*

applicant or his nominee giving such evidence of title and serving such notices, if any, as may for the time being be prescribed (s. 4). The registration of a person as first registered proprietor of freehold land with a possessory title only, does not affect or prejudice the enforcement of any estate, right or interest adverse to or in derogation of the title of the first proprietor, and subsisting or capable of arising, at the time of registration of that proprietor; but, save as aforesaid, has the same effect as registration of a person with an absolute title (s. 6). [ABSOLUTE TITLE.] For the effect of registration of leaseholds with a possessory title, see s. 11 of the Act.

It should be noted that if, on an application for registration with a possessory title, the registrar is satisfied as to the title to the freehold estate, he may register it as absolute, whether the applicants consent or not, but no higher fee is to be charged than would have been charged for registration with possessory title (s. 4, proviso (iii)).

POSSIBILITY. A chance or expectation. Possibilities are of two kinds:—

1. A bare possibility, such as that (which existed before 1926) of the eldest son succeeding, on his father's decease intestate, to the inheritance of his lands. -

2. A possibility *coupled with an interest*, or, in other words, a possibility recognised in law as an estate or interest; as the chance of B succeeding to an estate, held by A for his life, in the event of C not being alive at A's death. In this sense it includes a contingent remainder. See now s. 4 (2) of the Law of Property Act 1925, which provides that all rights and interests in land may be disposed of, including a possibility coupled with an interest. [CONTINGENCY WITH DOUBLE ASPECT.]

POST. After. Occurring in a book it refers to a later page or line.

POST ENTRY. When goods are weighed or measured, and the merchant has got an account thereof at the Custom House, and finds his entry already made too small, he must make a *post* or additional *entry* for the surplusage, in the same manner as the first was done. Post entries are usually confined to cargoes of grain.

POST FINE. A duty formerly paid to the king by the cognisee in a fine, when the same was fully passed. [FINE, 1.]

POST LITEM MOTAM. After a suit has been in contemplation; or, "after an issue has become, or appeared likely to become, a subject of judicial controversy".

POST MORTEM (after death), *e.g.*, a *post mortem* examination of a corpse, to ascertain the cause of death.

POST OBIT BOND. A bond executed by a person on the receipt of money from another, whereby the borrower binds himself to pay to the lender a sum exceeding the sum so received, and the ordinary interest thereof, upon the death of a person upon whose decease he (the borrower) expects to become entitled to some property.

POSTDATING AN INSTRUMENT. The dating of an instrument as of a date after that on which it is executed. A bill, note or cheque may be post-dated. See the Bills of Exchange Act 1882, s. 13.

POSTEA. According to the practice formerly observed in actions at common law, the *postea* was the record of that which was done subsequently to the joining of issue; it stated the appearance of the parties, judge and jury, at the place of trial, and the verdict of the latter on the issues joined, and was indorsed on the *nisi prius* record by the associate. The associate's certificate now forms the substitute for the postea. [NISI PRIUS RECORD.]

POSTLIMINIUM. A fiction in the Roman law by which a person who, having been taken captive by the enemy, returned from captivity, was deemed never to have lost his liberty or his *status* as a citizen. A similar fiction is applied in some cases in international law, *e.g.*, by prize courts in the case of goods captured in war by an enemy, and afterwards rescued.

POSTMASTER-GENERAL. The former title of the master of the Post Office. His powers included the establishment of posts and post offices, and the collection and delivery of postal packets. He had the exclusive privilege of collecting, despatching and delivering mail within the British postal area.

The office was abolished by s. 1 of the Post Office Act 1969, and his functions were, by s. 3, transferred to a Minister of Posts and Telecommunications. That

Ministry, in turn, was abolished in 1974, the functions of the Minister being transferred to a Secretary of State.

POST-NUPTIAL. After marriage; thus a post-nuptial settlement is a settlement made after marriage, and, not being made on the consideration of marriage, it is in general considered as *voluntary*, that is, as having been made on no valuable consideration. [CONSIDERATION.]

POSTPONEMENT OF TRIAL may be applied for on sufficient grounds which must appear by affidavit. See as to civil trials, R.S.C. 1965, Ord. 35, r. 3.

POSTREMOGENITURE. The right of the youngest born. [BOROUGH ENGLISH.]

POST WAR CREDITS. Amounts credited to individual taxpayers in respect of additional tax charged during the war years 1941–1946 and subsequently repaid.

POTENTIA PROPINQUA is a common possibility, which may reasonably be expected to happen.

POTENTIA REMOTA is a remote possibility, which cannot reasonably be expected to happen.

POTWALLERS, or **POT-WALLOPERS.** Such as cooked their own diet in a fireplace of their own, and were on that account entitled, by the custom of some boroughs, to vote in the parliamentary election for the borough. The rights of such persons as were entitled, on this account, at the time of the passing of the Representation of the People Act 1832, to exercise the franchise, were preserved during their lives.

POULTRY. Domestic fowls, ducks, geese, guinea-fowls, pigeons and turkeys: see s. 14 of the Protection of Birds Act 1954; also, for the purposes of the Diseases of Animals Act 1950, pheasants and partridges. [LIVESTOCK.]

POUND (Lat. *Parcus*) is an enclosure for keeping cattle or other goods distrained. By s. 10 of the Distress for Rent Act 1737 any person distraining for rent may turn any part of the premises, upon which a distress is taken, into a pound, *pro hac vice*, for securing of such distress. A pound is either pound *overt*, that is, open overhead; or pound *covert*, that is, close. [DISTRESS.]

POUNDAGE. 1. A subsidy to the value of twelve pence in the pound on all manner of merchandise, formerly granted to the king.

2. A sheriff's allowance on the amount levied by him in execution. See s. 20 of the Sheriffs Act 1887; and R.S.C. 1965, Ord. 47, r. 4.

POUNDBREACH. The destruction of a pound, or any part, lock, or bolt thereof, or the taking of cattle or other goods from the place where they are impounded. See the Distress for Rent Act 1689 and the Pound-Breach Act 1843.

POURSUIVANT. The Queen's messenger. Those formerly attending the kings in their wars were called *Poursuivants-at-Arms*.

There are four poursuivants in the Herald's Office, called respectively *Rouge Croix, Bluemantle, Rouge Dragon*, and *Portcullis*.

POWER is an authority to dispose of any real or personal property independently of or even in defeasance of any existing estate or interest therein. The person entitled to exercise the power (who is called the *donee of the power*) may have no interest in the property in question, in which case the power is called a power *collateral* or *in gross*; or he may himself have an interest in the property, and the power is then called a power *coupled with an interest*, or a power *appendant* or *appurtenant*, *e.g.*, in case of a parent having a life interest in property, with power to appoint the property (either by deed or will) to his children after his death. The exercise of the power is called an *appointment*; and the persons taking the property under such an appointment are called *appointees*, and not grantees or assigns.

Powers may be *general*, giving right to appoint as the donee may think fit, or *special* only in favour of some or all of certain persons or classes of persons. Also they may be powers of *revocation*, *e.g.*, in voluntary settlements, or of *revocation and new appointment*, *e.g.*, in marriage settlements to enable shares of children to be rearranged. After 1925 powers of appointment, with certain exceptions, will operate only in equity. See s. 1 (7) of the Law of

POWER—*continued.*

Property Act 1925. [ILLUSORY APPOINTMENT.]

POWER OF ATTORNEY. An authority given by one to another to act for him in his absence, *e.g.*, to convey land, receive debts, sue, etc. The party so authorised to act is called the *attorney* of the party giving the authority. See the Powers of Attorney Act 1971, which provides that a power of attorney must be made by deed. A form of general power of attorney is printed in Sch. 1 to the Act.

POYNINGS' LAW was an Act of Parliament (otherwise called the Statute of Drogheda) made in Ireland by Henry VII, in the year 1495, whereby it was enacted that all the statutes in England then in force should be in force in Ireland, It was called Poynings Law because Sir Edward Poynings was at that time Lord Lieutenant of Ireland. Other Poynings' laws are mentioned.

PRACTICE is the procedure in a court of justice, through the various stages of any matter, civil or criminal, depending before it.

The practice in the Supreme Court of Judicature is now regulated by the Supreme Court of Judicature (Consolidation) Act 1925, and the Rules of the Supreme Court 1965, and amending rules, which may be found in the "Annual Practice". As to the practice of the county courts see the County Courts Act 1959, and the County Court Rules 1936, which continue in force as if made under the Act of 1959.

PRACTICE COURT. [BAIL COURT.]

PRACTICE MASTER. One of the Queen's Bench Masters, sitting by rotation for the purpose of answering queries as to points of practice. One such Master is on duty each week day throughout the year (save on bank holidays and days when the courts are closed) according to a rota arranged from time to time. See R.S.C. 1965, Ord. 63, r. 2.

PRACTITIONER. A doctor, dentist or veterinary surgeon. See s. 132 of the Medicines Act 1968.

PRÆCIPE. 1. An original writ commanding a person to do a thing, or show the reason wherefore he has not done it. Abolished.

2. A note of instructions formerly delivered by a plaintiff or his solicitor to the officer of the court who stamped the writ of summons, specifying the county in which the defendant was supposed to reside, the nature of the writ, the names of the plaintiff and defendant, and the name of the solicitor issuing the writ, and the date. Still necessary in the County Court.

No writ of *execution* can be issued without the party issuing it, or his solicitor, filing a præcipe for the purpose. See R.S.C. 1965, Ord. 46, r. 6.

PRÆCIPE IN CAPITE. A writ of right, brought by one of the king's immediate tenants *in capite*, was called a *præcipe in capite.* [IN CAPITE; WRIT OF RIGHT.]

PRÆCIPE QUOD REDDAT (command that he restore). A writ by which a person was directed to restore the possession of land; a phrase used especially of the writ by which a *common recovery* was commenced. Abolished. [RECOVERY.]

PRÆCIPE, TENANT TO THE, signified a tenant in a real action, against whom a *præcipe* or writ was sued. But the phrase was especially used of the person against whom, in the proceeding called a *common recovery*, the fictitious action was to be brought. [RECOVERY.]

PRÆDIAL TITHES. Tithes paid out of the produce of land. [TITHES.]

PRÆFINE. The same as *primer fine.* [FINE, 1.]

PRÆMUNIRE. Under the Statute of Præmunire 1392 it was an offence to procure, at Rome or elsewhere, any translations, processes, excommunications, bulls, instruments or other things, against the king, his crown and realm, to which, by a further statute of 1400 (now repealed) was added the offence of accepting any provision of the Pope, to be exempt from obedience to the proper ordinary. The offence was so called from the words *præmunire facias* (cause him to be forewarned, *præmunire* being a barbarous word for *præmoneri*), by which the writ for the citation of the party charged with any such offence was commenced.

PRÆPOSITUS. 1. A person in authority; hence the word *provost.* A *præpositus regius* was an officer of a hundred.

2. The person from whom descent is traced under the old canons.

PRÆSCRIPTION. [PRESCRIPTION.]

PRAY IN AID is a phrase often used to signify "claiming the benefit of an argument". Especially in suits or actions in which there are several parties, the above phrase is sometimes used by a counsel who claims the benefit, on behalf of his own client, of an argument already used on behalf of some other party in the suit or action.

PREAMBLE OF A STATUTE. The recital at the beginning of some Acts of Parliament, to explain the minds of the makers of the Act, and the mischiefs they intend to remedy by the same.

In the case of private bills, if the Committee of either House, before whom the bill comes, find the preamble "not proven", the bill is lost.

PRE-AUDIENCE. The priority of right of being heard in a court of justice, as the Attorney and Solicitor General before Queen's Counsel, and Queen's Counsel before junior barristers, etc.

PREBEND. A fixed portion of the rents and profits of a cathedral church set apart for the maintenance of the prebendaries.

PRECATORY WORDS. These are words in a will or settlement "praying" or "desiring" that a thing shall be done. In some cases it is held that such words create a trust; and such a trust is sometimes called a *precatory trust.*

PRECEDENCE, PATENT OF. [PATENT OF PRECEDENCE.]

PRECEDENCE, TABLE OF. The table of rules regulating the respective priorities of the various orders and dignities within the realm.

PRECEDENT CONDITION. [CONDITIONS PRECEDENT AND SUBSEQUENT.]

PRECEDENTS are examples which may be followed. The word is used principally, though by no means exclusively, to indicate one of the two following things:—

1. A decision in a court of justice cited in support of any proposition for which it is desired to contend. A prior decision of the House of Lords is binding upon all inferior courts, though no longer necessarily upon the House of Lords itself, and nothing but an Act of Parliament can alter it.

2. Drafts of deeds, wills, mortgages, pleadings, etc., which may serve as patterns for future draftsmen and conveyancers.

PRECEPT. 1. A commandment in writing sent out by a justice of the peace or other like officer for the bringing of a person or record before him.

2. An instigation to murder or other crime. In this sense the word is quite obsolete.

3. The direction issued by a sheriff to the proper returning officers of cities and boroughs within his jurisdiction for the election of members to serve in parliament.

4. The direction by the clerk of the peace, judges or commissioners of assize to the sheriff for the summoning a sufficient number of jurors.

5. The direction formerly issued by the clerk of the peace to the overseers of parishes for making out the jury lists.

6. The demand for money made upon rating authorities by those local authorities which are not rating authorities.

PRECINCT. Boundary. Hence it signifies—

1. A certain limited district round some important edifice, as a cathedral.

2. The local district for which a high or petty constable is appointed. [CONSTABLE.]

3. A place formerly privileged from arrests.

PRE-CONTRACT. A contract made before another contract; especially with reference to a contract of marriage, which, according to the ancient law, rendered void a subsequent marriage solemnised in violation of it.

PREDIAL TITHES. [PRÆDIAL TITHES.]

PRE-EMPTION. 1. A right of purchasing before another; a privilege formerly allowed to the king's purveyor. As to registration of rights of pre-emption, see s. 2 (4) (iv) of the Land Charges Act 1972; and as to releases of such rights, see s. 186 of the Law of Property Act 1925, which provides that if not released they shall remain in force as equitable interests only.

2. A right given to the owner from whom lands have been acquired by compulsory powers in case such lands should become *superfluous* for the undertaking for which they were acquired. See ss. 127–129 of the Lands Clauses Consolidation Act 1845.

PRE-EMPTION—*continued*.

3. In international law it signifies the right of a belligerent compulsorily to purchase merchandise of a neutral at its mercantile value to prevent it falling into the hands of the enemy.

PREFER often means to bring a matter before a court of justice; as when it is said that A preferred a charge of assault against B.

PREFERENCE (FRAUDULENT). A term used in connection with payments, transfers, conveyances, etc., made by a person unable to pay his debts by way of preference to some of his creditors over others. All such payments, etc., are fraudulent and void as against the trustee in bankrupty if the debtor becomes bankrupt within three months. See s. 44 of the Bankruptcy Act 1914. As to fraudulent settlements, see *ibid.*, s. 27.

PREFERENCE SHARES in a company are shares entitling their holders to preferential dividend; so that a holder of preference shares is entitled to have the whole of his dividend (or so much thereof as represents the extent to which his shares are, by the constitution of the company, to be deemed preference shares) paid before any dividend is paid to the ordinary shareholders. Usually such shares have preference also in regard to capital in the event of winding up.

PREFERENTIAL PAYMENTS. Payments that are made in preference to the rights of others in bankruptcy, the winding up of companies, or the administration of estates of persons dying insolvent. On a winding up one year's rates and taxes, sums due for value added tax, four months' salaries of clerks and four months' wages of labourers up to two hundred pounds in each case, and certain amounts under the Social Security Acts, are payable in priority to all other debts. See Companies Act 1948, s. 319. [PREFERENCE, FRAUDULENT.]

PREGNANCY, PLEA OF. [JURY OF MATRONS.]

PREJUDICE. Prejudicing a matter. Thus, for instance, a court may decide that A is entitled for his life to the income of a fund "without prejudice" to any question between B and C, who claim adversely to each other the income of the fund after his

death. And generally, the expression "without prejudice" implies that the consideration of the question to which it refers is postponed to a future time. And the phrase is often used in a lawyer's letter for the purpose of guarding himself as to anything therein contained being construed as an admission of liability.

PRELIMINARY ACT. In actions for damage by collision between vessels a sealed document giving all particulars of the collision must be filed by the solicitor for each side before any pleadings are delivered; such document is called a preliminary act. See R.S.C. 1965, Ord. 75, r. 18.

PREMIER. [PRIME MINISTER.]

PREMISES (Lat. *Præmissa*). 1. The commencement of a deed, setting forth the number and names of the parties, with their additions or titles, and the recital, if any, of such deeds and matters of fact as are necessary to explain the reasons upon which the deed is founded; the consideration upon which it is made; and, if the deed be a disposition of property, the particulars of the property intended to be thereby transferred; also the operative words, with the exceptions and reservations (if any).

2. Hence it has come to signify the lands granted; and hence any specified houses or lands.

3. Propositions antecedently supposed or proved.

PREMIUM. 1. A reward.

2. The periodical payment for the insurance of life or property.

3. A lump sum or fine paid for the granting of a lease.

4. A sum paid in excess of the nominal value of shares or stock.

PREMUNIRE. [PRÆMUNIRE.]

PREPENSE. Aforethought. Thus, malice prepense is equivalent to malice-aforethought. [MALICE.]

PREROGATIVE. The special power, pre-eminence or privilege which the Queen has, over and above other persons, in right of her crown and independently of statute and the courts.

PREROGATIVE COURTS. The courts of the provinces of Canterbury and York respectively, presided over by judges appointed by the respective archbishops.

The jurisdiction of these courts has become practically obsolete as the testamentary jurisdiction of the ecclesiastical courts has now been transferred to the Chancery Division of the High Court.

PREROGATIVE WRITS are writs which in their origin arise from the extraordinary powers of the Crown. They differ from other writs mainly in the two following points:—

1. They do not issue as of mere course, nor without some probable cause being shown why the extraordinary powers of the Crown should be called in to the party's assistance.

2. They are generally directed, not to a sheriff or other public officer, but to the parties themselves whose acts are the subject of complaint.

They are, or were, the writs of *procedendo, mandamus, prohibition, quo warranto, habeas corpus,* and *certiorari.* See these titles and the Administration of Justice (Miscellaneous Provisions) Act 1938.

PRESCRIBE TO. To assert or claim anything by title or prescription. [PRESCRIPTION.]

PRESCRIPTION. 1. *Præscriptio,* in the Roman law, was an exception *written in front* of the plaintiff's pleading. Afterwards it became applied exclusively to the *præscriptio longi temporis,* etc., or the prescription founded on length of possession. Hence its modern meaning. It was allowed by way of equitable plea where a defendant, sued in reference to the possession of property, had complied with the main conditions of *usucapion,* without having acquired ownership by usucapion. [USUCAPION.]

2. Prescription at common law, as defined by Blackstone, is where a man can show no other title to what he claims than that he, and those under whom he claims, have immemorially used and enjoyed it. The difference between prescription and custom is, that custom is a *local* usage, and not annexed to any *person,* whereas prescription is a *personal* usage. Prescription may, perhaps, in this sense be defined as the presumption of a grant arising from long usage.

This still applies to the acquisition of rights not included in the Prescription Act 1832, *e.g.,* right of support for buildings.

The Act of 1832 provides that a thirty years' enjoyment of rights of *common,* and other profits or benefits to be taken or enjoyed upon any land, shall no longer be defeated by proof that the enjoyment commenced at a period subsequent to legal memory [LEGAL MEMORY]; and that a prescriptive claim of sixty years' enjoyment shall be absolute and indefeasible except by proof that such enjoyment took place under some deed, or written consent or agreement. In the case of *ways* and *watercourses,* the periods are twenty and forty years respectively. In the case of *lights,* the period is twenty years absolute, save for the purpose of certain proceedings under the Rights of Light Act 1959, when the period is twenty-seven years.

The above is styled *positive* or *acquisitive prescription,* namely, that by which a title is acquired (as the *usucapio* of the Roman law), and in the English law properly applies to incorporeal hereditaments only. *Negative* prescription is that by which a right of challenge is lost (as the prescription under the Statutes of Limitation), and this is applicable to corporeal rights; thus if an owner of land in the wrongful possession of another does not sue within twelve years from the time when such wrongful possession was obtained, he will usually lose his right to the property. See the Limitation Act 1939, the Rights of Way Act 1932, and the Law of Property Act 1925, s. 12, which provides that nothing in Part I of the Act shall affect the operation of any Statute of Limitation relating to land or any law with reference to the acquistion of easements or rights over or in respect of land.

PRESENTATION. The act of a patron in offering his clerk to the bishop, to be instituted in a benefice of his gift. It includes collation, nomination, and any other manner of filling vacant benefices. See the Pastoral Measure 1968. [ADVOWSON; PRESENTMENT.]

PRESENTATIVE ADVOWSON. [ADVOWSON.]

PRESENTEE. A clerk presented by the patron of a living to the bishop. [ADVOWSON; PRESENTATION.]

PRESENTMENT. 1. Presentation to a benefice. [PRESENTATION.]

PRESENTMENT—*continued*.

2. The formal information to the lord, by the tenants of a manor, of anything done out of court.

3. An information formerly made by a jury in a court before a judge who had authority to punish an offence. It was used of notice taken by a grand jury of anything from their own knowledge or observation. Such "presentment" is obsolete. The better known meaning of the term was when the grand jury, after hearing evidence in support of a bill of indictment found that there was sufficient ground to warrant its trial. This finding was known as the "presentment". Grand juries have been abolished.

4. The presenting a bill of exchange to the drawee for acceptance, or to the acceptor for payment. See the Bills of Exchange Act 1882, ss. 39 *et seq.* [ACCEPTANCE OF A BILL; BILL OF EXCHANGE.]

PRESENTS. A word in a deed signifying the deed itself, which is expressed by the phrase "these presents". It is especially used in a deed-poll, which cannot be described as "This Indenture". But see s. 57 of the Law of Property Act 1925, which provides that any deed may be described as a deed simply, or as a conveyance, mortgage, lease, or otherwise according to the nature of the transaction intended to be effected.

PRESIDENT OF THE COUNCIL. (Lord President of the Council.) A high officer of the State, whose office is to attend on the sovereign, and to propose business at the council table. He is a member of the Judicial Committee of the Privy Council, and of the Cabinet. [JUDICIAL COMMITTEE OF THE PRIVY COUNCIL.]

PRESUMPTION. That which comes near, in greater or less degree, to the proof of a fact. It is called violent, probable, or light, according to the degree of its cogency. Presumptions are also divided into— (1) *præsumptiones juris et de jure*, otherwise called irrebuttable presumptions (often, but not necessarily, fictitious), which the law will not suffer to be rebutted by any counter-evidence; as, that an infant under eight years is not responsible for his actions; (2) *præsumptiones juris tantum*, which hold good in the absence of counter-evidence, but against which counter-evidence may be admitted; and (3) *præsumptiones hominis*, which are not necessarily conclusive, though no proof to the contrary be adduced.

PRESUMPTION OF DEATH. The presumption that a man is dead where there is no direct evidence of the fact. This presumption takes place when a man has not been heard of for seven years; but the presumption is simply that the man is dead, and not that he died at the end of the seven years, or any other specified time. So that if B, a legatee under A's will, has been last heard of six years before A's death, B's representatives will not, after A has been dead a year, be entitled to presume that B survived A, so as to claim the legacy for themselves.

PRESUMPTION OF SURVIVORSHIP is the presumption that A survived B, or B survived A, when there is no evidence which died first, *e.g.*, when both perish in the same ship wreck. The law of England recognised no such presumption, and survivorship had to be proved. Under s. 184 of the Law of Property Act 1925 the presumption (subject to any order of the court) was that the younger survived. [COMMORIENTES.]

PRESUMPTIVE EVIDENCE. A term especially used of evidence which, if believed, would not be necessarily conclusive as to the fact in issue, but from which, according to the ordinary course of human affairs, the existence of that fact might be presumed. In this sense it is synonymous with circumstantial evidence.

PRESUMPTIVE HEIR. [HEIR APPARENT.]

PRESUMPTIVE TITLE. One which arises out of the mere occupation of property without any apparent right or pretence of right.

PRETENDED, or **PRETENSED, RIGHT** or **TITLE** (Lat. *Jus prætensum*) was the right or title to land set up by one who was out of possession against the person in possession. The Maintenance and Embracery Act 1540 (repealed by the Criminal Law Act 1967) forbade the sale of a pretended right or title to land, unless the vendor had received the profits for one whole year before the grant, or had been in actual possession of the land, or of the possession of the land, or of the reversion or remainder, on pain that both purchaser and vendor should each forfeit the value of such land to the king and the prosecutor. Compare the Law of Property Act 1925, s. 4.

PREVARICATION originally signified the conduct of an advocate who betrayed the cause of his client, and by collusion assisted his opponent, hence it signifies collusion between an informer and a defendant in a feigned prosecution; also any secret abuse committed in a public office or private commission. To say that a witness *prevaricates* means that he gives quibbling and evasive answers to questions put to him.

PREVENTIVE DETENTION. The court might formerly pass a sentence of corrective training upon a persistent offender with a view to his reformation and the prevention of crime. Preventive detention and corrective training were abolished by the Criminal Justice Act 1967, but s. 28 of the Powers of Criminal Courts Act 1973 empowers the court to impose an extended sentence of imprisonment upon any persistent offender. [PERSISTENT OFFENDER.]

PREVENTIVE JUSTICE is that portion of law which has reference to the direct prevention of offences. It generally consists in obliging those persons, whom there is probable ground to suspect of future misbehaviour, to give full assurance to the public that such offences as is apprehended shall not happen, by finding pledges or securities to keep the peace, or for their good behaviour. [GOOD BEHAVIOUR; KEEPING THE PEACE.]

PRICKING FOR SHERIFFS. The custom with regard to the appointment of sheriffs is, that all the judges, together with the other great officers, meet in the Court of Exchequer (*scil.*, Queen's Bench Division of the High Court of Justice) on the morrow of St. Martin (that is, on the 12th of November), and then and there the judges propose three persons for each county, to be reported (if approved of) to the king or queen, who afterwards appoints one of them for sheriff. This appointment is made by marking each name with the prick of a pin, and is therefore called "pricking for sheriffs". This mode of appointment was continued by the Sheriffs Act 1887, which

consolidated the law relating to sheriffs. The Sheriffs of London and Middlesex are now appointed by the Queen. See the Local Government Act 1972, s. 219.

PRIEST. A person in Holy Orders either in the Church of England or of Rome. Except by special dispensation, no person under 24 years of age can be ordained a priest.

PRIMA FACIE CASE. A litigating party is said to have a *prima facie* case when the evidence in his favour is sufficiently strong for his opponent to be called on to answer it. A *prima facie* case, then, is one which is established by sufficient evidence, and can be overthrown only by rebutting evidence adduced on the other side.

PRIMA FACIE EVIDENCE. A phrase sometimes used to denote evidence which established a *prima facie* case in favour of the party adducing it. [PRIMA FACIE CASE.]

PRIMÆ IMPRESSIONIS (of first impression). A case of first impression is one as to which there is no precedent directly in point.

PRIMAGE. A payment due to mariners and sailors, for the loading of a ship at the setting forth from any haven.

PRIMARY CONVEYANCES, as opposed to derivative conveyances, are conveyances which do *not* take effect by way of enlarging, confirming, altering, or otherwise affecting other conveyances; they are feoffments, grants, gifts, leases, exchanges, partitions.

PRIMARY EVIDENCE. The best evidence, *i.e.*, evidence which is not secondary, second-hand, or hearsay evidence. [SECONDARY EVIDENCE; SECOND-HAND EVIDENCE.]

PRIMATE. A title given to the archbishops of Canterbury and York, and of Dublin and Armagh.

PRIME MINISTER, or Premier, is a member of either one or other House of Parliament (by constitutional practice, now, of the House of Commons only) selected by the Queen as the person who is most likely to command a working majority in the House of Commons, to be head of the Government.

PRIMER FINE. [FINE, 1.]

PRIMER SEISIN. A burden incident to the king's tenants *in capite*, by which the king was entitled, when any of such tenants died, to receive of the heir, if he were of full age, one whole year's profits of the lands, if they were in immediate possession; and half a year's profits if they were in reversion expectant upon an estate for life. [IN CAPITE.]

PRIMITIÆ. The first year's profits of a benefice, formerly payable to the Crown. [FIRST FRUITS.]

PRIMOGENITURE. The title of the eldest son in right of his birth, whereby in the United Kingdom before 1926 he succeeded to all the real estate of an intestate parent.

Primogeniture was almost unknown except in the United Kingdom; it arose owing to the exigencies of military service under the feudal system. Under the provisions of Part IV of the Administration of Estates Act 1925, primogeniture was abolished.

PRINCE OF WALES. The eldest son of the reigning sovereign. Edward II, being born at Carnarvon, was the first English Prince of Wales. The heir apparent to the Crown is made Prince of Wales and Earl of Chester by special creation and investiture. He is also Duke of Cornwall by inheritance. The present Prince of Wales was invested at Carnarvon Castle in 1969.

PRINCIPAL. 1. An heirloom (*q.v.*).

2. The amount of money which has been borrowed, as opposed to the interest payable thereon. [INTEREST, 2.]

3. The head of a college or other institution.

4. In criminal law a principal of the first degree was one who committed a felony either directly or through an innocent agent; a principal in the second degree was one who did not commit a felony himself but was present at the time when the felony was committed and assisted the principal in the first degree. In treasons and misdemeanours there were no degrees and accessories before the fact were treated as principals.

The distinction between felony and misdemeanour has now been abolished. [ACCESSORY; FELONY.]

5. A person who employs an agent.

6. A person for whom another becomes surety.

PRINCIPAL CHALLENGE. A challenge to a juror for such a cause assigned as carries with it *prima facie* marks of suspicion. [CHALLENGE.]

PRINTING. As to the requirement of printing of pleadings, affidavits, etc., and the quality and size of paper to be used for documents in the Supreme Court, see R.S.C. 1965, Ord. 66.

PRIORITY. 1. An antiquity of tenure, in comparison with one not so ancient.

2. Any legal precedence or preference; as when we say that certain debts are paid in *priority* to others; or that certain incumbrancers of an estate are allowed *priority* over others, that is, are to be allowed to satisfy their claims out of the estate before the others can be admitted to any share therein, etc. [PREFERENTIAL PAYMENTS.]

PRISAGE. 1. An ancient hereditary duty belonging to the Crown, being the right of taking two tuns of wine from every ship importing into England twenty tuns or more. But, by charter of Edward I, this was exchanged into a duty of two shillings for every tun imported by merchant strangers, and was then called *butlerage* because paid to the king's butler. Abolished in 1811.

2. The share which belongs to the Crown of such merchandises as are taken at sea by way of lawful prize.

PRISON. A place of detention in safe custody, or for punishment after conviction. The law relating to prisons is consolidated in the Prison Act 1952 as amended by the Courts Act 1971.

PRISON BREACH. [BREACH, 5.]

PRIVATE ACT OF PARLIAMENT. A local or personal Act affecting particular persons and private concerns. By s. 9 of the Interpretation Act 1889 every state passed after the year 1850 is to be taken to be a public Act, and judicially noticeable as such, unless the contrary is expressly declared by the Act. [BILL, 4; LOCAL AND PERSONAL ACTS; PRIVATE BILLS.]

PRIVATE BILLS are bills brought into parliament, on the petition of parties interested and on payment of fees. Such bills are brought in generally in the interest of individuals, counties, or other localities, and are distinguished from measures of public policy in which the whole community are interested. *May.* [BILL, 4; LOCAL AND PERSONAL ACTS; PRIVATE ACT OF PARLIAMENT.]

PRIVATE CHAPELS are chapels owned by noblemen and other privileged persons, and used by themselves and their families. They are thus opposed to *public chapels*, otherwise called *chapels of ease*, which are built for the accommodation of particular districts within a parish, in *ease* of the original parish church. As to the licensing of ministers at university, school, etc., chapels, see s. 2 of the Extra-Parochial Ministry Measure 1967.

PRIVATE COMPANY. A private company is a company which by its articles (*a*) restricts the right to transfer its shares; and (*b*) limits the number of its members to fifty, not including persons who are in the employment of the company and persons who, having been formerly in the employment of the company, were while in that employment, and have continued after the determination of that employment to be, members of the company; and (*c*) prohibits any invitation to the public to subscribe for any shares or debentures of the company. See s. 28 of the Companies Act 1948.

PRIVATEERS are defined as armed ships fitted out by private persons, commissioned in time of war by the Lords of the Admiralty, or other lawful authority acting for the Crown in that behalf, to cruise against the enemy. These commissions, when granted, have been usually denominated "letters of marque". [DECLARATION OF PARIS; LETTERS OF MARQUE AND REPRISAL.]

PRIVATION. [DEPRIVATION.]

PRIVIES. [PRIVITY OF CONTRACT; PRIVITY OF ESTATE.]

PRIVILEGE. That which is granted or allowed to any person, or any class of persons, either against or beyond the course of ordinary law; as, for instance, the non-liability of a member of the legislature to any court other than the parliament itself, for words spoken in his place in parliament. Newspapers, too, have a qualified privilege as regards certain reports and other matters, by s. 7 of the Defamation Act 1952. Such qualified privilege extends to fair and accurate reports of proceedings in any dominion legislature,

international organisation or court, etc. (*ibid.*, Schedule).

PRIVILEGE, WRIT OF. A writ formerly in use whereby a member of parliament, when arrested in a civil suit, might claim his deliverance out of custody by virtue of his parliamentary privilege. 1 *Bl.*

PRIVILEGED COMMUNICATION. 1. A communication which, though *prima facie* libellous or slanderous, yet, by reason of the circumstances under which it is made, is protected either absolutely or in the absence of malice from being made the ground of proceedings for libel or slander; *e.g.*, confidential communications without malice, etc.

2. A communication which is protected from disclosure in evidence in any civil or criminal proceeding; *e.g.*, confidential communications between a party and his legal adviser in reference to the matter before the court.

PRIVILEGED COPYHOLDS. [CUSTOMARY FREEHOLD.]

PRIVILEGED DEBTS. [PREFERENTIAL PAYMENTS.]

PRIVILEGED VILLENAGE, otherwise called villein-socage, was a tenure described by Bracton, in which the services were *base* as in villenage, but were *certain*, as in free and common socage. It seems principally to have prevailed among the tenants of the king's demesnes: and was supposed by some to be the same as the tenure in *antient demesne*. [ANCIENT DEMESNE; FREEHOLD; SOCAGE.]

PRIVILEGIUM. 1. A law, *ex post facto*, conferring rights or inflicting a punishment in respect of an act already done.

2. *Property propter*, a qualified property in animals *feræ naturæ*, *i.e.*, a privilege of hunting and taking them in exclusion of others.

PRIVILEGIUM CLERICALE. [BENEFIT OF CLERGY.]

PRIVITY. Knowledge of something being done; knowledge beforehand, and concurrence in it. See *per* Lord Denning, M.R., in *The Eurysthenes*, [1976] 3 All E.R. 243.

PRIVITY OF CONTRACT is the relation subsisting between the parties to the same contract. Thus if A, B, and C mutually

PRIVITY OF CONTRACT
—continued.

contract, there is privity of contract between them; but if A contract with B, and B make an independent contract with C on that same subject matter, there is no privity of contract between A and C.

PRIVITY OF ESTATE between two persons is where their estates are so related to each other that they make but one estate in law, being *derived at the same time* out of the *same original seisin.* Thus if A, the owner of an estate, convey it to B for a term of years, with remainder to C for his life, there is privity of estate between A and C. But if A conveys to B for his life, and B makes a lease for years to C, there is no privity between A and C.

PRIVITY OF TENURE is the relation subsisting between a lord and his immediate tenant.

PRIVY. A partaker; one who has an interest in any action or thing. See the several titles immediately preceding this title.

PRIVY COUNCIL is in law the principal council belonging to the sovereign. Privy councillors are made such by the sovereign's nomination, without either patent or grant: and, on such nomination, they become privy councillors, with the title of Right Honourable during the life of the sovereign who has chosen them, but subject to removal at his or her discretion. The substantial importance of the Privy Council has given way to that of the Cabinet. [JUDICIAL COMMITTEE OF THE PRIVY COUNCIL.]

PRIVY PURSE. Her Majesty's Privy Purse is that portion of the public money voted to the Queen and her consort, which they may deal with as freely as any private individual may with his property. A certain sum per year is assigned by parliament for this purpose. Salaries and expenses of Her Majesty's Household are payable under separate allowances, and these expenses, together with the Privy Purse, a further allowance for Royal bounty, alms, and special Services, and supplementary provision for expenses of the duties of the Royal Family, etc., make up a total of £980,000 allowed annually in the Queen's Civil List by the Civil List Act 1972.

Additional sums may be made under the provisions of the Civil List Act 1975.

PRIVY SEAL and **PRIVY SIGNET.** The seal used for such grants from the Crown, or other things, as pass the Great Seal; first they pass the Privy Signet, then the Privy Seal, and lastly the Great Seal of England. The Privy Seal is also used in matters of small moment which never pass the Great Seal. The Privy Signet is one of the sovereign's seals used for private letters and for grants which pass her hand by bill signed; it is always in the custody of the Queen's secretaries. [LORD PRIVY SEAL.]

PRIZE COURT. An international tribunal created by a special commission under the Great Seal in time of war to settle questions of capture, prize, and booty. See the Naval Prize Acts 1864 to 1916; and see also the Judicature Act 1925, s. 23, declaring that the High Court shall be a Prize Court.

PRIZE OF WAR. A ship or goods captured at sea or seized in port, by maritime or air forces in time of war. When seized at sea, such goods are droits of the Crown; when seized in port they are droits of Admiralty. Prize differs from booty in that the former is taken by maritime or air forces, the latter by land forces.

If a ship, aircraft or goods belonging to a British subject, after being taken as prize by the enemy, is, or are, retaken by any of Her Majesty's ships of war or aircraft, the prize must be restored to the owner on his paying *prize salvage*, one-eighth of the value of the prize as ascertained by the Prize Court, or such other sum, not exceeding one-eighth, as may be agreed.

Formerly *prize bounty* could be granted by the Sovereign under proclamation or Order in Council, such prize bounty being money representing a proportion of captured prizes, and payable to officers and crew of Her Majesty's ships who were actually present at the taking or destroying of any armed enemy ship. Such payments were abolished as to future wars by s. 9 of the Prize Act 1948.

PRIZE-FIGHTING in a public place is an affray, and an indictable misdemeanour on the part both of combatants and backers. *Mere presence* at a prize-fight, however, would seem not to be sufficient to render a person guilty of assault.

PRO FORMA. For form's sake.

PRO HAC VICE. For this occasion. An appointment *pro hac vice* is an appointment for a particular occasion as opposed to a permanent appointment.

PRO INDIVISO. For an undivided part; a phrase used in reference to lands the occupation of which is in joint tenancy or in common. [COMMON, TENANCY IN; JOINT TENANCY.]

PRO INTERESSE SUO. For his own interest. These words are used, especially of a party being admitted to intervene *for his own interest* in a suit instituted between other parties.

PRO RATA. Proportionately.

PRO TANTO. For so much, or so far as it will go; as if a tenant for life make a lease for 100 years, the lease is good *pro tanto*, that is, for such an estate or interest as the tenant for life may lawfully convey.

PROBATE. The exhibiting and proving wills by executors in the High Court upon which the original is deposited in the registry of the court, and a copy, called the *probate copy*, is made out under the seal of the court, and delivered to the executor, together with a certificate of its having been proved. It may be either *in common form* or *in solemn form per testes*, where the will is disputed or irregular. For rules in regard to the granting of probates, see Part VII of the Judicature Act 1925. Contentious business is dealt with in the Chancery Division of the High Court; non-contentious business has been assigned to the Family Division. [SOLEMN FORM.]

PROBATE COURT. A court established by the Court of Probate Act 1857, and to which was transferred the testamentary jurisdiction which up to that time had been exercised by the ecclesiastical courts. The Probate Court was merged in the Supreme Court of Judicature in 1873. Its jurisdiction is now exercised partly by the Chancery Division (contentious business) and partly by the Family Division (non-contentious business).

PROBATE, DIVORCE AND ADMIRALTY DIVISION. A former division of the High Court of Justice. The High Court was reorganised by the Administration of Justice Act 1970. The Probate, Divorce and Admiralty Division was renamed the Family Division, to which the High Court's matrimonial and domestic business was assigned. Admiralty business was assigned to the Queen's Bench Division and contentious probate business was transferred to the Chancery Division.

PROBATION. In certain circumstances a court, instead of sentencing an offender, may make a *probation order*, that is, an order requiring him to be under the supervision of a probation officer for a period of from one to three years. Generally, as to probation and discharge therefrom, see ss. 2–13 of the Powers of Criminal Courts Act 1973.

PROCEDENDO. 1. The writ of *procedendo ad judicium* was a writ which issued when the judge of any subordinate court delayed the parties in refusing to give judgment. The writ commanded him, in the name of the Crown, to proceed to judgment, but without specifying any particular judgment.

2. A writ whereby a cause which was removed on insufficient grounds from an inferior to a superior court by *certiorari* or otherwise was removed back again to the inferior court. [CERTIORARI.]

3. A writ to revive a commission of the peace which has been superseded by writ of *supersedeas*. [COMMISSION OF THE PEACE; CONSERVATOR OF THE PEACE; JUSTICE OF THE PEACE.]

PROCEDURE. The steps taken in an action or other legal proceeding. [PRACTICE.]

PROCESS. 1. The writ commanding the defendant's appearance in an action. This is sometimes called *original* process. Since the Judicature Acts the process for the commencement of all actions is the same in all Divisions of the High Court. It is either a writ of summons or an originating summons. [SUMMONS, 4.]

2. The various writs formerly issued in the course of an action. Those issued subsequently to the first or original writ, and prior to the writs of execution, were called the *mesne process*, and the writs of execution were called the *final process*. [EXECUTION, 1.]

3. The steps taken upon an indictment or other criminal proceeding.

PROCESSUM CONTINUANDO. A writ for the continuance of a process after

PROCESSUM CONTINUANDO
—continued.

the death of the chief justice, or other justices, in the writ of *oyer and terminer*. [ASSIZE, COURTS OF; OYER AND TERMINER.]

PROCHEIN AMY. [NEXT FRIEND.]

PROCLAMATION. A notice publicly given of any thing whereof the Queen thinks fit to advertise her subjects. The Queen cannot by her Proclamation create any offence which was not an offence before, unless parliament confers upon her the power to do so.

PROCLAMATION OF FINES. The proclamation of a fine was a notice openly and solemnly given at all the assizes held in the county where the lands lay, within one year after engrossing the fine; all claims not put in within the time allowed subsequent to the proclamation were barred. [FINE, 1.]

PROCTOR. 1. One who manages another person's affairs.

2. One chosen to represent a cathedral or collegiate church, or the clergy of a diocese, in the Lower House of Convocation. [SYNOD.]

3. One who prosecutes or defends a suit for another; especially certain officers who formerly were exclusively entitled to conduct suits in the ecclesiastical and admiralty courts. [QUEEN'S PROCTOR.]

4. An executive officer of the University.

PROCURATION. [PER PROCURATIONEM; PROCURATIONS.]

PROCURATION FEE. The fee which a scrivener or broker was allowed to take for making a bond. Also the fee charged for obtaining a loan on mortgage.

PROCURATION OF WOMEN. The procuring of women for the purpose of illicit intercourse is an offence under ss. 22, 23 of the Sexual Offences Act 1956.

PROCURATIONS are certain sums of money which parish priests pay yearly to the bishop or archdeacon for his visitation. They were anciently paid in necessary victuals for the visitor and his attendants, but afterwards turned into money.

PROCURATOR FISCAL (*Scotland*). An officer of the sheriff court whose duty it is to inquire into suspected offences in his area. [CROWN SOLICITOR.]

He also acts as public prosecutor. [SHERIFF COURT.]

PROFITS À PRENDRE are rights exercised by one man in the soil of another, accompanied with participation in the profits of the soil thereof, as rights of pasture, or digging sand. *Profits à prendre* differ from easements in that the former are rights of profit, and the latter are mere rights of convenience without profit. [COMMON; EASEMENT.]

PROHIBITION. An order to forbid an inferior court from proceeding in a cause there depending, upon suggestion that the cognizance thereof belongs not to that court.

The order replaces the former prerogative writ, and application is made to the Divisional Court. See the Administration of Justice (Miscellaneous Provisions) Act 1938.

Prohibition differs from injunction, in that prohibition is directed to a court as well as to the opposite party, whereas an injunction is directed to the party alone.

By the Judicature Act 1925, s. 41, no cause or proceeding at any time pending in the High Court of Justice, or before the Court of Appeal, shall be restrained by prohibition or injunction.

PROLICIDE. The destruction of human offspring. [INFANTICIDE.]

PROLIXITY. Unnecessary, superfluous, or impertinent statement. It renders an affidavit liable to be taken off the file, and in pleadings the offending party may be made to pay the costs.

PROLOCUTOR. The officer who, in each House of Convocation, is chosen to preside over the deliberations of that House.

PROMISE. A voluntary engagement by one man to another for the performance or non-performance of some particular thing. It differs from a contract, in that a contract involves the idea of mutuality, which a promise does not. [CONTRACT; COVENANT.]

PROMISSORY NOTE, otherwise called a *note of hand*, is defined by s. 83 of the Bills of Exchange Act 1882 as an unconditional promise in writing, made by one person to another, signed by the maker, engaging to pay on demand or at a fixed or determinable future time, a sum certain in money, to or to the order of a specified person or to bearer. The person who makes the note is called the maker, and the person to whom it is payable is called the payee. It differs from a bill of exchange, in that the maker stands in the place of drawer and acceptor. [BILL OF EXCHANGE; INLAND BILL OF EXCHANGE.]

PROMOTERS. 1. Those who, in popular and penal actions, prosecute offenders in their own name and the Queen's; common informers. The term is now only applied to the prosecutor of an ecclesiastical suit. [ACTIONS, CIVIL AND PENAL; QUI TAM ACTIONS.]

2. Persons or corporations at whose instance private bills are introduced into and passed through parliament. *May.* [BILL, 4.]

3. Especially those who press forward bills for the taking of land for railways and other public purposes; who are then called *promoters of the undertaking.*

4. Persons who assist in establishing companies. See the Companies Act 1948, s. 38.

PROMOTING THE OFFICE OF JUDGE. [OFFICE OF A JUDGE.]

PROMOTION MONEY. Money paid to the promoters of a company for their services in launching the concern. [PROMOTERS, 4.]

PROMULGATION OF A LAW. The publication of a law already made.

PROOF, in Scotch law, corresponds to *evidence* in English law; and *to lead proof* is to produce evidence. [BURDEN OF PROOF; PROBATE; PROVE.]

PROOF OF DEBT means generally the establishment by a creditor of a debt due to him from an insolvent estate, whether of a bankrupt, a deceased person, or a partnership or company in liquidation. [PROVE, 2.]

PROPAGANDA. It is an offence under s. 20 of the London County Council (General Powers) Act 1954 to deface public streets, structures, walls, fences, etc., with "propaganda writings," *i.e.,* any writing, letter, device or sign intended . . . for the purpose of propagating, etc., any principles or views or the dissemination of information.

PROPER FEUDS. The genuine or original feuds in the hands of military persons, and held by military services.

PROPERTY. 1. The highest right a man can have in any thing; which right, according to *Cowel*, no man can have in any lands and tenements, save only the king in right of his crown; or according to *Blackstone*, the sole and despotic dominion which one man claims and exercises over the external things of the world, in total exclusion of the right of any other individual in the universe. Property may be either (*a*) absolute, (*b*) qualified, or (*c*) possessory.

The five following applications of the term have been enumerated by Austin:

(i) A right indefinite in point of user—unrestricted in point of disposition—and unlimited in point of duration. In this sense, it is merely synonymous with the meaning of the term as given above, and is distinguished from a life interest or an interest for years on the one hand, and from a servitude or easement on the other.

(ii) The subject of such a right: as when it is said, that horse or that field is a person's property.

(iii) A right indefinite in point of user, but limited in duration; as, for instance a life interest.

(iv) Right as opposed to possession.

(v) A right availing against the world at large, as opposed to right arising out of contract or quasi-contract.

2. For the purposes of the Law of Property Act 1925, property includes any thing in action, and any interest in real or personal property. See s. 205 (1) (xx).

3. The basic definition of theft in the Theft Act 1968, is the dishonest appropriation of "property" belonging to another with the intention of permanently depriving the other of it. [THEFT.]

Section 4 of the Act gives an elaborate exposition of what is meant, in this connection, by the word "property." It includes money and all other property, real or personal, including things in action and other intangible property. In certain cases it may include land; and wild creatures, tamed or untamed, are to be regarded as property, though wild creatures not tamed nor ordinarily kept in captivity cannot be stolen. The taking of mushrooms, black-

PROPERTY—*continued.*
berries, etc. is not stealing unless they are taken for sale.

PROPERTY IN ACTION, as opposed to property in immediate possession, is the right to recover any thing (if it should be refused) by suit or action at law. [CHOSE.]

PROPERTY TAX. [INCOME TAX.]

PROPOSITUS. An expression sometimes used of a person from whom, dying intestate, descent had to be traced under the old canons of descent so as to ascertain who was to inherit his land.

PROPOUNDER. The person who, as executor under a will, or claiming administration with a will annexed, proposes it as genuine in the Probate Division, or other court having jurisdiction for the purpose. [ADMINISTRATOR; EXECUTOR; PROBATE.]

PROPRIETARY CHAPELS. Chapels of ease, which are the property of private persons, who have purchased or erected them with a view to profit or otherwise. [PRIVATE CHAPELS; PUBLIC CHAPELS.]

PROPRIETATE PROBANDA. A writ which lay for a person upon whom a distress was made, where the distrainor claimed that the goods distrained were his own property. [DISTRESS.]

PROPRIO VIGORE. By its own force.

PROROGATION OF PARLIAMENT. A putting off by the Crown of the sittings of parliament, the effect of which is to put an end to the session. It differs from an *adjournment*, in that an adjournment is effected by each house separately (though it may be at the instigation of the Crown); and after it all things continue as they were at the time of the adjournment made; whereas, after a *prorogation*, bills introduced and not passed are as if they had never been begun at all. *May.*

PROSECUTION. 1. The proceeding with, or following up, any matter in hand.
2. The proceeding with any suit or action at law. By a caprice of language, a person instituting *civil* proceedings is said to prosecute *his action or suit*; but a person instituting *criminal* proceedings is said to prosecute *the party accused*.
3. The party by whom criminal proceedings are instituted; so it is said, such a course was adopted by the prosecution, etc.

PROSECUTOR means properly any person who prosecutes any proceeding in a court of justice, whether civil or criminal; but the caprice of language has confined the term so as to denote in general a party who institutes criminal proceedings by way of indictment or information on behalf of the Crown, who is nominally the prosecutor in all criminal cases. [PUBLIC PROSECUTOR.]

PROSPECTUS is defined by the Companies Act 1948, s. 455, as "any prospectus, notice, circular, advertisement, or other invitation offering to the public for subscription or purchase any shares or debentures of a company."

PROSTITUTION. The indiscriminate consorting of a woman with men for hire. It is an offence under s. 22 of the Sexual Offences Act 1956 to procure a woman to become a common prostitute; and under *ibid.*, ss. 30, 31, for a man to live on the earnings of prostitution, or for a woman to exercise control over a prostitute. It is also an offence for a person to keep a brothel (*q.v.*) or to manage, or act or assist in the management of, a brothel. Loitering or soliciting in a street or public place for the purpose of prostitution is punishable under s. 1 of the Street Offences Act 1959.

PROTECTION. 1. The benefit or safety which is secured to every subject by the laws.
2. A special exemption or immunity given to a person by the Queen, by virtue of her prerogative, against suits in law or other vexations, in respect of the party being engaged in the Queen's service. It is now rarely granted.
3. The giving advantages in respect of duties to home over foreign commodities.

PROTECTION ORDER. An order under s. 10 of the Licensing Act 1964, authorising a person to whom an intoxicating liquor licence has been transferred to carry on business until the next transfer sessions or any adjournment thereof.

PROTECTIVE TRUSTS. [ALIMENTARY TRUSTS.]

PROTECTOR OF SETTLEMENT. The person or persons whose consent, under the Fines and Recoveries Act 1833, is necessary to enable a tenant in tail in remainder to bar the subsequent estates in remainder or reversion. The protector takes the place of the old tenant to the *præcipe* and is generally the prior tenant for life, but the author of the settlement may, in lieu of such prior tenant, appoint any number of persons, not exceeding three, to be together protector of the settlement. A protector is under no restraint in giving or withholding his consent. As to cases in which a married woman is a protector of a settlement, see s. 3 of the Married Women's Property Act 1907. S. 32 of the Fines and Recoveries Act 1833 (relating to the appointment of special protectors of a settlement), was repealed as respect settlements made or coming into operation after 1925; see Sch. VII to the Law of Property Act 1925.

PROTECTORATE. 1. The period in English history during which Cromwell was Protector.

2. A relation sometimes adopted by a strong country towards a weak one, whereby the former protects the latter from hostile invasion, and interferes more or less in its domestic concerns.

PROTEST. 1. A caution, by which a person declares that he does either not at all, or only conditionally, yield his consent to any act to which he might otherwise be deemed to have yielded an unconditional assent.

2. The dissent of a peer to a vote of the House of Lords, entered on the journals of the house, with his reasons for such dissent.

3. A formal declaration by the holder of a bill of exchange, or by a notary public at his request, that the bill of exchange has been refused acceptance or payment, and that the holder intends to recover all the expenses to which he may be put in consequence thereof. In the case of a foreign bill, such a protest is essential to the right of the holder to recover from the drawer or indorser. See s. 51 of the Bills of Exchange Act 1882. [BILL OF EXCHANGE.]

4. A document drawn up by a master of a ship and attested by a justice of the peace, consul, or notary public, stating the circumstances under which injury has happened to the ship or cargo.

PROTHONOTARY. [PROTO-NOTARY.]

PROTOCOL (Fr. *Protocole*). 1. A Byzantine term applied to the first sheet pasted on a MS. roll, stating by whom it was written, etc.

2. The first or original copy of anything.

3. The entry of any written instrument in the book of a notary or public officer, which, in case of the loss of the instrument, may be admitted as evidence of its contents.

4. A document serving as the preliminary to, or opening of, any diplomatic transaction.

PROTONOTARY. A chief scribe in a court of law. There were formerly three of such officers in the Court of Common Pleas, and one in the Court of King's Bench. He of the King's Bench recorded all civil actions in that court. Those of the Common Pleas entered all declarations, etc., and made out judicial writs. These officers were abolished in 1837.

PROVE. 1. To establish by evidence.

2. To establish a debt due from an insolvent estate, and to receive a dividend thereon.

3. To prove a will. [PROBATE.]

PROVINCE. 1. The circuit of an archbishop's jurisdiction. *Cowel.*

2. A colony or dependency.

3. An administrative division of the country used by the Ministry of Agriculture.

PROVINCIAL COURTS. The ecclesiastical courts of the Archbishops of York and Canterbury.

PROVISION was a word applied to the providing a bishop or any other person (called the *provisor*) with an ecclesiastical living by the Pope, before the incumbent was dead. The word was subsequently applied to any right of patronage usurped by the Pope. The purchasing "provisions" at Rome or elsewhere exposed the offender to the penalties of *præmunire.* [PRÆ-MUNIRE.]

PROVISIONAL ASSIGNEE was an assignee formerly appointed provisionally by the bankruptcy court until regular assignees should be appointed by the creditors.

PROVISIONAL ORDERS. Orders by a Government department authorising public undertakings under the authority of Acts of Parliament. Such orders are termed "provisional" because they do not come into force until confirmed by a further Act

PROVISIONAL ORDERS
—*continued.*

of Parliament. [SPECIAL PARLIAMENTARY PROCEDURE.]

PROVISO. A condition inserted into a deed, upon the observance whereof the validity of the deed depends.

PROVISOR. [PROVISION.]

PROVOCATION. The goading of a person into losing his self-control. Where, on a charge of murder, there is evidence on which the jury can find that the person charged was provoked, *whether by things done or by things said or by both together*, to lose his self-control, the question whether the provocation was enough to make a reasonable man do as he did must be determined by the jury, according to their view of the effect that such words or actions would have upon a reasonable man. See s. 3 of the Homicide Act 1957.

PROVOST MARSHAL. 1. An officer in the Queen's navy having charge of prisoners at sea.

2. A military or air force officer in control of military or air force police and having charge of prisoners.

3. An officer appointed in time of martial law to arrest and punish offenders. Execution parties are placed under his orders.

PROXIES. 1. Payments made to a bishop by a religious house, or by parish priests, for the charges of his visitation. [PROCURATIONS.]

2. By a *proxy* is generally understood a person deputed to vote in the place or stead of the party so deputing him. As in the House of Lords; at meetings of creditors of a bankrupt; at meetings of the shareholders of a company; and on various other occasions.

PUBERTY. The age of fourteen in men and twelve in women, at which they were deemed formerly capable of contracting marriage.

PUBLIC ACT OF PARLIAMENT. An Act to be judicially noticed, which is now the case with all Acts of Parliament, except the very few in which a declaration is inserted to the contrary. See s. 9 of the Interpretation Act 1889. [ACT OF PARLIAMENT; PRIVATE ACT OF PARLIAMENT.]

PUBLIC ANALYST. An analyst of food and drugs for a particular area under s. 89 of the Food and Drugs Act 1955.

PUBLIC CHAPELS are chapels of ease designed for the benefit of particular districts within a parish. They are opposite to *private chapels*, which are erected for the use of persons of rank, to whom the privilege has been conceded by the proper authorities; also to *proprietary chapels*, which are the property of private persons, and are erected with a view to profit or otherwise.

PUBLIC MEETING. Any number of persons may meet for any lawful purpose in any place with the consent of the owner of the place, but there is no "right of public meeting" known to English law, and persons have only a right to pass and repass in the public streets, etc.

Newspaper reports of public meetings are protected by qualified privilege under s. 7 of and the Schedule to the Defamation Act 1952.

As to disturbance of public meetings, see the Public Meeting Act 1908 and the Public Order Act 1936; also s. 84 of the Representation of the People Act 1949, which makes it an illegal practice to cause a disturbance at an election meeting.

PUBLIC MISCHIEF. An offence which tends to the prejudice of the community. See *R.* v. *Manley*, [1933] 1 K.B. 529.

PUBLIC NUISANCE. [NUISANCE.]

PUBLIC PLACE. Under the Prevention of Crime Act 1953 (prohibiting the carrying of offensive weapons without lawful authority or reasonable excuse) includes any highway and any other premises or place to which at the material time the public have or are permitted to have access, whether on payment or otherwise. See also the statutory definitions, including the Criminal Justice Act 1972, s. 33, and the Prevention of Terrorism (Temporary Provisions) Act 1974, s. 2 .

PUBLIC PROSECUTOR. The Director of Public Prosecutions appointed under the Prosecution of Offences Acts 1879 to 1908, whose duty it is to undertake the prosecution in cases where the magnitude of the offence makes it desirable.

PUBLIC TRUSTEE. An official appointed pursuant to the Public Trustee Act

1906. His powers and duties are prescribed by that Act.

PUBLICATION. 1. The declaration by a testator that a given writing is intended to operate as his last will and testament. This was formerly necessary to give legal effect to a will. But, by s. 13 of the Wills Act 1837, no publication is necessary beyond the execution attested by two witnesses as required by s. 9 of that Act.

2. The communication of a defamatory statement to any person or persons other than the party of whom it is spoken.

PUBLICI JURIS. Of public right.

PUBLISH. [PUBLICATION.]

PUERITIA. The age from seven to fourteen years.

PUFFER. A person employed to bid at a sale by auction on behalf of the owner of the land or goods sold. The employment of a puffer is illegal, unless a right to bid is reserved to the owner by the conditions or particulars of sale. See, as to land, the Sale of Land by Auction Act 1867, and, as to goods, s. 58 of the Sale of Goods Act 1893.

PUIS DARREIN CONTINUANCE (since the last continuance). A plea *puis darrein continuance* was a plea alleging some matter of defence which had arisen since the last "*continuance*" of *adjournment* of the court. [CONTINUANCE.]

Now, under R.S.C. 1965, Ord. 18, r. 9, a party may in any pleading plead any matter which has arisen at any time, whether before or since the issue of the writ.

PUISNE. Younger; thus, *mulier puisne* is the younger legitimate brother. [MULIER PUISNE.] So, the judges of the High Court, other than those having a distinctive title, are called the *puisne* judges. [DIVISIONS OF THE HIGH COURT.]

PUISNE MORTGAGE is any legal mortgage not being a mortgage protected by a deposit of documents relating to the legal estate affected. Such a mortgage is included in the list of land charges registrable under the Land Charges Act 1972. See s. 2 (4) Class C (i).

PUR AUTRE VIE. For another's life; thus a tenant *pur autre vie* is a tenant whose estate is to last during another person's life.

PURCHASE, besides its ordinary meaning, has a more extensive technical meaning in reference to the law of real property. The meaning is twofold:—

1. The word signifies any lawful mode of coming to an estate by the act of the *party* as opposed to the act of *law*; that is to say, in any manner except by descent, escheat, curtesy, and dower.

2. Any mode, other than descent, of becoming seised of real estate. [PURCHASER.]

PURCHASER. 1. One who acquires real or personal estate by the payment of money.

2. One who acquires real estate otherwise than by descent. Thus, in s. 1 of the Inheritance Act 1833, the "purchaser" is defined as the person who last acquired the land otherwise than by descent.

3. Under the Law of Property Act 1925 the word means a purchaser in good faith for valuable consideration, and includes a lessee, mortgagee, or other person who for valuable consideration acquires an interest in property, except that in Part I of that Act and elsewhere as expressly provided, the word only means a person who acquires an interest in or charge on property for money or money's worth; and in reference to a legal estate includes a chargee by way of legal mortgage. See s. 205 (1) (xxi).

PURE VILLENAGE. Villenage in which the service was base in its nature and uncertain. [COPYHOLD; FREEHOLD; PRIVILEGED VILLENAGE.]

PURGATION was a word applied to the methods by which, in former times, a man cleared himself of a crime of which he was accused. This was either *canonical*, by the oaths of twelve neighbours that they believed in his innocence; or *vulgar*, by fire or water ordeal; or by combat. [BENEFIT OF CLERGY; COMPURGATORS.]

PURGING. Atoning for an offence. Thus *purging a contempt of Court* is atoning for a contempt. The party then ceases to be "in contempt" that is to say, liable to the disabilities of one who refuses to obey the orders of the court. [CONTEMPT.]

PURLIEU. A word variously derived from *pur lieu* (exempt place), or *pourallée* (perambulation), and signifying all that ground which, having been made forest by Henry I, Richard I, or John, was by Henry III *disafforested*, so as to remit to the former owners their rights.

PURSUER. The Scotch name for a plaintiff or prosecutor.

PURVIEW. 1. That part of an Act of Parliament which begins with the words, *Be it enacted.*

2. The scope of an Act of Parliament.

PUT. An option which a party has of delivering stock at a certain time, in pursuance of a contract, the other party to the contract being bound to take the stock at the price and time therein specified.

PUTATIVE FATHER. The man who is supposed to be the father of a bastard child; especially one who is adjudged to be so by order of justices, under the Affiliation Proceedings Act 1957.

PYX. [PIXING THE COIN.]

Q

Q.B. Queen's Bench.

Q.B.D. Queen's Bench Division.

Q.C. Queen's Counsel.

Q.V. (*Quod vide*, Latin for "which see"). This abbreviation directs a reader to consult some passage referred to.

QUÆ SERVITIA. [PER QUÆ SERVITIA.]

QUALIFICATION. That which makes a person eligible to do certain acts or to hold office.

QUALIFIED. Limited: thus a qualified fee is equivalent to a base fee, being one which has a qualification subjoined thereto, and which must be determined (*i.e.*, put an end to) whenever the qualification annexed to it is at an end.

QUALIFIED ACCEPTANCE in the case of a bill of exchange is an acceptance with some variation of the effect of the bill as drawn. See s. 19 of the Bills of Exchange Act 1882.

QUALIFIED INDORSEMENT, on a bill of exchange or promissory note, is an indorsement which restrains, limits, or enlarges the liability of the indorser, in a manner different from that which the law generally imports as his true liability, deducible from the nature of the instrument. [BILL OF EXCHANGE; INDORSEMENT; PROMISSORY NOTE.] A particular species of this indorsement is one whereby the indorser repudiates liability, which may be made by annexing in French the words *sans recours*, or in English "without recourse to me," or other equivalent expression. Bills of Exchange Act 1882, ss. 16 (1) and 35.

QUALIFIED PROPERTY. A limited right of ownership; as, for instance:—

1. Such right as a man has in animals, *feræ naturæ*, which he has reclaimed. [FERÆ NATURÆ; INDUSTRIAM, PER; PROPERTY.]

2. Such right as a bailee has in the chattel transferred to him by the bailment. [BAILMENT.]

QUALIFIED TITLE. Under the Land Registration Act 1925 land may be registered with a qualified title. Where an absolute title (*q.v.*) is applied for, and on examination of the title it appears that the title can be established only for a limited period, or only subject to certain reservations, the registrar may, on the application of the person applying to be registered, by an entry made in the register, except from the effect of registration any estate, right, or interest (*a*) arising before a specified date, or (*b*) arising under a specified instrument or otherwise particularly described in the register, and a title registered, subject to such excepted estate, right, or interest is called a "qualified" title. The registration of freehold land with a qualified title has the same effect as registration with an absolute title, save that registration with a qualified title does not affect or prejudice the enforcement of any estate, right, or interest appearing by the register to be excepted (s. 7). [ABSOLUTE TITLE.] For the effect of registration of leaseholds with a qualified title, see s. 12 of the Act.

QUALITY OF ESTATE. The nature of an estate so far as regards the time of its commencement, and the manner of its enjoyment.

QUAMDIU BENE SE GESSERIT (as long as he shall behave himself well). These words imply that an office or privilege is to be held during good behaviour (as opposed to *durante bene placito*, during the pleasure of the grantor), and therefore is not to be lost otherwise than by the misconduct of the occupant; except of course by his death or voluntary resignation. Judges hold their office thus. See s. 12 of the Judicature Act 1925.

This is otherwise expressed by the phrase *ad vitam aut culpam.*

QUANDO ACCIDERINT (when they shall fall in). A judgment by which the creditor of a deceased person, who, having brought an action against the executor or administrator, has been met with a plea of *plene administravit*, is entitled to any assets which may in future fall into the hands of the defendant as legal representative of the deceased. [PLENE ADMINISTRAVIT.]

QUANTUM MERUIT (how much he has deserved). An action on a *quantum meruit* is an action of *assumpsit* grounded on a promise, express or implied, to pay the plaintiff for work and labour so much as his trouble is really worth. It no longer exists as a special form of action, but the phrase is still in use.

QUANTUM VALEBAT (as much as it was worth). A phrase applied to an action on an implied promise to pay for goods sold as much as they were worth, where no price had been previously fixed.

QUARANTINE. Forty days. 1. The space of forty days after the death of a husband seised of land, during which his widow was entitled to remain in her husband's capital mansion-house, and during which time her dower was to be assigned. [ASSIGNMENT OF DOWER; DOWER, 2.] 2. Forty days' probation for ships coming from infected countries, or such other time as may be directed by Order in Council. 3. Forty perches of land.

QUARE CLAUSUM FREGIT (wherefore he broke the close). A phrase applied to an action for trespass in breaking and entering the plaintiff's close, which includes every unwarrantable entry on another's soil.

QUARE EJECIT INFRA TERMINUM (wherefore he ejected him within the term). A writ which lay for a lessee who had been ejected from his farm before the expiration of his term. It differed from the writ of *ejectment* in being brought, not against the original wrongdoer, but against a feoffee or other person in possession claiming under the wrongdoer, for keeping out the lessee during the continuance of the term. Long obsolete. [EJECTMENT.]

QUARE IMPEDIT (wherefore he hinders). A writ which formerly lay for him

whose right of advowson was disturbed. Abolished in 1860. [ADVOWSON.]

QUARREL. A word anciently used for an action.

QUARRY. An excavation or system of excavations made for the purpose of, or in connection with, the getting of minerals (whether in their natural state or in solution or suspension) or products of minerals, being neither a mine (*q.v.*) nor merely a well or bore-hole or a well and bore-hole combined. See s. 180 of the Mines and Quarries Act 1954, which Act establishes a code of safety and working conditions for quarries.

QUARTER DAYS are, in England, the four following days:—

1. The 25th of March, being the Feast of the Annunciation of the Blessed Virgin Mary, commonly called Lady Day. [LADY DAY.]

2. The 24th of June, being the Feast of St. John the Baptist, otherwise called Midsummer Day.

3. The 29th of September, being the Feast of St. Michael and All Angels, commonly called Michaelmas Day.

4. The 25th of December, being the Feast of the Nativity of Christ, commonly called Christmas Day.

QUARTER SESSIONS were the general sessions of the peace held quarterly before the whole body of the justices of the peace in counties, and before the recorder in boroughs.

Quarter sessions were abolished by the Courts Act 1971: That Act transferred to the Crown Court all appellate and other jurisdiction conferred on any court of quarter sessions, by or under any Act, and, subject to the the provisions of the Act of 1971, all other powers and duties of quarter sessions were similarly transferred (*Hals. Laws*).

QUASH (Lat. *Cassum facere*) signifies to make void or annul. As when we say that an order of justices, or a conviction in an inferior court, is *quashed* by the judgment of a superior court.

QUASI-CONTRACT is an act or event from which, though not a consensual contract, an obligation arises *as if* from a contract (*quasi ex contractu*). Thus, for instance, an executor or administrator is

QUASI-CONTRACT—*continued.*
bound to satisfy the liabilities of the deceased to the extent of his assets received, *as if* he had contracted to do so. [IMPLIED.]

QUASI-ENTAIL is an estate *pur autre vie* granted to a man and the heirs of his body. See the Law of Property Act 1925. [PUR AUTRE VIE.]

QUASI-PERSONALTY. Things which are movables in point of law, though fixed to things real, either actually, as emblements, etc., or fictitiously, as chattels real, leases for years, etc.

QUASI-REALTY. Things which are fixed in contemplation of law to realty, but are movable in themselves, *e.g.*, heirlooms, title deeds, etc.

QUASI-TRUSTEE. A person who reaps a benefit from a breach of trust, and so becomes answerable as a trustee.

QUE ESTATE was an expression formerly used in pleading to avoid prolixity in setting out titles to land, as if B, claiming a lawful title to land pleaded a conveyance of the land to A which estate (*quem statum*) B had, without setting out at length how the estate came from A to B. Hence the expression came to signify an estate acquired otherwise than by descent. Such an estate enabled a man, at common law, to acquire by prescription such rights as were appendant or appurtenant to lands enjoyed by himself and those whose estate he had. [PRESCRIPTION.]

QUEEN. 1. A queen regent, regnant, or sovereign, is one who holds the crown in her own right. [KING.]
2. A queen consort is the wife of a reigning king.
3. A queen dowager is the widow of a deceased king.

QUEEN ANNE'S BOUNTY. A perpetual fund for the augmentation of poor livings, created by a charter of Queen Anne, out of the tenths and first fruits formerly payable by the beneficed clergy to the Pope, and, after the Reformation, to the English sovereigns. The functions, rights and privileges of the Governors of the Bounty of Queen Anne were transferred to the Church Commissioners by s. 2 of the Church Commissioners Measure 1947.

QUEEN CAN DO NO WRONG. This maxim means that the Queen is not legally responsible for anything she may please to do, or for any forbearance or omission. It does not mean that everything done by the government is just and lawful: but that whatever is exceptional in the conduct of public affairs is not to be imputed to the Queen.

The impediment to suing the Crown which this maxim implies was removed by the Crown Proceedings Act 1947.

QUEEN CONSORT. [QUEEN, 2.]

QUEEN DOWAGER. [QUEEN, 3.]

QUEEN'S BENCH DIVISION. The jurisdiction of the former Court of Queen's Bench was assigned in 1873 to the then newly-constituted Queen's Bench Division of the High Court of Justice. This Division is still one of three which together form the High Court, the others being the Chancery Division and the Family Division.

The Queen's Bench Division consists of the Lord Chief Justice, who is president thereof, and not less than seventeen puisne judges. As to the assignment of business to the Queen's Bench Division, see s. 56 (2) of the Supreme Court of Judicature (Consolidation) Act 1925.

QUEEN'S CORONER AND ATTORNEY. An officer of the Queen's Bench Division whose office is now merged in that of Master of the Crown Office, and is held by one of the Masters of the Supreme Court. See s. 106 (2) of the Judicature Act 1925.

QUEEN'S COUNSEL. A name given to barristers appointed by letters patent to be Her Majesty's counsel learned in the law. Their selection and removal rests in practice with the Lord Chancellor. A Queen's Counsel, in taking that rank, renounces the preparation of written pleadings and other chamber practice.

QUEEN'S EVIDENCE. Evidence for the Crown. An accused person who "turns Queen's evidence" is a person who confesses his guilt and proffers himself as a witness against his accomplices. His admission, however, in that capacity requires the sanction of the court; and, unless his statements be corroborated in some material part by unimpeachable evidence, the jury must be warned by the judge of the danger of convicting. If his evidence is unsatisfactory he may still be convicted on his original confession or other evidence.

QUEEN'S PROCTOR. The proctor or solicitor representing the Crown in the Family Division. In petitions for dissolution of marriage, or for declarations of nullity of marriage, the Queen's Proctor may, under the direction of the Attorney-General, and by leave of the court, intervene in the suit. See s. 8 of the Matrimonial Causes Act 1973, which relates to the duties of the Queen's Proctor and his costs.

QUEEN'S REMEMBRANCER. [REMEMBRANCERS.]

QUERELA. An action preferred in a court of justice. [AUDITA QUERELA; DUPLEX QUERELA.]

QUEST. Inquest or inquiry. [INQUEST.]

QUI APROBAT NON REPROBAT. He who accepts cannot reject.

QUI FACIT PER ALIUM FACIT PER SE. He who does a thing through another does it himself.

QUI TAM ACTIONS were actions brought by a person, under a penal statute, to recover a penalty, partly for the king or the poor, or some other public use, and partly for himself; so called because it was brought by a person who, as well as his lord the king as for himself, sued in this behalf: "*Qui tam pro domino rege, etc., quam pro se ipso in hac parte sequitur.*"

QUIA EMPTORES. A statute of Edward I, passed in 1290 to put a stop to the practice of subinfeudation. The statute provided that it should be lawful for every freeman to sell at his own pleasure his lands and tenements, or part thereof, so nevertheless that the feoffee (or purchaser) should hold the same lands or tenements of the same chief lord of the fee, and by the same services and customs, as his feoffee held them before.

QUIA TIMET (because he fears). A *quia timet* bill was a bill filed in Chancery for guarding against a future injury of which a plaintiff was apprehensive; as by a person entitled to property in remainder, for the purpose of securing it against any accident which might befall it previously to the time when it should fall into possession;

or by a person who feared that some instrument really void but apparently valid might hereafter be used against him, and which he wished to be cancelled. The jurisdiction to entertain questions of this kind, so far as it consists in the rectification, setting aside, or cancellation of deeds and other written instruments was, by s. 56 of the Judicature Act 1925, assigned to the Chancery Division of the High Court. So far as it consists in the granting of a mandamus or injunction, it may, by s. 45, be exercised in any division.

QUICQUID PLANTATUR SOLO, SOLO CEDIT. Whatever is affixed to the soil, belongs to the soil. [FIXTURES.]

QUID PRO QUO. A compensation, or the giving of one thing of value for another thing of like value. [CONSIDERATION.]

QUIET ENJOYMENT is a phrase applied especially to the undisturbed enjoyment, by a purchaser of landed property, of the estate or interest so purchased. A general covenant, by a vendor or lessor, for quiet enjoyment by the purchaser or lessee, extends only to secure the covenantee against the acts of persons claiming under a *lawful* title, for the law will never adjudge that a lessor (or vendor) covenants against the wrongful acts of strangers, unless his covenant is express to that purpose. The construction, however, is different where an individual is named, for there the covenantor is presumed to know the person against whose acts he is content to covenant, and may therefore be reasonably expected to stipulate against any disturbance from him, whether by lawful title or otherwise. See also s. 76 of, and Sch. II to, the Law of Property Act 1925, which deal with covenants for title. *Hill and Redman.*

QUIETUS. 1. Acquitted or discharged; a word used especially of the sheriffs and other accountants to the Exchequer, when they had given in their accounts.

2. An aquittance or discharge.

QUIETUS REDDITUS. Quit rent. [QUIT RENT.]

QUINTO EXACTUS. The fifth and last call of a defendant sued for outlawry, when, if he appeared not, he was declared outlawed. [EXIGENT; OUTLAWRY.]

QUIT CLAIM. A release or acquitting of a man of any action or claim which might be had against him.

QUIT RENT. Fixed rent paid by the freeholders and copyholders (especially the latter) of a manor in discharge or acquittance of other services. Obsolete.

QUITTANCE. A release.

QUO ANIMO (with what intention). A phrase often used in criminal trials, where there is no question of certain overt acts having been committed by the accused, and the only question is with what intention (*quo animo*) they were done. [FURANDI ANIMUS.]

QUO JURE (by what right). A writ that lay for him in whose lands another claimed common of pasture time out of mind, calling on the latter to show by what title he claimed.

QUO MINUS. 1. A writ that lay for him who had a grant of housebote or haybote in another man's woods, to prevent the grantor making such waste that the grantee could not enjoy his grant. [HAYBOTE; HOUSEBOTE.]

2. The allegation formerly made in civil actions in the Exchequer, that the plaintiff was the king's lessee or debtor, and that the defendant had done him the injury complained of, *quo minus suficiens existeret, etc.*, "by reason whereof he was the less able to pay the king his rent or debt." By this fiction the Court of Exchequer usurped the jurisdiction of the ordinary courts of justice. [COURT OF EXCHEQUER.]

QUO WARRANTO. 1. A writ that lay against him that usurped any franchise or liberty against the king; also against him that intruded himself as heir into any land. This writ is now obsolete.

2. An information in the nature of a writ of *quo warranto* was originally a criminal information for the wrongful use of a franchise, but is now a method of trying the existence of the civil right, and is regarded practically as a civil proceeding. S. 48 of the Judicature Act 1925 provides that proceedings in *quo warranto* shall be deemed to be civil proceedings whether for purposes of appeal or otherwise.

QUOAD HOC (in respect of this matter). A term used in law reports to signify, *as to this matter* the law is so.

QUOD APPROBO NON REPROBO. That which I accept I do not reject.

QUORUM. 1. A word used in commissions of the peace, by which it is intended to indicate that some particular justices, or some or one of them are always to be included in the business to be done, so that no business can be done without their presence; the words being "*quorum aliquem vestrum*, A, B, C, D, etc., *unum esse volumus*." The particular justices so named are called justices of the *quorum*. Formerly it was the custom to appoint only a select number of such justices; but even in Blackstone's time it had become the custom to advance all of them to that dignity, except perhaps only some one inconsiderable person, for the sake of propriety.

2. The *minimum* number of persons necessarily present in order that business may be proceeded with, at any meeting for the dispatch of business, in the Houses of Parliament, or elsewhere. *May.*

QUOUSQUE. A word implying a temporary state of things. Thus the lord of a manor, after making due proclamation at three consecutive courts of the manor for a person to come in as heir or devisee of a deceased tenant, was entitled to seize the lands *quousque*, that is, until some person claimed admittance. So, a prohibition *quousque* is a prohibition which is to take effect until some act be performed or event happen, or time be elapsed, according as is specified in the prohibition.

R

R. *Rex* or *regina*, as in the Queen's signature, Elizabeth R.

R.S.C. Rules of the Supreme Court made by a Rule Committee of judges and lawyers under the authority of the Judicature Act 1881 and the Judicature (Rule Committee) Act 1909. The rules were revised in 1965. They may be found in "The Annual Practice of the Supreme Court."

(*Canada.*) R.S.C. stands for Revised Statutes of Canada.

RABBIT. A beast of warren, also termed a "coney." Unlawfully taking or destroying rabbits by night is an offence under s. 1 of the Night Poaching Act 1828; similarly, it is an offence to trespass in pursuit of rabbits in the daytime under ss. 30–32 of the Game Act 1831. As to the right of a tenant to shoot rabbits on his farm, see the Ground Game Act 1880. The destruction and control of rabbits is provided for under the Pests Act 1954.

RACIAL DISCRIMINATION. [Discrimination.]

RACK. Torture for the purpose of extorting confession from an accused person. It is also called *question.*

RACK-RENT. Rent of the full annual value of the tenement on which it is charged, or as near to it as possible.

RAILWAY AND CANAL COMMISSION. A body established in 1888 to supersede the Railway Commissioners and exercise their jurisdiction with enlarged powers. Abolished in 1948.

RAILWAY COMMISSIONERS. [Railway and Canal Commission.]

RANK MODUS. Every *modus* of tithes was presumably based on a composition on fairly equitable terms, by which the *modus* was substituted for the payment of tithe. [Modus Decimandi; Tithes.] If, then, a *modus* was so large that it, beyond dispute, exceeded the value of the tithes in the time of Richard I (the date of legal memory), the *modus* was called a *rank modus,* and was not accepted as a legal *modus.* For, as it would be destroyed by any direct evidence proving its non-existence at any time since that era, so also it was destroyed by carrying in itself this internal evidence of a much later origin.

RANSOM. 1. The sum paid for the redeeming of one taken prisoner. *T.L.; Cowel;* 2 *Bl.*

2. Formerly a fine in the king's court, or the redemption of corporal punishment due by law for any offence. *T.L.; Cowel;* 4 *Bl.*

RANSOM-BILL. A security given by the master of a captured vessel to the captor for the ransom of the vessel, or any goods therein.

RAPE. 1. Part of a county, being in a manner the same with a hundred. The county of Sussex is divided into six rapes: those of Chichester, Arundel, Bramber, Lewes, Pevensey, and Hastings; each of which, besides their hundreds, has a castle,

river, and forest belonging to it. They seem to have been military governments in the time of the Conqueror.

2. Trespass committed in the forest by violence. This is called *rape of the forest.*

3. The ravishment of a woman without her consent by force, fear of fraud. It is an offence under s. 1 of the Sexual Offences Act 1956, punishable with imprisonment for life. Attempted rape is punishable with imprisonment for seven years. A man who induces a married woman to have sexual intercourse by impersonating her husband is guilty of rape (*ibid.,* s. 1 (2)).

RAPINE. Robbery, *i.e.,* the unlawful taking of property from the owner by violence, or putting him in fear. *Cowel;* 4 *Bl.*

RAPTU HÆREDIS. A writ for taking away an heir who held in socage.

RASURE. An erasure or obliteration in a deed or other instrument.

RATE. A tax levied by local authorities upon the occupation of hereditaments, irrespective of a person's income generally, and irrespective of whether the ratepayer is in fact deriving profits or gains from such occupation.

Under Part VIII of the Local Government Act 1972 the London borough councils and district councils are rating authorities, each having power to levy a rate in the form of a certain amount in the £ of rateable value. County councils assist in constituting local valuation panels.

The Greater London Council, county councils, parish councils and community councils all have power to issue precepts upon the rating authorities; they do not levy rates direct. Each of them precepts on the district which collects the county and parish rates at the same time as its own and forwards their shares to the other authorities.

RATE SUPPORT GRANT. A grant payable to local authorities under the provisions of the Local Government Act 1974, s. 2, Sch. 2. The grant is based on needs and resources and makes up for deficiencies in the rates raised by an authority, particularly in the field of educational finance.

RATE TITHE. Tithe paid *pro rata,* according to the custom of the place, for sheep or other cattle kept in a parish for less time than a year.

RATIFICATION. Confirmation, *e.g.*, of a contract.

RATIO DECIDENDI. The ground of a decision; a phrase often used in opposition to *obiter dictum*. [OBITER DICTUM.]

RATIONABILE ESTOVERIUM Reasonable estovers or alimony. [ESTOVERS.]

RATIONE TENURÆ (by reason of tenure or occupation). An individual or particular borough may be liable to repair a bridge *ratione tenuræ* though such liability is in general upon the county at large.

RATTENING. The offence of depriving a workman of his tools for the purpose of forcing him to join a trade union.

RAVISHMENT. [ABDUCTION; RAPE.]

RE. In the matter of. [IN RE.]

READER. 1. The chaplain of the Temple.

2. A lecturer.

READING IN is a phrase used to denote the reading of the Thirty-nine Articles of Religion, and repeating the Declaration of Assent prescribed by the Clerical Subscription Act 1865, which is required to every incumbent on the first Lord's Day on which he officiates in the church of his benefice, or such other Lord's Day as the ordinary shall appoint and allow.

REAL, besides its ordinary meaning, has in law two special meanings:—

First, as being applicable to a thing in contradistinction to a person:

Secondly, as applicable to land, and especially freehold interests therein, as opposed to other rights and interests.

REAL AND PERSONAL PROPERTY. By *real property* or *real estate* is meant such interests in land as, on the death of their owner intestate, formerly descended to his heir-at-law; or, if the land were copyhold or customary freehold, to the heir or heirs pointed out by custom. By *personal property*, or *personal estate* is meant such property as, on the owner's death, devolved on his executor alone or administrator, to be distributed (in so far as the owner had not made any disposition thereof by will) among his next of kin according to the Statute of Distributions.

Real property is not, however, precisely synonymous with property in land, nor is personal property synonymous with movable property. Thus, a title of honour, though annexed to the person of its owner, is real property because in ancient times such titles were annexed to the ownership of various lands. On the other hand, shares in canals, railways and other property-owning companies are personal property. A lease for years is also personal property, because in ancient times an ejected lessee could not recover his lease by real action; but he could bring a personal action for damages against his landlord, who was bound to warrant him possession.

The new code of succession on intestacy which was enacted by Part IV of the Administration of Estates Act 1925 applies alike to real and personal property and many of the distinctions above referred to have become obsolete. [ACTIONS REAL AND PERSONAL; CHATTELS; EJECTMENT.]

REAL REPRESENTATIVE. 1. The representative (whether heir or devisee) of a deceased person in respect of his real property.

2. By Part I of the Land Transfer Act 1897 the executor or administrator of any person dying after the commencement of that Act was constituted the real representative. Real estate except copyhold vested in him as trustee for the person beneficially entitled. Part I of the Land Transfer Act 1897 was repealed and re-enacted with amendments by the Administration of Estates Act 1925 in regard to deaths occurring after 1925.

REALTY. Real estate; that is, freehold interests in land; or, in a larger sense (so as to include chattels real), things substantial and immovable, and the rights and profits annexed to or issuing out of these.

REASONABLE AND PROBABLE CAUSE. A phrase used in connection with the defence to an action for false imprisonment or a prosecution for blackmail, that the defendant had reasonable and probable cause for arresting the plaintiff or making the demand. Also in an action for malicious prosecution plaintiff must prove that there was no reasonable and probable cause for the prosecution. The question of reasonable and probable cause when the facts are found is, in England, a question for the judge, but in Scotland for the jury.

RE-ASSURANCE POLICY is a contract whereby an insurer seeks to relieve himself from a risk which he may have incautiously undertaken, by throwing it upon some other underwriter.

RE-ATTACHMENT. A second attachment of him that was formerly attached and dismissed the court *sine die*, as by the not coming of the justices, or some such casualty. [EAT INDE SINE DIE.]

REBATE. Discount; a deduction from a payment in consideration of its being made before due.

REBELLION. 1. The taking up of arms traitorously against the Crown whether by natural subjects or others when once subdued. 2. Disobedience to the process of the Courts.

REBELLIOUS ASSEMBLY. A gathering together of twelve persons or more, going about of their own authority to change any laws or statutes of the realm; or to destroy any park or ground enclosed, or the banks of any fish-pond, pool, or conduit, or to destroy any deer, or burn stacks of corn, or to abate rents, or prices of victuals, etc.

REBUTTER. The pleading by the defendant in answer to the plaintiff's surrejoinder. [REJOINDER.]

REBUTTING EVIDENCE is evidence adduced to *rebut* a presumption of fact or law, that is, to avoid its effect. But the word is also used in a larger sense to include any evidence adduced to destroy the effect of prior evidence, not only in explaining it away while admitting its truth, but also by direct denial, or by an attack upon the character of the witness who has given it.

RECAPTION signifies:—1. A second distress of one formerly distrained for the same cause. 2. A writ that lay for the party thus distrained twice over the same thing. 3. A reprisal taken by one man against another, who had deprived him of his property, or wrongfully detained his wife, child, or servant.

RECEIPT. 1. That branch of the Exchequer in which the royal revenue is managed. [COURT OF EXCHEQUER.]

2. A written acknowledgment of the payment of money. A receipt for the purchase-money of land may be embodied in the purchase-deed. See the Law of Property Act 1925, ss. 67, 68.

RECEIVER. 1. One who receives stolen goods, knowing them to be stolen. The term "receiving" has now been replaced by that of "handling" stolen goods under s. 22 of the Theft Act 1968. By this section, a person is said to "handle" stolen goods if (*otherwise* than in the course of stealing them) he dishonestly "receives" them, or assists in their removal, disposal, etc.

2. An officer appointed (usually by the Court of Chancery) to receive the rents and profits of property, and account for them to the court, *e.g.*, in actions for dissolution of partnership or for the administration of an estate. If there is a business to be carried on temporarily the receiver may also be appointed *manager*. Under s. 45 of the Judicature Act 1925, a receiver may be appointed by an interlocutory order of the court in all cases in which it shall appear to be just or convenient. As to the power of a mortgagee to appoint a receiver, see s. 101 of the Law of Property Act 1925.

3. Under s. 8 of the Bankruptcy Act 1914 the Official Receiver may be appointed to act as interim receiver of the debtor's property.

4. Under s. 105 of the Mental Health Act 1959 a judge may by order appoint a receiver for a mentally disordered person.

RECEIVERS OF WRECKS. Officers appointed to summon as many men as may be necessary, to demand help from any ship near at hand, or to press into their service any vehicles, for the purpose of preserving or assisting any stranded or distressed vessel, or her cargo, or for the saving of human life. See the Merchant Shipping Act 1894, ss 511–514. [WRECK.]

RECITAL. That part of a deed which recites the deeds, arguments, and other matters of fact, which may be necessary to explain the reasons upon which it is founded.

Recitals are not essential to the validity of a deed, and are often dispensed with.

RECLAIMED ANIMALS. Wild animals made tame by art, industry, and education. [FERÆ NATURÆ.]

RECOGNITORS. A word formerly used of a jury empanelled upon an assize or real action. [ASSIZE, WRIT OF.]

RECOGNIZANCE. An obligation of record, which a man enters into before some court of record, or magistrate duly authorised, binding himself under a penalty to do some particular act; as to appear before the Crown Court, to keep the peace, to pay a debt, or the like. See s. 31 of the Powers of Criminal Courts Act 1973; and as to recognizances given in courts of summary jurisdiction, see ss. 91–97 of the Magistrates' Courts Act 1952.

RECOGNIZEE. He to whom another is bound in a recognizance (q.v.).

RECOGNIZOR. A person bound in a recognizance (q.v.).

RECONCILIATION. If at any stage of proceedings for divorce it appears to the court that there is a reasonable possibility of a reconciliation between the parties to the marriage, the court may adjourn the proceedings to enable attempts to be made to effect such reconciliation. See s. 6 of the Matrimonial Causes Act 1973.

RE-CONVERSION. The restoration, in contemplation of equity, to its actual original quality of property which has been constructively converted. [CONVERSION.]

RE-CONVEYANCE. A deed by which, on the payment off of a mortgage, the legal estate in the mortgaged property is re-vested in the mortgagor. After 1925 a receipt indorsed on a mortgage usually will operate as a re-conveyance, as is also the case in regard to mortgages to building societies. See the Law of Property Act 1925, s. 115, and Sch. III, Form No. 2.

RECORD. 1. An authentic testimony in writing preserved in the archives of a court of record. [COURT OF RECORD.]

2. Of *nisi prius*—"the record." [NISI PRIUS RECORD.]

3. Any disc, tape, perforated roll or other device in which sounds are embodied so as to be capable of being automatically reproduced: Copyright Act 1956, s. 48.

RECORD AND WRIT CLERKS were officers of the Court of Chancery whose duty it was to file bills brought to them for that purpose. Business was distributed among them according to the initial letter of the surname of the first plaintiff in a suit.

These officers were transferred to the High Court of Justice under s. 77 of the Judicature Act 1873, and made "Masters" thereof by s. 8 of the Judicature Act 1879. See now ss. 104–106 of the Judicature Act 1925.

RECORD, CONVEYANCES BY, are conveyances evidenced by the authority of a court of record. [COURT OF RECORD.] The principal conveyances by matter of record are conveyances by private Act of Parliament and royal grants.

RECORD, COURT OF. [COURT OF RECORD.]

RECORD, DEBT OF. A sum of money which appears to be due by the evidence of a court of record, such as a judgment, etc.

RECORD OFFICE. An office for the keeping of public records, established by the Public Record Office Act 1838 (now repealed), under the direction of the Master of the Rolls. This direction was transferred to the Lord Chancellor by s. 1 of the Public Records Act 1958. The actual charge of the office is taken by the Keeper of Public Records appointed under s. 2 of the Act of 1958.

RECORD, TRIAL BY, was where some matter of record was alleged by one party, which the opposite party denied; then the party pleading the record had a day given him to bring in the record, which if he failed to do, judgment was given for his antagonist.

RECORDER. The principal legal officer of a city or town to which the right to have such an officer has been granted.

Under the Courts Act 1971 the Crown may from time to time appoint qualified persons as recorders, to act as part-time judges of the Crown Court and to carry out other judicial functions. They must have been recommended by the Lord Chancellor and must be barristers or solicitors of at least ten years standing. They must take the oath of allegiance and the judicial oath.

By virtue of his office and with his consent a recorder is capable of sitting as a judge for any county court district in England and Wales, and he may be requested to sit as a judge of the High Court (*Hals. Laws*).

RECOVERY is either a true or a feigned recovery.

1. A true recovery is an actual or real

recovery of a thing, or the value thereof, by judgment.

2. A feigned recovery, otherwise called a *common recovery*, was a proceeding formerly resorted to by tenants in tail for the purpose of barring their entails, and all remainders and reversions consequent thereon, and making a conveyance in fee simple of the lands held in tail. [ESTATE.] The common recovery was a supposed real action carried on through every stage of the proceeding, and was as follows:—

Suppose Daniel Edwards, tenant in tail in possession of land, to be desirous of suffering a common recovery for the purpose of conveying the land to Francis Golding in fee simple. Golding then sued out a writ against him called a *præcipe quod reddat* (command that he restore), alleging that Edwards had no legal title to the land. The tenant Golding then appeared, and called on one Jacob Morland, who was supposed to have warranted the title to the tenant; and thereupon the tenant prayed that Jacob Morland might be called in to defend the title which he had so warranted. This was called *vouching to warranty*, and Morland was called the *vouchee*. Morland appeared and defended the title, whereupon Golding desired leave of the court to *imparl* or donfer with the vouchee in private, which was allowed him; but the vouchee disappeared, and made default, whereupon judgment was given for the demandant Golding, and the tenant Edwards had judgment to recover from Jacob Morland lands of equal value in recompense for the land warranted by him, and lost by his default; which was called the recompense or recovery in value. But this recompense was only nominal, as Jacob Morland was a person having no land of his own, being usually the crier of the court. The land was then, by judgment of law, vested in the recoverer, Golding, in fee simple.

In later times it was usual to have a recovery with *double voucher*, by first conveying an estate of freehold to any indifferent person against whom the *præcipe* was brought (which was called making a tenant to the *præcipe*); and then the tenant, in *præcipe* vouched the tenant in tail, who vouched over the common vouchee.

This cumbrous fiction was abolished by the Fines and Recoveries Act 1833, by which a tenant in tail was, in all cases, empowered to convey lands in fee simple by deed, enrolled within six months in the Court of Chancery, now the Central Office. Under s. 133 of the Law of Property Act 1925, the necessity for enrolment was abolished.

RECTIFICATION. The correction of an instrument in writing so as to express the true intention of the parties. Actions for this purpose are assigned to the Chancery Division. See s. 56 (1) of the Judicature Act 1925.

RECTO. Writ of right. [WRIT OF RIGHT.]

RECTOR. 1. He that has full possession of the rights of a parochial church. As opposed to a *vicar*, a rector is an incumbent of an unappropriated church. A rector (or parson) has for the most part the whole right to all the ecclesiastical dues in his parish, both great and small tithes, and the chancel is vested in him: whereas, in theory of law, a vicar has an appropriator over him, entitled to the best part of the profits, to whom the vicar is, as it were, a perpetual curate, with a standing salary. Where the appropriator is a layman, he is called lay impropriator, or lay rector. [APPROPRIATION, 1; IMPROPRIATION; VICAR.]

2. In some of the colleges in Oxford, the head is called by the title of Rector.

RECTOR SINECURE. A rector who in former times had no spiritual duties in his parish, and did not reside there. His duties were performed by a vicar. [SINECURE.]

RECTORIAL TITHES are those tithes which, in a benefice unappropriated, were paid to the rector, and, in a benefice appropriated, to the appropriator. Great as opposed to small tithes, generally in respect of hay, corn and wood. [APPROPRIATION, 1; VICAR.]

RECTORY. 1. A parish church, with its rights, glebes, tithes, and other profits.

2. The rector's mansion or parsonage-house.

RECTUS IN CURIA. Right in court; said of a man who, having been outlawed, had obtained a reversal of the outlawry, so

RECTUS IN CURIA—*continued.*
as to be again able to participate in the benefit of the law. [OUTLAWRY.]

RECUSANTS. Those who separate from the church established by law, and wilfully absent themselves from the parish church; they were liable to penalties under the statutes of James I and Elizabeth I.

RECUSATIO JUDICIS, by the civil and canon law, was an objection to a judge on suspicion of partiality, or for other good cause.

REDDENDO SINGULA SINGULIS. A phrase indicating that different words in one part of a deed or other instrument are to be applied respectively to their appropriate objects in another part.

REDDENDUM. That clause in a lease whereby rent is reserved to the lessor. It usually specifies the periods at which the rent is to be paid or rendered. No special form of words is essential. *Hill & Redman.*

RE-DEMISE signifies a re-granting of lands demised or leased.
The old way of granting a rent-charge was by *demise* and *re-demise.* That is, A demised land to B, and B re-demised it to A, reserving the sum agreed upon by way of rent.

REDEMPTION. 1. A ransom.
2. Especially, the buying back a mortgaged estate by payment of the sum due on the mortgage. [EQUITY OF REDEMPTION.]
3. Redemption of land tax; which is the payment by the landowner of such a lump sum as shall exempt his land from the land tax. [LAND TAX.]
4. Redemption of rentcharge. See the Law of Property Act 1925, s. 191.

REDISSEISIN. A disseisin made by him that once before was found and adjudged to have disseised the same man of his lands and tenements. [DISSEISIN.]

REDITUS ALBI. Quit rents paid in silver. [ALBA FIRMA: QUIT RENT.]

REDITUS CAPITALES. Chief rents. [CHIEF-RENTS; RENT, 4.]

REDITUS NIGRI. Quit rents paid in grain or base money. [ALBA FIRMA; BLACK MAIL; QUIT RENT.]

REDITUS QUIETI. Quit rents. [QUIT RENT.]

REDITUS SICCUS. [RENT, 3.]

REDUCTIO AD ABSURDUM. A method of proving the fallacy of an argument by showing that it leads to an absurd result.

REDUCTION INTO POSSESSION. The turning of a *chose in action* into a *chose in possession*; as when a man takes money out of a bank at which he has a balance, or procures the payment of a debt due. [CHOSE.]

REDUCTION OF CAPITAL. As to the cases in which a company may reduce its capital see ss. 66, 71 of the Companies Act 1948. In all cases a special resolution must be passed, and in most cases an application to the court is necessary. The words "and reduced" may be ordered to be added to the title of the company.

REDUNDANCY. Matter introduced into the pleadings of an action which is foreign to the scope of the action.

REDUNDANCY PAYMENT. Payment made as compensation to a workman for loss of his job. It is based on length of service and is payable by the employer. See the Redundancy Payments Act 1965, as amended by the Employment Protection Act 1975.

RE-ENTRY. The resuming or retaking of possession lately had.
A *proviso for re-entry* is a clause in a deed of grant or demise providing that the grantor or lessor may re-enter on breach of condition by the grantee or lessee. A proviso for re-entry will be construed according to the letter, unless a decisive reason is shown for departing from it. The Schedule to the Law of Property (Amendment) Act 1926 provided that a fee simple subject to a right of entry or re-entry should be a fee simple absolute, *i.e.*, it was not converted into an equitable interest. And see the Law of Property Act 1925, s. 146, and the Landlord and Tenant Act 1927, s. 18 (2), which impose restrictions on the enforceability of rights of re-entry. *Hill & Redman.* [FORFEITURE.]

REEVE. A termination signifying an executive officer. Thus we have *shire-reeve* signifying sheriff; *church-reeve* for churchwarden, etc.

RE-EXAMINATION is the examination of a witness by the counsel of the party on whose behalf he has given evidence, in reference to matters arising out of his cross-examination. [EXAMINATION, 1.]

RE-EXCHANGE is the expense incurred by a bill being dishonoured in a foreign country where it is made payable and returned to that country in which it was drawn or endorsed. For this expense the drawer is liable. [BILL OF EXCHANGE.]

RE-EXTENT. A second extent (or valuation) made upon lands and tenements upon complaint that the former extent was but partially performed. [EXTENT.]

REFEREE. 1. A person to whose judgment a matter is referred, whether by consent of the parties or by compulsory reference under the Arbitration Act 1950. See also ss. 88–97 of the Judicature Act 1925. [OFFICIAL REFEREES.]

2. Persons to whom are referred questions as to the *locus standi* of petitioners against private parliamentary bills.

REFEREE IN CASE OF NEED. The drawer or indorser of a bill of exchange may insert therein the name of a person to whom the holder may resort in case of need, *i.e.*, in case the bill is dishonoured. See the Bills of Exchange Act 1882, s. 15.

REFERENCE. Referring a matter to an arbitrator, or to a master or other officer of a court of justice, for his decision thereon. [ARBITRATION; OFFICIAL REFEREES.]

REFERENDUM. 1. A note addressed by an ambassador to his own Government with regard to a matter upon which he is not instructed.

2. A mode of appealing from an elected body to the whole electorate. The Referendum Act 1975 provided for the holding of a referendum on whether the United Kingdom should remain a member of the European Economic Community, the result showing a substantial majority in favour.

REFORMATORY SCHOOLS, formerly institutions to which juvenile offenders under sixteen might be sent for not less than two nor more than five years. Later called approved schools, which were discontinued on the establishment of community homes under the Children and Young Persons Act 1969.

REFRESHER. A further or additional fee paid to counsel where a case is adjourned from one term or sittings to another, or where the hearing lasts over the first day and for more than five hours. It may be allowed on taxation.

REGAL FISHES. [FISH ROYAL.]

REGALIA. The royal rights of the Queen, comprising, according to the civilians:—

1. Power of judicature.
2. Power of life and death.
3. Power of war and peace.
4. Masterless goods.
5. Assessments.
6. Minting of money.

[MAJORA REGALIA; MINORA REGALIA.]
Also the crown, sceptre with the cross, and other jewels and ornaments used at a coronation, are called the *regalia*.

REGARDANT. A villein *regardant* was a villein *annexed to a manor*, having charge to do all base services within the same, and to see the same freed from all things that might annoy his lord. A villein *regardant* was thus opposed to a villein *in gross*, who was transferable by deed from one owner to another.

REGENT. A person appointed to conduct the affairs of State in lieu of the reigning sovereign, in the absence, disability or minority of the latter. See the Regency Acts 1937 to 1953.

REGICIDE. A slayer of a king; or the murder of a king.

REGISTER. 1. The name of a book, wherein are mentioned most of the forms of the writs used at common law. [ORIGINAL WRIT.]

2. The register of a parish church, wherein baptisms, marriages, and burials are registered. Instituted by Thomas Cromwell, vicar-general of Henry VIII, in the year 1538. The General Register of Births, Marriages and Deaths is at Somerset House. [REGISTRAR, 1.]

3. A record of deeds and other documents relating to land, such as exists in Yorkshire, and in Scotland and Ireland. See ss. 11, 197 of the Law of Property Act 1925; and s. 135 of the Land Registration Act 1925. [YORKSHIRE REGISTRIES.]

4. A record of titles to land. [LAND REGISTRATION.]

REGISTER—*continued.*

5. The General Register and Record Office for Seamen, containing, *inter alia*, the number and date of the register of each foreign-going ship and her registered tonnage; the length and general nature of her voyage or employment; the names, ages and places of birth of the master, the crew, and the apprentices; their qualities on board their last ships or other employment; and the dates and places of their joining the ship. Merchant Shipping Act 1894, s. 251 *et seq.*

6. And, generally, a register signifies an authentic catalogue of names or events, *e.g.*, the register of companies under the Companies Act 1948, or a register of electors.

REGISTERED LAND. In the Land Registration Act 1925 this means land or any estate or interest in land the title to which is registered under that Act.

REGISTER OF ORIGINAL WRITS. [ORIGINAL WRIT; REGISTER, 1.]

REGISTER OF PATENTS. A book of patents kept at the Patent Office for public use. See s. 73 of the Patents Act 1949. [PATENT.]

REGISTERED OFFICE. The office of a company to which notices and other communications, including writs, may be addressed or sent. The address must be registered with the Registrar of Companies: see s. 107 of the Companies Act 1948.

REGISTRAR. An officer appointed to register the decrees of a court of justice, or in any manner to keep a register of names and events. Of these may be mentioned:—

1. The Registrar-General of births, deaths and marriages in England, to whom, subject to such regulations as shall be made by a principal secretary of state, the general management of the system of registering births, deaths and marriages is entrusted. He is now controlled by the Treasury.

2. The superintendent registrars of births, marriages and deaths.

3. The Registrar of Solicitors, whose duty it formerly was to keep an alphabetical list or roll of solicitors, and to issue certificates to persons who had been duly admitted and enrolled. These duties are now performed by The Law Society. See the Solicitors Act 1974. [ATTORNEY-AT-LAW; SOLICITOR.]

4. The Registrar of Companies (an officer appointed by the Board of Trade), whose business it is to certify when a company is incorporated, etc.

5. The Registrars in Bankruptcy of the High Court, who are required to exercise such judicial powers as may be delegated to them from time to time by the judge of the court; and to perform various duties in connection with bankruptcy.

6. Chancery Registrars are officers of the Chancery Division whose duty it is to enter causes for trial, to attend in court and take minutes of decisions given, and afterwards draw the same up in proper form, and settle them in the presence of the different parties or their solicitors.

7. Registrars of the Family Division have power to transact all such business and to exercise all such authority and jurisdiction in respect of the same as a judge in chambers.

8. District Registrars. [DISTRICT REGISTRIES.]

9. The Registrar of a county court, who is an officer appointed by the judge, subject to the approval of the Lord Chancellor. If the county court be one having jurisdiction in bankruptcy, he will be a registrar in bankruptcy.

10. The Deputy-Registrar of a county court, who is an officer appointed by the registrar, subject to the approval of the judge.

11. The Registrar of Friendly Societies; an officer whose duty it is to examine the rules of friendly societies, and, if he find them comformable to law, to certify them as being so.

12. The Registrar of the Privy Council, whose duty it is to summon the members of the Judicial Committee when their attendance is required, and to transact other business relating to the Privy Council.

13. The Registrar-General of Shipping and Seamen. [REGISTER, 5.]

REGISTRATION OF TITLE. [LAND REGISTRATION.]

REGISTRY. A place where anything is laid up. *Cowel.*

Or it may be defined as a place where a register is kept.

REGIUS PROFESSOR. This title, when applied to a professor, or reader of lectures in the universities, indicates that his office was founded by the king. King Henry VIII was the founder of five professorships in the universities of Oxford and Cambridge, namely, the professorships of Divinity, Greek, Hebrew, Law, and Physic.

REGULÆ GENERALES (general rules). Published by the Courts from time to time for the regulation of their practice.

RE-HEARING was formerly a hearing again of a matter which had been decided by a judge in Chancery, either (1) by the same judge or his successor, or (2) by the Lord Chancellor or the Lords Justices. In the latter case, the hearing was spoken of as a hearing on appeal; but in strictness it was a re-hearing, being a hearing in the same Court of Chancery.

Now, by R.S.C. 1965, Ord. 59, r. 3, all appeals to the Court of Appeal are by way of *re-hearing*, and are brought by notice of motion. The term re-hearing as opposed to new trial indicates that the original hearing was before a judge alone, and not with a jury. [APPEAL.]

RE-INSURANCE. Re-assurance. [RE-ASSURANCE POLICY.]

REJOINDER. The defendant's answer to the plaintiff's reply, and therefore the fourth stage in pleading in an action at law in cases where the pleadings reach to this stage.

Pleadings subsequent to reply must be ordered if required.

RELATION. 1. Relation is where, in consideration of law, two times or other things are considered as if they were one, and by this the thing subsequent is said to take its effect *by relation* at the time preceding; as when it is said that an adjudication in bankruptcy has relation back to the act of bankruptcy upon which the adjudication is made. [ACT OF BANKRUPTCY; ADJUDICATION.]

2. The act of a *relator* at whose instance an information is filed. [RELATOR.]

RELATIVE. In relation to an infant, "relative" means a grandparent, brother, sister, uncle or aunt, whether of the full blood, of the half-blood or by affinity: Adoption Act 1958, s. 57.

RELATOR. A relator is a private person at whose instance the Attorney-General allows an information to be filed:—

1. A relator action is one in which a person or body claiming to be entitled to restrain interference with a public right or to abate a public nuisance must bring such action in the name of the Attorney-General. The action is expressed to be brought by "the Attorney-General *at the relation of* X." See R.S.C. 1965, Ord. 15, r. 11.

2. In strictly criminal cases, such person is generally called the *prosecutor* or the *private prosecutor*; but he might be called a *relator*. [INFORMATION.]

RELEASE (Lat. *Relaxatio*). 1. A discharge or conveyance by one who has a right or interest in lands, but not the possession, whereby he extinguishes his right for the benefit of the person in possession. The former is called the *releasor*, the latter the *releasee*. [LEASE AND RELEASE; PARTICULAR TENANT; PRIVITY OF ESTATE.]

2. An instrument whereby a party beneficially entitled to any estate held upon trust discharges his trustee from any further claim or liability in respect of the same.

RELEGATION. A temporary banishment, not involving civil death.

RELICT. A widow.

RELICTA VERIFICATIONE (his verification abandoned) is an old phrase denoting that a defendant having pleaded withdraws his plea, and confesses the plaintiff's right of action, and thereupon judgment is given for the plaintiff. [VERIFICATION.]

RELIEF. 1. A payment made by an heir who succeeded to a feud which his ancestors had possessed. It was in horses, arms, money, or the like; and was called a *relief*, because it raised up and re-established the inheritance. Reliefs, which originated while feuds were only life estates, were continued after feuds became hereditary. Abolished.

2. The specific assistance prayed for by a party who institutes an action in Chancery. [STATEMENT OF CLAIM; SUMMONS, 3.]

3. A tenant may apply to the court for relief against the forfeiture of a lease on

RELIEF—*continued.*
account of non-payment of rent or of other breach.

RELINQUISHMENT, DEED OF. Under the Clerical Disabilities Act 1870 any person admitted to holy orders, after having resigned his preferment, may execute and cause to be enrolled in Chancery a *deed of relinquishment.* By this means he divests himself of holy orders.

REM. [IN REM; INFORMATION IN REM; JUS IN REM.]

REMAINDER is where any estate or interest in land is granted out of a larger one, and an ulterior estate expectant on that which is so granted is at the same time conveyed away by the original owner. The first estate is called the *particular estate,* and the ulterior one the *remainder,* or the *estate in remainder.* Thus, if land be conveyed to A for life, and after his death to B, A's interest is called a *particular* estate, and B's a *remainder.* The word, though properly applied to estates in land, is also applicable to personalty. After 1925 remainders subsist only as equitable interests. See Part I of the Law of Property Act 1925. [CONTINGENT REMAINDER; REVERSION; VESTED REMAINDER.]

REMAINDERMAN. A person entitled to an estate in remainder. [REMAINDER.]

REMAND is the recommittal of an accused person to prison, or his readmission to bail, on the adjournment of the hearing of a criminal charge in a magistrates' court. A remand may be granted for securing the attendance of witnesses, for making inquiries into the previous career of the accused, or other reasonable cause.

Under s. 43 of the Prison Act 1952 *remand centres* may be provided for the detention of persons not less than fourteen but under twenty-one years of age who are remanded or committed in custody for trial or sentence.

Remand homes as formerly provided under the Children and Young Persons Act 1933 are replaced by community homes under the provisions of the Children and Young Persons Act 1969.

REMANENT PRO DEFECTU EMPTORUM (they remain unsold for want of buyers). This is a sheriff's return to a writ of *fi. fa.* when he finds himself unable to sell the goods destrained. [FIERI FACIAS.]

REMANET. A cause put off from one sitting or assizes to another.

REMEDIAL STATUTES are such as supply some defect in the existing law, and redress some abuse or inconvenience with which it is found to be attended, without introducing any provision of a penal character.

REMEDY. The means given by law for the recovery of a right, or of compensation for the infringement thereof.

REMEMBRANCERS. 1. Officers of the Exchequer, of which there were formerly three: the Queen's Remembrancer, the Lord Treasurer's Remembrancer, and the Remembrancer of First Fruits. Their duty was to put the Lord Treasurer and the justices of that court in remembrance of such things as were to be called on and dealt with for the sovereign's benefit.

The duty of the Queen's Remembrancer is to enter in his office all recognizances taken for debts due to the Crown, etc.; to take bonds for such debts, and to make out process for breach of them; also to issue process against the collectors of customs and other public payments for their accounts. He is now an officer of the Supreme Court. See ss. 122, 135 of the Judicature Act 1925; under the former section the Senior Master of the Supreme Court (Queen's Bench Division) is to hold and perform the duties of the Queen's Remembrancer.

2. The Remembrancer of the City of London is an ancient officer of the Corporation, whose original duties were mainly ceremonial, it being his office to see to the due observance of all presentations, public processions and other matters affecting the privileges of the Corporation. In this character he was their agent in Parliament, and at the Council and Treasury Boards, and to this day he performs the duty of parliamentary solicitor to the Corporation. He attends the Houses of Parliament, and examines bills likely to affect the privileges of the City, and reports upon the same to the Corporation. He also attends the Courts of Aldermen and Common Council, and committees, when required.

REMISSION. Pardon of an offence.

REMITTER is where he who has the true property or *jus proprietatis* in lands, but is wrongfully out of possession thereof, has afterwards the freehold cast upon him by some subsequent, and of course defective, title; in this case he is *remitted* or sent back, by operation of law, to his ancient and more certain title.

REMITTIT DAMNA, otherwise called a *remittitur damna,* was an entry on the record of an action whereby a plaintiff remitted the whole or a portion of the damages awarded to him by the verdict of a jury. It was held that where a jury gave greater damages than had been claimed by the plaintiff in his declaration, the error might be cured before judgment by entering a *remittitur* for the surplus. At the present time the statement of claim might be amended at the trial under R.S.C. 1965, Ord. 20, r. 5.

REMOTENESS. 1. Where an attempt is made by any instrument in writing to tie up, or to dictate the devolution of, property, or to keep the same in suspense without a beneficial owner, beyond the period allowed by law. [PERPETUITY.] 2. *Remoteness of damage.* This expression is used to denote a want of sufficiently direct connection between a wrong complained of and the injury alleged to have been sustained thereby.

REMOVAL OF ACTIONS. Actions may, in certain cases, be moved from the High Court to the county court, or *vice versa.* They may be transferred under various sections of the County Courts Act 1959 (*e.g.,* actions of contract and tort, within certain limits, may be transferred from the county court to the High Court under s. 43 thereof, or from the High Court to the county court under s. 44.) Similarly, actions commenced in the Central Office of the High Court may be removed to a district registry, or *vice versa,* for sufficient reason, under R.S.C. 1965, Ord. 4, r. 6.

REMUNERATION. Payment for services. Can include reasonable allowances in respect of expenses properly incurred in the pursuance of the duties of any office: see *e.g.* the Air Corporations Act 1967, s. 33.

RENDER. 1. To give up again; to restore.

2. A word used in connection with rents and heriots. Goods subject to rent or heriot-service are said to *lie in render,* when the lord may not only seize the identical goods, but may also distrain for them. [HERIOT.]

RENEWAL OF LEASE. A re-grant of an expiring lease for a further term. Leases may be surrendered in order to be renewed without a surrender of under-leases by virtue of the Law of Property Act 1925, s. 150. For rules in regard to renewal of leases, see *e.g.* the Landlord and Tenant Act 1954, which provides security of tenure for certain tenants occupying residential premises under ground leases, and for occupying tenants of business premises.

RENEWAL OF WRITS. No writ of summons remains in force for more than twelve months, but may be renewed before the expiration of the twelve months for a further period of six months, and so on from time to time: see R.S.C. 1965, Ord. 6, r. 8.

RENOUNCING PROBATE is where a person appointed executor of a will refuses to accept the office.

RENT (Lat. *Reditus*). A compensation, or return; that is, a profit issuing periodically out of lands or tenements. It does not necessarily consist in the payment of money. Rents are of various kinds:—1. *Rent-service,* which has some corporeal service incident to it; for non-performance of which the lord may distrain, if he has in himself the reversion after the lease or particular estate of the lessee or grantee is expired. This is the ordinary rent. 2. *Rent-charge,* which is where the owner has no future interest in the land, but is enabled to distrain by virtue of a clause in the grant or lease reserving the rent. 3. *Rent-seck* (*reditus siccus*), or barren rent, is where there is merely a rent reserved by deed, but without any clause of distress, nor any right of distress at the common law. 4. *Rents of assize,* which are certain established rents payable by freeholders and ancient copyholders of a manor. Those of the freeholders are called *chief rents* (*reditus capitales*); and both sorts are called *quit rents* (*quieti reditus*), because thereby the tenant goes quiet and free of other services. When these rents were reserved in silver or white money, they were anciently called *white rents,* or *blanch firmes* (*reditus albi*); in contra-distinction to rents reserved in

RENT—*continued.*

work, grain, or baser money, which were called *reditus nigri* or black-mail. 5. *Rack-rent* is a rent of the full value of a tenement, or near it. 6. *A fee farm rent* is a rent issuing out of an estate in fee, of at least one-fourth of the value of the lands at the time of its reservation. 7. *Forehand rent* is one payable in advance. The difference which formerly existed between the various kinds of rent is now of no practical importance.

Ss. 121, 191 of the Law of Property Act 1925 contain provisions for the remedies available for the recovery of annual sums charged on land by way of rent-charge, and for the redemption and apportionment of rents. As used in the Act, rent includes a rent-service or a rent-charge or other rent toll, duty, royalty, or annual or periodical payment in money or money's worth, reserved or issuing out of or charged upon land, but does not include mortgage interest, s. 205 (1) (xxiii).

Many enactments relating to rent control and related matters were consolidated by the Rent Act 1968. See also, as to furnished tenancies, the Rent Act 1974.

RENT ALLOWANCE. [RENT REBATE.]

RENT REBATE. Rent rebates and rent allowances may be granted to council house tenants and private tenants respectively under the provisions of the Housing Finance Act 1972, ss. 18, 19.

RENT TRIBUNALS. Tribunals established under s. 69 of the Rent Act 1968 (as substituted by s. 205 (4) of the Local Government Act 1972) to which contracts for furnished letting may be referred by either party for approval of, or reduction of, the rent. The constitution of such tribunals is laid down in Sch. 10 to the Act.

RENTS OF ASSIZE. [RENT, 4.]

REPATRIATION. The recovery of the rights of a natural-born subject by one who has become expatriated.

REPEAL (Fr. *Rappel*). A calling back. The revocation of one statute, or a part of it, by another. See the Interpretation Act 1889, ss. 11, 38.

REPLEADER was an order of the court that the parties *replead*; granted when the parties in the course of pleading raised an issue immaterial or insufficient to determine the true question in the case.

Repleaders are now out of use, as the courts have almost unlimited power of allowing amendments for the purpose of determining the real question in controversy between the parties. [AMENDMENT.]

REPLEGIARI FACIAS. A writ of replevin which issued out of Chancery, commanding the sheriff to deliver the distress (*i.e.*, the thing taken by way of distress) to the owner, and afterwards to do justice in respect of the matter in dispute in his own county court. Now superseded by ordinary action of replevin. [REPLEVIN.]

REPLEVIABLE, or **REPLEVISABLE.** Capable of being replevied. [REPLEGIARE FACIAS; REPLEVIN.]

REPLEVIN is defined as a redelivery to the owner of his cattle or goods distrained upon any cause upon security that he will prosecute the action against him that distrained, denominated an action of replevin. The "replevisor" is the party who takes back his goods. The action, if intended to be commenced in a county court, must, according to the condition of the bond, be commenced within a month; if in a superior court, then within a week. It should be brought in the latter where there is good ground for believing that the title to some corporeal or incorporeal hereditament, or to some toll, fair, market or franchise is in question, or that the rent or damage exceeds £20. The action is now tried in the same way as other actions. See Party IV of the County Courts Act 1959.

REPLEVISH. To let one to mainprise on surety. [MAINPRISE.]

REPLICATION signified generally a pleading of the plaintiff whereby he replied (otherwise than by a legal or formal objection) to a defendant's plea or answer. [REPLY.] In the action of replevin [REPLEVIN], the replication was the *defendant's* second pleading; the plaintiff's second pleading being called his *plea*. In divorce the replication is the reply to the respondent's *answer*.

REPLY. 1. The *reply* of a plaintiff is that statement in his pleading whereby he *replies* to the defence. See R.S.C. 1965, Ord. 18, r. 3.

2. The speech of counsel for the plaintiff in a civil case, or for the prosecution in a

criminal case, in answer in either case to the points raised by the defence, is generally called the *reply*.

REPORTS. 1. Histories of legal cases, with the arguments used by counsel and the reasons given for the decision of the court.

2. The reports of Chief Justice Coke are especially styled The Reports, and are in general cited without the author's name, as "Rep." [LAW REPORTS.]

The following is a catalogue of the principal Reports which have appeared up to the present time, together with the periods over which they extend and the abbreviations by which they are usually referred to. In the first column are given the names of the Reports in alphabetical order; in the second the abbreviation or abbreviations by which they are or may be referred to; in the third the period over which the Reports extend, or, in some cases, the date of publication; and in the fourth, the courts or jurisdictions whose decisions are embraced in the several series of Reports respectively.

Reports	Abbreviations	Date	Court
Action (Prize Causes)	Acton	1809–1811	Privy Council.
Adam	Adam	1893 to the present time	Court of Justiciary, Scotland.
Addams..	Add.	1822–1826	Ecclesiastical.
Adolphus & Ellis ...	Ad. & El. *or* A. & E.	1834–1842	King's (*or* Queen's) Bench.
Adolphus & Ellis New Series	Ad. & El., N.S. *or* Q.B. (for Queen's Bench.)	1841–1852	Queen's Bench.
Alcock & Napier ...	Alc. & N... ...	1831–1833	Common Law, Ireland.
Alcock's Registry Cases	Alc.	1832–1841	Common Law, Ireland.
Aleyn	Aleyn	1646–1649	King's Bench.
All England	All E.R. ...	1936 to the present time	All superior Courts.
All England Reprint	All E.R. Rep. ...	1558–1935	All Courts.
Ambler...	Amb. *or* Ambl. ...	1716–1783	Chancery.
Anderson, Sir E... ...	And.	16th century	Common Pleas.
Andrews, George ...	Andr.	1737–1740	King's Bench.
Annaly...	Ann.	... ...	King's Bench.
Anstruther	Anst.	1792–1797	Exchequer.
Arkley	Arkl.	1846–1848	Court of Justiciary, Scotland.
Armstrong, Macartney & Ogle	Arm. Mac. & O.	1840–1842	Civil and Criminal Courts, Ireland.
Arnold...	Arn.	1838–1839	Common Pleas.
Arnold & Hodges ...	Arn. & H.. ...	1840–1841	Queen's Bench.
Aspinall's Maritime Law Cases	Asp. M.L.C. ...	1870–1943	Admiralty.
Atkyns...	Atk.	1736–1754	Chancery.
Ball & Beatty	Ball & B. *or* B. & B.	1807–1814	Chancery, Ireland.
Bankruptcy and Companies Winding-up	B. & C.R.	1918–1941	Bankruptcy, etc.
Barnardiston (Ch.) ...	Barnard. (Ch.) ...	1740–1741	Chancery.
Barnardiston (K.B.) ...	Barnard. (K.B.)...	1726–1734	King's Bench.
Barnes' Notes of Cases	Barnes	1732–1760	Common Pleas.
Barnewall & Adolphus	Barn. & Ad. *or* B. & A.	1830–1834	King's Bench.

REPORTS—*continued.*

Reports	Abbreviations	Date	Court
Barnewall & Cresswell	Barn. & Cress. *or* B. & C.	1822–1830	King's Bench.
Barron & Arnold ...	Bar. & Arn. ...	1843–1846	Election Committees.
Barron & Austin ...	Bar. & Aust. ...	1842 ..	Election Committees.
Batty	Batt.	1825–1826	King's Bench, Ireland.
Beatty	Beat.	1813–1830*	Chancery, Ireland.
Beavan...	Beav.	1838–1866	Rolls.
Bell (Crown Cases) ...	Bell, C.C...	1858–1860	Crown Cases Reserved.
Bell (Scotch Appeals)	Bell, Sc. App.	1842–1850	House of Lords.
Bell (Scotch Decisions)	Bell, Ct. of Sess.	1790–1792	Court of Sessions.
	Bell, Ct. of Sess. fol.	1794–1795	
Bellewe's Reports (published 1585)	Bellewe	1377–1400	Common Law.
Belt's Supplement to Vesey, sen.	Belt's Sup. ...	1746–1756	Chancery.
Benloe	Benl.	1440–1627	King's Bench.
Benlow...	Ben.	1357–1579	Common Pleas.
Best & Smith	B. & S.	1861–1870	Queen's Bench.
Bingham.	Bing.	1822–1834	Common Pleas.
Bingham's New Cases	Bing. N.C. ...	1834–1840	Common Pleas.
Blackham, Dundas & Osborne	B. D. & O. ...	1846–1848	Exchequer, Ireland.
Blackstone, Henry ...	H. Bl.	1788–1796	Common Pleas.
Blackstone, Sir W. ...	W. Bl.	1746–1779	Common Law.
Bligh	Bli..	1819–1821	House of Lords.
Bligh's New Series ...	Bli. N.S.... ...	1827–1837	House of Lords.
Bluett's Notes of Cases	Blu.	1720–1847	Isle of Man Courts.
Bosanquet & Puller	Bos. & P. *or* B. & P.	1796–1804	Common Pleas.
Bosanquet & Puller's ... New Reports	Bos. & P.N.R.	1804–1807	Common Pleas.
Bridgman, Sir John	J. Bridg.... ...	1613–1621	Common Pleas.
Bridgman, Sir Orlando	O. Bridg... ...	1660–1666	Common Pleas.
British & Colonial Prize Cases	Br. & Col. Pr. Cas.	1914–1919	Prize Courts.
Broderip & Bingham	Bro. & B. *or* B. & B.	1819–1822	Common Pleas.
Brooke's New Cases ...	Brooke, N.C. *or* B.N.C.	1515–1558	Common Law.
Broun	Broun	1842–1845	Court of Justiciary, Scotland.
Brown's Reports of Cases in Chancery	Bro. C.C... ...	1778–1794	Chancery.
Brown's Reports of Cases in Parliament	Bro. P.C... ...	1702–1800	House of Lords.
Browne & Macnamara Railway Cases	Bro. & Mac. ...	1881–1900	Railway and Canal Cases.
Browning & Lushington	B. & L.	1863–1866	Admiralty and Privy Council.

* Including also some earlier cases.

Reports	Abbreviations	Date	Court
Brownlow & Goldes-borough	B. & G.	1569–1624	Common Pleas.
Bruce's Reports	Bruce	1714–1715	Court of Session.
Buck's Cases in Bank-ruptcy	Buck	1816–1820	Bankruptcy, etc.
Bulstrode	Bulstr.	1610–1626	King's Bench.
Bunbury	Bunb.	1713–1741	Exchequer.
Burrow's Reports ...	Burr.	1756–1772	King's Bench.
Burrow's Settlement Cases	Burr. S.C. ...	1733–1776	King's Bench.
Butterworths Workmen's Compensation Cases	B.W.C.C... ...	1907–1949	King's Bench.
Cababe & Ellis	Cab. & El. ...	1882–1885	Queen's Bench.
Caldecott's Settlement Cases	Cald. S.C.	1776–1885	King's Bench.
Calthrop's Cases on the Customs of London	Calthrop	1609–1618	King's Bench.
Campbell	Camp.	1807–1816	Nisi Prius.
Carpmael's Patent Cases	Carp. P.C. ...	1602–1842	All the Courts.
Carrington & Kirwan	Carr. & K. or C. & K.	1843–1853	Nisi Prius and Criminal Courts.
Carrington & Marsh-man	Car. & M. or C. & M.	1841–1842	Nisi Prius and Criminal Courts.
Carrington & Payne	Car. & P. or C. & P.	1823–1841	Nisi Prius and Criminal Courts.
Carrow, Hamerton & Allen's New Sess. Cases	C. H. & A. or New Sess. Cas.	1844–1851	All the Courts.
Carter	Cart.	1664–1673	Common Pleas.
Carthew	Carth.	1687–1700	King's Bench.
Cary	Cary	1557–1602	Chancery.
Cases in Chancery ...	Ch. Ca.	1660–1697	Chancery.
Cases in Equity Abridged	Cas. Eq. Ab. or Eq. Cas. Abr.	1667–1744	Chancery.
Cases in the time of Finch	Cas. temp. Finch	1673–1680	Chancery.
Cases in the time of Lord Hardwicke	Cas. temp. Hard-wicke	1733–1737	King's Bench.
Cases in the time of Lord Talbot	Cas. temp. Talbot	1730–1737	Chancery.
Cases of Practice, King's Bench	Cas. Pra. K.B. ...	1655–1775	King's Bench.
Chitty	Chit.	1770–1822*	King's Bench.
Choice Cases in Chancery	Cho. Ca. Ch. ...	1558–1605	Chancery.
Clark & Finnelly ...	Cl. & Fin.	1831–1846	House of Lords.
Clayton	Clay.	1631–1650	York Assizes.

* Including also some earlier cases.

REPORTS—*continued.*

Reports	Abbreviations	Date	Court
Cockburn & Rowe ...	C. & R.	1833 ...	Election Committees.
Cohen	Cr. App. Rep. ...	1908 to the present time	Criminal Appeal.
Coke, Sir Edward ...	Co. Rep. *or* Rep.	1572–1616	Common Law.
Colles	Colles	1697–1713	House of Lords.
Collyer...	Coll.	1844–1846	Chancery.
Coltman's Registration Cases	Colt.	1879–1885	Registration Cases.
Comberbach	Comb.	1685–1698	King's Bench.
Commercial Cases ...	Com. Cas.. ...	1895–1941	The Commercial Court.
Common Bench Reports	C.B.	1845–1856	Common Pleas.
Common Bench Reports, New Series	C.B., N.S. ...	1856–1865	Common Pleas.
Common Law Reports	C.L.R.	1853–1855	Common Law Courts.
Common Market Law Reports	C.M.L.R. ...	1962 to the present time	European Court.
Comyns..	Com. Dig.. ...	1695–1740	Common Law Courts.
Connor & Lawson ...	Conn. & Law., *or* C. & L.	1841–1843	Chancery, Ireland.
Cooke	Cooke Pr. Cas.	1706–1747	Common Pleas.
Cooke & Alcock ...	C. & A.	1833–1834	King's Bench, Ireland.
Cooper, George ...	Coop. G... ...	1792–1815	Chancery.
Cooper's Cases in Chancery	Coop. temp. Brough.	1833–1834	Chancery (Lord Brougham).
„ „ „	„ Pr. Cas.	1837–1838	Chancery.
„ „ „	„ temp. Cott.	1846–1848	Chancery (Lord Cottenham).
Corbett & Daniell ...	Corb. & D. ...	1819 ...	Election Committees.
County Court Cases ...	C.C. Cas... ...	1847–1852	Common Law Courts.
Couper...	Coup.	1868–1885	Court of Justiciary, Scotland.
Court of Session Cases	Court Sess. Ca.	1821 to the present time	Court of Session, Scotland.
Cowell's Indian Appeals (Law Rep. vol. ii)	L.R., 2 Ind. App.	Publication commenced March, 1875	Privy Council.
Cowper	Cowp.	1774–1778	King's Bench.
Cox & Atkinson's Registration Appeals	Cox & Atk. ...	1843–1846	Common Pleas.
Cox (Chancery)	Cox	1783–1797	Chancery.
Cox (Criminal Law)	Cox's C.C. ...	1843–1945	Criminal Courts.
Craig & Phillips. ...	Cr. & Ph.	1840–1841	Chancery.
Craigie Stewart & Paton's Scotch Appeals	Cr. St. & P. ...	1726–1822	House of Lords.
Crawford & Dix. ...	Cr. & D... ...	1838–1846	Irish Courts.
Cresswell's Insolvent Cases	Cress. Insolv. Cas.	1827–1829	Insolvency.
Cripps' Church Cases	Cripps' Church Cas.	1847–1850	Ecclesiastical.
Croke, time of Charles I	Cro. Car... ...	1625–1641	Common Law.

Reports	Abbreviations	Date	Court
Croke, time of Elizabeth	Cro. Eliz. ...	1582–1603	Common Law.
Crock, time of James I	Cro. Jac.	1603–1625	Common Law.
Crompton & Jervis ...	Cr. & J. or C. & J.	1830–1832	Exchequer.
Crompton & Meeson	Cr. & M... ...	1832–1834	Exchequer.
Crompton, Meeson & Roscoe	Cr. M. & R. ...	1834–1835	Exchequer.
Cunningham	Cunn.	1734–1735	King's Bench.
Curteis...	Curt.	1834–1844	Ecclesiastical.
Dalrymple, Sir Hew ...	Dalr.	1698–1720	Court of Session, Scotland.
Daniell...	Dan.	1817–1823	Exchequer, Equity.
Danson & Lloyd ...	D. & L.	1828–1829	Common Law.
Davies' Patent Cases ...	D.P.C.	1785–1816	Common Law Courts.
Davis, Sir John.. ...	Davis	1604–1611	Common Law, Ireland.
Davison & Merivale ...	D. & M.... ...	1843–1844	Queen's Bench.
Deacon	Deac.	1834–1840	Bankruptcy, etc.
Deacon & Chitty ...	Deac. & Chit. ...	1832–1835	Bankruptcy.
Deane's Reports completed by Swabey	Deane or Dea. & Sw.	1855–1857	Ecclesiastical.
Dearsly	Dears. C.C. ...	1852–1856	Criminal Courts.
Dearsly & Bell... ...	Dearsl. & B. or D. & B.	1856–1858	Criminal Courts.
Deas & Anderson ...	Deas. & And. ...	1829–1832	Court of Session.
De Gex...	De G.	1844–1848	Bankruptcy.
De Gex & Jones. ...	De G. & Jo. or D. & J.	1857–1859	Chancery (Appeals).
De Gex & Smale ...	De G. & Sm. ...	1846–1852	Chancery.
De Gex, Fisher & Jones	De G. F. & Jo. or D. F. & J.	1859–1862	Chancery (Appeals).
De Gex, Jones & Smith	De G. J. & Sm. or D. J. & S.	1862–1865	Chancery (Appeals).
De Gex, Macnaghten & Gordon	De G. Mac. & G. or D.M. & G.	1851–1857	Chancery (Appeals).
Delane...	Delane	1832–1835	Revising Barristers.
Denison..	Den. C.C. ...	1844–1852	Criminal Courts.
Dickens..	Dick.	1559–1798	Chancery.
Dodson	Dods.	1811–1822	Admiralty.
Douglas' Election Cases	Doug. El. Cas.	1774–1776	Election Committees.
Douglas' King's Bench	Dougl. K.B. ...	1778–1785	King's Bench.
Dow	Dow	1812–1818	House of Lords.
Dow & Clarke	Dow & Cl. ...	1827–1832	House of Lords.
Dowling's Practice Reports	Dowl. or D.P.C.	1830–1841	Bail Court.
Dowling's Practice Reports, New Series	Dowl., N.S. ...	1841–1843	Bail Court.
Dowling Lowndes ...	Dowl. & L. or D. & L.	1843–1849	Bail Court.
Dowling & Ryland, King's Bench	Dowl. & Ry. or D. & R.	1822–1827	King's Bench.
Dowling & Ryland, Nisi Prius	D. & R., N.P. ...	1822–1823	Nisi Prius Cases.

REPORTS—*continued.*

Reports	Abbreviations	Date	Court
Dowling & Rylands' Magistrates' Cases	D. & R.M.C. ...	1822–1827	King's Bench.
Drewry...	Drew.	1852–1859	V.-C. Kindersley.
Drewry & Smale ...	Dr. & Sm.. ...	1859–1865	V.-C. Kindersley.
Drinkwater	Drink.	1840–1841	Common Pleas.
Drury	Dru.	1841–1844	Chancery, Ireland.
Drury & Walsh ...	Dru. & Wal. ...	1837–1841	Chancery, Ireland.
Drury & Warren ...	Dru. & War. ...	1841–1843	Chancery, Ireland.
Dunlop, Bell & Murray	... ...	1834–1840	Court of Session.
Durie	Durie	1621–1642	Court of Session.
Durnford & East's Term Reports	Durn. & E. *or* T.R.	1785–1800	King's Bench.
Dyer	Dy.	1513–1581	Common Law.
Eagle and Young's Collection of Tithe Cases	E. & Y.	1204–1825	All the Courts.
East	East	1800–1812	King's Bench.
Eden	Eden	1757–1766	Chancery.
Edgar	Edg.	1724–1725	Court of Session.
Edwards	Edw.	1808–1812	Admiralty.
Elchie	Elch.	1733–1754	Court of Session.
Ellis & Blackburn ...	Ell. & Bl. *or* E. & B.	1852–1858	Queen's Bench.
Ellis & Ellis ...	Ell. & E.... ...	1858–1861	Queen's Bench.
Ellis, Blackburn & Ellis	Ell. Bl. & Ell. *or* E. B. & E.	1858–1860	Queen's Bench.
Equity Cases ... Abridged	Eq. Cas. Abr.	1667–1744	Chancery.
Equity Reports.. ...	Eq. R.	1853–1855	Chancery.
Espinasse	Esp.	1793–1810	Nisi Prius.
Exchequer Reports	Exch.	1847–1856	Exchequer.
Faculty Decisions ...	Fac. Dec... ...	1752–1841	Court of Session.
Falconer	Falc.	1744–1751	Court of Session.
Falconer & Fitzherbert	Falc. & F.. ...	1835–1838	Election Committees.
Ferguson.	Ferg.	1738–1752	Court of Session.
Ferguson's Consistorial Reports	Ferg.	1811–1817	Consistorial Court, Scotland (now abolished).
Finch	Finch	1673–1680	Chancery.
Finch's Precedents ...	Prec. Ch... ...	1689–1722	Chancery.
Finlason's Leading Cases	Finl. L.C.	Publd. 1847	Common Law.
Fitzgibbons	Fitz-G.	1727–1731	King's Bench.
Flannagan & Kelly	Fl. & K.... ...	1840–1842	Rolls Court, Ireland.
Fonblanque	Fonb.	1849–1852	Bankruptcy.
Forbes	Forb.	1705–1713	Court of Session.
Forester's Cases t. Talbot	Cas. temp. Talbot.	1730–1737	Chancery.
Forrest...	Forr.	1800–1801	Exchequer.

Reports	Abbreviations	Date	Court
Fortescue	Fort.	1692–1736	All the Courts.
Foster (Crown Law) ...	Fost. C.L.. ...	1708–1760	Criminal Courts.
Foster & Finlayson ...	F. & F. ...	1856–1867	Nisi Prius and Criminal Courts.
Fountainhall ...	Fount.	1678–1712	Court of Session.
Fox & Smith ...	Fox & S... ...	1822–1825	King's Bench, Ireland.
Fox & Smith, Registration Cases	Fox. & S., Reg. ...	1886–1895	Registration Cases.
Fraser	Fras.	1776–1777	Election Committees.
Freeman ...	Freem. (Ch.) ...	1660–1706	Chancery.
Freeman ...	Freem. (K.B.)	1670–1704	Common Law.
Gale	Gale	1835–1836	Exchequer.
Gale and Davidson ...	G. & D. ...	1841–1843	Queen's Bench.
Gibson...	Gibs. ...	1621–1642	Court of Session.
Giffard	Giff. or Gif.	1857–1865	V.-C. Stuart.
Gilbert	Gilb. (Ch.)	1706–1726	Chancery, etc.
Gilmour & Falconer	Gil. & Fal.	1661–1686	Court of Session.
Glascock.	Glasc. ...	1831–1832	Irish Courts.
Glyn & Jameson ...	G. & J. ...	1819–1828	Bankruptcy, etc.
Godbolt.. ...	Godb. ...	1574–1637	Queen's or King's Bench.
Gouldsborough	Gouldsb. ...	1586–1601	Common Law.
Gow	Gow	1818–1820	Nisi Prius.
Gwillim..	Gwill. ...	1224–1824	All the Courts.
Haggard (Adm.). ...	Hagg. Adm. ...	1822–1838	Admiralty.
Haggard's Consistorial Reports	Hagg. Cons. ...	1789–1821	Court of Session.
Haggard's Ecclesiastical Reports	Hagg. Eccl. ...	1827–1833	Ecclesiastical.
Hailes	Hail.	1766–1791	Court of Session.
Hall & Twells	Hall & Tw. or H. & Tw.	1848–1850	Chancery.
Hanmer's Lord Kenyon's Notes	Ld. Ken... ...	1753–1759	King's Bench.
Hansell...	H. B. R.	1915–1917	Bankruptcy and Companies Winding-up.
Harcarse.	Harc.	1681–1691	Court of Session.
Hardres..	Hardr.	1655–1669	Exchequer.
Hare	Hare or Ha. ...	1841–1853	Vice-Chancellors' Courts.
Harrison & Rutherfurd	Har. & Ruth. ...	1865–1866	Common Pleas.
Harrison & Wollaston	Har. & W. ...	1835–1836	King's Bench.
Hayes	Hayes	1830–1832	Exchequer, Ireland.
Haynes & Jones. ...	Haynes & Jo. ...	1832–1834	Exchequer, Ireland.
Hemming & Miller ...	Hem. & Mill. or H. & M.	1862–1865	V.-C. Wood.
Hetley	Het.	1627–1631	Common Pleas.
Hobart...	Hob.	1613–1625	Common Law.
Hodges...	Hodg.	1835–1837	Common Pleas.

REPORTS—*continued.*

Reports	Abbreviations	Date	Court
Hogan	Hog.	1816–1834	Rolls Court, Ireland.
Holt (L. C. J.)	Holt (K.B.) ...	1688–1710	King's *or* Queen's Bench.
Holt's Nisi Prius ...	Holt	1815–1817	Nisi Prius.
Holt, Wm.	Holt, Eq... ...	1845 ...	Vice-Chancellors' Courts.
Home	Home Ct. of Sess.	1735–1744	Court of Session.
Hopwood & Coltman	Hop. & C..	1868–1878	Common Pleas.
Hopwood & Philbrick	Hop. & Ph. ...	1863–1867	Common Pleas.
Horn & Hurlstone ...	H. & H.	1838–1839	Exchequer.
House of Lords' Cases	H. L. Cas.. ...	1847–1866	House of Lords.
Hovenden's Supplement to Vesey, Junr.	Hov. Suppl. ...	1753–1817	Chancery.
Howell's State Trials	How. St. Tr. *or* State Tr.	1163–1820	All the Courts.
Hudson & Brooke ...	H. & B.	1827–1831	Common Law, Ireland.
Hume	Hume	1781–1822	Court of Session.
Hunt's Annuity Cases	Hunt	1777–1794	All the Courts.
Hurlstone & Coltman	H. & C.	1862–1866	Exchequer.
Hurlstone & Gordon	Included in Exch. Reports	1854–1856	Exchequer.
Hurlstone & Norman	H. & N.	1856–1862	Exchequer.
Hurlstone & Walmsley	H. & W. ...	1840–1841	Exchequer.
Hutton	Hutt.	1617–1638	Common Pleas.
Irish Chancery	Ir. Ch.	1850–1867	Chancery.
Irish Circuit Cases ...	Ir. Cir. Ca. ...	1841–1843	Assize Courts, Ireland.
Irish Common Law Reports	Ir. C.L.R... ...	1849–1866	Common Law, Ireland.
Irish Equity Reports	Ir. Eq. R... ...	1838–1851	Chancery, Ireland.
Irish Jurist	Ir. Jur.	1849–1866	Irish Courts.
Irish Law Recorder	Ir. L. Rec. ...	1827–1831	Irish Courts.
Irish Law Reports	Ir. L. Rep. ...	1838–1851	Common Law Courts, Ireland.
Irish Reports, Common Law	I.C.L.R.	1849–1866	Common Law Courts, Ireland.
Irish Reports, Equity	I.Eq. R.	1838–1851	Chancery, Ireland.
Jacob	Jac.	1821–1823	Chancery.
Jacob & Walker ...	Jac. & W. *or* J. & W.	1819–1821	Chancery.
Jebb	Jebb C.C.	1822–1840	Criminal Courts, Ireland.
Jebb & Bourke	J. & B.	1841–1842	Queen's Bench, Ireland.
Jebb & Symes	J. & S.	1838–1841	Queen's Bench, Ireland.
Jenkins' Centuries (*i.e.*, Hundreds) of Reports	Jenk. Cent. ...	1220–1623	Exchequer Chamber.
Johnson	Johns. *or* Jo. ...	1858–1860	Chancery, V.-C. Wood.
Johnson & Hemming	John. & H. *or* J. & H.	1859–1862	Chancery, V.-C. Wood.
Jones	Jon. Ex. R. ...	1834–1838	Exchequer, Ireland.
Jones & Carey	Jones & C. ...	1838–1839	Exchequer, Ireland.
Jones & Latouche ...	Jo. & Lat.. ...	1844–1846	Chancery, Ireland.

Reports	Abbreviations	Date	Court
Jones, Sir T.	Jo. *or* T. Jo. ...	1667–1685	Common Law.
Jones, Sir W.	Jo. *or* W. Jo. ...	1620–1640	Common Law.
Jurist Reports	Jur.	1837–1854	All the Courts.
Jurist Reports, New Series	Jur., N.S... ...	1855–1867	All the Courts.
Jurist (Scottish) ...	Sc. Jur.	1829–1873	Scotch Courts.
Justice of the Peace	J.P.	1837 to the present time	All the Courts.
Kay	Kay	1853–1854	Chancery, V.-C. Wood.
Kay & Johnson ...	Kay & J... ...	1854–1858	Chancery, V.-C. Wood.
Keane & Grant ...	K. & G. ...	1854–1862	Registration Cases in the Common Pleas.
Keble	Keb.	1661–1677	King's Bench.
Keen	Keen *or* Kee ...	1836–1838	Rolls Court.
Keilwey	Keil.	1327–1578	Common Law.
Kelynge..	Kel. W. ...	1730–1732	Chancery.
Kenyon's Notes of Cases	Ld. Ken. *or* Keny.	1753–1759	King's Bench.
Knapp	Knapp	1829–1836	Privy Council.
Knapp & Ombler ...	Knapp & O. ...	1834–1835	Election Committees.
Lane	Lane	1605–1611	Exchequer.
Latch	Lat.	1625–1628	King's Bench.
Law Journal	L.J.O.S.	1822–1831	All the Courts.
Law Journal, New Series	L.J., N.S., *or* L. J. Rep., N.S.*	1832–1949	All the Courts.
Law Recorder (Ireland)	Ir. L. Rec.. ...	1827–1831	Irish Courts.

* (1) As the Old Series of the Law Journal Reports consisted of but nine volumes, it is not necessary to append the initials "N.S." to the references to volumes of the New Series later than the ninth, and in fact they are often omitted in such references, the omission not involving any risk of confusion.

(2) As the Law Journal Reports consist of several sections, according to the jurisdiction in which any given case is heard, the abbreviations representing the section or jurisdiction should, in referring, be added to the initials "L.J." Thus, "L.J.,Ch." is a reference to the Chancery section of the Reports; "L.J., Bank." *or* "L.J.,Bkcy." to the Bankruptcy section, etc. Cases in the House of Lords and Exchequer Chamber are arranged according to the courts from which they originally come. From the commencement of the 45th volume in January 1876, the Queen's Bench, Common Pleas and Exchequer Reports form one section; so do the Probate, Divorce and Admiralty Reports. From 1947 the Law Journal Reports consist of one volume covering all courts and they are cited as [1947] L.J.R.

In reference to the Law Reports, the figure representing the volume is placed between "L. R." and the abbreviation representing the particular division or series; thus, a reference to the first page of the ninth volume of the Queen's Bench series should be given as "L.R., 9 Q.B. 1." Three new series of the Law Reports commenced in 1876, of which the first (Chancery, Bankruptcy and Lunacy) series was cited as "Ch.D."; the second (Common Law) series was divided into four sections, cited as "Q.B.D.," "C.P.D.," "Ex.D." and "P.D." respectively; and the third (Appellate) series was cited as "App. Cas." Since 1891 they have been cited as [1891] 1 Ch., 2 Ch.; [1891] 1 Q.B., 2 Q.B. (or K.B.); [1891] P., etc.

REPORTS—*continued.*

Reports	Abbreviations	Date	Court
Law Reports	Law Rep. *or* L.R.	1865 to the present time	All the Courts.
Law Times Reports ...	L.T.O.S.... ...	1843–1860	All the Courts.
Law Times, New Series	L. T.	1859–1947	All the Courts.
Leach	Leach	1730–1814	Criminal Courts.
Lee	Lee	1752–1758	Ecclesiastical.
Lee's Cases, tempore Hardwicke	Lee *temp.* Hard.	1733–1738	King's Bench.
Legal Observer.. ...	Leg. Ob.	1830–1856	All the Courts.
Leigh & Cave ...	L. & C.	1861–1865	Crown Cases Reserved.
Leonard..	Leon.	1552–1615	Common Law.
Levinz	Lev.	1660–1696	Common Law.
Lewin's Crown Cases	Lew. C.C.. ...	1822–1838	Criminal Courts (Northern Circuit).
Ley	Ley	1608–1629	Common Law.
Lilly's "Cases in Assize"	Lil..	Publd. 1719	Common Law.
Littleton	Litt.	1627–1631	Common Pleas and Exch.
Lloyd & Goold, tempore Plunkett	L. & G. *temp.* Plunk. *or* Ll. & G. *t.* Pl.	1834–1839	Chancery, Ireland.
Lloyd & Goold, tempore Sugden	L. & G. *temp.* Sug. *or* Ll. & G. *t.* Sugd.	1835 ...	Chancery, Ireland.
Lloyd & Welsby ...	L. & Welsb. ...	1829–1930	Common Law.
Lloyd's...	Lloyd's Rep. ...	1951 to the present time	Admiralty.
Lloyd's List Law Reports	Lloyd L. Rep.	1919–1950	Admiralty.
Lloyd's Prize Cases ...	Lloyd Pr. Cas.	1914–1924	Prize Court.
Lofft	Lofft	1772–1774	King's Bench.
Longfield & Townshend	L. & T.	1841–1842	Exchequer, Ireland.
Lowndes & Maxwell	L. & M.... ...	1852 ...	Bail Court.
Lowndes, Maxwell & Pollock	L. M. & P. ...	1850–1851	Bail Court, etc.
Luders	Luders	1784–1787	Election Committees.
Lumley's Poor Law Cases	Lumley P.L.C.	1834–1842	All the Courts.
Lushington	Lush	1859–1862	Admiralty.
Lutwyche	Lutw.	1682–1704	Common Pleas.
Lutwyche's Registration Cases	Lutw. Reg. Cas.	1843–1853	Common Pleas.
Macfarlane	Macf.	1838–1839	Jury Court, Scotland.
Maclaurin	Macl.	1670–1773	Scotch Criminal Courts.
Maclean & Robinson	Macl. & R. ...	1839 ...	House of Lords (Sc. App.)
Macnaghten & Gordon	Macn. & Gor.	1849–1852	Chancery Appeals.

Reports	Abbreviations	Date	Court
Macpherson's Court of Session Cases	Macph. (Ct. of Sess.)	1862–1873	Court of Session.
Macpherson's Indian Appeals (in connection with the Law Reports [vol. i.])	Macph. Ind. Ap. or L.R., 1 Ind. App.	1873–1874	Privy Council (see "Cowell's Indian Appeals").
Macqueen's	Macq. Sc. App.	1849–1865	House of Lords.
Macrea & Hertslet ...	Mac. & H. ...	1847–1852	Insolvent Debtor's Court.
Macrory's Patent Cases	Mac. P.C.. ...	1847–1856	All the Courts.
Maddock	Madd.	1815–1821	Chancery.
Maddock & Geldart	Madd. & Gel. or 6 Mad.	1819–1822	Chancery.
Magistrate, The ...	Mag.	1848–1852	All the Courts.
Manning & Granger	Man. & Gr. or M. & G.	1840–1845	Common Pleas.
Manning & Ryland ...	M. & R. (K.B.)	1827–1830	King's Bench.
Manning & Ryland's Magistrates' Cases	M. & R. (M.C.)	1827–1830	King's Bench.
Manning, Granger & Scott (C.B., 1st nine volumes)	C. B. (for Common Bench)	1845–1856	Common Pleas (see "Common Bench Reports").
Manson's Reports ...	Mans.	1893–1914	Bankruptcy and Company Winding-up.
March's New Cases ...	Mar.	1639–1642	Common Law.
Marriot	Marr.	1776–1779	Admiralty.
Marshall	Marsh.	1813–1816	Common Pleas.
Maule & Selwyn ...	M. & S.	1813–1817	King's Bench.
Maclean & Robinson's Scotch Appeals	Mac. & Rob. ...	1839 ...	House of Lords.
M'Cleland	M'Clel	1824 ...	Exchequer, Equity.
M'Cleland & Younge	M'Clel. & Y. ...	1824–1825	Exchequer, Equity.
Meeson & Welsby ...	Mees. & Wels. or M. & W.	1836–1847	Exchequer.
Megone's Company Cases	Meg.	1889–1891	Company Cases.
Merivale	Mer.	1815–1817	Chancery.
Milward	Milw.	1819–1843	Ecclesiastical Courts, Ireland.
Modern Reports (Leach's)	Mod.	1669–1755	All the Courts.
Molloy...	Moll.	1808–1831	Chancery, Ireland.
Montagu	Mont.	1829–1832	Bankruptcy.
Montagu & Ayrton	Mont. & Ayr. or M. & A.	1832–1838	Bankruptcy.
Montagu & Bligh ...	Mont. & B. or M. & B.	1832–1833	Bankruptcy.
Montagu & Chitty ...	Mont. & Chit. or M. & C.	1838–1840	Bankruptcy.
Montagu & M'Arthur	Mont. & M'A.	1826–1830	Bankruptcy.

REPORTS—*continued.*

Reports	Abbreviations	Date	Court
Montagu & M'Arthur	Mont. & M'A.	1826–1830	Bankruptcy.
Montagu, Deacon & De Gex	Mont. D. & De G.	1840–1844	Bankruptcy.
Moody...	Mood. C. C. ...	1824–1844	Criminal Courts.
Moody & Malkin ...	Mood. & M. *or* M. & M.	1826–1830	Nisi Prius.
Moody & Robinson	Mood. & Rob. *or* M. & R.	1830–1844	Nisi Prius.
Moore (see also the following names)	Moore (K.B.) ...	1485–1620	Common Law.
Moore	Moore (C.P.) ...	1817–1827	Common Pleas.
Moore & Payne. ...	Moore & P. *or* M. & P.	1827–1831	Common Pleas.
Moore & Scott	Moo. & S. *or* M. & Scott	1831–1834	Common Pleas.
Moore's Indian Appeals	Moo. Ind. App.	1836–1872	Privy Council.
Moore's Privy Council Cases	Moo. P.C.C. ...	1836–1863	Privy Council.
Moore's Privy Council Cases, New Series	Moo. P.C.C., N.S.	1862–1873	Privy Council.
Morrel, Bankruptcy Reports	Morr. B.R. ...	1884–1893	Bankruptcy.
Mosely...	Mos.	1726–1730	Chancery.
Murphy & Hurlstone	M. & H.... ...	1837 ...	Exchequer.
Murray's Reports ...	Murr.	1816–1830	Jury Court, Scotland.
Mylne & Craig	My. & Cr. ..	1835–1841	Chancery Appeals.
Mylne & Keen	My. & K.	1832–1835	Chancery Appeals.
Nelson	Nels.	1625–1693	Chancery.
Neville & Macnamara's Railway and Canal Cases	Nev. & M. ...	1855–1874	All the Courts.
Neville & Manning ...	Nev. & M. (K.B.)	1832–1836	King's Bench.
Neville & Manning (Mag. Cas.)	N. & M. (M.C.)	1832–1836	King's Bench.
Neville & Perry ...	Nev. & P. (K.B.) *or* N. & P. (K.B.)	1836–1838	King's Bench.
New County Court Cases	N.C.C. Cas. ...	1848–1851	Common Law Courts.
New Magistrates' Cases	N.M.C. *or* New Mag. Cas.	1844–1850	Common Law Courts.
New Practice Cases	N.P.C. *or* New Pract. Cas.	1844–1848	Common Law Courts.
New Reports	N.R. *or* New Rep.	1862–1865	All the Courts.
New Sessions Cases ...	New Sess. Cas.	1844–1851	Common Law Courts.
Nisbet	Nisb.	1665–1677	Court of Session.
Nolan (Magistrates' Cases)	Nolan	1791–1793	King's Bench.

Reports	Abbreviations	Date	Court
Notes of Cases	Notes of Cases	1841–1850	Ecc. & Adm. Courts.
Noy	Noy	1558–1649	Common Law.
O'Malley & Hardcastle	O'Malley & H.	1869–1934	Election Cases.
Owen	Owen	1557–1614	Common Law.
Palmer...	Palm.	1619–1629	King's Bench.
Parker	Park.	1743–1767	Exchequer.
	App.	1678–1717	
Paton's Scotch Appeals	Pat. App... ...	1726–1822	House of Lords.
Peake	Peake	1790–1794	Nisi Prius.
Peake's Additional Cases	Peake, Add. Cas.	1795–1812	Nisi Prius.
Peckwell	Peckw.	1803–1806	Election Committees.
Peere Williams	P. Wms.... ...	1695–1735	Chancery.
Perry & Davidson ...	Per. & Dav. ...	1838–1841	Queen's Bench.
Perry & Knapp	Per. & Kn. ...	1833	Election Committees.
Philipps..	Phil. El. Cas. ...	1780 ...	Election Committees.
Phillimore	Phil. Eccl.. ...	1809–1821	Ecclesiastical.
Phillips...	Phill.	1841–1849	Chancery Appeals.
Pigot & Rodwell (Reg. Cas.)	Pig. & Rod. ...	1843–1845	Common Pleas.
Pitcairn's Criminal Trials	Pitc.	1488–1624	Court of Justiciary.
Plowden	Plowd.	1550–1580	Common Law.
Pollexfen	Pollexf.	1670–1682	King's Bench.
Popham..	Poph.	1591–1627	Common Law.
Power, Rodwell & Dew	P.R. & D.. ...	1848–1856	Election Committees.
Precedents in Chancery	Prec. Ch... ...	1689–1722	Chancery.
Price	Price	1814–1824	Exchequer.
Queen's Branch Reports	Q.B.	1841–1852	Queen's Bench.
Railway and Canal Cases	Rail. Cas. *or* Rail & Can. Cas.	1835–1854	All the Courts.
Railway and Canal Traffic Cases	Ry. & Can. Tr. Cas.	1855–1950	All the Courts.
Raymond, Lord ...	Ld. Raym. ...	1694–1732	Common Law.
Raymond, Sir T.. ...	Raym. *or* T. Raym.	1660–1683	Common Law.
Rayner's Tithe Cases	Reyn.	1575–1782	All the Courts.
Real Property Cases	R.P. Cas... ...	1843–1847	All the Courts.
Reilly's Albert Arbitration	... ...	1871–1873	Lord Cairns.
Reilly's European Arbitration	... ...	1872 ...	Lord Westbury.

REPORTS—*continued.*

Reports	Abbreviations	Date	Court
Reports of Patent Cases	R.P.C.	1884 to the present time	All the Courts.
Reports in Chancery ...	Ch. Rep. *or* Rep. Ch.	1615–1710	Chancery.
Revised Reports. ...	R.R.	1785–1866	All the Courts.
Ridgway, Lapp & Shoales	R. L. & S. ...	1793–1795	King's Court, Ireland.
Ridgway's Case in the time of Lord Hardwicke	Ridg. *temp.* Hard.	1733–1736 1744–1746	King's Bench. Chancery.
Ridgway's Parliamentary Reports	Ridg. P.C. ...	1784–1796	House of Lords, Ireland.
Robertson (Eccl. Reports)	Rob. Eccl. ...	1844–1853	Ecclesiastical.
Robertson (Scotch Appeals)	Rob. Sc. App.	1707–1727	House of Lords.
Robinson (Chr.). ...	Ch. Rob. ...	1798–1808	Admiralty.
Robinson, Geo. (Scotch Appeals)	G. Rob. *or* Robin. App.	1840–1841	House of Lords.
Robinson, W.	Wm. Rob. ...	1838–1850	Admiralty.
Rolle, Sir. H.	Roll. Rep., *or* Rolle	1614–1625	King's Bench.
Rose	Rose	1810–1816	Bankruptcy.
Ross' Leading Cases on Commercial Law	Ross, L.C. ...	Publd. 1853	All the Courts.
Ross' Leading Cases on the Law of Scotland	... ...	Publd. 1849	Scotch Courts.
Russell	Russ.	1824–1829	Chancery Appeals.
Russell & Mylne ...	Russ. & Myl. *or* R. & M.	1829–1833	Chancery Appeals.
Russell & Ryan.. ...	Russ. & Ry. ...	1800–1823	Criminal Courts.
Ryan & Moody	Ry. & M. ...	1823–1826	Nisi Prius.
Salkeld...	Salk.	1689–1712	King's Bench (principally).
Saunders.	Saund.	1666–1672	King's Bench.
Saunders & Cole (Bail Ct.)	B.C.R.	1846–1848	Bail Court.
Sausse & Scully	Sau. & Sc. ...	1837–1840	Rolls Court, Ireland.
Saville	Sav.	1580–1591	Common Law.
Sayer	Say.	1751–1756	King's Bench.
Shoales & Lefroy ...	Sch. & Lef. *or* S. & L.	1802–1806	Chancery, Ireland.
Scott	Scott	1834–1840	Common Pleas.
Scott's New Reports ...	Scott, N.R. ...	1840–1845	Common Pleas.
Searle & Smith.. ...	Se. & Sm. ...	1859–1860	Probate and Divorce.
Select Cases in Chancery	Sel. Ca. Ch. ...	1685–1698	Chancery.
Sessions Cases... ...	Sess. Cas. (K.B.)	1710–1747	King's Bench.
Shaw	Shaw	1848–1852	Court of Justiciary.

Reports	Abbreviations	Date	Court
Shaw & Dunlop ...	S. & D. or Sh. Just.	1819–1831	Court of Justiciary.
Shaw, Dunlop, Napier & Bell	S., D., N. & B. or Sh. Teind Ct.	1821–1831	Court of Teinds.
Shaw & M'Clean's Scotch Appeals	Sh. & M'C. ...	1835–1838	House of Lords.
Shaw's Scotch Appeals	Sh. Sc. App. ...	1821–1824	House of Lords.
Shower...	Show.	1678–1695	King's Bench.
Shower's Cases in Parl.	Show. P.C. ...	1694–1699	House of Lords.
Siderfin	Sid.	1657–1670	King's Bench.
Simons...	Sim.	1826–1852	Chancery.
Simons & Stuart ...	Sim. & St. or S. & S.	1822–1826	Chancery.
Simons, New Series ...	Sim., N.S. ...	1850–1852	Chancery.
Skinner	Skin.	1681–1697	King's Bench.
Smale & Giffard. ...	Sm. & Giff. ...	1852–1857	Chancery, V.-C. Stuart.
Smith	Smith (K.B.) ...	1803–1806	King's Bench.
Smith & Batty... ...	Sm. & Bat. ...	1824–1825	King's Bench, Ireland.
Smith's Leading Cases	Smith, L.C. ...		Common Law Courts.
Smith's (Lacey) Registration Cases	Smith, Reg. Cas.	1895–1914	Registration Cases.
Smythe...	Smythe	1839–1840	Common Pleas, Ireland.
Solicitors' Journal and Reporter	S.J. or Sol. Jo. ...	Jan. 1857 to the present time	All the Courts.
Spinks	Spinks or Ecc. & Ad.	1853–1855	Ecclesiastical and Admiralty.
Spinks' Prize Cases ...	Spinks' Pr. Cas.	1854–1856	Admiralty.
Stair	Stair Rep. ...	1661–1681	Court of Session.
Starkie...	Stark.	1814–1823	Nisi Prius.
State Trials (ed. Howell)	How. St. Tr. or State Tr.	1163–1820	All the Courts.
Strange...	Stra.	1716–1747	King's Bench.
Stuart, Milne & Peddie	Stu. M. & P. ...	1851–1853	Scotch Courts.
Style	Sty.	1646–1655	King's or Upper Bench.
Swabey...	Swab.	1855–1859	Admiralty.
Swabey & Tristram ...	Sw. & Tr. ...	1858–1865	Probate and Divorce.
Swanston	Swanst.	1818–1821	Chancery.
Swinton..	Swint.	1835–1841	Court of Justiciary.
Syme	Sym.	1826–1829	Court of Justiciary.
Tamlyn	Taml.	1829–1830	Rolls Court.
Taunton	Taunt.	1807–1819	Common Pleas.
Tax Cases	Tax Cas... ...	1875 to the present time	All the Courts.
Temple & Mew ...	T. & M.... ...	1848–1851	Crown Cases Reserved.
Term Reports, by Durnford & East	Term Rep. or T. Rep.	1785–1800	King's Bench.

REPORTS—*continued.*

Reports	Abbreviations	Date	Court
Thornton's Notes of Cases	Thorn. *or* Notes of Cases	1841–1850	Ecclesiastical and Admiralty.
Times Law Reports ...	T.L.R.	1884–1952	All the Courts.
Tothill	Toth.	1559–1646	Chancery.
Traffic Cases	Traff. Cas. ...	1951 to the present time	All the Courts.
Tudor's Leading Cases:—			
Mercantile and Maritime Law	Tudor L.C. Merc. Law		All the Courts.
Real Property and Conveyancing	Tudor L.C.R.P.		All the Courts (see also "White & Tudor").
Turner & Russell ...	Turn. & Russ. *or* T. & R.	1822–1825	Chancery.
Tyrwhitt	Tyr.	1830–1835	Exchequer.
Tyrwhitt & Granger ...	Tyr. & Gr. ...	1835–1836	Exchequer.
Vaughan	Vaugh.	1666–1673	Common Pleas.
Ventris	Vent.	1668–1691	All the Courts.
Vernon	Vern.	1680–1719	Chancery.
Vernon & Scriven ...	V. & S. *or* Vern. & Scr.	1786–1788	Common Law, Ireland.
Vesey	... ...		(See next three names.)
Vesey & Beames ...	V. & B. *or* Ves. & B.	1812–1814	Chancery.
Vesey junior	Ves. jun. *or*, after the first two vols., Ves. simply.	1789–1817	Chancery.
Vesey senior	Ves. Sen.	1747–1756	Chancery.
Wallis	Wall.	1766–1791	Chancery, Ireland.
Webster's Patent Cases	Webst. Pat. Cas.	1602–1855	All the Courts.
Weekly Law Reports ...	W.L.R.	1953 to the present time	All the Courts.
Weekly Notes	W.N.	1866–1952	All the Courts.
Weekly Reporter ...	W.R.	1852–1906	All the Courts.
Welsby, Hurlstone & Gordon	Exch. (for Exchequer)	1847–1856	Exchequer.
Welsh	Welsh Reg. Cas.	1832–1840	Registry Cases, Ireland.
West (Chancery) ...	West (Ch.) *or* West *temp.* Hard.	1736–1740	Chancery.
West (House of Lords)	West (H.L.) ...	1839–1841	House of Lords.
White & Tudor's Leading Cases	Wh. & Tud. L.C. *or* L.C. Eq.		Chancery.
Wightwick	Wight	1810–1811	Exchequer.
Willes	Willes	1737–1758	Common Pleas.
Williams (Peere) ...	P. Wms.	1695–1735	Chancery.
Willmore, Wollaston & Davison	W. W. & D. *or* Will. Woll. & Dav.	1837 ...	Queen's Bench and Bail Court.

Reports	Abbreviations	Date	Court
Willmore, Wollaston & Hodges	W. W. & H. *or* Will. Woll. & H.	1838–1839	Queen's Bench.
Wilmot's Opinions ...	Wilm.	1757–1770	All the Courts.
Wilson, George	Wils. *or* G. Wils.	1742–1774	Common Law.
Wilson, John ...	Wils. Ch. ...	1818–1819	Chancery.
Wilson, John ...	Wils. Ex. Eq. ...	1817 ...	Exchequer (Equity).
Wilson & Shaw's Scotch Appeals	Wils. & S. *or* W. & S.	1825–1834	House of Lords.
Winch	Winch	1621–1625	Common Pleas.
Wolferstan & Bristow	Wolf. & B. *or* W. & B.	1859–1864	Election Committees.
Wolferstan & Dew ...	Wolf. & D. *or* W. & D.	1857–1858	Election Committees.
Wollaston's Practice Cases	W.P.C. *or* Woll.	1840–1841	Common Law Courts.
Wood's Tithe Cases ...	Wood	1650–1798	Exchequer.
Workmen's Compensation Cases (Minton-Senhouse)	W.C.C.	1898–1907	All the Courts.
Year Books	Y.B.	1273–1535	Common Law.
Yelverton	Yelv.	1602–1613	King's Bench.
Younge	Younge	1830–1832	Exchequer (Equity).
Younge & Collyer (Chancery)	You. & Coll. C.C. *or* Y. & C.C.C.	1841–1843	Chancery.
Younge & Collyer (Exchequer, Equity)	You. & Coll. Ex. Eq. *or* Y. & C. Ex.	1833–1841	Exchequer (Equity).
Younge & Jervis ...	Y. & J.	1826–1830	Exchequer.

REPRESENTATION. 1. For the purposes of intestate succession to anyone, the children of a deceased relative are, within certain degrees, allowed to *represent* their parents: thus, if a man dies leaving a brother A, and the children of a deceased brother B, the children of B are said to take by *representation*. See now Part IV of the Administration of Estates Act 1925.

2. The character borne by an heir or devisee, or an executor or administrator. [PERSONAL REPRESENTATIVE; REAL REPRESENTATIVE.]

3. A statement. [MISREPRESENTATION.]

4. A system by which electors choose representatives in an assembly. British election law is principally contained in the Representation of the People Act 1949.

REPRIEVE. The suspension of the execution of a criminal sentence.

REPRISAL. A taking in return; that is to say, taking the goods of a wrongdoer to make compensation for the wrong he has done, or as a pledge for amends being made. [LETTERS OF MARQUE AND REPRISAL; RECAPTION.]

REP-SILVER. Money anciently paid by servile tenants to their lord to free them from the duty of reaping his corn.

REPUBLICATION OF WILL. The revival of a will revoked, either by re-execution or by a codicil adapted to the purpose. [PUBLICATION, 1.]

REPUDIATION. A rejection or disclaimer; especially of a man's disclaiming a

REPUDIATION—*continued.*

share in a transaction to which he might otherwise be bound by tacit acquiescence.

REPUGNANT. Inconsistent; generally used of a clause in a written instrument inconsistent with some other clause or with the general object of the instrument.

REPUTATION. 1. A person's good name.

2. That which generally has been and many men have said and thought.

REPUTED OWNER. A bankrupt, in reference to goods and chattels in his apparent possession with the consent of the true owner, is called the *reputed owner* of such goods.

The doctrine of reputed ownership, by which a bankrupt trader is deemed the reputed owner of goods in his apparent possession, was introduced into the bankrupt laws in 1623 for the purpose of protecting the creditors of a trader from the consequences of the false credit which he might acquire by being suffered to have in his possession, as apparent owner, property which did not really belong to him. Such property may in general be claimed by the trustee in the bankruptcy for the benefit of the creditors. See the Bankruptcy Act 1914, s. 38. [ORDER AND DISPOSITION.]

REQUEST, COURT OF. [COURT OF REQUEST.]

REQUEST, LETTERS OF. [LETTERS OF REQUEST.]

REQUISITIONS ON TITLE are written inquiries made by the solicitor of an intending purchaser of land, or of any estate or interest therein, and addressed to the vendor's solicitor, in respect of some apparent insufficiency in the abstract of title. [ABSTRACT OF TITLE.]

RES GESTÆ. The material facts of a case as opposed to mere hearsay. The phrase is generally used in reference to that which is apparently hearsay, and yet is in fact immediately relevant to the matter in question. Thus proof may be received of the language used at seditious meetings, in order to show the objects and character of such meetings.

RES INTEGRA. An affair not broached or meddled with; one on which no action had been taken, or deliberation had.

RES INTER ALIOS ACTA ALTERI NOCERE NON DEBET. *A matter litigated between two parties ought not to prejudice a third party.* That is the general rule; but it must be taken with this important qualification, that though a decision, in a case between A and B, cannot directly prejudice C, yet if there be a legal point at issue in C's case identical with one which was in controversy between A and B, the court will generally regard itself as bound by the prior decision, at least if the court which pronounced it was the same, or one of equal or superior authority.

RES IPSA LOQUITUR. The matter itself speaks; or, "the thing speaks for itself." A phrase used in actions for injury occasioned by negligence where no proof is required of negligence beyond the accident itself.

RES JUDICATA. A matter which has been adjudicated upon.

RES NULLIUS. A thing which has no owner.

RESCOUS or **RESCUE** is a resistance against lawful authority, in taking a person or thing out of the custody of the law; as if a bailiff or other officer, upon a writ, arrests a man, and others by violence take him away, or procure his escape; this is a *rescous in fact.* So if one distrains beasts for damage feasant [DAMAGE FEASANT] in his ground, and as he drives them, they enter the owner's house, and he will not deliver them up upon demand; this is a *rescous in law.*

RESCUSSOR. A person committing a *rescous* or *rescue.* [RESCOUS.]

RESERVATION. A keeping back, as when a man lets his land, *reserving* a rent. Sometimes it signifies an exception; as when a man lets a house, and *reserves* to himself one room. And see the Law of Property Act 1925, s. 65, which provides that a reservation of a legal estate shall operate at law without any execution of the conveyance by the grantee of the legal estate out of which the reservation is made.

RESERVING A POINT OF LAW. It was formerly the practice for a judge at the assizes (now the Crown Court) to reserve points of law for consideration of the full court of Westminster. There is now provision for appeals in both civil and criminal cases.

RESIANCE. A man's abode, residence, or continuance in a place.

RESIANT ROLLS. Rolls containing the *resiants* in a tithing, etc., which were called over by the steward on holding courts leet. [COURT LEET; TITHING.]

RESIDENCE. A continuance of a spiritual person upon his benefice. Now used generally for any person's continuance in a place, and defined for various purposes by different Acts of Parliament, *e.g.*, in the case of parliamentary franchise. [SETTLEMENT.]

RESIDUARY ACCOUNT. The account which an executor or administrator, after paying the debts and particular legacies of the deceased, and before paying over the *residuum*, prepares, setting forth the particulars of the assets of the estate and of the payments made thereout; formerly this was necessary in order to assess legacy and succession duty, both of which were abolished by the Finance Act 1949.

RESIDUARY DEVISEE. A person entitled under a will to the *residue* of the testator's lands; that is, to such as are not specifically devised by the testator's will. By s. 25 of the Wills Act 1837 it is provided that, unless a contrary intention shall appear by the will, such real estate or interest as shall be comprised, or intended to be comprised, in any devise in such will contained, which shall fail or be void by reason of the death of the devisee in the lifetime of the testator, or by reason of such devise being contrary to law, or otherwise incapable of taking effect, shall be included in the residuary devise (if any) contained in such will.

RESIDUARY ESTATE is a term used variously to mean:—

1. A testator's property not specifically devised or bequeathed. See s. 33 (4) of the Administration of Estates Act 1925.

2. Such part of the personal estate as is primarily liable to the payment of debts.

3. That which remains after debts and legacies have been paid.

RESIDUARY LEGATEE is one to whom the residue, or a proportionate share in the residue, of a testator's personal property is left, after debts, funeral expenses, and specific and pecuniary legacies have been satisfied.

RESIDUUM, or **RESIDUE.** The residue of the personal estate of a deceased person after payment of debts and specific and pecuniary legacies.

RESIGNATION. 1. The giving up of a benefice into the hands of the ordinary.

2. The giving up of any office by letter or other instrument in writing delivered to the party lawfully authorised to receive it. See s. 84 of the Local Government Act 1972.

RESIGNATION BOND. A bond or other engagement in writing which might formerly be taken by a patron from the clergyman presented by him to a living, to resign the benefice at a future period. Abolished under s. 5 of the Benefices Act 1898 (Amendment) Measure, 1923.

RESOLUTION. Any matter resolved upon, especially at a public meeting.

I. *Resolutions of Creditors.*—These are resolutions passed at meetings of the creditors of a bankrupt or one whose property is in liquidation. Resolutions thus passed are of three kinds:—

1. An *ordinary resolution*, which is decided by a majority in value of the creditors present personally or by proxy at the meeting and voting upon such resolution.

2. A *special resolution*, which is decided by a majority in number and three-fourths in value of the creditors present personally or by proxy at the meeting and voting upon such resolution.

3. A resolution (to which no name is given) which is required for the approval of a composition or scheme. This must be passed by a majority in number representing three-fourths in value of all creditors who have proved. See s. 167 of the Bankruptcy Act 1914.

II. *Resolutions of Companies.*—An extraordinary resolution is defined to be a resolution passed by a majority of not less than three-fourths of the members of the company present in person or by proxy at a general meeting of which notice specifying the intention to propose the extraordinary resolution has been duly given.

A special resolution is defined as one which has been (*a*) passed in manner required for extraordinary resolution, and (*b*) confirmed by a majority of such members as may be present at a subsequent meeting of which not less than twenty-one

RESOLUTION—*continued.*
days' notice has been given. See s. 141 of the Companies Act 1948.

III. *Resolutions in Parliament.*—In Parliament, every question, when agreed to, assumes the form of an *order*, or a *resolution* of the House. By its *orders*, the House directs its committees, its members, its officers, the order of its own proceedings and the acts of all persons whom they concern. By its *resolutions*, the House declares its own opinions and purposes. *May.*

RESORT, COURT OF LAST. A court from which there is no appeal.

RESPECTUM, CHALLENGE PROPTER. [CHALLENGE.]

RESPITE. Delay or forbearance. Thus:—

1. *Respite of homage* was the forbearing or excusing of the homage which ought first of all to be performed by the tenant that held by homage. [HOMAGE.]

2. *Respite of a jury* signifies the adjournment of the sittings of the jury for defect of jurors.

3. *Respite of a sentence* signifies a delay, or putting off of the execution of the sentence.

RESPONDEAT OUSTER. Let him answer over; that is to say, when a dilatory plea put in by the defendant has been overruled by the court, let him put in a more substantial plea, or *answer over* in some better manner. [DILATORY PLEA; PLEADING OVER.]

RESPONDEAT SUPERIOR. Let the superior be held responsible. In pursuance of this maxim, a principal is liable in damages for the act of his agent, and a master for the act of his servant; provided that in each case the act of the inferior, whether specifically authorised or not, was within the scope of the duties imposed by the superior.

RESPONDENT. A party called upon to *answer* a petition or an appeal.

RESPONDENTIA. A loan upon the security of the goods and merchandise in a vessel, or upon the mere hazard of a voyage. [BOTTOMRY.] Such a loan is insurable.

RESTAUR. 1. The remedy which different assurers have against each other according to the date of their assurances.

2. The remedy a person has against another who has agreed to indemnify him against any damage sustained.

RESTITUTIO IN INTEGRUM. The rescinding of a contract or contracts (*e.g.,* on the ground of fraud) so as to restore parties to their original position.

RESTITUTION. The restoring of anything unlawfully taken from another. It is most frequently used in the common law for the setting him in possession of lands and tenements that has been unlawfully disseised of them.

RESTITUTION OF CONJUGAL RIGHTS. A petition for restitution of conjugal rights might formerly be presented in the High Court by either husband or wife when one lived separately from the other without any sufficient reason, to compel the party so living separately to return to the other. The court, if satisfied that the allegations contained in the petition were true, and that there was no legal ground why a decree for restitution of conjugal rights should not be granted, might make the decree accordingly, ordering the other to return to cohabitation within the time limited by the order. Abolished by the Matrimonial Proceedings and Property Act 1970.

RESTITUTION ORDER. An order for the restitution of stolen property. See s. 28 of the Theft Act 1968, as amended by the Criminal Justice Act 1972.

RESTRAINING ORDER was an order restraining the Bank of England, or some public company, from allowing any dealing with some stock or shares specified in the order. [DISTRINGAS.]

RESTRAINING STATUTES. Those which restrict previous rights or powers; a phrase used especially of the Acts of Parliament passed to restrain simoniacal practices in presentations to livings.

RESTRAINT OF MARRIAGE. Conditions attached to a gift or bequest in *general* restraint of marriage are void on grounds of public policy, but not so conditions against second marriage, or if the restraint be *partial* only.

RESTRAINT OF TRADE. Contracts in general restraint of trade, *i.e.,* unlimited as to time or area, are void. Contracts in partial restraint may, however, be upheld.

RESTRAINT ON ANTICIPATION. [ANTICIPATION.]

RESTRICTIVE INDORSEMENT is an indorsement on a bill or note which restricts the negotiability of the bill to a particular person, or a particular purpose; as "pay to I. S. only," or "pay John Holloway for my use." It is to be distinguished from a *blank indorsement*, which consists merely of the signature of the indorser; from a *full indorsement*, which makes the bill or note payable to a given person or his order; and from a *qualified indorsement*, which qualifies the liability of the indorser. See s. 35 of the Bills of Exchange Act 1882. [INDORSEMENT; QUALIFIED INDORSEMENT.]

RESTS are periodical balancings of an account made for the purpose of converting interest into principal, and charging the party liable thereon with compound interest.

RESULTING TRUST is a trust raised by implication in favour of the author of the trust himself, or his representatives. This generally happens where an intended trust fails. See ss. 53 (2) and 60 (3) of the Law of Property Act 1925, under which resulting trusts may still be created.

RESULTING USE. A use returning by way of implication to the grantor himself. Since 1925 there can be no resulting "use" but only a resulting "trust." [RESULTING TRUST; USE.]

RETAINER. 1. A servant, but not menial or familiar, that is, not continually dwelling in the house of his master, but only wearing his livery, and attending sometimes upon special occasions.

2. The right which an executor (and at common law an administrator), who was a creditor of his testator, had to *retain* so much of the testator's assets as would pay his own debt.

3. A counsel's retaining fee. Retainers in this sense are either general or special. For rules as to retainer, see the *Annual Practice*.

4. An authority given to a solicitor to proceed in an action. This may be given verbally; but a written retainer is always preferable. A retainer of this kind is either *general* or *special*. The solicitor of a person has an implied authority from his client to accept service of process, but he cannot in general commence an action for him without a special retainer.

RETIRING A BILL. The word "retire" in its application to bills of exchange, is an ambiguous word. In its ordinary sense it is used of an indorser who takes up the bill by handing the amount to a transferee, and thereupon holds the instrument, with all his remedies intact. But it is sometimes used of an acceptor who pays a bill at maturity, and thereby extinguishes all remedies upon it.

RETORNO BREVIUM. The return of writs. [RETURN, 1.]

RETOUR SANS PROTET or **SANS FRAIS.** A request or direction by the drawer of a bill of exchange, that, in case the bill should be dishonoured by the drawee, it be returned without protest and without expense (*sans frais*). The effect of such a request is to disable the drawer of the bill (and perhaps also the indorsers) from resisting payment of the bill on the ground that it has not been protested. [BILL OF EXCHANGE; PROTEST, 3.]

RETRAXIT (he has retracted). This was an open and voluntary renunciation of his suit by the plaintiff in court, by which he for ever lost his right of action upon the matter in question. A *retraxit* differed from a non-suit in that a nonsuit was properly a neglect by the plaintiff to appear when called upon to do so. 3 *Bl.* [NOLLE PROSEQUI; NONSUIT.]

RETURN. 1. The return of a writ by a sheriff or bailiff, or other party to whom a writ is directed, is a certificate made to the court of that which he has done, touching the execution of the writ directed to him.

2. The return of a member to serve in parliament for a given constituency. This is the return of the writ which directed the sheriff or other officer to proceed to the election. [RETURNING OFFICER.]

3. A certificate or report by commissioners on a matter on which they have been directed to inquire. The word is especially so used in reference to matters of statistic detail; thus "the returns of the census," etc.

4. The return of goods replevied. [REPLEVIN.]

RETURNING OFFICER. The officer to whom a writ is directed, requiring him to proceed to the election of a member to serve in parliament or some other public body. See s. 40 of the Local Government Act 1972.

REVELAND. Land of the king not granted out to any, but resting in charge of the *reve* or bailiff of the manor. It is said to have been the thane-land of Domesday.

REVENUE signifies properly the yearly rent that accrues to every man from his lands and possessions. But it is applied especially to the general income received by the State in taxes, etc., and to the hereditary revenues of the Crown.

REVENUE SIDE OF THE EX-CHEQUER. That jurisdiction of the Court of Exchequer, or of the Exchequer Division of the High Court of Justice, by which it ascertained and enforced the proprietary rights of the Crown against the subjects of the realm. By Order in Council, (1881) the Exchequer Division was merged in the Queen's Bench Division. In 1947 the Revenue List was substituted for the Revenue Side of the Q.B.D., which was in effect abolished.

REVERSAL OF JUDGMENT is the annulling of a judgment on appeal therefrom, by the court to which the appeal is brought.

REVERSION. 1. A reversion signifies properly the residue of an estate *left in the grantor* to commence in possession after the determination of some particular estate granted out by him.

2. But it is frequently, though improperly, used so as to include any future estate, whether in reversion or remainder. [ESTATE, II; REMAINDER.]

REVERSIONARY INTEREST. An interest in real or personal property in remainder or reversion. As to the powers of married women to dispose of such interests, see the Married Women's Property Act 1882, and s. 169 of the Law of Property Act 1925. The latter section gives the court power, with the married woman's consent, to bind her interest in property (including reversionary interests), which she is by law unable to dispose of or bind herself. [REVERSION.]

REVERSIONARY LEASE. 1. A lease to take effect *in futuro*. Such a lease must now take effect within twenty-one years from the date of the instrument purporting to create it; otherwise it is void. See s. 149 (3) of the Law of Property Act 1925.

2. A general lease to take effect after the expiration of a former lease.

REVERSIONER means strictly a person entitled to an estate in reversion [REVERSION, 1]; but the word is used generally to signify any person entitled to any future estate in real or personal property, as *e.g.* dealings with expectant non-reversioners, etc.

REVERTER. Returning or reversion.

REVIEW, BILL OF. A *bill of review* was a bill sometimes brought in Chancery for the purpose of reviewing a cause already heard. This bill might be brought after the decree had been signed and enrolled (1) if error of law appeared on the face of the decree; (2) if new evidence was discovered which could not have been had or used when the decree passed; but in the latter case only by leave of the court. Proceedings in error have been abolished and the procedure would now be by appeal to the court of appeal.

REVIEW OF TAXATION is the reconsideration by the taxing master, or by a judge in chambers, of the items allowed or disallowed in the taxation of costs, or any of them. [TAXATION OF COSTS.]

REVISING BARRISTERS were junior barristers of not less than seven years' standing, appointed every year to revise the register of parliamentary electors in each district. Such appointments were discontinued after 1918.

REVIVING is a word metaphorically applied to rents, debts and rights of action, signifying a renewal of them after they are extinguished, *e.g.*, debts barred by the Statutes of Limitation are revived by acknowledged in some cases.

REVIVOR was a proceeding to revive a suit or action which, according to the old practice, became abated by the death of one of the parties, the marriage of a female party, or some other cause. In Chancery this was formerly done by *bill of revivor*, now abolished. [ABATEMENT, 4.]

REVIVOR, WRIT OF, was a writ to revive a judgment in an action at common law, which could not be enforced directly by writ of execution, in consequence of lapse of time or change of parties. A procedure for obtaining leave to issue execution after lapse of time, change of parties, etc., is now provided by R.S.C. 1965, Ord. 46, r. 2. [ABATEMENT, 4.]

REVOCATION is the reversal by any one of a thing done by himself. Thus, when it is provided in a marriage settlement or other instrument, that an appointment may be made "with or without power of revocation," it is implied that the party making the appointment may, if he think fit, reserve the power of annulling what he has done. A power granted or reserved in a deed or other instrument to revoke an appointment already made, and to make a fresh one, is called a *power of revocation and new appointment*. Any act or instrument which is capable of being annulled by its author is said to be *revocable*. Some instruments are in their nature revocable, as wills. Deeds under seal are not in general revocable, unless a power to revoke be therein expressly reserved. A will may be revoked (1) by marriage (unless it is expressed to have been made in contemplation of marriage); (2) by the execution of another will or codicil or by some writing of revocation executed as a will; (3) by the burning, tearing, or other destruction of the original will (*animo revocandi*) by the testator, or by some other person in his presence and by his direction. See ss. 19, 20, of the Wills Act 1837. In case the whole property is disposed of during the testator's lifetime the will ceases to have effect.

REVOCATION OF PROBATE is where probate of a will, having been granted, is afterwards recalled by the court on proof of a subsequent will, or other sufficient cause.

RHODIAN LAW. An ancient code of maritime law used by the people of Rhodes, some of the principles of which have been adopted in our own maritime code.

RIDER. 1. A clause proposed to be added to a motion before a meeting.

2. An addition to the verdict of a jury.

RIDINGS. Three former divisions of the county of York, called the North, the East, and the West Riding. The word "riding" was a corruption of "trithing," a name indicating a threefold division of a county.

Under the reorganisation of local government areas under the Local Government Act 1972, the ridings were incorporated into the metropolitan counties of South Yorkshire and West Yorkshire, and the non-metropolitan county of North Yorkshire.

RIGHT. A lawful title or claim to anything. The word is frequently used to denote a claim to a thing of which one is not in possession.

RIGHT IN COURT. [RECTUS IN CURIA.]

RIGHT OF ACTION. The right to bring an action in any given case. But the phrase is frequently used in a more extended sense, as identical with *chose in action*, to mean all rights which are not rights of possession, and to include the large class of rights over things in the possession of others, which must be asserted by action in cases where the qualified or temporary possessor refuses to deliver them up. [CHOSE.]

RIGHT OF SEARCH. The right of a belligerent to examine and inspect the papers of a neutral vessel on the high seas, and the goods therein contained, to see whether the ship is neutral or an enemy, and to ascertain whether she has contraband of war or enemies' property on board.

RIGHT OF WAY. A right enjoyed by one man (either in his specific character or as one of the public) of passing over another's land, subject to such conditions and restrictions as are specified in the grant, or sanctioned by the custom, by virtue of which the right exists. Rights of way are susceptible of almost infinite variety; they may be limited both as to the intervals at which they may be used (as a way to church) and as to the actual extent of the user authorised (as a footway, horseway or carriageway). As to public rights of way, and dedication of ways, see ss. 34–36 of the Highways Act 1959.

RIGHT, PETITION OF. [PETITION OF RIGHT.]

RIGHT TO BEGIN. The right to commence the argument on a trial, which belongs to that side on whom the burden of proof rests. The party beginning has also the right to reply to his adversary's case. The appellant begins all civil appeals.

RIGHT, WRIT OF. [WRIT OF RIGHT.]

RIGHTS, BILL OF. [BILL OF RIGHTS.]

RINGING THE CHANGES. A trick by which a criminal, on receiving a piece of money in payment of an article, pretends that it is not good, and, changing it in such a manner as not to be seen by the buyer,

RINGING THE CHANGES
—continued.

returns to the latter a spurious coin. This is held to be an uttering of false money. *Frank's case* (1794), Leach, 644. The phrase is also generally applied to fraudulent exchanges of coin, effected in the course of paying money or receiving money in payment.

RIOT. A tumultuous disturbance of the peace by three or more persons assembling together of their own authority, mutually to assist one another against any who shall oppose them in the execution of some unlawful purpose or of some lawful purpose by unlawful means of a private nature, and afterwards actually executing the same in a violent and turbulent manner, to the terror of at least one person of reasonable firmness and courage. This is held to be a riot, whether the act be of itself lawful or unlawful.

RIOTOUS ASSEMBLY. The unlawful assembling of twelve persons or more to the disturbance of the peace. In such cases it was provided by the Riot Act 1714 (repealed), that if any justice of the peace, sheriff, under-sheriff, or mayor of a town, should command them by proclamation in the Queen's name to disperse, then if they contemned his orders, and continued together for one hour afterwards, such contempt should be felony. Persons whose property is damaged by the acts of rioters may recover compensation out of the police rate of the district. See the Riot (Damages) Act 1886. In order to constitute an offence, the riotous act had formerly to consist in demolishing, or beginning to demolish, some house or other building, machinery, etc.: Malicious Damage Act 1861 (repealed by the Criminal Damage Act 1971).

RIPARIAN PROPRIETORS. Proprietors of the banks of a river.

RIPARIAN STATES. States whose jurisdictions are bounded by the banks of a river.

RIVER BOARDS. Bodies established under the River Boards Act 1948 to deal with polution, fishing and flood control in place of local authorities, fishery boards, drainage boards and catchment boards. Their functions were transferred to river authorities established under the Water Resources Act 1963.

ROAD. [SPECIAL ROAD.]

ROBBERY. A person is guilty of robbery if he steals, and immediately before or at the time of doing so, and in order to do so, he uses force on any person or puts or seeks to put any person in fear of being then and there subjected to force. A person guilty of robbery, or of an assault with intent to rob, is liable to imprisonment for life. See s. 8 of the Theft Act 1968.

ROE, RICHARD. A fictitious personage who often appeared in actions at law prior to 1852; sometimes as one of the pledges for the due prosecution of an action, and sometimes as the casual ejector in an action of ejectment. [EJECTMENT.]

ROGUE. An idle wandering beggar, vagrant or vagabond. [INCORRIGIBLE ROGUE.]

ROLL. A schedule of paper or parchment, which may be turned or wound up. [See the following titles.]

ROLL OF COURT. The court-roll of a manor, wherein the business of the court, the admissions, surrenders, names, rents, and services of the tenants are copied and enrolled. Copyholds were abolished by the Law of Property Act 1922. [COURT ROLLS; MANOR.]

ROLLS COURT. The office appointed for the custody of the rolls and records of the Chancery, the master whereof is called the Master of the Rolls. The phrase is especially used to signify the court-room in which the Master of the Rolls sat as judge. [MASTER OF THE ROLLS.]

ROLLS OF PARLIAMENT. The manuscript registers of the proceedings of parliament.

ROLLS OFFICE OF THE CHANCERY. [ROLLS COURT.]

ROMNEY MARSH. A tract of land in Kent, governed by certain ancient and equitable laws of sewers, composed by Henry De Bathe, a judge of the reign of Henry III.

ROOT OF TITLE. It is the duty of a vendor in making title, on a sale of land, to show what has happened to the absolute ownership of the land during thirty years, and to prove that it now resides in him. It is necessary, therefore, that the abstract of title (*q.v.*) should contain what is called a "good root of title," that is, some document which deals with the absolute ownership, both at law and in equity, and which contains nothing to cast doubts on the title of the disposing party. A good root of title deals with the legal and the equitable interest contracted to be sold in such a fashion that the property is adequately identified.

A mortgage deed or a purchase deed, thirty years old, is usually a good root of title, but a general devise in a will is not sufficient.

ROUT is where three or more meet under circumstances which constitute an unlawful assembly and make some advances towards carrying out their object. [Riot; Unlawful Assembly.]

ROYAL ASSENT (Lat. *Regius assensus*). The assent given by the sovereign to a bill passed in both Houses of parliament. The royal assent to a bill had formerly to be given either in person, or by commission by letters patent under the Great Seal, signed with the sovereign's hand, and notified to both Houses assembled together in the upper House. The procedure has been modified by the Royal Assent Act 1967. A bill, upon receiving the royal assent, becomes an Act of Parliament. *May*. [La Reyne le veult; La Reyne S'Avisera.]

ROYAL FISH. [Fish Royal.]

ROYAL GRANTS. Grants by letters patent or letters close from the Crown. These are always matters of record.

ROYAL MINES. Mines of silver and gold.

ROYAL STYLE AND TITLES. These were made by Proclamation in 1953, and are: "Elizabeth II, by the Grace of God of the United Kingdom of Great Britain and Northern Ireland and of Her other Realms and Territories Queen, Head of the Commonwealth, Defender of the Faith." (*Elizabeth II, Dei Gratia Brittaniarum Regnorumque Suorum Ceterorum Regina, Consortionis Populorum Princeps, Fidei Defensor.*)

ROYALTY. 1. The royal dignity and prerogatives.

2. A *pro rata* payment to a grantor or lessor, on the working of the property leased, or otherwise on the profits of the grant or lease. The word is especially used in reference to mines, patents and copyrights.

RUBRIC. Directions and instructions contained in the Book of Common Prayer (*q.v.*).

RULE. 1. A regulation for the government of a society agreed to by the members thereof.

2. A rule of procedure made by a lawful judicial authority for some court or courts of justice, *e.g.*, the Orders and Rules under the Judicature Acts, consolidated in the Rules of the Supreme Court, 1965. See also s. 99 of the Judicature Act 1925.

3. An order made by a superior court upon motion in some matter over which it has summary jurisdiction. A rule is either granted absolutely in the first instance, or as a *rule nisi*, or a *rule to show cause*, that is, a rule that the thing applied for be granted, *unless* the opposite party show sufficient reason against it, on a day assigned for that purpose. The rule is *served* upon the opposite party, and when it comes on for argument, the court, having heard counsel, *discharges* the rule or makes it *absolute*. [Rule of Court.]

4. A rule obtained, as of course, on the application of counsel.

5. A rule obtained at chambers without counsel's signature to a motion paper, on a note of instructions from an attorney, was called a *side-bar rule*.

6. A point of law settled by authority; as *e.g.* the *Rule in Shelley's case*, etc. [See next title.]

RULE IN SHELLEY'S CASE, so called from having been quoted and insisted on in *Shelley's case*, is the following rule:— That wherever a man by any gift or conveyance takes an estate of freehold, and in the same gift or conveyance an estate is limited, either mediately or immediately, to his *heirs* in fee or in tail, the word *heirs* is a word of *limitation*, and not of purchase. In other words, it is to be understood as expressing the quantity of estate which the party is to take, and not as conferring any distinct estate on his heirs, or the heirs of his body, as the case may be. The rule was abolished in regard to instruments coming into operation after 1925. See s. 131 of the Law of Property Act 1925.

RULE NISI. [RULE, 3.]

RULE OF COURT. 1. An order made on motion, generally in open court, or else made generally to regulate the practice of the court. [RULE, 2, 3.]

2. A submission to arbitration, or the award of an arbitrator, is said to be made a *rule of court*, when the court makes a rule that such submission or award shall be conclusive. See now ss. 1, 26 of the Arbitration Act 1950.

RULES OF GOOD HUSBANDRY. Rules under which the occupier of an agricultural unit is deemed to be fulfilling his responsibilities under the Agriculture Act 1947. They include properly mowing or grazing permanent pasture, the maintaining of crops and livestock free from disease, etc. See s. 11 of the Act.

RULE OF LAW. The doctrine that all men are equal before the law, and that acts of officials in carrying out government orders are cognizable in the ordinary courts of law.

RUNNING DAYS. [LAY DAYS.]

RUNNING DOWN CASE. An action against the driver of one vehicle for running into another; or against a ship or boat for damaging another by a collision.

RUNNING WITH THE LAND. A covenant is said to *run with the land* when each successive owner of the land is entitled to the benefit of the covenant, or liable (as the case may be) to its obligation. As to such covenants, see s. 80 of the Law of Property Act 1925.

RURAL DEAN. An officer of the church, generally a parochial clergyman, appointed to act under the bishop or archdeacon; his proper duty being to inspect the conduct of the parochial clergy, to inquire into and report dilapidations, and to examine candidates for confirmation.

RURAL DEANERY. The circuit of the jurisdiction of a rural dean. Every diocese is divided into archdeaconries, each archdeaconry into rural deaneries, and each rural deanery into parishes. [RURAL DEAN.]

RURAL DISTRICT COUNCIL. Formerly the council of a county district which was rural in character. Abolished in the reorganisation of local authorities under the Local Government Act 1972. [DISTRICT COUNCIL.]

S

S. Section (of an Act).

S.C. An abbreviation frequently used for "same case", in giving a second reference to any case which may be cited.

S.I. Statutory instrument (*q.v.*).

S.J. Solicitors' Journal.

S.L.R. Statute Law Revision Act.

S.P. *Sine prole*, without issue.

S.R. & O. Statutory rules and orders; now called statutory instruments.

S.S.C. Solicitor of the Supreme Court.

SAC signifies the liberty of holding pleas (*i.e.*, assuming jurisdiction) in the court of lordship or manor, and of imposing mulcts and forfeitures upon transgressors. [LIBERTIES.]

SACCULARII. Cutpurses; that is, those who privately steal from a man's person, as by picking his pocket.

SACRILEGE. 1. Stealing things dedicated to the offices of religion.

2. Breaking into a church, chapel, meeting house, or other place of divine worship, and committing an offence therein; or, being in such place, committing an offence therein, and breaking out. Formerly punishable under the Larceny Act 1916, which was repealed by the Theft Act 1968.

SAFE CONDUCT. A security given by the sovereign, under the Great Seal of England, for enabling a foreigner of a nation at war with us quietly to come in and pass out of the realm.

SAFE PLEDGE. A surety given for a man's appearance at a day assigned.

SAILING INSTRUCTIONS are written or printed directions delivered by the commanding officer of a convoy to the masters of ships under his care, by which they are enabled to understand and answer his signals, and also to know the place of rendezvous in case of dispersion. Without these sailing instructions, no vessel can have the full protection and benefit of a convoy.

SALE. A transmutation of property from one man to another in consideration of a price paid in money. Under the Sale of Goods Act 1893 a contract of sale of goods is defined to be "a contract whereby the seller transfers or agrees to transfer the property in goods to the buyer for a money consideration called the price".

The freedom of parties to exclude by agreement the statutory warranties and conditions in contracts for the sale of goods was limited by the Supply of Goods (Implied Terms) Act 1973.

SALIC or **SALIQUE LAW.** An ancient law of Pharamond, King of the Franks, excluding women from inheritances, and from succession to the crown.

SALVAGE or **SALVAGE MONEY.** A reasonable reward payable by owners of goods saved at sea from pirates, enemies, or the perils of the sea, to those who have saved them.

Claims for salvage may be made in the High Court of Justice, or in county courts having Admiralty jurisdiction.

SALVO (*Salvo jure*). Without prejudice to.

SALVOR. A person who saves goods at sea. [SALVAGE.]

SANCTION OF A LAW. The provision for enforcing it.

SANCTUARY. A place privileged for the safeguard of men's lives that were offenders. The sanctuary was allowed to shelter the party accused, if within forty days he acknowledged his fault, swore to abjure the realm, and submitted himself to banishment.

The privilege of sanctuary was abolished in 1623.

SANS FRAIS. Without incurring any expense. [RETOUR SANS PROTET.]

SANS NOMBRE. Without stint. A term sometimes applied to the case of common for cattle *levant et couchant*. But a common *sans nombre* generally means a common of pasture without any limit to the number of beasts which may be turned on it to feed there; which can only happen if it be a common in gross. [COMMON; LEVANT AND COUCHANT; SURCHARGE OF COMMON.]

SANS RECOURS. Without recourse; meaning "without recourse to me". These words are appended to an indorsement on a bill or note to qualify it, so as not to make the indorser responsible for any payment thereon. This is the proper mode of indorsing a bill where an agent indorses on behalf of his principal. [BILL OF EXCHANGE; QUALIFIED INDORSEMENT.]

SATISFACTION. 1. The acceptance by a party injured of a sum of money, or other thing, in bar of any action he might otherwise have had in respect of such injury. Payment of a sum of money will not operate as satisfaction of a larger sum owing; but payment in any other form, *e.g.*, even by cheque or bill of exchange, will. [ACCORD; SATISFACTION ON THE ROLL.]

2. The making of a donation with the express or implied intention that it shall be taken as an extinguishment of some claim which the donee has upon the donor. This generally happens under one of the two following states of circumstances:—(1) When a father, or person *in loo parentis*, makes a double provision for a child, or person standing towards him in a filial relation, *i.e.*, satisfaction of portions by legacies, or legacies by portions; (2) When a debtor confers, by will or otherwise, a pecuniary benefit on his creditor. In the first case the question arises whether the later provision is *in satisfaction* of the former, or intended to be added to it. In the second, the question is whether the benefit conferred is intended *in satisfaction* of the debt, or whether the creditor is to be allowed to take advantage of it, and nevertheless claim independently against other assets of the debtor.

Satisfaction differs from *performance*, in that satisfaction implies the substitution of something different from that agreed to be given, while in cases of performance the thing agreed to be done is taken to be in truth wholly or in part performed.

SATISFACTION ON THE ROLL is the entry on the roll or record of a court that a judgment is satisfied, whether by the voluntary payment of the judgment debtor, or the compulsory process of law.

SAXON LAGE. The laws of the West Saxons. *Cowel.* [MERCEN LAGE.]

SCACCARIUM. The exchequer. [COURT OF EXCHEQUER.]

SCANDAL. 1. A report or rumour, or action whereby one is affronted in public.

2. An irrelevant and abusive statement introduced into the pleadings in an action. By R.S.C. 1965, Ord. 18, r. 19, the court or a judge may order scandalous statements to

SCANDAL—*continued.*
be struck out of the pleadings, and out of affidavits by Ord. 41, r. 6.

SCANDALUM MAGNATUM. Words spoken in derogation of a peer, judge, or other great officer of the realm; which were subjected to peculiar punishments by a statute of Edward I, passed in 1275, and by divers other ancient statutes. Obsolete.

SCHEDULE. An appendix to an Act of Parliament or instrument in writing, for the purpose of facilitating reference in the Act or instrument itself.

SCHEME OF ARRANGEMENT. An arrangement between a debtor and his creditors whereby it is agreed that the debts shall be paid or partly paid under an agreed scheme, instead of the debtor being adjudged bankrupt.

SCIENTER. Knowingly; a word applied especially to that clause in a declaration in certain classes of actions in which the plaintiff alleged that the defendant *knowingly* did or permitted that from whence arose the damage of which the plaintiff complained. In an action of deceit the *scienter* must be averred and proved. *Scienter* formerly had also to be proved in cases of injuries done by animals, except in the case of injury done by dogs to sheep, cattle, etc. See now the Animals Act 1971.

SCILICET. "That is to say"; or, as it is sometimes expressed, "to wit". [VIDE-LICET.]

SCINTILLA JURIS. A spark or shadow of right formerly said to subsist in a feoffee or grantee in certain cases under the repealed Statute of Uses 1535.

SCIRE FACIAS (that you cause him to know). A *scire facias* is a judicial writ, founded upon some matter of record, and requires the person against whom it is brought to show cause why the party bringing it should not have advantage of such record, or (as in the case of a *scire facias* to repeal grants of the Crown and letters patent, except for inventions) why the record should not be annulled and vacated. A *scire facias* may be issued against a shareholder of a company on a judgment against the company, and in various other cases.

SCIRE FECI. The sheriff's return on a *scire facias*, that he has caused notice to be given to the party against whom the writ was issued.

SCOLD. A troublesome and angry woman, who, by brawling and wrangling amongst her neighbours, broke the public peace, increased discord, and became a public nuisance to the neighbourhood. Scolds were punished by means of the castigatory or duckingstool.

SCOT AND LOT. A customary contribution laid upon all subjects according to their ability. In some boroughs, the *scot and lot inhabitants* (that is, such as paid the poor rate as inhabitants) were allowed to vote in parliamentary elections for the borough; these rights were reserved by the Representation of the People Act 1832, but only so far as regarded the persons who then enjoyed them.

SCOTCH PEERS. 1. The ancient peers of Scotland.

2. Formerly representative peers were elected to sit in the House of Lords; but the Peerage Act 1963 conferred upon the holders of *all* Scottish peerages the right to receive writs of summons to attend the Lords. [HOUSE OF LORDS; PARLIAMENT.]

SCRIP. Certificates of shares in a public company. A scrip certificate is a certificate entitling the holder to apply for shares in a public company, either absolutely or on the fulfilment of specified conditions.

SCRIPT. A testamentary document of any kind, whether a will, codicil, draft of a will or codicil, or written instructions for the same.

SCRIVENER. An old word, signifying—
1. One who receives money to place it out at interest, and who supplies those who want to raise money on security.
2. One who draws contracts.

SCRUTINY. In regard to elections, the examination and checking of votes. Obtained by means of the presentation of an election petition. [ELECTION PETITION.]

SCUTAGE, or **SCUTAGIUM.** The payment made by tenants in chivalry, in lieu of personal service. [ESCUAGE; KNIGHT-SERVICE.]

SE DEFENDENDO (in defending himself). A plea for one charged with the slaying of another, that he did so in his own defence. [HOMICIDE, 2.]

SEA LETTER. A document which should be found on board of every neutral ship, specifying the nature and quantity of the cargo, the place whence it comes, and its destination.

SEA MARKS. Lighthouses, buoys and beacons.

SEAL. Wax impressed with a device, and attached as a mark of authenticity to letters and other instruments in writing. A contract under seal is called a *specialty contract* or *covenant*. It needs no valuable consideration to support it, as a contract not under seal does. An instrument under seal is necessary to pass all freehold and leasehold interests in land, except in the case of leases for periods not exceeding three years, where the rent reserved amounts at least to two-thirds of the full improved value of the land. See ss. 52 and 54 (2) of the Law of Property Act 1925. [CONSIDERATION; CONTRACT; GREAT SEAL; PRIVY SEAL.]

SEAL DAYS. Motion days in the Court of Chancery used to be so called.

SEARCH, RIGHT OF. [RIGHT OF SEARCH.]

SEARCH WARRANT is a warrant granted by a judge or magistrate to search a house, shop or other premises, e.g., a warrant may be granted by a justice under s. 26 of the Theft Act 1968 for the purpose of searching for stolen goods.

SEARCHES. Usually made by purchasers to find out incumbrances. Such searches are made at the Land Registry (generally by obtaining an official certificate of search) for land charges, and at the offices of local authorities for local land charges, etc.

SEAWORTHY. A ship is said to be seaworthy when it is in a fit condition to perform the voyage on which it is sent. By s. 457 of the Merchant Shipping Act 1894 every person who sends, or who is party to any attempt to send, any ship to sea in an unseaworthy state, so as to endanger the life of any person, is guilty of a misdemeanour, unless he can prove that he used all reasonable means to keep the ship seaworthy and was ignorant of such unseaworthiness; or that the going to sea of such ship in an unseaworthy state was, under the circumstances, reasonable and justifiable.

SECK RENT. [RENT.]

SECONDARY. 1. An officer who is second or next to the chief officer.

2. An under-sheriff of London, so called especially in reference to his jurisdiction in the assessment of damages under writs of inquiry. [INTERLOCUTORY JUDGMENT; WRIT OF INQUIRY.]

SECONDARY CONVEYANCE. [DERIVATIVE CONVEYANCE.]

SECONDARY EVIDENCE is evidence not of the best and most direct character; which is admissible in certain cases where the circumstances are such as to excuse a party from giving the proper or primary proof. Thus a copy of a deed is secondary evidence of its contents. Secondary evidence is receivable in many cases. There are no degrees in secondary evidence. The testimony of a witness is as sufficient secondary evidence of the contents of a written instrument as a copy of such instrument would be although the latter would be more satisfactory.

Secondary evidence must not be confounded with secondhand evidence. [SECONDHAND EVIDENCE.]

SECONDARY USE. The same as a shifting use. [SHIFTING USE.]

SECONDHAND EVIDENCE is the same as *hearsay evidence*, the ordinary meaning of which is the oral or written statement of a person who is not produced in court, conveyed to the court either by a witness or by the instrumentality of a document. The general rule is that hearsay or secondhand evidence is not admissible; but there are certain exceptions to this rule. Thus, in matters of public or general interest, popular reputation or opinion or the statements of deceased witnesses made against their own interest will be received as evidence. And on charges of homicide the declarations of the deceased, made in expectation of death, are admissible in evidence for or against the accused. [HEARSAY EVIDENCE.]

SECRET TRUST. A trust created by a testator who leaves property to a person on a promise, express or implied, that such legatee will hold it in trust for another.

SECRETARY OF STATE. The ordinary method of communication between Sovereign and subject is through a Sec-

SECRETARY OF STATE
—continued.

retary of State. There are now fifteen principal secretaries of state: the Secretary of State for Foreign and Commonwealth Affairs; the Secretary of State for the Home Department; the Secretary of State for Social Services; the Secretary of State for Defence; the Secretary of State for Scotland; the Secretary of State for Employment; the Secretary of State for Education and Science; the Secretary of State for Wales; the Secretary of State for Trade; the Secretary of State for Industry; the Secretary of State for the Environment; the Secretary of State for Northern Ireland; the Secretary of State for Energy; the Secretary of State for Prices and Consumer Protection and Paymaster-General; and the Secretary of State for Transport.

SECTA, or **SUIT.** By these words were anciently understood the witnesses or followers of the plaintiff which he brought to support his case.

SECTA CURIÆ. Suit of court; that is to say, the attendance at the lord's court, to which the tenant was bound in time of peace.

SECURED CREDITOR. A creditor who holds some special security for his debt, as a mortgage or lien. A secured creditor in bankruptcy may either give up his security or give credit for its value and prove for his whole debt, or else realise his security and prove for the balance and receive a dividend *pari passu* with the other creditors. See the Bankruptcy Act 1914, and Rules thereunder.

SECURITATE PACIS. [KEEPING THE PEACE.]

SECURITY FOR COSTS. As to the cases in which security for costs is now required see R.S.C. 1965, Ord. 23, and the notes thereon in the *Supreme Court Practice.*

SECURITY FOR GOOD BEHAVIOUR. [GOOD BEHAVIOUR.]

SECURITY FOR KEEPING THE PEACE. [KEEPING THE PEACE.]

SECUS. Otherwise; not so.

SEDITION consists in attempts made, by meetings or speeches, or by publications, to disturb the tranquillity of the State, which do not amount to treason.

SEDUCTION. An action for damages for seduction might formerly be brought by a parent, master, or one *in loco parentis* for the debauching of his daughter or servant; *per quod servitium amisit.* The woman herself had no action. The action was abolished by the Law Reform (Miscellaneous Provisions) Act 1970, s. 5.

SEE (Lat. *Sedes*). The circuit of a bishop's jurisdiction; or his office or dignity as being bishop of a given diocese.

SEIGNIORY. A lordship or manor.

SEISED. Feudally possessed of a freehold.

SEISED IN HIS DEMESNE AS OF FEE. This technical expression describes a tenant in fee simple in possession of a corporeal hereditament. The expression means that the land to which it refers is a man's *dominicum*, or property, since it belongs to him and his heirs for ever; yet this *dominicum*, property, or demesne is strictly not absolute or allodial, but qualified or feudal; it is his demesne *as of fee*, that is, it is not purely and simply his own, since it is held of a superior lord, in whom the ultimate property resides.

SEISIN (Scotch, *Sasine*; French, *Saisine*) is the feudal possession of a freehold estate in land. It is opposed—(1) To a merely beneficial or equitable title; (2) To the possession of a mere leasehold estate.

Seisin is of two kinds—*seisin in deed*, and *seisin in law.* Seisin in deed is when an actual possession is taken. Seisin in law is where lands descend, and no one has actually entered on them; or where one is by wrong disseised of them.

SEISIN, LIVERY OF. The delivery of feudal possession sometimes called investiture. [FEOFFMENT.]

SEISINA FACIT STIPITEM (seisin makes the stock of descent). This was the maxim of law by which, before the Inheritance Act 1833, the title by descent was traced from the person who died last seised. By s. 2 of that Act, descent is traced from the last person entitled who did not inherit. The old canons of descent were abolished as regards persons dying after 1925, and a new code enacted by Part IV of the Administration of Estates Act 1925. [DESCENT; SEISIN.]

SEIZING OF HERIOTS is when the lord of a manor, on the death of a tenant, seizes the beast or other chattel due by way of heriot. Provision is made by the Law of Property Act 1922 for the extinction of manorial incident including heriots. [HERIOT.]

SEIZURE QUOUSQUE. By the custom of most manors, if no heir to copyhold lands came to the court to be admitted in the place of a deceased tenant, the lord of the manor after proclamation at three consecutive customary courts might seize the land *quousque, i.e.,* until some person claimed to be admitted. [QUOUSQUE.]

SELECT COMMITTEE. A parliamentary committee, composed of certain members appointed by the house, to consider or inquire into any matters, and to report their opinion for the information of the house. *May.*

SELECTIVE EMPLOYMENT TAX. A former tax on employers, of short duration; having been introduced by the Finance Act 1966, it was abolished by the Finance Act 1972.

SELF-DEFENCE. If a person, in order to defend himself or his family or property, uses force which is reasonable in the circumstances and unintentionally kills his assailant, the killing is excusable. In defending himself, in such a case, a person must retreat as far as he can before resorting to force, though a person defending his house apparently need not do so (*R.* v. *Hussey* (1924), 89 J.P. 28). He must demonstrate by his actions that he does not want to fight (*R.* v. *Julien,* [1969] 2 All E.R. 856).

SEMBLE. It appears; an expression often used in reports, to indicate that such was the opinion of the court on a point not directly before them.

SEMI-NAUFRAGIUM. Half-shipwreck; a term used by Italian lawyers, by which they understood the casting merchandise into the sea to prevent shipwreck. The word is also used to signify the state of a vessel which has been so much injured by a tempest or accident, that to repair the damage would cost more than the ship is worth. [TOTAL LOSS.]

SENESCHAL. 1. A steward.

2. Also, one who dispenses justice.

SENTENCE OF A COURT. A definitive judgment pronounced in a civil or criminal proceeding. [DEFERMENT OF SENTENCE; SUSPENDED SENTENCE.]

SENTENCE OF DEATH RECORDED. This was the recording of a sentence of death not actually pronounced, on the understanding that it would not be executed. Under s. 1 of the Judgment of Death Act 1823 it was competent for the judge to do this in capital felonies other than murder. By s. 2, such a record was to have the same effect as if the judgment had been pronounced, and the offender reprieved by the court. No longer in use.

SEPARATE ESTATE. Such estate as was enjoyed by a married woman to her *separate use,* independently of her husband, so that she might dispose of it by will, and bind it by her contracts as if she were unmarried, provided she was not, by any instrument under which she took it, restrained from anticipating the income thereof. The common law did not allow a married woman to possess any property independently of her husband, but the Married Women's Property Act 1882 almost abolished the distinction between married and unmarried women in respect of property. By the Law Reform (Married Women and Tortfeasors) Act 1935, all property of a married woman belongs to her in all respects as if she were a *feme sole.* Restraints on anticipation were abolished by the Married Women (Restraint upon Anticipation) Act 1949. [HUSBAND AND WIFE.]

SEPARATE MAINTENANCE. Maintenance provided by a husband for his wife on the understanding that she is to live separate from him.

SEPARATE USE. [SEPARATE ESTATE.]

SEPARATION. A deed of separation is a deed made between husband and wife, whereby each covenants not to molest the other, and the husband agrees to pay so much to trustees for her separate maintenance, the trustees covenanting to indemnify him against his wife's debts.

Though the law allows provision to be made for a separation already determined on, yet it will not sanction any agreement to provide for the contingency of a future separation.

SEPARATION—*continued.*

A *decree* for judicial separation may be granted under s. 17 of the Matrimonial Causes Act 1973. An *order* for separation (now known as a "matrimonial order") may be obtained from justices under s. 2 of the Matrimonial Proceedings (Magistrates' Courts) Act 1960.

SEPARATISTS. 1. A sect of dissenters, allowed by a repealed statute of 1833 to make affirmation in lieu of oaths.

2. Dissenters generally.

SEQUELA VILLANORUM. The family retinue and appurtenances to the goods and chattels of villeins, which were at the absolute disposal of the lord.

SEQUESTER. A term used in the civil law for renouncing. The word also signifies the setting apart of a man's property, or a portion thereof, for the benefit of creditors.

SEQUESTRARI FACIAS DE BONIS ECCLESIASTICIS. A writ of execution in an action against a beneficed clergyman, commanding the bishop to enter into the rectory and parish church, and take and sequester the same, until of the rents, tithes and profits thereof, and of the other ecclesiastical goods of the defendant, he has levied the plaintiff's debt. This writ is in the nature of a *levari facias.* See R.S.C. 1965, Ord. 47, r. 5. [LEVARI FACIAS.]

SEQUESTRATION. 1. The order sent out by a bishop in execution of the writ of *sequestrari facias,* whereby the bishop directs the churchwardens to collect the profits of the defendant's benefice, and pay the same to the plaintiff, until the full sum be raised.

2. A writ directed by the court to commissioners, usually four in number, commanding them to enter the lands and take the rents and profits and seize the goods of the person against whom it is directed. This may be issued against a defendant who is in contempt by reason of neglect or refusal to appear or answer, or to obey a decree of the court. This writ may be issued under the Judicature Acts in whatever division of the High Court the action may be brought. R.S.C. 1965, Ord. 45.

SERIATIM. Individually, separately and in order.

SERJEANT, or **SERGEANT** (Lat. *Serviens*), is a word used variously as follows:—

1. *Serjeants at arms,* whose office is to attend the person of the sovereign; to arrest traitors and persons of quality offending, and to attend the Lord High Steward of England sitting in judgment upon any traitor. Two of them, by allowance of the sovereign, attend on the two houses of parliament. Their duties are to execute the commands of the house in arresting offenders. *May.*

2. *Serjeant at Law.* This was the highest degree in the legal profession. A serjeant at law was so made by the royal mandate or writ, commanding him to take that degree by a certain day. Their privilege of exclusive audience in the Court of Common Pleas was abolished in 1846, when that court was thrown open to all barristers.

A serjeant, on being so created, retired from the Inn of Court by which he was called to the bar, and became a member of Serjeants' Inn. The degree of serjeant is never taken now, though it has not been formally abolished.

3. *The Common Serjeant,* a judicial officer in the City of London. He acts as a circuit judge by virtue of his office.

SERJEANTS' INN. [SERJEANT, 2.]

SERJEANTY. An ancient tenure. [GRAND SERJEANTY; PETIT SERJEANTY.]

SERVANT. Servants are of several descriptions:—1. Menial servants: being persons retained by others to live within the walls of the house, and to perform the work and business of the household. 2. Persons employed by men of trades and professions under them, to assist them in their particular callings. 3. Apprentices, who are placed with a master to learn his trade. 4. Servants in husbandry, who used to be hired by the year. The following points may be mentioned in connection with the law of master and servant:—1. A master may *maintain,* that is, abet and assist, his servant in any action at law against a stranger: whereas in general to do this is an offence against the law. [MAINTENANCE, 1.] 2. A master might formerly bring an action against any man for injuring his servant, or for seducing his female servant; but in such case he had to allege his own damage by the loss of his servant, and such damage had to be proved at the trial. [SEDUCTION.] 3. If a servant by his negligence does any damage to a stranger, the master is liable for his neglect, provided the damage be done while the servant is acting in his master's employment.

SERVI. Bondmen, or servile servants.

SERVICE (*Servitium*). 1. That duty which a tenant, by reason of his fee, owes to his lord.

2. The duty which a servant owes to his master.

3. *Service of Process.*—This is the delivery of a writ, summons, or notice in any action or suit being instituted, or notice of any step or process therein, to the party to be affected thereby, or his solicitor, or other party having an interest in the subject-matter of the suit. It is now regulated by R.S.C. 1965, Ords. 10, 11 and 65. An *address for service* is an address at which such notice may be served, so as to bind the party whom it is thereby intended to serve.

4. Of notices by landlord or tenant.

SERVIENT TENEMENT. A tenement subject to an easement or servitude. [DOMINANT TENEMENT; EASEMENT; SERVITUDES.]

SERVITIUM LIBERUM. Free service such as to find a man and horse, or to go with the lord into the army, or to attend his court; as opposed to base services, such as ploughing the lord's land, or hedging his demesnes, which a freeman would be unwilling to perform. [FREEHOLD.]

SERVITUDES. The name in the Roman and Scotch law for *easements*. The property subject to the easement was called the *servient tenement*; and, in the case of an easement appurtenant, the property to which the enjoyment of the easement was attached was called the *dominant tenement*. [EASEMENT.]

SESS. A tax.

SESSION. 1. The sitting of parliament from its meeting to its prorogation, of which there is in general but one in each year.

2. The sitting of justices in court upon commission. [SESSIONS.]

SESSION, COURT OF. [COURT OF SESSION.]

SESSIONS. A sitting of justices in court upon commission, as the Sessions of Oyer and Terminer, the Petty Sessions, Special Sessions, etc. The Sessions of Oyer

and Terminer were held before the former justices of assize, the Quarter Sessions were held in counties before the justices of the peace, and in boroughs which had a separate court of quarter sessions before the recorder. Both assizes and quarter sessions have been abolished, their place being taken by the Crown Court. [CROWN COURT.]

SET-OFF may be defined generally to be the merging (wholly or partially) of a claim of one person against another in a counter-claim by the latter against the former. Thus, a plea of set-off is a plea whereby a defendant acknowledges the justice of the plaintiff's demand, but sets up another demand of his own, to counterbalance that of the plaintiff, either in whole or in part. This was a defence created by a statute of 1728 (since repealed), and was unknown to the common law.

By R.S.C. 1965, Ord. 18, r. 17, where a claim by a defendant to a sum of money is relied on as a defence to the whole or part of a claim made by the plaintiff, it may be included in the defence and set off against the plaintiff's claim, whether or not it is also added as a counterclaim.

SETS OF BILLS are exemplars or parts of a bill of exchange made on separate pieces of paper; each part referring to the other parts, and containing a condition that it shall continue payable only so long as the others remain unpaid: the set or parts constitute one bill. See the Bills of Exchange Act 1882, s. 71.

SETTLED ESTATES. [SETTLEMENT; SETTLED LAND.]

SETTLED LAND. Land limited *by way of succession*, to a person other than the person for the time being entitled to the beneficial enjoyment thereof. Such lastmentioned person is called a limited owner (*q.v.*). See the Settled Land Act 1925.

SETTLEMENT. 1. A deed whereby property is *settled*, that is, subjected to a string of limitations. In this sense one speaks of *marriage settlements* and *family settlements*. [STRICT SETTLEMENT.]

2. The termination of a disputed matter by the adoption of terms agreeable to the parties thereto.

3. A colony or plantation.

SETTLEMENT, ACT OF. [ACT OF SETTLEMENT.]

SETTLING DAYS, on the Stock Exchange, are the days appointed for the settlement of accounts arising from purchases and sales of stock. The settling days for English and foreign stocks and shares occur twice in every month, the middle and the end. The settling days for Consols are once in every month, generally near the commencement of the month.

SETTLOR. A person who makes a settlement of his land or personal property. [SETTLEMENT.]

SEVER. [SEVERANCE.]

SEVERAL COVENANTS are covenants entered into with several persons in such a manner or under such circumstances that they are construed as separate. If the interest of several parties in a deed appears to be separate, the covenants will be construed as separate, unless the language expressly and unequivocally indicates a joint covenant. *Hill & Redman.*

SEVERAL FISHERY. A fishery of which the owner is also the owner of the soil, or derives his right from the owner of the soil. Generally an exclusive right. [FISHERY.]

SEVERAL TAIL. This expression is used to denote a limitation whereby land is given and entailed severally to two. For example, land is given to two men and their wives, and the heirs to their bodies begotten; the donees have a joint estate for their two lives, and yet they have several inheritances, because the issue of the one shall have his moiety and the issue of the other his moiety. [ENTAIL; ESTATE; JOINT TENANCY; LIMITATION OF ESTATES.]

SEVERALTY, or **SEVERAL TENANCY,** is the holding of lands by a person in his own right only, without any other person being joined or connected with him in point of interest during his estate therein. It is thus opposed to holding in joint tenancy, in coparcenary, and in common. [COMMON, TENANCY IN; COPARCENARY; JOINT TENANCY.]

SEVERANCE. 1. The singling or severing of two or more that are joined in one writ, action or suit. As when two persons made defendants in a suit in respect of the same interest *sever* their defences, that is, adopt independent defences.

2. The dissolution or termination of a joint tenancy, or a tenancy in coparcenary or in common. A severance of a joint tenancy may be effected by partition or by any of the tenants disposing of his shares. See also s. 36 of the Law of Property Act 1925. There can never be a severance of a legal joint tenancy after 1925 so as to create a tenancy in common.

SEWER. A pipe which takes the drainage from more than one building. Regulated principally by ss. 14–52 of the Public Health Act 1936; but sewerage functions were transferred from local authorities to water authorities by ss. 14–16 of the Water Act 1973.

SEX DISCRIMINATION. [DISCRIMINATION.]

SHACK. *Common of shack* is the right of persons, occupying lands lying together in the same common field, to turn out their cattle after harvest to feed promiscuously in that field.

SHAM PLEA. A plea manifestly frivolous and absurd, pleaded for the purpose of vexation and delay. Under R.S.C., 1965, Ord. 18, r. 19, the court or a judge may order to be struck out or amended any matter in the pleadings which may tend to prejudice, embarrass or delay the fair trial of the action. [IMPERTINENCE.]

SHARE. A share or proportion of the capital of a company, entitling the holder to a share in the profits of the company. Shares may be of different classes, the principal among which are:
(1) *Preference shares*, the holders of which have preference over other classes as regards dividends and the repayment of capital. These may be either *non-cumulative* or *cumulative*, the latter entitling the holders to arrears of dividend, as well as to current dividends, in priority to other shareholders; they may also be *redeemable* at a future date.
(2) *Ordinary shares*, which carry no such special rights or privileges.
(3) *Deferred shares*, the holders of which are entitled to any residue after payment of dividends to the other classes of shareholders in accordance with the terms laid down in the memorandum and articles of the company.

SHEADING. A riding, tithing or division in the Isle of Man, of which there are six in the island.

SHELLEY'S CASE. [Rule in Shelley's Case.]

SHEPWAY, COURT OF. A court held before the Lord Warden of the Cinque Ports. [Cinque Ports.]

SHERIFF, or SHIRE-REVE. The chief bailiff or officer of the *shire*; an officer of great antiquity in the kingdom. He is called in Latin *vice-comes*, as being the deputy of the earl, or *comes*, to whom the custody of the shire is said to have been committed at the first division of the kingdom into counties. But the earls gradually withdrew from the county administration, and now the sheriff is the chief officer of the Crown in the county, and does all the Queen's business therein; the Crown committing the custody of the county to the sheriff, and to him alone.

For many centuries the bulk of the administrative work in the county was done by the justices and since 1888 by the county council. The sheriff's duties now are few; to superintend parliamentary elections, to execute process, to attend on the judges at the Crown Court, and to return the jury in criminal trials. Even these duties are carried out by deputies.

Sheriffs were formerly chosen by the inhabitants of the several counties, in confirmation of which it was enacted by a statute of Edward I (1300) that the people should have election of sheriffs in every shire where the shrievalty is not of inheritance; for anciently, in some counties the sheriffs were hereditary. As to the present mode of appointing sheriffs, see the Local Government Act 1972, s. 219.

SHERIFF COURT. (*Scotland.*) County courts in Scotland, the judges of which are sheriffs. The office of sheriff was formerly hereditary. The courts have both civil and criminal jurisdiction. The offices of sheriff and sheriff substitute were renamed sheriff principal and sheriff, respectively, by the Sheriff Courts (Scotland) Act 1971.

SHERIFF'S COURT. 1. [City of London Court.]

2. The court held by the sheriff of a county, or his deputy, either in virtue of a writ of inquiry, to assess the damages which the plaintiff had sustained in an undefended action, or to try issues sent to him for that purpose by a writ of trial. This latter

jurisdiction was granted in 1833, but abolished in 1867.

The two ancient sheriffs' courts for the Poultry Compter and the Giltspur Street Compter in the City of London have never been formally abolished. No judges have been appointed since 1929 (*Hals. Laws*).

SHERIFF'S OFFICERS. Bailiffs; either bailiffs of hundreds, or bound-bailiffs.

SHERIFF'S POUNDAGE. [Poundage, 2.]

SHERIFF'S TOURN was a court of record, appointed to be held twice in every year, within a month after Easter and Michaelmas, before the sheriff in different parts of the county; being, indeed, only the *turn* of the sheriff to keep a court leet, in each respective hundred. The sheriff's tourn was abolished by s. 18 (4) of the Sheriffs Act 1887. [Court Leet; Frank-Pledge.]

SHEW CAUSE. [Rule, 3.]

SHIFTING USE was a use in land, limited in derogation of a preceding estate or interest, as when land was limited to A and his heirs to the use of B and his heirs with a proviso that when C returns from Rome, the land shall be to the use of C and his heirs, in derogation of the use previously vested in B. The Statute of Uses was repealed by the Law of Property Act 1925. After 1925, a shifting use subsists only as an equitable interest. The equitable interest can still be made to shift from one person to another, but the legal estate cannot be limited in such a manner.

SHIP. Under s. 742 of the Merchant Shipping Act 1894 the term includes "every description of vessel used in navigation not propelled by oars." By s. 57 of the Harbours Act 1964 it includes seaplanes and hover vehicles.

The ownership of every British ship is divided into 64 shares, all of which may belong to one person, or they may be divided amongst two or more persons. Not more than 64 persons can be registered as part owners, except that five persons may be regarded as joint owners of one share.

SHIP-BROKER. One whose business it is to procure freights or charter-parties, and to negotiate the sale of ships.

SHIP MONEY. An ancient imposition that was charged upon the ports, towns, cities, boroughs and counties of the realm. Having lain dormant for many years, it was revived by King Charles I in 1635 and 1636; but by the Ship Money Act 1640 it was declared to be contrary to the laws and statutes of the realm.

SHIPPER. A consignor of goods to be sent by sea.

SHIP'S HUSBAND is the general agent of the owners of a vessel in its use and employment. His duty is in general to exercise an impartial judgment in the employment of tradesmen and the appointment of officers; to see that the ship is properly repaired, equipped and manned; to procure freights and charter-parties; to preserve the ship's papers, make the necessary entries, adjust freight and averages, disburse and receive moneys, and keep and make up the accounts as between all parties interested.

SHIP'S PAPERS. The papers or documents required for the manifestation of property in a ship or cargo.

They are of two kinds:—

1. Those required by the law of a particular country, as the certificate of registry, bills of lading, etc., required by the law of England.

2. Those required by the law of nations to be on board neutral ships, to vindicate their title to that character, such as the pass-port, muster-roll, etc.

SHIRE, derived from the Saxon *scyran*, to divide, is a portion of land called a county.

SHIRE-REEVE. [SHERIFF.]

SHORT BILL. [ENTERING BILLS SHORT.]

SHORT CAUSE. Where a writ is specially indorsed and leave, whether conditional or unconditional, is given to defend, a special list, called the Short Cause List, is kept for the trial of causes in which the judge is of opinion that a long trial will not be requisite. See R.S.C., Ord. 14, r. 6, and notes thereto in the *Supreme Court Practice.*

SHORT ENTRY. [ENTERING BILLS SHORT.]

SHORT TITLE. Every Act of Parliament now contains a section or subsection giving a short title, *i.e.*, a title that can be conveniently and easily cited, to such Act. Many former statutes were given short titles by the Short Titles Act 1896.

SHRIEVALTY. 1. The sheriff's office.

2. As used with reference to any given person, it means the period during which he was sheriff.

SI NON OMNES (if not all). A writ, on association of justices, by which, if all in commission cannot meet at the day assigned, it is allowed that two or more of them may finish the business.

SIGHT, BILLS PAYABLE AT, are equivalent to bills payable on demand. See s. 10 of the Bills of Exchange Act 1882.

SIGNATURE. An indication, by sign, mark, or generally by the writing of a name or initials, that a person intends to bind himself to the contents of a document.

SIGNET. 1. One of the Queen's seals with which her private letters are sealed.

2. Writers to the signet in Scotland perform substantially the same functions as solicitors in England.

SIGN-MANUAL. The signature of the sovereign.

SIGNIFICAVIT. A name by which the writ *de excommunicato capiendo* was known, because it expressed that the bishop *signified* to the sovereign in Chancery the contempt committed by the party to whom the writ referred.

SIGNING JUDGMENT. [ENTERING JUDGMENT.]

SILK GOWN. A phrase used especially of the silk gowns worn by Queen's Counsel; hence, "to take silk" means to attain the rank of Queen's Counsel.

SILVER. [BRITANNIA; HALLMARK; STERLING.]

SIMILITER (in like manner). A phrase indicating that when a defendant puts himself upon the country, that is, upon trial by jury (by plea of not guilty or otherwise), the plaintiff or Crown prosecutor *doth the like.* All joinders of issue were formerly called the similiter.

SIMONY is the corrupt presentation of, or the corrupt agreement to present, any person to an ecclesiastical benefice for money, gift or reward, and is generally committed in one of the two following ways:—

1. By the purchase of the next presentation to a living actually vacant.

2. By a clergyman purchasing, either in his own name or another's, the next presentation to a living, and afterwards presenting, or causing himself to be presented, thereto. But the purchase by a clergyman of an entire advowson, or even of a limited interest therein, is not simony, though the purchaser afterwards present himself. See now the declaration contained in the Schedule to the Benefices Act 1898.

SIMPLE CONTRACT. A contract, express or implied, which is created by verbal promise, or by writing not under seal. [CONTRACT.]

SIMPLE CONTRACT DEBT. A debt arising out of a simple contract. [ASSET.]

SIMPLE TRUST is a trust which requires no act to be done by the trustee except conveyance or transfer to his *cestui que trust* on request by the latter. [CESTUI QUE TRUST.]

SINE DIE. Without day; that is to say, without any day appointed for the resumption of the business on hand. Thus, an adjournment *sine die* is an adjournment without appointing any day for meeting again. [EAT INDE SINE DIE.]

SINE PROLE. Without issue; frequently abbreviated into "s.p.".

SINECURE. Without cure of souls; a word used in former times of a rector who by custom was relieved from residence, and had no spiritual duties, these being performed by the vicar. By the Ecclesiastical Commissioners Act 1840 provision was made for the abolition of sinecure rectories. [RECTOR; VICAR.] And a sinecure office is generally understood to mean a nominal office, with no duties attaching to it.

SINGLE BOND (Lat. *Simplex obligatio*). A bond whereby a party obliges himself to pay to another a certain sum of money on a day specified, without any condition for making void the obligation. This hardly ever occurs in practice. [BOND.]

SINGLE COMBAT. A species of trial. [WAGER OF BATTEL.]

SINGLE ENTRY is a system of bookkeeping according to which each entry in the day-book, invoice-book, cash-book and bill-book is posted or entered *once* to some account in the ledger; whereas, in *double entry* each entry is posted to *two* different accounts. [DOUBLE ENTRY.]

SINKING FUND. A fund for the reduction of the National Debt, regulated by various Acts of Parliament.

SITTINGS. The division of the legal year into terms was abolished by the Judicature Act 1873, and *sittings* were substituted. There are now four sittings in each year, *viz.*, the Michaelmas, Hilary, Easter, and Trinity sittings. See R.S.C., 1965, Ord. 64, r. 1.

SITTINGS IN BANC. [BANC.]

SITTINGS IN CAMERA are sittings other than sittings in open court. This course is often adopted for the hearing of cases where a public hearing would defeat the ends of justice, or on the grounds of public decency, *e.g.*, as in the hearing of evidence as to impotence, etc., in nullity cases; see s. 48 (2) of the Matrimonial Causes Act 1973. The court may also sit in camera where it is necessary for the public safety. [CAMERA.]

SIX CLERKS IN CHANCERY were six officers in the Court of Chancery, whose duties were to receive and file all bills, answers, replications and other records in all causes on the equity side of the Court of Chancery. Their office was abolished in 1842, and their functions were thenceforth discharged by the Record and Writ Clerks. [CLERK OF RECORDS AND WRITS.]

SIX-DAY LICENCE. One granted under s. 65 of the Licensing Act 1964, containing a condition that the licensed premises shall be closed during the whole of Sunday.

SKILLED WITNESS, also called an *expert* or *professional witness*, is a person called to give evidence in a matter relating to his own trade or profession, as when a medical man is called to give evidence on the effects of poison. As to the rules of court relating to, and the admissibility of, such evidence, see s. 3 of the Evidence Act 1972.

SLANDER. Defamatory language used of another. It is *oral*, not in writing or print. See the Defamation Act 1952. [DEFAMATION: LIBEL, 5.]

SLIP. An unstamped memorandum of an intended marine insurance policy. Such a document, even where it is invalid as a legal contract, is admissible in evidence for certain collateral purposes. See s. 21 of the Marine Insurance Act 1906. It has been held that the non-disclosure of facts material to the risk, discovered subsequently to the execution of the "slip", does not vitiate a policy afterwards executed.

SMALL DEBTS COURTS. Courts of requests or of conscience for the recovery of small debts, now superseded by the county courts. [CONSCIENCE, COURTS OF; COUNTY COURT; COURT OF REQUEST.]

SMALL TITHES were the tithes which generally vested in the *vicar* as opposed to the *rector* or *appropriator*. They included tithes mixed and personal; that is, tithes of wool, milk, pigs, of manual occupations, trades, and fisheries, and other fruits of the personal industry of the inhabitants. [TITHES.]

SMUGGLING is the offence of importing or exporting prohibited goods, or importing or exporting goods not prohibited without paying the duties imposed thereon by the laws of the customs and excise.

SOCAGE in its most general signification denoted a tenure of land by a certain and determinate service, as opposed to chivalry or knight-service, where the tenure was precarious and uncertain. It was of two kinds: *free-socage*, where the services were not only certain but honourable; and *villein socage* or *privileged villenage*, where the services, though certain, were of a baser nature. All tenures (with a few exceptions) were, by the Tenures Abolition Act 1660, turned into free and common socage. [FREEHOLD: KNIGHT-SERVICE.]

SOCAGERS, SOCMANS, SOKEMANS or **SOCMEN** (Lat. *Socmanni*). Tenants in socage.

SOCIAL SECURITY. Most of the former national insurance legislation was repealed by the Social Security Act 1973 and replaced by a scheme of social security contributions and benefits under that Act.

The main provisions of the Act of 1973, together with the National Insurance (Industrial Injuries) Acts 1965 to 1974, and certain other enactments relating to social security, were consolidated by the Social Security Act 1975. See also the Social Security Pensions Act 1975.

SOIT FAIT COMME IL EST DÉSIRÉ. Let it be as it is desired. [LA REYNE LE VEULT.]

SOLD NOTE. [BOUGHT AND SOLD NOTES.]

SOLE. Not married, single.

SOLE CORPORATION. [CORPORATION.]

SOLE TENANT (Lat. *Solus tenens*). One that holds in severalty; that is, in his own sole right, and not with another. [SEVERAL TENANCY.]

SOLEMN FORM. There are two kinds of probate, namely, probate in *common form*, and probate in *solemn form*. Probate in common form is granted in the registry, without any formal procedure in court, upon an *ex parte* application made by the executor. Probate in solemn form is in the nature of a final decree pronounced in open court, all parties interested having been duly cited. The difference between the effect of probate in common form and probate in solemn form is, that probate in common form is revocable, whereas probate in solemn form is irrevocable as against all persons who have been cited to see the proceedings, or who can be proved to have been privy to these proceedings, except in the case where a will of subsequent date is discovered, in which case probate of an earlier will, though granted in solemn form, would be revoked. [PROBATE.]

SOLICITATION. Incitement or inducement to commit an offence.

The solicitation to the commission of an offence is a misdemeanour at common law, and punishable by fine and imprisonment, even though no offence be in fact committed.

SOLICITING. [STREET OFFENCES.]

SOLICITOR. Solicitors were formerly regarded specially as officers of the Court of Chancery; but by the Judicature Act 1873, s. 87, all attornies, solicitors, and proctors were to be styled solicitors of the Supreme Court. To become a solicitor a person must now be articled to a practising solicitor, generally for five years, pass the necessary examinations conducted by the Law Society, and be admitted by the Master of the Rolls. A certificate to practice must be taken out annually. A solicitor may act as advocate in the Bankruptcy Court, in county courts, petty sessions, in certain proceedings in the Crown Court, and in most other inferior courts. Also in chambers, in the Supreme Court. A solicitor can sue for costs, but is liable for negligence. See the Solicitors Act 1974. [ADVOCATE; ARTICLED CLERK.]

SOLICITOR-GENERAL. The second law office of the Crown, next to the Attorney-General.

SOLIDUM. To be bound *in solidum* is to be bound for a whole debt jointly and severally with others, as opposed to being bound, *pro rata*, for a proportionate part only.

SORCERY. [WITCHCRAFT.]

SOUL-SCOT. An ecclesiastical heriot. [HERIOT.] In many parishes, on the death of a parishioner, after the lord's heriot or best chattel was taken out, the second best chattel was reserved to the church as a mortuary. This mortuary was, in the laws of Canute, called *soul-scot.* [MORTUARY, 1.]

SOUNDING IN DAMAGES. This phrase is used of an action which is brought in point of form for damages.

SOVEREIGN. [KING; QUEEN.]

SPEAKERS OF THE HOUSES OF PARLIAMENT. The Speaker is the officer who is, as it were, the common mouth of the rest; and as there are two Houses, so there are two speakers. The one, the Lord Speaker of the House of Peers, who is most commonly the Lord Chancellor, or Lord Keeper of the Great Seal of England. The other, being a member of the House of Commons, is called the Speaker of the House of Commons. The Speaker of the House of Commons holds office till the dissolution of parliament in which he was elected. It is the duty of the Speaker to preside over the debates of the house, and manage the formality of business. He has also special duties in regard to giving certificates under the provisions of the Parliament Act 1911. The Speaker of the House of Commons may not give his opinion or argue any question in the house; but the Speaker of the House of Lords, if he be a lord of parliament (which is generally but not necessarily the case), may do so. In the House of Commons the Speaker never votes, except when the votes are equal; but in the House of Lords the Speaker has a vote with the rest of the house, but no casting vote, for should the votes be equal the non-contents prevail. *May.*

SPEAKING WITH PROSECUTOR. This is in the nature of an imparlance by a defendant convicted of a misdemeanour immediately affecting an individual, as a battery, imprisonment, or the like; in which case the court may permit the defendant to speak with the prosecutor, before any judgment is pronounced; and, if the prosecutor declares himself satisfied, may inflict but a trivial punishment.

SPECIAL ACCEPTANCE OF A BILL OF EXCHANGE means the acceptance of a bill as payable at some specified place, and not elsewhere. [ACCEPTANCE OF A BILL; BILL OF EXCHANGE.]

SPECIAL ADMINISTRATION is the administration of certain specific effects of a deceased person; otherwise called a *limited* administration. [ADMINISTRATION; LIMITED ADMINISTRATION.]

SPECIAL AGENT. An agent empowered to act as such in some particular matter, and not generally. [GENERAL AGENT.]

SPECIAL BAIL. Formerly used to denote substantial sureties, as opposed to the imaginary beings John Doe and Richard Roe, who did duty as *common bail*, both for the plaintiff's prosecution of the suit, and for the defendant's attendance and obedience. [COMMON BAIL.]

SPECIAL BAILIFFS. 1. The same as bound bailiffs.
2. Persons named by a party in a civil suit for the purpose of executing some particular process therein, and appointed by the sheriff on the application of such party. For the conduct of such officers the sheriff is not responsible. [BAILIFF.]

SPECIAL BASTARD. One born of parents who afterwards intermarry. Such a person is legitimated by subsequent marriage, even where born in adultery: Legitimacy Act 1959. See also the Children Act 1975, Sch. 1, Part III. [LEGITIMATION.]

SPECIAL CASE. 1. A statement of facts agreed to on behalf of two or more litigant parties, and submitted for the opinion of a court of justice as to the law bearing upon the facts so stated.

2. By the Crown Cases Act 1848 any court of oyer and terminer, gaol delivery, or quarter sessions might reserve any question of law arising in a case and state it in the form of a special case for the Court of Crown Cases Reserved. The jurisdiction of this court was transferred to the Court of Criminal Appeal, the jurisdiction of which has, in turn, been transferred to the criminal division of the Court of Appeal under the Criminal Appeal Acts 1966 and 1968.

3. A case stated by justices or by a police magistrate for the opinion of the High Court under s. 87 of the Magistrates' Courts Act 1952.

SPECIAL COMMISSION. An extraordinary commission of oyer and terminer and gaol delivery, confined to certain offences which stood in need of immediate inquiry and punishment.

SPECIAL CONSTABLES. [CONSTABLE, 6.]

SPECIAL DAMAGE. Damage which in a given case may be shown to have arisen to the plaintiff from the conduct of the defendant. In some cases, as for instance in cases of assault and false imprisonment, an action will lie without showing special damage; in others it is necessary to show special damage in order to maintain the action.

SPECIAL DEMURRER. A demurrer showing the special grounds on which the party demurs to the pleading of his adversary. Abolished. [DEMURRER.]

SPECIAL EXAMINER. A person formerly appointed to take evidence in a particular suit.

Now by R.S.C. 1965, Ord. 39, r. 1, the court or a judge may, in any cause or matter where it appears necessary for the purposes of justice, make an order for the examination upon oath before the court or a judge or any officer of the court, or any other person, and at any place, of any person, and may empower any party to any such cause or matter to give on deposition any evidence therein.

SPECIAL JURY was a jury consisting of persons who were of a certain station in society; namely, esquires or persons of higher degree, or bankers, or merchants, or persons who occupied a house or premises of a certain rateable value. Now abolished.

SPECIAL LICENCE. [MARRIAGE LICENCE.]

SPECIAL OCCUPANT. [OCCUPANT.]

SPECIAL PARLIAMENTARY PROCEDURE. A procedure to which certain ministerial orders are subjected by various statutes. Prescribed by the Statutory Orders (Special Procedure) Acts 1945 and 1965.

SPECIAL PERSONAL REPRESENTATIVE. One who is appointed as a special or additional representative to act in respect of settled land only. See s. 7 (1) of the Settled Land Act 1925.

SPECIAL PLEA. A plea in bar, not being the plea of the general issue. [PLEA.]

SPECIAL PLEADER. A lawyer whose professional occupation it is to give verbal or written opinions upon statements submitted to him, and to draw pleadings, civil and criminal, and such practical proceedings as may be out of the usual course.

Special pleaders are not necessarily at the bar; but those that are not are required to take out annual certificates. The number of special pleaders is now very small.

SPECIAL PLEADING. The science of pleading which formerly constituted a distinct branch of the law, with treatises and professors of its own. It had the merit of developing the points in controversy with the severest precision. But its strictness and subtlety were a frequent subject of complaint; and now the drawing up or preparation of pleadings must be undertaken by a barrister or solicitor. See the Solicitors Act 1974.

SPECIAL PROPERTY. A limited or qualified right in any subject of property. Thus, one who hires a horse to ride has a special property in the horse.

SPECIAL RESOLUTION. [RESOLUTION.]

SPECIAL SESSIONS. A sessions held by justices acting for a division of a county for the transaction of special business. A special sessions is generally held by virtue of a provision of some Act of Parliament. Due notice of it is usually given to all the justices resident within the division for which it is held; and in some cases this is required by Act of Parliament. A special sessions is sometimes called a *special petty sessions*; and a special sessions held for the purpose of licensing public houses is sometimes called a *Brewster Sessions*. [SESSIONS.]

SPECIAL TAIL. [TAIL SPECIAL.]

SPECIAL TRAVERSE. A form of traverse formerly in use in action by which a party sought to explain or qualify his denial of his opponent's pleading, instead of putting his denial in a direct form. Abolished in 1852.

SPECIAL TRUST. A trust imposing active duties on the trustee; otherwise called an *active trust*.

SPECIAL VERDICT. A verdict in which the jury state the facts of a case, as they find them to be proved, leaving it to the court to draw the proper legal inferences therefrom. Special verdicts in criminal cases are very rare.

SPECIALTY, or **SPECIALTY DEBT,** is an obligation contracted by matter of record, or by bond or other instrument under seal. [ASSET.]

SPECIFIC DEVISE. A devise of specific land. [RESIDUARY DEVISEE.]

SPECIFIC LEGACY. A legacy of a specific fund or of a specific chattel.

If the subject of such a legacy be sold or otherwise made away with in the testator's lifetime, the legacy is adeemed. [ADEMPTION OF A LEGACY.]

SPECIFIC PERFORMANCE. A suit for specific performance is one in which a person with whom another has made a contract prays that the latter may be decreed specifically to perform it. The specific performance of a contract has in general been decreed in equity, where the contract is not a positive contract of a personal nature (as to sing at a theatre), nor one for the non-performance of which damages would be a sufficient compensation (as to pay a liquidated sum of money).

By s. 56 (1) of the Judicature Act 1925 actions for the specific performance of

contracts between vendors and purchasers of real estates, including contracts for leases, were assigned to the Chancery Division of the High Court. See also s. 52 of the County Courts Act 1959.

SPECIFICATION. The particular description of an invention in respect of which a patent is sought. See s. 3 of the Patents Act 1949.

SPIRITS. Volatile liquids obtained by distillation, *e.g.*, brandy, whisky. The manufacture of spirits, their importation and exportation, the duties thereon, etc., are regulated by the Customs and Excise Act 1952, under s. 307 of which "spirits" includes all liquors mixed with spirits and all mixtures, compounds or preparations made with spirits, but not including methylated spirits or angostura bitters.

SPIRITUAL LORDS. [LORDS SPIRITUAL.]

SPIRITUALITIES OF A BISHOP are those profits which he receives as a bishop, and not as a baron of parliament, as the duties of his visitation, etc. *Cowel.* By s. 2 of the Ecclesiastical Commissioners Act 1860 provision was made for the payment of these duties to the Church Commissioners.

SPLITTING A CAUSE OF ACTION signifies the bringing of separate actions for the different parts of a claim; or otherwise bringing several actions where one would suffice. This is prohibited in the county courts by s. 69 of the County Courts Act 1959.

SPOLIATION. 1. An injury done by one clerk or incumbent to another, in taking the fruits of his benefice without any right thereunto, but under a pretended title; which, when the right of advowson does not come into debate, is cognizable in the spiritual court.

2. Also the writ that lies in such case for the one incumbent against the other.

SPRINGING USE. A use limited to commence *in futuro*, independently of any preceding estate; as if land be conveyed to A and his heirs, to the use of B and his heirs on the death of C. In this case, while C lives, the use limited to B and his heirs is still *in futuro*. Such a use is also called an *executory use* or *executory interest*. As the Statute of Uses was repealed by the Law of Property

SPRINGING USE—*continued.*

Act 1925 a springing use now subsists only in regard to equitable interests. The equitable interest can still be made to spring up in a person, but the legal estate cannot be limited in such a manner.

STADIUM, in Domesday Book, is a furlong, or an eighth of a mile.

STAKEHOLDER. One with whom a stake is deposited pending the decision of a wager, etc. [WAGER.]

The term is also used in relation to a sum of money paid as a deposit on a contract for purchase of property. Such sum is often paid to some person as a stakeholder as between the two parties, not as agent for the vendor.

STALLAGE. Money paid for pitching stalls in fairs or markets; or the right to do so.

STAMP DUTIES are taxes imposed upon written instruments such as conveyances, etc., and are either *ad valorem* duties, or are fixed in amount.

Where a stamp is essential to the legal validity of a writing, that writing cannot be given in evidence in civil proceedings if it be unstamped, or be insufficiently stamped, except upon complying with the conditions and the payment of the penalties specified in ss. 14 and 15 of the Stamp Act 1891. But this rule does not apply to criminal proceedings.

STANDARD TIME. [SUMMER TIME.]

STANDING MUTE. [MUTE; PEINE FORTE ET DURE.]

STANDING ORDERS are orders framed by each House of parliament for the permanent guidance and order of its proceedings. Such orders, if not vacated or repealed, endure from one parliament to another, and are of equal force in all. They occasionally fall into desuetude, but by the law and custom of parliament they are binding until their operation is concluded by another vote of the House upon the same matter. *May.*

STANNARIES. The mines and works where tin metal is worked. [COURT OF STANNARIES OF CORNWALL AND DEVON.]

STANNARY COURTS. [COURT OF STANNARIES OF CORNWALL AND DEVON.]

STAPLE signifies the public mart in certain towns or cities, whither the merchants of England were, by Act of Parliament, to carry their *staple commodities*, for the purpose of disposing of them wholesale. [STATUTE, 2.]

STAPLE INN. One of the Inns of Chancery, between Holborn Bars and Southampton Buildings, Chancery Lane. [INNS OF CHANCERY.]

STAR-BOARD. [LARBOARD.]

STAR-CHAMBER, or **CAMERA STELLATA.** A court of very ancient origin, but new-modelled by a statute of Henry VII in 1487. It consisted of various lords spiritual and temporal, being privy councillors, together with two judges of the courts of common law, without the intervention of any jury. Their jurisdiction extended legally over riots, perjury, misbehaviour of sheriffs, and other notorious misdemeanours contrary to the laws of the land.

It wrongfully extended its jurisdiction and was abolished by the Habeas Corpus Act 1640.

STARE DECISIS. Abiding by precedent.

STATEMENT OF AFFAIRS. A statement by a debtor in bankruptcy proceedings, listing his debtors, creditors, assets, etc. See s. 14 of the Bankruptcy Act 1914.

STATEMENT OF CLAIM is the statement by the plaintiff, in an action brought in the High Court of Justice, of the ground of his complaint and of the relief or remedy to which he claims to be entitled.

STATEMENT OF DEFENCE is the statement delivered by a defendant in answer to the plaintiff's statement of claim. It must be delivered within fourteen days after the plaintiff's delivery of his statement of claim, or from the time limited for appearance, whichever is last, unless the time be extended by a court or judge. The defendant may, in his statement of defence, adduce any facts on which he seeks to reply as supporting a right of set-off or counter-claim; in which case he must state specifically that he does so by way of set-off or counter-claim. R.S.C., 1965, Ord. 18. [STATEMENT OF CLAIM.]

STATIONERS' HALL. The hall of the Stationers' Company, in the City of London, at which every person claiming copyright in a book formerly had to register his title in order to be able to bring actions against persons infringing it. Such registration is now unnecessary.

STATIONERY OFFICE. A government office controlling the printing of Acts of Parliament and other books and publications required by Parliament and the public departments.

STATUS. The condition of a person in the eye of the law. In Roman law the term had reference to freedom, citizenship and the capacity to contract.

STATUS OF IRREMOVABILITY. Under the former poor law this was the right acquired by a pauper, by one whole year's residence in any parish, not to be removed therefrom.

STATUS QUO. The state in which any thing is already. Thus, when it is said that, provisionally, matters are to remain *in statu quo*, it is meant that, for the present, matters are to remain as they are. Sometimes, however, the phrase is used retrospectively: and, if so, this will generally be indicated by the context; as when, on a treaty of peace, matters are to *return* to the *status quo*, this means the *status quo ante bellum*, their state prior to the war.

STATUTE. 1. An Act of Parliament made by the Queen in Parliament. It normally requires the consent of the Lords and Commons; but see the Parliament Act, 1911, for circumstances in which a bill may become law without the consent of the Lords.

A *statute*, in the ancient sense of the word, means the legislation of a session; the various Acts of Parliament passed in it being so many *chapters* of the entire statute. Thus, by the Statute of Gloucester, the Statute of Merton, etc., is meant a body of legislation comprising various chapters on different subjects. But in reference to modern legislation the word *statute* denotes a *chapter* of legislation, or what is otherwise called an *Act of Parliament*. [DE-CLARATORY ACT; ENABLING STATUTE; KING.]

2. A short writing called a *statute merchant* or *statute staple*. These are in the nature of bonds of record, and are called *statutes*, because made according to the forms expressly provided by statutes, which direct both before what persons, and in what manner they ought to be made. Obsolete.

STATUTE MERCHANT. [STATUTE, 2.]

STATUTE OF FRAUDS, LIMITATIONS, etc. [FRAUDS, STATUTE OF, etc.]

STATUTE OF WESTMINSTER, 1931, defines the constitutional position of the older dominions and their relationship with the United Kingdom.

STATUTE STAPLE. [STATUTE, 2.]

STATUTES AT LARGE. A phrase used to denote an edition of the statutes printed *verbatim*.

STATUTORY DECLARATION. A declaration made before a magistrate or commissioner for oaths in the form prescribed by the Statutory Declarations Act 1835, by which voluntary affidavits, in matters where no judicial inquiry is pending, are prohibited. Any person making a statutory declaration falsely is guilty of a misdemeanour under s. 5 of the Perjury Act 1911.

STATUTORY INSTRUMENT. The most important form of delegated legislation including all Orders in Council and all statutory rules and orders which have to be laid before Parliament.

STATUTORY OWNER. As used in the Settled Land Act 1925, this term means "the trustees of the settlement or other person who during a minority or at any other time when there is no tenant for life, have the powers of a tenant for life under this Act, but does not include the trustees of the settlement where by virtue of an order of the court or otherwise the trustees have power to convey the settled land in the name of the tenant for life". See s. 117 (1) (xxvi).

STATUTORY TRUSTS. It is enacted by s. 47 of the Administration of Estates Act 1925 that in the case of a person dying intestate, a certain part of his property shall be held by the personal representative upon what are called the "statutory trusts". Under the "statutory trusts" for issue, the property must be divided equally among the children who are alive at the death of the intestate, as soon as they attain twenty-one or marry. The share of any child who dies before the intestate goes to the issue of that child on the "per stirpes" principle, as soon as such issue attain twenty-one or

STATUTORY TRUSTS—*continued.*
marry. See also s. 35 of the Law of Property
Act 1925.

STAY OF PROCEEDINGS is the putting an end to the proceedings in an action
by a summary order of the court. It differs
from an injunction and from a prohibition,
as follows:
1. Staying proceedings is effected by the
court in which the action is brought, or by
some other court on appeal therefrom.
2. An injunction to restrain proceedings
is an order of an independent court
restraining the plaintiff from proceeding in
the action.
3. A prohibition is an order of a superior
court, prohibiting the court in which the
action is brought from taking cognizance
thereof.
Under s. 41 of the Judicature Act 1925 no
cause or proceedings pending in the High
Court of Justice or Court of Appeal shall be
restrained by prohibition or injunction, but
the courts have power on motion in a
summary way to stay proceedings in cases
where an injunction or prohibition could
formerly have been obtained.

STEALING. The dishonest appropriation of property belonging to another
with the intention of permanently depriving the other of it. [THEFT.]

STEALING AN HEIRESS. [HEIRESS.]

STERLING. A word used to indicate
that silver is of a standard of fineness of 925
parts to 1,000. Formerly also used of the
currency, *e.g.* "the pound sterling". The
former silver currency is now debased.

STET PROCESSUS, in an action, is an
entry on the roll, in the nature of a judgment, that by consent of the parties all
further proceedings are stayed. It cannot be
ordered without the consent of the parties.

STETHE. A bank of a river.

STEVEDORE. A person whose occupation it is to stow packages and goods in a
ship's hold, and discharge cargoes.

STEWARD (Lat. *Senescallus*).
1. *The Lord High Steward of England*,
etc.[HIGH STEWARD.]
2. The *Steward of a Manor* is an officer of

the lord of the manor, appointed to hold his
courts, to admit tenants, to accept surrenders, etc.
3. *Stewards of the Barmote Courts.* [BAR-
MOTE COURTS.]

STINT. [SANS NOMBRE.]

STIPEND. By this word we generally
understand any periodical payment for
services; especially the income of an
ecclesiastical living or curacy.

STIPENDIARY. A feudatory to whom
an estate was granted in return for services
to his lord.

STIPENDIARY MAGISTRATES are
paid, full-time magistrates appointed to act
alone, or with other justices, by s. 2 of the
Administration of Justice Act 1973. They
must be barristers or solicitors of seven
years standing. In London the place of the
stipendiary magistrate is taken by the
Metropolitan Police Magistrate.

STIPULATION, in the Roman law,
was a solemn form giving legal validity to
an agreement; in the Admiralty Courts it is
a recognizance of fidejussors in the nature
of bail.

STIRPES, DISTRIBUTION PER. A
distribution *per stirpes* is a division of
property among families according to
stocks, *i.e.*, taking into consideration the
representatives of deceased persons who if
they had survived would themselves have
taken. This division is called a distribution
per stirpes, as opposed to a distribution *per
capita.* For the present code of succession
on intestacy applying alike to real and
personal property, see Part IV of the
Administration of Estates Act 1925.
[CAPITA, DISTRIBUTION PER.]

STOCK. 1. A race or family.
2. In reference to the investment of
money, the term "stock" implies those sums
of money contributed towards raising a
fund whereby certain objects, as of trade or
commerce, may be effected. It is also
employed to denote the moneys advanced
to the Government, which constitute a part
of the National Debt, whereupon a certain
amount of interest is payable. Since the
introduction of the system of borrowing
upon interminable annuities, the meaning
of the word "stock" has gradually changed;
and instead of signifying the security upon

which loans are advanced, it has for a long time signified the principal of the loans themselves. In this latter sense we speak of the sale, purchase, and transfer of stock. [STOCK BROKER; STOCK EXCHANGE.]

STOCK BROKER is a person who, for a commission, negotiates for other parties the buying and selling of stocks, according to the rules of the Stock Exchange. The members of the Stock Exchange are called *jobbers* and *brokers*. The jobber is the dealer, who buys and sells at the market prices, and acts as an intermediary between the broker who buys and the broker who sells. The broker, on behalf of his principal, deals with the jobber. [STOCK EXCHANGE.]

STOCK EXCHANGE. An association of stock brokers and jobbers in the city of London. [STOCK BROKER.]

The regulations of the Stock Exchange are, like other usages of trade, recognised by courts of law as evidence of the course of dealing between the parties to a contract.

STOCK JOBBER. [STOCK BROKER.]

STOP ORDER is an order to restrain dealing with any money or stock standing to the credit of any cause or matter. This is the means by which the assignee of a fund in court may give notice of the assignment, and prevent the transfer or payment of such money or stock without notice to him although not a party to the cause or matter in which the fund is standing. See R.S.C., 1965, Ord. 50. [PAYMENT OF MONEY INTO COURT, 2.]

STOPPAGE IN TRANSITU. The right which an unpaid vendor of goods has, on hearing that the buyer is insolvent, to stop and reclaim the goods while in their transit and not yet delivered to the buyer. This right will not be affected by the mere fact that the vendor has consigned the goods to the buyer under a bill of lading; but if the buyer has indorsed the bill of lading to a third party for valuable consideration, and without notice of the facts, such party's claim, as assignee of the property under the bill of lading, is paramount to the vendor's right to stop *in transitu*. The leading case on the subject of *stoppage in transitu* is *Lickbarrow* v. *Mason* (1787), 6 East 21. See also ss. 44–46 of the Sale of Goods Act 1893.

STOWAGE. 1. A place where goods are laid.

2. The money paid for such a place.
3. The act of stowing cargo in a vessel. The stowage of the cargo is primarily a duty of the shipowner and master, and nothing absolves them from this obligation short of express agreement with the charterer, or the unambiguous usage of the port.

STRANDING. A ship is said to be *stranded* within the meaning of a policy of insurance when, by tempest, by bad steering, or by violence, it is forced or driven on shore. The circumstances must be accidental, and the ship must remain on shore for a certain time, *i.e.*, a mere striking against a rock or bank would not appear to be a *stranding*.

STRANGER. One not party or privy to any act.

STRANGER IN BLOOD. One who is no relation in blood. The term was used chiefly in reference to the different scales of the former legacy or succession duty.

STRAY, otherwise **ESTRAY,** is a beast gone astray, of which the owner is not known. [ESTRAYS.]

STREET. A generic term embracing any highway and any footpath, road, lane, square, court, alley or passage, whether a thoroughfare or not. See s. 295 of the Highways Act 1959.

STREET BETTING. An offence under the Betting, Gaming and Lotteries Act, 1963.

STREET OFFENCES. Various offences capable of being committed in streets are specified in s. 54 of the Metropolitan Police Act 1839 and s. 28 of the Town Police Clauses Act 1847. Such offences include sliding on ice or snow, ringing doorbells, making bonfires, blowing horns, etc. The Street Offences Act 1959 makes loitering or soliciting for the purposes of prostitution an offence punishable with a fine or imprisonment or both.

STRICT SETTLEMENT. 1. This phrase was formerly used to denote a settlement whereby land was limited to a parent for life, and after his death to his first and other sons or children in tail, with trustees interposed to preserve contingent remainders.

2. Generally, a settlement in which land is limited to, or is held in trust for, any person by way of succession unless it is

STRICT SETTLEMENT—*continued.*
subject to "an immediate binding trust for sale." Its object is to keep lands in a particular family. Important alterations in the mode of creating strict settlements are contained in the Settled Land Act 1925. Under that Act a settlement of a legal estate in land *inter vivos* is to be effected (except as provided in the Act) by two deeds, namely, a vesting deed declaring that the land is vested in the tenant for life or statutory owner for the legal estate the subject of the intended settlement, and a trust instrument declaring the trusts affecting the settled land. [VESTING DEED.]

STRIKE. The cessation of work by a body of persons employed acting in combination, or a concerted refusal or a refusal under a common undertaking of any number of persons employed in consequence of a dispute. See more fully the Contracts of Employment Act 1972, Sch. 1.

STRIKING OFF THE ROLL. This phrase is used to denote the removal of a solicitor of the Supreme Court from the roll of solicitors of that court. It takes place either at the party's own request, or for misconduct. [SOLICITOR.]

STRIKING OUT PLEADINGS. By R.S.C. 1965, Ord. 18, r. 19, the court or a judge may at any stage of the proceedings order to be struck out or amended anything in the pleadings which is unnecessary, scandalous, or which tends to embarrass or delay the fair trial of the action. By Ords. 24, r. 16, and 26, r. 6, a defence may be struck out as a punishment for the defendant for default in making discovery or allowing inspection after order to do so.

STUFF GOWN. The gown of a member of the junior bar. Hence the phrase is used of junior barristers, as opposed to Queen's Counsel. [SILK GOWN.]

SUB MODO. Under condition or restriction.

SUB SILENTIO. In silence.

SUBDUCT. To withdraw. A term used in probate proceedings, *e.g.*, to subduct a caveat.

SUBINFEUDATION signifies a feudal subletting, under which persons, holding estates under the king or other superior lord, carved out in their turn portions of such estates to be held of them by *tenants paravail*, or inferior tenants. This practice was forbidden, as regards England, by the Statute *Quia Emptores*, passed in 1290, except as regards the king's tenants *in capite*, for whom a similar law was enacted some years afterwards. [FEE; IN CAPITE; PARAMOUNT; PARAVAIL; QUIA EMPTORES.]

SUBMISSION is a word especially used with reference to the submission of a matter in dispute to the judgment of an arbitrator or arbitrators.

SUBNORMALITY. [DEFECTIVE.]

SUBORNATION OF PERJURY is the offence of instructing or procuring another to commit perjury. [PERJURY.]

SUBPOENA (Lat. *Sub poena*, under a penalty).

1. A writ whereby formerly all persons under the degree of peerage were called upon to appear and answer to a bill in Chancery. Abolished in 1852.

2. A writ directed to a person commanding him, under a penalty, to appear and give evidence. This is called a *subpoena ad testificandum.*

3. A writ directed to a person, requiring him not only to give evidence, but to bring with him such deeds or writings as the party who issues the *subpoena* may think material for his purpose. This is called a *subpoena duces tecum*, being a species of the *subpoena ad testificandum.* See R.S.C., 1965, Ord. 38, rr. 14 *et seq.*

SUBROGATION. Substitution. Used particularly of the right of an insurer who has paid a claim to succeed to the rights of the insured.

SUBSCRIBING WITNESS is a person who puts his name to an instrument as attesting witness. [ATTESTATION.]

SUBSEQUENT CONDITION. [CONDITIONS PRECEDENT AND SUBSEQUENT.]

SUBSIDY. 1. An aid, tax or tribute granted by parliament to the Queen for the urgent occasions of the kingdom, to be levied of every subject upon his property, at such rate as parliament may think fit.

2. A species of custom payable upon exports and imports of staple commodities.

3. A payment made out of taxation to producers of goods for the purpose of

keeping down the price. See, *e.g.* as to food subsidies, the Prices Acts 1974 and 1975. As to housing subsidies, see the Housing Rents and Subsidies Act 1975.

SUBSTANTIAL DAMAGES, given by the verdict of a jury, are damages which amount to a substantial sum, as opposed to merely nominal damages. [NOMINAL DAMAGES.]

SUBSTITUTED SERVICE is where a writ or other process is served upon some person other than the person upon whom the service ought more properly to be effected, by reason of its being impossible to effect personal service. See R.S.C. 1965, Ord. 65, r. 4.

SUBTRACTION is when any person who owes any suit, duty, custom or service to another, withdraws it or neglects to perform it; as in the cases of (1) the neglect of a tenant to attend his lord's court, or otherwise to perform the duties of his tenancy; (2) the neglect by a landowner to pay tithes or ecclesiastical dues; (3) the neglect or refusal by husband or wife to live with the other; and in various other cases.

SUCCESSION is where one comes to property previously enjoyed by another. It is either *singular* or *universal*. Singular succession is where the purchaser, donee, or legatee of a specific chattel, or other specific property, succeeds to the right of the vendor, donor, or testator. Universal succession is the succession to an indefinite series of rights, as the succession by the trustee of a bankrupt to the estate and effects of the bankrupt, or by an executor or administrator to the estate of the deceased.

For the present rules of succession on intestacy applying alike to real and personal estate, see Part IV of the Administration of Estates Act 1925.

SUE. To take legal proceedings claiming a civil right against anyone.

SUFFERANCE. An estate at sufferance is where one comes into possession of land under a lawful title, and, after the title has come to an end, keeps it without any title at all, by the sufferance of the rightful owner. The party continuing in possession is called a *tenant at sufferance.*

SUFFERANCE WHARF. [WHARF.]

SUFFERING A RECOVERY. The tenant in tail, who procured a common recovery of his land to be effected, to the intent that a conveyance might be made of the land in fee simple, was said to *suffer a recovery.* [RECOVERY.]

SUFFRAGAN. A word signifying *deputy.*

A suffragan bishop is a titular bishop appointed to aid and assist the bishop of the diocese in his spiritual function.

Bishops are also called *suffragan* in respect of their relation to the archbishops of their province.

SUFFRAGE. Vote, elective franchise; aid, assistance.

SUGGESTIO FALSI. A suggestion or insinuation of something false. Normally used in conjunction with *suppressio veri.* [MISREPRESENTATION.]

SUI JURIS is a phrase used to denote a person who is under no disability affecting his legal power to make conveyances of his property, to bind himself by contracts, and to sue and be sued; as opposed to persons wholly or partially under disability, as infants, mentally disordered persons, prisoners, etc.

SUICIDE. Self-killing, no longer a crime. Formerly in the case of a suicide pact between two persons, where one died and the other survived the survivor was guilty of murder. He is now liable to a sentence of imprisonment only: see Suicide Act, 1961, s. 2.

SUIT. A following. The word is, or has been, used as follows:—

1. *Suit of Court*; that is, the attendance which tenants owed to the court of their lord. [SECTA CURIÆ.] 2. *Suit covenant*; which is, when your ancestor hath covenanted with mine to sue to his court. 3. *Suit custom*; when I and my ancestors have been entitled to you and your ancestors' suit time out of mind. 4. *Suit regal*; when men come to the sheriff's tourn or leet. 5. The following any one in chase. 6. A petition made to the king or any great person. 7. *Suit of the king's peace*; that is, pursuing a man for having broken the king's peace by treasons, insurrections, or trespasses. 8. The witnesses or followers of the plaintiff in an action at law. 9. The legal proceeding itself; hence, any litigation. In legal documents and treatises it is most usual to speak of *an action at law* and *a suit in equity.*

SUIT—*continued.*

Otherwise the word suit may include action; and commonly the word "lawsuit" denotes any contentious litigation. See s. 225 of the Judicature Act 1925. Many of the above terms are now obsolete.

SUITOR. A party to a suit or litigation.

SUITORS' FEE FUND. A fund formed from the payment of the fees of suitors in the Court of Chancery. The suitors' fee fund was the primary fund from which were paid the salaries of some of the officers of the court and other expenses connected therewith.

SUMMARY CONVICTION is a conviction before magistrates without the intervention of a jury. To this head may, perhaps, be added the committal of an offender by a judge for contempt of court.

SUMMARY JURISDICTION. The power of a court to give judgment or make an order forthwith. Specially, in criminal cases, the power of magistrates to hear or dispose of a case without sending it for trial at the Crown Court.

SUMMER TIME. The time (being one hour in advance of Greenwich mean time) originally fixed by Order in Council under the Summer Time Act 1947. That Act was repealed by the British Standard Time Act 1968, which established the time in the United Kingdom, for an experimental period, one hour in advance of Greenwich mean time throughout the year.

After three years it was decided not to make the Act of 1968 permanent. Accordingly Greenwich mean time was restored from 1 November 1971; but the Summer Time Act 1972 allows time to be advanced by one hour in summer, or by two hours if so directed by Order in Council.

SUMMING UP, in a civil or criminal trial before a judge and jury, is the charge of the judge to the jury, re-capitulating in greater or less detail the statements of the witnesses and the contents of the documents (if any) adduced on either side, commenting upon the manner in which they severally bear upon the issue, and giving his direction upon any matter of law that may arise upon them.

SUMMING UP EVIDENCE. This may be done by the judge, of whom it is

more properly said [see the previous title], or by a counsel summing up his own case at the close of the evidence which he has adduced.

SUMMONS may be defined generally as:—A citation to appear before a judge or magistrate. The word is used variously, as follows:—

1. A citation summoning a person to appear before a police magistrate or bench of justices.

2. An application to a judge at chambers, whether at law or in equity. [ADJOURNED SUMMONS.]

3. The writ of summons which is the commencement of an action. It is a writ calling on the defendant to cause an appearance to the action to be entered for him within eight days after service, in default whereof the plaintiff may proceed to judgment and execution. There are different forms of it, according as the defendant does or does not reside within the jurisdiction, and if he does not, the period of eight days may be enlarged, with reference to the distance he may be from England.

By R.S.C. 1965, Ord. 6, r. 2, every writ of summons, before it is issued, must be indorsed with a statement of claim, or with a concise statement of the nature of the claim made on the relief or remedy required in the action; or where the claim is for a liquidated demand only, with a statement of the amount claimed in respect of the debt on demand and for costs. [ORIGINATING SUMMONS; STATEMENT OF CLAIM.]

SUMMONS FOR DIRECTIONS. [DIRECTIONS, SUMMONS FOR.]

SUMPTUARY LAWS are laws made to restrain excess in apparel and other luxuries; of which there were formerly many in England, but they were mostly repealed in 1603.

SUPER VISUM CORPORIS (on view of the body). A phrase applied to the view had by a coroner's jury of the body of the deceased concerning whose death they are appointed to inquire. The Coroners Act 1887 allows a view to be dispensed with on a second inquest. See also s. 14 of the Coroners (Amendment) Act 1926. As to the appointment of coroners, see s. 220 of the Local Government Act 1972.

SUPERCARGO. A factor or agent who goes with a ship beyond the seas by order of the owner of the wares therein, and disposes of the same to the best advantage.

SUPERFLUOUS LANDS. [Preemption.]

SUPERINSTITUTION signifies one institution upon another; as where A is admitted and instituted to a benefice upon one title, and B is admitted, instituted, etc., upon the presentment of another, claiming under an adverse title. [Institution.]

SUPERINTENDENT REGISTRAR. A local officer whose business it is to supervise the registrars of births, deaths and marriages in the registration districts within his jurisdiction. [Registrar, 2.]

SUPERIOR COURTS. An expression formerly used to denote the Court of Chancery, the Courts of Queen's Bench, Common Pleas, and Exchequer. These courts, with the old courts of Probate, Divorce, and Admiralty, were consolidated together in the Supreme Court of Judicature.

Today the Court of Appeal, the High Court and the Courts-Martial Appeal Court are superior courts; so too is the Crown Court, although it is in some respects subject to the supervisory jurisdiction of the High Court.

No matter is deemed to be beyond the jurisdiction of a superior court unless it is expressly shown to be so. The unreversed judgment of a superior court is conclusive as to all relevant matters decided by it. [Inferior Court; Supreme Court of Judicature.]

SUPERSEDEAS. A writ in divers cases, signifying in general a command to stay or forbear the doing of anything. The word is especially used with reference to the superceding of a commission of the peace, which suspends the power of the justices therein mentioned, but does not totally destroy it.

SUPERSTITIOUS USES. A superstitious use has been defined as "one which has for its object the propagation of the rites of a religion not tolerated by the law", e.g., a gift of money for saying prayers for the dead. Superstitious uses are opposed to charitable uses which are recognised by law.

SUPER-TAX. [Surtax.]

SUPPLEMENTAL BILL was a bill filed in equity by way of supplement to one previously filed, when new matter arose which did not exist when the first bill was filed. Such a bill set forth the whole of the original bill, together with the new matter. Amendments of the pleadings may now be allowed at any stage of the proceedings in an action by R.S.C. 1965, Ord. 20, rr. 5 et seq. [Amendment.]

SUPPLEMENTAL DEED. Recitals (q.v.) are often used when the deed in which they occur is effectual only by virtue of its complying with the terms of some other deed, to show that the terms have been duly complied with. But lengthy recitals of a previous instrument may be avoided by expressing the deed to be "supplemental" to the previous instrument. Such a supplemental deed has to be read in conjunction with the deed to which it is expressed to be made supplemental in order to see that the terms of the latter deed have been duly complied with.

SUPPLETORY OATH. An oath administered to a party in the spiritual and civil law courts in order to turn the *semiplena probatio*, which consists in the testimony of but *one witness*, into the *plena probatio*, afforded by the testimony of *two witnesses*.

SUPPLIANT. The claimant in a petition of right. [Petition of Right, 1.]

SUPPLICAVIT was a writ issuing out of Chancery or the Queen's Bench, for taking surety of the peace against a man. It was directed to the justices of the peace for the county, and to the sheriff. Now almost obsolete. [Keeping the Peace.]

SUPPORT. The right of support is the right of a person to have his buildings or other landed property supported by his neighbour's house or land.

Every man is entitled to have his land in its natural state supported by the adjoining land of his neighbour, against whom an action will lie if, by digging on his own land, he removes that support. This right to lateral support from adjoining soil is not held to be an easement, but is a right of property passing with the soil. Thus, if the owner of two adjoining closes conveys away one of them, the alienee, without any grant for that purpose, is entitled to the lateral support of the other close the very instant when the conveyance is executed, as

SUPPORT—*continued.*

much as he would be after the expiration of twenty years or of any longer period.

But, where a person builds to the utmost extremity of his own land, and thereby increases the lateral pressure on the soil of his neighbour, if the latter digs his own ground, so as to remove some part of the soil, an action will not lie for the injury occasioned to the former, unless he has, by grant or prescription, acquired a right to the support of the house by the soil of his neighbour.

SUPPRESSIO VERI. The suppression of truth; that is, the suppression, in a one-sided statement, of some material fact on the other side. [MISREPRESENTATION; SUGGESTIO FALSI.]

SUPRA. Above. Often used to refer a reader to a previous part of a book.

SUPRA PROTEST. [ACCEPTANCE SUPRA PROTEST.]

SUPREME COURT OF JUDICATURE. A court which was first established by the Judicature Act 1873, by s. 3 of which it was provided that the High Court of Chancery, the Courts of Queen's Bench, Common Pleas, and Exchequer, the High Court of Admiralty, the Court of Probate, the Divorce Court, and the London Court of Bankruptcy, should be united, and constitute one Supreme Court of Judicature in England. By s. 4, the Supreme Court was to consist of two divisions, one to be called Her Majesty's High Court of Justice, and the other, Her Majesty's Court of Appeal. To the High Court of Justice, under s. 16 of the Act, was transferred the jurisdiction exercised by the Courts of Chancery, Queen's Bench, Common Pleas, Exchequer, Admiralty, Probate, Divorce, Bankruptcy, the Court of Common Pleas at Lancaster, the Court of Pleas at Durham and the assize courts; with certain exceptions mentioned in s. 17 of the Act, of which the most conspicuous was the appellate jurisdiction exercised by the Court of Appeal in Chancery. To Her Majesty's Court of Appeal was transferred the jurisdiction exercised by the Lord Chancellor and Lords Justices of the Court of Appeal in Chancery, also the jurisdiction of the Court of Exchequer Chamber, and the jurisdiction exercised by the Judicial Committee of the Privy Council on appeal from the High Court of Admiralty, or from any order in lunacy made by the Lord Chancellor, or any other person having jurisdiction in lunacy. By s. 31, the High Court was divided, for the more convenient dispatch of business, into five divisions: (1) the Chancery Division; (2) the Queen's Bench Division; (3) the Common Pleas Division; (4) the Exchequer Division; (5) the Probate, Divorce, and Admiralty Division; but subsequently Nos. (3) and (4) were merged into the Queen's Bench Division, and by s. 94 of the Bankruptcy Act 1883 the business of the London Court of Bankruptcy was transferred to the High Court.

In ss. 56 *et seq.* of the Act of 1873, provisions were made for the trial of causes before official and special referees.

The whole Act of 1873, with the exception of a very few provisions, was repealed by the Supreme Court of Judicature (Consolidation) Act 1925, but the scheme of the prior Act was untouched and its provisions were re-enacted.

The Supreme Court now consists of Her Majesty's Court of Appeal and Her Majesty's High Court of Justice, together with the Crown Court.

The Court of Appeal was reconstituted by the Criminal Appeal Act 1966, and now consists of two divisions, the civil division and the criminal division.

The High Court was also reorganised by the Administration of Justice Act 1970, and now consists of three divisions: the Queen's Bench Division, the Chancery Division and the Family Division.

The Crown Court was established by the Courts Act 1971, superseding the criminal jurisdiction of the courts of assize and all the judicial jurisdiction of courts of quarter sessions. It is part of the Supreme Court, with jurisdiction throughout England and Wales, and is a superior court of record (*Hals. Laws*).

SURCHARGE. If the funds of a local authority have been used for a purpose for which there is no legal sanction, a district auditor may usually surcharge the members or officials responsible.

SURCHARGE AND FALSIFY. If, in an account stated, there is any mistake, omission, accident, or fraud, by which the account stated is vitiated, it has been held that a court of equity would interfere; in some cases, by directing the whole account to be opened and taken *de novo*; in others, by allowing it to stand, with liberty to the plaintiff to surcharge and falsify. To *surcharge* is to show an omission of something for which credit ought to have been given; and to *falsify* is to prove an item to have been wrongly inserted. [ACCOUNT.]

SURCHARGE OF COMMON is when a commoner puts more beasts in a forest, or in pasture, than he has a right to do. [ADMEASUREMENT OF PASTURE.]

SURETY is a man who contracts to be answerable for another in such a manner that the latter is primarily answerable. As, if money be advanced to A; and B, his friend, joins with him in giving a bond for its repayment; then B is surety for A.

SURETY OF GOOD BEHAVIOUR. [GOOD BEHAVIOUR; KEEPING THE PEACE.]

SURETY OF THE PEACE. [KEEPING THE PEACE.]

SURPLUSAGE. A superfluity, or addition of something unnecessary, in any legal document.

SURREBUTTER was the plaintiff's answer to the defendant's rebutter, and was the plaintiff's fourth pleading.

SURREJOINDER. The answer by the plaintiff to the defendant's rejoinder. [SURREBUTTER.]

SURRENDER (Lat. *Sursum reditio*) is the falling of a less estate into a greater.

1. *Surrender in deed.* This takes place by the yielding up of an estate for life or years to him that has the immediate reversion or remainder. To constitute a valid express surrender, it is essential that it should be made to, and accepted by, the owner (in his own right) of the reversion or remainder.

2. *Surrender by operation of law.* This phrase is properly applied to cases where the tenant for life or years has been a party to some act the validity of which he is by law afterwards estopped from disputing, and which would not be valid if his particular estate continued to exist; thus, when a lessee for years accepts a new lease from his lessor, he is estopped from saying that his lessor had not the power to make the new lease, so that the acceptance of the new

lease amounts in law to a surrender of the former one. The effect of a surrender by operation of law is expressly reserved by s. 54 (2) of the Law of Property Act, 1925. [ESTOPPEL.]

3. *Surrender of copyholds.* This was the yielding up by a copyholder of his interest to his lord, according to the custom of the manor, generally in order that the same might be granted out again to such person or persons, and for such use or uses, as are named in the surrender. The lord was compellable by *mandamus* to admit the surrenderee, that is, the person to whose use the surrender is made. Under the Law of Property Act 1922, copyholds have become extinct. [COPYHOLD.]

SURROGATE is one that is substituted or appointed in the room of another. The word is most commonly used of a person who is appointed by the bishop for granting marriage licences.

SURTAX. A tax, formerly payable in respect of incomes exceeding a certain amount per annum. Last charged in the financial year 1972–73. Replaced by higher rate tax.

SURVIVORSHIP is a word used not merely of the *fact* of survivorship, but of the rights arising therefrom; that is to say, of the right of the survivor or survivors of joint tenants to the estate held in joint tenancy, in exclusion of the representatives of the deceased. [JOINT TENANCY; PRESUMPTION OF SURVIVORSHIP.]

SUS. PER COLL. An abbreviation for *suspendatur per collum* (let him be hanged by the neck); the note formerly written by the judge, in the calendar of prisoners, against the name of a prisoner sentenced to death, as a warrant to the sheriff to do execution.

SUSPEND. 1. To forbid a solicitor, or a person in Holy Orders, to carry on his vocation for a certain period of time.

2. To declare an Act of Parliament to be of no effect. Declared illegal by the Bill of Rights, 1688.

SUSPENDED SENTENCE. By s. 22 of the Powers of Criminal Courts Act 1973, a court which passes a sentence of imprisonment for not more than two years for an offence may order that the sentence shall not take effect unless, during a period

SUSPENDED SENTENCE
—continued.

specified in the order, the offender commits another offence punishable with imprisonment, in which case the original sentence may be revised.

SUSPENSION. 1. A temporary stop or cessation of a man's right. Or, of his exercise of an office, *e.g.*, of a clergyman by an ecclesiastical court.

2. A temporary revocation of any law by proper authority.

SUSPENSION, PLEA IN, is a species of dilatory plea in an action, showing some matter of temporary incapacity to proceed with the suit. [ABATEMENT, 6.]

SYMBOLIC DELIVERY. A delivery of any small thing in token of a transfer of something else. Thus, in Saxon times, the delivery of a turf was a necessary solemnity to establish the conveyance of lands. Until 1926 the conveyance of copyhold estates was usually made by the delivery, on the part of the vendor, of a rod or verge to the lord or his steward, and then by the re-delivery of the same from the lord to the purchaser. By the Law of Property Act 1922 copyholds became extinct. [FEOFF-MENT.]

SYNDIC. An agent or attorney who acts for a corporation or university. By s. 161 (2) of the Judicature Act 1925 probate or administration is not to be granted to a syndic or nominee on behalf of a trust corporation.

SYNGRAPH. 1. The name given by the canonists to deeds of which *both parts* (that is to say, the copies corresponding to each party) were written on the same piece of parchment, with some word or letters of the alphabet written between them, through which the parchment was cut in such a manner as to leave half the word on one part and half on the other.

2. Hence, a deed or writing under the hand and seal of all the parties.

SYNOD. A meeting or assembly of ecclesiastical persons concerning religion, of which there were originally four kinds:—

1. General, when bishops, etc., of all nations met together.

2. National, when those of one nation only came together.

3. Provincial, when they of one province

met, being what was called the Convocation.

4. Diocesan, when those of but one diocese met.

5. Under the Synodical Government Measure 1969 the functions, authorities, right and privileges of the Convocations of Canterbury and York were vested in the General Synod of the Church of England. This has had the effect of renaming and reconstituting the former Church Assembly.

T

TABLE A. A code of regulations for the management of a company limited by shares. These regulations are set out in Sch. I to the Companies Act 1948. Articles of association may adopt, exclude, or modify Table A.

TACK, in Scotland, signifies a lease.

TACK DUTY. The rent reserved on a lease.

TACKING. A means whereby, when a third or subsequent mortgagee of land, by getting a conveyance to himself of the legal estate of the first mortgagee, was enabled to obtain for his own security, priority over the second mortgagee.

TAIL. [ESTATE.]

TAIL FEMALE. Where a real estate was settled on A B and the heirs female of his or her body. Under such words of limitation, females alone could succeed and would inherit together; nor could any female claim except through females. In practice it never now occurs.

TAIL GENERAL. Where an estate is limited to a man and the heirs of his body, without any restriction at all.

TAIL MALE. Where an estate is limited to a man and the heirs male of his body; that is, so far as regards the first generation, to males; and, so far as regards subsequent generations, to males claiming exclusively through males.

TALES. A supply of jurymen to make up a deficiency. If a sufficient number of jurors did not appear, or if by means of challenges or exemptions a sufficient number of unexceptionable ones did not remain, either party might pray a *tales*. The judge who tried the cause could award a *tales de circumstantibus*; that was, to command the sheriff to return so many other men duly qualified as should be present, or could be found, to make up the number required, and to add their names to the former panel.

TALLEY, or **TALLY.** A stick cut in two parts, on each whereof was marked, with notches or otherwise, what was due between debtors and creditors. This was the ancient way of keeping accounts, one part being kept by the creditor, the other by the debtor. Hence the *tallier* of the Exchequer, also called the *teller*. The use of tallies in the Exchequer was abolished in 1783; and in consequence of changes introduced in 1834 in the keeping of the public accounts, the old tallies were ordered to be destroyed. They were accordingly employed to heat the stoves in the House of Lords, and are said to have been the cause, from having been burned in too large quantities, of the fire which broke out in October 1834, and consumed the two Houses of parliament.

TALLIAGE. A tax laid upon cities and burghs.

TALTARUM'S CASE, which was decided in Michaelmas Term, 1472 (the twelfth year of Edward IV), is known as the case in which the judges by implication laid down those principles on which "common recoveries" were sanctioned for so many centuries, as a means of converting estates tail into fees simple. [RECOVERY.]

TAM QUAM. An old writ of error, from inferior courts, when the error was supposed to be in giving the judgment as well as in awarding execution upon it.

TANGIBLE PROPERTY is property which may be touched and is the object of sensation, corporeal property; this kind of property is opposed to intangible rights or incorporeal property, such as patents, copyrights, advowsons, rents, etc.

TAXATION OF COSTS. The settlement by a taxing master of the amount payable by a party in respect of costs in any action or suit.

TAXING MASTER. An officer appointed to tax costs.

TELEVISION. The broadcasting of pictures as well as sound. Programmes are sent out by the British Broadcasting Corporation, incorporated by Royal Charter in 1926 and operating under the licence of the Secretary of State; and also by the Independent Broadcasting Authority. As to the latter, see the Independent Broadcasting Authority Act 1973.

TELLERS. 1. Four officers of the Exchequer, formerly appointed to receive moneys due to the king and to pay moneys payable by the king. Abolished in 1834.

2. Members of parliament appointed by the Speaker to count the numbers in a parliamentary division. *May.*

TEMPLES. Two of the Inns of Court. [INNS OF COURT.]

At the suppression of the order of Knights Templars their dwelling was purchased by the professors of the common law, and converted into inns of court in the year 1340. They are called the Inner and Middle Temple. Essex House, built in 1185, was formerly a part of the house of the Templars, and was called the Outer Temple because it was situated without Temple Bar.

TEMPORALITIES OF BISHOPS are the revenues, lands, tenements and lay-fees belonging to the bishops' sees.

TENANCY IN COMMON. [COMMON, TENANCY IN.]

TENANT. 1. One who holds or possesses lands or tenements by any right, be it for life, years, at will or at sufferance, in dower, custody or otherwise; all lands being considered as *holden* of the king or in the past of some superior lord.

2. Especially, a tenant under a lease from year to year, or other fixed period.

3. The word is sometimes used in reference to interests in pure personalty, as e.g. of a tenant for life of a fund, etc.

TENANT AT SUFFERANCE. A person who, having been in lawful possession of land, wrongfully continues in possession after his title has come to an end, without the agreement or disagreement of the person then entitled.

TENANT AT WILL is a person in possession of lands let to him to hold at the will of the lessor. Such a tenancy may arise under an express lease or by implication of

TENANT AT WILL—*continued.*

law. It is implied wherever a person is in possession of land with the permission of the owner, provided that he is neither a freeholder nor the holder of a term of years absolute, and provided that he does not hold possession in his capacity as servant of the owner. A copyhold tenant was originally a tenant at will, and he remained nominally so, being said to hold *at the will of the lord according to the custom of the manor*; but, as the lord's will was controlled by the custom, the so-called tenancy at will was hardly less beneficial than a freehold.

TENANT BY COPY OF COURT ROLL. A copyholder.

TENANT BY SUFFERANCE. [TENANT AT SUFFERANCE.]

TENANT BY THE CURTESY. [CURTESY OF ENGLAND.]

TENANT FOR LIFE. A person who holds an estate for his life and under the Settled Land Act 1925 is given wide and unfettered powers of dealing with land. [ESTATE.]

TENANT FOR YEARS. One who holds for a term of years.

TENANT FROM YEAR TO YEAR. A tenancy from year to year is now fixed, by general usage, to signify a tenancy determinable at half a year's notice (or in an agricultural tenancy, one year's notice) on either side, ending with the current year of the tenancy. If the tenancy commences on one of the quarterly feast days the half-year may be computed from one of such feast days to another; otherwise, the half-year must consist of 182 days. See the Agricultural Holdings Act 1948.

TENANT IN TAIL. [ESTATE.]

TENANT RIGHT. The right of a tenant on termination of tenancy to compensation for unexhausted improvements effected on his holding. Formerly governed by custom, but now by the Agricultural Holdings Act 1948. Also used to indicate the moneys so paid.

TENANT TO THE PRÆCIPE. [PRÆCIPE, TENANT TO THE.]

TENANTABLE REPAIR. Such a state of repair in houses or buildings as renders them fit for the occupation of a tenant.

A tenant from year to year of a house is bound to keep it wind and water tight, to use it in a tenant-like manner, and to make fair and tenantable repairs, such as putting in windows or doors that have been broken by him, so as to prevent waste and decay of the premises. *Hill and Redman.*

TENANTS IN COMMON. [COMMON, TENANCY IN.]

TENDER. 1. An offer of money or any other thing in satisfaction of a debt or liability. See next title.

2. Coin or paper money, which, so far as regards the nature and quality thereof, a creditor may be compelled to accept in satisfaction of his debt, is called *legal tender.* [LEGAL TENDER.]

TENDER, PLEA OF. A plea by a defendant that he has been always ready to satisfy the plaintiff's claim, and now brings the sum demanded into court.

TENEMENT. 1. A house or homestall.

2. Land holden of a superior lord; and in this sense *tenement* is one of the technical words applicable to all real estates, and includes offices and dignities which concern lands and profits issuing out of lands.

TENENDUM. The clause in a deed which was formerly used to signify the tenure by which the estate granted was to be holden; as by knight service, etc. But such tenures being now reduced to free and common socage, the tenure is never specified; and the *tenendum* in a deed is of very little use, and only kept in by custom.

TENOR. 1. By the *tenor* of a deed, or other instrument in writing, is signified the matter contained therein, according to the true intent and meaning thereof.

2. The word *tenor*, in reference to writs and records, signifies a copy or transcript, whereas *effect* signifies that the substance only is set out.

TENTERDEN'S ACT. The Statute of Frauds Amendment Act 1828, passed at the instance of Lord Tenterden, Justice of the King's Bench.

The following provision of Lord Tenterden's Act is still in operation: "No action is to be brought whereby to charge any person upon or by reason of any assurance made concerning the character, conduct, credit, ability, trade or dealings of any person, to the intent that such person may obtain credit, money, or goods, unless such representations be in writing and signed by the party to be charged therewith": see s. 6 of the Act.

TENTHS. 1. The tenth part of all spiritual preferments in the kingdom, originally payable to the Pope, and, after the Reformation, to the Crown, until applied by Queen Anne for the purposes of Queen Anne's Bounty, that is, to make up the deficiencies of smaller benefices. [QUEEN ANNE'S BOUNTY.]

2. A temporary aid issuing out of personal property anciently granted from time to time by parliament.

TENURE. The manner whereby tenements were holden of their lords. To hold land by *the tenure* of any given service is to hold land on the condition of a faithful performance of that service; so that the non-performance thereof would be a cause of forfeiture to the lord. This forfeiture might be enforced by writ of *cessavit*. The word is now used in conjunction with freehold and leasehold. [ESTATE; FEE; KNIGHT-SERVICE; MILITARY TENURES; SOCAGE; TENENDUM.]

TERM. 1. The period of time in which alone the superior courts of common law were formerly open for the redress of injuries. [SITTINGS.]

2. *A term of years.* This phrase is often used to denote a fixed period of time extending over several years; but in the law of real property it is especially used to signify an estate or interest in land to be enjoyed for a fixed period. For definition of "term of years absolute" as used in the Law of Property Act 1925, see s. 205 (1) (xxvii) thereof. [OUTSTANDING TERM.]

TERM FEE. A fee in respect of each term in which any proceedings in a cause or matter in the Supreme Court have taken place after appearance. This is to cover attendance and other matters which cannot be specially charged.

TERM IN GROSS. A phrase used to designate an estate for years in land *not* held in trust for the party who would be entitled to the land on the expiration of the term. [OUTSTANDING TERM; TERM, 2.]

TERMINUS A QUO. The starting point.

TERMINUS AD QUEM. The terminating point.

TERMOR. He that holds lands or tenements for a term of years or life.

TERMS, TO BE UNDER. A party in an action or other legal proceeding is said to be *under terms,* when an indulgence is granted to him by the court in exercise of its discretion, on condition of his observing certain things.

TERRA TESTAMENTALIS. Gavelkind land; so called from being formerly devisable by will, when other lands were not so devisable. Gavelkind was abolished by the Law of Property Act 1922, as respects enfranchised land, and generally in regard to land by the Administration of Estates Act 1925, s. 45. [DEVISE; GAVELKIND.]

TERRAR. The same as *Terrier.* [TERRIER.]

TERRE TENANT. He who has the actual possession or occupation of land.

TERRIER (Lat. *Terrarium.*) A land roll or survey of lands, containing the quantity of acres, tenants' names, and such like; and in the Exchequer there is a terrier of all the glebe lands in England, made in 1338. In general, an ecclesiastical terrier contains a detail of the temporal possessions of the Church in every parish.

TERRITORIAL WATERS. Those within a marine league of the coast of a country were, by international law, held to be within the jurisdiction of that country: Territorial Waters Jurisdiction Act 1878, and *R* v. *Kent Justices, Ex p. Lye,* [1967] 2 Q.B. 153.

The question of the extent of territorial waters has become much disputed. It is still generally agreed that such waters extend to at least three nautical miles, measured from low-water mark. Some countries now claim greater limits, based on claims to exclusive fishery rights, or to the extent of the continental shelf.

TERRORISM. The use of violence for political ends, including any violence for the purpose of putting the public or any

TERRORISM—*continued.*

section of the public in fear: Prevention of Terrorism (Temporary Provisions) Act 1974, s. 9 (1).

TESTAMENT. The true declaration of a man's last will as to that which he would have to be done after his death. Strictly speaking, a testament is a disposition of *personal* property only. [WILL.]

TESTAMENTARY CAUSES are causes relating to the validity and execution of wills. The phrase is generally confined to those causes which were formerly matters of ecclesiastical jurisdiction, and are now dealt with by the Chancery Division.

TESTAMENTARY GUARDIAN. A guardian appointed by will. See now, generally as to guardianship, the Guardianship of Minors Act 1971 and the Guardianship Act 1973. [GUARDIAN.]

TESTATE. Having made a will.

TESTATOR. He who makes a will. [WILL.]

TESTATRIX. She who makes a will. [WILL.]

TESTATUM. The witnessing part of a deed, beginning "Now this Deed witnesseth."

TESTES, PROOF OF WILL PER, is a proof of a will by witnesses, in a more solemn form than ordinary, in cases where the validity of the will is disputed. It is by action in the Chancery Division or in some cases in the county court. [SOLEMN FORM.]

TESTIMONIUM CLAUSE. The final clause in a deed or will, commencing "In witness, etc."

TESTIMONY. Evidence. [EVIDENCE; PERPETUATING TESTIMONY.]

THANE. A nobleman. In Anglo-Saxon times thanes were of two orders, king's thanes and ordinary thanes.

THAVIE'S INN. Once an Inn of Chancery. [INNS OF CHANCERY.]

THEFT. The basic definition of theft is given in s. 1 of the Theft Act, 1968, which enacts that "a person is guilty of theft if he dishonestly appropriates property belonging to another with the intention of permanently depriving the other of it," it being

immaterial whether the appropriation is made with a view to gain or is made for the thief's own benefit.

Sections 2–6 of the Act then expand and explain this basic definition by stating what is meant by *dishonestly* (s. 2); *appropriates* (s. 3); *property* (s. 4); *belonging to another* (s. 5); and *with the intention of permanently depriving the other of it* (s. 6).

Other sections of the Theft Act (which repeals the former Larceny Acts of 1861 and 1916) define robbery, burglary, blackmail, etc. [APPROPRIATION; BURGLARY; DISHONEST; PROPERTY; ROBBERY.]

THEFT BOTE. The receiving, by a party robbed, of his goods back again, or other amends, upon an agreement not to prosecute. Theft bote was a species of the offence called *compounding a felony*, and was punishable by fine and imprisonment. [COMPOUNDING.]

THESAURUS INVENTUS. [TREASURE TROVE.]

THINGS. The subjects of property, which may be either *in action* or *in possession*. Things *in action* are not immediately available to the owner without the consent of some other person, whose refusal will give a right of *action*. Things *in possession* may be used immediately without the concurrence of any other person. [CHOSE.]

THIRD PARTY. One who is a stranger to a proceeding between two other persons. A third party may, by leave of the court or a judge, be introduced into an action by a defendant claiming an indemnity or other remedy over against him, by means of a notice called a "third party notice" being given him. See R.S.C. 1965, Ord. 16.

THIRD PARTY INSURANCE. A policy of insurance which insures the insured person in respect of any liability which may be incurred by him in respect of damage or injury to any person not a party to the policy. Such insurance is compulsory in the case of users of motor vehicles: see Part VI of the Road Traffic Act 1972.

THIS DAY SIX MONTHS. An expression used in parliament to mean "never." Thus a proposal to read a bill "this day six months" is a proposal to reject it, because parliament would not be sitting six months hence. "This day three months" has the same meaning. The term fixed in either case is one beyond the probable duration of the session. If, however, the session should last to the time so nominally specified, it seems that the bill or bills will appear amongst the orders of the day. *May.*

THREAT. Any menace of such a nature and extent as to unsettle the mind of the person on whom it operates, and to take away from his acts that free voluntary action which alone constitutes consent. [BLACKMAIL.]

TICKET OF LEAVE. A written licence to a prisoner serving a life sentence to be at large, upon such conditions as the Home Secretary thinks fit. The present provisions as to release on licence will be found in s. 61 of the Criminal Justice Act 1967.

TIMBER. Wood fitted for building or other such-like uses. Oak, ash and elm are timber in all places; and, by the custom of some particular counties, in which other kinds of trees are generally used for building, they are also for that reason considered as timber; and for a tenant for life (unless he be unimpeachable for waste) to cut down timber trees, or to do any act whereby they may decay, is waste, timber being part of the inheritance. But even where a tenant for life is impeachable for waste he has a statutory power to cut and sell timber which is ripe and fit for cutting provided that he obtains the consent of the trustees or an order of the court. In such a case, however, three-quarters of the net proceeds become capital money, and one-quarter becomes income. See s. 66 of the Settled Land Act 1925. [WASTE.]

TIME. [SUMMER TIME.]

TIME BARGAIN was a contract for the sale of a certain amount of stock at a certain price on a future day, the vendor not in general having such stock to sell at the time of the contract, but intending to purchase it before the time appointed for the execution of the contract. Time bargains were forbidden by an Act of 1733, under a penalty of £500. Such contracts could not, therefore, be enforced by the courts of law. As, however, any party failing to meet his engagement was stigmatised in the Stock Exchange as a *lame duck*, and his name exhibited as a defaulter, the disgrace attending upon a breach of such contracts

secured their general observance. The Act above mentioned was, therefore, repealed in 1860. [BULL, 2.]

TIME IMMEMORIAL. TIME OUT OF MIND. These expressions denote time beyond legal memory; that is, the time prior to the commencement of the reign of Richard I, A.D. 1189. But see the Prescription Act 1832. [LEGAL MEMORY.]

TIME POLICY is a policy of marine insurance in which the risk is limited, not to a given voyage, but to a certain fixed term or period of time. In such policies the risk insured is entirely independent of the voyage of the ship. [MIXED POLICY; VOYAGE POLICY; WARRANTY.]

TIME THE ESSENCE OF THE CONTRACT. Where a contract specifies a time for its completion, or something to be done towards it, then, if time be of the essence of the contract, the non-performance by either party of the act in question by the time so specified will entitle the opposite party to regard the contract as broken. Whether time be or be not of the essence of the contract must, in the absence of express words, be gathered from the general character of the contract and the surrounding circumstances. By the Law of Property Act 1925, s. 41, stipulations in a contract as to time, or otherwise, which according to rules of equity are not deemed to be or to have become of the essence of the contract, are also construed and have effect at law in accordance with the same rules.

TINPENNY. A tribute once paid for the liberty of digging in tin mines.

TIPSTAFF. An officer who attends the courts, his duty being to take charge of prisoners committed by the court.

TITHES. The tenth part of the fruits, prædial, personal and mixed, formerly due to the ministers of the Church for their maintenance. Tithes arose from the profits and stock of lands, or from the personal industry of the inhabitants of a parish. The former class were either *prædial*, among which were tithes of corn, grass, hops and wood; or *mixed*, as of wool, milk, pigs, etc.; the latter *personal*, as of occupations, trades, fisheries and the like. Of *prædial* and *mixed* tithes the tenth had to be paid in gross; but of *personal* tithes only the tenth

TITHES—*continued*.

part of the clear profits was due; nor were tithes of this latter kind generally due at all, except so far as the particular custom of the place might authorise the claim. Hence it may be inferred, that whatever was of the substance of the earth, as stone, lime, chalk and the like, was not in its nature titheable; nor, except by force of special custom, was tithe demandable in respect to animals which are *feræ naturæ*. [Feræ Naturæ.]

Tithes were also divided into *great* and *small* tithes. *Small* tithes included tithes mixed and personal, whereas tithes of corn, hay and wood were generally comprised under *great* tithes; but no clear line of demarcation seems to have been drawn between them.

All tithes *prima facie* by presumption of law belonged to the *rector*; but any part of the tithes might be shown, by evidence, to belong to the *vicar*. [Rector; Vicar.] Such evidence might consist either of a deed of endowment, vesting certain tithes in the vicar, or of such proof of long usage as was sufficient to raise a presumption that an endowment of that description, though lost, was anciently made. Not infrequently an endowment vested all the *small* tithes in the vicar.

Tithe was commuted over a period of years into tithe rent-charge which in its turn was extinguished by the Tithe Act 1936, and a tithe redemption annuity is payable which will terminate in due course unless previously commuted.

TITHING (Lat. *Decuria*). The number or company of ten men with their families knit together in a society, all being bound to the king for the peaceable behaviour of each other. Of these companies, there was one chief or principal person called teothing-man or tithing-man, who was in fact a constable.

TITHING-MAN. A constable or head of a tithing. [Tithing.]

TITLE. 1. A title of honour; which is in addition to a person's name, implying that he has some honour, office, or dignity.

2. A title to orders; which is a certificate of preferment or provision required by the 33rd Canon, in order that a person may be admitted into holy orders; unless he be a fellow or chaplain in Oxford or Cambridge, or master of arts of five years' standing in either of the universities, and living there at his sole charges; or unless the bishop himself intends shortly to admit him to some benefice or curacy.

3. *Title to Lands or Goods*. This signifies either (1) a party's right to the enjoyment thereof; *or* (2) the means whereby such right has accrued, and by which it is evidenced; or, as it is defined by Blackstone, the means whereby an owner has the just possession of his property.

When we speak of a man having a *good title* to his property we mean that the evidence of his right is cogent and conclusive, or nearly so; and when we speak of a *bad title* we mean that the evidence is weak and insufficient. A thirty years' title is in general sufficient in the case of sale of lands, under s. 44 of the Law of Property Act 1925. [Document of Title.]

4. The title of an Act of Parliament is its heading, and in modern times it has also a "short title," more condensed than the heading, mentioned in the body of the Act as the name by which it is to be known. See the Short Titles Act 1896.

5. The title of an affidavit consists of two parts: (1) the style of the court (or division of the High Court of Justice) in which the affidavit is to be used, and (2) the names of the parties to the action or other proceeding.

TITLE, COVENANTS FOR. On dispositions of real estate the transferee is entitled to covenants for title. These were formerly express and varied according to the nature of the disposition, *e.g.*, a vendor gave *limited* covenants extending to all acts done by him or any one through whom he derived title otherwise than by purchase for value; a mortgagor gave *absolute* covenants, not confined to the above acts. They are now implied by the use of the proper words, *e.g.*, beneficial owner, trustee, etc. See s. 76 of, and Sch. II to, the Law of Property Act 1925, and s. 38 (2) of the Land Registration Act 1925.

TITLE DEEDS. Deeds evidencing a person's right or title to lands, otherwise called *muniments of title*.

The possession of the title deeds is of importance, as the land cannot be sold without them. Thus, what is called an "equitable mortgage" is generally effected by a deposit of title deeds. Moreover, any mortgagee who negligently allows his mortgagor to retain the title deeds, and to raise money on a second mortgage of the land by fraudulently concealing the first mortgage, will have his security postponed to that of the second mortgagee. For the present rules relating to the priority of mortgagees, see ss. 97 *et seq.* of the Law of Property Act 1925.

TOFT. A messuage or house, or rather a place where a messuage has stood and is not rebuilt.

TOLL. 1. A liberty to buy and sell within the precincts of a manor or market.

2. A tribute or custom paid for passage.

3. A liberty to take, or to be free from such tribute. See also the following titles.

TOLL THOROUGH. Money paid for the passage of man or beast in or through highways, or over ferries, bridges, etc.

TOLL TRAVERSE. A toll paid for passing over a private person's ground. It is thus opposed to *toll thorough*, which is paid for passing over a public highway.

TOLLED. To *toll* is to take away; thus, when a man's right of entry upon lands was barred or taken away by lapse of time, or otherwise, it was said to be *tolled.*

TONNAGE. 1. A custom or impost paid to the king for merchandise carried out or brought in in ships, at a certain rate for every ton. It was at first granted for the defence of the realm, the safeguard of the seas, and the safe passage of merchandise.

2. The number of tons burden that a ship will carry, or the number of tons of water displaced thereby.

TONNAGE-RENT. A royalty payable on every ton of mineral gotten.

TONTINE is a species of loan in which the parties who invest receive life annuities, with benefit of survivorship; so called from Lorenzo Tonti, a Neapolitan, who lived in the 17th century. The nature of the plan is this: An annuity, after a certain rate of interest is granted to a number of people, divided into classes according to their respective ages; so that the whole annual fund of each class is regularly divided among the survivors of that class; and, on the death of the last survivor, reverts to the power by which the tontine was erected.

TOOLS are those implements which are commonly used by the hand of man in some labour necessary for his subsistence. The tools of a person's trade are, by s. 38 of the Bankruptcy Act 1914, excepted to a limited amount from the general property which on his bankruptcy passes to his creditors. To a certain extent they were also privileged from distress.

TORT. A wrong; so called because it is wrested (*tortum*), wrung, or crooked. The word "tort" is especially used to signify a civil wrong independent of contract; that is to say, an actionable wrong not consisting exclusively in a breach of contract, the infringement of a purely equitable right, or a crime. An action for such a wrong is called an *action of tort*. Of this class are actions of libel, assault, trespass, etc. [WRONG.]

TORT FEASOR. A wrong-doer, a trespasser.

TORTIOUS. Wrongful.

TORTIOUS OPERATION OF A FEOFFMENT. When a *tenant for life* made a feoffment in fee of the lands of which he was tenant for life, a freehold of inheritance passed to the feoffee, but a freehold *by wrong*, thus divesting the person in reversion or remainder of his *estate*, and leaving him a *right of entry*, of which he might avail himself *at once*.

But feoffments by *tenants in tail* (or *discontinuances*, as they were called) operated to take away not merely the *estate* of the party entitled in remainder, but also his *right of entry without action*; so that he was driven to his action to recover his estate when the time came. This effect of a discontinuance was abolished in 1833; and such meaning as was left in the doctrine of the tortious operation of a feoffment was abolished in 1845. [FEOFFMENT.]

TORTURE. A cruel and wanton infliction of pain on any living being.

The word is used especially in our law books of the rack or question which was sometimes applied to extort confessions from criminals. [RACK.]

TOTAL LOSS is the entire loss of an insured vessel, or of goods insured, so as to render the underwriters liable to the owner. [UNDERWRITER.]

Total loss is either *actual* or *constructive*; actual, when the thing is actually destroyed, or so damaged that it cannot ever arrive in

TOTAL LOSS—*continued.*
specie at the port of destination; constructive, when the injury, though short of actual loss, is yet so great as to make the subject of it useless to its owner.

When the subject of the insurance, though not wholly destroyed, is placed in such peril as to render the successful prosecution of the venture improbable, the insured may treat the case as a total loss, and demand the full sum insured. In such case, however, he must, within a reasonable time, give notice to the insurer of his intention, and of his abandonment to the insurer of all right in the thing insured. See ss. 55 *et seq.* of the Marine Insurance Act 1906. [ABANDONMENT.]

TOTIDEM VERBIS. In so many words.

TOTIES QUOTIES. As often as occasion shall require.

TOURN. [SHERIFF'S TOURN.]

TOUT TEMPS PRIST. *Always ready*; a plea, by way of defence to an action, brought by a plaintiff whose claim has never been disputed, to the effect that the defendant is, and always has been, ready to satisfy the plaintiff's demand.

TOWAGE. Money paid for towing a ship.

TOWN. A tithing or vill; any collection of houses larger than a village.

TOWN CLERK. A person (usually a solicitor) formerly appointed by a local authority to manage their affairs under the repealed Local Government Act 1933.

TOWN COUNCIL. [MUNICIPAL CORPORATION.]

TOWN PLANNING. Town and country planning is now governed by the Town and Country Planning Act 1971. The Act primarily imposes a control over all land by making it unlawful to develop land without planning permission, which must first be granted either by the local planning authority (*e.g.*, the county council) or by the Minister of Housing and Local Government.

TRADE DESCRIPTION. Any description, statement, etc., as to number, quantity, gauge or weight of any goods, or as to their standard of quality or fitness, as to their country of origin or mode of manufacture, etc. See the Trade Descriptions Acts 1968 and 1972.

TRADE DISPUTE. A dispute between employers and workers or between workers and workers, connected with one or more of the following: (*a*) terms and conditions of employment, or the physical conditions in which workers are required to work; (*b*) engagement or non-engagement, or termination or suspension of employment or the duties of employment, of one or more workers; (*c*) allocation of work or the duties of employment as between workers or groups of workers; (*d*) matters of discipline; (*e*) the membership or non-membership of a trade union on the part of a worker; (*f*) facilities for officials of trade unions; and (*e*) machinery for negotiation or consultation, etc. See s. 29 of the Trade Union and Labour Relations Act 1974.

TRADE EFFLUENT. An outflow of dirty water or waste matter from trade premises, by discharge into a sewer, river, etc. See the Control of Pollution Act 1974.

TRADE FIXTURES, in a house or other premises occupied for the purposes of business, include machinery and utensils of a chattel nature, such as saltpans, vats, etc., for soap-boiling; engines for working collieries; also buildings of a temporary description erected by the tenant for the purpose of carrying on his business.

TRADE MARK. A mark, signature or device affixed to an article to show that it is manufactured, etc., by some particular person or firm. As to trade marks and the registration thereof, see the Trade Marks Act 1938.

TRADE UNION. By the Trade Union and Labour Relations Act 1974 a trade union means an organisation (whether permanent or temporary) which either (*a*) consists wholly or mainly of workers of one or more descriptions and is an organisation whose principal purposes include the regulation of relations between workers of that description or those descriptions and employers or employers' associations; or (*b*) consists wholly or mainly of (i) constituent or affiliated organisations which fulfil the conditions specified in paragraph (*a*) above . . . or (ii) representatives of such constituent or affiliated organisations. In either case it must be an organisation whose principal purposes include the regulation of relations between workers and employers or between workers and employers' associations, or include the regulation of relations between its constituent or affiliated organisations.

A somewhat simpler definition is contained in Sch. 20 to the Social Security Act 1975: "An association of employed earners".

TRADER. One engaged in merchandise or commerce. Formerly there was a distinction between traders and non-traders under the bankruptcy laws, but this distinction has been abolished. [BANKRUPT.]

TRANSCRIPT. A copy. Used particularly of a copy (in longhand) of a shorthand note. Also used in reference to a copy of an account in the books of the Paymaster-General.

TRANSFER OF CAUSE is the removal of a cause from one court or judge to another by lawful authority. See R.S.C. 1965, Ord. 4, and s. 59 of the Judicature Act 1925.

In certain cases, also, under the County Courts Act 1959 and the Judicature Act 1925, an action may be ordered to be transferred to the county court, or from an inferior court to the High Court.

TRANSIRE. A warrant from the custom-house to let goods pass.

TRANSITORY ACTION. An action, the venue of which could be laid in any county as opposed to local actions. Formerly, transitory actions might be tried anywhere, but in local actions, the venue must have been laid, and the trial held, in the county where the trespass or other cause of action took place. Now, there is no local venue for the trial of any action. [VENUE.]

TRANSITU (STOPPAGE IN). [STOPPAGE IN TRANSITU.]

TRANSLATION. 1. A version of a book or publication out of one language into another. Where the laws of copyright require a *translation* to be made of a foreign work for which copyright is claimed, this requirement is not satisfied by mere *adaptation*.

2. The removal of a bishop from one diocese to another.

TRANSPORTATION was the banishing or sending away a person convicted of crime, either pursuant to the express terms of a judicial sentence, or as a condition of pardon by the Crown, to some place out of the United Kingdom, there to remain during the term for which he was ordered to be transported.

Transportation was superseded by penal servitude, and now by imprisonment. See the Criminal Justice Act 1948.

TRAVERSE is a denial, in pleading, of facts alleged on the other side.

TRAVERSE OF AN INDICTMENT.
1. The denial of an indictment by plea of not guilty.
2. The postponement of the trial of an indictment after a plea of not guilty thereto. This was formerly customary in indictments for misdemeanours, but was prohibited by s. 27 of the Criminal Procedure Act 1851 (repealed by the Courts Act 1971).

TRAVERSE OF AN OFFICE. The challenging, by a subject, of an inquest of office, as being defective and untruly made. [INQUEST; OFFICE FOUND.]

TRAVERSE TOLL. [TOLL TRAVERSE.]

TRAVERSING NOTE. A note filed by a plaintiff in Chancery on behalf of a defendant who had refused or neglected to answer interrogatories, the effect of which was to deny the statements of the bill, and to put the plaintiff upon proof of the whole.

The traversing note was not expressly abolished under the Judicature Acts, but the provisions contained in R.S.C. in reference to default in pleading, render it unnecessary.

TREASON. A betraying, treachery, or breach of faith, especially against the sovereign or liege lord. Treason against the sovereign has always been regarded as *high* treason, in contradistinction to certain offences against private superiors, which were formerly ranked as *petty* treason. [PETIT TREASON.]

Treason is defined by the Treason Act 1351 as consisting in one or other of the following acts:—
1. When a man compasses or imagines the death of our lord the king, of our lady

TREASON—*continued.*
his queen, or of their eldest son and heir. These words include a queen regnant.

2. If a man do violate the king's companion, or the king's eldest daughter unmarried, or the wife of the king's eldest son and heir.

3. If a man do levy war against our lord the king in his realm.

4. If a man be adherent to the king's enemies in his realm, giving to them aid and comfort in the realm, or elsewhere.

5. If a man counterfeit the king's great or privy seal.

6. If a man counterfeit the king's money; and if a man bring false money into the realm counterfeit to the money of England, knowing the money to be false, to merchandise and make payment withal.

7. If a man slay the chancellor, treasurer, or the king's justices of the one bench or the other, justices in eyre, or justices of assize, and all other justices assigned to hear and determine, being in their places doing their offices.

Of the above branches Nos. 5 and 6 are no longer treason; counterfeiting the great or privy seal being an ordinary offence under s. 3 of the Forgery Act 1913; and No. 6 being the offence of coining under the Coinage Offences Act 1936.

In addition to the treasons specified in the Treason Act 1351 it is treason to attempt to hinder the succession to the Crown of the person entitled thereto under the Act of Settlement: s. 3 of the Treason Act 1702.

It is now sufficient to speak of high treason as treason simply, seeing that petty treason, as a distinct offence, has been abolished, and many acts which are treason under the above statutes are also treason-felonies under the Treason Felony Act, 1848, and now prosecuted thereunder.

Men convicted of high treason were formerly sentenced to be drawn on a hurdle to the place of execution, and to be there hanged and disembowelled alive, and then beheaded and quartered. Women, for all kinds of treason, were sentenced to be burned alive.

By the Treason Act 1790 hanging was substituted for burning in the case of women convicted of high or petty treason; and by the Treason Act 1814 men convicted of treason were to be drawn to the place of execution, and hanged till dead, and then beheaded and quartered. Finally, by the Forfeiture Act 1870, the punishment of treason was reduced to hanging.

The procedure in all trials for treason or misprision of treason is the same as in that for murder. See the Treason Act 1945.

TREASON FELONY, under the Treason Felony Act 1848, is the offence of compassing, devising, etc., to depose Her Majesty from the Crown; or to levy war in order to intimidate either House of parliament, etc.; or to stir up foreigners by any printing or writing to invade the kingdom. This offence is punishable with imprisonment for life. By the above statute the Government is enabled to treat as lesser offences many offences which must formerly have been treated as high treason.

TREASURE TROVE (Lat. *Thesaurus inventus*) consists of money, coin, gold, silver, plate or bullion found hidden in the earth or other private place, the owner thereof being unknown. In such case the treasure belongs to the Crown, and any person concealing the same from the Crown is liable to fine and imprisonment.

TREASURER. [LORD TREASURER; TREASURY.]

TREASURER'S REMEM-BRANCER. [REMEMBRANCERS.]

TREASURY. The Lords Commissioners of the Treasury, being the department of State under whose control the royal revenue is administered. [LORD TREASURER.]

TREATING, providing food, drink, or entertainment before, during, or after an election for corruptly influencing votes renders the person providing it liable to penalties, and a voter corruptly receiving it incapable of voting, and renders his vote void; it also may invalidate the election on petition. See s. 100 of the Representation of the People Act 1949.

TREATY. 1. A negotiation.

2. A compact between nations.

TRESPASS (Lat. *Transgressio*). 1. Any transgression or offence against the law.

2. Any misfeasance or act of one man whereby another is injuriously treated or damnified.

3. The action brought for injury done to

person or property with violence. This action, when brought for an unwarrantable entry upon land of the plaintiff, was called trespass *quare clausum fregit*. [CLOSE; QUARE CLAUSUM FREGIT.]

4. *Trespass on the case.* This was a form of action for some unlawful act, negligence or omission, whereby indirect or consequential damage had resulted to the plaintiff. [ACTION ON THE CASE.]

TRIAL. The examination of a cause, civil or criminal, before a judge who has jurisdiction over it, according to the laws of the land.

The rules with regard to trials in the High Court are to be found in R.S.C. 1965, Ords. 33–35. Actions may be tried in one of the following ways:—(1) Before a judge or judges; (2) before a judge sitting with assessors; (3) before a judge and jury; (4) before an official or special referee; (5) before a master; or (6) before a special referee.

Criminal trials generally take place before a judge and jury in the Crown Court or at the Central Criminal Court. Minor offences are in general dealt with summarily before magistrates.

TRIAL AT BAR. [BAR, 6.]

TRIAL BY CERTIFICATE. [CERTIFICATE, TRIAL BY.]

TRIAL BY RECORD. [RECORD, TRIAL BY.]

TRIBUNAL. A body appointed to adjudicate or arbitrate on some disputed question or matter, as *e.g.* lands tribunal, rent tribunal. See the Tribunals and Inquiries Act 1971.

TRINA ADMONITIO. Threefold warning. [PEINE FORTE ET DURE.]

TRINITY HOUSE. A company of masters of ships incorporated in the reign of Henry VIII, and charged by many successive Acts of Parliament with numerous duties relating to the marine, especially the appointment and licensing of pilots, and the superintendence of lighthouses, buoys and beacons.

Trinity House is a self-elected body, and is composed of *elder brethren* and *younger brethren.* The elder brethren manage the affairs of the society, being for the most part elected from the younger brethren.

TRINITY TERM. [SITTINGS.]

TRINODA NECESSITAS was the threefold obligation to which every man's estate was by the ancient law subject, *pontium reparatio, arcium constructio, et expeditio contra hostem*; that is, repairing bridges, building castles, and repelling invasions.

TRIORS, TRIOURS or **TRIERS.** 1. The lords formerly selected to try a peer, when indicted for felony, in the Court of the Lord High Steward. [HIGH STEWARD.]

2. Two indifferent persons formerly named by the court to try the reasonableness of a challenge made by a party to a juror on the ground of some alleged probable circumstances of suspicion, as acquaintance and the like; or to the whole panel of jurors, on account of a like objection to the sheriff. [CHALLENGE.]

TRIPARTITE. Divided into three parts, having three corresponding copies; a deed to which there are three distinct parties.

TRITHING, TRIDING or **TRI-HING.** In ancient times, when a county was divided into three jurisdictions, each of them was called a trithing, triding or trihing. These divisions subsisted until recently in the county of Yorkshire, where by an easy corruption they were denominated *ridings.* They were abolished in the reorganisation of local government by the Local Government Act 1972.

TROVER (from Fr. *Trouver*, to find) was one of the forms of action at law, being originally a kind of action of trespass on the case, based on the finding by defendant of the plaintiff's goods, and converting them to his own use. But in time the suggestion of the finding became mere matter of form, and all that it became necessary to prove was that the goods were the plaintiff's, and that the defendant converted them to his own use. In this action the plaintiff could not recover the specific chattel, but only damages for its conversion. The fictitious suggestion of the "finding" was abolished by the Common Law Procedure Act 1852, by which a simple form of declaration was introduced for such cases. [CONVERSION; DETINUE.]

TRUCK SYSTEM. A name given to the practice of paying the wages of workmen in goods instead of money. The

TRUCK SYSTEM—*continued.*

plan had been for the masters to establish warehouses or shops, and the workmen in their employment had either (1) got their wages accounted for to them by supplies of goods from such depôts, without receiving any money, or (2) they had got the money, with a tacit or express understanding that they were to resort to the warehouses or shops of their masters for such articles as they were furnished with.

This system of dealing being considered open to grave abuses, it was abolished by the Truck Acts 1831 to 1940.

TRUE BILL. [BILL, 3.]

TRUST. 1. A confidence reposed by one person in conveying or bequeathing property to another, that the latter will apply it to a purpose or purposes desired by the former. These purposes are generally indicated in the instrument, whether deed or will, by which the disposition is made.

2. Hence it signifies the beneficial interest created by such a transaction. In this sense it may be defined as a beneficial interest in, or ownership of, real or personal property, unattended with the legal or possessory ownership thereof. [USE.]

For the various kinds of trusts, see under their respective titles.

TRUST CORPORATION. The Public Trustee or a corporation either appointed by the court in any particular case to be a trustee or entitled by rules made under s. 4 (3) of the Public Trustee Act 1906 to act as custodian trustee. See s. 68 of the Trustee Act 1925.

TRUST INSTRUMENT. The Settled Land Act 1925 provides that all settlements of land created *inter vivos* must be effected by two deeds, namely a vesting deed and a trust instrument, otherwise the settlement will not operate to transfer or create a legal estate (s. 4 (1)). The trust instrument sets out the trusts upon which the person who for the time being is entitled to the actual enjoyment of the land must hold the fee simple which has been transferred to him by the vesting deed (*q.v.*). See s. 4 (3) and Sch. I, Form No. 3.

TRUSTEE. A person to whom an estate is conveyed, devised, or bequeathed, in trust for another, called the *cestui que trust.*

TRUSTEE, PUBLIC. [PUBLIC TRUSTEE; TRUST CORPORATION.]

TUNNAGE. [TONNAGE.]

TURBARY (Lat. *Turbagium*). The right to dig turf on another man's ground. And *common of turbary* is a liberty which some tenants have by prescription to dig on the lord's waste. [COMMON.]

TURN. [SHERIFF'S TOURN.]

TURPIS CAUSA. An illegal or immoral consideration by which a contract is vitiated.

TYTHES. [TITHES.]

TYTHING. [TITHING.]

U

UBERRIMA FIDES. The most perfect frankness. This is essential to the validity of certain contracts between persons bearing a particular relationship to one another, *e.g.*, guardian and ward, solicitor and client, insurer and insured.

UBI JUS, IBI REMEDIUM. Where there is a right, there is a remedy.

ULPIAN. Domitius Ulpianus was one of the five great Roman jurists, upon whose writings the compilations of Justinian are mainly founded. The greater part of his works were written in the reign of Caracalla. On the accession of Alexander Severus, in A.D. 222, he became the emperor's chief adviser.

ULTIMATUM. A final proposal in a negotiation in which it is intimated that, in case of its rejection, the negotiation must be broken off.

ULTRA VIRES. Beyond their powers; a phrase applied especially to directors of companies exceeding their legal powers under the articles of association or the Acts of Parliament by which they are governed; though it is equally applicable to excess of authority of any kind.

UMPIRE. 1. An arbitrator.

2. Especially a referee called in to decide when two arbitrators cannot agree. See the Arbitration Act 1950. [ARBITRATION.]

UNCERTAINTY is where a deed or will is so obscure and confused that the judges can make nothing of it, which sometimes occurs in wills made by testators without legal advice. Any disposition or conveyance to which it is impossible to affix a meaning is said to be *void for uncertainty*; but the judges will use every effort to affix a meaning to the language used where it is possible to do so.

UNCONSCIONABLE BARGAIN. A bargain so one-sided and inequitable in its terms as to raise a presumption of fraud and oppression. [USURY, 2; MONEY-LENDER.]

UNDEFENDED. 1. When a person sued in a civil cause or accused of a crime has no counsel to speak for him on his trial, and has to make his defence himself, he is sometimes said to be *undefended*, that is, undefended by counsel.

2. An undefended cause is one in which a defendant makes default (1) in not putting in an appearance to the plaintiff's action; (2) in not putting in his statement of defence; (3) in not appearing at the trial, either personally or by counsel, after having received due notice of trial. R.S.C. 1965, Ords. 13, 19 and 35, r.1.

UNDERLEASE. A lease by a lessee for years, for a period less than the residue of the term, as opposed to an *assignment* by which the entire residue is conveyed. A lessee who grants a sublease or underlease still remains liable on the covenants to the lessor, but the sub-lessee is not liable to the original lessor, whereas an *assignee* is so liable. As used in the Law of Property Act 1922 the term "underlease", unless the context otherwise requires, includes a sub-term created out of a derivative leasehold interest. See s. 190 (4). And see s. 146 (5) of the Law of Property Act 1925, whereby "underlease" includes an agreement for an underlease where the underlessee has become entitled to have his underlease granted.

UNDER-SHERIFF is an officer who acts directly under the high sheriff, and performs all the duties of the sheriff's office except his functions as returning officer at parliamentary elections. The high sheriff is civilly responsible for the acts or omissions of his under-sheriff. As to the appointment of under-sheriffs, see s. 219 of the Local Government Act 1972. [SHERIFF.]

UNDERTAKING. A promise; especially one given in the course of legal proceedings, which may be enforced by attachment or otherwise. By R.S.C. 1965, Ord. 10, r. 1, a solicitor may give an undertaking to appear on behalf of a defendant, and in this case personal service of the writ on the defendant is not required. A solicitor not appearing according to his undertaking is by Ord. 75, r. 9, liable to attachment.

UNDERWRITER is a person who *underwrites* or subscribes his name to a policy of insurance, thereby undertaking to indemnify the assured against the losses referred to in the policy, to the extent therein mentioned. The word is used especially with reference to *marine insurance*. Underwriters of shares in a company are persons who, for a commission, offer to take up any shares offered to but not taken up by the public. [INSURANCE; LLOYD'S.]

UNDUE INFLUENCE. Any improper pressure put upon a person to induce him to confer a benefit upon the party pressing. A gift or will may be set aside by the courts where such pressure has been exercised. In elections undue influence to induce persons to vote or refrain from voting by violence, restraint, threats, etc., renders the person using it guilty of a misdemeanour, and if by a candidate, disqualifies him from sitting in that parliament for the constituency. See s. 101 of the Representation of the People Act 1949. [CORRUPT PRACTICES.]

UNFAIR DISMISSAL. [WRONGFUL DISMISSAL.].

UNIFORMITY, ACT OF. [ACT OF UNIFORMITY.]

UNILATERAL. One-sided; a word used especially of a bond or contract by which one party is bound.

UNION. The consolidation of two or more bodies or areas into one. This may (or might) be done:—

1. In the past for the better administration of the poor laws. Under these laws, now repealed, any two or more parishes could be consolidated into one union under the government of a single board of guardians, to be elected by the owners and ratepayers of the component parishes. Each of such unions was to have a common workhouse, provided and maintained at the common expense. Such workhouse was frequently called "the union workhouse", or, more briefly, "the union".

2. For ecclesiastical purposes, under the Acts for the union of benefices.

UNITY OF POSSESSION signifies:—
1. The joint possession by one person of two rights by several titles.
2. The holding of the same estate in undivided shares by two or more. [COMMON, TENANCY IN; COPARCENARY.]

UNIVERSAL AGENT. A person appointed to do all the acts which the principal may lawfully do, and the power to do which he may lawfully delegate to another.

UNIVERSITY COURTS were courts established in the Universities of Oxford and Cambridge, by ancient charters, confirmed in Queen Elizabeth I's reign by the Oxford and Cambridge Act 1571.
The courts in each university were:—
1. The Chancellor's court, having jurisdiction in personal actions affecting members of the university, and in cases of misdemeanours and minor offences committed by them. This court still sits at Oxford.
2. The court of the lord high steward, having jurisdiction in cases of treason, felony, and mayhem, when committed by a member of the university. [CHANCELLOR, 4; HIGH STEWARD, 3.]

UNLAWFUL ASSEMBLY. A meeting of three or more persons to do an unlawful act or a lawful act by unlawful means under such circumstances as to cause apprehension of a breach of the peace.

UNLIMITED COMPANY. A company, the liability of whose members is unlimited. [LIMITED COMPANY.]

UNLIQUIDATED DAMAGES. Damages the amount of which in money is not settled, as in cases of libel, slander, assault, etc. [LIQUIDATED DAMAGES.]

UNSOUND MIND. [MENTAL DISORDER.]

UNWRITTEN LAW. [LEX NON SCRIPTA.]

UPPER BENCH was the name given, during the protectorate of Oliver Cromwell, to the Court of King's Bench. [COURT OF KING'S (or QUEEN'S) BENCH.]

URBAN DISTRICT COUNCIL. Formerly each administrative county in England and Wales was divided into a number of districts of which some were non-county boroughs, others urban or rural districts. These were abolished in the reorganisation of local authorities under the Local Government Act 1972. [COUNTY; DISTRICT COUNCIL.]

URBAN SERVITUDES are city servitudes, or servitudes of houses; that is to say, easements appertaining to the building and construction of houses; as, for instance, the right to light and air, or the right to build a house so as to throw the rain-water on a neighbour's house. [EASEMENT; SERVITUDE.]

USAGE. Practice long continued. It must always be proved, thus differing from custom, which is in some cases judicially noticed. [CUSTOM.]

USANCE, in reference to foreign bills of exchange, is the common period, fixed by the usage or habit of dealing between the country where the bill is drawn and that where it is payable, for the payment of bills.

USE. 1. A *use*, before the Statute of Uses (1535) consisted in the equitable right to receive the profit or benefit of lands and tenements, which was, in cases of lands conveyed to uses, divorced from the legal ownership thereof. The object of such conveyances was principally to evade the Statutes of Mortmain, by which lands were prohibited from being given directly to religious houses. The ecclesiastics obtained grants to persons *to the use* of religious houses, which the clerical chancellors of those days declared to be binding. Another supposed advantage of uses was that they could be dealt with and disposed of without the formalities required for the transfer of the legal estates.
2. After the Statute of Uses, the *use* of the land involved the *legal* ownership, for by that statute it was provided that where any person or persons should stand seised of any lands or other hereditaments to the use, confidence or trust of any other person or persons, the persons that had any such use, confidence or trust should be deemed in lawful seisin and possession of the same lands and hereditaments for such estates as they had in the use, trust or confidence. The Statute of Uses was repealed by s. 207 of, and Sch. VII to, the Law of Property Act, 1925. The provisions in any statute or other instrument requiring land to be conveyed

to uses shall take effect as directions that the land shall (subject to creating or reserving thereout any legal estate authorised by the Act of 1925 which may be required) be conveyed to a person of full age upon the requisite trusts. Interests in land which could previously have been created as legal interests shall be capable of being created as equitable interests.

3. If, since the Statute of Uses, land should be conveyed to A to the use of B to the use of C, B would have the legal estate, the use to C being *a use upon a use*, which the courts of law refused to recognise. But C would, nevertheless, be recognised in a court of equity as the party entitled. Practically, however, the relation between B and C would be expressed by the word *trust* and not by the word *use*. See, however, the effect of the Law of Property Act 1925, as noted in paragraph 2, *supra*.

USE AND OCCUPATION. An action for use and occupation is an action brought by a landlord against a tenant for the profits of land. This action is allowed by s. 14 of the Distress for Rent Act 1737 where there has been no demise by deed. It is also maintainable against a tenant holding over after a lease by deed has expired, in respect of such holding over. The measure of damages recoverable in this action is the rent, where a rent has been agreed upon; and where no rent has been agreed upon, then such sum as the jury may find the occupation to be worth.

USER. The enjoyment of property.

USES, STATUTE OF. [USE.]

USES, SUPERSTITIOUS. [SUPERSTITIOUS USES.]

USES TO BAR DOWER. A form of conveyance of land to a man married before the Dower Act 1833 came into operation so as to prevent the wife's right to dower attaching, he taking only a life estate and a power of appointment. Now obsolete.

USHER. A door-keeper of a court.

USQUE AD FILUM AQUÆ, or more fully, "usque ad medium filum aquæ" (up to the middle thread of the water), is a phrase used to express half the land covered by a stream; which, in the case of a stream not navigable, belongs to the proprietor of the adjoining bank.

USUCAPION, or **USUCAPTION.** The enjoying a thing by long continuance of time or title by prescription. [PRESCRIPTION.]

USUFRUCT, in Roman law, was a temporary right of using a thing without having the full dominion over the substance. But in practice a usufruct was generally understood to signify a right of enjoyment of anything for the life of the usufructuary, *i.e.*, of the party entitled to the usufruct. And the word is so understood in the law of Scotland.

USURA MARITIMA. Maritime usury; that is, the loan of money on the hazard of a voyage; otherwise called *fœnus nauticum*. [BOTTOMRY; FŒNUS NAUTICUM.]

USURPATION. The using that which is not one's own. It is a word used especially in the common law to signify the *usurpation of an advowson*; that is, when a stranger, who is not the patron, presents a clergyman to the living, and the clergyman so presented is thereupon admitted and instituted.

So, an usurpation of a franchise is the use of a franchise by a person who has no right to it.

USURY. 1. The gain of anything in consideration of a loan beyond the principal or thing lent; otherwise called interest.

2. Especially any such gain above mentioned as is illegal or excessive. The laws against usury were repealed by the Usury Laws Repeal Act 1854; but this repeal does not affect the jurisdiction of the High Court in granting relief to persons who have obtained loans of money on exorbitant and iniquitous terms. [MONEY-LENDER.]

UTERINE BROTHER (Lat. *Uterinus frater*). A brother by the mother's side only.

UTTER BAR. The outer or junior bar, as opposed to the serjeants-at-law and Queen's counsel. [OUTER BAR.]

UTTER BARRISTERS. [OUTER BAR.]

UTTERING. To *utter* coins or documents (a phrase especially used in reference to false coin and forged documents) is to pass them off as genuine. Any person knowingly uttering false coin is guilty of

UTTERING—*continued.*
misdemeanour. See the Forgery Act 1913, s. 6; and the Coinage Offences Act 1936.

V

V. Versus (*q.v.*).

V.-C. Vice-Chancellor.

VACANT POSSESSION is where a tenant has virtually abandoned the premises which he held. Thus where the tenant of a house locked it up and quitted it, the court held that the landlord should treat it as a vacant possession. Where an action of ejectment was brought for the recovery of a vacant possession, the writ might be served by posting a copy of it on the door of the dwelling-house, or other conspicuous part of the property. See now R.S.C. 1965, Ord. 10, r. 4. The term is normally used to describe premises which are for sale or have been sold without being subject to any lease or underlease.

VACANT SUCCESSION is where, on the death of a sovereign or other person of title, there is no one appointed by law to succeed. Or the phrase might be applied to an *hæreditas jacens*, where there was no one to succeed the deceased.

VACATION. The time between the end of one sittings and the beginning of another. [SITTINGS.]

By R.S.C. 1965, Ord. 64, r. 1 the vacations to be observed in the courts and offices of the Supreme Court are four in number:—(1) The Long Vacation, from August 1st to September 30th (Order of 1950); (2) the Christmas Vacation, from the 22nd of December to the 10th of January; (3) the Easter Vacation, from the Thursday before Easter Sunday to the second Monday after; (4) and a vacation beginning on the Saturday before the spring holiday and ending on the Monday after. The days of the commencement and termination of each vacation are included in such vacation.

The county courts are normally closed during September. See s. 38 of the County Courts Act 1959.

VACATION SITTINGS. Two judges of the High Court ("vacation judges") sit during the Long Vacations for the hearing of applications requiring immediate attention. R.S.C. 1965, Ord. 64, r. 2.

VACATURA. An avoidance of an ecclesiastical benefice.

VADIUM MORTUUM. Dead pledge. [MORTGAGE.]

VAGABOND. One who wanders about and has no certain dwelling. By various statutes it is provided that certain acts shall constitute their perpetrator a rogue and vagabond. See s. 4 of the Vagrancy Act 1824. [VAGRANT; WITCHCRAFT.]

VAGRANT. A person belonging to one of the following classes:—(1) Idle and disorderly persons; (2) rogues and vagabonds; (3) incorrigible rogues. These several classes are defined by various Acts of Parliament. See principally the Vagrancy Act 1824.

VALOR BENEFICIORUM (value of benefices) was the name of an assessment of the value of ecclesiastical livings, made in the reign of Elizabeth I, for the purpose of regulating the payment of first fruits. It was commonly called the *King's books*, and the clergy were rated in accordance with it. [FIRST FRUITS.]

VALOR MARITAGII. The *value of the marriage*, which wards in knight-service forfeited, in case they refused a suitable marriage, without *disparagement* or inequality, tendered by the lord.

VALUABLE CONSIDERATION. A consideration for a grant, contract or other act which the law deems an equivalent for the same, must consist of money or money's worth. A court of justice will not in general enter into the question of the *adequacy* of a consideration which is *bona fide* intended as an equivalent. For the purposes of the Law of Property Act 1925 "valuable consideration" includes marriage, but does not include a nominal consideration in money. See s. 205 (1) (xxi). [CONSIDERATION.]

VALUE ADDED TAX. A tax charged on the supply of goods and services in the United Kingdom and on the importation of goods into the United Kingdom. It was imposed by the Finance Act 1972, which Act abolished purchase tax.

VALUE RECEIVED. A phrase implying the existence of a valuable consideration. The phrase is especially used to indicate that a bill of exchange has been accepted for value and not by way of accommodation. [ACCOMMODATION BILL.]

VALUED POLICY. A policy in which the sum to be recovered under it is agreed upon beforehand between the parties, and expressed on the face of the policy. The value thus agreed on is binding as between the parties, assuming that the transaction is *bona fide*. See s. 27 of the Marine Insurance Act 1906. [OPEN POLICY.]

VARIANCE. A discrepancy between the statement of the cause of action in writ, and a count in the declaration or statement of claim; or between a statement in a pleading and the evidence adduced in its support. Power is given to the court, under different statutes, for the amendment of variances. [AMENDMENT.]

VASSAL. A tenant holding lands under a lord, and bound by his tenure to feudal services.

VAVASOUR was anciently the first dignity, next to a peer; now quite obsolete.

VENDEE. A buyer, to whom lands or goods are sold.

VENDITIONI EXPONAS. A writ judicial directed to a sheriff or under-sheriff, who had taken goods into his hands under a writ of execution, and could not sell them at a reasonable price, commanding him to sell them for the best price he could get, however inadequate, in order to satisfy the judgment debt.

VENDOR. A seller. In sales of lands the party selling is almost always spoken of as "the vendor"; but in sales of goods he is quite as frequently spoken of as "the seller".

VENDOR'S COVENANTS FOR TITLE. [TITLE, COVENANTS FOR.]

VENDOR'S LIEN is the hold which an unpaid vendor of land has over the land for the payment of the purchase-money. This lien exists against the vendee and his heirs, and against persons claiming by a voluntary conveyance from the vendee; also against purchasers under him, with notice that the purchase-money due from such vendee has not been paid. Now, to remain enforceable against subsequent purchasers of land, it must be registered as a "general equitable charge" under s. 2 (4) (iii) of the Land Charges Act 1972. [LIEN.] As to the lien of an unpaid seller of goods, see Sale of Goods Act 1893, ss. 31–43.

VENERY. Chase, hunting. Beasts of venery are beasts of chase, and were formerly held to belong to the king, or to such as were authorised under him.

VENIA ÆTATIS was a privilege granted by a prince or sovereign, in which a minor was entitled to act as if he were of full age.

VENIRE DE NOVO. This is a form of motion for a new trial; the words implying that a new *venire facias* was directed to the sheriff. It was formerly grantable as a matter of right whenever it appeared on the face of the record that there had been a mistrial.

VENIRE FACIAS (that you cause to come). A writ in the nature of a summons to cause a party to appear, who is indicated for a petty misdemeanour, or on a penal statute.

VENIRE FACIAS JURATORES was a writ judicial directed to the sheriff, when issue was joined in an action, commanding him to summon a jury. Abolished in 1852.

VENIRE FACIAS TOT MATRONAS (cause so many matrons to come). A former writ directing the summoning of a jury of matrons to see if a woman be with child. [JURY OF MATRONS.]

VENTRE INSPICIENDO. [AD VENTREM INSPICIENDUM.]

VENUE (Lat. *Vicinetum*). The neighbourhood from whence a jury come for the trial of an action or indictment. In former times the direction to the sheriff was to summon a jury, not from the *body of the county* but from the *immediate neighbourhood* where the facts occurred, and from among those persons who best knew the truth of the matter; the jurors being formerly regarded as witnesses, or as persons in some measure cognizant, of their own knowledge, of the matter in dispute, and of the credit to be given to the parties; and, in order to know into what county the *venire facias* [VENIRE FACIAS JURATORES] should issue, it was necessary that the issue in the action, and the pleadings out of which it arose, should show particularly what that place or neighbourhood was. Such place was called the *visne* or *venue*; and the statement of it, in the pleadings,

VENUE—*continued.*

obtained the same name; to allege the place being, in the language of pleading, to *lay the venue.*

A venue was either *transitory* or *local.* It was transitory when the cause of action was of a sort that might have happened anywhere, which was generally the case where the locality was not the gist of the action, as in a case of assault. It was local when it could have happened in one county only, as in an action for trespass in breaking and entering the plaintiff's close. Changing the venue meant changing the place of trial, which, in civil actions before the Judicature Acts, might be done by a special order of the judge, or by consent of the parties to the action.

Now, by R.S.C. 1965, Ord. 33, r. 4, the determination of the place and mode of trial is by order made on the summons for directions.

VERBA ACCIPIENDA SUNT SEC- UNDUM SUBJECTAM MATERIAM. Words are to be understood with reference to the subject-matter.

VERBA CHARTARUM FORTIUS ACCIPIUNTUR CONTRA PRO- FERENTEM. The words of a deed are construed more strongly against the grantor.

VERDICT is the answer given to the court by the jury, in any cause, civil or criminal, committed to their trial, and is either general or special: *general* when they give it in general terms, as guilty or not guilty; *special* when they find it at large according to the evidence given, and pray the direction of the court as to what the law is upon the facts so found. It is now possible for a jury to give a majority verdict: see the Juries Act 1974.

VERGE. 1. The compass about the king's court, which bounded the jurisdiction of the lord steward, and of the corner of the king's house. It extended for twelve miles from the royal residence. [COURT OF MARSHALSEA.]

2. An uncertain quantity of land from fifteen to thirty acres.

3. A stick or rod by which a copyhold tenant of a manor was admitted; and, holding it in his hand, took the oath of fealty to the lord of the manor.

4. Land at the side of a road which is part of the highway but not paved.

VERIFICATION was the concluding averment, "and this he is ready to verify", which was formerly necessary in every pleading which contained new affirmative matter. Since 1852, no longer necessary.

VERSUS. Against. Smith *versus* Jones is the cause of Smith against Jones. Usually abbreviated to "v".

VEST (Lat. *Vestire*). 1. To deliver to a person the full possession of land, and so to clothe him with the legal estate therein. [INVESTITURE.]

2. To become a vested interest. See the following titles.

VESTED IN INTEREST. A phrase used to indicate a present fixed right of future enjoyment, as reversions, vested remainders, and other future interests which do not depend on a period or event uncertain.

VESTED IN POSSESSION. A phrase used to indicate that an estate is an estate in possession, as opposed to an estate in reversion or remainder.

VESTED REMAINDER, in the law of real property, is a remainder which is always ready, from its beginning to its end, to come into possession at once, subject only to the determination of some prior particular estate or estates.

The two following characteristics of every vested remainder may be adduced, by one or other of which it may be distinguished from any given contingent remainder:—1. A vested remainder is limited to some specific person, and not to a dubious or uncertain person. 2. A vested remainder cannot be prevented from taking effect in possession by any condition extrinsic to the limitation by which it is created. But a remainder is none the less a vested remainder merely because it may fail to take effect by virtue of some condition implied in the limitation by which it exists. [LIMITATION OF ESTATES.] Thus, if land be granted to A for life, remainder to B for life, B's estate is a vested remainder, though, if B dies before A, it will never come into possession. But if land be granted to A for life, remainder to B and his heirs if B survive A, B's estate is then called a contingent remainder, because the condition that B shall survive A is extrinsic to the limitation to B and his heirs. After 1925, remainders subsist only as equitable interests. See s. 1 of the Law of Property Act 1925. [REMAINDER.]

VESTING ASSENT. This means, in relation to settled land, the instrument whereby a personal representative, after the death of a tenant for life or statutory owner, or the survivor of two or more tenants for life or statutory owners, vests settled land in a person entitled as tenant for life or statutory owner. See s. 117 of the Settled Land Act 1925.

VESTING DECLARATION. This is a declaration made by the appointor in a deed of appointment of new trustees to the effect that the trust property shall vest in the persons who become or are the trustees. If the deed of appointment contains such a vesting declaration, the deed operates, without any conveyance or assignment, to vest in the persons named, as joint tenants and for the purposes of the trust, the estate, interest or right to which the declaration relates. See s. 40 of the Trustee Act 1925.

VESTING DEED. Since 1st January 1926, all settlements of land created *inter vivos* must be effected by two different deeds, namely, a vesting deed and a trust instrument (*q.v.*); see s. 4 of the Settled Land Act 1925. The function of the vesting deed is to vest the legal fee simple in the person who for the time being is to have the actual enjoyment of the land, or, if he is a minor or otherwise incapable, then to vest it in some other person who is denominated a "statutory owner" (*q.v.*). For the contents of the vesting deed, see s. 5 of the Settled Land Act 1925, and for specimen forms, see *ibid.*, Sch. I, Forms Nos. 1 and 2.

VESTING ORDER is an order of the Chancery Division of the High Court of Justice, vesting the legal estate in property (generally land) in any person specified in the order. This can be done, *e.g.*, under the Trustee Acts, when the trustees appointed are unwilling or unable to act in the execution of the trusts; or when for any reason it is desirable to appoint new trustees, and it is found impracticable or inconvenient to procure a conveyance to them in the ordinary way.

VESTRY. 1. The place in a church where the priest's vestures are deposited.

2. An assembly of the minister, church-wardens and parishioners, so called because it is still very often usually held in the vestry of the church.

VESTURE signifies—(1) a garment; (2) the possession of seisin of land; (3) the profit of land.

VETERA STATUTA. Old statutes. This phrase is applied to the statutes from Magna Charta to the end of the reign of Edward II.

VEXATA QUÆSTIO. A question much discussed and not settled.

VEXATIOUS ACTION. An action brought merely for the sake of annoyance or oppression. The court has an inherent power to stay such an action. See s. 51 of the Judicature Act 1925.

VI ET ARMIS. With force and arms; a phrase formerly used in declarations for trespass, and in indictments.

VIA, in the Roman law, was the servitude (or easement) of a carriage road enjoyed by one man through another's property. [EASEMENT; SERVITUDE.]

VIA REGIA. The king's highway or common way.

VIABILITY. Capability of living after birth; possibility of continued existence.

VICAR, a substitute; one who performs the functions of another. The priest of every parish was called *rector*, unless the prædial tithes were impropriated, and then he was called vicar, *quasi vice fungens rectoris* (as if vicariously discharging the duty of a rector).

A vicar was originally the substitute of the appropriator in those parishes where the fruits of the living had been appropriated either by religious houses or by laymen. He took only the *small* tithes, and the chancel was not vested in him. [APPROPRIATION, 1; RECTOR.]

VICAR GENERAL was, in ancient times, an officer *occasionally* constituted, when the bishop was called out of the diocese by foreign embassies or attendances in parliament, or other affairs; and his commission contained in it the whole administration of the diocese, except the hearing of causes in the Consistory Court, which was the province of the *official*, otherwise called the *official principal*. [OFFICIAL.] In time, the vicar general came to be a fixed and standing officer, who

VICAR GENERAL—*continued.*

should be ready (without the trouble of a special commission for every occasion) to execute the episcopal power, when the bishop himself was hindered by infirmities, avocations or other impediments. The office of *vicar general* came by degrees to be united with that of *official*; and the person in whom the two offices are united is called the bishop's *chancellor*. [CHANCELLOR, 5.]

VICARAGE. The benefice, office or parsonage house of a vicar.

VICARIAL TITHES. Tithes appropriated to a vicarage. [TITHES; VICAR.]

VICE-CHANCELLOR. 1. A judicial officer having jurisdiction in equity under the Lord Chancellor. The first vice-chancellor was appointed in 1813, and two additional vice-chancellors in 1841.

In 1873, the vice-chancellors were transferred to the High Court of Justice, and appointed judges of the Chancery Division; and no more vice-chancellors were thereafter to be appointed under that style.

2. A principal officer in the universities of Oxford and Cambridge. He must be selected from among the heads of colleges in the university.

VICE-COMES signifies properly the sheriff of a county, being the deputy of the count or earl.

VICEROY. A person in place of the Queen; hence a governor of a dependency.

VICE-WARDEN OF THE STANNARIES. The local judge of the Stannary Courts. [COURT OF STANNARIES OF CORNWALL AND DEVON.]

VICINAGE. Neighbourhood.

VIDELICET. Namely; often abbreviated in "viz." or "vizt." To state a time or other matter in a pleading with the phrase "to wit", or "that is to say", was formerly called *laying it with a videlicet.*

VIEW. The act of viewing; a word especially applicable in speaking of a jury viewing any person or thing in controversy. In some cases, when the cause concerns lands or messuages, of which it is thought expedient that the jury should have a *view*, the officer of the court will, on application, draw up a rule for one. Two persons will be appointed as *showers*, and six jurymen as *viewers*, and the sheriff will return their

names to the associate for the purpose of being called at the trial. By R.S.C. 1965, Ord. 35, r. 8, the court or a judge may make an order for the inspection of any property or thing being the subject of any cause or matter before him, or the judge may inspect it himself.

So, if it is required to stop up or divert a highway a magistrates court may, after a view, if it thinks fit, by two or more justices, order the highway to be stopped up or diverted.

So a coroner's inquisition into the death of a person is held *super visum corporis* (on view of the body). [SUPER VISUM CORPORIS.]

VIEW OF FRANKPLEDGE (Lat. *Visus Franci Plegii*). [COURT LEET; FRANKPLEDGE.]

VIEWERS. [VIEW.]

VILL was sometimes taken for a manor; sometimes for a parish, or part of it; sometimes of collections of houses consisting of ten freemen or frankpledges. [FRANK-PLEDGE; MANOR; PARISH.]

VILLAIN or **VILLEIN.** A person of servile degree. There were two sorts of villains in England. The one was termed a *villain in gross*, who was immediately bound to the person of the lord and his heirs, and transferable by deed from one owner to another. The other was a *villain regardant* to a manor, as being a member belonging and annexed to a manor, and bound to the lord thereof.

VILLENAGE. 1. The condition of a villain or villein. [VILLAIN.]

2. A base tenure. [PRIVILEGED VILLENAGE.]

VINCULO MATRIMONII. From the bond of marriage.

VINDICTIVE DAMAGES, in an action, are damages given by way of punishing the defendant over and above the actual amount of injury suffered by the plaintiff. [EXEMPLARY DAMAGES.]

VIOLENT PRESUMPTION, in the law of evidence, is a presumption of such a nature as almost to amount to proof. [PRESUMPTION.]

VIRTUTE OFFICII. By virtue of his office. [EX OFFICIO.]

VIS MAJOR. Irresistible force; such an interposition of human agency as is from its nature and power absolutely uncontrollable; *e.g.*, the inroads of a hostile army, or forcible robberies, may relieve from liability from contract.

VISCOUNT. The degree of nobility next to an earl.

VISITATION. 1. The office that is performed by a bishop in every diocese once every three years, or by the archdeacon once a year, in visiting the churches and their rectors, etc.

2. The office of inquiring into and correcting the irregularities of corporations. [VISITOR.]

VISITOR. 1. A person appointed to visit, inquire into, and correct irregularities arising in a society or corporation. The ordinary is the visitor of ecclesiastical corporations; that is, of corporations composed entirely of spiritual persons, as bishops, etc. In the colleges of Oxford and Cambridge, the visitor is generally either the Crown, acting by the Lord Chancellor, or some bishop of the Church of England, or the chancellor or vice-chancellor of the university, or the head of some college *ex officio*. The errors and abuses of civil lay incorporations are inquired into and redressed by the Queen's Bench Division of the High Court of Justice.

2. An official visitor of mental patients. Such visitors are appointed by the Lord Chancellor under s. 108 of the Mental Health Act 1959, and are known as Lord Chancellor's Visitors. Their functions, set out in s. 109 of the Act, are to visit patients for the purpose of investigating matters relating to the capacity of patients to administer their property and affairs, etc. Both medical and legal visitors are appointed.

3. Boards of visitors to prisons were established by the Courts Act 1971, replacing the former visiting committees.

VIVA VOCE. Orally. [WITNESS.]

VIVARY. A park, warren or fishery.

VIVUM VADIUM. [WELSH MORTGAGE.]

VOID AND VOIDABLE. A transaction is said to be *void* when it is a mere nullity and incapable of confirmation; whereas a *voidable* transaction is one which may be either avoided or confirmed by matter arising *ex post facto*.

Thus, prior to the Infants' Relief Act 1874, the contract of a minor (otherwise than for necessaries) was merely voidable, as it might be confirmed by him on coming of age; but since that Act such a contract is generally void, and incapable of confirmation.

As to void or voidable marriages, see the Matrimonial Causes Act 1973, ss. 11–16.

VOIDANCE. The state of an ecclesiastical benefice without an incumbent.

VOIR DIRE or **VOIRE DIRE** (Lat. *Veritatem dicere*). A corruption of *vrai dire*. An examination of a witness upon the *voir dire* is a series of questions by the court and is usually in the nature of an examination as to his competency to give evidence, or some other collateral matter, and generally takes place prior to his examination in chief. It was formerly used in cases where a witness was suspected of an interest in the cause, which, until the Evidence Act 1843, rendered his testimony inadmissible. The *voir dire* was used by the Court of Star Chamber.

VOLENTI NON FIT INJURIA. No injury is done to one who consents.

VOLUNTARY CONFESSION. A confession of crime made by an accused person, without any promise of worldly advantage held out to him as obtainable by confession, or any harm threatened to him if he refuses to confess, the promise or threat being made by a person in authority. Such a confession is always admissible in evidence against the party.

VOLUNTARY CONVEYANCE. This phrase denotes a conveyance not founded upon a valuable consideration. [VALUABLE CONSIDERATION.] S. 173 of the Law of Property Act 1925 provides that every voluntary disposition of land made with intent to defraud a subsequent purchaser is void at the instance of that purchaser.

VOLUNTARY OATH. An oath not taken before a magistrate or other proper officer in some civil or criminal proceeding. Voluntary oaths were prohibited by the Statutory Declarations Act 1835 and statutory declarations substituted for them. [STATUTORY DECLARATION.]

VOLUNTARY SETTLEMENT. A settlement made without valuable consideration.

VOLUNTARY WASTE. Waste committed on lands by the voluntary act of the tenant, as opposed to waste which is merely permissive. [WASTE.]

VOUCH (Lat. *Vocare*). 1. To call or summon.

2. To answer for.

VOUCHEE (Lat. *Vocatus*). A person "vouched" or summoned. [RECOVERY; VOUCHER, 1.]

VOUCHER. 1. *Vouching to warranty*. This, in the old form of real action for the recovery of land, was the calling in of some person to answer the action, who had warranted the title of the tenant or defendant to the land in question. [RECOVERY.]

2. A book of accounts, wherein are entered the acquittances or warrants for the accountant's discharge. Also an acquittance or receipt discharging a person, as being evidence of payment.

VOYAGE POLICY. A policy of insurance on a ship against losses incurred during a voyage specified in the policy. [TIME POLICY.]

WAGE. The giving security for the due performance of anything. [GAGE.]

WAGER. A mutual contract for the future payment of money by A to B, or by B to A, according as some unknown fact or event, otherwise of no interest to the parties contracting, shall turn out. Wagers are void in law by s. 18 of the Gaming Act 1845. General provisions as to gaming are now contained in the Betting, Gaming and Lotteries Act 1963, as amended, and the Gaming Act 1968.

WAGER OF BATTEL. A mode of trial, in the nature of an appeal to Providence, to give the victory to him who had the right. It was introduced into England by William the Conqueror, and was available only in three cases: one military, one criminal, and the third, civil.

1. In the court-martial, or court of chivalry and honour. [COURT OF CHIVALRY.]

2. In appeals of felony, and upon approvements. [APPEAL; APPROVER.]

3. Upon issue joined in a writ of right. [WRIT OF RIGHT.]

In wager of battel on a writ of right, the parties fought by their champions; but on appeals they fought in their own proper persons, the party losing in the battle losing in the cause or appeal.

Wagers of battel were abolished in 1819.

WAGER OF LAW (Lat. *Vadiatio legis*). This was a proceeding which consisted in the defendant's discharging himself from a claim on his own oath, bringing with him at the same time into court eleven of his neighbours to swear that they believed his denial to be true. Abolished in 1833.

WAGERING POLICIES were policies of assurance, in the subject-matter whereof the assured had no interest; as, for instance, an insurance on the life of a stranger. They were rendered void by the Life Assurance Act 1774. As to marine insurance, see the Marine Insurance (Gambling Policies) Act 1909.

WAGES. Any money or salary paid or payable to any clerk or servant, labourer or workman. A minor can recover wages up to £1,000 in the county court without a next friend, under s. 80 of the County Courts Act 1959. When a master becomes bankrupt, a clerk or servant is entitled to be paid any sum owing to him, limited to a certain amount, in priority to the general creditors; and any labourer or workman is entitled to be paid any sum due not exceeding four months' wages, in priority to the general creditors. [PREFERENTIAL PAYMENTS; TRUCK SYSTEM.]

WAIFS (Lat. *Bona waviata*). Goods stolen and thrown away by the thief in his flight, for fear of being apprehended. Waifs were formerly forfeited to the king or lord of the manor, unless they belonged to a foreign merchant. Their forfeiture was intended as a punishment to the owner for not bringing the thief to justice.

WAIN-BOTE. Timber for waggons or carts.

WAIVER. The abandonment of a right by one party, so that afterwards he is estopped from claiming it. Thus it is said that a party waives a claim, or waives an objection, meaning that he does not put it forward. So, a man is said to *waive a tort* when he foregoes his right of treating a wrongful act as such; which he does, when he expressly, or by implication, adopts the act of the wrongdoer. Thus, if goods have been wrongfully taken and sold, and the owner thinks fit to receive the price or part thereof, he adopts the transaction, and cannot afterwards treat it as wrong.

WAPENTAKE. From *weapon* and *take*; the name in the northern counties for a hundred. [HUNDRED.]

WAR RISKS. Risks arising from hostilities, rebellion, revolution, and civil war, etc., including piracy. Insurance of such risks is now largely governed by the Marine and Aviation Insurance (War Risks) Act 1952.

WARD (Lat. *Custodia*) signifies *care* or *guard*, and is used variously to denote:

1. A portion of a city or town. See the Local Government Act 1972, s. 6.

2. The heir of the king's tenant, that held by knight's service *in capite*, was called a ward during his nonage. [IN CAPITE; WARDSHIP.]

3. A minor under the protection of the Chancery Division of the High Court, called a ward of court.

4. And, generally, a minor under the protection or tutelage of a guardian. [GUARDIAN; WATCH AND WARD.]

WARDEN. A guardian; he who has the custody of any person or things by his office; as the Warden of the Cinque Ports; the warden of a college, etc.

WARDMOTE. A court anciently kept in every ward in the city of London.

WARDSHIP. The custody of a ward; a word used especially with reference to wardship in chivalry; but also applicable to any form of the relation between guardian and ward.

WAREHOUSING SYSTEM. The system of allowing goods imported to be deposited in public warehouses, at a reasonable rent, without payment of the duties on importation if they are re-exported; or, if they are to be withdrawn for home consumption, then without payment of such duties until they are so removed.

WARNING OF A CAVEAT. A notice to a person who has entered a caveat in the Chancery Division, to appear and set forth his interest. [PROBATE.]

WARRANT. 1. A precept under hand and seal directed to some officer authorising him to arrest an offender to be dealt with according to law.

2. A writ conferring some right or authority.

3. A citation or summons. [DOCK WARRANT; SEARCH WARRANT.]

WARRANTOR. A person who warrants, or gives a warranty. [WARRANTY.]

WARRANTY. A promise or covenant offered by a bargainor, to warrant or secure the bargainee against all men in the enjoyment of anything agreed on between them. The word is used especially with reference to any promise (express or implied by law, according to circumstances) from a vendor to a purchaser, that the thing sold is the vendor's to sell and is good and fit for use, or at least for such use as the purchaser intends to make of it. As to warranty on sale of goods, see s. 62 of the Sale of Goods Act 1893. [CAVEAT EMPTOR; VOUCHER.]

In marine insurances an *express* warranty is an agreement expressed in the policy, whereby the assured stipulates that certain facts are or shall be true, or that certain acts shall be done relative to the risk. It may relate to an existing or past fact, or be promissory and relate to the future; and the fact or act warranted need not be material to the risk. A formal expression is not necessary to give effect to a warranty. An *implied* warranty is such as necessarily results from the nature of the contract, as that the ship is seaworthy.

WARREN (Lat. *Vivarium*). 1. A place in which birds, fishes, or wild beasts are kept. 2. A franchise or privilege, either by prescription or grant from the king, to keep beasts and fowls of warren, which are hares, coneys, partridges, pheasants, etc. 3. Also any place to which such privilege extends. [FREE WARREN.]

WASTE. 1. Spoil and destruction done or allowed to be done, by a tenant for life or other particular tenant, to houses, woods, lands, or other corporeal hereditaments, during the continuance of his particular estate therein. Waste is either *voluntary*, if it be a matter of commission, as by pulling down a house; or *permissive*, as if a house be allowed to fall into ruin for want of necessary repairs.

2. *Waste of a manor* is the uncultivated or common ground, over which the tenants enjoyed rights of pasturage for their animals.

3. The verges at the sides of roads are called roadside wastes.

WATCH AND WARD. *Watch* was the word applicable to the night duty of constables; *ward* to their duties in the daytime, in apprehending rioters and robbers on the highways, etc. [CONSTABLE.]

WATCH COMMITTEE. A committee once chosen from the council of a borough with a separate police force, not exceeding in number one-third of the members of the council, to appoint and control the borough constables. [OBSOLETE.]

WATER. Under the word "water", in a conveyance, it seems that a right of fishing will pass, but the soil will not pass. The term "land" includes water, but the term "water" does not include the land upon which it stands.

WATER BAILIFFS. 1. Officers in port towns for the searching of ships.

2. Keepers appointed under the Salmon Fishery Acts to prevent poaching.

WATER COURSE. A right which a man may have to the benefit of flow of a river or stream. This right includes that of having the course of the stream kept free from any interruption or disturbance to the prejudice of the proprietor, by the act of persons without his own territory; whether owing to a diversion of the water, or to its obstruction, or pollution by offensive commixture. Also used to describe the stream itself.

WATER-GAVIL. A rent paid for fishing in, or other benefit received from, some river.

WATER ORDEAL. [ORDEAL.]

WATERWAY. A lake, river, canal, etc., suitable for sailing, boating, bathing or fishing. See National Parks and Access to the Countryside Act 1949, s. 114.

WAVESON. Such goods as after shipwreck appear swimming upon the waves. [FLOTSAM; WRECK.]

WAY. [HIGHWAY; RIGHT OF WAY; WAYS.]

WAY-BILL. A document setting out the names of passengers carried in a public conveyance or a description of goods sent with a public carrier by land.

WAY-GOING CROP. [AWAY-GOING CROP.]

WAYS. 1. Paths. Of these there are various kinds:—(1) A foot-way (Lat. *iter*). (2) A bridle road for horse and man (Lat.

actus). (3) A cart-way, containing also the two preceding. (4) A drift-way or a way for driving cattle. (5) A highway. [HIGHWAY.]

2. Rights of way: either private or public rights of way over a man's ground. [RIGHT OF WAY.]

WEAPON. [OFFENSIVE WEAPON.]

WEAR AND TEAR. The waste of any substance by the ordinary use of it. The words "reasonable use, wear and tear excepted", are sometimes used in connection with the covenants in a lease.

WELSH LANGUAGE. The Welsh language may be used in any court in Wales by any party, witness or other person who desires to use it (Welsh Language Act 1967, s. 1 (1)).

WELSH MORTGAGE is a mortgage in which there is no condition or proviso for repayment at any time. The agreement is that the mortgagee, to whom the estate is conveyed, shall receive the rents till his debt is paid, and in such case the mortgagor and his representatives are at liberty to redeem at any time.

WEREGILD. The fine formerly paid for killing a man, when such crimes were punished with a pecuniary mulct, and not with death. This fine was paid partly to the king, for the loss of his subject, partly to the lord whose vassal he was, and partly to the next of kin of the slain man.

WESTMINSTER, STATUTES OF. (1) A statute of Edward I, passed in 1275. It contains fifty-one chapters, each of which would in modern times be regarded as a separate statute, or Act of Parliament. In fact it represents the whole of the legislation for the year 1275. (2) A later statute of Edward I, 1285. It contains fifty chapters, the first being the celebrated enactment *De donis conditionalibus*. (3) A third statute of Edward I, 1290, known as the statute of *Quia Emptores*. (4) A modern statute of 1931, with provisions relating to the Dominions.

WHARF. A broad plain place near a river, canal, or other water to lay wares on that are brought to or from the water.

There are two kinds of wharf—*legal quays* and *sufferance wharfs*. The former are established by Act of Parliament, or exist as such by immemorial usage. The latter are places where goods may be landed and shipped by special permission of the Crown.

WHARFAGE. Money paid for landing wares at a wharf, or for shipping or taking goods thence into a boat or barge.

WHITE RENTS (Lat. *Reditus albi*). [ALBA FIRMA; BLACK MAIL.]

WHOLE BLOOD. The relation between two persons descended from a pair of nearest common ancestors; as opposed to the relation of the half blood, in which there is but one nearest common ancestor, whether male or female.

WIDOW BENCH. The share of her husband's estate which a widow was allowed besides her jointure.

WIDOW'S QUARANTINE. [QUARANTINE.]

WIFE'S EQUITY TO A SETTLE-MENT. [EQUITY TO A SETTLEMENT.]

WILL. The legal declaration of a man's intention which he wills to be performed after his death. It is revocable during the testator's life. [WILLS ACT.] It has been said that a will and testament are, strictly, not of the same meaning; that a will is limited to land, and a testament to personal estate. But this distinction, if it ever existed, is now quite obsolete.

WILL, ESTATE AT. The estate of a tenant holding lands at the will of the lessor. [ESTATE; TENANT AT WILL.]

WILLS ACT. The Wills Act 1837 permits of the disposition by will of every kind of interest in real and personal estate, and provides that all wills, whether of real or of personal estate, shall be in writing signed at the foot or end thereof by the testator or by some person in his presence and by his direction, and shall be attested by two witnesses present together at the same time, and that such attestation shall be sufficient.

WINDING UP AN ESTATE is the putting it in liquidation for the purpose of distributing the assets among creditors and others who may be found entitled thereto. "Winding up" is a phrase most frequently used in connection with public companies unable to satisfy their liabilities. See Part V of the Companies Act 1948.

WINDOW TAX. A tax formerly levied on houses which contained more than six windows and were worth more than £5 per annum.

WIRELESS TELEGRAPHY. Signalling or communicating through space, without the use of wires. See the Wireless Telegraphy Acts 1949 to 1967, and the Sound Broadcasting Act 1972. [BROADCASTING; TELEVISION.]

WITCHCRAFT. Supposed intercourse with evil spirits; formerly punishable with death under Acts of 1541 and 1603, both of which were repealed in 1735. The last execution for witchcraft in England, that of a woman and her daughter of nine, took place by hanging in 1716. The Witchcraft Act 1735 was repealed by the Fraudulent Mediums Act 1951.

WITENAGEMOTE. [WITTENAGEMOTE.]

WITH COSTS. A phrase which, when used with reference to the result of an action, implies that the successful party is entitled to recover his costs from his opponent. [COSTS.]

WITHDRAWAL OF JUROR. A practice occasionally adopted by consent of the parties to an action, when neither party feels sufficient confidence to render him anxious to persevere until verdict, or where the case has been settled between the parties, or where the jury are unable to agree upon a verdict. If, after the withdrawal of a juror, the plaintiff should proceed with the action, the defendant may apply to stay the proceedings. [STAY OF PROCEEDINGS.]

WITHDRAWING THE RECORD was where a plaintiff revoked the entry of a cause for trial, and thus discontinued the action. Now by R.S.C. 1965, Ord. 21, a party who has entered an appearance in an action may withdraw the appearance at any time with the leave of the court. A plaintiff may discontinue an action, or withdraw any particular claim, without leave, at any time not later than 14 days after service of the defence on him; a defendant may, without leave, withdraw his defence or any part of it at any time. Leave is required to withdraw a claim (or counter claim) if such discontinuance is not within 14 days.

WITHERNAM (Lat. *Vetitum namium*). An unlawful distress, or forbidden taking,

WITHERNAM—*continued.*

as the taking or driving a thing distrained out of the county, so that the sheriff cannot upon the replevin make deliverance thereof to the party distrained. Hence it signifies also the *reprisals* for such forbidden taking as above mentioned, which was enforced by ·a writ of *capias in withernam.* [REPLEVIN.]

WITHOUT DAY. [EAT INDE SINE DIE.]

WITHOUT IMPEACHMENT OF WASTE. A phrase used in conveyance to tenants for life or other particular tenants, to indicate that the tenant is not to be held responsible for waste. At law the tenant could not be impeached for any form of waste, but in equity he was liable if the waste was of a serious character, hence called *equitable waste*; that is, the commission of wanton injury, as the pulling down of the family mansion house, or felling timber left standing for ornament. [WASTE.]

WITHOUT PREJUDICE to any matter in question means that a decision come to, or action taken, is not to be held to affect such question, but to leave it open. Thus, when a lawyer writes on behalf of a client to offer a compromise of a question in dispute, he guards himself from being supposed to make any admission, beyond the mere fact of his willingness to compromise, by stating that what he offers is without prejudice to any question in dispute.

WITHOUT RECOURSE TO ME. [SANS RECOURS.]

WITHOUT RESERVE. A term applied to a sale by auction, indicating that no price is reserved. In such case the seller may not employ any person to bid at the sale, and the auctioneer may not knowingly take any bidding from any such person. See the Sale of Land by Auction Act 1867, and the Sale of Goods Act 1893, s. 58.

WITNESS. A person who, on oath or solemn affirmation, gives evidence in any cause or matter. [EVIDENCE.]

By R.S.C. 1965, Ord. 38, r. 1, any fact required to be proved at the trial of any action begun by writ by the evidence of witnesses shall be proved by the examination of the witnesses orally and in open court.

By Ord. 38, r. 2, the court may order that the affidavit of any witness may be read at the trial if in the circumstances of the case it thinks it reasonable so to order. By r. 4 the number of medical or other expert witnesses may be limited; and r. 9 makes provision for the receiving in evidence of depositions. See also, as to depositions, R.S.C. 1965, Ord. 39. In criminal cases evidence must almost always be given orally; sometimes evidence by certificate is accepted: Criminal Justice Act 1948, s. 41; the depositions may occasionally be read.

WITTENAGEMOTE, or **WITENA-GEMOTE.** The great meeting of wise men, or common council of England under the Saxons. Sometimes called Michelgemote.

WOOLSACK. The seat of the Lord Chancellor in the House of Lords. It is not strictly within the House, for the lords may not speak from that part of the chamber. *May.*

WORDS OF LIMITATION. Words following the name of an intended grantee or devisee under a deed or will, which are intended to "limit" or mark out the estate or interest taken by the party. See now s. 60 of the Law of Property Act 1925, which abolishes technicalities in regard to conveyances and deeds and words of limitation. [LIMITATION OF ESTATES; RULE IN SHELLEY'S CASE.]

WORK EXPERIENCE. Children who are in their last year of schooling may obtain work experience as part of their education under the provisions of the Education (Work Experience) Act 1973.

WORKHOUSE. [UNION.]

WORKMAN. [SERVANT.]

WOUNDING. An aggravated species of assault and battery, consisting in one person giving another some dangerous hurt. To constitute a wound, the continuity of the skin must be broken.

WRECK, (Lat. *Wreccum maris*) by the ancient common law, was where any ship was lost at sea, and the goods or cargo were thrown upon the land; in which case the goods so wrecked were adjudged to belong to the king.

In order to constitute a legal wreck the goods had (in the original sense) to come to land. The law distinguished goods lost at sea by the old names of *jetsam, flotsam* and *ligan.* See under those titles. By s. 510 of the

Merchant Shipping Act 1894, "wreck" for the purposes of that Act includes *jetsam*, *flotsam*, *ligan* and *derelict*.

Provision is made by ss. 465, 466 of that Act for inquiring into losses of ships by inspecting officers of coastguard.

Modern diving equipment has enabled people to explore the sea bed, and many "wrecks" (in the sense of sunken ships which have remained, in some cases for centuries, beneath the sea) have been discovered. The Protection of Wrecks Act 1973 enables wreck sites within United Kingdom waters to be protected from unauthorised interference on account of their historic, archaeological or historic importance.

WRIT. The Queen's precept, whereby any thing is commanded to be done touching a suit or action. Writs were distinguished into original and judicial writs. Original writs were those that were sent out for the summoning of a defendant in an action, and bore in the *teste* the name of the sovereign. Judicial writs were those that were sent out by order of the court where the cause depended, and the *teste* bore the name of the chief justice of that court whence it issued. [ORIGINAL WRIT; PREROGATIVE WRITS.]

Specimen forms of writs of summons appear in Appendix A to the Rules of the Supreme Court.

WRIT IN AID. One issued after a writ of execution has passed, *e.g.*, *venditioni exponas*.

WRIT OF CAPIAS. [CAPIAS.]

WRIT OF ENTRY. [ENTRY, WRIT OF.]

WRIT OF ERROR. [ERROR.]

WRIT OF INQUIRY. A former process in an action at common law, by which, after judgment by default for the plaintiff, the sheriff inquired, by the oaths of twelve honest and lawful men, what amount of damages the plaintiff had really sustained. The inquiry was undertaken by the undersheriff before a jury; and when their verdict was given, the sheriff returned the inquisition, which was entered upon the roll; and thereupon execution issued for the amount so assessed. The writ of inquiry has been abolished.

WRIT OF RIGHT was the old writ in the law for asserting the right to lands in fee simple unjustly withheld from the true proprietor. This writ was properly brought, in the first instance, in the court baron of the lord of whom the lands were holden, and then it was called a *writ of right patent*; but if the lord held no court, or had waived his right, it might be brought in the king's courts in the first instance, *quia dominus remisit curiam*, and then it was called a *writ of right close*, and was directed to the sheriff and not to the lord.

Also, when one of the king's immediate tenants *in capite* [IN CAPITE] was deforced (*i.e.*, unjustly deprived of his land), his writ of right was called a *writ of right close*.

The writ of right was considered the highest writ in the law. But it could not be sued out at any distance of time, for by a statute of 1540, it was enacted that the seisin claimed in a writ of right should be within sixty years.

There were also various writs which were said to be in the nature of a writ of right. These writs resembled the writ of right in that they were droitural and not merely possessory actions, but differed from it in some other respects. In some of these writs the fee simple was not demanded; and in others not land, but some incorporeal hereditament. In others land was claimed in fee simple, but was so claimed under peculiar circumstances, to which the writ of right proper did not apply.

The writ of right was abolished in 1833.

WRIT OF RIGHT CLOSE. [WRIT OF RIGHT.]

WRIT OF RIGHT OF ADVOWSON. A writ of right framed for the purpose of trying a right to an advowson, but in other respects corresponding with other writs of right, except that the Statutes of Limitations did not apply to it. Abolished in 1833. [WRIT OF RIGHT.]

WRIT OF RIGHT PATENT. [WRIT OF RIGHT.]

WRIT OF SUMMONS. [SUMMONS, 3; WRIT.]

WRITER TO THE SIGNET. W.S. The writers to the signet are the oldest body of law practitioners in Scotland. They perform in the Supreme Courts of Scotland duties corresponding to those of solicitors in England.

WRITINGS OBLIGATORY. This phrase is sometimes used for bonds. [BOND.]

WRONG. That which is *wrung* or turned aside from the right or straight way to the desired end. It corresponds to the French *tort*, from the Latin *tortum*, twisted. [TORT.]

The words *wrong* and *tort* may be used in law to signify any injury; but they are used especially to denote such civil injuries as are independent of contract, and are not breaches of trust.

WRONGFUL DISMISSAL. The unjustifiable dismissal of a servant or employee in breach of a contract of service or before the expiration of a period of notice. The servant may sue for damages for loss of employment and wages or salary.

As to remedies for *unfair* dismissal (which include reinstatement or compensation) see ss. 71–80 of The Employment Protection Act 1975.

Y

YARDLAND (Lat. *Virgata terræ*). A quantity of land containing in some counties twenty acres, in others twenty-four, and in others thirty acres of land.

YEAR. [OLD STYLE.]

YEAR AND DAY. 1. Where the law of Scotland requires any act to be performed within a year, a day is generally added *in majorem evidentiam*, that it may appear with greater certainty that the year is completed.

2. The same reason will probably account for the frequent mention of the year and day in the old English law; for instance, in reference to the time within which appeals might be brought; also in reference to the time within which death must follow upon a mortal wound, in order to constitute the crime murder; and in various other cases. [YEAR, DAY, AND WASTE.]

YEAR BOOKS were reports of cases in a regular series from the reign of King Edward I to the reign of King Henry VIII inclusive. They were taken down by the protonotaries, or chief scribes of the courts, at the expense of the Crown, and published annually,.whence they were known under the denomination of *Year Books*.

YEAR, DAY, AND WASTE was part of the king's prerogative, whereby he was entitled to the profits for a *year and a day* of persons attainted of petty treason or felony, together with the right of wasting the said tenements; afterwards restoring it to the lord of fee. Now abolished.

YEAR TO YEAR. [TENANT FROM YEAR TO YEAR.]

YEARS, ESTATE FOR. An estate demised or granted for a term of years.

YEOMAN. (Sax. *Geman*; Lat. *Communis*). He that had free land of forty shillings a year; who was anciently thereby qualified to serve on juries, vote for knights of the shire, and do any other act, where the law required one that was *probus et legalis homo*.

YEOMANRY. The small freeholders and farmers. [YEOMAN.] The name was also given to certain local forces raised by individuals with the approbation of the king, who accepted their voluntary service. It survives in some Territorial units.

YIELDING AND PAYING are words used at the beginning of the *reddendum* clause in a lease, with reference to the rent intended to be payable under the lease. [REDDENDUM.]

YORKSHIRE REGISTRIES are the registries of documents and transactions relating to land first provided by Acts of Parliament for the ridings of the county of York. These Acts were repealed and re-enacted with certain modifications by the Yorkshire Registries Act 1884. Under s. 11 of the Law of Property Act 1925 it is necessary to register in the Yorkshire Registry only instruments which operate to transfer or create a legal estate; and, under s. 197, this registration is deemed to constitute actual notice of the transfer or creation of the legal estate, or charge by way of legal mortgage, to all persons, and for all purposes whatsoever.

Further, it is provided by the Law of Property (Amendment) Act 1926, Schedule (amending the Land Charges Act 1925, s. 10 (6)), that the registration of a general equitable charge, restrictive covenant, equitable easement or estate contract affecting land in any of the three Ridings, shall be effected at the appropriate Registry

YORKSHIRE REGISTRIES—
continued.
in Yorkshire, and not at the Land Registry in London. See also the ss. 135, 136 of the Land Registration Act 1925.

The Yorkshire ridings disappeared, as such, in the reorganisation of Local Government under The Local Government Act 1972.

YOUNG PERSON. A person who has attained the age of fourteen years but who is under seventeen years. See s. 107 of the Children and Young Persons Act 1933.

Z

ZERO-RATING. Relief from payment of value added tax on the supply of certain goods and services, *e.g.* food (with exceptions), books and newspapers, coal, fuel, etc. See the Finance Act 1972, s. 12, Sch. 4 (as varied from time to time by order).

ZOONOSES. Animal diseases which can be transmitted to man, *e.g.* bovine tuberculosis, brucellosis, rabies. Provisions for the control of such diseases are made in the Agriculture (Miscellaneous Provisions) Act 1972, s. 1.